OF MARKETING

FOURTH EDITION

PRENTICE HALL
ENGLEWOOD CLIFFS,
NEW JERSEY 07632

Library of Congress Cataloging-in-Publication Data

KOTLER, PHILIP.
    Principles of marketing / Philip Kotler, Gary Armstrong. — 4th
ed.
        p.   cm.
    Includes bibliographies and indexes.
    ISBN 0–13–705360–6
    1. Marketing.   I. Armstrong, Gary.   II. Title.
HF5415.K636   1989
658.8–dc19   88–27432
                                            CIP

Principles of Marketing, fourth edition: Philip Kotler and Gary Armstrong
Editorial/production supervision: Esther S. Koehn
Interior design and cover design: Kenny Beck
Photo research: Teri Stratford
Photo editor: Lorinda Morris
Manufacturing buyer: Margaret Rizzi

© 1989, 1986, 1983, 1980 by Prentice-Hall, Inc.
A Division of Simon & Schuster
Englewood Cliffs, New Jersey 07632

Printed in the United States of America
10 9 8 7 6 5 4 3 2 1

ISBN 0-13-705360-6

Prentice-Hall International (UK) Limited, *London*
Prentice-Hall of Australia Pty. Limited, *Sydney*
Prentice-Hall Canada Inc., *Toronto*
Prentice-Hall Hispanoamericana, S.A., *Mexico City*
Prentice-Hall of India Private Limited, *New Delhi*
Prentice-Hall of Japan, Inc., *Tokyo*
Simon & Schuster Asia Pte. Ltd., *Singapore*
Editora Prentice-Hall do Brasil, Ltda., *Rio de Janeiro*

To

Nancy, Amy, Melissa, and Jessica Kotler

Kathy, Casey, and Mandy Armstrong

ABOUT THE
Authors

PHILIP KOTLER

GARY ARMSTRONG

AS a team, Philip Kotler and Gary Armstrong provide a blend of skills uniquely suited to writing an introductory marketing text. Professor Kotler is one of the world's leading authorities on marketing. Professor Armstrong is an award-winning teacher of undergraduate business students. Together they make the complex world of marketing practical, approachable, and enjoyable.

Philip Kotler is S. C. Johnson & Son Distinguished Professor of International Marketing at the Kellogg Graduate School of Management, Northwestern University. He received his master's degree at the University of Chicago and his Ph.D. at M.I.T., both in economics. Dr. Kotler is author of *Marketing Management: Analysis, Planning, Implementation, and Control* (Prentice Hall), now in its sixth edition and the most widely used marketing textbook in graduate schools of business. He has authored several other successful books, and he has written over eighty articles for leading journals. Dr. Kotler's numerous honors include the *Paul D. Converse Award* given by the American Marketing Association to honor "outstanding contributions to science in marketing" and the *Stuart Henderson Britt Award* as Marketer of the Year. In 1985, he was named the first recipient of two major awards: the *Distinguished Marketing Educator of the Year Award* given by the American Marketing Association and the *Philip Kotler Award for Excellence in Health Care Marketing* presented by the Academy for Health Care Services Marketing. Dr. Kotler has served as chairman of the College on Marketing of the Institute of Management Sciences (TIMS) and as director of the American Marketing Association. He has consulted with many major American companies on marketing strategy.

Gary Armstrong is Professor and Chairman of Marketing in the Graduate School of Business Administration at the University of North Carolina at Chapel Hill. He holds undergraduate and masters degrees in business from Wayne State University in Detroit, and he received his Ph.D. in marketing from Northwestern University. Dr. Armstrong has contributed numerous articles to leading business journals, and his doctoral dissertation received the American Marketing Association's first-place award. As a consultant and researcher, he has worked with many companies on marketing research, sales management, and marketing strategy. But Professor Armstrong's first love is teaching. He is currently very active in the teaching and administration of North Carolina's undergraduate business program. His recent administrative posts include Associate Director of the Undergraduate Business Program and Director of the Business Honors Program, among others. He works closely with business-student groups and has received several campus-wide and School of Business teaching awards. He is the only two-time recipient of the school's Award for Excellence in Undergraduate Teaching.

Contents

5 CONSUMER MARKETS: INFLUENCES ON CONSUMER BEHAVIOR 114

6 CONSUMER MARKETS: BUYER DECISION PROCESSES 140

7 ORGANIZATIONAL MARKETS AND ORGANIZATIONAL BUYER BEHAVIOR 162

PART 3   SELECTING TARGET MARKETS

8 MEASURING AND FORECASTING DEMAND 194

9 MARKET SEGMENTATION, TARGETING, AND POSITIONING 212

PART 4   DEVELOPING THE MARKETING MIX

10 DESIGNING PRODUCTS: PRODUCTS, BRANDS, PACKAGING, AND SERVICES   240

16 PROMOTING PRODUCTS: COMMUNICATIONS AND PROMOTION STRATEGY 412

17 PROMOTING PRODUCTS: ADVERTISING, SALES PROMOTION, AND PUBLIC RELATIONS 432

PART 6   EXTENDING MARKETING

APPENDICES

Preface

"MARKETING is too important to be left to the marketing department," states David Packard of Hewlett-Packard. And Professor Stephen Burnett of Northwestern adds, "In a truly great marketing organization, you can't tell who's in the marketing department. Everyone in the organization has to make decisions based on the impact on the consumer."

Marketing is the business function that identifies customer needs and wants, determines which target markets the organization can best serve, designs appropriate products, services, and programs to serve these markets, and calls upon everyone in the organization to "think and serve customers." From a societal point of view, marketing is the link between a society's material requirements and its economic patterns of response.

Yet to many people marketing is seen narrowly as the art of finding clever ways to dispose of the company's products. Many see marketing only as advertising or selling. But real marketing is not the art of selling what you make so much as knowing what to make! Organizations gain market leadership by understanding consumer needs and finding solutions that satisfy these needs through product innovation, product quality, and customer service. If these are absent, no amount of advertising or selling can compensate.

Principles of Marketing is designed to help students learn about the basic concepts and practice of modern marketing in an enjoyable and practical way. Marketing is all around us, and we all need to know something about it. Most students are surprised to find that marketing is so widely used. Marketing is used not only by manufacturing companies, wholesalers, and retailers, but by all kinds of individuals and organizations. Lawyers, accountants, and doctors use marketing to manage demand for their services. So do hospitals, museums, and performing arts groups. No politician can get the needed votes and no resort the needed tourists without developing and carrying out marketing plans.

People throughout these organizations need to know how to define and segment a market and develop need-satisfying products and services for chosen target markets. They must know how to price their offerings to make them attractive and affordable, and how to choose middlemen to make their products available to customers. And they need to know how to advertise and promote products so that customers will know about them and want them. Clearly, marketers need a broad range of skills in order to sense, serve, and satisfy consumer needs.

Students also need to know marketing in their roles as consumers and citizens. Someone is always trying to sell us something, so we need to recognize the methods they use. And when students enter the job market, they must do "marketing research" to find the best opportunities and the best ways to "market themselves" to prospective employers. Many will start their careers with marketing jobs in salesforces, in retailing, in advertising, in research, or in one of a dozen other marketing areas.

APPROACH AND OBJECTIVES

Principles of Marketing is designed to present the complex and fascinating world of marketing in an easy to grasp, lively, and enjoyable way. The book is comprehensive and innovative. It covers all of the basics of marketing and provides fresh insights into the latest marketing developments. It applies marketing thinking to products and services, consumer and industrial markets, profit and nonprofit organizations, domestic and foreign companies, and small and large firms. It covers important marketing principles and concepts that are supported by research and evidence from economics, the behavioral sciences, and modern management theory.

In addition to its comprehensive and innovative coverage, *Principles of Marketing* takes a practical, managerial approach to marketing. It provides a rich depth of practical examples and applications, showing the major decisions that marketing managers face in their efforts to balance the organization's objectives and resources against needs and opportunities in the marketplace. Each chapter opens with a major example describing an actual company situation. Boxed Marketing Highlights, short examples, cases, and color illustrations highlight high-interest ideas, stories, and marketing strategies.

Finally, *Principles of Marketing* makes learning marketing easy and enjoyable. Its writing style and level are well suited to the beginning marketing student. It tells stories that reveal the drama of modern marketing: Kellogg's abrupt repositioning to meet changing baby-boomer life styles; the rise and fall of New Coke, the Edsel of the eighties; how Oshkosh found a niche with "designer trucks"; Beecham's marketing malpractice suit; 3M's legendary emphasis on new product development; tiny Vernor's success in the shadows of giants Coke and Pepsi; Procter & Gamble's fight to hold share in the diaper and toothpaste markets; how Revlon sells not just products, but hopes and dreams; Caterpillar's price war with Komatsu and Kodak's attack on Fuji Film in Japan; Century City Hospital's use of marketing to capture demand in key market segments; and Gerber's difficult social responsibility decisions following a product tampering scare. These and dozens of other examples and illustrations throughout each chapter reinforce key concepts and bring marketing to life for the student.

Thus *Principles of Marketing* gives the marketing student a comprehensive and innovative, managerial and practical introduction to marketing. Its style and extensive use of examples and illustrations make the book straightforward, easy to read, and enjoyable.

CHANGES IN THE FOURTH EDITION

The fourth edition of *Principles of Marketing* offers several improvements in organization, content, and style. The text is a chapter shorter. Strategic planning and the marketing process are now presented in a single, streamlined chapter (Chapter 2), providing an early overview of marketing elements and marketing's role in the organization. Marketing planning is now combined with the other marketing management functions—implementation, organization, and control—in a single chapter (Chapter 19). This chapter and a substantially revised Chapter 20 (Competitor Analysis and Competitive Strategy) combine to help integrate the material at the end to the course.

The fourth edition has been thoroughly edited to improve readability. Dozens of new color illustrations add to the book's visual appeal. All tables, facts, figures, and references have been thoroughly updated. Hundreds of new examples have been added within the text materials. Half the book's cases are new to this edition. Chapter objectives and lists of key term definitions have been added to each chapter to enhance learning.

The fourth edition of *Principles of Marketing* offers substantial new or improved material on several important topics: identifying and analyzing competitors, marketing strategies for service firms, responding to the marketing environment, regionalizing marketing strategies, industrial market segmentation, finding competitive advantage, test marketing, "off-price" retailing, direct marketing, consumer and trade promotion tools, inside sales and telemarketing and international pricing and countertrade.

*L*EARNING AIDS

Many aids are provided within this book to help students learn about marketing. The main ones are:

- *Opening Examples.* Each chapter starts with a dramatic marketing story that introduces the chapter material and arouses student interest.
- *Chapter Objectives.* Each chapter presents objectives that prepare the student for the chapter material and point out learning goals.
- *Full-Color Figures, Photographs, and Illustrations.* Throughout each chapter, key concepts and applications are illustrated with strong, full-color visual materials.
- *Marketing Highlights.* Additional examples and important information are highlighted in boxed exhibits throughout the text.
- *Summaries.* Each chapter ends with a summary that wraps up the main points and concepts.
- *Review Questions.* Each chapter has a set of review questions covering the main chapter points.
- *Key Terms.* Key Terms are highlighted within each chapter, and a list of key term definitions is provided at the end of each chapter.
- *Case Studies.* Cases for class discussion or written assignment are provided at the end of each major part of the book. The twenty cases challenge students to apply marketing principles to real companies in real situations.
- *Appendices.* Two appendices, "Marketing Arithmetic" and "Careers in Marketing," provide additional, practical information for students.
- *Glossary.* At the end of the book, an extensive glossary provides quick reference to the key terms found in the text.
- *Indexes.* An author index and a subject index help students quickly find information and examples in the book.

*S*UPPLEMENTS

A successful marketing course requires more than a well-written book. It requires a dedicated teacher and a complete set of supplemental learning and teaching aids. The following aids support *Principles of Marketing*.

Annotated Instructor's Edition
The Annotated Instructor's Edition, prepared by George Franke of Virginia Polytechnic Institute and State University, is an innovative, new teaching resource that combines the student text with a comprehensive set of teaching materials. Prepared especially

for the instructor, it contains suggestions for organizing and teaching the introductory marketing course, teaching tips, case commentaries, and much more. Page-by-page annotations provide references to color transparencies, discussion ideas, and hundreds of recent examples and anecdotes for use in class.

Test Item File

The Test Item File contains about 3000 multiple choice, true-false, and essay questions. The questions are available in the Test Item File booklet, on computer tape, or through the Prentice Hall Computerized Testing Service. The Diploma I Test Generating System is also provided for preparing and editing tests containing test-bank or teacher designed questions on IBM, Apple II, and Macintosh personal computers.

Study Guide and Applications Manual

An important learning tool, this improved study guide provides review questions for each chapter, together with carefully designed application exercises.

Full-Color Transparencies

The Transparencies Package includes over 100 full-color transparencies—about 40 with important figures and illustrations from the book, and 60 with advertisements and illustrations not found in the book. More than 140 black-and-white transparency masters are also provided.

Audio-Visual Materials

An extensive new video series containing dozens of marketing features, examples, case histories, television advertisements, and other items has been assembled for adopters to help enrich and enliven their classes. For complete information, contact your local Prentice Hall representative or write to Whitney Blake, College Book Division, Prentice Hall.

Personal Computer Application Software

A wide range of computer applications have been developed to accompany this new edition. Software includes spreadsheet applications for text examples as well as outside case examples.

Additional Supplements

Additional supplements include *Readings in Marketing* (by Cox and Blair), and "Product Manager," a practical marketing simulation game that operates on microcomputer.

ACKNOWLEDGMENTS

No book is the work only of its authors. We owe much to the pioneers of marketing, who first identified its major issues and developed its concepts and techniques. Our thanks also go to our colleagues at the J. L. Kellogg Graduate School of Management, Northwestern University, and the Graduate School of Business Administration, University of North Carolina at Chapel Hill, for ideas and suggestions. We owe special thanks to George Franke, who prepared the *Annotated Instructor's Edition* and coordinated the book's many supplements, and to Richard Clewett and Charles Lamb for their work on the timely, lively, and practical cases for the text. We also want to acknowledge the contributions of Thomas Paczkowski and Ronald Weir in preparing the *Study Guide* and *Test Item File*, respectively.

Many reviewers at other colleges provided valuable comments and suggestions. We are indebted to the following colleagues:

Gerald Albaum
University of Oregon

David Anderson
Wheaton College

David L. Appel
University of Notre Dame

Boris W. Becker
Oregon State University

Michael Belch
San Diego State University

Donald Bergh
University of Colorado

Robert L. Berl
Memphis State University

Paul N. Bloom
University of North Carolina

Robert Boris
Bryant and Stratton Business Institute

Jane Bradlee-Durfee
Mankato State University

Candida Brush
Boston College

Austin Byron
Northern Arizona University

Dennis Cahill
Cleveland State University

Helen Caldwell
Providence College

Charles R. Canedy, III
University of Hartford

Paul Cohen
CUNY of Staten Island—Sunnyside

Keith Cox
University of Houston

Robert Dalton
Russell Sage College

Ronald Decker
University of Wisconsin—Eau Claire

Rohit Deshpande
Dartmouth College

Richard English
San Diego State University

Thomas Falcone
Indiana University of Penna.

David Georgoff
Florida Atlantic University

Thomas J. Hickey
SUNY-Oswego

Kathryn Hunnicutt
University of Georgia

Ralph Jackson
University of Tulsa

Denise Johnson
Indiana University

Raymond F. Keyes
Boston College

Irene Lange
California State University at Fullerton

Frederick Langrehr
Brigham Young University

Jean Lefebvre
University of Hartford

Frank Marion
Loyola University in New Orleans

John Martin
Boston University

Charlotte Mason
University of North Carolina—Chapel Hill

Douglas W. Mellott, Jr.
Louisiana Tech University

Ronald Michaels
University of Kansas

Chem Narayana
University of Illinois at Chicago

Robert Olsen
California State University, Fullerton

Linda Parry
Russell Sage College

William Piper
University of Wisconsin

Christopher P. Puto
University of Michigan

Abdul Qastin
Lakeland College

Juanita Roxas
University of Georgia

David R. Rink
Northern Illinois University

Dennis W. Rook
University of Southern California

Robert E. Thompson
Indiana State University

Deepak Sainanee
Purdue University

Jerry Wilson
Memphis State University

Dean Siewers
Rochester Institute of Technology

Peter Wilton
University of California, Berkeley

Clint B. Tankersley
Syracuse University

John Zietlow
Liberty University

John Tanner
University of Georgia

We also owe a great deal to the people at Prentice Hall who helped to develop this book. Whitney Blake, marketing editor, provided strong advice and fresh insights. Esther Koehn, production editor, skillfully guided the book through production. Ann Torbert provided developmental assistance. Additional thanks go to Lori Morris for photo research and Marjorie Winters for assistance with permissions.

Finally, we owe many thanks to our families—Nancy, Amy, Melissa, and Jessica Kotler, and Kathy, Casey, and Mandy Armstrong—for their constant understanding, support, and encouragement.

PHILIP KOTLER
GARY ARMSTRONG

PRINCIPLES OF MARKETING

1 Social Foundations of Marketing: Meeting Human Needs

MARKETING touches all of us every day of our lives. We wake up to a Panasonic radio alarm clock, which plays a Lionel Richie song followed by a United Airlines commercial advertising a Bahamas vacation. We enter the bathroom, where we brush our teeth with Colgate, shave with Gillette, gargle with Scope, and use other toiletries and appliances produced by manufacturers around the world. We put on our Levi's jeans and Nike shoes. We enter the kitchen and drink Minute Maid orange juice and pour Borden milk into a bowl of Kellogg's Rice Krispies. Later we drink a cup of Maxwell House coffee with two teaspoons of Domino sugar while munching on a slice of Sara Lee coffee cake.

We consume oranges grown in California, coffee imported from Brazil, a newspaper made of Canadian wood pulp, and radio news coming from as far away as Australia. We pick up our mail and find a Metropolitan Museum of Art shoppers' catalog, a letter from a Prudential insurance salesperson offering services, and coupons saving us money on our favorite brands. We step out of our home and drive to the Northbrook Court Shopping Center with its Neiman-Marcus, Lord & Taylor, Sears, and hundreds of other stores filled with goods from floor to ceiling. Later we exercise at a Nautilus Fitness Center, grab a McDLT at McDonald's, and plan a trip to Disney World at a Thomas Cook travel agency.

The marketing system has made all this possible, with little effort on our part. It has given us a standard of living that our ancestors could not have imagined.

1. Define marketing and discuss its role in the economy.
2. Compare the five marketing management philosophies.
3. Identify the goals of the marketing system.
4. Explain how marketing can be used by different kinds of business and nonbusiness organizations.

THE MARKETING system that delivers our high standard of living consists of many large and small companies, all seeking excellence. What makes a company excellent? This question exploded across America in the early 1980s, and for good reason. Several of America's blue chip companies—Chrysler, International Harvester, Harley Davidson—were slipping badly. Markets changed at dizzying rates, yet many U.S. companies failed to respond to these changes. Like dinosaurs, they flirted with extinction.

A handful of other American companies continued to record healthy sales and profits. Two business researchers, Peters and Waterman, studied many such successful companies—companies like Hewlett-Packard, Frito-Lay (PepsiCo), Procter & Gamble, 3M, McDonald's, Marriott—to find out what made them tick. They reported the results in what became the best selling business book of all times, *In Search of Excellence.*[1] They found that these companies shared a set of basic marketing principles. Each had a keen understanding of its customers, strongly defined markets, and the ability to motivate its employees to produce high quality and value for customers. Half of what they found related to what marketers call the "marketing concept."

In a second book, Peters offers more stories about companies doing smart and wonderful things to improve their customers' satisfaction.[2] He describes how IBM collects customer ratings of its sales and service people and gives awards to IBM employees who satisfy customers most. He talks about how The Limited studies women's clothing needs and creates appropriate store systems for different segments (The Limited, Limited Express, Victoria's Secret, Sizes Unlimited). And he tells of Stew Leonard's supermarket in Norwalk, Connecticut, where Stew sits down with eight customers for a few hours each Saturday to talk about how he can improve customer service.

The critical need for marketing in today's companies is dramatically documented in a recent study in which senior managers of major American companies identified their foremost problem as "developing, improving, and implementing competitive marketing strategies."[3] As a further sign, executive recruiting firms report a large increase in demand for top marketing executives. One such firm found that more current top executives have come out of marketing than out of any other field—31 percent of the chief executives of the *Fortune 1000* companies had mostly marketing backgrounds, up 28 percent from four years earlier.[4]

Marketing has become a key factor producing business success. And it must be understood not in the old sense of making a sale—selling—but rather in the new sense of satisfying customer needs—marketing. Today's companies face increasingly stiff and sophisticated competition, and the rewards will go to those who can best read customer wants and deliver the greatest value to their target consumers. Marketing skills will separate the amateurs from the professionals in the marketplace.

In this chapter, we will define marketing and its core concepts, describe the major philosophies underlying marketing thinking and practice, discuss the goals of the marketing system, and explain how marketing is used by different kinds of organizations.

WHAT IS MARKETING?

What does the term *marketing* mean? Most people mistakenly think of marketing only as selling and promotion. And no wonder! Americans are bombarded with television commercials, newspaper ads, direct mail, and sales calls. Someone is always trying to sell something. It seems that we cannot escape death, taxes, or selling.

Therefore many students are surprised to learn that selling is only the tip of the marketing iceberg. It is but one of several marketing functions, and often not the most important one. If the marketer does a good job of identifying consumer needs, developing good products, and pricing, distributing, and promoting them effectively, these goods will sell very easily.

Everyone knows about "hot" products to which consumers flock in droves. When Polaroid designed its Spectra camera, when Coleco first sold Cabbage Patch dolls, when Ford introduced its Taurus car, these manufacturers were swamped with orders. They had designed the "right" products—not me-too products, but ones offering new benefits. Peter Drucker, a leading management thinker, put it this way: "The aim of marketing is to make selling superfluous. The aim is to know and understand the customer so well that the product or service fits him and sells itself."[5]

This does not mean that selling and promotion are unimportant, but rather that they are part of a larger "marketing mix," a set of marketing tools that work together to affect the marketplace. Here is our definition of *marketing*:

> **Marketing** is a social and managerial process by which individuals and groups obtain what they need and want through creating and exchanging products and value with others.[6]

To explain this definition, we will look at the following core concepts: *needs, wants, demands, products, exchange, transactions,* and *markets.* These concepts are shown in Figure 1-1 and discussed below.

Needs   The most basic concept underlying marketing is that of human needs. A **human need** is a state of felt deprivation in a person. Humans have many complex needs. They include basic physical needs for food, clothing, warmth, and safety; social needs for belonging and affection; and individual needs for knowledge and self-expression. These needs are not created by Madison Avenue, but are a basic part of human makeup.

Wants   A second basic concept in marketing is that of **human wants,** which are the form human needs take as shaped by culture and individual personality. A hungry person in Bali wants mangoes, suckling pig, and beans. A hungry person in the United States stops at McDonald's for a hamburger, French fries, and a Coke. Wants are described in terms of objects that will satisfy a need. As a society evolves, the wants of its members expand. People are exposed to an increasing number of objects

FIGURE 1-1
Core marketing concepts

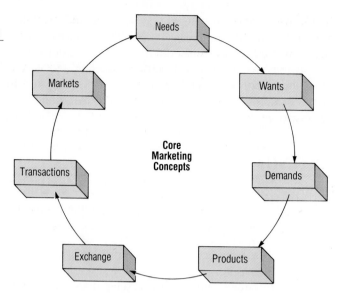

that arouse their interest and desire. Producers try to provide the things that people need.

Sellers often confuse wants and needs. A manufacturer of drill bits may think that the customer needs a drill bit, but what the customer really needs is a *hole*. These sellers suffer from "marketing myopia."[7] They concentrate so much on their products that they focus only on existing wants and lose sight of underlying customer needs. They forget that a physical product is only a tool to solve a consumer problem. These sellers have trouble if a new product comes along that serves the need better or cheaper. The customer will have the same need but will want the new product. As a classic example, Hollywood fell on hard times because it concentrated on its products (movies) rather than underlying consumer needs (entertainment). The television industry grew rapidly at Hollywood's expense because it found a new and better way to serve consumers' entertainment needs.

Kaiser Sand & Gravel Company's marketing mission is to "find a need and fill it."

Demands   People have almost unlimited wants but limited resources. They therefore choose products that produce the most satisfaction for their money. When backed by buying power, wants become **demands.**

It is easy to list a society's demands at a given time. In a single year, for example, 240 million Americans might purchase 67 billion eggs, 2 billion chickens, 5 million hair dryers, 133 billion domestic air passenger miles, and over 20 million lectures by college English professors. These and other consumer goods and services lead, in turn, to a demand for more than 150 million tons of steel, 4 billion tons of cotton, and many other industrial goods. These are a few of the demands in a $3.5 trillion economy.

Consumers view products as bundles of benefits and choose products that give them the best bundle for their money. An inexpensive Toyota means basic transportation, a low price, and fuel economy. A Cadillac means comfort, luxury, and status. People choose the product whose benefits add up to the most satisfaction, given their wants and resources.

Products   Human needs, wants, and demands suggest that there are products to satisfy them. A **product** is anything that can be offered to a market for attention, acquisition, use, or consumption that might satisfy a need or want.

Suppose a person feels the need to be more attractive. We will call all the products that can satisfy this need the *product choice set*. They may include new clothes, hair styling services, a Caribbean suntan, exercise classes, and many others. These products are not all equally desirable. The more available and less expensive products, such as clothing and a new haircut, are likely to be purchased first. The closer products come to matching consumers' wants, the more successful they will be. Producers need to know what consumers want and then provide products that come as close as possible to satisfying these wants.

The concept of product is not limited to physical objects. Anything capable of satisfying a need or want can be called a product. In addition to goods and services, products include *persons*, *places*, *organizations*, *activities*, and *ideas*. A consumer decides which entertainers to watch on television, places to go on a vacation, organizations to contribute to, and ideas to support. To the consumer, these are all products.

Products do not have to be physical objects. Here, the "product" is a trip to the zoo.

If the term product does not seem to fit at times, we can use the terms *satisfier*, *resource*, or *offer*. All describe something of value to someone.

Exchange   Marketing occurs when people decide to satisfy needs and wants through exchange. **Exchange** is the act of obtaining a desired object from someone by offering something in return. Exchange is only one of many ways people can obtain a desired object. For example, hungry people can find their own food by hunting, fishing, or fruit gathering. They can beg for food or take food away from someone else. Finally, they can exchange money, another good, or a service for the food.

Of these ways of satisfying needs, exchange has much in its favor. People do not have to prey on others or depend on donations. Nor do they have to have the skills to produce every necessity for themselves. They can concentrate on making things they are good at making and trade them for needed items made by others. The society ends up producing much more than under any other alternative.

Exchange is the core concept of marketing.[8] For an exchange to take place, several conditions must be satisfied. There must be at least two parties, and each must have something of value to the other. Each party must want to deal with the other party; each must be free to accept or reject the other's offer. Finally, each party must be able to communicate and deliver.

These conditions make exchange possible. Whether exchange actually takes place depends on the parties' coming to an agreement. If they agree, we conclude that the act of exchange leaves all of them better off (or at least not worse off) because each was free to reject or accept the offer. In this sense, just as production creates value, exchange creates value. It gives people more consumption possibilities.

Transactions   As exchange is the core concept of marketing, a transaction is its unit of measurement. A **transaction** consists of a trade of values between two parties. In a transaction, A gives X to B and gets Y in return. For example, you pay Sears $400 for a television set. This is a classic *monetary transaction*, but not all transactions involve money.

MARKETING HIGHLIGHT 1–1

GOING BACK TO BARTER

With today's high prices, many companies are returning to the primitive practice of barter—trading goods and services they make for other goods and services they need. Companies barter billions of dollars worth of goods and services each year, and the practice is growing at 25 percent annually. Barter now accounts for a quarter of the world's international trade.

Companies use barter to increase sales, unload extra goods, and save cash. For example, when Shell Oil was stuck with 5 million Can Care strips—a product for killing insects in garbage cans—it exchanged with a Caribbean resort for a load of unrefined sugar. When Climaco Corporation was overstocked with bubble bath, it swapped the excess for $300,000 worth of advertising for one of its other products. McDonnell Douglas traded planes to Yugoslavia for canned hams and tools, and Pierre Cardin served as a consultant to China in exchange for silks and cashmeres.

Many kinds of specialty companies have appeared to help companies with bartering. Retail trade exchanges and trade clubs arrange barter for small retailers. Larger corporations use trade consultants and brokerage firms. Media brokerage houses provide advertising space in exchange for products, and international barter is handled by countertrade organizations. One trading company, Barter Systems, Inc., operates sixty-two trading centers around the United States. A letter that it sent to some of its twenty-five thousand clients stated: "Wanted: $300,000 worth of dried milk or cornflakes in exchange for an airplane of equal value."

In a *barter transaction* you might give your old refrigerator to a neighbor in return for a second-hand television set. A barter transaction can also include services instead of goods, as when a lawyer writes a will for a doctor in return for a medical exam (see Marketing Highlight 1–1). A transaction involves at least two things of value, conditions that are agreed to, a time of agreement, and a place of agreement.

In the broadest sense, the marketer tries to bring about a response to some offer. And the response may be more than "buying" or "trading" goods and services in the narrow sense. A political candidate wants a response called "votes," a church wants "joining," a social action group wants "adopting the idea." Marketing consists of actions taken to obtain a desired response from a target audience toward some product, service, idea, or other object.

Markets   The concept of transactions leads to the concept of a market. A **market** is the set of actual and potential buyers of a product. To understand the nature of a market, imagine a primitive economy with only four persons: a fisherman, a hunter, a potter, and a farmer. Figure 1-2 shows three different ways in which these traders could meet their needs. In the first case, *self-sufficiency*, they gather the needed goods for themselves. Thus the hunter spends most of the time hunting, but also takes time to fish, make pottery, and farm to obtain the other goods. The hunter is less efficient at hunting, and the same is true of the other traders.

In the second case, *decentralized exchange*, each person sees the other three as potential "buyers" who make up a market. Thus the hunter may make separate trips to trade meat for the goods of the fisherman, the potter, and the farmer. In the third case, *centralized exchange*, a new person called a merchant appears and locates in a central area, called a marketplace. Each trader brings goods to the merchant and trades for other needed goods. Thus the hunter transacts with one "market" to obtain all the needed goods, rather than with three other persons. Merchants and central marketplaces greatly reduce the total number of transactions needed to accomplish a given volume of exchange.[9]

As the number of persons and transactions increases in a society, the number of merchants and marketplaces also increases. In advanced societies, markets need not be physical places where buyers and sellers interact. With modern communications and transportation, a merchant can advertise a product on late evening television, take orders from hundreds of customers over the phone, and mail the goods to the buyers on the following day without having had any physical contact with the buyers.

A market can grow up around a product, a service, or anything else of value. For example, a labor market consists of people who are willing to offer their work

FIGURE 1-2
Evolution toward centralized exchange

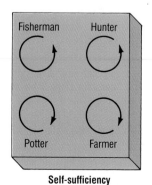
Self-sufficiency

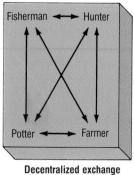
Decentralized exchange

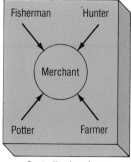
Centralized exchange

in return for wages or products. Various institutions such as employment agencies and job-counseling firms will grow up around a labor market to help it function better. The money market is another important market that emerges to meet the needs of people so that they can borrow, lend, save, and protect money. And the donor market emerges to meet the financial needs of nonprofit organizations.

Marketing
The concept of markets finally brings us full circle to the concept of marketing. Marketing means working with markets to bring about exchanges for the purpose of satisfying human needs and wants. Thus we return to our definition of marketing as a process by which individuals and groups obtain what they need and want through creating and exchanging products and value with others.

Exchange processes involve work. Sellers have to search for buyers, identify their needs, design good products, promote them, store and deliver them, set prices, and provide service after the sale. Such activities as research, product development, communication, distribution, pricing, and service are core marketing activities.

Although we normally think of marketing as being carried on by sellers, buyers also carry on marketing activities. Consumers do "marketing" when they search for the goods they need at prices they can afford. Company purchasing agents do "marketing" when they track down sellers and bargain for good terms. In a *seller's market*, sellers have more power and buyers have to be the more active "marketers." In a *buyer's market*, buyers have more power and sellers have to be more active "marketers."

In the early 1950s the supply of goods began to grow faster than the demand. Marketing became identified with sellers trying to find buyers. This textbook will take that point of view and examine the marketing problems of sellers in a buyers' market.

MARKETING MANAGEMENT

Most people think of market management as finding enough customers for the company's current output. But this is too limited a view. The organization has a desired level of demand for its products. At any point in time, there may be no demand, adequate demand, irregular demand, or too much demand, and marketing management must find ways to deal with these different demand states (see Marketing Highlight 1–2). Marketing management is concerned not only with finding and increasing demand, but also with changing or even reducing it. Thus marketing management seeks to affect the level, timing, and nature of demand in a way that will help the organization achieve its objectives. Simply put, marketing management is *demand management*.

We define marketing management as follows:

Marketing management is the analysis, planning, implementation, and control of programs designed to create, build, and maintain beneficial exchanges with target buyers for the purpose of achieving organizational objectives.

Marketing managers include sales managers and salespeople, advertising executives, sales promotion people, marketing researchers, product managers, pricing specialists, and others. We will say more about these marketing jobs in Chapters 2 and 20, as well as in Appendix B, "Careers in Marketing."

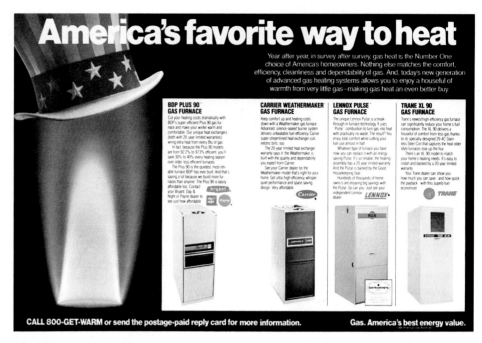

Managing demand: During the gas shortages of the 1970s, the American Gas Association demarketed natural gas by telling people how to conserve. Then when gas supplies grew in the 1980s, the AGA ran ads to stimulate sales while continuing to emphasize energy efficiency.

VARIOUS STATES OF DEMAND

Marketing managers in different organizations might face any of the following states of demand. The marketing task is to manage demand effectively.

Negative Demand. A major part of the market dislikes the product and may even pay to avoid it. Examples are vaccinations, dental work, and seat belts. Marketers must analyze why the market dislikes the product, and whether product redesign, lower prices, or more positive promotion can change the consumer attitudes.

No Demand. Target consumers may be uninterested in the product. Thus farmers may not care about a new farming method, and college students may not be interested in taking foreign language courses. The marketer must find ways to connect the product's benefits with the market's needs and interests.

Latent Demand. Consumers have a want that is not satisfied by any existing product or service. There is strong latent demand for nonharmful cigarettes, safer neighborhoods, and more fuel-efficient cars. The marketing task is to measure the size of the potential market and develop effective goods and services that will satisfy the demand.

Falling Demand. Sooner or later, every organization faces falling demand for one of its products. Churches have seen their membership decline, and private colleges have seen fewer applications. The marketer must find the causes of market decline and restimulate demand by finding new markets, changing product features, or creating more effective communications.

Irregular Demand. Demand varies on a seasonal, daily, or even hourly basis, causing problems of idle or overworked capacity. In mass transit, much equipment is idle during slow travel hours and too little is available during peak hours. Museums are undervisited during weekdays and overcrowded during weekends. Marketers must find ways to change the time pattern of demand through flexible pricing, promotion, and other incentives.

Full Demand. The organization has just the amount of demand it wants and can handle. The marketer works to maintain the current level of demand in the face of changing consumer preferences and increasing competition. The organization maintains quality and continually measures consumer satisfaction to make sure it is doing a good job.

Overfull Demand. Demand is higher than the company can or wants to handle. Thus the Golden Gate Bridge carries more traffic than is safe; and Yellowstone National Park is overcrowded in the summertime. The marketing task, called *demarketing*, is to find ways to reduce the demand temporarily or permanently. Demarketing involves such actions as raising prices and reducing promotion and service. Demarketing does not aim to destroy demand, but only to reduce it.

Sources: See Demos Vardiabasis, ''Countertrade: New Ways of Doing Business,'' *Business to Business*, December 1985, pp. 67–71; Linda A. Dickerson, ''Barter to Gain a Competitive Edge in a Cash-Poor Economy, *Marketing News*, March 16, 1984, pp. 1–2; and Arthur Bragg, ''Bartering Comes of Age,'' *Sales & Marketing Management*, January 1988, pp. 61–63.

MARKETING MANAGEMENT PHILOSOPHIES

We have described marketing management as carrying out tasks to achieve desired exchanges with target markets. What philosophy should guide these marketing efforts? Very often the interests of the organization, customers, and society conflict. What weights should be given to each? Clearly, marketing activities should be carried out under some philosophy.

There are five competing concepts under which organizations conduct their marketing activity: the production, product, selling, marketing, and societal marketing concepts.

The Production Concept

The **production concept** holds that consumers will favor products that are available and highly affordable, and therefore management should focus on improving production and distribution efficiency. This concept is one of the oldest philosophies guiding sellers.

The production concept is a proper philosophy in two types of situations. In the first, the demand for a product is bigger than the supply. In this case, management should look for ways to increase production. The second situation is one in which the product's cost is high and improved productivity is needed to bring it down. Henry Ford's whole philosophy was to perfect the production of the Model T so that its cost could be brought down and more people could afford it. He joked about offering people any color car as long as it was black. Today Texas Instruments (TI) follows this philosophy of increased production and lower costs in order to bring down prices. It won a major share of the American hand-calculator market with this philosophy. But when TI used the same strategy in the digital watch and home computer markets, it failed. In its drive to bring down prices, TI lost sight of what its customers wanted.

Some service organizations also follow the production concept. Many medical and dental practices use assembly-line principles, as do some government agencies such as unemployment offices and license bureaus. Although this way of operating results in handling many cases per hour, it is often thought to be unfriendly and impersonal.

The Product Concept

Another major concept guiding sellers, the **product concept** holds that consumers will favor products that offer the most quality, performance, and features, and therefore the organization should devote its energy to making continuous product improvements. Many manufacturers believe that if they can build a better mousetrap, the world will beat a path to their door.[10] But they are often rudely shocked. Buyers are looking for a solution to a mouse problem, but not necessarily a better mousetrap. The solution might be a chemical spray, an exterminating service, or just a good old house cat. Furthermore, a better mousetrap will not sell unless the manufacturer designs, packages, and prices the new product attractively, places it in convenient distribution channels, brings it to the attention of people who need it, and convinces them that it is a better product.

The product concept leads to marketing myopia. Railroad management thought that users wanted *trains* rather than *transportation* and overlooked the growing challenge of airlines, buses, trucks, and automobiles. Colleges assume that high school graduates want a liberal arts education rather than specific job skills and overlook the increasing challenge of vocational schools.

The Selling Concept

Many organizations follow the **selling concept**, which holds that consumers will not buy enough of the organization's products unless the organization undertakes a large selling and promotion effort. The selling concept is practiced hardest with *unsought goods*, those that buyers normally do not think of buying, such as insurance, encyclopedias, and funeral plots. These industries are good at tracking down prospects and hard-selling them on product benefits. Hard-selling also occurs with sought goods, such as automobiles.

From the moment the customer walks into the showroom, the auto salesman "psychs him out." If the customer likes the floor model, he may be told that there is another customer about to buy it and that he should decide on the spot. If the customer balks at the price, the salesman offers to talk to the manager to get a special concession. The customer waits ten minutes and the salesman returns with "the boss doesn't like it but I got him to agree." The aim is to "work up the customer" to buy on the spot.[11]

The selling concept is also practiced in the nonprofit area. A political party will vigorously sell its candidate to the voters as being a fantastic person for the job. The candidate works in voting precincts from early morning to late evening shaking hands, kissing babies, meeting donors, making speeches. Many dollars are spent on radio and television advertising, posters, and mailings. Any flaws in the candidate are hidden from the public because the aim is to get the sale, not worry about satisfaction after the sale.

The Marketing Concept

The **marketing concept** holds that achieving organizational goals depends on determining the needs and wants of target markets and delivering the desired satisfactions more effectively and efficiently than competitors. This concept is a relatively recent business philosophy. The marketing concept has been stated in colorful ways, such as "Find a need and fill it"; "Make what you can sell instead of trying to sell what you can make"; and "We're not satisfied until you are" (GE). J. C. Penney's motto summarizes this concept: "To do all in our power to pack the customer's dollar full of value, quality, and satisfaction."

The marketing concept: GE promises consumer satisfaction.

FIGURE 1-3
The selling and marketing concepts contrasted

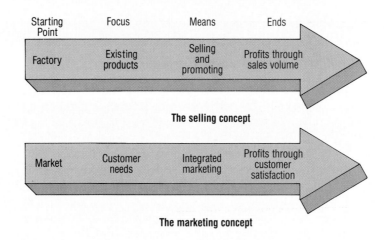

The selling concept and the marketing concept are frequently confused. Theodore Levitt contrasts the two:

> Selling focuses on the needs of the seller; marketing on the needs of the buyer. Selling is preoccupied with the seller's need to convert his product into cash; marketing with the idea of satisfying the needs of the consumer by means of the product and the whole cluster of things associated with creating, delivering and finally consuming it.[12]

Figure 1-3 compares the selling and marketing concepts. The selling concept takes an *inside-out* perspective. It starts with the factory, focuses on the company's existing products, and calls for heavy selling and promoting as a means to achieve profitable sales. The marketing concept takes an *outside-in* perspective. It starts with a well-defined market, focuses on customer needs, coordinates all the marketing activities that affect customers, and produces profits by creating customer satisfaction. Under the marketing concept, companies produce what consumers want and, in this way, satisfy consumers and make profits.

Many companies have adopted the marketing concept. We know that Procter & Gamble, IBM, and McDonald's follow this concept faithfully (see Marketing Highlight 1–3). We also know that the marketing concept is practiced more in consumer-goods companies than in industrial-goods companies and more in large companies than in small companies. Also, many companies claim they practice the concept but do not. They have the forms of marketing—such as a marketing vice-president, product managers, marketing plans, marketing research—but not the substance. Several years of hard work are needed to turn a sales-oriented company into a market-oriented company.[13]

The **societal marketing concept** holds that the organization should determine the needs, wants, and interests of target markets and deliver the desired satisfactions more effectively and efficiently than competitors in a way that maintains or improves the consumer's and the society's well-being. The societal marketing concept is the newest of the five marketing management philosophies.

The societal marketing concept questions whether the pure marketing concept is adequate in an age of environmental problems, resource shortages, rapid population growth, world hunger and poverty, and neglected social services. It asks if the firm that senses, serves, and satisfies individual wants is always doing what is best for

McDonald's Applies the Marketing Concept

McDonald's Corporation, the fast-food hamburger retailer, is a master marketer. With over 10,000 outlets in 50 countries, and over $14 billion in annual sales, McDonald's doubles the sales of its nearest rival, Burger King, and triples those of Wendy's. Nineteen million customers pass through the golden arches every day, and an astounding 96 percent of all Americans ate at McDonald's last year. McDonald's now serves 145 hamburgers per second. Credit for this amazing success belongs to a strong marketing orientation. McDonald's knows how to serve people and to adapt to changing consumer wants.

Before McDonald's, Americans could get hamburgers in restaurants or diners. But consumers often encountered poor-tasting hamburgers, slow and unfriendly service, unattractive decor, unclean conditions, and a noisy atmosphere. In 1955 Ray Kroc, a fifty-two-year-old salesman of milkshake-mixing machines, became excited about a string of seven restaurants owned by Richard and Maurice McDonald. Kroc liked their fast-food restaurant concept and bought the chain for $2.7 million.

Kroc decided to expand the chain by selling franchises to others. As times changed, so did McDonald's. It expanded its sit-down sections, improved decor, launched a breakfast menu, added new food items, and opened new outlets in high-traffic areas.

Kroc's marketing philosophy is captured in McDonald's motto of "Q.S.C. & V.," which stands for quality, service, cleanliness, and value. Customers enter a spotlessly clean restaurant, walk up to a friendly counterperson, quickly receive a good-tasting hamburger, and eat it there or take it out. There are no jukeboxes or telephones to create a teenage hangout. Nor are there any cigarette machines or newspaper racks. McDonald's is a family affair, appealing strongly to children.

McDonald's has mastered the art of serving consumers, and it carefully teaches the basics to all its franchisees and employees. They all take training courses at McDonald's "Hamburger University" in Elk Grove Village, Illinois. They emerge with a degree in "Hamburgerology," with a minor in "French Fries."

McDonald's closely monitors product and service quality through continuous customer surveys and puts great energy into improving hamburger production methods to simplify operations, bring down costs, speed up service, and bring greater value to customers. Beyond this, each McDonald's restaurant works to become a part of its neighborhood through community involvement and service projects.

McDonald's focus on consumers has made it the world's largest food service organization. The company's huge success has been reflected in the increased value of its stock over the years: 250 shares of McDonald's stock purchased for less than $6,000 in 1965 would be worth over a million dollars today!

Source: See Phil Pruitt, "Bigwig of the Burger Biz," *USA Weekend*, November 14–16, 1986, pp. 4–5; and Kathleen Deveny, "Meet Mike Quinlan, Big Mac's Attack CEO," *Business Week*, May 9, 1988, pp. 92–97.

McDonald's motto is "quality, service, cleanliness, and value."

FIGURE 1-4
Three considerations
underlying the societal
marketing concept

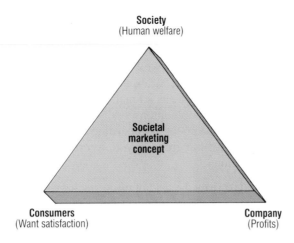

Society
(Human welfare)

Societal
marketing
concept

Consumers
(Want satisfaction)

Company
(Profits)

consumers and society in the long run. The pure marketing concept overlooks possible conflicts between short-run consumer wants and long-run consumer welfare.

Consider the Coca-Cola Company. People see it as being a highly responsible corporation producing fine soft drinks that satisfy consumer tastes. Yet consumer and environmental groups have voiced concerns that Coke has little nutritional value, can harm people's teeth, contains caffeine, and adds to the litter problem with one-way disposable bottles.

This is the kind of situation that led to the societal marketing concept. As Figure 1-4 shows, the societal marketing concept calls upon marketers to balance three considerations in setting their marketing policies. Originally, companies based their marketing decisions largely on short-run company profit. Then they began to recognize the long-run importance of satisfying consumer wants, and this recognition introduced the marketing concept. Now they are beginning to think of society's interests when making decisions. The societal marketing concept calls for balancing all three considerations—company profits, consumer wants, and society's interests. Many companies have made large sales and profit gains by practicing the societal marketing concept.

THE GOALS OF THE MARKETING SYSTEM

Our marketing system consists of the collective marketing activities of tens of thousands of profit and nonprofit organizations. This marketing system affects everyone—buyers, sellers, and many public groups with common characteristics. And the goals of these groups may conflict. *Buyers* want good-quality products at reasonable prices in convenient locations. They want wide brand and feature assortments; helpful, pleasant, and honest salespeople; and strong warranties backed by good follow-up service. The marketing system can greatly affect buyer satisfaction.

Sellers face many challenging decisions when preparing an offer for the market. What consumer groups should be targeted? What do target consumers need, and how should products be designed and priced to meet these needs? What wholesalers and retailers should be used? And what advertising, personal selling, and sales promotion would help sell the product? The market demands a lot. Sellers must apply modern marketing thinking to develop an offer that attracts and satisfies customers.

Legislators, public interest groups, and other *publics* have a strong interest in the marketing activities of business. Do manufacturers make safe and reliable products? Do they describe their products accurately in ads and packaging? Is competition working in the market to provide a reasonable range of quality and price choice? Are manufacturing and packaging activities hurting the environment? The marketing system has a major impact on the quality of life, and various groups of citizens want to make the system work as well as possible. They act as watchdogs of consumer interests and favor consumer education, information, and protection.

The marketing system affects so many people in so many ways that it inevitably stirs controversy. Some people intensely dislike modern marketing activity, charging it with ruining the environment, bombarding the public with senseless ads, creating unnecessary wants, teaching greed to youngsters, and committing several other sins. Consider the following:

> For the past 6,000 years the field of marketing has been thought of as made up of fast-buck artists, con-men, wheeler-dealers, and shoddy-goods distributors. Too many of us have been "taken" by the touts or con-men; and all of us at times have been prodded into buying all sorts of "things" we really did not need, and which we found later on we did not even want.[14]

Others vigorously defend marketing:

> Aggressive marketing policies and practices have been largely responsible for the high material standard of living in America. Today through mass, low-cost marketing we enjoy products which once were considered luxuries, and which still are so classified in many foreign countries.[15]

What should society seek from its marketing system? Four alternative goals have been suggested: maximize consumption, maximize consumer satisfaction, maximize choice, and maximize life quality.

Maximize Consumption

Many business executives believe that the marketing system should stimulate maximum consumption, which will in turn create maximum production, employment, and wealth. This view comes across in such headlines as "IBM Woos Home Computer Buyers With New Generation Models"; "New Pepsi Ads and Promotions Hype Sales"; "Circuit City Moves West, Serves New Markets."

The assumption is that the more people buy and consume, the happier they are. "More is better" is the war cry. Yet some people doubt that increased material goods mean more happiness; they see too many affluent people leading unhappy lives.

Maximize Consumer Satisfaction

Another view holds that the goal of the marketing system is to maximize consumer satisfaction, not consumption. Buying a new car or owning more clothes counts only if this results in more consumer satisfaction. Unfortunately, consumer satisfaction is difficult to measure. First, nobody has figured out how to measure the total satisfaction created by a particular product or marketing activity. Second, the satisfaction that individual consumers get from the "goods" of a product or service must be offset by the "bads," such as pollution and environmental damage. Third, the satisfaction people get from consuming certain goods, such as status goods, depends on few other people having these goods. Thus it is hard to evaluate the marketing system in terms of how much satisfaction it delivers.

Maximize Choice

Some marketers believe that the goal of a marketing system should be to maximize product variety and consumer choice. The marketing system would enable consumers to find those goods that exactly satisfy their tastes. Consumers would be able to maximize their life styles and, therefore, their satisfaction.

Maximizing consumer choice, unfortunately, comes at a cost. First, goods and services will be more expensive, since great variety will increase production and inventory costs. Higher prices will reduce consumers' real income and consumption. Second, the increase in product variety will require greater consumer search and effort. Consumers will have to spend more time learning about and evaluating the different products. Third, more products will not necessarily increase the consumer's real choice. There are many brands of beer in the United States, but most of them taste the same. When a product category contains many brands with few differences, consumers face false choice. Finally, great product variety is not always welcomed by all consumers. For some consumers, too much choice leads to confusion and frustration.

Maximize Life Quality

Many people believe that the goal of a marketing system should be to improve the "quality of life." The quality of life includes the quality, quantity, availability, and cost of goods; the quality of the physical environment; and the quality of the cultural environment. People judge marketing systems not just by the amount of direct consumer satisfaction that is created, but also by the impact of marketing on the quality of the physical and cultural environment. Most people would agree that quality of life is a worthwhile goal for the marketing system, but they recognize that it is not easy to measure and that it means different things to different people.

*T*HE RAPID ADOPTION OF MARKETING

Most people think that marketing is carried on only in large companies operating in capitalistic countries. The truth is that marketing is carried on within and outside the business sector in all kinds of countries.

In the Business Sector

In the business sector, different companies become interested in marketing at different times. General Electric, General Motors, Sears, Procter & Gamble, and Coca-Cola saw marketing's potentialities almost immediately. Marketing spread most rapidly in consumer packaged goods companies, consumer durables companies, and industrial equipment companies—in that order. Producers of such commodities as steel, chemicals, and paper adopted marketing later, and many still have a long way to go.

More recently, consumer service firms, especially airlines and banks, have moved toward modern marketing. Marketing has also attracted the interest of insurance and stock brokerage companies. The latest business groups to take an interest in marketing are professionals such as lawyers, accountants, physicians, and architects. Until recently, professional associations have not allowed their members to engage in price competition, client solicitation, and advertising. But the U.S. antitrust division ruled that these restraints are illegal. Accountants, lawyers, and other professional groups are now allowed to advertise and to price aggressively.

In the International Sector

Marketing is practiced not only in the United States, but in the rest of the world. In fact, several European and Japanese multinationals—companies like Nestle, Siemens, Toyota, and Sony—have often outperformed their U.S. competitors. Multinationals have introduced and spread modern marketing practices throughout the world. As a result, management in smaller countries is beginning to ask: What is marketing? How does it differ from plain selling? How can we introduce marketing into the firm? Will it make a difference?

In socialist countries, marketing has traditionally had a bad name. However, such marketing functions as marketing research, branding, advertising, and sales promotion are now spreading rapidly. The USSR now has over one hundred state-operated advertising agencies and marketing research firms. Soviet consumers regularly see newspaper, magazine, and television ads touting everything from high-fashion to high-tech. Retail stores hold government sponsored sales. Several companies in Poland and Hungary have marketing departments, and several socialist universities teach marketing.[16]

In the Nonprofit Sector

Marketing is currently attracting the interest of nonprofit organizations such as colleges, hospitals, police departments, museums, and symphonies. Consider the following developments:

> Facing low enrollments and rising costs, many private colleges are using marketing to attract students and funds. St. Joseph's College in Renssalaer, Indiana, obtained a 40 percent increase in freshman enrollments by advertising in Seventeen and on several rock radio stations. Some other institutions are designing more complete marketing programs by analyzing their environments and markets, selecting target segments, and preparing complete marketing plans to position themselves in chosen markets.
>
> As hospital costs and room rates soar, many hospitals face underutilization, especially in their maternity and pediatrics sections. Many are taking steps toward marketing. A Philadelphia hospital, competing for maternity patients, offered a steak and champagne dinner with candlelight for new parents. St. Mary's Medical Center in Evanston, Indiana, uses innovative billboards to promote its emergency care service. Other hospitals, in an effort to attract physicians, have installed services such as saunas, chauffeurs, and private tennis courts.[17]

Marketing in the nonprofit sector: the United States government is now one of the country's largest advertisers.

These organizations have marketplace problems. Their administrators are struggling to keep them alive in the face of changing consumer attitudes and smaller financial resources. Many such institutions have turned to marketing as a possible answer to their problems.

Even U.S. government agencies are showing an increased interest in marketing. The U.S. Postal Service and Amtrak have marketing plans for their operations. The U.S. Army has a marketing plan to attract recruits and is one of the top advertising spenders in the country. Other government agencies are now marketing energy conservation, nonsmoking, and other public causes.

■ SUMMARY

Marketing touches everyone's life. It is the means by which a standard of living is developed and delivered to a people. Many people confuse marketing with selling, but marketing occurs long before and after the selling event. Marketing actually combines many activities—marketing research, product development, distribution, pricing, advertising, personal selling, and others—designed to sense, serve, and satisfy consumer needs while meeting the organization's goals.

Marketing is the social and managerial process by which individuals and groups obtain what they need and want through creating and exchanging products and value with others. The key concepts of marketing are needs, wants, demands, products, exchange, transactions, and markets.

Marketing management is the analysis, planning, implementation, and control of programs designed to create, build, and maintain beneficial exchanges with target markets for the purpose of achieving organizational objectives. Marketers must be good at managing the level, timing, and composition of demand, since actual demand can be different from what the organization wants.

Marketing management can be conducted under five different marketing philosophies. The production concept holds that consumers will favor products that are available at low cost, and therefore management's task is to improve production efficiency and bring down prices. The product concept holds that consumers favor quality products, and therefore little promotional effort is required. The selling concept holds that consumers will not buy enough of the company's products unless they are stimulated through heavy selling and promotion. The marketing concept holds that a company should research the needs and wants of a well-defined target market and deliver the desired satisfactions. The societal marketing concept holds that the company should generate customer satisfaction and long-run societal well-being as the key to achieving organizational goals.

Marketing practices have a major impact on people in our society. Different goals have been proposed for a marketing system, such as maximizing consumption, consumer satisfaction, consumer choice, or life quality. Many people believe that marketing's goal should be to enhance the quality of life and that the means should be the societal marketing concept.

Interest in marketing is growing as more organizations in the business sector, in the international sector, and in the nonprofit sector recognize how marketing can improve performance.

■ QUESTIONS FOR DISCUSSION

1. Why should *you* study marketing?

2. Do you intend to *market* yourself or to *sell* yourself when looking for a job after graduation? *In Search of Excellence* describes marketing principles practiced by many top companies. How can you apply these principles to improve your chances of landing the job you want?

3. In Figure 1–1, are there different "starting points" on the circle for different marketing management philosophies? Are there points on the circle where the arrows could go both ways? Give an example.

4. Historian Arnold Toynbee and economist John Kenneth Galbraith have argued that the desires stimulated by marketing efforts are not genuine: "A man who is hungry need never be told of his need for food." Is this a valid criticism of marketing? Why or why not?

5. How do the notions of products, exchanges, transactions, and markets apply when you buy a soft drink from a vending machine? Do they also apply when you vote for the political candidate of your choice? Explain your answers.

6. How can an organization practice the marketing concept when it is faced with negative demand? Latent demand? Overfull demand? Give examples.

7. Identify organizations in your town that practice the production concept, the product concept, and the selling concept. Choose one of these organizations and suggest how it could become more marketing oriented. Be specific.

8. Procter & Gamble is credited with being a good "listener." In what ways might a company listen to the

consumer? How does this relate to a company's record of success?

9. According to economist Milton Friedman, "Few trends could so thoroughly undermine the very foundations of our free society as the acceptance by corporate officials of a social responsibility other than to make as much money for their stockholders as possible." Do you agree or disagree? How would society be affected if marketers decided that their only responsibility was to maximize profits?

10. Florida and other states have attempted to tax advertising, many proposals have been made to end advertising for cigarettes, and the Supreme Court in 1986 upheld a ban on advertising for a legal service. Do these efforts conflict with the goals of our marketing system? Does your answer depend on which goal you think is appropriate for our society?

11. Why have many nonprofit organizations adopted marketing techniques in recent years? How does your school market itself to attract new students?

■ KEY TERMS

Demands Human wants that are backed by buying power.

Exchange The act of obtaining a desired object from someone by offering something in return.

Human need A state of felt deprivation in a person.

Human want The form that a human need takes as shaped by culture and individual personality.

Market The set of actual and potential buyers of a product.

Marketing A social and managerial process by which individuals and groups obtain what they need and want through creating and exchanging products and value with others.

Marketing concept The marketing management philosophy that holds that achieving organizational goals depends on determining the needs and wants of target markets and delivering the desired satisfactions more effectively and efficiently than competitors.

Marketing management The analysis, planning, implementation, and control of programs designed to create, build, and maintain beneficial exchanges with target markets for the purpose of achieving organizational objectives.

Product Anything that can be offered to a market for attention, acquisition, use, or consumption that might satisfy a need or want.

Product concept The marketing management philosophy that consumers will favor products that offer the most quality, performance, and features, and therefore the organization should devote its energy to making continuous product improvements.

Production concept The marketing management philosophy that consumers will favor products that are available and highly affordable, and therefore management should focus on improving production and distribution efficiency.

Selling concept The marketing management philosophy that consumers will not buy enough of the organization's products unless the organization undertakes a large selling and promotion effort.

Societal marketing concept The marketing management philosophy that the organization should determine the needs, wants, and interests of target markets and deliver the desired satisfactions more effectively and efficiently than competitors in a way that maintains or improves the consumer's and society's well-being.

Transaction A trade between two parties that involves at least two things of value, agreed upon conditions, a time of agreement, and a place of agreement.

■ REFERENCES

1. Thomas J. Peters and Robert H. Waterman, Jr., *In Search of Excellence: Lessons from America's Best-Run Companies* (New York: Harper & Row, 1982).

2. Thomas J. Peters and Nancy Austin, *A Passion for Excellence: The Leadership Difference* (New York: Random House, 1985).

3. "Business Planning in the Eighties: The New Competitiveness of American Corporations," a study conducted by Yankelovich, Skelly, & White for Coopers and Lybrand, 1984.

4. See E. S. Ely, "Room at the Top: American Companies Turn to Marketers to Lead Them Through the '80s," *Madison Avenue*, September 1984, p. 57.

5. Peter F. Drucker, *Management: Tasks, Responsibilities, Practices* (New York: Harper & Row, 1973), pp. 64–65.

6. Here are some other definitions: "Marketing is the performance of business activities that direct the flow of goods and services from producer to consumer or user." "Marketing is getting the right goods and services to the right people at the right place at the right time at the right price with the right communication and promotion." "Marketing is the creation and delivery of a standard of living." In 1985, the American Marketing Association approved this definition: "Marketing is the process of planning and executing the conception, pricing, promotion, and distributing of ideas, goods, and services to create exchanges that satisfy individual and organizational objectives."

7. See Theodore Levitt's classic article, "Marketing Myopia," *Harvard Business Review*, July–August 1960, pp. 45–56.

8. For more discussion on marketing as an exchange

process, see Franklin S. Houston and Jule B. Gassenheimer, "Marketing and Exchange," *Journal of Marketing*, October 1987, pp. 3–18.

9. The number of transactions in a decentralized exchange system is given by N(N-1)/2. With four persons, this means 4(4 - 1)/2=6 transactions. In a centralized exchange system, the number of transactions is given by N, here 4. Thus a centralized exchange system reduces the number of transactions needed for exchange.

10. Ralph Waldo Emerson offered this advice: "If a man . . . makes a better mousetrap . . . the world will beat a path to his door." Several companies, however, have built better mousetraps yet failed. One was a laser mousetrap costing $1,500. People do not automatically learn about new products, believe product claims, or willingly pay a higher price.

11. See Irving J. Rein, *Rudy's Red Wagon: Communication Strategies in Contemporary Society* (Glenview, IL: Scott-Foresman, 1972).

12. Levitt, "Marketing Myopia."

13. For more on the marketing concept, see Theodore Levitt, "Marketing and Its Discontents," *Across the Board*, February 1984, pp. 42–48; and Franklin S. Houston, "The Marketing Concept: What It Is and What It Is Not," *Journal of Marketing*, Vol. 50 (April 1986), pp. 81–87.

14. Richard N. Farmer, "Would You Want Your Daughter to Marry a Marketing Man?" *Journal of Marketing*, January 1967, p. 1.

15. William J. Stanton and Charles Futrell, *Fundamentals of Marketing*, 8th ed. (New York: McGraw-Hill, 1987), p. 7.

16. See Elisa Tinsley, "The Soviet Promise of Expanded Markets: Consumer Demand Growing," *Advertising Age*, January 6, 1986, p. 38.

17. For other examples, and for a good review of nonprofit marketing, see Philip Kotler and Alan R. Andreasen, *Strategic Marketing for Nonprofit Organizations* (Englewood Cliffs, NJ: Prentice Hall, 1987).

2 Strategic Planning and Marketing's Role in the Organization

IN the 1970s, slow growth and low profits sent many food companies on the acquisition trail, seeking to add more promising nonfood products and businesses to their portfolios. Following this trend, Kraft Inc. merged in 1980 with Dart Industries to become Dart & Kraft, a huge company made up of many smaller companies, divisions, and brands with sales totaling almost $10 billion a year. Kraft's strategic planners hoped that Dart's nonfood businesses would add zip to Kraft's then-stodgy food operations, producing more rapid growth and higher profits.

Most consumers knew a lot about the Kraft in Dart & Kraft. Brands such as Miracle Whip, Velveeta, Kraft Salad Dressings, Parkay, Cracker Barrel, Philadelphia Brand, Sealtest, and Breyers are household words to most of us. Most consumers knew little about the Dart in Dart & Kraft. Some of the brands are familiar, but few of us would have connected them with Dart & Kraft. They included Tupperware, Duracell, Hobart, Kitchen Aid, and West Bend. Dart & Kraft also included many little-known companies such as Universal Packaging (cardboard cartons), Wilsonart (laminates and adhesives), Hospital Products Company (disposable medical and surgical products), and Absorbent Cotton Company (cotton and gauze dressings).

The new Dart & Kraft faced many difficult strategic planning questions. What new businesses should be added to the company's portfolio, and which old ones should be dropped? Which current business units should receive more emphasis, and which should receive less? Each unit had special strengths and needs. Some were very successful in mature markets—for example, Dart & Kraft held almost half of the U.S. cheese market. Other units were strong in smaller but faster growing markets—Celestial Seasonings had 40 percent of the growing herbal teas market. Still other units were mired in less attractive, slow-growth markets, such as bulk edible oils and cardboard cartons.

Dart & Kraft set out to shed less attractive products while building or buying more profitable ones in more attractive markets. Between 1980 and 1986, Dart & Kraft pruned its product lines by 25 percent, sold off 30 businesses (such as its fluid milk business, and its Kitchen Aid appliances), and used the cash to buy twenty-five more promising companies (in areas such as fitness equipment food service distributing and frozen foods).

By 1986, because of more efficient operations and a number of successful new food products, Kraft's food business was surging and profitable. The retail food division, though producing only about 37 percent of the company's sales, contributed nearly 60 percent of company profits. Earnings from Tupperware, West-Bend, and other former Dart businesses, however, were falling off. The Dart nonfood businesses that Kraft had acquired to stimulate growth and profits were now holding the company back. So in 1986, Kraft management made its biggest strategic planning move yet. Like many other food companies that had diversified broadly in the 1970s, Kraft now moved back to the basics. Only six years after merging Kraft with Dart, the two were split into separate companies again. The new Kraft Inc. consisted of the Kraft food operations plus the fast-growing Duracell battery business, totaling about $9.5 billion in annual sales. The remaining Dart & Kraft businesses, including Tupperware, Hobart, West Bend, and Wilsonart, were spun off to shareholders as a separate $1.8 billion company called Premark International. Kraft completed its move back to food when it shed Durcell in 1988.

The splitting apart of the two companies after so short a time made some analysts question the wisdom of the original merger. Kraft managers, however, claim that the merger worked well. They point out that shareholders profited handsomely—a $1 investment in Dart & Kraft stock in 1980 was worth over $5 by mid-1986. But new challenges and opportunities called for new strategic directions. By splitting up the company, Kraft shed some slower growing, less profitable businesses and concentrated its resources on its more promising core food businesses. The postmerger Kraft is healthier, faster-growing, and more profitable than the premerger Kraft.

Thus in only six years, Kraft made two dramatic strategic planning shifts in an attempt to best match the company to changing market opportunities. And it will continue to plan for market changes yet to come. Large companies cannot survive in their fast-changing environments by making last-minute decisions and trusting to luck. They must use flexible strategic planning to position their companies for long-run success.[1]

Chapter Objectives   *After reading this chapter, you should be able to:*

1. Discuss company-wide strategic planning and its four steps.
2. Describe how companies develop mission statements and objectives.
3. Explain how companies evaluate and develop their "business portfolios."
4. Discuss marketing's role in strategic planning.
5. Describe the marketing management process and the forces that influence it.

ALL companies must look ahead and develop long-term strategies to meet the changing conditions in their industries. No one strategy is best for all companies. Each company must find the game plan that makes the most sense given its situation, opportunities, objectives, and resources. The hard task of selecting an overall company strategy for long-run survival and growth is called *strategic planning*.

Marketing plays an important role in strategic planning. It provides information and other inputs to help prepare the strategic plan. In turn, strategic planning defines marketing's role in the organization. Guided by the strategic plan, marketing works with other departments in the organization to help achieve overall strategic objectives.

In this chapter, we will look first at the organization's overall strategic planning. Next we will discuss marketing's role in the organization as defined by the overall strategic plan. Then we will look at the marketing management process—the process that marketers undertake to carry out their role in the organization.

OVERVIEW OF PLANNING

Benefits of Planning

Many companies operate without formal plans. In new companies, many managers are so busy that they have no time for planning. In mature companies, many managers argue that they have done well without formal planning and therefore it cannot be too important. They resist taking the time to prepare a written plan. They argue that the marketplace changes too fast for a plan to be useful—it would end up collecting dust.

Yet formal planning can yield many benefits. It encourages management to think ahead systematically and improves interactions between company executives. It causes the company to sharpen its objectives and policies, leads to better coordination of company efforts, and provides clearer performance standards for control. And sound planning better prepares the company for sudden developments.

Approaches to Planning

Management can adopt one of three possible approaches to planning. In the first approach, *top-down planning*, top management sets goals and plans for all the lower levels of management. It assumes that employees cannot or will not take responsibility and prefer to be directed. In the opposite approach, *bottom-up planning*, the various organizational units prepare their own goals and plans and send them on to higher management levels for approval. This approach assumes that employees like responsibility and that they will be more creative and committed if they participate in the planning. Most companies use a third approach known as *goals down-plans up planning*. In this approach, top management looks at the company's opportunities and requirements and sets corporate goals for the year. The various company units then develop plans to help the company reach the corporate goals. These plans, when approved by top management, become the final plan.

Kinds of Plans

Companies usually prepare annual plans, long-range plans, and strategic plans. The *annual plan* describes the current marketing situation, company objectives, the marketing strategy for the year, the action program, budgets, and controls. Top management approves this plan and uses it to coordinate marketing activities with production, finance, and other areas of the company.

The *long-range plan* describes the major factors and forces affecting the organization over the next several years. It includes long-term objectives, the major marketing strategies that will be used to attain them, and the resources required. The long-range plan is reviewed and updated each year so that the company always has a current long-range plan. For example, American Hospital Supply has a "rolling" five-year plan. Its annual plan is a detailed version of the first year of the long-range plan. Managers prepare a five-year plan for each product early in the year and an annual plan later in the year. The five-year plan is revised each year because the marketing environment changes and planning assumptions need to be reviewed.

The company's annual and long-range plans deal with current businesses and how to keep them going. Management must also plan which businesses the company should stay in and which new ones it should pursue. The environment is full of surprises, and management must design the company to withstand shocks. *Strategic planning* involves adapting the firm to take advantage of opportunities in its constantly changing environment.

S TRATEGIC PLANNING

Strategic planning sets the stage for the rest of the planning in the firm. We define it as follows:

> **Strategic planning** is the process of developing and maintaining a strategic fit between the organizations' goals and capabilities and its changing marketing opportunities. It relies on developing a clear company mission, supporting objectives, a sound business portfolio, and coordinated functional strategies.

The steps in the strategic planning process are shown in Figure 2-1. At the corporate level, the company first defines its overall purpose and mission. This mission is then turned into detailed supporting objectives that guide the whole company. Next, top management decides what portfolio of businesses and products is best for the company, and how much support to give each one. Each business and product unit must in turn develop detailed marketing and other functional plans that support the company-wide plan. Thus marketing planning occurs at the business unit, product, and market levels. It supports company strategic planning with more detailed planning for specific marketing opportunities. We discuss each of the strategic planning steps in more detail below.

Defining the Company Mission

An organization exists to accomplish something. At first it has a clear purpose or mission, but over time, as the organization grows and adds new products and markets, its mission may become unclear. Or the mission may remain clear, but some managers may no longer be interested in it. Or the mission may remain clear, but may no longer be best given new conditions in the environment.

When management senses that the organization is drifting, it must renew its search for purpose. It is time to ask: What is our business? Who is the customer? What is value to the customer? What will our business be? What should our business be? These simple-sounding questions are among the most difficult the company will ever have to answer. Successful companies continuously raise these questions and answer them carefully and fully.

Many organizations develop formal mission statements that answer these questions. A **mission statement** is a statement of the organization's purpose, what it wants to accomplish in the larger environment. Writing a formal company mission statement is not easy. Some organizations will spend a year or more trying to prepare a good statement of their firm's purpose. In the process they will discover a lot about themselves and their potential opportunities. A clear mission statement guides people in the organization so that they can work independently and yet collectively toward overall organizational goals.

FIGURE 2-1
Steps in strategic planning

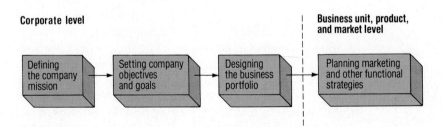

Companies traditionally defined their business in product terms, such as "We manufacture video games," or in technological terms, such as "We are a chemical-processing firm." But some years ago, Theodore Levitt proposed that *market definitions* of a business are better than product or technological definitions.[2] Products and technologies eventually become out of date, but basic market needs may last forever. A market-oriented mission statement defines the business in terms of serving particular customer groups or needs. Consider this example:

> In the early 1980s, consumers began to tire of video games. In 1983 alone, the industry lost over $1.5 billion. Many companies which had defined themselves as "video game producers" fell on hard times or withdrew from the market. But Bally Manufacturing, a leader in video arcade games and famous for such video games as PacMan and Space Invaders, had defined its business as "leisure and entertainment." Guided by this definition it had purchased Health and Tennis Corporation of America (a chain of health clubs) and Six Flags Corporation (entertainment parks). When the crunch hit the video games industry, the impact on Bally was lessened by the fact that video games provided less than 50 percent of sales.[3]

Bally defines its mission as leisure and entertainment.

Management should avoid making its mission too narrow or too broad. A lead pencil manufacturer that says it is in the communication equipment business is stating its mission too broadly. Mission statements should be specific, realistic, and motivating. Many mission statements are written for public relations purposes and lack specific, workable guidelines. The statement "We want to be the leading company in this industry producing the highest-quality products with the best service at the lowest prices" sounds good but is vague and full of contradictions. It will not help the company make tough decisions.

Setting Company Objectives and Goals

The company's mission can be turned into detailed supporting objectives for each level of management. Each manager will have objectives and be responsible for reaching them.

As an illustration, the International Minerals and Chemical Corporation is in many businesses, including the fertilizer business. The fertilizer division does not say that its mission is to produce fertilizer. Instead, it says that its mission is to "increase agricultural productivity." This mission leads to a hierarchy of objectives: business objectives, marketing objectives, and, finally, a marketing strategy (see Figure 2-2). The mission of increasing agricultural productivity leads to the company's business objective of researching new fertilizers that promise higher yields. But research is expensive and requires improved profits to plow back into research programs. So a major objective becomes "to improve profits."

Profits can be improved by increasing sales or reducing costs. Sales can be increased by enlarging the company's share of the U.S. market and by entering new foreign markets. These become the company's current marketing objectives.

Marketing strategies must be developed to support these marketing objectives. To raise its U.S. market share, the company will increase its product's availability and promotion. To enter new foreign markets, the company will cut prices and call on large farms abroad. These are the broad marketing strategies.

FIGURE 2-2
Hierarchy of objectives for the International Minerals and Chemical Corporation, Fertilizer Division

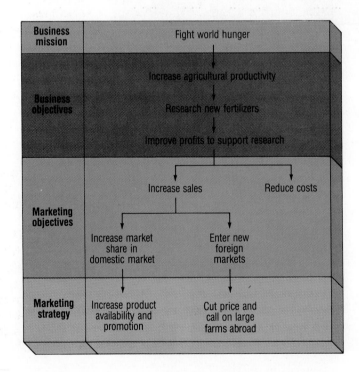

Each marketing strategy would have to be outlined in greater detail. For example, increasing the product's promotion will call for more salespeople and advertising. In this way the firm's mission is translated into a set of objectives for the current period. The objectives should be as specific as possible. The objective "increase our market share" is not as useful as "increase our market share to 15 percent by the end of the second year."

Designing the Business Portfolio

Guided by the company's mission statement and objectives, management must then plan its business portfolio. A company's **business portfolio** is the collection of businesses and products that make up the company. The best business portfolio is the one that best fits the company's strengths and weaknesses to opportunities in the environment. The company must (1) analyze the current business portfolio and decide which businesses should receive more or less investment, and (2) develop growth strategies for adding new products or businesses to the portfolio.

Analyzing the Current Business Portfolio

The major tool in strategic planning is business *portfolio analysis*, whereby management evaluates the businesses making up the company. The company will want to put strong resources into its more profitable businesses and phase down or drop its weaker businesses. It can keep its portfolio of businesses up-to-date by withdrawing from declining businesses and strengthening or adding growing businesses. For example, in recent years, Kraft has strengthened its portfolio by selling off many less attractive nonfood businesses while adding such promising ones as Lender's Bagel Bakery, Frusen Gladje and Charl's ice creams, Tombstone frozen pizza, and All-American Gourmet frozen foods.

Management's first step is to identify the key businesses making up the company. These can be called the strategic business units. A **strategic business unit (SBU)** is a unit of the company that has a separate mission and objectives and that can be planned independently from other company businesses. An SBU can be a company division, a product line within a division, or sometimes a single product or brand.

Identifying SBUs can be very difficult. In a large corporation, should SBUs be defined at the level of companies, divisions, product lines, or brands? At Kraft, for example, is the U.S. Retail Food Division an SBU, or is the Miracle Whip brand an SBU? Many companies use a hierarchy of portfolios. For example, General Electric has a five-level portfolio structure—individual products combine to make up product-line portfolios, which combine to form market-segment portfolios, which make up SBUs, which are combined into business-sector portfolios. The corporate portfolio includes all lower-level portfolios. Defining basic business units for portfolio analysis is often a complex task.

The next step in business portfolio analysis calls for management to assess the attractiveness of its various SBUs and decide how much support each deserves. In some companies, this process takes place informally. Management looks at the company's collection of businesses or products and judges how much each SBU should contribute and receive. Other companies use formal portfolio planning methods. The purpose of strategic planning is to find ways in which the company can best use its strengths to take advantage of attractive opportunities in the environment. Most standard portfolio analysis methods, therefore, evaluate SBUs on two important dimensions—the attractiveness of the SBU's market or industry, and the strength of the SBU's position in that market or industry. The two best-known of these portfolio planning methods are those developed by the Boston Consulting Group, a leading management consulting firm, and by General Electric.[4]

FIGURE 2-3
The BCG growth-share
matrix

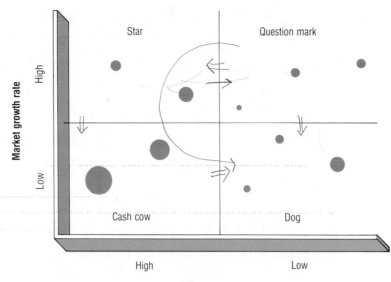

THE BOSTON CONSULTING GROUP APPROACH. Using the Boston Consulting Group (BCG) approach, a company classifies all its SBUs in the **growth-share matrix** shown in Figure 2-3. On the vertical axis, *market growth rate* provides a measure of market attractiveness. On the horizontal axis, *relative market share* serves as a measure of company strength in the market. By dividing the growth-share matrix in the way indicated, four types of SBUs can be distinguished.

- **Stars.** Stars are high-growth, high-share businesses or products. They often need heavy investment to finance their rapid growth. Eventually their growth will slow down, and they will turn into cash cows.

- **Cash cows.** Cash cows are low-growth, high-share businesses or products. These established and successful SBUs need less investment to hold their market share. They produce a lot of cash that the company uses to pay its bills and to support other SBUs that need investment.

- **Question marks.** Question marks are low-share business units in high-growth markets. They require a lot of cash to hold their share, let alone increase it. Management has to think hard about which question marks it should try to build into stars and which should be phased out.

- **Dogs.** Dogs are low-growth, low-share businesses and products. They may generate enough cash to maintain themselves, but do not promise to be large sources of cash.

The ten circles in the growth-share matrix represent a company's ten current SBUs. The company has two stars, two cash cows, three question marks, and three dogs. The areas of the circles are proportional to the SBU's dollar sales. This company is in fair shape, although not in good shape. Fortunately it has two good-sized cash cows, whose income helps finance the company's question marks, stars, and dogs. The company should take some decisive action concerning its dogs and its question marks. The picture would be worse if the company had no stars, or had too many dogs, or had only one weak cash cow.

Once it has classified its SBUs, the company must determine what role each will play in the future. One of four strategies can be pursued for each SBU. The company can invest more in the business unit in order to *build* its share. Or it can invest just enough to *hold* the SBU's share at the current level. It can *harvest* the SBU, milking its short-term cash flow regardless of the long-term effect. Finally, the company can *divest* the SBU by selling it or phasing it out and using the resources elsewhere.

As time passes, SBUs change their positions in the growth-share matrix. Each SBU has a life. Many SBUs start out as question marks, and move into the star category if they succeed. They later become cash cows as market growth falls, then finally die off or turn into dogs toward the end of their life cycle. The company needs to add new products and units continuously so that some of them will become stars and, eventually, cash cows to help finance other SBUs.

THE GENERAL ELECTRIC APPROACH. General Electric introduced a comprehensive portfolio planning tool called a **strategic business-planning grid** (see Figure 2-4). Like the BCG approach, it uses a matrix with two dimensions—one representing industry attractiveness (the vertical axis) and one representing company strength in the industry (the horizontal axis). The best businesses are those located in highly attractive industries where the company has high business strength.

The GE approach considers many factors besides market growth rate as part of industry attractiveness. It uses an industry attractiveness index made up of market size, market growth rate, industry profit margin, amount of competition, seasonality and cyclicality of demand, and industry cost structure. Each of these factors is rated and combined in an index of industry attractiveness. For our purposes, an industry's attractiveness will be described as high, medium, or low. As an example, Kraft has identified numerous highly attractive industries—natural foods, specialty frozen foods, physical fitness products, and others. It has withdrawn from less attractive industries such as bulk oils and cardboard packaging.

For *business strength*, the GE approach again uses an index rather than simply a measure of relative market share. The business strength index includes such factors as the company's relative market share, price competitiveness, product quality, customer and market knowledge, sales effectiveness, and geographic advantages. These factors are rated and combined in an index of business strength. Business strength can be described as strong, average, or weak. Thus Kraft has substantial business strength in food and related industries but is relatively weak in the home appliances industry.

The grid is divided into three zones. The green cells at the upper left show strong SBUs in which the company should invest and grow. The yellow diagonal cells contain SBUs that are medium in overall attractiveness. The company should maintain its level of investment in these SBUs. The three red cells at the lower

FIGURE 2-4
General Electric's strategic business-planning grid

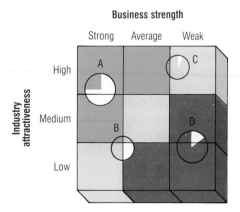

right indicate SBUs that are low in overall attractiveness. The company should give serious thought to harvesting or divesting them.

The circles represent four company SBUs; the areas of the circles are proportional to the sizes of the industries in which these SBUs compete. The pie slices within the circles represent each SBU's market share. Thus circle A represents a company SBU with a 75 percent market share in a good-sized, highly attractive industry in which the company has strong business strength. Circle B represents an SBU that has a 50 percent market share, but the industry is not very attractive. Circles C and D represent two other company SBUs in industries where the company has small market shares and not much business strength. Altogether, the company should build A, maintain B, and make some hard decisions on what to do with C and D.

Management would also plot the projected positions of the SBUs with and without changes in strategies. By comparing current and projected business grids, management can identify the major strategic issues and opportunities it faces.

PROBLEMS WITH MATRIX APPROACHES. The BCG, GE, and other matrix approaches revolutionized strategic planning in the 1970s. But such approaches have limitations. They can be difficult, time-consuming, and costly to implement. Management may find it hard to define SBUs and to measure market share and growth. Also, these approaches focus on classifying current businesses, but they provide little advice for future planning. Management must still use judgment to set the business objectives for each SBU, to decide what resources each will be given, and to figure out which new businesses should be added. These formal approaches can also lead the company to place too much emphasis on market-share growth or growth through entry into attractive new markets. Using these approaches, many companies plunged into unrelated and new high-growth businesses that they did not know how to manage, with very bad results. At the same time, they were often too quick to abandon, sell, or milk to death their healthy mature businesses.

Despite these and other problems, and though many companies have dropped formal matrix methods in favor of more customized approaches better suited to their situations, most companies remain firmly committed to strategic planning. Roughly 75 percent of the *Fortune 500* companies practice some form of portfolio planning.[5] Such analysis is no cure-all for finding the best strategy. But it can help management to understand the company's overall situation, to see how each business or product contributes, to assign resources to its businesses, and to orient the company for future success. When used properly, strategic planning is just one important aspect of overall strategic management, a way of thinking about how to manage a business.[6]

Developing Growth Strategies

In designing the business portfolio, management goes beyond evaluating current businesses. It also finds future businesses and products the company should consider. One useful device for identifying growth opportunities is the **product/market expansion grid**.[7] This grid is shown in Figure 2-5. Below, we apply it to Kraft.

MARKET PENETRATION. First, Kraft management considers whether the company's major brands can achieve deeper **market penetration**—more sales to present customers without changing the products in any way. For example, to increase Kraft's dairycase sales, the company might cut prices, increase advertising, get Kraft products into more stores, or obtain better shelf positions for Kraft. Basically, Kraft management would like to increase usage by current customers and attract customers of other brands to Kraft.

MARKET DEVELOPMENT. Second, Kraft management considers possibilities for **mar-

FIGURE 2-5
Market opportunity
identification through
the product/market
expansion grid

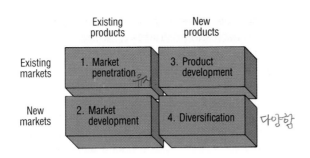

ket development—identifying and developing new markets for current products. For example, managers at Kraft review *demographic markets*—infants, preschoolers, teenagers, young adults, senior citizens—to see if any of these groups can be encouraged to buy or to buy more Kraft products. The managers look at *institutional markets*—restaurants, food services, hospitals—to see if sales to these buyers can be increased. And the managers review *geographical markets*—France, Thailand, India—to see if these markets can be developed. All of these are market development strategies.

PRODUCT DEVELOPMENT. Third, management considers **product development**—offering modified or new products for current markets. Kraft products could be

Market development: Jockey enters the women's market.

AMERICAN BUSINESS GETS BACK TO THE BASICS

During the sixties and seventies, strategic planners in many American companies got expansion fever. It seemed that everyone wanted to get bigger and grow faster by broadening their business portfolios. Companies milked their stodgy but profitable core businesses to get cash needed to acquire glamorous, faster-growing businesses in more attractive industries. It didn't seem to matter that many of the acquired businesses fit poorly with old ones, or that they operated in markets unfamiliar to company management.

Thus many firms exploded into huge conglomerates, sometimes containing hundreds of unrelated products and businesses operating in a dozen diverse industries. Managing these smorgasbord portfolios often proved difficult. The conglomerate managers soon learned that it was tough to run businesses in industries they knew little about. Many newly acquired businesses bogged down under added layers of corporate management and increased administrative costs. Meanwhile, profitable core businesses that financed the acquisitions withered from lack of investment and management attention.

By the mid-eighties, as attempt after attempt at scatter-gun diversification foundered, acquisition fever gave way to a new philosophy—getting back to the basics. The new trend has many names—narrowing the focus, sticking to your knitting, the contraction craze, restructuring, the urge to purge. They all mean narrowing the company's market focus and getting the firm back to the basics of serving one or a few core industries that it knows best. The company sheds businesses that don't fit its narrowed focus, and rebuilds by concentrating resources on other businesses that do. The result is a smaller but more focused company, a more muscular firm serving fewer markets but serving them much better. Companies in all industries are getting back in focus and shedding unrelated operations. According to one survey, 56 percent of all Fortune 500 companies have begun the slimming-down process during the last five years. Some companies have taken drastic steps. For example, during the 1970s huge Gulf & Western acquired businesses in dozens of diverse industries ranging from auto products and industrial equipment to apparel and furniture, from cement and cigars to race-tracks and video games. But since 1983, it has focused on entertainment, information, and financial services, purging the company of over fifty operations that made up nearly half its sales. Similarly, ITT, after diversifying wildly during the sixties and seventies, is divesting $1.7 billion worth of businesses that don't fit its new focus.

Several food companies have made strong moves back to the bread-and-butter basics. Cured of its acquisition fever, Kraft refocused on food, divesting most of the nonfood businesses acquired when it merged with Dart Industries. Quaker Oats sold off its specialty retailing businesses—Jos. A. Banks (clothing), Brookstone (tools), and Eyelab (optical)—and will probably sell its profitable Fisher-Price toy operation. It used the proceeds to strengthen current food brands and to acquire the Golden Grain Macaroni Company (Rice-a-Roni and Noodle-a-Roni) and Gaines Foods (pet foods), whose products strongly complement Quaker's. General Mills ended twenty years of diversification by lopping off most of its nonfood businesses and moving back to the kitchen. It sold such companies as Izod (fashions), Monet (jewelry), Parker Brothers (games), and Kenner (toys) while increasing investment in its basic consumer food brands (Wheaties and other cereals, Betty Crocker cake mixes, Gorton's seafoods, Gold Medal flour), restaurants (Red Lobster, Darryl's), and specialty retailing (Talbots, Eddie Bauer).

These and other companies have concluded that bigger is not always better and that fast-growing businesses in attractive industries are not good investments if they spread the company's resources too thin, or if the company's managers can't run them properly. They've learned that a company without market focus—one that tries to serve too many diverse markets—might end up serving few markets well.

Sources: See Stewart Toy, "Splitting Up: The Other Side of Merger Mania," *Business Week*, July 1, 1985, pp. 50–55; Myron Magnet, "Restructuring Really Works," *Fortune*, March 2, 1987, pp. 38–46; Thomas Moore, "Old-Line Industry Shapes Up," *Fortune*, April 27, 1987, pp. 23–32; David Lieberman and Joe Weber, "Gulf & Western: From Grab Bag to Lean, Mean, Marketing Machine," *Business Week*, September 14, 1987, pp. 152–56; and Walter Kiechel III, "Corporate Strategy for the 1990s," *Fortune*, February 29, 1988, pp. 34–42.

offered in new sizes, or with new ingredients, or in new packaging, all representing possible product modifications. Kraft could also launch new brands to appeal to different users, or it could launch other food products that its current customers might buy. All these are product development strategies.

DIVERSIFICATION. Fourth, Kraft considers **diversification,** starting up or buying businesses that are entirely outside of its current products and markets. For example, the company's recent moves into such "hot" industries as fitness equipment and health foods represent diversification. Some companies try to identify the most attractive emerging industries. They feel that half the secret of success is to enter attractive industries instead of trying to be efficient in an unattractive industry. But many companies that diversified too broadly in the sixties and seventies are now narrowing their market focus and getting back to the basics of serving one or a few industries that they know best (see Marketing Highlight 2–1).

Planning Functional Strategies

The company's strategic plan establishes what kinds of businesses the company will be in and its objectives for each. Then within each business unit, more detailed planning must take place. Each functional department—marketing, finance, accounting, purchasing, manufacturing, personnel, and others—plays an important role in the strategic planning process. First, the departments provide information for strategic planning. Then management in each business unit prepares a plan that states the role each department will play. The plan shows how all the functional areas will work together to accomplish strategic objectives.

Each functional department deals with different publics to obtain the inputs the business needs, inputs such as cash, labor, raw materials, research ideas, manufacturing processes, and others. For example, marketing brings in revenues by negotiating exchanges with consumers. Finance arranges exchanges with lenders and stockholders to obtain cash. Thus the marketing and finance departments should work together to obtain funds for the business. Similarly, the personnel department supplies labor, and purchasing obtains materials needed for operations and manufacturing.

Marketing's Role in Strategic Planning

There is much overlap between overall company strategy and marketing strategy. Marketing looks at consumer needs and the company's ability to satisfy them; these same factors guide the company mission and objectives. Because most company strategy planning deals with marketing variables—such as market share, market development, growth—it is sometimes hard to separate strategic planning from marketing planning. In fact, in some companies, strategic planning is called "strategic marketing planning."

Marketing plays a key role in the company's strategic planning in several ways. First, marketing provides a guiding philosophy—company strategy should revolve around serving the needs of important consumer groups. Second, marketing provides inputs to strategic planners by helping to identify attractive market opportunities and to assess the firm's potential for taking advantage of them. Finally, within individual business units marketing designs strategies for reaching the unit's objectives.[8]

Within each business unit, marketing management must figure out the best way it can help to achieve strategic objectives. Some marketing managers will find that their objective is not necessarily to build sales. Their job may be to hold existing sales with a smaller marketing budget, or actually to reduce demand. Thus marketing management must manage demand to the level decided by the strategic planning done at headquarters. Marketing helps to assess each business unit's potential, but once the unit's objective is set, marketing's task is to carry it out profitably.

FIGURE 2-6
Alternate views of
marketing's role in the
company

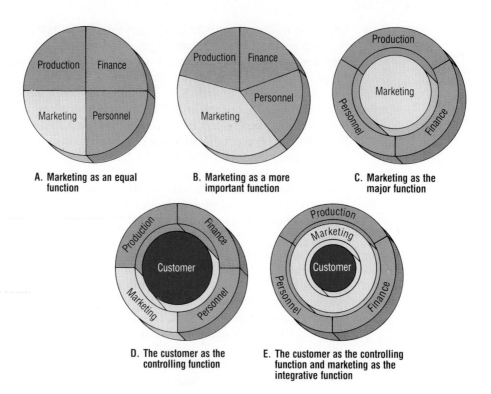

A. Marketing as an equal
   function

B. Marketing as a more
   important function

C. Marketing as the
   major function

D. The customer as the
   controlling function

E. The customer as the controlling
   function and marketing as the
   integrative function

Marketing and the Other Business Functions

There is much confusion about marketing's importance in the firm. In some firms it is just another function—all functions count in the company, and none takes leadership. This view is illustrated in Figure 2-6A. If the company faces slow growth or a sales decline, marketing may become more important for the time being (Figure 2-6B).

Some marketers claim that marketing is the major function of the firm. They quote Drucker's statement: "The aim of the business is to create customers." They say it is marketing's job to define the company's mission, products, and markets and to direct the other functions in the task of serving customers (Figure 2-6C).

Other marketers prefer to put the customer at the center of the company. They argue that all functions should work together to sense, serve, and satisfy the customer (Figure 2-6D).

Finally, some marketers say that marketing still needs to be in a central position in order to be certain that customers' needs are understood and satisfied (Figure 2-6E). These marketers argue that the firm cannot succeed without customers, so the key task is to attract and hold customers. Customers are attracted by promises and held through satisfaction, and marketing defines the promise and ensures its delivery. But actual consumer satisfaction is affected by the performance of other departments, so marketing plays an integrative role to help assure that all departments work together toward consumer satisfaction.

Conflict Between Departments

Each business function has a different view of which publics and activities are most important. Manufacturing focuses on suppliers and production; finance is concerned with stockholders and sound investment; marketing emphasizes consumers and prod-

DEPARTMENT	EMPHASIS	MARKETING EMPHASIS
R&D (Research & Development)	Basic research Intrinsic quality Functional features	Applied research Perceived quality Sales features
Engineering	Long design lead time Few models Standard components	Short design lead time Many models Custom components
Purchasing	Narrow product line Standard parts Price of material Economical lot sizes Purchasing at infrequent intervals	Broad product line Nonstandard parts Quality of material Large lot sizes to avoid stockouts Immediate purchasing for customer needs
Manufacturing	Long production lead time Long runs with few models No model changes Standard orders Ease of fabrication Average quality control	Short production lead time Short runs with many models Frequent model changes Custom orders Aesthetic appearance Tight quality control
Inventory	Fast-moving items, narrow product line Economical level of stock	Broad product line High level of stock
Finance	Strict rationales for spending Hard and fast budgets Pricing to cover costs	Intuitive arguments for spending Flexible budgets to meet changing needs Pricing to further market development
Accounting	Standard transactions Few reports	Special terms and discounts Many reports
Credit	Full financial disclosures by customers Low credit risks Tough credit terms Tough collection procedures	Minimum credit examination of customers Medium credit risks Easy credit terms Easy collection procedures

uct, pricing, promotion, and distribution. Ideally, all the functions should blend to reach the firm's overall objectives. But in practice, departmental relations are full of conflicts and misunderstandings. Some conflict results from differences of opinion on what is in the best interests of the firm. Some results from real trade-offs between departmental well-being and company well-being. And some conflict results from unfortunate departmental stereotypes and biases.

Under the marketing concept, the company wants to blend all the different functions toward consumer satisfaction. The marketing department takes the consumer's point of view. But other departments stress the importance of their own tasks, and they may resist bending their efforts to the will of the marketing department. Because departments tend to define company problems and goals from their own points of view, conflicts are inevitable. Table 2-1 shows the main point of view differences between marketing and other departments.

When marketing tries to develop customer satisfaction, it often causes other departments to do a poorer job *in their terms*. Marketing department actions can increase purchasing costs, disrupt production schedules, increase inventories, and create budget headaches. Yet marketers must get all departments to think "consumer," to look through the customer's eyes, and to put the consumer at the center of company activity.

Marketing management can best gain support for its goal of consumer satisfaction

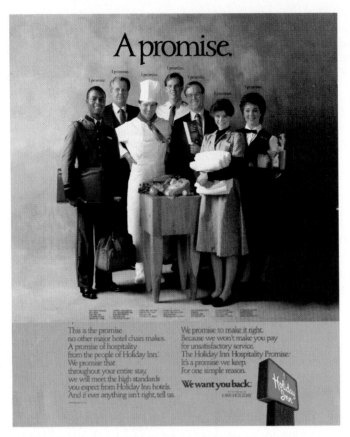

Holiday Inns recognizes that all of the company's people must work to sense, serve, and satisfy customer needs.

by working to understand the other functions. Marketing managers must work closely with other managers to develop a system of functional plans under which the different departments can work together to accomplish the company's overall strategic objectives.[9]

THE MARKETING MANAGEMENT PROCESS

The strategic plan defines the company's overall mission and objectives. Within each business unit, marketing plays a role in helping to accomplish the overall strategic objectives. Alert companies rely on marketing as the main system for monitoring and adapting to the changing marketplace. Marketing is not simply selling or advertising but, rather, a whole process for matching the company to its best opportunities. We define the marketing management process as follows:

> The **marketing management process** consists of (1) analyzing marketing opportunities, (2) selecting target markets, (3) developing the marketing mix, and (4) managing the marketing effort.

These steps are shown in Figure 2-7, along with the chapters dealing with each step. The rest of this chapter summarizes the entire process. Later chapters discuss each step in detail.

FIGURE 2-7
The marketing
management process

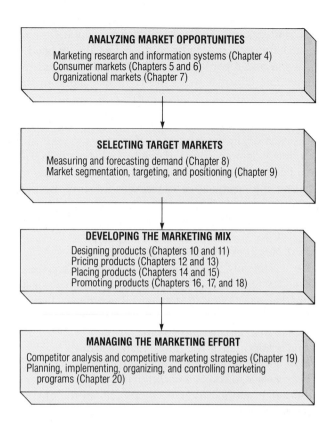

ANALYZING MARKET OPPORTUNITIES

Marketing research and information systems (Chapter 4)
Consumer markets (Chapters 5 and 6)
Organizational markets (Chapter 7)

SELECTING TARGET MARKETS

Measuring and forecasting demand (Chapter 8)
Market segmentation, targeting, and positioning (Chapter 9)

DEVELOPING THE MARKETING MIX

Designing products (Chapters 10 and 11)
Pricing products (Chapters 12 and 13)
Placing products (Chapters 14 and 15)
Promoting products (Chapters 16, 17, and 18)

MANAGING THE MARKETING EFFORT

Competitor analysis and competitive marketing strategies (Chapter 19)
Planning, implementing, organizing, and controlling marketing
   programs (Chapter 20)

Analyzing Market Opportunities

Every company needs to be able to identify new market opportunities. No company can depend on its present products and markets to last forever. The complex and changing environment constantly offers new opportunities and threats. The company must carefully analyze its consumers and the environment so that it can avoid the threats and take advantage of the opportunities. To survive, it must continually seek new ways to offer value to consumers.

Companies may think that they have few opportunities, but this belief is only a failure to think strategically about what business they are in and what strengths they have. Every company faces many opportunities. Companies can search for new opportunities casually or systematically. Many companies find new ideas by simply keeping their eyes and ears open to the changing marketplace. Other organizations use formal methods for analyzing the marketing environment.

Not all opportunities are right for the company. A marketing opportunity must fit the company's objectives and resources. Personal computers are an attractive industry, but not for every company. For example, we sense that personal computers would not be right for McDonald's. McDonald's seeks a high level of sales, growth, and profits from the fast-food business. And even though McDonald's has very large resources, it lacks the technical know-how, industrial marketing experience, and special distribution channels needed to sell personal computers successfully.

In analyzing market opportunities—in fact, throughout the marketing management process—managers need a plentiful supply of information. They need information about consumers and how they make buying decisions. They need to know about key actors in the marketing environment—competitors, suppliers, resellers, and publics. They also need to know about broader environmental forces that affect the company and its consumers—demographic, economic, natural, technological, political, and cultural. The marketing information system assesses the information needs of marketing managers and obtains the needed information from several sources—internal records, marketing intelligence, and marketing research. It then distributes this information to the right managers, in the right form, at the right time.

Selecting Target Consumers

Companies know that they cannot satisfy all consumers in a given market, at least not all consumers in the same way. There are too many different kinds of consumers with too many different kinds of needs. And some companies are in a better position to serve certain segments of the market. Each company must study the total market and choose the segments it can profitably serve better than its competitors can. This involves four steps: demand measurement and forecasting, market segmentation, market targeting, and market positioning.

Demand Measurement and Forecasting

Suppose a company is looking at possible markets for a potential new product. The company first needs to make a careful estimate of the current and future size of the market and its various segments. To estimate current market size, the company would identify all competing products, estimate their current sales, and determine whether the market is large enough.

Equally important is the future market growth. Companies want to enter markets that show strong growth prospects. Growth potential may depend on the growth rate of certain age, income, and nationality groups that use the product more. Growth may also be related to larger developments in the environment, such as economic conditions, the crime rate, and life style changes. For example, the future market for quality children's toys and clothing is strongly related to current birth rates, trends in consumer affluence, and projected family life styles. Forecasting the effect of these environmental forces is difficult, but it must be done in order to make a decision about the market. The company's marketing information specialists will probably use complex techniques to measure and forecast demand.

Market Segmentation

Suppose the demand forecast looks good. The company now has to decide how to enter the market. The market consists of many types of customers, products, and needs, and the marketer has to determine which segments offer the best chance to achieve company objectives. Consumers can be grouped in various ways based on geographic factors (regions, cities), demographic factors (sex, age, income, education), psychographic factors (social classes, life styles), and behavioral factors (purchase occasions, benefits sought, usage rates). The process of classifying customers into groups with different needs, characteristics, or behavior is called **market segmentation.**

Every market is made up of market segments, but not all ways of segmenting the market are equally useful. For example, Tylenol would gain little by distinguishing between male and female users of pain relievers if both respond the same way to marketing stimuli. A **market segment** consists of consumers who respond in a similar way to a given set of marketing stimuli. In the car market, consumers who choose the biggest, most comfortable car no matter what its price make up one market segment. Other segments include buyers who care mainly about price and operating economy, those looking for style and status, those wanting high performance and sportiness, or those wanting safety and durability. It would be very difficult to make one model of car that would be the first choice of buyers in each of these segments. Companies are wise to focus their efforts on meeting the distinct needs

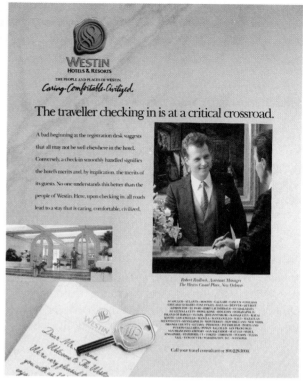

Positioning: Here Embassy Suites positions itself on price/ value with "You don't have to be a fat cat to enjoy The Suite Life." Alternatively, Westin Hotels and Resorts positions itself as "caring, comfortable, and civilized."

of one or more market segments. Thus, they study the geographic, demographic, behavioral, and other characteristics of each market segment to evaluate its attractiveness as a marketing opportunity.

Market Targeting

After a company has evaluated market segments, it can enter one or many segments of a given market. A company with limited skills or resources might decide to serve only one or a few special segments. This strategy limits sales but can be very profitable (see Marketing Highlight 2–2). Or a company might choose to serve several related segments, perhaps those that have different kinds of customers but with the same basic wants. Or a large company might decide to offer a complete range of products to serve all the market segments.

Most companies enter a new market by serving a single segment, and if this proves successful, they add segments. Honda, Toyota, and Nissan first entered the U.S. market successfully with small economy cars, then added mid-price and higher-price cars. Large companies eventually seek full market coverage. They want to be the "General Motors" of their industry. GM says that it makes a car for every "person, purse, and personality." The leading company normally has different products designed to meet the special needs of each segment.

Market Positioning

Once a company has decided which market segments to enter, it must decide what "positions" it wants to occupy in those segments. A product's *position* is the place the product occupies in consumers' minds relative to competitors. If a product is

MARKET SEGMENTATION AND TARGETING: "DESIGNER TRUCKS" BY OSHKOSH

Have you ever heard of the Oshkosh Truck Corporation? Perhaps not. But chances are good that you've seen some Oshkosh trucks around without realizing it. Oshkosh is the world's largest producer of crash, fire, and rescue trucks for airports. It also makes those "forward placement" concrete carriers, the ones that pour conveniently from the front but look as though they were put together backwards. In an environment where large, diversified truck manufacturers are having trouble, the smaller and more focused Oshkosh is thriving. The reason: smart marketing segmentation and targeting.

Oshkosh produces specialized heavy-duty trucks for customers that need unique, innovative designs for specific uses in adverse operating conditions. "Oshkosh is to trucks what Armani is to clothes. It builds designer trucks: heavy-duty, off-road, all-wheel drive, frequently custom-designed vehicles that sell

for anywhere from $36,000 to $750,000." Until the early 1980s, Oshkosh focused on special municipal and commercial segments with its unique concrete carriers and crash, fire, and rescue vehicles. But then, in 1981, it added a new target—the U.S. military. It began with a contract for 2,450 Heavy Expanded Mobility Tactical Trucks (HEMTT). The $120,000 HEMTT, an eight-wheel drive, all-terrain vehicle that carries up to 11 tons, quickly won the respect of military users and buyers. Since 1982, Oshkosh's defense business has soared, with contracts totaling more than $1.5 billion. Military orders now account for 84 percent of total Oshkosh sales.

Oshkosh's focused segmentation and targeting strategy has produced spectacular sales and profit results. The company's sales jumped from $72 million in 1981 to over $400 million in 1987. Over the last five years, profits have grown an average 64 percent

Oshkosh Trucking specializes in "designer trucks" for use in adverse operating conditions.

perceived to be exactly like another product on the market, consumers would have no reason to buy it.

Market positioning is arranging for a product to occupy a clear, distinctive, and desirable place relative to competing products in the minds of target consumers. Thus marketers plan positions that distinguish their products from competing products and that give them the greatest strategic advantage in their target markets. For example, the Hyundai automobile is positioned on low price as "the car that makes sense." Chrysler offers the "best built, best backed American cars"; Pontiac says "we build excitement"; and at Ford "quality is job one." Jaguar is positioned as "a blending of art and machine," while Saab is "the most intelligent car ever built." Mercedes is "engineered like no other car in the world"; the luxurious Bentley is "the closest a car can come to having wings." Such deceptively simple statements form the backbone of a product's marketing strategy.

To plan a product's position, the company first identifies the existing positions per year; return on equity last year reached 38 percent. In fact, Oshkosh has been so successful that numerous competitors have begun to invade its snug specialty truck niche, hoping to share in the sumptuous returns.

With competition increasing rapidly in current segments, Oshkosh is developing new ones. For example, it's targeting municipal markets with new crash, fire, and rescue vehicles modified for emergency snow removal. And Oshkosh is working to establish itself in international specialty truck segments."It built a set of powerful low-gear trucks to haul a 3,000-ton Saudi desalinization plant from the sea to the sands miles inland. For a Brazilian job, it created another set of monsters to carry 18 massive turbine generators, each weighing in at over six million pounds, at three miles an hour for 90 days," a feat that won Oshkosh a mention in *The Guinness Book of World Records*. Such projects testify to the company's versatility in meeting the needs of the special segments it serves. Says one Oshkosh executive, "We could build [a vehicle] in volumes of as low as one and as high as a thousand and still make money on it."

Thus, Oshkosh has built a strong position in a number of small, highly specialized market segments. Compared to truck industry giants such as General Motors, Ford, or Navistar, Oshkosh is a fairly small operator. But it's faster-growing and more profitable than its larger, less-focused competitors. And in its designer-truck segments, Oshkosh is the major player. Through smart market segmentation and targeting, Oshkosh has proven that small can be beautiful.

Sources: See Stuart Gannes, "The Riches in Market Niches," *Fortune*, April 27, 1987, p. 228. Extracts from Jagannath Dubashi, "Designer Trucks," *Financial World*, May 19, 1987, pp. 35–36.

of all the products and brands currently serving its market segments. It next figures out what consumers want with respect to major product attributes. The company then selects a position based on its product's ability to satisfy consumer wants better than competitors' products. Finally, it develops a marketing program that communicates and delivers the product's position to target consumers.

<table>
<tr><td>**Developing the Marketing Mix**</td><td>Once the company has decided upon its positioning strategy, it is ready to begin planning the details of the marketing mix. The marketing mix is one of the major concepts in modern marketing. We define it as follows:</td></tr>
</table>

The **marketing mix** is the set of controllable marketing variables that the firm blends to produce the response it wants in the target market.

The marketing mix consists of everything the firm can do to influence the demand for its product. The many possibilities can be collected into four groups of variables

FIGURE 2-8
The four Ps of the marketing mix

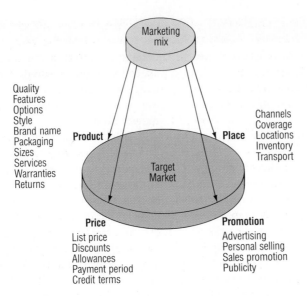

known as the "four Ps:" *product, price, place,* and *promotion.*[10] The particular marketing variables under each P are shown in Figure 2-8.

Product stands for the "goods-and-service" combination the company offers to the target market. Thus a Ford Taurus automobile "product" consists of nuts and bolts, spark plugs, pistons, headlights, and thousands of other parts. Ford offers several Taurus styles and dozens of optional features. The car comes fully serviced and with a comprehensive warranty, which is as much a part of the product as the tailpipe.

Price stands for the amount of money customers have to pay to obtain the product. Ford calculates suggested retail prices that its dealers might charge for each Taurus. But Ford dealers rarely charge the full sticker price. Instead, they negotiate the price with each customer, offering discounts, trade-in allowances, and credit terms to adjust for the current competitive situation and to bring the price into line with the buyer's perceptions of the car's value.

Place stands for company activities that make the product available to target consumers. Ford maintains a large body of independently owned dealerships that sell the company's many different car models. Ford selects its dealers carefully and supports them strongly. The dealers keep an inventory of Ford automobiles, demonstrate them to potential buyers, negotiate prices, close sales, and service the cars after the sale.

Promotion stands for activities that communicate the merits of the product and persuade target customers to buy it. Ford spends more than $600 million each year on advertising to tell consumers about the company and its products. Dealership salespeople assist potential buyers and persuade them that Ford is the best car for them. Ford and its dealers offer special promotions—sales, cash rebates, low financing rates—as added purchase incentives.

An effective marketing program blends all of the marketing mix elements into a coordinated program designed to achieve the company's marketing objectives.[11]

Managing the Marketing Effort

So far, we have looked at how the company analyzes consumers and selects target markets and at the marketing mix tools the company can use to meet consumer needs. But when developing a marketing strategy, managers must consider more than consumer needs—they must also consider the company's industry position relative to competitors. Marketing managers must design competitive marketing strategies that match the company's position and resources against those of competitors, then effectively manage and adapt these strategies to meet changing conditions.

Competitive Marketing Strategies

To be successful, the company must do a better job than its competitors of satisfying target consumers. Thus marketing strategies must be adapted to the needs of consumers and also to the strategies of competitors. Based on its size and industry position, the company must find the strategy that gives it the strongest possible competitive advantage.

Designing competitive marketing strategies begins with thorough competitor analysis. The company constantly compares its products, prices, channels, and promotion with its close competitors. In this way it can discern areas of potential advantage and disadvantage. The company must formally or informally monitor the competitive environment to answer these and other important questions: Who are our competitors? What are their objectives and strategies? What are their strengths and weaknesses? And how will they react to different competitive strategies we might use?

Which competitive marketing strategy a company adopts depends on its industry position. A firm that dominates a market can adopt one or more of several *market-leader* strategies. General Motors is the automobile industry leader. Other well-known leaders include IBM (computers), Caterpillar (large construction equipment), Kodak (photographic film), Sears (retailing), and Boeing (aircraft). Leaders can try to expand the total market by looking for new users and more use from current customers. Because the leader has the largest market share, it gains the most when the total market is expanded. Or the company might try to increase its market share by investing heavily to attract customers away from competitors. The dominant company can also design strategies to defend its current business against competitor attacks. It can lead the industry in innovation, competitive effectiveness, and value to consumers. It can carefully assess potential threats, counterattacking when necessary. Or the market leader may launch new products or marketing programs to strike down competitors before they become major threats.

Market challengers are runner-up companies that aggressively attack competitors to get more market share. Ford and Toyota are among the challengers in the automobile industry. The challenger might attack the market leader, other firms its own size, or smaller local and regional competitors. Challengers can choose from several *market-challenger* strategies. If the challenger is strong enough, it can pit its resources directly against those of competitors. A weaker challenger can concentrate its strengths against the competitor's weaknesses. Or the challenger can bypass the competitor and develop new products, new markets, or new technologies. In the automobile industry in recent years, Ford and several Japanese challengers have eaten heavily into General Motors' industry lead.

Some runner-up firms will choose to follow rather than challenge the market leader. Firms using *market-follower* strategies seek stable market shares and profits by following competitor's product offers, prices, and marketing programs. They may follow closely or at a distance, or they may follow closely in some ways and sometimes go their own ways. The market follower's goal is to keep current customers and to attract a fair share of new ones without drawing retaliation from the market leader or other competitors. Many market followers are more profitable than the leaders in their industries. For many years, Ford and Chrysler were content to follow General

Motors. But recently, slow sales and increasing foreign competition have forced these companies into more aggressive strategies.

Smaller firms in a market, or even larger firms that lack established positions, often adopt *market-nicher* strategies. They specialize in serving market niches that major competitors overlook or ignore. Nichers avoid direct confrontations with the majors by specializing along market, customer, product, or marketing-mix lines. Through smart "niching," low-share firms in an industry can be as profitable as their larger competitors. In the auto industry, Hyundai niches in the very-low-price segment, Mercedes in the luxury segment, and Porsche in the high-performance, high-price segment.

Thus the company must choose its competitive marketing strategies based on its industry position and its strengths and weaknesses relative to competitors. And strategy must change to meet changes in the competitive situation.

The Marketing Management Functions

Marketing management's job is to field effective marketing programs which will give the company a strong competitive advantage in its target markets. This involves four key marketing management functions—analysis, planning, implementation, and control.

Marketing *analysis* and *planning*, discussed earlier in this chapter, involve looking at the company's markets and marketing environment to find attractive opportunities, than deciding on marketing strategies that will help the company attain its overall strategic objectives. Good marketing analysis and planning are only a start toward successful company performance—the marketing plans must also be implemented well. It is often easier to design good marketing strategies than to put them into action.

People at all levels of the marketing system must work together to *implement* marketing strategies and plans. People in marketing must work closely with people in finance, purchasing, manufacturing, and other company departments. And many outside people and organizations must help with implementation—suppliers, resellers, advertising agencies, research firms, the advertising media. To successfully implement its marketing plans and strategies, the company must blend all elements into a cohesive program.

Many surprises are likely to occur as marketing plans are being implemented. The company needs *control* procedures to make sure that its objectives will be achieved. Companies want to make sure that they are achieving the sales, profits, and other goals set in their annual plans. This involves measuring ongoing market performance, determining the causes of any serious gaps in performance, and deciding on the best corrective action to take to close the gaps. Corrective action may call for improving the ways in which the plan is being implemented, or even changing the goals.

Companies also should stand back from time to time and look at their overall approach to the marketplace. The purpose is to make certain that the company's objectives, policies, strategies, and programs remain appropriate in the face of rapid environmental changes. Giant companies such as Chrysler, International Harvester, Singer, and A&P all fell on hard times because they did not watch the changing marketplace and make the proper adaptations. A major tool used for such strategic control is the *marketing audit*, which is described in Chapter 20.

Figure 2-9 summarizes the entire marketing management process and the forces influencing company marketing strategy. Target consumers stand in the center. The company identifies the total market, divides it into smaller segments, selects the

FIGURE 2-9
Factors influencing company marketing strategy

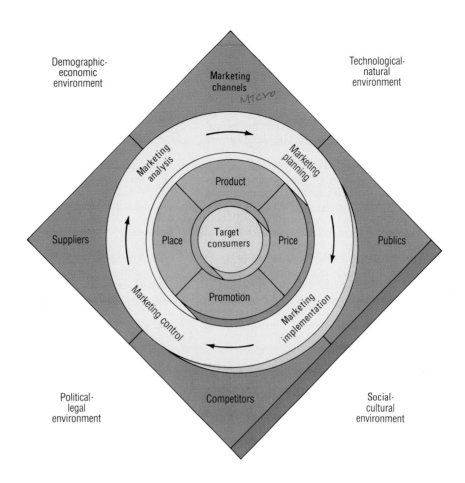

most promising segments, and focuses on serving and satisfying these segments. It designs a marketing mix made up of factors under its control—product, price, place, and promotion. To find the best marketing mix and put it into action, the company engages in marketing analysis, planning, implementation, and control. Through these activities, the company watches and adapts to the actors and forces in the marketing environment.

■ SUMMARY

Strategic planning involves developing a strategy for long-run survival and growth. Marketing helps in strategic planning, and the overall strategic plan defines marketing's role in the company. Marketers undertake the marketing management process to carry out their role in the organization.

Not all companies use formal planning or use it well. Yet formal planning offers several benefits, including systematic thinking, better coordination of company efforts, sharper objectives, and improved performance measurement, all of which can lead to improved sales and profits. Companies develop three kinds of plans—annual plans, long-range plans, and strategic plans.

Strategic planning sets the stage for the rest of company planning. The strategic planning process consists of developing the company's mission, objectives and goals, business portfolio, and functional plans.

Developing a sound mission statement is a challenging undertaking. The mission statement should be market-oriented, feasible, motivating, and specific if it is to direct the firm to its best opportunities. The mission statement then leads to supporting objectives and goals.

From here, strategic planning calls for analyzing the company's business portfolio and deciding which businesses should receive more or less resources. The company might use a formal portfolio planning method such as the BCG growth-share matrix or the General Electric strategic business grid. But most companies are now designing more customized portfolio planning approaches that better suit their unique situations.

Beyond evaluating current strategic business units, management must plan for growth into new businesses and products. The product-market expansion grid shows four avenues for growth. Market penetration involves more sales of current products to current customers. Market development involves identifying new markets for current products. Product development involves offering new or modified products to current markets. Finally, diversification involves starting businesses entirely outside of current products and markets.

Each of the company's functional departments provides inputs for strategic planning. Once strategic objectives have been defined, management within each business must prepare a set of functional plans that coordinates the activities of the marketing, finance, manufacturing, and other departments. Each department has a different idea about which objectives and activities are most important. The marketing department stresses the consumer's point of view. Other departments stress different things, and this generates conflict between departments. Marketing managers must understand the points of view of the other functions and work with other functional managers to develop a system of plans that will best accomplish the firm's overall strategic objectives.

To fulfill their role in the organization, marketers engage in the marketing management process, which consists of analyzing marketing opportunities, selecting target markets, developing the marketing mix, and managing the market effort. The company first carefully analyzes consumers and the environment, looking for threats to avoid and opportunities to exploit. Consumers are at the center of the marketing management process. The marketer divides the total market into smaller segments and selects the segments it can best serve. It then designs its marketing mix to attract and satisfy these target segments. Marketing strategies must be based on consumer needs, and also on the company's industry position and resources relative to competitors. The company must continually monitor competitors' products, prices, channels, and promotion. Depending on the company's position and strengths, it may choose market-leader, market-challenger, market-follower, or market-nicher strategies and programs.

To find the best competitive marketing strategy and put it into action, marketing managers perform four important marketing management functions—marketing analysis, marketing planning, marketing implementation, and marketing control. Through these activities, the company watches and adapts to the marketing environment.

■ QUESTIONS FOR DISCUSSION

1. What are the benefits of a "rolling" five-year plan—that is, why should managers take time to write a five-year plan that will be changed every year?

2. In a series of job interviews, you ask three recruiters to describe the missions of their companies. One says, "To make profits." Another says, "To create customers." The third says, "To fight world hunger." What do these mission statements tell you about the companies?

3. Choose a local radio station, and state what its mission, objectives, and strategies appear to be. In addition to its current activities, what else could the station do to accomplish its mission?

4. A producer of polyester fiberglass parts obtains the Styrene Monomer necessary for production from a company subsidiary that also sells to other companies. The subsidiary is much smaller than several other producers of Styrene Monomer and has lost money for the past five years. What cell of the BCG growth-share matrix does this strategic business unit fall in? What should the parent company do with this SBU?

5. Rank the four cells in the product/market expansion grid according to how much *risk* and how much *profit potential* each has. What market opportunities in each

of these cells has Burger King pursued? What future opportunities would you suggest?

6. In 1978 the chairman of AT&T announced to company employees that "we will become a marketing company." What did he mean by this? What company changes might have been necessary for this transformation to take place? Give examples of how its finance and accounting departments could have contributed to making AT&T a marketing company.

7. Marketers must take into account factors beyond their control that affect their ability to profitably serve their customers. What uncontrollable factors must be considered during strategic marketing planning?

8. Assume you are considering starting a business after graduation. What is the opportunity for a new music store selling records, tapes, and compact discs in your town? What target market or markets would you pursue, and what marketing mix would you develop for your store? Justify your answers.

9. Which competitive marketing strategies are the major fast-food chains using? Describe the strategies used by the market leaders, the market challengers, the market followers, and the market nichers.

■ KEY TERMS

BCG growth-share matrix A portfolio planning method that evaluates a company's strategic business units in terms of their market growth rate and relative market share. SBUs are classified as stars, cash cows, question marks, or dogs.

Business portfolio The collection of businesses and products that make up the company.

Cash cows Low-growth, high-share businesses or products—established and successful units that generate cash which the company uses to pay its bills and support other business units that need investment.

Diversification A strategy for company growth by starting up or acquiring businesses outside the company's current products and markets.

Dogs Low-growth, low-share businesses and products that may generate enough cash to maintain themselves, but do not promise to be a large source of cash.

GE strategic business-planning grid A portfolio planning method that evaluates a company's strategic business units using indexes of industry attractiveness and the company's strength in the industry.

Market development A strategy for company growth by identifying and developing new market segments for current company products.

Market penetration A strategy for company growth by increasing sales of current products to current market segments without changing the product in any way.

Market positioning Arranging for a product to occupy a clear, distinctive, and desirable place relative to competing products in the minds of target consumers.

Market segment A group of consumers who respond in a similar way to a given set of marketing stimuli.

Market segmentation The process of classifying customers into groups with different needs, characteristics, or behavior.

Marketing management process The process of (1) analyzing marketing opportunities, (2) selecting target markets, (3) developing the marketing mix, and (4) managing the marketing effort.

Marketing mix The set of controllable marketing variables that the firm blends to produce the response it wants in the target market.

Mission statement A statement of the organization's purpose, what it wants to accomplish in the larger environment.

Product development A strategy for company growth by offering modified or new products to current market segments.

Product/market expansion grid A portfolio planning tool for identifying company growth opportunities through market penetration, market development, product development, or diversification.

Question marks Low-share business units in high-growth markets, which require a lot of cash to hold their share or build into stars.

Stars High-growth, high-share businesses or products, which often require heavy investment to finance their rapid growth.

Strategic business unit (SBU) A unit of the company that has a separate mission and objectives, and that can be planned independently of other company businesses. An SBU can be a company division, a product line within a division, or sometimes a single product or brand.

Strategic planning The process of developing and maintaining a strategic fit between the organization's goals and capabilities and its changing marketing opportunities. It relies on developing a clear company mission, supporting objectives, a sound business portfolio, and coordinated functional strategies.

■ REFERENCES

1. For more information see "Dart & Kraft Turns Back to Its Basic Business—Food," *Business Week*, June 11, 1984, pp. 100-05; Kenneth Dreyfack, "Kraft, Minus Some Extra Baggage, Is Picking Up Speed," *Business Week*, March 9, 1987, pp. 74–75; and Beth Austin, "Kraft's Hungry . . . and Wants More," *Advertising Age*, July 20, 1987, pp. 3, 50.

2. Theodore Levitt, "Marketing Myopia," *Harvard Business Review*, July-August 1960, pp. 45–56.

3. Kathleen Deveny, "Bally Is On a Winning Streak," *Business Week*, December 2, 1985, pp. 30–31; and Michael Oneal and Christopher S. Ecklund, "For Bally, Dumping Trump Raises the Ante," *Business Week*, March 9, 1987, p. 45.

4. For additional reading on these and other portfolio analysis approaches, see Philippe Haspeslagh, "Portfolio Planning: Limits and Uses," *Harvard Business Review*, January–February 1982, pp. 58–73; and Yoram Wind, Vijay Mahajan, and Donald J. Swire, "An Empirical Comparison of Standardized Portfolio Models," *Journal of Marketing*, Spring 1983, pp. 89–99.

5. Richard G. Hamermesh, "Making Planning Strategic," *Harvard Business Review*, July–August 1986, pp. 115–20.

6. See Daniel H. Gray, "Uses and Misuses of Strategic Planning," January–February 1986, pp. 89–96.

7. H. Igor Ansoff, "Strategies for Diversification," *Harvard Business Review*, September–October 1957, pp. 113–24.

8. For more reading on marketing's role, see Paul F. Anderson, "Marketing, Strategic Planning and the Theory of the Firm," *Journal of Marketing*, Spring 1982, pp. 15–26; and Yoram Wind and Thomas S. Robertson, "Marketing Strategy: New Directions for Theory and Research," *Journal of Marketing*, Spring 1983, pp. 12–25.

9. For more reading, see Yoram Wind, "Marketing and the Other Business Functions," in *Research in Marketing*, vol. 5, Jagdish N. Sheth, ed. (Greenwich, CT: JAI Press, 1981), pp. 237–56; and Robert W. Ruekert and Orville C. Walker, Jr., "Marketing's Interaction with Other Functional Units: A Conceptual Framework and Empirical Evidence," *Journal of Marketing*, Vol. 51, January 1987, pp. 1–19.

10. The four P classification was first suggested by E. Jerome McCarthy, *Basic Marketing: A Managerial Approach*, (Homewood, IL: Irwin, 1960).

11. See Benson P. Shapiro, "Rejuvenating the Marketing Mix," *Harvard Business Review*, September–October 1985, pp. 28–34.

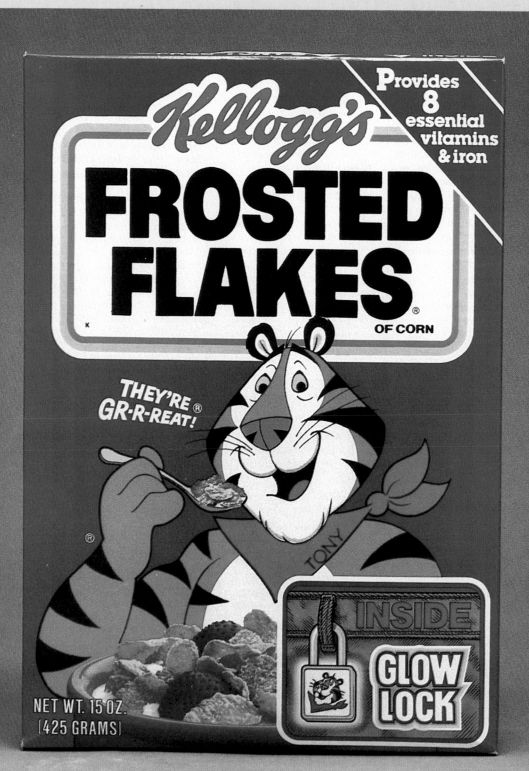

3 The Marketing Environment

IN 1894 vegetarian Will Kellogg of Battle Creek, Michigan, found a way to make nutritious wheat meal more appealing to patients in his brother's sanitarium. He invented a process to convert the unappetizing wheat meal into attractive, tasty little cereal flakes. The crunchy flakes quickly became popular. In 1906 Will founded the Kellogg Company to sell his cereal to the world at large, and the breakfast table would never again be the same. Will Kellogg's modest invention spawned the giant ready-to-eat cereal industry, in which half a dozen large competitors now battle for shares of $4.6 billion in yearly sales. Since the very beginning, the Kellogg Company has been atop the heap, leading the industry with innovative technology and marketing.

During the 1950s and 1960s, Kellogg and other cereal makers prospered. The post-World-War-II baby boom created lots of kids, and kids eat lots of cereal. As the baby boom generation passed through its childhood and teen years, cereal sales grew naturally with increases in the child population. Kellogg and its competitors focused heavily on the glut of young munchers. They offered pre-sweetened cereals in fetching shapes and colors, pitched by memorable animated characters. Remember Tony the Tiger, Toucan Sam, the Trix Rabbit, Sugar Bear, and Snap, Crackle, and Pop?

But by 1980, the marketing environment had changed. The aging baby boomers, concerned about their spreading waistlines and declining fitness, launched a national obsession with clean living and good nutrition. They began giving up the cereals they'd loved as kids, and industry sales growth flattened. After decades of riding natural market growth, Kellogg and its competitors now had to fight for profitable shares of a stagnant market. But through the good years, Kellogg had grown complacent and sluggish. The company stumbled briefly in the early eighties, and its market share dropped off.

To counter slow cereal-industry growth, most of Kellogg's competitors—General Mills, General Foods, Quaker Oats, Ralston-Purina—diversified broadly into faster-growing nonfood businesses. But Kellogg chose a different course. It implemented an aggressive marketing strategy to revive industry sales by persuading baby boomers to eat cereal again.

Kellogg advertised heavily to reposition its old products and bring them more in line with changing adult life styles. New ad campaigns for the company's old brands stressed taste and nutrition. A Kellogg's Corn Flakes ad showed adults discussing professional athletes who eat the cereal. In another spot, a young medical student told his mom that Rice Krispies have more vitamins and minerals than her oatmeal. In a Kellogg's Frosted Flakes ad, consumers sitting at a breakfast table, their features obscured by shadows, confessed that they still ate the Frosted Flakes they loved as kids. "That's OK," they're told, "Frosted Flakes have the taste adults have grown to love."

Beyond repositioning the old standards, Kellogg invested heavily in new brands aimed at adult taste buds and life styles. Crispix, Raisin Squares, the Nutri-Grain line, and many other innovative adult Kellogg brands sprouted on grocers' shelves. But the heart of Kellogg's push to capture the adult market was its growing line of high-fiber, bran cereals—All-Bran, 40 Percent Bran Flakes, Bran Buds, Raisin Bran, and Cracklin' Oat Bran. Kellogg's advertising made some

serious health pitches for these brands, tying them to high-fiber, low-fat diets and healthy living. One long-running ad campaign even linked Kellogg's All-Bran with reduced risks of cancer. The controversial campaign drew sharp criticism from competitors, strong praise from the National Cancer Institute, and sales from consumers. Kellogg did not make such strong claims for all its bran products. Its ads for Bran Flakes stated simply: "You take care of the outside; Kellogg's 40 Percent Bran Flakes will help you take care of the inside."

Kellogg's quick and aggressive reaction to its changing marketing environment paid off handsomely. The company's high-powered marketing attack more than doubled the growth rate for the entire cereal industry. And while diversified competitors are now spending time and money fixing or unloading their nonfood businesses, Kellogg is sharply focused on cereals. In only four years, Kellogg's overall market share grew from 35 percent to 42 percent, and the company's share of the fast-growing bran segment exceeds 50 percent. Four of the nation's five best-selling cereals are Kellogg brands, and Kellogg is once again one of America's most profitable companies. As Tony the Tiger would say, at Kellogg things are going *G-r-r-reat!*[1]

Chapter Objectives   *After reading this chapter, you should be able to:*

1. Describe the environmental forces that affect the company's ability to serve its customers.

2. Explain how changes in the demographic and economic environments affect marketing decisions.

3. Identify the major trends in the firm's natural and technological environments.

4. Discuss the key changes occurring in the political and cultural environments.

THE marketing environment consists of forces that surround the marketing department. To be successful, the company must adapt its marketing mix to trends and developments in this marketing environment. We define a company's marketing environment as follows:

> A **company's marketing environment** consists of the actors and forces outside of marketing that affect marketing management's ability to develop and maintain successful transactions with its target customers.

The uncertain marketing environment deeply affects the company. Instead of changing slowly and predictably, the environment can produce major surprises and shocks. How many managers at Gerber Foods foresaw the end of the baby boom? Which auto companies foresaw the huge impact consumerism and environmentalism would have on their business decisions? The marketing environment offers both opportunities and threats, and the company must use its marketing research and marketing intelligence systems to watch the changing environment.

The marketing environment is made up of a microenvironment and a macroenvironment. The **microenvironment** consists of the forces close to the company that affect its ability to serve its customers—the company, marketing channel firms, customer markets, competitors, and publics. The **macroenvironment** consists of the larger societal forces that affect the whole microenvironment—demographic, economic, natural, technological, political, and cultural forces. We will first look at the company's microenvironment and then at its macroenvironment.

THE COMPANY'S MICROENVIRONMENT

The job of marketing management is to create attractive offers for target markets. However, marketing management's success will be affected by the rest of the company, middlemen, competitors, and various publics. These actors in the company's microenvironment are shown in Figure 3-1. Marketing managers cannot simply focus on the target market's needs. They also must watch all actors in the company's microenvironment. We will look at the company, suppliers, middlemen, customers, competitors, and publics—in that order. We will illustrate the role and impact of these actors by referring to the Schwinn Bicycle Company, a major U.S. bicycle producer.

The Company In making marketing plans, marketing management at Schwinn takes other company groups into account, groups such as top management, finance, R&D, purchasing, manufacturing, and accounting. All these groups form the company microenvironment (see Figure 3-2).

Top management at Schwinn consists of the bicycle division's general manager, the executive committee, the chief executive officer, the chairman of the board, and the board of directors. These higher levels of management set the company's mission, objectives, broad strategies, and policies. Marketing managers make decisions within the plans made by top management. And marketing plans must be approved by top management before they can be implemented.

Marketing managers also work closely with other company departments. Finance is concerned with finding and using funds to carry out the marketing plan. R&D focuses on the problems of designing safe and attractive bicycles. Purchasing worries about getting supplies and materials, while manufacturing is responsible for producing the desired number of bicycles. Accounting has to measure revenues and costs to

FIGURE 3-1
Major actors in the company's microenvironment

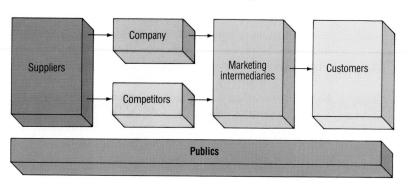

FIGURE 3-2
Company
microenvironment

help marketing know how well it is achieving its objectives. All these departments have an impact on the marketing department's plans and actions.

Suppliers

Suppliers are firms and individuals that provide the resources needed by the company to produce goods and services. For example, Schwinn must obtain steel, aluminum, rubber tires, gears, seats, and other materials to produce bicycles. It also must obtain labor, equipment, fuel, electricity, computers, and other factors of production.

Supplier developments can seriously affect marketing. Marketing managers need to watch price trends of their key inputs. Rising supply costs may force price increases that can harm the company's sales volume. Marketing managers must also watch supply availability. Supply shortages, labor strikes, and other events can lose sales in the short run and damage customer goodwill in the long run.

Marketing Intermediaries

Marketing intermediaries are firms that help the company to promote, sell, and distribute its goods to final buyers. They include middlemen, physical distribution firms, marketing service agencies, and financial intermediaries.

Middlemen

Middlemen are business firms that help the company find customers or make sales to them. These include wholesalers and retailers who buy and resell merchandise (they are often called *resellers*). Schwinn's primary method of marketing bicycles is to sell them to hundreds of independent dealers who resell them at a profit.

Why does Schwinn use middlemen? The answer is that middlemen perform important functions more cheaply than Schwinn can by itself. They stock bicycles where customers are located. They show and deliver bicycles when consumers want them. They advertise the bikes and negotiate terms of sale. Schwinn finds it better to work through independent middlemen than to try to own and operate its own massive system of outlets.

Selecting and working with middlemen is not easy. No longer do manufacturers have many small, independent middlemen from which to choose. They now face large and growing middlemen organizations. More and more bicycles are being sold through large corporate chains (such as Sears and K mart) and large wholesaler,

Middlemen perform important functions for Schwinn. They stock, display, promote, sell, service, and deliver Schwinn's bicycles.

retailer, and franchise-sponsored voluntary chains. These groups have great power to dictate terms or shut the manufacturer out of large markets. Manufacturers must work hard to get "shelf space."

Physical Distribution Firms (보관. 배달)
Physical distribution firms help the company to stock and move goods from their origin to their destination. Warehouses are firms that store and protect goods before they move to the next destination. Transportation firms include railroads, truckers, airlines, barges, and other companies that specialize in moving goods from one location to another. A company has to decide on the best ways to store and ship goods, balancing such factors as cost, delivery, speed, and safety.

Marketing Services Agencies
Marketing services agencies—marketing research firms, advertising agencies, media firms, and marketing consulting firms—help the company to target and promote its products to the right markets. When the company decides to use one of these agencies, it must choose carefully, since these firms vary in creativity, quality, service, and price. The company has to review the performance of such firms regularly and consider replacing those that no longer perform well.

Financial Intermediaries
Financial intermediaries include banks, credit companies, insurance companies, and other companies that help finance transactions or insure risk associated with the

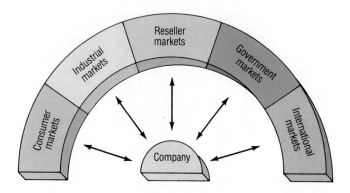

FIGURE 3-3
Types of customer markets

Industrial markets

Reseller markets

Government markets

Consumer markets

International markets

Company

buying and selling of goods. Most firms and customers depend on financial intermediaries to finance their transactions. The company's marketing performance can be seriously affected by rising credit costs or limited credit or both. For this reason, the company has to develop strong relationships with important financial institutions.

Customers
The company needs to study its customer markets closely. It can operate in five types of customer markets. These are shown in Figure 3-3 and defined below:

* **Consumer markets:** individuals and households that buy goods and services for personal consumption
* **Industrial markets:** organizations that buy goods and services for further processing or for use in their production process
* **Reseller markets:** organizations that buy goods and services in order to resell them at a profit
* **Government markets:** government agencies that buy goods and services in order to produce public services or transfer these goods and services to others who need them
* **International markets:** foreign buyers, including consumers, producers, resellers, and governments

Schwinn sells bicycles in most these markets. It sells some bicycles directly to consumers through factory outlets. It sells bicycles to producers who use them to deliver goods or to ride throughout their large plant complexes. It sells bicycles to bicycle wholesalers and retailers who resell them to consumer and producer markets. And it sells bicycles to foreign consumers, producers, resellers, and governments. Each market type has special characteristics that call for careful study by the seller.

Competitors
Every company faces a wide range of competitors. The marketing concept states that to be successful, the company must satisfy the needs and wants of consumers better than competitors do. Thus marketers must do more than simply adapt to the needs of target consumers. They must also adapt to the strategies of competitors who are serving the same target consumers. Companies must gain strategic advantage by strongly positioning their offerings against competitors' offerings in the minds of consumers.

No single competitive marketing strategy is best for all companies. Each firm must consider its size and industry position compared to those of competitors. Large firms with dominant positions in an industry can use certain strategies that smaller firms cannot afford. But being large is not enough. There are winning strategies for large firms; there are also losing strategies for large firms. And small firms can find strategies that give them better rates of return than large firms. Both large and

FIGURE 3-4
Types of publics

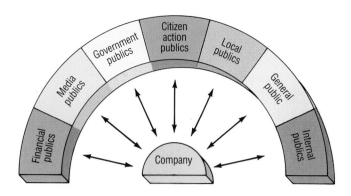

small firms must find marketing strategies that best position them against competitors in their markets.

Publics　The company's marketing environment also includes various publics. We define public as follows:

> A **public** is any group that has an actual or potential interest in or impact on an organization's ability to achieve its objectives.

Every company is surrounded by seven types of publics (see Figure 3-4):

Types of publics

- *Financial publics.* Financial publics influence the company's ability to obtain funds. Banks, investment houses, and stockholders are the major financial publics. Schwinn seeks the goodwill of these groups by issuing annual reports and showing the financial community that its "house is in order."

- *Media publics.* Media publics are those that carry news, features, and editorial opinion. They include newspapers, magazines, and radio and television stations. Schwinn holds press conferences, issues press releases, and stages publicity events to get more and better media coverage.

- *Government publics.* Management takes government developments into account. Schwinn's marketers consult the company's lawyers on issues of product safety, truth-in-advertising, dealers' rights, and others. Schwinn must consider joining with other bicycle manufacturers to lobby for more advantageous laws.

- *Citizen action publics.* A company's marketing decisions may be questioned by consumer organizations, environmental groups, minority groups, and others. For example, parent groups are lobbying for greater safety in bicycles, which are the nation's number-one hazardous product. Schwinn has the opportunity to be a leader in product safety design. Schwinn's public relations department can help it to stay in touch with consumer groups.

- *Local publics.* Every company has local publics such as neighborhood residents and community organizations. Large companies usually appoint a community relations officer to deal with the community, attend meetings, answer questions, and contribute to worthwhile causes.

- *General public.* A company needs to be concerned about the general public's attitude toward its products and activities. The public's image of the company affects its buying. To build a strong "corporate citizen" image, Schwinn will lend its officers to community fund drives, make large contributions to charity, and set up systems for consumer complaint handling.

- *Internal publics.* A company's internal publics include blue-collar workers, white-collar workers, volunteers, managers, and the board of directors. Large companies have newsletters and other ways to inform and motivate their internal publics. When employees feel good about their company, this positive attitude spills over to external publics.

STAKEHOLDERS

We believe in building mutually beneficial and enduring relationships with all of our stakeholders, based on conducting business activities with integrity and respect.

NCR's Mission: Create Value for Our Stakeholders

CUSTOMERS

We take customer satisfaction personally: we are committed to providing superior value in our products and services on a continuing basis.

NCR's Mission: Create Value for Our Stakeholders

EMPLOYEES

We respect the individuality of each employee and foster an environment in which employees' creativity and productivity are encouraged, recognized, valued and rewarded.

NCR's Mission: Create Value for Our Stakeholders

SHAREHOLDERS

We are dedicated to creating value for our shareholders and financial communities by performing in a manner that will enhance returns on investments.

NCR's Mission: Create Value for Our Stakeholders

SUPPLIERS

We think of our suppliers as partners who share our goal of achieving the highest quality standards and the most consistent level of service.

NCR's Mission: Create Value for Our Stakeholders

COMMUNITIES

We are committed to being caring and supportive corporate citizens within the worldwide communities in which we operate.

NCR's Mission: Create Value for Our Stakeholders

In these corporate image ads, NCR communicates with its customer, employee, shareholder, supplier, and community publics (which it calls stakeholders).

A company can prepare marketing plans for its major publics as well as its customer markets. Suppose the company wants some response from a particular public, such as its goodwill, favorable word of mouth, or donations of time or money. The company would have to design an offer to this public attractive enough to produce the desired response.

THE COMPANY'S MACROENVIRONMENT

The company and its suppliers, marketing intermediaries, customers, competitors, and publics all operate in a larger macroenvironment of forces that shape opportunities and pose threats to the success of the company. The company must carefully watch and respond to these forces. The macroenvironment consists of the six major forces shown in Figure 3-5. The remaining sections of this chapter will examine these forces and show how they affect marketing plans.

Demographic Environment　**Demography** is the study of human populations in terms of size, density, location, age, sex, race, occupation, and other statistics. The demographic environment is of

FIGURE 3-5
Major forces in the
company's
macroenvironment

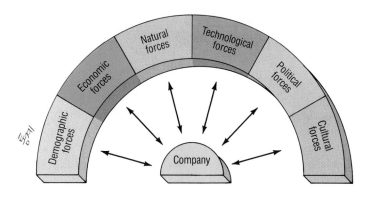

major interest to marketers because people make up markets. The most important demographic trends in the United States are described below.

Changing Age Structure of the U.S. Population

The U.S. population stood at over 240 million in 1987 and may reach 300 million by the year 2020. The single most important demographic trend in the United States is the changing age structure of the population. The U.S. population is getting older for two reasons. First, there has been a slowdown in the *birthrate* in the last two decades, so there are fewer young people to pull the population's average age down. Second, *life expectancy* is increasing, so there are more older people to pull the average age up.

During the **baby boom** that followed World War II and lasted until the early 1960s, the annual birthrate reached an all-time high. The baby boom created a huge "bulge" in the U.S. age distribution—the 75 million baby boomers account for more than one-third of the nation's population. And as the baby boom generation ages, it pulls the average age up with it. Because of its sheer size, most major demographic and socioeconomic changes occurring during the next half decade will be tied to the baby-boom generation (see Marketing Highlight 3–1).

The baby boom was followed by a "birth dearth," and by the mid-1970s the birthrate had fallen sharply. This decrease was caused by smaller family sizes resulting from the desire to improve personal living standards, improved birth control, and the increasing desire of women to work outside the home. Though family sizes are expected to remain smaller, the birthrate is climbing again, as the baby boom generation moves through the childbearing years and creates a second but smaller baby boom (the "echo boom"). The birthrate is expected then to decline in the 1990s.

The second factor in the general aging of the population is increased life expectancy. Current average life expectancy is 76 years, a 27-year increase since 1900. Increasing life expectancy and the declining birthrate are producing an aging population. The U.S. median age is now 32 and is expected to reach 36 by the year 2000 and 40 by 2030.[2]

The changing age structure of the population will result in different growth rates for various age groups over the decade, and these differences will strongly affect marketers' targeting strategies. Expected growth trends for six age groups are described below.[3]

CHILDREN. The number of preschoolers will increase dramatically through 1990, then taper off slightly through the 1990s as the baby boomers move out of childbearing years. Markets for children's toys and games, clothes, furniture, and food are enjoying a short "boom" after years of "bust." Sony and other electronics firms are now

THE BABY BOOMERS

The postwar baby boom, which began in 1946 and ran through the early 1960s, produced 75 million babies. Since then, the baby boomers have become one of the biggest forces shaping the marketing environment. The boomers have presented a moving target, creating new markets as they moved through infancy, preadolescence, teens, young adulthood, and now middle age. They created markets for baby products and toys in the '50s; jeans, records, and cosmetics in the '60s; fun and informal fashions in the '70s; and fitness, new homes, and child care in '80s.

Today the baby boomers are starting to gray at the temples and spread at the waist. And they are reaching their peak earning and spending years—the boomers account for a third of the population but make up 40 percent of the workforce and earn over half of all personal income. They are settling into homeownership, starting to raise families, and maturing into the most affluent generation in history. They constitute a lucrative market for housing, furniture and appliances, low-calorie foods and beverages, physical fitness products, high-price cars, convenience products, and financial services.

Boomers cut across all walks of life, but marketers have recently paid the most attention to the small upper crust of the boomer generation—its more educated, mobile, and wealthy segments. These segments have gone by many names. In the early to mid-'80s, they were called yuppies (young urban professionals), yumpies (young upwardly mobile professionals), bumpies (black upwardly mobile professionals), yummies (young upwardly mobile mommies). The latest term is DINKs, dual-income, no-kids couples. The DINKs work long hours, make hefty incomes, spend money to save time, and buy lavishly.

> The members of this . . . species can best be spotted after 9 P.M. in gourmet groceries, their Burberry-clothed arms reaching for arugula or a Le Menu frozen flounder dinner. In the parking lot, they slide into their BMWs and lift cellular phones to their ears before zooming off to their architect-designed homes in the exurbs. . . . Then they consult the phone-answering machine, pop dinner into the microwave, and finally sink into their Italian leather sofa to watch a videocassette of, say, last week's *L.A. Law* or *Cheers* on their high-definition, large-screen stereo television.

Moving into the '90s, the yuppies and DINKs are giving way to a new breed. The boomers are evolving from the "youthquake generation" to the

offering products designed for children. Many retailers are adding new children's brands. For example, Sears has joined with McDonald's to market McKid's clothing. Other retailers are opening separate children's clothing chains such as GapKids, Kids 'R' Us, and Esprit Kids. Such markets will continue strongly through the coming decade but will again decrease as the century closes.[4]

YOUTHS. The number of 10- to 19-year-olds will drop through the early 1990s, then begin to increase again as the century closes. This means first a slowdown then a gradual increase in sales growth for jeans manufacturers, movie and record companies, cosmetics producers, colleges, and others who target the teen market.

YOUNG ADULTS. This group will decline during the nineties as the "birth dearth" generation moves in. Marketers who sell to the 20-to-34 age group—furniture makers, life insurance companies, sports equipment manufacturers—will no longer rely on increasing market size for increases in sales. They will have to work for bigger shares of smaller markets.

EARLY MIDDLE AGE. The baby boom generation will continue to move into the 35-to-49 age group, creating huge increases. For example, the number of 40- to 44-year-olds will increase by 50 percent. This group is a major market for larger homes, new automobiles, clothing, entertainment, and investments.

LATE MIDDLE AGE. The 50-to-64 age group will continue to shrink until the end of the century. Then it will begin to increase as the baby boomers move in. This

The baby boomers: a prime target for marketers.

"backache generation"—they're slowing up, having children, and settling down. They are approaching life with a new reasonableness, in the way they live, think, eat, and spend. Staying home with the family and being a "couch potato" is becoming their favorite way to spend an evening. The upscale boomers still exert their affluence, but they indulge themselves in more subtle and sensible ways. They spend heavily on convenience and high-quality products, but they have less of a taste for lavish or conspicuous buying.

Some marketers think that upscale boomers are tiring of all the attention, or that focusing on affluent boomer groups is diverting companies from other profitable segments. Some marketers are using subtler approaches that avoid stereotyping these consumers or tagging them as yuppies, or DINKS, or something else. But whatever the you call them, you can't ignore them. The baby boomers have been the most potent market force for the last 40 years, and they will continue to be for the next 40.

Source: See Fay Rice, "Wooing the Aging Baby Boomers," *Fortune*, February 1, 1988, pp. 68–77; and Bill Barol, "The Eighties Are Over," *Newsweek*, January 4, 1988, pp. 40–48. The quoted material is from Martha Smilgis, "Here Come the DINKs," *Time*, April 20, 1987, p. 75.

group is a major market for eating out, travel, clothing, recreation, and financial services.

RETIREES. Between 1980 and 2000, the over-65 group will have increased by over one-third. By the year 2000, this group will comprise almost 13 percent of all Americans; by 2020 there will be twice as many elderly as there are teenagers. This group has a demand for retirement communities, quieter forms of recreation, single-portion food packaging, life care and health care services, and travel.

Thus the changing age structure of the U.S. population will strongly affect future marketing decisions. In particular, the baby boom generation will continue to be a prime target for marketers.

The Changing American Family

The American ideal of the two-children, two-car suburban family has been losing some of its luster. There are many forces at work.[5] People are marrying later and having fewer children. Although 96 percent of all Americans will marry, the average age of couples marrying for the first time has been rising over the years. Couples with no children under 18 now make up almost half of all families. And of those families that have children, the average number of children is under 2, down from 3.5 in 1955.

There has also been an increase in the number of working mothers. The percent-

Lipton and other companies target smaller households with single-serve or individually-portioned packaging.

age of mothers of children under age 18 who hold some kind of job has increased since 1960 from about 25 percent to over 64 percent. Their incomes contribute 40 percent of the household's income and influence the purchase of higher-quality goods and services. Marketers of tires, automobiles, insurance, travel, and financial services are increasingly directing their advertising to working women. These changes are accompanied by a shift in the traditional roles and values of husbands and wives, with the husband assuming more domestic functions such as shopping and childcare. As a result, husbands are becoming more of a target market for food and household appliance marketers.

Finally, the number of nonfamily households is increasing. Many young adults leave home and move into apartments. Other adults choose to remain single. Still others are divorced or widowed people living alone. By the year 2000, 47 percent of all households will be nonfamily or single-parent households. These groups have their own special needs. For example, they need smaller apartments; inexpensive and smaller appliances, furniture, and furnishings; and food packaged in smaller sizes. Marketers must increasingly consider the special needs of nonfamily households, since they are now growing more rapidly than family households.

Geographic Shifts in Population
Americans are a mobile people, with about 17 percent, or 41 million Americans, moving each year. Among the major trends are the following:[6]

MOVEMENT TO THE SUNBELT STATES. During the 1980s, the populations in the West and South grew. Most of the Midwest and Northeast states, on the other hand, lost population (see Figure 3-6). These population shifts interest marketers because people in different regions buy differently. For example, the movement to the Sunbelt states will lessen the demand for warm clothing and home heating equipment and increase the demand for air conditioning.

MOVEMENT FROM RURAL TO URBAN AREAS. Except for a short period during the early 1970s, people have been moving from rural to metropolitan areas for over a century. The metropolitan areas show a faster pace of living, more commuting, higher incomes, and greater variety of goods and services than can be found in the small towns and rural areas that dot America. The largest cities, such as New York, Chicago, and San Francisco, account for most of the sales of expensive furs, perfumes, luggage, and works of art. These cities also support the opera, ballet, and other forms of "high culture."

MOVEMENT FROM THE CITY TO THE SUBURBS. In the 1950s, Americans made a massive exit from the cities to the suburbs. Big cities became surrounded by even bigger suburbs. The U.S. Census Bureau calls sprawling urban areas *MSAs* (Metropolitan Statistical Areas).[7] Companies use the MSAs in researching the best geographical segments for their products and in deciding where to buy advertising time. MSA research shows, for example, that people in Seattle buy more toothbrushes per capita than any other U.S. city; people in Salt Lake City eat more candy bars; folks from New Orleans use more ketchup, and those in Miami drink more prune juice.[8]

Americans living in the suburbs have more casual, outdoor living, greater neighbor interaction, higher incomes, and younger families. Suburbanites buy station wag-

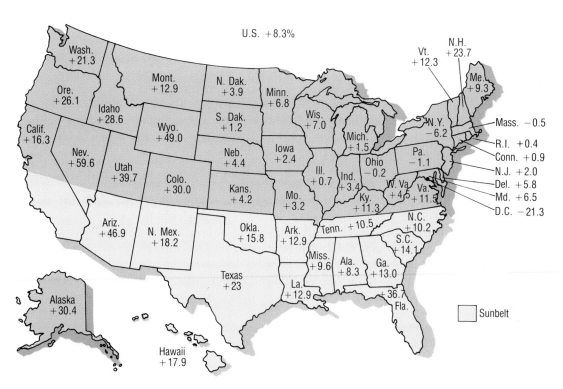

FIGURE 3-6 Population growth rates: 1980–1990
Source: U.S. Department of Commerce, Bureau of Census.

ons, home workshop equipment, outdoor furniture, lawn and gardening tools, and outdoor cooking equipment.

A Better-Educated and More White-Collar Population

In 1950, only half of all U.S. adults had gone beyond the ninth grade. By 1985, 72 percent of all Americans age 18 had completed high school. And by 1990 more than 20 percent of Americans over 24 will have completed college.[9] The rising number of educated people will increase the demand for quality products, books, magazines, and travel. It suggests a decline in television viewing, because college-educated consumers watch less TV than the population at large.

The workforce is becoming more white-collar. Between 1950 and 1985, the proportion of white-collar workers rose from 41 to 54 percent, blue-collar workers declined from 47 to 33 percent, and service workers increased from 12 to 14 percent. Through 1995, the most growth will come in the following occupational categories: computers, engineering, science, medicine, social service, buying, selling, secretarial, construction, refrigeration, health service, personal service, and protection.[10]

Demographic trends are highly reliable for the short- and intermediate-run. There is little excuse for a company's being suddenly surprised by a demographic development. Companies can list the major demographic trends, then spell out what the trends mean for them.

Economic Environment

The **economic environment** consists of factors that affect consumer purchasing power and spending patterns. Markets require buying power as well as people. Total purchasing power depends on current income, prices, savings, and credit. Marketers should be aware of major trends in income and of changing consumer spending patterns.

Changes in Income

Real income per capita declined during the 1970s and early 1980s, as inflation, high unemployment, and increased taxes reduced the amount of money people had to spend. As a result, many Americans turned to more cautious buying. They bought more store brands and fewer national brands to save money. Many companies introduced economy versions of their products and turned to price appeals in their advertising. Some consumers postponed purchases of durable goods, while others purchased them out of fear that prices would be 10 percent higher the next year. Many families began to feel that a large home, two cars, foreign travel, and private higher education were beyond their reach.

In the mid-1980s, however, economic conditions improved. And current projections suggest that real income will increase modestly through the mid-1990s.[11] This increase will largely result from rising income in certain important segments. The baby boom generation will be moving into its prime wage-earning years, and the number of small families headed by dual-career couples will increase greatly. These more affluent groups will demand higher quality and better service, and they will be willing to pay for it. These consumers will buy more time-saving products and services, more travel and entertainment, more physical fitness products, more cultural activities, and more continuing education.

Marketers must pay attention to income distribution as well as average income. Income distribution in the United States is still very skewed. At the top are upper-class consumers, who are a major market for luxury goods. The comfortable middle class has to be somewhat careful about its spending but can still afford the good life some of the time (see Marketing Highlight 3–2). The working class must stick

THE HIGH-LIVING MIDDLE CLASS

Some 3.3 million American households have incomes that enable them to live affluent or rich lives. But far more—26 million—partake of the good life some of the time, treating themselves to Godiva chocolates, Giorgio Armani cologne, and long weekends in St. Thomas and Jamaica. They are the Joneses of the Eighties, and most have incomes of less than $40,000.

Market researchers at Grey Advertising, a New York agency with billings of $2 billion a year, discovered this new mass of "ultra consumers" while trying to figure out who has been buying so many $380 Burberry raincoats, $250 Louis Vuitton purses, and $200 Mont Blanc fountain pens. There simply aren't enough affluent or near-affluent Americans to account for all the spending on luxury goods.

The ad agency interviewed people across the country between the ages of 21 and 50 with household incomes of more than $25,000 a year, a slice representing about a quarter of the adult population. Of those surveyed, just over half said they bought the top of the line whenever they could afford it. Only 5% of these ultra consumers had incomes above $75,000, *Fortune*'s minimum for an affluent lifestyle.

The vast majority of these folks obviously aren't in the market for Rolls-Royces or complete designer wardrobes. But they do *rent* limos from time to time and are devotees of designer-label accessories like Hermès scarves and Gucci loafers. "This is more an attitude of the mind than the pocketbook," says Barbara Feigin, an executive vice president at Grey.

Wanting it all has long been a hallmark of the middle class. Ultra consumers also want the best. Buying the best is a way to set themselves apart and bolster their self-image. Madison Avenue strives to reinforce that desire. Ads for premium-priced products as varied as Ultress hair coloring and Mitsubishi

The comfortable middle class partakes of the good life some of the time.

cars have a cloying sameness: sensual, provocative, and elegant, no matter what's for sale.

Since they cannot afford across-the-board extravagance, most ultra consumers splurge on a few items and scrimp elsewhere. They get by with fewer clothes to afford the Toshiba DX-7 digital VCR with hi-fi sound and do without the new bed so they can sleep between all-cotton sheets. "They don't have all that many wonderful things at once," says Feigin. Small doses of opulence must suffice.

Source: Reprinted with permission from Jaclyn Fierman, "The High-Living Middle Class, *Fortune*, April 13, 1987, p. 28.

---

close to the basics of food, clothing, and shelter and must try hard to save. Finally, the underclass (persons on welfare and many retirees) have to count their pennies when making even the most basic purchases.

Changing Consumer Spending Patterns

Table 3-1 shows the proportion of their total expenditures that households at different income levels spend on major categories of goods and services. Food, housing, and transportation use up most household income. Consumers at different income

	INCOME LEVEL		
EXPENDITURE	$10,000–15,000	$20,000–30,000	Over $40,000
Food	17.3%	15.5%	13.0%
Housing	22.4	21.9	22.3
Utilities	9.3	7.8	5.9
Clothing	4.8	4.9	6.2
Transportation	21.2	21.1	20.0
Health care	5.6	4.0	3.2
Entertainment	4.0	4.6	5.5
Personal care	1.0	0.9	0.9
Reading	0.7	0.7	0.6
Education	1.1	1.0	1.4
Tobacco	1.6	1.2	0.6
Alcohol	1.6	1.4	1.3
Contributions	2.6	3.7	4.5
Insurance and pensions	5.3	9.9	13.2
Other	1.4	1.4	1.3

Source: *Consumer Expenditure Survey: Interview Survey*, 1984, U.S. Department of Labor, Bureau of Labor Statistics, Bulletin 2267, August 1986, pp. 18–21.

levels, however, have different spending patterns. Some of these differences were noted over a century ago by Ernst Engel, who studied how people shifted their spending as their income rose. He found that as family income rises, the percentage spent on food declines, the percentage spent on housing remains constant (except for such utilities as gas, electricity, and public services, which decrease), and the percentage spent on other categories and savings increases. Engel's "laws" have generally been supported by later studies.

Changes in such major economic variables as income, cost of living, interest rates, and savings and borrowing patterns have a large impact on the marketplace. Companies use economic forecasting to watch these variables. Businesses do not have to be wiped out by an economic downturn or caught short in a boom. With adequate warning, they can take advantage of changes in the economic environment.

Natural Environment

The **natural environment** involves natural resources that are needed as inputs by marketers or that are affected by marketing activities. During the 1960s, public concern grew over whether the natural environment was being damaged by the industrial activities of modern nations. Popular books raised concerns about shortages of natural resources and about the damage to water, earth, and air caused by certain industrial activity. Watchdog groups such as the Sierra Club and Friends of the Earth sprang up, and legislators proposed measures to protect the environment. Marketers should be aware of four trends in the natural environment.

Shortages of Raw Materials

Air and water may seem to be infinite resources, but some groups see a long-run danger to these supplies. Environmental groups have lobbied for a ban on certain propellants used in aerosol cans because of their potential damage to the ozone layer. Water shortage is already a problem in some parts of the world.

Renewable resources, such as forests and food, have to be used wisely. Companies in the forestry business are required to reforest timberlands in order to protect the soil and to ensure enough wood supplies to meet future demand. Food supply can be a major problem in that the amount of farmable land is limited, and more and more of it is being developed for urban areas.

Nonrenewable resources, such as oil, coal, and various minerals, pose a serious problem:

> . . . it would appear at present that the quantities of platinum, gold, zinc, and lead are not sufficient to meet demands . . . silver, tin, and uranium may be in short supply even at higher prices by the turn of the century. By the year 2050, several more minerals may be exhausted if the current rate of consumption continues.[12]

The marketing implications are many. Firms using scarce materials face large cost increases, even if the materials remain available. If consumers are unwilling to pay higher prices, these firms must find new materials. For example, facing the rising costs and reduced supplies of quality hardwoods, furniture manufacturers have increasingly used less costly plastics and synthetic laminates to hold furniture prices down. Firms engaged in research and development and in exploration can help by developing new sources and materials.

Increased Cost of Energy

One nonrenewable resource, oil, has created the most serious problem for future economic growth. The major industrial economies of the world depend heavily on oil, and until economical energy substitutes can be developed, oil will continue to dominate the world political and economic picture. Large increases in the price of oil during the 1970s (from about $2 per barrel in 1970 to $34 per barrel in 1982) created a frantic search for alternative forms of energy. Though oil prices have moderated to under $20 per barrel, coal is again popular, and companies are searching for practical ways to harness solar, nuclear, wind, and other forms of energy. In solar energy alone, hundreds of firms are putting out products to use solar energy for heating homes and other uses.

As energy costs increase, companies search for alternatives. Here General Motors experiments with a solar powered car.

Increased Levels of Pollution

Industrial activity will almost always damage the quality of the natural environment. Consider the results of recent industrial activity: the disposal of chemical and nuclear wastes, the dangerous mercury levels in the ocean, the quantity of DDT and other chemical pollutants in the soil and food supply, and the littering of the environment with nonbiodegradable bottles, plastics, and other packaging materials.

The public's concern for a nonpolluted environment creates a marketing opportunity for alert companies. It creates a large market for pollution control solutions such as scrubbers and recycling centers. It leads to a search for new ways to produce and package goods that do not cause environmental damage.[13]

Government Intervention in Natural Resource Management

Various government agencies play an active role in environmental protection. For example, the Environmental Protection Agency (EPA) was set up in 1970 to deal with pollution. The EPA sets pollution standards and enforces them and conducts research on the causes and effects of pollution.

Marketing management needs to pay attention to the natural environment. Business can expect strong controls from government and pressure groups. Instead of opposing regulation, business should help develop solutions to the material and energy problems facing the nation.

Technological Environment

The most dramatic force shaping people's destiny is technology. The **technological environment** consists of forces that affect new technology, creating new product and market opportunities. Technology has released such wonders as penicillin, open-heart surgery, and the birth control pill. It has released such horrors as the hydrogen bomb, nerve gas, and the submachine gun. It has released such mixed blessings as the automobile, television, and white bread. Our attitude toward technology depends on whether we are more impressed with its wonders or with its blunders.

Every new technology replaces an older technology. Transistors hurt the vacuum-tube industry, xerography hurt the carbon-paper business, the auto hurt the railroads, and television hurt the theaters. Instead of the older industries adopting the new technologies, they fought or ignored them, and their businesses declined.

New technologies create new markets and opportunities. The marketer should watch the following trends in technology.

Faster Pace of Technological Change

Many of today's common products were not available even a hundred years ago. Abraham Lincoln did not know of automobiles, airplanes, phonographs, radios, or the electric light. Woodrow Wilson did not know of television, aerosol cans, home freezers, automatic dishwashers, room air conditioners, antibiotics, or electronic computers. Franklin Delano Roosevelt did not know of xerography, synthetic detergents, tape recorders, birth control pills, or earth satellites. And John F. Kennedy did not know of personal computers, digital watches, VCRs, or word processors. Companies that do not keep up with technological change will soon find their products out of date. And they will miss new product and market opportunities.

Unlimited Opportunities

Scientists today are working on a wide range of new technologies that will revolutionize our products and production processes. The most exciting work is being done in biotechnology, solid-state electronics, robotics, and materials science.[14] Scientists today are working on the following promising new products and services:

Practical solar energy	Commercial space shuttle	Effective superconductors
Cancer cures	Tiny but powerful computers	Electric cars
Chemical control of mental health	Household robots that do cooking and cleaning	Electronic anesthetic for pain killing
Desalinization of seawater	Nonfattening, tasty, nutritious foods	Totally safe and effective contraceptives

Scientists also speculate on fantasy products, such as small flying cars, single-person rocket belts, three-dimensional television, space colonies, and human clones. The challenge in each case is not only technical but commercial—to make practical, affordable versions of these products.

High R&D Budget

The United States leads the world in research and development spending. In 1987, R&D expenditures exceeded $123 billion, and they have been increasing steadily

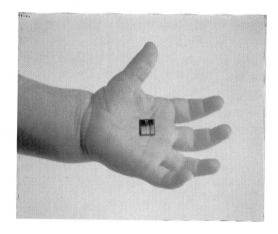

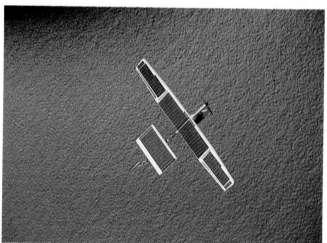

Technology brings exciting new products and services.

NASA: AN IMPORTANT SOURCE OF TECHNOLOGY FOR BUSINESS

Since 1958, the National Aeronautics and Space Administration (NASA) has sponsored billions of dollars' worth of aerospace research that has brought us thousands of new products. In 1962, NASA set up a program to help pass its aerospace technology along to other state and federal government agencies, public institutions, and private industry. Nine NASA applications centers across the country provide information about existing NASA technology and help in applying this technology.

NASA-backed aerospace research has had a great impact on industrial and consumer products. For example, NASA's need for small space systems resulted in startling advances in microcircuitry, which in turn revolutionized consumer and industrial electronics with new products ranging from home computers and video games to computerized appliances and medical systems. NASA was the first to develop communications satellites, which now carry over two-thirds of all overseas communications traffic. Here are just a few of countless other applications.

- NASA's need for lightweight and very thin reflective materials led to research that changed the previously small-scale plastics metalization business into a flourishing industry. Using such technology, the Metalized Products Division of King-Seeley Thermos Company now makes a large line of consumer and industrial products ranging from "insulated outdoor garments to packaging materials for frozen foods, from wall coverings to aircraft covers, from bedwarmers to window shades, labels to candy wrappings, reflective blankets to photographic reflectors."

- NASA's efforts to develop tasty, nutritional, lightweight, compactly packaged, nonperishable food for astronauts in outer space have found many applications in the food industry. Many commercial food firms

are now producing astronaut-type meals for public distribution—freeze-dried foods and "retort-pouch" meals that can be used for a number of purposes.

- NASA's need for a superstrong safety net to protect people working high in the air on space shuttles led to a new fiber. A relatively small net made of this fiber's twine can support the average-size automobile. The twine is now used to make fishing nets more than a mile long and covering more than 86 acres. The twine is thinner and denser than nylon cord, so the new nets offer less water resistance, sink faster, go deeper, and offer 30 percent productivity gains.

- A portable X-ray machine developed by NASA uses less than 1 percent of the radiation required by conventional X-ray devices. About the size of a thermos, the unit gives instant images and is ideal for use in emergency field situations such as on-the-spot scanning for bone injuries to athletes. It can also be used for instant detection of product flaws or for security uses such as examining parcels in mailrooms and business entrances.

- Special high-intensity lights developed by NASA to simulate the effect of sunlight on spacecraft resulted in several types of flashlights for professional and home use. One such hand-held light, which operates on a 12-volt auto or boat battery, is 50 times brighter than a car's high-beam headlights and projects a beam of light more than a mile. As a signal, it can be seen for over 30 miles.

- Bioengineering and physiological research to design cooling systems for astronaut space clothing has led to numerous commercial and consumer products—cooler athletic clothing, lightweight and heat-resistant clothing for firefighters, survival gear for hikers and campers, and dozens of others.

Source: Based on information found in *Spinoff* (Washington, DC: U.S. Government Printing Office), various issues between 1977 and 1986.

since the start of the 1980s.[15] The federal government supplied almost half of total R&D funds, while American industry supplied the rest. Government research can be a rich source of new product and service ideas (see Marketing Highlight 3–3).

The five industries spending the most R&D money are aircraft and missiles, electrical equipment and communication, chemicals and allied products, machinery, and motor vehicles and other transportation. Such companies as General Motors, IBM, AT&T, DuPont, and General Electric spend millions of dollars each year on R&D. Some high-technology companies spend as much as 25 percent of their sales on research. Today's research is mostly carried out by laboratory teams rather than by lone inventors like Thomas Edison, Samuel Morse, or Alexander Graham Bell. Managing company scientists is a major challenge. They tend to resent too much cost control. They are often more interested in solving scientific problems than in coming up with marketable products. Companies are adding marketing people to R&D research teams to try to obtain a stronger marketing orientation.

Concentration on Minor Improvements (R&D). 회사내에서의 기술개발의 대량투자.

As a result of the high cost of developing and introducing new technologies and products, many companies are making minor product improvements instead of gambling on major innovations. General Motors, Ford, and other car manufacturers focus most of their R&D efforts on improving current product features—more fuel-efficient engines, more durable transmissions, roomier trunks, more modern and attractive styling. They spend much less on creating major innovations, such as new types of engines or entirely new transportation systems. Even basic research companies like Du Pont, Bell Laboratories, and Pfizer are being cautious. Most companies are content to put their money into copying competitors' products and making minor feature and style improvements. Much of the research is defensive rather than offensive.

Increased Regulation (정부의 통제강화) 검사.

As products become more complex, the public needs to know that products are safe. Thus government agencies investigate and ban potentially unsafe products. The Federal Food and Drug Administration has set up complex regulations on testing new drugs. The Consumer Product Safety Commission sets safety standards for consumer products and penalizes companies that fail to meet these standards. Such regulations have resulted in much higher industry research costs and in longer times between new product ideas and their introductions. Marketers must be aware of these regulations when finding and developing new products.

Technological change faces opposition from those who see it as threatening nature, privacy, simplicity, and even the human race. Various groups have opposed such changes as the construction of nuclear plants, high-rise buildings, and recreational facilities in national parks. They have called for assessment of new technologies before allowing their commercial use.

Marketers need to understand the changing technological environment and how new technologies can serve human needs. They need to work closely with R&D people to encourage more market-oriented research. They must be alert to possible negative aspects of any innovation that might harm users and bring about opposition.

Political Environment

Marketing decisions are strongly affected by developments in the political environment. The **political environment** is made up of laws, government agencies, and pressure groups that influence and limit various organizations and individuals in society. We will look at some main political trends and what they mean to marketing management.

Legislation Regulating Business (법을 만듬)

Legislation affecting business has increased steadily over the years. This legislation has been enacted for a number of reasons. The first is to *protect companies* from each other. Business executives all praise competition but try to neutralize it when it touches them. 회사내의 강한 경쟁을 막기위해

TABLE 3-2
Milestone U.S.
Legislation Affecting
Marketing

Sherman Antitrust Act (1890)
Prohibits (a) "monopolies or attempts to monopolize" and (b) "contracts, combinations, or conspiracies in restraint of trade" in interstate and foreign commerce.

Federal Food and Drug Act (1906)
Forbids the manufacture, sale, or transport of adulterated or fraudulently labeled foods and drugs in interstate commerce. Supplanted by the Food, Drug, and Cosmetic Act, 1938; amended by Food Additivies Amendment in 1958 and the Kefauver-Harris Amendment in 1962. The 1962 amendment deals with pretesting of drugs for safety and effectiveness and labeling of drugs by generic name.

Meat Inspection Act (1906)
Provides for the enforcement of sanitary regulations in meat-packing establishments and for federal inspection of all companies selling meats in interstate commerce.

Federal Trade Commission Act (1914)
Establishes the commission, a body of specialists with broad powers to investigate and to issue cease-and-desist orders to enforce Section 5, which declares that "unfair methods of competition in commerce are unlawful."

Clayton Act (1914)
Supplements the Sherman Act by prohibiting certain specific practices (certain types of price discrimination, tying clauses and exclusive dealing, intercorporate stockholdings, and interlocking directorates) "where the effect . . . may be to substantially lessen competition or tend to create a monopoly in any line of commerce." Provides that violating corporate officials can be held individually responsible; exempts labor and agricultural organizations from its provisions.

Robinson-Patman Act (1936)
Amends the Clayton Act. Adds the phrase "to injure, destroy, or prevent competition." Defines price discrimination as unlawful (subject to certain defenses) and provides the FTC with the right to establish limits on quantity discounts, to forbid brokerage allowances except to independent brokers, and to prohibit promotional allowances or the furnishing of services or facilities except where made available to all "on proportionately equal terms."

Miller-Tydings Act (1937)
Amends the Sherman Act to exempt interstate fair-trade (price fixing) agreements from antitrust prosecution. (The McGuire Act, 1952, reinstates the legality of the nonsigner clause.)

Wheeler-Lea Act (1938)
Prohibits unfair and deceptive acts and practices regardless of whether competition is injured; places advertising of foods and drugs under FTC jurisdiction.

Antimerger Act (1950)
Amends Section 7 of the Clayton Act by broadening the power to prevent intercorporate acquisitions where the acquisition may have a substantially adverse effect on competition.

Automobile Information Disclosure Act (1958)
Prohibits car dealers from inflating the factory price of new cars.

National Traffic and Safety Act (1958)
Provides for the creation of compulsory safety standards for automobiles and tires.

Fair Packaging and Labeling Act (1966)
Provides for the regulation of the packaging and labeling of consumer goods. Requires manufacturers to state what the package contains, who made it, and how much it contains. Permits industries' voluntary adoption of uniform packaging standards.

Child Protection Act (1966)
Bans sale of hazardous toys and articles. Amended in 1969 to include articles that pose electrical, mechanical, or thermal hazards.

Federal Cigarette Labeling and Advertising Act (1967)
Requires that cigarette packages contain the following statement: "Warning: The Surgeon General Has Determined That Cigarette Smoking is Dangerous to Your Health."

Truth-in-Lending Act (1968)
Requires lenders to state the true costs of a credit transaction, outlaws the use of actual or threatened violence in collecting loans, and restricts the amount of garnishments. Established a National Commission on Consumer Finance.

National Environmental Policy Act (1969)
Establishes a national policy on the environment and provides for the establishment of the Council on Environmental Quality. The Environmental Protection Agency was established by Reorganization Plan No. 3 of 1970.

Fair Credit Reporting Act (1970)
Ensures that a consumer's credit report will contain only accurate, relevant, and recent information and will be confidential unless requested for an appropriate reason by a proper party.

TABLE 3-2 (Continued)

Consumer Product Safety Act (1972)
Establishes the Consumer Product Safety Commission and authorizes it to set safety standards for consumer products as well as exact penalties for failure to uphold the standards.

Consumer Goods Pricing Act (1975)
Prohibits the use of price maintenance agreements among manufacturers and resellers in interstate commerce.

Magnuson-Moss Warranty/FTC Improvement Act (1975)
Authorizes the FTC to determine rules concerning consumer warranties and provides for consumer access to means of redress, such as the "class action" suit. Also expands FTC regulatory powers over unfair or deceptive acts or practices.

Equal Credit Opportunity Act (1975)
Prohibits discrimination in a credit transaction because of sex, marital status, race, national origin, religion, age, or receipt of public assistance.

Fair Debt Collection Practice Act (1978)
Makes it illegal to harass or abuse any person and make false statements or use unfair methods when collecting a debt.

FTC Improvement Act (1980)
Provides the House of Representatives and Senate jointly with veto power over FTC Trade Regulation Rules. Enacted to limit FTC's powers to regulate "unfairness" issues.

Until recently, antitrust worries kept IBM from playing too rough in the computer industry. Through the sixties and seventies the company had fought off antitrust suits and federal attempts to break it up. IBM took it easy on competitors by selling a product for four or five years and holding prices stable. This let competitors survive profitably against the industry giant. "As long as they came out with products fairly soon after IBM did, they could come look forward to a few years of easy money." But in the late seventies, a more favorable regulatory climate let IBM flex its marketing muscle. IBM flooded the market with new products and made deep price cuts in all major market segments. The result was devastating to many of IBM's big, traditional rivals. Fearing total domination by IBM, competitors are screaming loudly. Charging IBM with harmful competitive practices, they are filing antitrust suits and urging federal regulators to step in and restore industry competitive balance.[16]

So laws are passed to define and prevent unfair competition. These laws are enforced by the Federal Trade Commission and the Antitrust Division of the attorney general's office.

The second purpose of government regulation is to *protect consumers* from unfair business practices. Some firms, if left alone, would make bad products, tell lies in their advertising, and deceive through their packaging and pricing. Unfair consumer practices have been defined and are enforced by various agencies. Many managers see red with each new consumer law, and yet a few have said that "consumerism may be the best thing that has happened . . . in the past 20 years."[17]

The third purpose of government regulation is to *protect the interests of society against unrestrained business behavior.* Profitable business activity does not always create a better quality of life. For example, selling more and bigger cars can be profitable to the auto industry but can also lead to more gas consumption, air pollution, traffic jams, and fatal car accidents. Regulation arises to make certain that firms take responsibility for the social costs of their production or products.

The amount of government regulation tapered off during the 1980s. Yet laws and their enforcement will continue be an important factor in marketing decision making. Business executives have to watch these developments when planning their products and marketing programs. Marketers need to know about the major laws protecting competition, consumers, and society. The main federal laws are listed in Table 3-2. Marketers should also know the state and local laws that affect their local marketing activity.[18]

Changing Government Agency Enforcement 법을 집행하기 위해 여러기관을 만듬

To enforce the laws, Congress established several federal regulatory agencies—the Federal Trade Commission, the Food and Drug Administration, the Interstate Commerce Commission, the Federal Communications Commission, the Federal Power Commission, the Civil Aeronautics Board, the Consumer Products Safety Commission, the Environmental Protection Agency, and the Office of Consumer Affairs. These agencies can have a major impact on a company's marketing performance. Government agencies have some discretion in enforcing the laws. From time to time, they appear to be overly eager and unpredictable. The agencies are dominated by lawyers and economists, who often lack a practical sense of how business and marketing works. In recent years the Federal Trade Commission has added staff marketing experts to better understand the complex issues. The degree of enforcement lessened during the eighties under the Reagan administration, with a strong trend toward deregulation.

Growth of Public Interest Groups (압력단체의 증가)

The number and power of public interest groups have increased during the past three decades. The most successful is Ralph Nader's Public Citizen group, which watchdogs consumer interests. Nader lifted consumerism into a major social force, first with his successful attack on unsafe automobiles (resulting in the passage of the National Traffic and Motor Vehicle Safety Act of 1962), and then through investigations of meat processing (resulting in the passage of the Wholesome Meat Act of 1967), truth-in-lending, auto repairs, insurance, and X-ray equipment. Hundreds of other consumer interest groups—private and governmental—operate at the national, state, and local levels. Other groups that marketers need to consider are those seeking to protect the environment and to advance the "rights" of women, blacks, and senior citizens.

The volume of laws, agency enforcement, and growing pressure groups have put restraints on marketer freedom. Marketers often have to clear their plans with the company's legal and public relations departments. Private marketing transactions have moved into the public domain.

> There is some evidence that the consumer may not be king, nor even queen. The consumer is but a voice, one among many. Consider how General Motors makes its cars today. Vital features of the motor are designed by the United States government; the exhaust system is redesigned by certain state governments; the production materials used are dictated by suppliers who control scarce material resources. For other products, other groups and organizations may get involved. Thus, insurance companies directly or indirectly affect the design of smoke detectors; scientific groups affect the design of spray products by condemning aerosols; minority activist groups affect the design of dolls by requesting representative figures. Legal departments also can be expected to increase their importance in firms, affecting not only product design and promotion but also marketing strategies. At a minimum, marketing managers will spend less time with their research departments asking "What does the consumer want" and more and more time with their production and legal people asking "What can the consumer have?"[19]

Cultural Environment

The **cultural environment** is made up of institutions and other forces that affect society's basic values, perceptions, preferences, and behaviors. People grow up in a particular society that shapes their basic beliefs and values. They absorb a world view that defines their relationship to themselves and others. The following cultural characteristics can affect marketing decision making.

Secondary cultural values: the shift toward physical fitness and well-being has created a need for new products and services.

Persistence of Cultural Values (국민성)

People in a given society hold many beliefs and values. Their core beliefs and values have a high degree of persistence. For example, most Americans believe in work, getting married, giving to charity, and being honest. These beliefs shape more specific attitudes and behaviors found in everyday life. Core beliefs and values are passed on from parents to children and are reinforced by schools, churches, business, and government.

People's *secondary* beliefs and values are more open to change. Believing in marriage is a core belief; believing that people should get married early is a secondary belief. Thus family planning marketers could argue more effectively that people should get married later than that they should not get married at all. Marketers have some chance of changing secondary values, but little chance of changing core values.

Subcultures

Each society contains *subcultures*—groups of people with shared value systems based on common life experiences or situations. Episcopalians, teenagers, and working women all represent separate subcultures whose members share common beliefs, preferences, and behaviors. To the extent that subcultural groups show different wants and buying behavior, marketers can choose subcultures as their target markets.

Shifts in Secondary Cultural Values

Although core values are fairly persistent, cultural swings do take place. Consider the impact of popular music groups, movie personalities, and other culture heroes on young people's hair styling, clothing, and sexual norms. Marketers want to predict cultural shifts in order to spot new opportunities or threats. Several firms offer "futures" forecasts. For example, the Yankelovich marketing research firm tracks forty-one cultural values, such as "anti-bigness," "mysticism," "living for today," "away from possessions," and "sensuousness." The firm describes the percentage of the population who share the attitude as well as the percentage who are antitrend. For example, the percentage of people who value physical fitness and well-being has gone up steadily over the years. Marketers will want to cater to this trend with appropriate products and communication appeals.

The major cultural values of a society are expressed in people's relationship to themselves, others, institutions, society, nature, and the universe.

PEOPLE'S RELATION TO THEMSELVES. People vary in their emphasis on serving themselves versus serving others. In the 1960s and 1970s, many people focused on self-satisfaction. Some were pleasure seekers, wanting fun, change, and escape. Others sought self-realization by joining therapeutic or religious organizations. The marketing implications of a "me-society" are many. People use products, brands, and services as a means of self-expression. They buy their "dream cars" and "dream vacations." They spend more time in outdoor health activities (jogging, tennis), in thought, and on arts and crafts. The leisure industry (camping, boating, arts and crafts, sports) faces good growth prospects in a society where people seek self-fulfillment.

PEOPLE'S RELATION TO OTHERS. More recently, observers have noted a shift from a "me-society" to a "we-society" in which more people want to be with and serve others. A recent survey showed that more people are becoming involved in charity or social-service activities.[20] And among adults widespread concern about social isolation and a strong desire for human contact have been growing. This suggests a bright future for "social support" products and services that improve direct communication between people, such as health clubs, vacations, and games. It also suggests a growing market for "social substitutes," things that allow people who are alone to feel that they are not alone, such as home videotape recorders and computers.

PEOPLE'S RELATION TO INSTITUTIONS. People vary in their attitudes toward corporations, government agencies, trade unions, universities, and other institutions. Most people accept these institutions, although some people are highly critical of particular ones. By and large, people are willing to work for the major institutions and expect them to carry out society's work. There is, however, a decline in institutional loyalty. People are giving a little less of themselves to these institutions and are trusting them less.

Several marketing implications follow. Organizations need to find new ways to win consumer confidence. They need to review their advertising communications to make sure their messages are honest. They need to review their various activities to make sure that they are being "good corporate citizens." More organizations are turning to social audits and to public relations to build a positive image with their publics.

PEOPLE'S RELATION TO SOCIETY. People vary in their attitudes toward their society, from patriots who defend it, to reformers who want to change it, to discontents who want to leave it. The trend through the 1960s and 1970s was toward declining patriotism and more criticism of where the country was going. The 1980s, however, have seen a substantial increase in patriotism. People's attitudes about their society

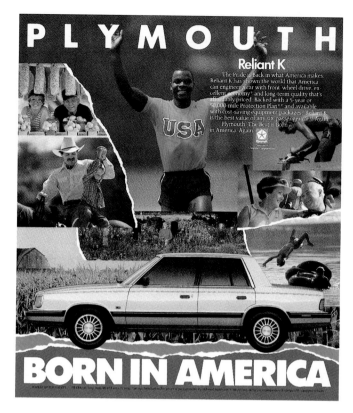

Plymouth responds to renewed consumer patriotism with its "Born in America" theme.

will influence their consumption patterns, levels of savings, and attitudes toward the marketplace.

Marketers need to watch consumers' changing social orientations and adapt their strategies accordingly. For example, U.S. companies have responded to renewed consumer patriotism with "made in America" themes and flag-waving promotions. At Chrysler, "the pride is back, born in America." The latest Sears catalog cover contains a photograph of the Statue of Liberty and the message "Thank You America." The American textile industry blitzed consumers with a $40 million "Crafted with Pride in the USA" advertising campaign featuring Bob Hope, Diann Carroll, Cathy Lee Crosby, and other celebrities insisting that "made in the USA" matters.[21]

PEOPLE'S RELATION TO NATURE. People vary in their attitudes toward the natural world. Some feel ruled by it or fearful of it, others are in harmony with it, and still others seek to master it. A long-term trend has been people's growing mastery over nature through technology, and the belief that nature is bountiful. More recently, however, people have recognized that nature can be destroyed or spoiled by human activities.

Love of nature is leading to more camping, hiking, boating, fishing and other outdoor activities. Business has responded with hiking gear, camping equipment, better insect repellents and sunscreens, and other products for outdoors enthusiasts. Tour operators are offering more tours to wilderness areas. Food producers have found growing markets for "natural" products such as natural cereal, natural ice-cream, and health foods. Marketing communicators are using appealing natural backgrounds in advertising their products.

PEOPLE'S RELATION TO THE UNIVERSE. People vary in their beliefs about the origin of the universe and their place in it. Most Americans practice religion, but religious conviction and practice have been dropping off through the years. Church attendance has been falling steadily, with the exception of certain evangelical movements reaching out to bring people back to organized religion. As people lose their religious orientation, they seek to enjoy their life on earth as fully as possible. They seek goods and experiences that offer fun and pleasure. In the meantime, religious institutions start turning to marketers for help in reworking their appeals so they can compete with the worldly attractions of modern society.

In summary, cultural values are showing the following long-run trends:

"Me society" ⟶	"We society"
Postponed satisfaction ⟶	Immediate satisfaction
Hard work ⟶	The easy life
Formal relationships ⟶	Informal relationships
Religious orientation ⟶	Worldly, nonreligious orientation
Declining patriotism ⟶	Increasing patriotism

RESPONDING TO THE MARKETING ENVIRONMENT

Many companies view the marketing environment as an "uncontrollable" force to which they must adapt. They passively accept the marketing environment and do not try to change it. They analyze the environmental forces and design strategies that will help the company avoid the threats and take advantage of the opportunities the environment provides.

Other companies take an *environmental management* perspective.[22] Rather than simply watching and reacting, these firms take aggressive actions to affect the publics and forces in their marketing environment. They hire lobbyists to influence legislation affecting their industries and stage media events to gain favorable press coverage. They run "advertorials" (ads expressing their editorial point of view) to shape public opinion. They press lawsuits and file complaints with regulators to keep competitors in line. And they form contractual agreements to better control their distribution channels. The following example shows how one company overcame a seemingly uncontrollable environmental constraint.

> Citicorp, the U.S. banking giant, had been trying for years to start full-service banking in Maryland. It had only credit card and small service operations in the state. Under Maryland law, out-of-state banks could provide only certain services and were barred from advertising, setting up branches, and other types of marketing. In March 1985, Citicorp offered to build a major credit card center in Maryland that would create 1,000 white-collar jobs and further offered the state $1 million in cash for the property where it would locate. By imaginatively designing a proposal to benefit Maryland, Citicorp became the first out-of-state bank to provide full banking services there.[23]

Marketing management cannot always affect environmental forces—in many cases, it must settle for simply monitoring and reacting to the environment. For example, a company would have little success trying to influence geographic population shifts, the economic environment, or major cultural values. But whenever possible, smart marketing managers take a pro-active rather than reactive approach to the marketing environment.

■ SUMMARY

The company must start with the marketing environment in searching for opportunities and monitoring threats. The marketing environment consists of all the actors and forces that affect the company's ability to transact effectively with the target market. The company's marketing environment can be divided into the microenvironment and the macroenvironment.

The microenvironment consists of five components. The first is the company's internal environment—its several departments and management levels—as it affects marketing management's decision making. The second component includes the marketing channel firms that cooperate to create value: the suppliers and marketing intermediaries (middlemen, physical distribution firms, marketing service agencies, financial intermediaries). The third component consists of the five types of markets in which the company can sell: the consumer, producer, reseller, government, and international markets. The fourth component consists of the competitors facing the company. The fifth component consists of all the publics that have an actual or potential interest in or impact on the organization's ability to achieve its objectives: financial, media, government, citizen action, local, general, and internal publics.

The company's macroenvironment consists of major forces that shape opportunities and pose threats to the company: demographic, economic, natural, technological, political, and cultural.

The demographic environment shows a changing age structure in the U.S. population, a changing American family, geographic population shifts, and a better-educated and more white-collar population. The economic environment shows changing real income and changing consumer spending patterns. The natural environment shows coming shortages of certain raw materials, increased energy costs, increased pollution levels, and increasing government intervention in natural resource management. The technological environment shows rapid technological change, unlimited innovational opportunities, high R&D budgets, concentration on minor improvements rather than major discoveries, and increased regulation of technological change. The political environment shows substantial business regulation, strong government agency enforcement, and the growth of public interest groups. The cultural environment shows long-run trends toward a "we-society," immediate satisfaction, the easy life, greater patriotism, informal relationships, and a more worldly, nonreligious orientation.

Many companies treat the marketing environment as an uncontrollable force, passively analyzing the environment and reacting to it without trying to change it. Other companies take an environmental management perspective, designing strategies whenever possible to affect the marketing environment.

■ QUESTIONS FOR DISCUSSION

1. Some companies are so large that their purchase volume gives them the power to dictate terms to their suppliers. What are the advantages and disadvantages of marketing to companies that have the ability to "make or break" their suppliers?

2. How would an automobile manufacturer's marketing mix vary for different types of customer markets? Describe similarities and differences in the marketing mixes for consumer, industrial, reseller, government, and international markets.

3. Assume you are the communications director for a small regional airline. What publics would be affected by a news report that your company had a maintenance schedule that was considerably less frequent than competing airlines? How would you communicate with these different publics, and what would you say?

4. What environmental trends will affect the success of Walt Disney Productions through the 1990s? If you were the vice-president of marketing for the company, what plans would you make to deal with these trends?

5. Immigration is an important component of U.S. population growth. Currently, there is one legal immigrant for every six or seven people born in the United States, twice the ratio of twenty years ago. How will this trend affect marketing over the next five years? Over the next fifty years?

6. Recent life-style studies have shown an increasing trend in the attitude that "meal preparation should take as little time as possible." What products and businesses are being affected by this trend? What future marketing opportunities are suggested by this trend?

7. If Union Carbide developed a battery that made practical electric cars feasible, how do you think U.S. auto manufacturers would respond to this technological development? Would foreign manufacturers respond the same way? What kind of company do you think would be the first to market an electric car to the general public?

8. If Ralph Nader became president, what changes would you expect to see in the climate for marketing in the

United States? What changes would you look for if Lee Iacocca became president?

9. A major alcoholic-beverage marketer is planning the introduction of a mildly alcoholic "adult soft drink" that would be a socially acceptable substitute for stronger drinks. What environmental factors might affect the introduction decision, marketing plan, and success of this product?

10. Discuss steps a hospital could take to "manage" its supplier, competitive, customer, and political environments.

■ KEY TERMS

Baby boom The major increase in the annual birthrate following World War II and lasting until the early 1960s. The "baby boomers," now moving into middle age, are a prime target for marketers.

Company marketing environment The actors and forces outside of marketing that affect marketing management's ability to develop and maintain successful transactions with its target customers.

Cultural environment Institutions and other forces that affect society's basic values, perceptions, preferences, and behaviors.

Demography The study of human populations in terms of size, density, location, age, sex, race, occupation, and other statistics.

Economic environment Factors that affect consumer purchasing power and spending patterns.

Macroenvironment The larger societal forces that affect the whole microenvironment—demographic, economic, natural, technological, political, and cultural forces.

Marketing intermediaries Firms that help the company to promote, sell, and distribute its goods to final buyers; they include middlemen, physical distribution firms, marketing service agencies, and financial intermediaries.

Microenvironment The forces close to the company that affect its ability to serve its customers—the company, marketing channel firms, customer markets, competitors, and publics.

Natural environment Natural resources that are needed as inputs by marketers or that are affected by marketing activities.

Political environment Laws, government agencies, and pressure groups that influence and limit various organizations and individuals in society.

Public Any group that has an actual or potential interest in or impact on an organization's ability to achieve its objectives.

Suppliers Firms and individuals that provide the resources needed by the company to produce goods and services.

Technological environment Forces that affect new technologies, creating new product and market opportunities.

■ REFERENCES

1. For more information, see Russell Mitchell, "The Health Craze has Kellogg Feeling G-r-r-reat," *Business Week*, March 30, 1987, pp. 52–53; J. S. Richards, "Cereal Makers Reposition Products to Lure Adults," *Adweek*, May 26, 1986, p. 29; "Kellogg: Snap, Crackle, Profits," *Dun's Business Month*, December 1985, pp. 32–33; and John C. Maxwell, Jr., "Cereals Report Crisp Gains," *Advertising Age*, September 28, 1987, p. 88.

2. See Richard Kern, "USA 2000," *Sales and Marketing Management*, October 27, 1986, pp. 8–29, here p. 8.

3. See "The Year 2000: A Demographic Profile of Consumer Market," *The Marketing News*, May 25, 1984, Sec. 1, pp. 8–10; and Kern, "USA 2000," pp. 10–12.

4. See Paul B. Brown, Pete Engardio, Kirven Ringe, and Steve Klinkerman, "Bringing Up Baby: A New Kind of Marketing Boom," *Business Week*, April 22, 1985, pp. 58–65; and Horst H. Stipp, "Children or Consumers," *American Demographics*, February 1988, pp. 27–32.

5. For more reading, see Paul C. Glick, "How American Families Are Changing," *American Demographics*, January 1984, pp. 21–25; Fabian Linden, "In the Rearview Mirror," *American Demographics*, April 1987, pp. 4–5; and Richard Kern, "USA 2000," pp. 16–17.

6. See Joe Schwartz, "On the Road Again," *American Demographics*, April 1987, pp. 39–42.

7. The MSA (Metropolitan Statistical Area) concept classifies heavily populated areas as MSAs or PMSAs (Primary Metropolitan Statistical Areas). MSAs and PMSAs are defined in the same way, except that PMSAs are also components of larger "megalopolies" called CMSAs (Consolidated Metropolitan Statistical Areas). MSAs and PSMAs are areas consisting of (1) a city of at least 50,000 in population, or (2) an urbanized area of at least 50,000 with a total metropolitan area of at least 100,000.

8. See Thomas Moore, "Different Folks, Different Strokes," *Fortune*, September 16, 1985, pp. 65–68.

9. "The Year 2000: A Demographic Profile," *The Marketing News*, May 25, 1984, Sec. 1, p. 10.

10. See Fabian Linden, "In the Rearview Mirror," p. 4. For more reading, see Bryant Robey and Cheryl Russell, "A Portrait of the American Worker," *American Demographics*, March 1984, pp. 17–21.

11. See Thomas G. Exter, "Where the Money Is," *American Demographics*, March 1987, pp. 26–32; William Lazer, "How Rising Affluence Will Reshape Markets," *Ameri-*

can Demographics, February 1984, pp. 17–20; and "USA Tomorrow," p. 19.

12. *First Annual Report of the Council on Environmental Quality* (Washington, DC: Government Printing Office, 1970), p. 158.

13. See Karl E. Henion II, *Ecological Marketing* (Columbus, OH: Grid, 1976).

14. See Charles Panat, *Breakthroughs* (Boston: Houghton Mifflin, 1980); and "Technologies for the '80s," *Business Week*, July 6, 1981, pp. 48ff.

15. See "America's R&D Performance: A Mixed Review," *Business Week*, April 20, 1987, p. 59; Sana Siwolop, "Research Spending is Building Up to a Letdown," *Business Week*, June 22, 1987, pp. 139–140; and Stuart Gannes, "The Good news About U.S. R&D," *Fortune*, February 1, 1988, pp. 48–56.

16. See Bro Uttal, "Is IBM Playing Too Rough?" *Fortune*, December 10, 1984, pp. 34–37; and "Personal Computers: IBM Will Keep Knocking Heads," *Business Week*, January 10, 1985, p. 67.

17. Leo Greenland, "Advertisers Must Stop Conning Consumers," *Harvard Business Review*, July–August 1974, p. 18.

18. For a summary of legal developments in marketing, see Louis W. Stern and Thomas L. Eovaldi, *Legal Aspects of Marketing Strategy: Antitrust and Consumer Protection Issues* (Englewood Cliffs, NJ: Prentice Hall, 1984).

19. Extracts from Gerald R. Salancik and Gregory D. Upah, "Directions for Interorganizational Marketing" (unpublished paper, School of Commerce, University of Illinois, Champaign, August 1978).

20. See Natalie de Combray, "Volunteering in America," *American Demographics*, March 1987, pp. 50–52; Annetta Miller, "The New Volunteerism," *Newsweek*, February 8, 1988, pp. 42–44; and Bill Barol, "The Eighties are Gone," *Newsweek*, January 14, 1988, p. 48.

21. See Kenneth Dreyfack, "Draping Old Glory Around Just About Everything," *Business Week*, October 27, 1986, pp. 66–67; and Pat Sloan, "Ads Go All-American," *Advertising Age*, July 28, 1986, pp. 3, 52.

22. See Carl P. Zeithaml and Valerie A. Zeithaml, "Environmental Management: Revising the Marketing Perspective," *Journal of Marketing*, Vol. 48 (Spring 1984), pp. 46–53.

23. Philip Kotler, "Megamarketing," *Harvard Business Review*, March–April 1986, p. 117.

CASE 1

KODAK DISK CAMERA

Eastman Kodak Co. said it has suspended production of its compact disk camera, hailed when introduced in 1982 as the "new engine that will drive amateur photography."

The Rochester, N.Y.–based photographic-product and chemical concern cited poor sales for its decision to halt production, at least temporarily, of the mass-marketed disk camera. The company will continue to produce film for the camera.

Camera industry specialists had anticipated the Kodak action, citing problems with picture quality from the disks as well as the increasing popularity of easy-to-use 35mm cameras. Kodak had said it would review its extensive product line and discontinue those products that weren't profitable.

Wilbur Prezzano, the general manager of Kodak's photographic products group, told an industry publication that the company was committed to disk film and photofinishing. "But how committed we are to the hardware side of it—that in large measure will be guided by consumer demand and economics," he told Photo Marketing Association International's magazine. He noted that Kodak left the 8mm video camera business because of flagging sales. A Kodak spokesman said no date has been set for resuming production. "We have enough inventory for at least a month," he said. "I don't see a return to production in the next month or so."

Kodak estimates it has sold 30 million disk cameras since 1982, when it launched the camera with the largest advertising campaign in its history. The small cameras fit in the palm of a person's hand. Film for the camera is mounted in 15 frames on a disk that clicks automatically to the next frame each time an exposure is made.

Alta Cools, publisher of an industry newsletter, said that although millions of disk cameras were sold, the camera didn't do as well as planned. The main flaw with it was the size of the negatives, she said: "The negatives were too small to give a good quality picture."

Ms. Cools said she suspected Kodak might exit the business because it hadn't introduced an improved version of the disk since February 1986. A Kodak product announcement included everything but disk cameras—two new 35mm camera lines, a new 110 camera, and a new disposable camera. Furthermore, one of the new 35mm cameras is expected to sell below $50, less than the disk sold for when it was first introduced in 1982. "Now you can buy a 35mm camera almost as cheaply as a disk and with better results," said Ms. Cools.

Former Kodak Chairman Walter A. Fallon believed that the disk would be the camera of the 1980s, saying at its unveiling: "The new engine that will drive amateur photography is here." But while the company concentrated on the easy-to-use, inexpensive, but lower-quality disks, other camera makers were simplifying the high-quality 35mm camera.

"I think Kodak misread the market when they introduced the disk," said Eugene Glazer, an analyst with Dean

Witter Reynolds, Inc. "Kodak always viewed cameras as a mass-market product, which by nature means very low prices. They failed to see customers are willing to pay significantly higher prices to get higher quality."

He said he doesn't expect Kodak will resume production of the disk. He expects the current disk manufacturing capacity to be shifted to produce a line of recently introduced 35mm cameras.

1. Identify and discuss the factors that led to a decline in sales of the Kodak disk camera.

2. What macroenvironmental forces should Kodak carefully monitor?

3. Discuss the idea of viewing cameras as a mass-market product.

Source: Claire Ansberry, "Kodak Suspends Its Production of Disk Cameras," *The Wall Street Journal*, February 2, 1988. Reprinted by permission of *The Wall Street Journal*. © Copyright Dow Jones & Company, Inc. 1988. All rights reserved.

CASE 2

SONY CORPORATION: WALKMAN/WATCHMAN

Sony introduced the Walkman at the end of 1979, and in 1980, it shipped 550,000 of these gadgets worldwide. The product has now become widely accepted and imitated. At least twenty companies have entered the market with similar products. The Walkman provides high-quality playback through lightweight earphones attached to a lightweight cassette player worn on the belt or around the neck. Sony management must now determine how it should compete in this maturing market for Walkman type products. The first step is to reassess who are the buyers, why they buy, and how the product is used.

The Walkman was created by a young engineer who made it for fun. In time, it was shown to Akio Morita, Sony's chairman, who adopted it for his personal use and enthusiastically served as the product development project leader, reducing the time between product planning and marketing to six months instead of the usual one to two years. Product development and marketing ideas were obtained from high-school and university students during focus group sessions.

Competition brought imitators and price cutting. Walkman stereo cassette players are being sold in mass, retailing outlets for as low as $29. Competitors' products are sold for as much as 50 percent lower. Sony's response to this intense competition has been to maintain its premium prices, expand the line, and improve its products. Sony's innovative skills in trying to keep ahead of competition are evident in the new Walkman stereo cassette player. It incorporates a new earphone concept and is as small as the plastic box that holds a standard cassette (¾ inch by 2⅔ inches by 4¼ inches) and uses one AA-cell battery. Each earphone fits into the ear sideways, with the speaker facing toward the front of the ear. The earphone does not slide around on the head, sounds better than most earphones, feels comfortable, and lets the user hear more environmental sounds.

In planning its future marketing efforts for Walkman, Sony is interested in knowing whether the market will continue to grow and at what rate. This involves assessing what groups of consumers will use the product and for what purposes. The eventual total market could be very large and offer many market segmentation opportunities. Sony must also consider how competing technologies (for example, portable compact disc players) will affect the future market. In any event, Sony will have to decide what, if any, competitive advantages it has and how best to use them in search of profit, avoiding price competition as much as possible. It could concentrate on one or two models for all parts of the market or offer models designed especially for different segments.

A related Sony innovation is Watchman, a personal hand-held or vestpocket black-and-white TV. The Watchman was priced to sell for about $200, but has been advertised for as little as $149. Its 2-inch screen gives clarity and picture definition that rival many larger conventional sets. Its brightness and luminance can easily be seen at a football game, and words are easy to read. The Watchman uses a miniaturized cathoderay tube, just like most TVs. It is palm-sized—9½ inches by 3 inches by 6 inches—and weighs 18 ounces. It is powered by 4 AA-cell batteries or an optional voltage adapter and is equipped with a telescoping antenna and a carrying strap.

In marketing the Watchman, Sony faces the same basic problems it does with the Walkman, but in a different phase of the product life cycle. The apparent similarity of the marketing characteristics of the two products suggests that they should be marketed to consumers in the same way. On the other hand, care must be taken to avoid the pitfall of reasoning by analogy.

1. What groups of buyers exist for the Walkman, and what can Sony do to increase sales of the product to each of these groups?

2. Who are the potential buyers of the Watchman? Under what circumstances would they use it? How should the Watchman be marketed?

4 Marketing Research and Information Systems

IN 1985 the Coca-Cola Company made a spectacular marketing blunder. After 99 successful years, it set aside its long-standing rule—"don't mess with Mother Coke"—and dropped its original formula Coke! In its place came *New* Coke with a sweeter, smoother taste. The company boldly announced the new taste with a flurry of advertising and publicity.

At first, amid the introductory fanfare, New Coke sold well. But sales soon went flat, and the stunned public reacted. Coke began receiving over 1,500 phone calls and many sacks of mail each day from angry consumers. A group called Old Cola Drinkers staged protests, handed out tee-shirts, and threatened a class-action suit unless Coca-Cola brought back the old formula. Most marketing experts predicted that New Coke would be the "Edsel of the Eighties."

After just two months, the Coca-Cola Company brought old Coke back. Called Coke Classic, it sold side-by-side with New Coke on supermarket shelves. The company said that New Coke would remain its "flagship" brand, but consumers had a different idea. By the end of 1985, Classic was outselling New Coke in supermarkets by two to one. By mid-1986, the company's two largest fountain accounts, McDonald's and Kentucky Fried Chicken, had returned to serving Coke Classic in their restaurants.

Quick reaction saved the company from potential disaster. It stepped up efforts for Coke Classic and slotted New Coke into a supporting role. By 1987, Coke Classic was again the company's main brand, and the country's leading soft drink, with a 19 percent market share versus Pepsi's 18.5 percent. New Coke became the company's "attack brand"—its Pepsi stopper. With computer-enhanced star Max Headroom leading the charge, company ads boldly compared New Coke's taste with Pepsi's. Still, New Coke managed only a 2 percent market share.

Why was New Coke introduced in the first place? And what went wrong? Many analysts blame the blunder on poor marketing research.

In the early 1980s, though Coke was still the leading soft drink, it was slowly losing market share to Pepsi. For years, Pepsi had successfully mounted the "Pepsi Challenge," a series of televised taste tests showing that consumers preferred the sweeter taste of Pepsi. By early 1985, though Coke led in the overall market, Pepsi led in share of supermarket sales by 2 percent. (That doesn't sound like much, but 2 percent of the huge soft-drink market amounts to $600 million in retail sales.) Coca-Cola had to do something to stop its loss of market share—the solution appeared to be a change in Coke's taste.

Coca-Cola began the largest new product research project in the company's history. It spent over two years and $4 million on research before settling on a new formula. It conducted some 200,000 taste tests—30,000 on the final formula alone. In the blind tests, 60 percent of consumers chose the new Coke over the old, and 52 percent chose it over Pepsi. Research showed that New Coke would be a winner, and the company introduced it with confidence. What happened?

Looking back, Coke's marketing research was too narrowly focused. The research looked only at taste; it did not explore how consumers felt about dropping the old Coke and replacing it with a new version. It took no account of the intangibles—Coke's name, history, packaging, cultural heritage, and image. But to many people, Coke stands beside baseball, hot dogs, and apple pie as an American institution; it represents the very fabric of America. Coke's symbolic meaning turned out to be more important to many consumers than its taste. More complete marketing research would have detected these strong emotions.

Coke's managers may also have used poor judgment in interpreting the research and planning strategies around it. For example, they took the finding that 60 percent of consumers preferred New Coke's taste to mean that the new product would win in the marketplace—as when a political candidate wins with 60 percent of the vote. But it also meant that 40 percent still wanted the old Coke. By dropping the old Coke, the company trampled the taste buds of its large core of loyal Coke drinkers who did not want a change. The company might have been wiser to leave the old Coke alone and introduce New Coke as a brand extension, as was later done successfully with Cherry Coke.

The Coca-Cola Company has one of the largest, best managed, and most advanced marketing research operations in America. Good marketing research has kept the company atop the rough-and-tumble soft-drink market for decades. But marketing research is far from an exact science. Consumers are full of surprises, and figuring them out can be awfully tough.[1]

Chapter Objectives   *After reading this chapter, you should be able to:*

1. Discuss the importance of information to the company.
2. Define the marketing information system and discuss its parts.
3. Describe the four steps in the marketing research process.
4. Identify the different kinds of information a company might use.
5. Compare the advantages and disadvantages of various methods of collecting information.

IN carrying out marketing analysis, planning, implementation, and control, marketing managers need information at almost every turn. They need information about customers, competitors, dealers, and other forces in the marketplace. One marketing executive put it this way: "To manage a business well is to manage its future; and to manage the future is to manage information."[2]

During the past century, most companies were small and knew their customers firsthand. Managers picked up marketing information by being around people, observing them, and asking questions. In this century, many factors have increased the need for more and better information. As companies become national in scope, they need more information on larger, more distant markets. As incomes increase and buyers become more selective, sellers need better information about how buyers respond to different products and appeals. As sellers use more complex marketing approaches and face more competition, they need information on the effectiveness of their marketing tools. Finally, in today's rapidly changing environments, managers need more up-to-date information to make timely decisions.

The supply of information has also increased greatly. John Naisbitt suggests that the United States is undergoing a "megashift" from an industrial to an information-based economy.[3] He found that over 65 percent of the U.S. work force is now employed in producing or processing information, compared to only 17 percent in 1950. Using improved computer systems and other technologies, companies can now provide information in great quantities. In fact, today's managers sometimes receive too much information. For example, one study found that with all the companies offering data and with all the information now available through supermarket scanners, a packaged goods brand manager is bombarded with one million to one *billion* new numbers each week.[4] As Naisbitt points out: "Running out of information is not a problem, but drowning in it is."[5]

Yet marketers frequently complain that they lack enough information of the right kind or have too much of the wrong kind. Or marketing information is so spread throughout the company that it takes a great effort to locate simple facts. Subordinates may withhold information they believe will reflect badly on their performance. Important information often arrives too late to be useful, or on-time information is not accurate. Companies have greater capacity to provide managers with information, but often have not made good use of it. Many companies are now studying their managers' information needs and designing information systems to meet these needs.

THE MARKETING INFORMATION SYSTEM

We define the marketing information system as follows:

> A **marketing information system (MIS)** consists of people, equipment, and procedures to gather, sort, analyze, evaluate, and distribute needed, timely, and accurate information to marketing decision makers.

The marketing information system is illustrated in Figure 4-1. The MIS begins and ends with marketing managers. First it interacts with these managers to assess their information needs. Next it develops the needed information from internal company records, marketing intelligence activities, and marketing research. Information analysis processes the information to make it more useful. Finally, the MIS distributes information to managers in the right form and at the right time to help them in marketing analysis, planning, implementation, and control.

We will now take a closer look at the functions of the company's marketing information system.

ASSESSING INFORMATION NEEDS

A good marketing information system balances the information managers would *like* to have against what they really *need* and what is *feasible* to offer. The company begins by interviewing managers to find out what information they would like. Table

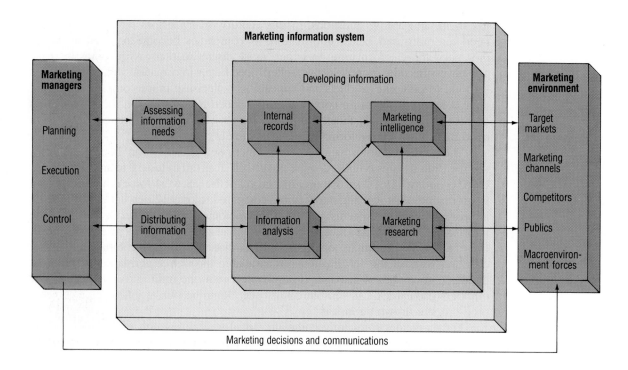

FIGURE 4-1   The marketing information system

4-1 lists a useful set of questions. But managers do not always need all the information they ask for, and they may not ask for all they really need. Moreover, sometimes the MIS cannot supply all the information managers request.

Some managers will ask for whatever information they can get without thinking carefully about what they really need. With today's information technology, most companies can provide much more information than managers can actually use. Too much information can be as harmful as too little.

Other busy managers may omit things they ought to know. Or managers may not know to ask for some types of information they should have. For example, managers might need to know that a competitor plans to introduce a new product during the coming year. Because they do not know about the new product, they do not think to ask about it. The MIS must watch the marketing environment and provide decision makers with information they should have to make key marketing decisions.

TABLE 4-1 **Questions for** **Assessing Marketing** **Information Needs**	1. What types of decisions are you regularly called upon to make? 2. What types of information do you need to make these decisions? 3. What types of information do you regularly get? 4. What types of special studies do you periodically request? 5. What types of information would you like to get that you are not now getting? 6. What information would you want daily? Weekly? Monthly? Yearly? 7. What magazine and trade reports would you like to see routed to you on a regular basis? 8. What specific topics would you like to be kept informed of? 9. What types of data analysis programs would you like to see made available? 10. What do you think would be the four most helpful improvements that could be made in the present marketing information system?

Information abounds—the problem is to give managers the *right information* at the *right time.*

Sometimes the company cannot provide the needed information, because it is not available or because of MIS limitations. For example, a brand manager might want to know how much competitors will change their advertising budgets next year and how these changes will affect industry market shares. The information on planned budgets is probably not available. Even if it is, the company's MIS may not be advanced enough to forecast resulting changes in market shares.

Finally, the company must decide whether the benefits of having an item of information are worth the costs of providing it, and both value and cost are often hard to assess. By itself, information has no worth—its value comes from how it is used. Though ways have been developed for calculating the value of information,[6] executives often must rely on subjective judgment. Similarly, while the company can add up the costs of the people and equipment that make up a marketing information system, or the costs of a marketing research project, figuring the cost of a specific item of information may be difficult.

The costs of obtaining, processing, storing, and delivering information can add up quickly. In many cases, additional information will do little to change or improve a manager's decision, or the costs of the information will exceed the returns from the better decision that results. For example, suppose a company estimates that launching a new product without any further information will yield a profit of $500,000. The manager believes that additional information will improve the marketing mix and allow the company to make $525,000. It would be foolish to pay $30,000 to obtain the extra information.

DEVELOPING INFORMATION

The information needed by marketing managers can be obtained from internal company records, marketing intelligence, and marketing research. The information analysis system then processes this information to make it more useful for managers.

Internal Records Most marketing managers use internal records and reports regularly, especially for making day-to-day planning, implementation, and control decisions. The company's accounting department makes financial statements and keeps detailed records of sales and orders, costs, and cash flows. Manufacturing reports on production schedules, shipments, and inventories. The sales force reports information on reseller reactions and competitor activities. Information on customer satisfaction or service problems is reported by the Customer Service Department. Research studies done for one department may provide useful information for several others. Managers can use information gathered from these and other sources within the company to evaluate performance and to detect problems and opportunities.

Here are examples of how companies use internal records information in making marketing decisions:

> Sears uses internal records as a powerful marketing tool. Marketing managers use computerized information on Sears' 40 million customers to promote special product and service offers to such diverse target segments as gardeners, appliance buyers, and expectant mothers. For example, Sears keeps track of the appliance purchases of each customer and promotes special service-package deals to customers who have bought several appliances but have not purchased maintenance contracts for them. Soon managers at other Sears subsidiaries—Allstate Insurance, Dean Witter Reynolds, and Coldwell Banker (real estate brokers)—will be able to develop sales leads using the same data.[7]
>
> Mead Paper's sales representatives can obtain on-the-spot answers to customers' questions about paper availability by dialing the company's computer center. The computer determines whether paper is available at the nearest warehouse and when it can be shipped. If it is not in stock, the computer checks the inventory at other nearby warehouses until one is located. If the paper is nowhere in stock, the computer determines where and when the paper can be produced. The sales representative gets an answer in seconds and thus has an advantage over competitors.

Information from internal records can usually be obtained more quickly and cheaply than information from other sources, but it also presents some problems. Because it was collected for other purposes, the information may be incomplete or in the wrong form for making marketing decisions. For example, accounting department sales and cost data used for preparing financial statements must be adapted for use in evaluating product, sales force, or reseller performance. Also, the many different areas of a large company produce great amounts of information; keeping track of it all is difficult. The marketing information system must gather, organize, process, and index this mountain of information so that managers can find it easily and get it quickly.

Marketing Intelligence **Marketing intelligence** is everyday information about developments in the marketing environment that helps managers prepare and adjust marketing plans. The marketing intelligence system determines what intelligence is needed, collects it by searching the environment, and delivers it to marketing managers who need it.

Marketing intelligence can be gathered from many sources. Much intelligence can be collected from the company's own personnel—executives, engineers and scientists, purchasing agents, and the salesforce. Yet company people are often busy and fail to pass on important information. The company must "sell" its people on their importance as intelligence gatherers, train them to spot new developments, and urge them to report intelligence back to the company.

The company also benefits when suppliers, resellers, and customers pass along important intelligence about competitors. Information on competitors can be obtained from what they say about themselves in annual reports, speeches and press releases, and advertisements. The company also can learn about competitors from what others say about them in business publications and at trade shows. Or the company can watch what competitors do—it can buy and analyze their products, monitor their sales, and check for new patents (see Marketing Highlight 4–1).

Companies also buy intelligence information from outside suppliers. The A. C. Nielsen Company sells data on brand shares, retail prices, and percentage of stores stocking different brands. Market Research Corporation of America sells reports on weekly movements of brand shares, sizes, prices, and deals. For a fee, companies can subscribe to one or more of over 3,000 online databases or information search services. For example, the *Adtrack* online database tracks all advertisements of a quarter page or larger from 150 major consumer and business publications. Companies can use it to assess their own and competitors' advertising strategies and style, share of advertising space, media usage, and ad budgets. The *Donnelly Demographics* database provides demographic data from the U.S. census plus Donnelly's own demographic projections by state, city, or zip code. Companies can use it to measure markets and develop segmentation strategies. The *Electronic Yellow Pages,* containing listings from nearly all the nation's 4,800 phone books, is the largest directory of American companies available. A firm like Burger King might use this database to count McDonald's restaurants in different geographic locations. A readily available online database exists to fill almost any marketing information need.[8]

Marketing intelligence can work in two directions, so companies must sometimes take steps to protect themselves from the snooping of competitors. For example, Kellogg had treated the public to tours of its Battle Creek, Michigan, plant since 1906, but recently closed its newly upgraded plant to outsiders to prevent competitors from getting any intelligence on its high-tech cereal equipment. In its corporate offices, Du Pont displays a poster showing two people at a lunch table and warns, "Be careful in casual conversation. Keep security in mind."[9]

Some companies set up an office to collect and circulate marketing intelligence. The staff scans major publications, summarizes important news, and sends news bulletins to marketing managers. It develops a file of intelligence information and helps managers to evaluate new information. These services greatly improve the quality of information available to marketing managers.

Marketing Research

Managers cannot always wait for information to arrive in bits and pieces from the marketing intelligence system. They often require formal studies of specific situations. For example, Hewlett-Packard wants to know how many and what kinds of people or companies will buy its new ultralight personal computer. Or Barat College in Lake Forest, Illinois, needs to know what percentage of its target market has heard of Barat, what they know about it, how they heard about Barat, and how they feel about the college. In such situations, the marketing intelligence system will not provide the detailed information needed. And managers normally do not have the skills or time to obtain the information on their own. They need formal marketing research.

We define marketing research as follows:

> **Marketing research** is the function that links the consumer, customer, and public to the marketer through information—information used to identify and define marketing opportunities and problems; generate, refine, and evaluate marketing actions; monitor marketing performance; and improve understanding of the marketing process.[10]

Marketing research specifies the information required to address marketing issues; designs the method for collecting information; manages and implements the data collection process; analyzes the results; and communicates the findings and their implications.

INTELLIGENCE GATHERING: SNOOPING ON COMPETITORS

Competitive intelligence gathering has grown dramatically as more and more companies need to know what their competitors are doing. Such well-known companies as Ford, Westinghouse, General Electric, Gillette, Revlon, Del Monte, General Foods, Kraft, and J.C. Penney are known to be busy snooping on their competitors.

A recent article in *Fortune* lists over twenty techniques companies use to collect their own intelligence. The techniques fall into four major groups.

- *Getting Information from Recruits and Competitors' Employees.* Companies can obtain intelligence through job interviews or from conversations with competitors' employees. According to *Fortune:*

When they interview students for jobs, some companies pay special attention to those who have worked for competitors, even temporarily. Job seekers are eager to impress and often have not been warned about divulging what is proprietary. They sometimes volunteer valuable information.

Companies send engineers to conferences and trade shows to question competitors' technical people. Often conversations start innocently—just a few fellow technicians discussing processes and problems . . . [yet competitors'] engineers and scientists often brag about surmounting technical challenges, in the process divulging sensitive information.

Companies sometimes advertise and hold interviews for jobs that don't exist in order to entice competitors' employees to spill the beans. . . . Often applicants

have toiled in obscurity or feel that their careers have stalled. They're dying to impress somebody.

- *Getting Information from People Who Do Business with Competitors.* Key customers can keep the company informed about competitors and their products:

For example, a while back Gillette told a large Canadian account the date on which it planned to begin selling its new Good News disposable razor in the United States. The Canadian distributor promptly called Bic and told it about the impending product launch. Bic put on a crash program and was able to start selling its razor shortly after Gillette did.

Intelligence can also be gathered by infiltrating customers' business operations:

Companies may provide their engineers free of charge to customers. . . . The close, cooperative relationship that the engineers on loan cultivate with the customer's design staff often enables them to learn what new products competitors are pitching.

- *Getting Information from Published Materials and Public Documents.* Keeping track of seemingly meaningless published information can provide competitor intelligence. For example, the types of people sought in help wanted ads can indicate something about a competitor's new strategies and products. Government agencies are another good source. For example:

Although it is often illegal for a company to photograph a competitor's plant from the air there are legitimate ways to get the photos. . . . Aerial photos

Marketing researchers have steadily expanded their activities (see Table 4-2). The most common activities are measurement of market potentials, market share analysis, the determination of market characteristics, sales analysis, studies of business trends, short-range forecasting, long-range forecasting, competitive product studies, management information system pricing studies, and testing of existing products.

Every marketer needs research. A company can do marketing research in its own research department or have some or all of it done outside. Whether a company uses outside firms depends on the skills and resources within the company. Most large companies have their own marketing research departments. A company with no research department will have to buy the services of research firms. But even companies with their own departments often use outside firms to do special research tasks or special studies.

Collecting intelligence: Xerox engineers tear apart a competitor's product to assess its design and to estimate costs.

often are on file with the U.S. Geological Survey or Environmental Protection Agency. These are public documents, available for a nominal fee.

• *Getting Information by Observing Competitors or Analyzing Physical Evidence.* Companies can get to know competitors better by buying their products or examining other physical evidence:

Companies increasingly buy competitors' products and take them apart to . . . determine costs of production and even manufacturing methods.

In the absence of better information on market share and the volume of product competitors are shipping, companies have measured the rust on rails of railroad sidings to their competitors' plants or have counted the tractor-trailers leaving loading bays.

Some companies even buy their competitors' garbage:

Once it has left the competitors' premises, refuse is legally considered abandoned property. While some companies now shred the paper coming out of their design labs, they often neglect to do this for almost-as-revealing refuse from the marketing or public relations departments.

Though most of these techniques are legal, and some might be considered shrewd competitiveness, many involve questionable ethics. The company should take advantage of publicly available information, but avoid practices that might be considered illegal or unethical. A company does not have to break the law or accepted codes of ethics to get good intelligence information.

Source: Based on Steven Flax, "How to Snoop on Your Competitors," *Fortune*, May 14, 1984, pp. 29–33. © 1984 Time Inc. All rights reserved.

The Marketing Research Process

This section describes the four steps in the marketing research process, shown in Figure 4-2: defining the problem and research objectives, developing the research plan, implementing the research plan, and interpreting and presenting the findings.

Defining the Problem and Research Objectives

The marketing manager and the researcher must work closely together to define the problem carefully and agree on the research objectives. The manager best understands the problem or decision for which information is needed; the researcher best understands marketing research and how to obtain the information. Managers must know enough about marketing research to help in the planning and to interpret research results. If they know little about marketing research, they may obtain the wrong information, accept wrong conclusions, or ask for information that costs too

TABLE 4-2 Research Activities of 599 Companies

TYPE OF RESEARCH	PERCENTAGE DOING IT	TYPE OF RESEARCH	PERCENTAGE DOING IT
Advertising research		**Product research**	
1. Motivation research	47%	1. New product acceptance and potential	76
2. Copy research	61	2. Competitive product studies	87
3. Media research	68	3. Testing of existing products	80
4. Studies of ad effectiveness	76	4. Packaging research: design or physical characteristics	65
5. Studies of competitive advertising	67		
Business economics and corporate research		**Sales and market research**	
1. Short-range forecasting (up to 1 year)	89	1. Measurement of market potentials	97
2. Long-range forecasting (over 1 year)	87	2. Market share analysis	97
3. Studies of business trends	91	3. Determination of market characteristics	97
4. Pricing studies	83	4. Sales analysis	92
5. Plant and warehouse location studies	68	5. Establishment of sales quotas, territories	78
6. Acquisition studies	73	6. Distribution channel studies	71
7. Export and international studies	49	7. Test markets, store audits	59
8. MIS (Management Information System)	80	8. Consumer panel operations	63
9. Operations Research	65	9. Sales compensation studies	60
10. Internal company employees	76	10. Promotional studies of premiums, coupons, sampling, deals, etc.	58
Corporate responsibility research			
1. Consumer "right to know" studies	18		
2. Ecological impact studies	23		
3. Studies of legal constraints on advertising and promotion	46		
4. Social values and policies studies	39		

Source: Dik Warren Twedt, ed., *1983 Survey of Marketing Research* (Chicago: American Marketing Association, 1983), p. 41.

much. Experienced marketing researchers who understand the manager's problem should also be involved at this stage. The researcher must be able to help the manager define the problem and to suggest ways that research can help the manager make better decisions.

Defining the problem and research objectives is often the hardest step in the research process. The manager may know that something is wrong, but not the specific causes. For example, managers of a discount retail chain store hastily decided that falling sales were caused by poor advertising and ordered research to test the company's advertising. When this research showed that the current advertising was reaching the right people with the right message, the managers were puzzled. It turned out that the stores themselves were not providing what the advertising promised. More careful problem definition would have avoided the cost and delay of doing the advertising research. It would have suggested research on the real problem of consumer reactions to the products, service, and prices offered in the chain's stores.

When the problem has been carefully defined, the manager and researcher must set the research objectives. A marketing research project can be one of three

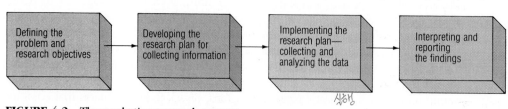

FIGURE 4-2 The marketing research process

types. Sometimes the research is **exploratory**—to gather preliminary information that will help to better define the problem and suggest hypotheses. Sometimes the research is **descriptive**—to describe things such as the market potential for a product or the demographics and attitudes of consumers who buy the product. Sometimes the research is **causal**—to test hypotheses about cause-and-effect relationships. For example, would a 10 percent decrease in tuition for a private college result in more than the increase in enrollments needed to break even financially? Managers often start with exploratory research and later follow with descriptive or causal research.

The statement of the problem and research objectives will guide the entire research process. The manager and researcher should put the statement in writing to be certain that they agree on the purpose and expected results of the research.

Developing the Research Plan

The second step of the marketing research process calls for determining the information needed and developing a plan for gathering it efficiently.

DETERMINING SPECIFIC INFORMATION NEEDS. The research objectives must be translated into specific information needs. For example, suppose the Campbell Soup Company decides to do research to find out how consumers will react to a new bowl-shaped plastic container that costs more but allows consumers to heat soup in a microwave oven and eat it without using dishes. This research might call for the following specific information:

- The demographic, economic, and life style characteristics of current soup users. (Busy working couples might find the convenience of the new package worth the price; families on a tight budget might want to pay less and wash the pan and bowls.)
- Consumer usage patterns for soup—how much soup consumers eat, where, and when. (The new package might be ideal for adults eating lunch on the go but less convenient for parents feeding lunch to several children.)
- The number of microwave ovens in consumer and commercial markets. (The number of microwaves in homes and business lunchrooms will limit the demand for the new container.)
- Retailer reactions to the new package. (Failure to get retailer support could hurt sales of the new package.)
- Forecasts of sales of the new and current packages. (Will the new package increase Campbell's profits?)

Campbell managers will need these and many other types of information to decide whether or not to introduce the new product.

SURVEYS OF SECONDARY INFORMATION. To meet the manager's information needs, the researcher can gather secondary data, primary data, or both. **Secondary data** consist of information that already exists somewhere, having been collected for another purpose. **Primary data** consist of information collected for the specific purpose at hand.

Researchers usually start by gathering secondary data. Table 4-3 shows the many secondary data sources, including *internal* and *external* sources.[11] Secondary data can usually be obtained more quickly and at a lower cost than primary data. For example, a visit to the library might provide all the information Campbell needs on microwave oven usage at almost no cost. A study to collect primary information might take weeks or months and cost thousands of dollars. Also, secondary sources can sometimes provide data an individual company cannot collect on its own—information not directly available or too expensive to collect. For example, it would be too expensive for Campbell to conduct a continuing retail store audit to find

TABLE 4-3
Sources of Secondary
Data

A. Internal sources

Internal sources include company profit and loss statements, balance sheets, sales figures, sales call reports, invoices, inventory records, and prior research reports.

B. Government publications

Statistical Abstract of the U.S., updated annually, provides summary data on demographic, economic, social, and other aspects of the American economy and society.

County and City Data Book, updated every three years, presents statistical information for counties, cities, and other geographical units on population, education, employment, aggregate and median income, housing, bank deposits, retail sales, etc.

U.S. Industrial Outlook provides projections of industrial activity by industry and includes data on production, sales, shipments, employment, etc.

Marketing Information Guide provides a monthly annotated bibliography of marketing information.

Other government publications include the *Annual Survey of Manufacturers*; *Business Statistics*; *Census of Manufacturers*; *Census of Population*; *Census of Retail Trade, Wholesale Trade, and Selected Service Industries*; *Census of Transportation*; *Federal Reserve Bulletin*; *Monthly Labor Review*; *Survey of Current Business*; and *Vital Statistics Report*.

C. Periodicals and books

Business Periodicals Index, a monthly, lists business articles appearing in a wide variety of business publications.

Standard and Poor's Industry Surveys provide updated statistics and analyses of industries.

Moody's Manuals provide financial data and names of executives in major companies.

Encyclopedia of Associations provides information on every major trade and professional association in the United States.

Marketing journals include the *Journal of Marketing, Journal of Marketing Research*, and *Journal of Consumer Research*.

Useful trade magazines include *Advertising Age, Chain Store Age, Progressive Grocer, Sales and Marketing Management, Stores*.

Useful general business magazines include *Business Week, Fortune, Forbes*, and *Harvard Business Review*.

D. Commercial data

A. C. Nielsen Company provides data on products and brands sold through retail outlets (Retail Index Services), supermarket scanner data (Scantrack), data on television audiences (Media Research Services), and others.

MRCA Information Services provides data on weekly family purchases of consumer products (National Consumer Panel) and data on home food consumption (National Menu Census).

Information Resources, Inc., provides supermarket scanner data (InfoScan) and data on the impact of supermarket promotions (PromotionScan).

SAMI/Burke provides reports on warehouse withdrawals to food stores in selected market areas (SAMI reports) and supermarket scanner data (Samscam).

Simmons Market Research Bureau (MRB Group) provides annual reports covering television markets, sporting goods, and proprietary drugs, giving demographic data by sex, income, age, and brand preferences (selective markets and media reaching them).

Other commercial research houses selling data to subscribers include the *Audit Bureau of Circulation, Arbitron, Audits and Surveys, Dun and Bradstreet, National Family Opinion, Standard Rate and Data Service*, and *Starch*.

out about the market shares, prices, and displays of competitors' brands. But it can buy the Nielsen Retail Index, which provides this information from regular audits of 1,300 supermarkets, 700 drug stores, and 150 mass merchandisers.[12]

Secondary data also present problems. The needed information may not exist—researchers can rarely obtain all the data they need from secondary sources. For example, Campbell may find little existing data about soup consumption patterns, and it will not find any existing information about consumer reactions to its new package. Even when the data can be found, they might not be very usable. The researcher must evaluate secondary information carefully to make certain it is *relevant* (fits research project needs), *accurate* (reliably collected and reported), *current* (up to date enough for current decisions), and *impartial* (objectively collected and reported).

Secondary data provide a good starting point for research and often help to define the problem and research objectives. In most cases, however, secondary sources cannot provide all the needed information, and the company must collect primary data.

PLANNING PRIMARY DATA COLLECTION. Some managers collect primary data by dreaming up a few questions and finding some people to interview. Data collected in this way might be useless or—even worse, misleading. Table 4-4 shows that designing a plan for primary data collection calls for decisions on research approaches, contact methods, sampling plan, and research instruments. _exploratory_

RESEARCH APPROACHES. **Observational research** is the gathering of primary data by observing relevant people, actions, and situations. For example:

* A food products manufacturer sends researchers into supermarkets to find out the prices of competing brands or how much shelf space and display support retailers give its brands.
* A bank evaluates possible new branch locations by checking the locations of competing branches, traffic patterns, and neighborhood conditions.
* A maker of personal care products pretests its ads by showing them to people and measuring eye movements, pulse rates, and other physical reactions.
* A department store chain sends observers posing as customers to its stores to check on store conditions and customer service.
* A museum checks the popularity of various exhibits by noting the amount of floor wear around them.

Several companies sell information collected through mechanical observation. For example, the A.C. Nielsen Company attaches "people meters" to television sets in selected homes to record who watches which programs. Nielsen then provides summaries of the size and demographic make-up of audiences for different television programs. The television networks use these ratings to judge program popularity and to set charges for advertising time. Advertisers use the ratings when selecting programs for their commercials.

Check-out scanners in retail stores also provide observation data. These scanners record consumer purchases in detail. Several companies collect and process scanner data for their subscribers. For example, Information Resources, Inc., through its BehaviorScan service, maintains consumer panels of households in major markets. Each household receives an identification number. When household members shop for groceries, they give their identification number to the check-out clerk. All the information about the family's purchases—brands bought, package sizes, prices paid—is recorded by the scanner and immediately entered by computer into the family's purchase file. The file also contains information about the household, such as income and age of children. Finally, the system monitors in-store factors that might affect buying, such as special price promotions and shelf displays. Thus BehaviorScan provides companies with quick and detailed information about how their products are selling, who is buying them, and what factors affect purchase.[13]

Observational research can be used to obtain information that people are unwilling or unable to provide. In some cases, observation may be the only way to obtain the needed information. On the other hand, some things simply cannot be observed—

TABLE 4-4 Planning Primary Data Collection	RESEARCH APPROACHES	CONTACT METHODS	SAMPLING PLAN	RESEARCH INSTRUMENTS
	Observation Survey Experiment	Mail Telephone Personal	Sampling unit Sample size Sampling procedure	Questionnaire Mechanical instruments

Information Resources, Inc.'s, BehaviorScan provides detailed information about how products are selling and who is buying them.

things such as feelings, attitudes and motives, or personal behavior. Long-run or infrequent behavior is also difficult to observe. Because of these limitations, researchers often use observation in combination with other data collection methods.

descriptive **Survey research** is the approach best suited for gathering descriptive information. A company that wants to know about people's knowledge, attitudes, preferences, or buying behavior can often find out by asking them directly. Survey research can be structured or unstructured. *Structured* surveys use formal lists of questions asked of all respondents in the same way. *Unstructured* surveys let the interviewer probe respondents and guide the interview according to their answers.

Survey research may be direct or indirect. In the *direct* approach, the researcher asks direct questions about behavior or thoughts—for example, "Why don't you buy clothes at K mart?" Using the *indirect* approach, the researcher might ask, "What kinds of people buy clothes at K mart?" From the response to this indirect question, the researcher may be able to discover why the consumer avoids K mart clothing—in fact, it may suggest reasons the consumer is not consciously aware of.

Survey research is the most widely used method for primary data collection, and it is often the only method used in a research study. The biggest advantage of survey research is its flexibility. It can be used to obtain many different kinds of information in many different marketing situations. Depending on the survey design, it may also provide information more quickly and at lower cost than the observational or experimental research.

Survey research also has some problems. Sometimes people are unable to answer survey questions because they cannot remember or never thought about what they do and why. Or people may be unwilling to answer questions asked by unknown interviewers or about things they consider private. Busy people may not take the time. To appear smarter or more informed respondents may answer survey questions even when they do not know the answer. Or they may try to help the interviewer by giving pleasing answers. Careful survey design can help to minimize these problems.

Whereas observation is best suited for exploratory research and surveys for descriptive research, **experimental research** is best suited for gathering causal information. Experiments involve selecting matched groups of subjects, giving them different treatments, controlling unrelated factors, and checking for differences in group responses. Thus experimental research tries to explain cause-and-effect relationships. Observation and surveys may be used to collect information in experimental research.

Researchers at McDonald's might use experiments before adding a new sandwich to the menu to answer such questions as the following:

* How much will the new sandwich increase McDonald's sales?
* How will the new sandwich affect the sales of other menu items?
* Which advertising approach would have the greatest effect on sales of the sandwich?
* How would different prices affect the sales of the product?
* Should the new item be targeted toward adults, children, or both?

For example, to test the effects of two different prices, McDonald's could set up the following simple experiment. It could introduce the new sandwich for one price at restaurants in one city, and for another price at restaurants in another similar city. If the cities are very similar, and if all other marketing efforts for the sandwich are the same, then differences in sales in the two cities could be related to the price charged. More complex experiments could be designed to include other variables and other locations.

CONTACT METHODS. Information can be collected by mail, telephone, or personal interview. Table 4-5 shows the strengths and weaknesses of each of these contact methods.

Mail questionnaires have many advantages. They can be used to collect large amounts of information at a low cost per respondent. Respondents may give more honest answers to more personal questions on a mail questionnaire than to an unknown interviewer in person or over the phone. No interviewer is involved to bias or influence the respondent's answers.

Mail questionnaires also have some disadvantages. They are not very flexible— they require simple and clearly worded questions, all respondents answer the same questions in a fixed order, and the researcher cannot adapt the questionnaire based on earlier answers. Mail surveys usually take longer to complete, and the response rate—the number of people returning completed questionnaires—is often very low. The researcher often has little control over the mail questionnaire sample—the

TABLE 4-5
Strengths and Weaknesses of the Three Contact Methods

	MAIL	TELEPHONE	PERSONAL
1. Flexibility	Poor	Good	Excellent
2. Quantity of data that can be collected	Good	Fair	Excellent
3. Control of interviewer effects	Excellent	Fair	Poor
4. Control of sample	Fair	Excellent	Fair
5. Speed of data collection	Poor	Excellent	Good
6. Response rate	Poor	Good	Good
7. Cost	Good	Fair	Poor

Source: Adapted with permission of Macmillan Publishing Company from *Marketing Research: Measurement and Method*, 4th ed., by Donald S. Tull and Del I. Hawkins. Copyright © 1987 by Macmillan Publishing Company.

Researchers watch a focus group session.

people who fill out the questionnaire. Even with a good mailing list, it is often hard to control *who* at the mailing address fills out the questionnaire.

Telephone interviewing is the best method for gathering information quickly, and it provides greater flexibility than mail questionnaires. Interviewers can explain questions that are not understood. They can skip some questions or probe more on others, depending on the respondent's answers. Telephone interviewing allows greater sample control. Interviewers can ask to speak to respondents with the desired characteristics or even by name, and response rates tend to be higher than with mail questionnaires.

Telephone interviewing also has drawbacks. The cost per respondent is higher than for mail questionnaires, and people may not want to discuss personal questions with an interviewer. Using an interviewer increases flexibility but also introduces interviewer bias. The way interviewers talk, small differences in how they ask questions, and other differences may affect respondents' answers. Interviewers may interpret and record responses differently, or under time pressures some interviewers might cheat by recording answers without asking questions.

Personal interviewing takes two forms, individual and group interviewing. *Individual interviewing* involves talking with people in their homes or offices, on the street, or in shopping malls. The interviewer must gain their cooperation, and the time involved can range from a few minutes to several hours. Sometimes a small payment is given to people in return for their time.

Group interviewing consists of inviting six to ten people to gather for a few hours with a trained interviewer to talk about a product, service, or organization. The interviewer needs objectivity, knowledge of the subject and industry, and some understanding of group and consumer behavior. The participants are normally paid a small sum for attending. The meeting is held in a pleasant place, and refreshments are served to make things informal. The interviewer starts with broad questions before moving to more specific issues, and he or she encourages free and easy discussion, hoping that the group dynamics will bring out actual feelings and thoughts. At the same time, the interviewer "focuses" the discussion—hence the name **focus group interviewing.** The comments are recorded through note taking, tape recording, or videotaping and are later studied to understand the consumers' buying process. Focus group interviewing has become one of the major marketing research tools for gaining insights into consumers thoughts and feelings.[14]

Personal interviewing is very flexible and can be used to collect large amounts of information. Trained interviewers can hold the respondent's attention for a long time and can explain difficult questions. They can guide interviews, explore issues, and probe as the situation requires. Personal interviews can be used with any type of questionnaire. Interviewers can show subjects actual products, advertisements, or packages and observe reactions and behavior. In most cases, personal interviews can be conducted fairly quickly.

The main drawbacks of personal interviewing are costs and sampling problems. Personal interviews may cost three to four times as much as telephone interviews. Group interview studies usually use small sample sizes to keep time and costs down, and it may be hard to generalize from the results. Because interviewers have more freedom in personal interviews, there is a greater problem of interviewer bias.

Which contact method is best depends on what information the researcher wants, and on the number and types of respondents to be contacted. Advances in computers and communications have had an impact on methods of obtaining information. For example, many research firms do Computer Assisted Telephone Interviewing (CATI) using a combination of WATS (Wide Area Telephone Service) lines and data entry terminals. The interviewer reads a set of questions from a video screen and types the respondent's answers right into the computer. This process eliminates data editing and coding, reduces errors, and saves time. Many research firms also conduct on-site computer interviewing. They set up microcomputers in shopping centers or at conventions—respondents sit down at the computer, read questions from its screen, and type in their own answers.

SAMPLING PLAN. Marketing researchers usually draw conclusions about large groups of consumers by studying a small sample of the total consumer population. A **sample** is a segment of the population selected to represent the population as a whole. Ideally, the sample should be representative so that the researcher can make accurate estimates of the thoughts and behaviors of the larger population.

Computer assisted telephone interviewing (CATI): The interviewer enters respondent's answers directly into the computer.

Designing the sample calls for three decisions. First, who is to be surveyed (what *sampling unit*)? The answer is not always obvious. For example, to study the decision-making process for a family automobile purchase, should the researcher interview the husband, wife, other family members, dealership salespeople, or all of these? The researcher must determine what information is needed and who is most likely to have it.

Second, how many people should be surveyed (what *sample size*)? Large samples give more reliable results than small samples. However, it is not necessary to sample the entire target market or even a large portion to get reliable results. If well chosen, samples of less than 1 percent of a population can often give good reliability.

Third, how should the people in the sample be chosen (what *sampling procedure*)? Table 4-6 describes different types of samples. To obtain a representative sample, one of the three types of probability samples should be drawn. But when probability sampling costs too much or takes too much time, marketing researchers will take nonprobability samples. Nonprobability samples can serve well in many research situations, even though the sampling error cannot be measured. These varied ways of drawing samples have different costs and time limitations, as well as different accuracy and statistical properties. Which method is best depends on the needs of the research project.

RESEARCH INSTRUMENTS. In collecting primary data, marketing researchers have a choice of two main research instruments—the questionnaire or mechanical devices.

The *questionnaire* is by far the more common instrument. Broadly speaking, a questionnaire consists of a set of questions presented to a respondent for his or her answers. The questionnaire is very flexible—there are many ways to ask questions. Questionnaires need to be carefully developed and tested before they can be used on a large scale. Experienced researchers can usually spot several errors in a carelessly prepared questionnaire (see Marketing Highlight 4–2).

In preparing a questionnaire, the marketing researcher must decide what questions to ask, the form of the questions, the wording of the questions, and the ordering of the questions. Questionnaires too often leave out questions that should be answered and include questions that cannot be answered, or will not be answered, or need not be answered. Each question should be checked to see that it contributes to the research objectives. Questions that are merely interesting should be dropped.

The *form* of the question can influence the response. Marketing researchers distinguish between closed-end and open-end questions. *Closed-end questions* include all the possible answers, and subjects make choices among them. Table 4-7A shows the most common forms of closed-ended questions as they might appear in a Delta Airlines survey of airline users. *Open-end questions* allow respondents to answer in

TABLE 4-6 **Types of Samples**		
	Probability sample	
	Simple random sample	Every member of the population has a known and equal chance of selection.
	Stratified random sample	The population is divided into mutually exclusive groups (such as age groups), and random samples are drawn from each group.
	Cluster (area) sample	The population is divided into mutually exclusive groups (such as blocks), and the researcher draws a sample of the groups to interview.
	Nonprobability sample	
	Convenience sample	The researcher selects the easiest population members from which to obtain information.
	Judgment sample	The researcher uses his or her judgment to select population members who are good prospects for accurate information.
	Quota sample	The researcher finds and interviews a prescribed number of people in each of several categories.

A "QUESTIONABLE" QUESTIONNAIRE

Suppose the following questionnaire had been prepared by a summer camp director to be used in interviewing parents of prospective campers. What do you think of each question?

1. What is your income to the nearest hundred dollars?

   People don't necessarily know their income to the nearest hundred dollars, nor do they want to reveal their income that closely. Furthermore, a questionnaire should never open with such a personal question.

2. Are you a strong or a weak supporter of overnight summer camping for your children?

   What do "strong" and "weak" mean?

3. Do your children behave themselves well in a summer camp? Yes ( ) No ( )

   "Behave" is a relative term. Besides, will people want to answer this? Furthermore, is "yes" or "no" the best way to allow a response to the question? Why is the question being asked in the first place?

4. How many camps mailed literature to you last April? This April?

   Who can remember this?

5. What are the most salient and determinant attributes in your evaluation of summer camps?

   What are "salience" and "determinant attributes"? Big, undefined words will only confuse the reader.

6. Do you think it is right to deprive your child of the opportunity to grow into a mature person through the experience of summer camping?

   Loaded question. How can one answer "yes," given the bias?

their own words. The main forms are shown in Table 4-7B. Open-end questions often reveal more because respondents are not limited in their answers. Open-end questions are especially useful in exploratory research, where the researcher is trying to find out how people think and is not measuring how many people think in a certain way. Closed-end questions, on the other hand, provide answers that are easier to interpret and tabulate.

Care should be used in the *wording* of questions. The researcher should use simple, direct, unbiased wording. The questions should be tested before they are widely used. Care should also be used in the *ordering* of questions. The first question should create interest if possible. Difficult or personal questions should be asked last so that respondents do not become defensive. The questions should come up in a logical order.

Although questionnaires are the most common research instrument, *mechanical instruments* are also used. For example, a galvanometer measures the strength of a subject's interest or emotions aroused by an exposure to an ad or picture. The galvanometer picks up the minute degree of sweating that accompanies emotional arousal. The tachistoscope flashes an ad to a subject for a length of time ranging from less than one-thousandth of a second to several seconds. After each exposure, the respondents describe everything they recall. Eye cameras are used to study respondents' eye movements to determine at what points their eyes land first in an ad and how long they linger on a given item.

Presenting the Research Plan. At this stage, the marketing researcher summarizes the research plan in a written proposal. A written proposal is especially important when the research project will be large and complex, or when an outside firm carries out the research. The proposal should cover the management problems addressed and the research objectives, the information to be obtained, sources of secondary information or methods for collecting primary data, and how the results will help management decision making. The proposal should also include research

TABLE 4-7 Types of Questions

A. CLOSED-END QUESTIONS

Name	Description	Example
Dichotomous	A question offering two answer choices.	"In arranging this trip, did you personally phone Delta?" Yes ☐ No ☐
Multiple choice	A question offering three or more answer choices.	"With whom are you traveling on this flight?" No one ☐ Children only ☐ Spouse ☐ Business associates/friends/relatives ☐ Spouse and children ☐ An organized tour group ☐
Likert scale	A statement with which the respondent shows the amount of agreement/disagreement.	"Small airlines generally give better service than large ones." Strongly disagree / Disagree / Neither agree nor disagree / Agree / Strongly agree 1 ☐ 2 ☐ 3 ☐ 4 ☐ 5 ☐
Semantic differential	A scale is inscribed between two bipolar words, and the respondent selects the point that represents the direction and intensity of his or her feelings.	*Delta Airlines* Large X : __ : __ : __ : __ : __ Small Experienced __ : __ : __ : __ : X : __ Inexperienced Modern __ : __ : __ : X : __ : __ Old-fashioned
Importance scale	A scale that rates the importance of some attribute from "not at all important" to "extremely important."	"Airline food service to me is" Extremely Important / Very important / Somewhat important / Not very important / Not at all important 1 __ 2 __ 3 __ 4 __ 5 __
Rating scale	A scale that rates some attribute from "poor" to "excellent."	"Delta's food service is" Excellent / Very good / Good / Fair / Poor 1 __ 2 __ 3 __ 4 __ 5 __

B. OPEN-END QUESTIONS

Name	Description	Example
Completely unstructured	A question that respondents can answer in an almost unlimited number of ways.	"What is your opinion of Delta Airlines?"
Word association	Words are presented, one at a time, and respondents mention the first word that comes to mind.	"What is the first word that comes to your mind when you hear the following?" Airline _____ Delta _____ Travel _____
Sentence completion	Incomplete sentences are presented, one at a time, and respondents complete the sentence.	"When I choose an airline, the most important consideration in my decision is _____"
Story completion	An incomplete story is presented, and respondents are asked to complete it.	"I flew Delta a few days ago. I noticed that the exterior and interior of the plane had very bright colors. This aroused in me the following thoughts and feelings." *Now complete the story.*
Picture completion	A picture of two characters is presented, with one making a statement. Respondents are asked to identify with the other and fill in the empty balloon.	WELL HERE'S THE FOOD. Fill in the empty balloon.
Thematic Apperception Tests (TAT)	A picture is presented, and respondents are asked to make up a story about what they think is happening or may happen in the picture.	Make up a story about what you see.

costs. A written research plan or proposal makes sure that the marketing manager and researchers have considered all important aspects of the research, and that they agree on why and how the research will be done. The manager should review the proposal carefully before approving the project.

Implementing the Research Plan （실시）

The researcher next puts the marketing research plan into action. This step involves collecting, processing, and analyzing the information. Data collection can be done by the company's marketing research staff or by outside firms. The company keeps more control over the collection process and data quality by using its own staff. However, outside firms that specialize in data collection can often do the job more quickly and at lower cost.

The data collection phase of the marketing research process is generally the most expensive and the most subject to error. The researcher should watch the fieldwork closely to make sure that the plan is correctly implemented and to guard against problems with contacting respondents, respondents who refuse to cooperate or who give biased or dishonest answers, and interviewers who make mistakes or take shortcuts.

The collected data must be processed and analyzed to pull out important information and findings. Data from questionnaires are checked for accuracy and completeness and then coded for computer analysis. The researcher applies standard computer programs to prepare tabulations of results and to compute averages and other measures for the major variables.

Interpreting and Reporting the Findings

The researcher must now interpret the findings, draw conclusions, and report them to management. The researcher should not try to overwhelm managers with numbers and fancy statistical techniques—this will lose them. The researcher should present major findings that are useful in the major decisions faced by management.

Interpretation should not be left only to the researchers. They are often experts in research design and statistics, but the marketing manager knows more about the problem and the decisions that must be made. In many cases, findings can be interpreted in different ways, and discussions between researchers and managers will help point to the best interpretations. The manager will also want to check that the research project was properly carried out and that all the necessary analysis was done. Or, after seeing the findings, the manager may have additional questions that can be answered using the research data collected. Finally, the manager is the one who must ultimately decide what action the research suggests. The researchers may even make the data directly available to marketing managers so that they can do new analyses and test new relationships on their own.

Interpretation is a very important phase of the marketing research process. The best research is meaningless if the manager blindly accepts wrong interpretations from the researcher. Similarly, managers may have biased interpretations. They tend to accept research results that show what they expected and to reject those that they did not expect or hope for. Thus managers and researchers must work together closely when interpreting research results, and both share responsibility for the research process, outcomes, and resulting decisions (see Marketing Highlight 4–3).

Marketing Research in Smaller Organizations

In this section we have looked at the marketing research process—from defining research objectives to interpreting and reporting results—as a lengthy, formal process

DELICARE: A CASE OF RESEARCH MALPRACTICE?

In early 1986, Beecham Products launched its new cold-water detergent for delicate fabrics, Delicare, with much confidence. Yankelovich Clancy Shulman, a large research firm, had conducted simulated test-market research and predicted that Delicare would quickly surpass the market leader, Woolite, capturing a 45 to 52 percent market share. Beecham paid $75,000 for the research and spent over $6 million on introductory advertising for the product. Yet in the end, Delicare leveled off at less than 20 percent of the market, far short of the 30 percent Beecham needed to recoup its investment. Beecham claimed that Yankelovich's faulty forecasts had caused it to suffer huge losses. In a move that rocked the marketing research industry, Beecham sued Yankelovich for negligence and marketing malpractice, seeking $24 million in damages.

Simulated test markets like the one used in the Delicare research provide a quick and inexpensive method for estimating consumer responses to a new product. Sample consumers view ads for the new product and others, then shop in a simulated store containing a variety of products. The researcher keeps track of how many consumers buy the new product being tested and how many buy competing products. The data are fed into a sophisticated computer model, which projects national sales from the results of the simulated test market. The Yankelovich model based its Delicare prediction on an important underlying statistic obtained from Beecham—the percentage of all U.S. homes that use a delicate-fabric detergent. Beecham claims it told Yankelovich to use a 30 percent figure but that the research firm used 75 percent. Yankelovich, however, claims that Delicare failed because Beecham provided inaccurate information, stopped advertising too soon, and ran ads different from those used in the research.

Regardless of the outcome, the Delicare case makes an important point for marketing managers and researchers—both must be closely involved in the entire research process. Beecham and Yankelovich managers share the blame for the Delicare research failure. If, as Yankelovich claims, Beecham provided inaccurate information, the researchers should have checked the data more carefully. And Beecham's marketers, rather than simply accepting the highly optimistic Delicare forecasts, should have reviewed the research outcomes and interpretations more critically. Ultimately, Beecham must take responsibility for its own marketing decisions. But if the company had worked more closely with Yankelovich throughout the research process, it might have avoided the Delicare fiasco.

Sources: See Matt Rothman, "A Case of Malpractice—in Marketing Research?" *Business Week*, August 10, 1987, pp. 28–29; and Annetta Miller and Dody Tsiantar, "A Test for Market Research," *Newsweek*, December 18, 1987, pp. 32–33.

carried out by large marketing companies. But many small businesses and nonprofit organizations also use marketing research. Almost any organization can find informal, low-cost alternatives to the formal and complex marketing research techniques used by research experts in large firms (see Marketing Highlight 4–4).

Information Analysis

Information gathered by the company's marketing intelligence and marketing research systems often requires more analysis, or managers need more help to apply it to marketing problems and decisions. Advanced statistical analysis of research data enables researchers to learn more about the relationships within a set of data and their statistical reliability. Such analysis allows management to go beyond means and standard deviations in the data and answer such questions as:

- What are the major variables affecting my sales, and how important is each one?
- If I raised my price 10 percent and increased my advertising expenditures 20 percent, what would happen to sales?

MARKETING HIGHLIGHT 4-4

MARKETING RESEARCH IN SMALL BUSINESSES AND NONPROFIT ORGANIZATIONS

Managers of small businesses and nonprofit organizations often think that marketing research can be done only by experts in large companies with big research budgets. But many of the marketing research techniques discussed in this chapter can also be used less formally by smaller organizations—and at little or no expense.

Managers of small businesses and nonprofit organizations can obtain good marketing information simply by *observing* things around them. For example, retailers can evaluate new locations by observing vehicle and pedestrian traffic. They can visit competing stores to check on facilities and prices. They can evaluate their customer mix by recording how many and what kinds of customers shop in the store at different times. Competitor advertising can be monitored by collecting advertisements from local media.

Managers can conduct informal *surveys* using small convenience samples. The director of an art museum can learn what patrons think about new exhibits by conducting informal "focus groups"—inviting small groups to lunch and having discussions on topics of interest. Retail salespeople can talk with customers visiting the store; hospital officials can interview patients. Restaurant managers might make random phone calls during slack hours to interview consumers about where they eat out and what they think of various restaurants in the area.

Managers can also conduct their own simple *experiments*. For example, by changing the themes in regular fund-raising mailings and watching results, a nonprofit manager can find out much about which marketing strategies work best. By varying newspaper advertisements, a store manager can learn the effects of things such as ad size and position, price coupons, and media used.

Small organizations can obtain most of the secondary data available to large businesses. In addition, many associations, local media, chambers of commerce, and government agencies provide special help to small organizations. The U.S. Small Business Administration offers dozens of free publications giving advice on topics ranging from planning advertising to ordering business signs. Local newspapers often provide information on local shoppers and their buying patterns.

Sometimes volunteers and colleges are willing to help carry out research. Nonprofit organizations can often use volunteers from local service clubs and other sources. Many colleges are seeking small businesses and nonprofit organizations to serve as cases for projects in marketing research classes.

Thus secondary data collection, observation, surveys, and experiments can be used effectively by small organizations with small budgets. Though such informal research is less complex and costly, it must still be done carefully. Managers must carefully think through the objectives of the research, formulate questions in advance, recognize the biases introduced by smaller samples and less skilled researchers, and conduct the research systematically. If carefully planned and implemented, such low-cost research can provide reliable information for improving marketing decision making.

Source: Based on information found in Alan R. Andreasen, "Cost-Conscious Marketing Research," *Harvard Business Review*, July–August, 1983, pp. 74–79, and other sources.

---

* What are the best predictors of consumers who are likely to buy my brand versus my competitor's brand?
* What are the best variables for segmenting my market, and how many segments exist?

Information analysis might also involve a collection of mathematical models that will help marketers make better decisions. Each model represents some real system, process, or outcome. These models can help answer the questions of *what if* and *which is* best. In the past twenty years, marketing scientists have developed a great number of models to help marketing managers make better marketing mix decisions, design sales territories and sales call plans, select sites for retail outlets, develop optimal advertising mixes, and forecast new product sales.[15]

*D*ISTRIBUTING INFORMATION

Marketing information has no value until managers use it to make better marketing decisions. The information gathered through marketing intelligence and marketing research must be distributed to the right marketing managers at the right time. Most companies have centralized marketing information systems that provide managers with regular performance reports, intelligence updates, and reports on the results of studies. Managers need these routine reports for making regular planning, implementation, and control decisions. But marketing managers may also need nonroutine information for special situations and on-the-spot decisions. For example, a sales manager having trouble with a large customer wants a summary of the account's sales and profitability over the past year. Or a retail store manager whose store has run out of a best-selling product wants to know the current inventory levels in the chain's other stores. In companies with centralized information systems, these managers must request the information from the MIS staff and wait; often the information arrives too late to be useful.

Recent developments in information handling have caused a revolution in information distribution. With recent advances in microcomputers, software, and communications, many companies are decentralizing their marketing information systems. They are giving managers direct access to information stored in the system. One survey found that 53 percent of the marketing and advertising managers in *Fortune* 1500 companies have personal computers in their offices.[16] In many of these companies, marketing managers can use a desk-top or lap-top computer to tie into the company's information network. Without leaving their desks, they can obtain information from internal records or outside information services, analyze the information

An advanced office network ties the manager directly into the company's information system.

INFORMATION NETWORKS: DECENTRALIZING THE MARKETING INFORMATION SYSTEM

New information technologies are making it possible to help managers obtain, process, and send information directly through machines rather than relying on the services of information specialists. The last decade's centralized information systems are giving way to systems that take information management out of the hands of staff specialists and put it into the hands of managers. Many companies are developing *information networks* that link separate technologies such as word processing, data processing, and image processing into a single system.

For example, envision the working day of a future marketing manager. On arriving at work, the manager turns to a desk terminal and reads any message that arrived during the night, reviews the day's schedule, checks the status of an ongoing computer conference, reads several intelligence alerts, and browses through abstracts of relevant articles from the previous day's business press. To prepare for a late-morning meeting of the new-products committee, the manager calls up a recent marketing research report from microfilm storage to the screen, reviews relevant sections, edits them into a short report, sends copies electronically to other committee members

who are also connected to the information network, and has the computer file a copy on microfilm. Before leaving for the meeting, the manager uses the terminal to make lunch reservations at a favorite restaurant and to buy airline tickets for next week's trip to Chicago.

The afternoon is spent preparing sales and profit forecasts for the new product discussed at the morning meeting. The manager obtains test market data from company data banks and information on market demand, sales of competing products, and expected economic conditions from external data bases to which the company subscribes. These data are used as inputs for the sales forecasting model stored in the company's model bank. The manager "plays" with the model to see how different assumptions affect predicted results.

At home later that evening, the manager uses a portable personal computer to contact the network, prepare a report on the product, and send copies to the terminals of other involved managers, who can read them first thing in the morning. When the manager logs off, the computer automatically sets the alarm clock and puts out the cat.

using statistical packages and models, prepare reports on a word processor, and communicate with others in the network through telecommunications (see Marketing Highlight 4–5).

Such systems offer exciting prospects. They allow the managers to get the information they need directly and quickly and to tailor it to their own needs. As more managers develop the skills needed to use such systems, and as improvements in the technology make them more economical, more and more marketing companies will use decentralized marketing information systems

■ SUMMARY

In carrying out their marketing responsibilities, marketing managers need information. Despite the growing supply of information, managers often lack enough information of the right kind or have too much of the wrong kind. To overcome these problems, many companies are taking steps to improve their marketing information systems.

A well-designed marketing information system begins and ends with the user. It first assesses information needs by interviewing marketing managers and surveying their

decision environment to determine what information is desired, needed, and feasible to offer.

The MIS next develops information and helps managers to use it more effectively. Internal records provide information on sales, costs, inventories, cash flows, and accounts receivable and payable. Such data can be obtained quickly and cheaply but must often be adapted for marketing decisions. The marketing intelligence system supplies marketing executives with everyday information about developments in the external marketing environment. Intelligence can be collected from company employees, customers, suppliers, and resellers, or by monitoring published reports, conferences, advertisements, competitor actions, and other activities in the environment.

Marketing research involves collecting information relevant to a specific marketing problem facing the company. Every marketer needs marketing research, and most large companies have their own marketing research departments. Marketing research involves a four-step process. The first step consists of the manager and researcher carefully defining the problem and setting the research objectives. The objective may be exploratory, descriptive, or causal. The second step consists of developing the research plan for collecting data from primary and secondary sources. Primary data collection calls for choosing a research approach (observation, survey, experiment); choosing a contact method (mail, telephone, personal); designing a sampling plan (who to survey, how many to survey,

and how to choose them); and developing research instruments (questionnaire, mechanical). The marketing manager should review the written research plan carefully before approving the project. The third step consists of implementing the marketing research plan by collecting, processing, and analyzing the information. The fourth step consists of interpreting and reporting the findings. Further information analysis helps marketing managers to apply the information and provides advanced statistical procedures and models to develop more rigorous findings from information.

Finally, the marketing information system distributes information gathered from internal sources, marketing intelligence, and marketing research to the right managers at the right times. More and more companies are decentralizing their information systems through distributed processing networks that allow managers to have direct access to information.

■ QUESTIONS FOR DISCUSSION

1. What are some kinds of information that managers would *like* to have to make better decisions about product development, distribution, advertising, and pricing? What kinds of information would a marketing information system be likely to provide?

2. List some internal and environmental factors that would call for marketing research by a company.

3. As a sales representative calling on industrial accounts, you would learn a lot that would help decision makers in your company. What kinds of information would you pass on to your company? How would you decide whether something is worth reporting?

4. The president of a campus organization has asked you to conduct a marketing research project on why membership is declining. Discuss how you would apply the steps in the research process to this project.

5. You are a research supplier, designing and conducting studies for different clients. What is the *most* important thing you can do to ensure that your clients will get their money's worth from your services?

6. What research problem did Coke appear to be investigating prior to the introduction of New Coke? What were the company's research objectives? What problem *should* Coke have investigated instead?

7. What type of research would be appropriate in the following situations, and why?
   a. Post cereals wants to investigate the effect young children have on parents' decisions to buy its products.
   b. Your college bookstore wants to get some insights into how students feel about the store's merchandise, prices, and service.

c. McDonald's is considering locating a new outlet in a fast-growing suburb.
d. Gillette wants to determine whether a new line of deodorant for children will be profitable.

8. In several test communities in the United States, it is possible to send different versions of a commercial to different consumers' homes, record the viewers' purchases at grocery checkout counters, and see which version produced the greatest sales. Participation in this testing is voluntary. The ACLU claims that this is an invasion of privacy; marketers claim that it will lead to better marketing decisions. What do you think?

9. Focus-group interviewing has become one of the most common research techniques in marketing, but it is also a widely criticized research technique. What are the advantages and disadvantages of focus groups? What are some kinds of questions that focus groups can be used to investigate.

10. What kinds of information would you need in order to develop a mathematical model of how marketing mix decisions affect sales? Would this information be supplied by the firm's marketing information system, or would you need to collect additional data?

11. A product-use study showed that many people were wasting their money by using more of a product at a time than they needed to. The company's advertising actually encouraged this overuse. The marketing research director sent a memo to the advertising manager suggesting that the advertising be modified, but no changes were made. Was the director's action appropriate? What else should he or she have done?

■ KEY TERMS

Causal research   Marketing research to test hypotheses about cause-and-effect relationships.

Descriptive research   Marketing research to better describe marketing problems, situations, or markets—such as the market potential for a product, or the demographics and attitudes of consumers.

Experimental research   The gathering of primary data by selecting matched groups of subjects, giving them different treatments, controlling related factors, and checking for differences in group responses.

Exploratory research   Marketing research to gather preliminary information that will help to better define problems and suggest hypotheses.

Focus group interviewing   Personal interviewing that consists of inviting six to ten people to gather for a few hours with a trained interviewer to talk about a product, service, or organization. The interviewer "focuses" the group discussion on important issues.

Marketing information system (MIS)   People, equipment, and procedures to gather, sort, analyze, evaluate, and distribute needed, timely, and accurate information to marketing decision makers.

Marketing intelligence   Everyday information about developments in the marketing environment that helps managers prepare and adjust marketing plans.

Marketing research   The function that links the consumer, customer, and public to the marketer through information—information used to identify and define marketing opportunities and problems; generate, refine, and evaluate marketing actions; monitor marketing performance; and improve understanding of the marketing process.

Observational research   The gathering of primary data by observing relevant people, actions, and situations.

Primary data   Information collected for the specific purpose at hand.

Sample   A segment of the population selected for marketing research to represent the population as a whole.

Secondary data   Information that already exists somewhere, having been collected for another purpose.

Survey research   The gathering of primary data by asking people questions about their knowledge, attitudes, preferences, and buying behavior.

■ REFERENCES

1. Based on numerous sources including "Coke 'Family' Sales Fly as New Coke Stumbles," *Advertising Age*, January 17, 1986, p. 1ff; Scott Scredon and Marc Frons, "Coke's Man on the Spot: The Changes Goizueta Is Making Outweigh the Spectacular Blunder," *Business Week*, July 29, 1985, pp. 56–61; Jack Honomichl, "Missing Ingredients in 'New' Coke's Research," *Advertising Age*, July 22, 1985, p. 1ff; and "He Put The Kick Back in Coke," Fortune, October 26, 1987, pp. 46–56.

2. Marion Harper, Jr., "A New Profession to Aid Management," *Journal of Marketing*, January 1961, p. 1.

3. John Naisbitt, *Megatrends: Ten New Directions Transforming Our Lives* (New York: Warner Books, 1984).

4. "Harnessing the Data Explosion," *Sales and Marketing Management*, January 1987, p. 31.

5. Naisbitt, *Megatrends*, p. 16.

6. Donald S. Tull and Del I. Hawkins, *Marketing Research: Measurement and Method*, 4th ed. (New York: MacMillan, 1987), pp. 40–41, 750–60.

7. See "Business Is Turning Data into a Potent Strategic Weapon," *Business Week*, August 22, 1983, p. 92.

8. See Tim Miller, "Focus: Competitive Intelligence," *Online Access Guide*, March/April 1987, pp. 43–57.

9. Ibid., p. 46.

10. The American Marketing Association officially adopted this definition in 1987.

11. For an excellent annotated reference to major secondary sources of business and marketing data, see Thomas C. Kinnear and James R. Taylor, *Marketing Research: An Applied Approach* (New York: McGraw-Hill, 1983), pp. 146–56, 169–84. Also see "The Nation's Top Research Companies Profiled," *Advertising Age*, May 11, 1987, pp. S2-S26.

12. Ibid., p. 150.

13. See Leonard M. Lodish and David J. Reibstein, "New Gold Mines and Minefields in Market Research," *Harvard Business Review*, January–February 1986, pp. 168–82.

14. See Bobby J. Calder, "Focus Groups and the Nature of Qualitative Marketing Research," *Journal of Marketing*, August 1977, pp. 353–64; and J. L. Welch, "Researching Marketing Problems and Opportunities with Focus Groups," *Industrial Marketing Management*," November 1985, pp. 245–54.

15. For more on statistical analysis, consult a standard text such as Tull and Hawkins, *Marketing Research*. For a review of marketing models, see Gary L. Lilien and Philip Kotler, *Marketing Decision Making: A Model Building Approach* (New York: Harper & Row, 1983); also see John D. C. Little, "Decision Support Systems for Marketing Managers," *Journal of Marketing*, Summer 1979, pp. 9–26.

16. "Marketing Managers No Stranger to the PC," *Sales and Marketing Management*, May 13, 1985. Also see Peter Nulty, "How Personal Computers Change Managers' Lives," *Fortune*, September 3, 1984, pp. 38–48.

5

Consumer Markets: Influences on Consumer Behavior

PETER SCHUTZ, chief executive at Porsche, spends a full 25 percent of his time talking with customers. He wants to truly know who they are, what they think and how they feel, and why they buy a Porsche

rather than a Jaguar, or a Ferrari, or a big Mercedes coupe. These are difficult questions—even Porsche owners themselves don't know exactly what motivates their buying. But Schutz puts top priority on understanding customers and what makes them tick.

Porsche appeals to a very narrow segment of financially successful people, achievers who set extraordinarily high goals for themselves, then work doggedly to meet them. They expect no less from "their hobbies, or the clothes they wear, or the restaurants they go to, or the cars they drive." These achievers see themselves not as a regular part of the larger world, but as exceptions. They buy a Porsche because it mirrors their self-image—the car stands for the things owners like to see in themselves and in their lives.

Most of us buy what Schutz calls utility vehicles, that is, "cars to be used: to go to work, to deliver the kids, to go shopping." We buy on facts like price, size, function, fuel economy, and other practical con-

siderations. But a Porsche is a nonutility car, one to be enjoyed, not just used. Porsche buyers are moved not by facts, but by feelings. They are trying to match their dreams. To most Porsche owners, a car is more than mere transportation. It's like a piece of clothing, "something the owner actually wears and is seen in. . . . It's a very personal relationship, one that has to do with the way the car sounds, the way it vibrates, the way it feels." People buy a Porsche because they enjoy driving it, just being in it. "Just to get there, they could do it a lot less expensively. The car is an expression of themselves."

A Porsche runs from $25,000 to well over $65,000, but price isn't much of an issue with most buyers. The company deals often with folks who can buy anything they want. To many Porsche owners, the car is a hobby. In fact, Porsche's competition comes not just from other cars, but from such things as sailboats, summer homes, and airplanes. But "most of those objects require a lot of one thing these folks don't have, and that's time. If you have a Porsche and make *it* your hobby, you can enjoy it every day on your way to work and on your way to the airport, something you can't do with a sailboat or summer home."

Surprisingly, many Porsche owners are not car enthusiasts—not interested in racing or learning how to drive a high-performance car. They simply like the way a Porsche makes them feel or what the car tells others about their achievements, life style, and station. Schutz tells of a very successful career woman who owned an expensive Porsche. Like many Porsche buyers, "she had a lot of everything in the world except time. And she also had a 14-year-old daughter whom she adored. She said, 'Mr. Schutz, when I drive this car to the high school to pick my daughter up after school, I end up with five youngsters in the car. If I drive any other car, I can't even find her; she doesn't want to come home.' "

Porsche works hard to meet its buyers' demanding expectations. The car itself features progressive engineering, high performance, and tasteful, timeless styling. Porsche sells only about 50,000 cars a year— less than a month's production at Chevrolet. Schutz claims the company looks for only moderate growth; he wants to make one less Porsche than the demand. He says, "You get to see too many of them around, and all of a sudden it's nothing special." The company does all it can to make Porsche ownership very special. It's even hired a representative to sell celebrities, executives of large companies, top athletes, and other notables on its cars. Having these high-profile Americans driving Porsches and talking to their friends about them at cocktail parties is the best advertising the company could get.

Understanding Porsche buyers is an essential but difficult task for the company. Buyers are moved by a complex set of deep and subtle motivations. Their behavior springs from deeply held values and attitudes, from their view of the world and their place in it, from what they think of themselves and what they want others to think of them, from rationality and common sense, and from whimsy and impulse. Schutz sums it up this way: "If you really want to understand our customers, you have to understand the phrase, 'If I were going to be a car, I'd be a Porsche.' "[1]

Chapter Objectives   *After reading this chapter, you should be able to:*

1. Define the consumer market and construct a simple model of consumer buying behavior.
2. Tell how culture, subculture, and social class influence consumer buying behavior.
3. List the major social factors that affect consumer buying behavior.
4. Describe how consumers' personal characteristics influence their buying decisions.
5. Discuss the four major psychological factors that affect the buying process.

THE PORSCHE example shows that many different factors affect consumer buying behavior. Buying behavior is never simple, yet understanding it is the essential task of marketing management.

This chapter and the next will explore the dynamics of consumer behavior and the consumer market. The **consumer market** consists of all the individuals and households who buy or acquire goods and services for personal consumption. The American consumer market consists of more than 240 million people who consume over $2 trillion of goods and services—that's almost $9,000 worth for every man, woman, and child. Each year this market grows by several million persons and over $100 billion, making it one of the most attractive consumer markets in the world.

The attractive American consumer market: the annual consumption of an American family of four.

American consumers vary tremendously in age, income, education level, and tastes. And they buy an incredible variety of goods and services. We will now look at how consumers make their choices among these products.

*M*ODEL OF CONSUMER BEHAVIOR

In earlier times, marketers could understand consumers well through the daily experience of selling to them. But as firms and markets have grown in size, many marketing decision makers have lost direct contact with their customers. Most marketers have had to turn to consumer research. They are spending more money than ever to study consumers, trying to learn more about consumer behavior. Who buys? How do they buy? When do they buy? Where do they buy? Why do they buy?

The central question is this: How do consumers respond to various marketing stimuli the company might use? The company that really understands how consumers will respond to different product features, prices, and advertising appeals has a great advantage over its competitors. Therefore companies and academics have heavily researched the relationship between marketing stimuli and consumer response. Their starting point is the stimulus-response model of buyer behavior shown in Figure 5-1. This figure shows that marketing and other stimuli enter the consumer's "black

FIGURE 5-1
Model of buyer behavior

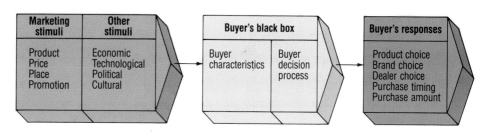

box" and produce certain responses. Marketers must figure out what is in the buyer's "black box."

On the left, <u>marketing stimuli consist of the four Ps—product, price, place, and promotion</u>. Other stimuli include major forces and events in the buyer's environment—economic, technological, political, and cultural. All these stimuli enter the buyer's black box, where they are turned into a set of observable buyer responses shown on the right—product choice, brand choice, dealer choice, purchase timing, and purchase amount.

The marketer wants to understand how the stimuli are changed into responses inside the consumer's black box. The black box has two parts. First, the buyer's characteristics influence how he or she perceives and reacts to the stimuli. Second, the buyer's decision process itself affects outcomes. This chapter looks at buyer characteristics as they affect buying behavior. The next chapter examines the buyer decision process.

PERSONAL CHARACTERISTICS AFFECTING CONSUMER BEHAVIOR

Consumer purchases are strongly influenced by cultural, social, personal, and psychological characteristics. These factors are shown in Figure 5-2. For the most part they cannot be controlled by the marketer, but they must be taken into account. We want to examine the influence of each factor on a buyer's behavior. We will illustrate these characteristics for the case of a hypothetical consumer named Jennifer Smith. Jennifer Smith is a married college graduate who works as a brand manager in a leading consumer packaged goods company. She currently wants to find a new leisure time activity that will offer some contrast to her working day. This need has led her to consider buying a camera and taking up photography. Many characteristics in her background will affect the way she goes about looking at cameras and choosing a brand. The remainder of the chapter will examine the personal characteristics that affect a consumer's behavior.

Cultural Factors   Cultural factors exert the broadest and deepest influence on consumer behavior. We will look at the role played by the buyer's culture, subculture, and social class.

FIGURE 5-2
Factors influencing behavior

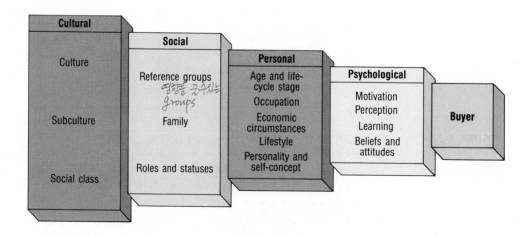

Culture

Culture is the most basic cause of a person's wants and behavior. Human behavior is largely learned. The child growing up in a society learns basic values, perceptions, wants, and behaviors from the family and other key institutions. An American child learns or is exposed to the following values: achievement and success, activity and involvement, efficiency and practicality, progress, material comfort, individualism, freedom, external comfort, humanitarianism, youthfulness, and fitness and health.[2]

Jennifer Smith's wanting a camera is a result of being raised in a modern society where camera technology and a whole set of consumer learnings and values have developed. Jennifer knows what cameras are. She knows how to read instructions on how to operate cameras, and her society has accepted the idea of women photographers. In another culture, say a primitive tribe in central Australia, a camera may mean nothing. It may simply be a curiosity.

Marketers are always trying to spot cultural shifts in order to imagine new products that might be wanted. Several cultural shifts are occurring in America. For example, people today want more leisure time to spend in such activities as sports, vacationing, and camping. To increase their leisure time, they are adopting more time-saving products and services such as microwave ovens and fast food. The shift toward increased leisure has spawned a huge catalog shopping industry. More than 6,500 catalog companies bombard American households with 8.5 billion catalogs each year. These catalogers range from large retailers like Sears and Spiegel to upscale specialty retailers like L. L. Bean, Sharper Image, Royal Silk, and Land's End.

People are also becoming more concerned about their health, creating a huge new industry. To stay healthier, they are putting more time into physical exercises such as jogging and weight lifting, eating lighter and more natural foods, and learning how to relax. With today's emphasis on youthfulness, older people want to look and feel younger. They are spending more on physical exercise, youthful clothing, formulas to restore color to graying hair, and cosmetic surgery. Finally, there has been a cultural shift toward informality—people today want a more relaxed and informal style. They are choosing more casual clothing, furnishing their homes more simply, and entertaining with a lighter touch.

Subculture

Each culture contains smaller **subcultures,** or groups of people with shared value systems based on common life experiences and situations. Nationality groups such as the Irish, Polish, Italians, and Hispanics are found within large communities and have distinct ethnic tastes and interests. Religious groups such as the Catholics, Mormons, Baptists, and Jews are subcultures with their own preferences and taboos. Racial groups such as blacks and Orientals have distinct culture styles and attitudes. Age subcultures include baby boomers, teens, and seniors. Geographical areas such as the South, California, and New England are distinct subcultures with characteristic life styles. Many of these subcultures make up important market segments, and marketers often find it worthwhile to design products and marketing programs tailored to the needs of these subculture groups (see Marketing Highlight 5–1).[3]

Jennifer Smith's interest in various goods will be influenced by her nationality, religion, race, and geographical background. These factors will affect her food preferences, clothing choices, recreation, and career goals. Subcultures attach different meanings to picture taking, and her subculture could affect Jennifer's interest in cameras and the brand she buys.

MARKETERS TARGET IMPORTANT SUBCULTURE GROUPS

When subcultures grow large and affluent enough, companies often design special marketing programs to serve their needs. Here are examples of three important subculture groups.

Hispanic Consumers

For years marketers have viewed the Hispanic market—Americans of Mexican, Cuban, and Puerto Rican descent—as small and poverty-stricken, but these perceptions are badly out of date. Expected to number 40 million by the year 2000, Hispanics are the second largest and fastest-growing U.S. minority. Annual Hispanic purchasing power totals $134 billion.

Over half of all Hispanics live in one of six metropolitan areas—Los Angeles, New York, Miami, San Antonio, San Francisco, and Chicago. They are easy to reach through the growing selection of Spanish-language broadcast and print media that cater to Hispanics. Hispanics have long been a target for marketers of food, beverages, and household care products. But as the segment's buying power increases, Hispanics are now emerging as an attractive market for pricier products such as computers, financial services, photography equipment, large appliances, life insurance, and automobiles. Hispanic consumers tend to be brand-conscious and quality-conscious—generics don't sell well to Hispanics. Perhaps more important, Hispanics are very brand-loyal, and they favor companies who show special interest in them. Many companies are devoting larger ad budgets and preparing special appeals to woo Hispanics. Because of the segment's strong brand loyalty, companies that get the first foothold have an important head start in this fast-growing market.

Black Consumers

With an total personal income of almost $205 billion annually, if the U.S. population of 30 million black Americans were a separate nation, their buying power would rank 12th in the free world. The black population in the United States is growing in affluence and sophistication. Blacks spend relatively more than whites on clothing, personal care, home furnishings, and fragrances; and relatively less on medical care, food, transportation, education, and recreation. Blacks place more importance than whites on brand

Social Class

Almost every society has some form of social class structure. **Social classes** are relatively permanent and ordered divisions in a society whose members share similar values, interests, and behaviors. Social scientists have identified the seven American social classes, which are shown in Table 5-1.

Social class is not determined by a single factor such as income but is measured as a combination of occupation, income, education, wealth, and other variables. In some social systems, members of different classes are reared for certain roles and cannot change their social positions. But in the United States, the lines between social classes are not fixed and rigid; over their lifetimes, people can move to a higher social class or drop into a lower one. Marketers are interested in social class because people within a given social class tend to have similar behavior—including buying behavior.

Social classes show distinct product and brand preferences in such areas as clothing, home furnishings, leisure activity, and automobiles. Jennifer Smith's social class may affect her camera decision. She may have come from a higher social class background. In this case, her family probably owned an expensive camera and may have dabbled in photography. The fact that she thinks about "going professional" is also in line with a higher social class background.

names, are more brand loyal, do less "shopping around," and shop more at neighborhood stores.

In recent years, many large companies—Sears, McDonald's, Procter & Gamble, Coca-Cola—have stepped up their efforts to tap this lucrative market. They employ black-owned advertising agencies, use black models in their ads, and place ads in black consumer magazines. Some companies develop special products, packaging, and appeals for the black consumer market.

Senior Consumers

As the U.S population ages, "seniors"—people 65 and older—are becoming a very attractive market. The seniors market will grow to over 40 million consumers by the year 2000. Seniors are better off financially than other consumer segments—they spend about $200 billion each year and they average twice the disposable income of consumers in the under-35 group.

Seniors have long been the target of the makers of laxatives, tonics, and denture products. But many marketers know that not all seniors are poor and feeble. Most are healthy and active, and they have many of the same needs and wants as younger consumers. Because seniors have more time and money, they are an ideal market for exotic travel, restaurants, high-tech home entertainment products, leisure goods and services, designer furniture and fashions, financial services, and life and health care services. Their desire to look as young as they feel makes seniors good candidates for specially designed cosmetics and personal care products, health foods, and home physical fitness products.

Several companies are hotly pursuing the seniors market. For example, Sears 40,000-member "Mature Club" offers older consumers 25 percent discounts on everything from eyeglasses to lawnmowers. Southwestern Bell publishes the "Silver Pages," crammed full of ads offering discounts and coupons to 20 million seniors in ninety markets. To appeal more to mature consumers, McDonald's employs older folks as hosts and hostesses in its restaurants and casts them in its ads. As the seniors segment grows in size and buying power, and as the stereotypes of seniors as doddering, creaky, and impoverished shut-ins fade, more and more marketers will develop special strategies for this important market.

Social Factors   A consumer's behavior is also influenced by social factors, such as the consumer's reference groups, family, and social roles and status.

Reference Groups

A person's behavior is influenced by many reference groups. **Reference groups** are groups that have a direct (face-to-face) or indirect influence on the person's attitudes or behavior. Reference groups that have a direct influence and to which a person belongs are called *membership groups*. Some are *primary groups* with whom there is regular informal interaction, such as family, friends, neighbors, and co-workers. Some are *secondary groups*, which are more formal and have less regular interaction. They include organizations such as religious groups, professional associations, and trade unions.

People are also influenced by groups to which they do not belong. An *aspirational group* is one to which the individual wishes to belong. For example, a teenage football player may aspire to play someday for the Dallas Cowboys. He identifies with this group although there is no face-to-face contact. A *dissociative group* is one whose values or behavior a person rejects. The same teenager might want to avoid any relationship with street gangs.

Marketers try to identify the reference groups of the target market they are

TABLE 5-1
Characteristics of
Seven Major American
Social Classes

Upper uppers (less than 1 percent)

Upper uppers are the social elite who live on inherited wealth and have well-known family backgrounds. They give large sums to charity, run debutante balls, own more than one home, and send their children to the finest schools. They are a market for jewelry, antiques, homes, and vacations. They often buy and dress conservatively rather than showing off their wealth. While small in number, upper uppers serve as a reference group for others to the extent that their consumption decisions trickle down and are imitated by the other social classes.

Lower uppers (about 2 percent)

Lower uppers have earned high income or wealth through exceptional ability in the professions or business. They usually begin in the middle class. They tend to be active in social and civic affairs and buy for themselves and their children the symbols of status, such as expensive homes, schools, yachts, swimming pools, and automobiles. They include the new rich who consume conspicuously to impress those below them. They want to be accepted in the upper-upper stratum, a status more likely to be achieved by their children than by themselves.

Upper middles (12 percent)

Upper middles possess neither family status nor unusual wealth. They are primarily concerned with "career." They have attained positions as professionals, independent businesspersons, and corporate managers. They believe in education and want their children to develop professional or administrative skills so that they will not drop into a lower stratum. Members of this class like to deal in ideas and "high culture." They are joiners and highly civic-minded. They are the quality market for good homes, clothes, furniture, and appliances. They seek to run a gracious home, entertaining friends and clients.

Middle class (32 percent)

The middle class is made up of average-pay white- and blue-collar workers who live on "the better side of town" and try to "do the proper things." To keep up with the trends, they often buy products that are popular. Twenty-five percent own imported cars, and most are concerned with fashion, seeking the better brand names. Better living means owning a nice home in a nice neighborhood with good schools. The middle class believes in spending more money on worthwhile experiences for their children and aiming them toward a college education.

Working class (38 percent)

The working class consists of average-pay blue-collar workers and those who lead a "working class life style," whatever their income, school background, or job. The working class depends heavily on relatives for economic and emotional support, for tips on job opportunities, for advice on purchases, and for assistance in times of trouble. The working class maintains sharper sex role divisions and stereotyping. Car preferences include standard size and larger cars, rejecting domestic and foreign compacts.

Upper lowers (9 percent)

Upper lowers are working (are not on welfare), although their living standard is just above poverty. They perform unskilled work for very poor pay although they strive toward a higher class. Often, upper lowers are educationally deficient. Although they fall near the poverty line financially, they manage to "present a picture of self-discipline" and "maintain some effort at cleanliness."

Lower lowers (7 percent)

Lower lowers are on welfare, visibly poverty stricken, and usually out of work or have "the dirtiest jobs." Often they are not interested in finding a job and are permanently dependent on public aid or charity for income. Their homes, clothes, and possessions are "dirty," "raggedy," and "broken-down."

Source: See Richard P. Coleman, "The Continuing Significance of Social Class to Marketing," *Journal of Consumer Research*, December, 1983, pp. 265–280; and Richard P. Coleman and Lee P. Rainwater, *Social Standing in America: New Dimension of Class* (New York: Basic Books, 1978).

selling to. Reference groups influence a person in at least three ways. They expose the person to new behaviors and life styles. They influence the person's attitudes and self-concept because he or she want to "fit in." And they create pressures to conform that may affect the person's product and brand choices (see Marketing Highlight 5–2).

The importance of group influence varies across products and brands, but it tends to be strongest for conspicuous purchases.[4] A product or brand can be conspicuous for one of two reasons. First, it may be noticeable because the buyer is one of few people who own it—luxuries are more conspicuous than necessities because fewer people own the luxuries. Second, a brand can be conspicuous because it is

USING REFERENCE GROUPS TO SELL: HOME-PARTY AND OFFICE-PARTY SELLING

Many companies capitalize on reference-group influence to sell their products. Home-party and office-party selling involve throwing sales parties in homes or workplaces and inviting friends and neighbors or coworkers to see products demonstrated. Companies such as Mary Kay Cosmetics, Avon, and Tupperware are masters at this form of selling.

Mary Kay Cosmetics provides a good example of home-party selling. A Mary Kay beauty consultant

Reference group selling: Tupperware office-party selling and Mary Kay home-party selling.

(of which there are 170,000) asks different women to host small beauty shows in their homes. Each hostess invites her friends and neighbors for a few hours of refreshments and informal socializing. Within this congenial atmosphere, the Mary Kay representative gives a two-hour beauty plan and free makeup lessons to the guests, hoping that many of them will buy some of the demonstrated cosmetics. The hostess receives a commission on sales plus a discount on personal purchases. Usually, about 60 percent of the guests buy something, partly because of the influence of the hostess and the other women attending the party.

In recent years, changing demographics have adversely affected home-party selling. An increasing proportion of women are working, which leaves fewer women with the time for shopping and fewer women at home to host or attend home sales parties. To overcome this problem, most party-plan sellers have followed their customers into the workplace with office-party selling. For example, Avon now trains its 400,000 salespeople to sell through office parties during coffee and lunch breaks and after hours. The company once sold only door-to-door but currently picks up a quarter of its sales from buyers at businesses. The well-known suburban Tupperware party has also invaded the office, in the form of Tupperware "rush-hour parties" held at the end of the workday in business offices around the country. At these parties, office workers meet in comfortable, familiar surroundings, look through Tupperware catalogs, watch product demonstrations, and discuss Tupperware products with their friends and associates. Tupperware's 85,000 sales representatives now make about 20 percent of their sales outside the home.

Home-party and office-party selling are now being used to market everything from cosmetics, kitchenware, and lingerie to exercise instruction and handmade suits. Such selling requires a sharp understanding of reference groups and how people influence each other in the buying process.

Sources: See Shannon Thurman, "Mary Kay Still in the Pink," *Advertising Age*, January 4, 1988, p. 32; Len Strazewski, "Tupperware Locks in a New Strategy," *Advertising Age*, February 8, 1988, p. 30; and Kate Ballen, "Get Ready for Shopping at Work," *Fortune*, February 15, 1988, pp. 95–98.

consumed in public where it can be seen by others. Figure 5-3 shows how group influence might affect product and brand choices for four types of products—public luxuries, private luxuries, public necessities, and private necessities.

A person considering the purchase of a public luxury such as a sailboat will be strongly influenced by others. Many people will notice the sailboat because few people own one. They will notice the brand because the boat is used in public. Thus both the product and the brand will be conspicuous, and the opinions of others will strongly influence decisions about whether to own a boat and what brand to buy. At the other extreme, group influences do not much affect decisions for private necessities because neither the product nor the brand will be noticed by others.

Manufacturers of products and brands subject to strong group influence must figure out how to reach the opinion leaders in the relevant reference groups. **Opinion leaders** are people within a reference group who, because of special skills, knowledge, personality, or other characteristics, exert influence on others. At one time, sellers thought that opinion leaders were primarily community social leaders whom the mass market imitated because of "snob appeal." But opinion leaders are found in all strata of society, and one person may be an opinion leader in certain product areas and an opinion follower in others. Marketers try to identify the personal characteristics of opinion leaders for their products, determine what media they use, and direct messages at them.

If Jennifer Smith buys a camera, both the product and the brand will be visible to others she respects, and her decision to buy the camera and her brand choice may be strongly influenced by some of her groups. Friends who belong to a photography club may influence her to buy a good camera.

Family

Family members can strongly influence buyer behavior. We can distinguish between two families in the buyer's life. The buyer's parents make up the *family of orientation*. From parents a person acquires an orientation toward religion, politics, and economics and a sense of personal ambition, self-worth, and love. Even if the buyer no longer interacts very much with his or her parents, the parents can still significantly influence the buyer's unconscious behavior. In countries where parents continue to live with their children, their influence can be crucial.

The *family of procreation*—the buyer's spouse and children—have a more direct influence on everyday buying behavior. The family is the most important consumer-

FIGURE 5-3
Extent of group influence on product and brand choice
Source: Adapted from William O. Bearden and Michael J. Etzel, "Reference Group Influence on Product and Brand Purchase Decisions," *The Journal of Consumer Research*, September 1982, p. 185.

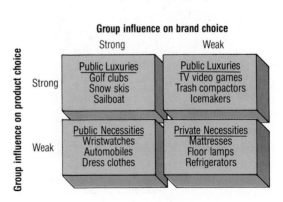

buying organization in society, and it has been researched extensively. Marketers are interested in the roles and relative influence of the husband, wife, and children on the purchase of a large variety of products and services.

Husband-wife involvement varies widely by product category and by stage in the buying process. And buying roles change with evolving consumer life styles. The wife has traditionally been the main purchasing agent for the family, especially in the areas of food, household products, and clothing. But this is changing with the increasing number of working wives, later first marriages, and changing cultural norms. For example, women now buy 45 percent of all cars, and men account for about 40 percent of food shopping dollars.[5]

In the case of expensive products and services, husbands and wives engage more in joint decision making. The marketer needs to determine which member normally has the greater influence on the purchase of a particular product or service. Either the husband has more influence, or the wife, or they have equal influence. The following products and services fall under each:

- *Husband*: insurance, automobiles, television
- *Wife*: washing machines, carpeting, furniture, kitchenware, financial management
- *Equal*: living-room furniture, vacation, housing, outside entertainment, choice of doctor

Understanding the dynamics of husband-wife decision making can help marketers to aim their marketing strategies toward the right family members.

In the case of Jennifer Smith buying a camera, her husband will play an influencer role. He may have an opinion about her buying a camera and the kind of camera to buy. At the same time, she will be the primary decider, purchaser, and user.[6]

Family buying decisions: depending on the product and situation, individual family members exert different amounts of influence.

Roles and Status

A person belongs to many groups—family, clubs, organizations. The person's position in each group can be defined in terms of *role* and *status*. With her parents, Jennifer Smith plays the role of daughter; in her family, she plays the role of wife; in her company, she plays the role of brand manager. A **role** consists of the activities a person is expected to perform according to the people around him or her. Each of Jennifer's roles will influence some of her buying behavior.

Each role carries a **status** reflecting the general esteem given to it by society. The role of brand manager has more status in this society than the role of daughter. As a brand manager, Jennifer will buy the kind of camera that reflects her role and status. People often choose products that show their status in society. Thus a company president will drive a Mercedes or Cadillac and wear expensive clothes. An office worker will drive a Taurus or Toyota and wear less expensive clothes.

Personal Factors

A buyer's decisions are also influenced by personal characteristics such as the buyer's age and life-cycle stage, occupation, economic situation, life style, and personality and self-concept.

Age and Life-Cycle Stage

People change the goods and services they buy over their lifetimes. They eat baby food in the early years, most foods in the growing and mature years, and special diets in the later years. People's taste in clothes, furniture, and recreation is also age-related.

Buying is also shaped by the stage of the *family life cycle*. The stages of the family life cycle are listed in Table 5-2. Marketers often define their target markets in terms of life-cycle stages and develop appropriate products and marketing plans accordingly.

Psychological life-cycle stages have also been identified. Adults experience certain passages or transformations as they go through life.[7] Thus Jennifer Smith may move from being a satisfied brand manager and wife to personally dissatisfied, causing her to search for a new way to fulfill herself. Such a change may have stimulated her strong interest in photography. Marketers should pay attention to the changing buying interests that might be associated with various adult passages.

Occupation

A person's occupation affects the goods and services bought. A blue-collar worker will buy work clothes, tools, and American-made cars. A company president will buy expensive clothes, air travel, country club membership, and a large sailboat. Marketers try to identify the occupational groups that have an above-average interest in their products and services. A company can even specialize in making products needed by a given occupational group.

Economic Situation

A person's economic situation will greatly affect product choice. People's economic circumstances consist of their level of spendable income, savings and assets, borrowing power, and attitudes toward spending and saving. Jennifer Smith can consider buying an expensive Nikon camera if she has enough spendable income, savings, or borrowing power. Marketers of income-sensitive goods closely watch trends in personal income, savings, and interest rates. If economic indicators point to a boom or recession, marketers can take steps to redesign, reposition, and reprice their products.

TABLE 5-2
Family Life Cycle
Stages

Young:
  Single
  Married without children
  Married with children
          Infant children
          Young children
          Adolescent children
  Divorced with children

Middle-aged:
  Single
  Married without children
  Married with children
          Young children
          Adolescent children
  Married without dependent children
  Divorced without children
  Divorced with children
          Young children
          Adolescent children
  Divorced without dependent children

Older:
  Older married
  Older unmarried

Source: Adapted from Patrick E. Murphy and William A. Staples, "A Modernized Family Life Cycle," *Journal of Consumer Research*, June 1979, p. 16. Also see Janet Wagner and Sherman Hanna, "The Effectiveness of Family Life Cycle Variables in Consumer Expenditure Research," *Journal of Consumer Research*, December 1983, pp. 281–91.

Life Style

People coming from the same subculture, social class, and even occupation may have quite different life styles. **Life style** is a person's pattern of living as expressed in his or her activities, interests, and opinions. Life style captures something more than the person's social class or personality. If we know a person's social class, we can infer many things about likely behavior but fail to see him or her as a complete individual. If we know someone's personality, we can infer several things about his or her unique psychological characteristics but not much about activities, interests, and opinions. Life style profiles a person's whole pattern of acting and interacting in the world.

The technique of measuring life styles is known as *psychographics*.[8] It involves measuring the major dimensions shown in Table 5-3. The first three are known as

TABLE 5-3
Life Style Dimensions

ACTIVITIES	INTERESTS	OPINIONS	DEMOGRAPHICS
Work	Family	Themselves	Age
Hobbies	Home	Social issues	Education
Social events	Job	Politics	Income
Vacation	Community	Business	Occupation
Entertainment	Recreation	Economics	Family size
Club membership	Fashion	Education	Dwelling
Community	Food	Products	Geography
Shopping	Media	Future	City size
Sports	Achievements	Culture	Stage in life cycle

Source: Joseph T. Plummer, "The Concept and Application of Life-Style Segmentation," *Journal of Marketing*, January 1974, p. 34.

the AIO dimensions (activities, interests, opinions). Consumer life styles are measured using long questionnaires—sometimes as long as twenty-five pages—that ask people how strongly they agree or disagree with such statements as:

- I am the kind of person who plans whatever I do very carefully.
- For fun, I would rather go out than stay home.
- I usually dress for fashion, not for comfort.
- I enjoy watching sports on television.

The data are then analyzed to find distinctive life style groups. Marketers often design marketing programs or appeals to fit specific life style groups.

Several research firms have developed life style classifications. The best known is the SRI values and life styles (VALS) typology, which classifies the American public into nine life style groups.[9] These groups are described in Table 5-4, along with the percentage of the U.S. population in each. A person may progress through several of these life style groups over the course of a lifetime. People's life styles affect their buying behavior.

TABLE 5-4
The VALS Nine
American Life Styles

Survivors (4 percent)
People marked by poverty and little education who have given up on life. They find little satisfaction in life and concentrate on just making it from day to day. They tend to be conservative and are "despairing, depressed, and withdrawn."

Sustainers (7 percent)
People also marked by poverty but who are striving to move ahead toward a better life. They are "angry, distrustful, rebellious, and combative" and have a deep distrust of the system. Despite their strong need for status and group acceptance, they see themselves as having less social status.

Belongers (33 percent)
Traditional, conforming, and family-oriented people. They have a strong need for acceptance and would rather be followers than leaders. They prefer the status quo and tend to lead happy and contented lives.

Emulators (10 percent)
"Ambitious, competitive, and ostentatious" people who are striving to move ahead by emulating the richer and more successful. They tend to be hard-working, less conservative, and fairly successful but less satisfied with life.

Achievers (23 percent)
The "driving and driven" people who made the system and are now at the top. They are hard-working, successful, and self-confident, and they tend to feel good about the system, themselves, and their accomplishments.

I-am-mes (5 percent)
Typically young people in transition between the old and the new. They find life confusing, contradictory, and uncertain; experience emotional ups and downs; and live life "intensely, vividly, and experientially." They are seeking and finding new interests and new life goals.

Experientials (7 percent)
Those seeking intense personal experiences and emotions. Action and interaction are the important things in their lives. They are politically and socially liberal, independent and self-reliant, and fairly happy with life. They appreciate nature and seek spiritual meaning in things.

Societally conscious (9 percent)
People driven by social ideals—by concern with societal issues and events such as consumerism, conservation, pollution, and wildlife protection. They tend to be well-educated; "successful, influential, and mature"; and sophisticated and politically effective.

Integrateds (2 percent)
Mature and balanced people who have a broad perspective and can find solutions to opposing views. They combine inner directedness and outer directedness. They lead when action is called for, and they have high social status even though they do not seek it.

Source: Arnold Mitchell, *The Nine American Life Styles* (New York: Macmillan, 1983). Used by permission of the author and publisher.

Several companies have used the VALS typology to improve their marketing strategies. For example, based on VALS, Merrill Lynch changed its ad theme from "Bullish on America" (with ads showing a herd of bulls) to "A breed apart" (with ads showing a single bull taking its own lead). VALS analysis showed that the original ads attracted Belongers, but that the heavy investors Merrill Lynch wanted to reach are Achievers. Further, Achievers don't want to be part of the crowd—they want to stand out. Thus Merrill Lynch's target market found the "breed apart" theme featuring a single, independent bull more compelling.[10] In another example, Bank of America found that the business people they were targeting consisted mainly of Achievers who were strongly competitive individualists. The bank designed highly successful ads showing people engaged in solo sports such as sailing, jogging, and water skiing.[11]

The life style concept, when used carefully, can help the marketer gain an understanding of changing consumer values and how they affect buying behavior.[12] Jennifer Smith, for example, can choose to live like a capable homemaker, a career woman, or a free spirit. She plays several roles, and her way of reconciling them expresses her life style. If she becomes a professional photographer, her life style will change, in turn changing what and how she buys. When preparing marketing strategy, the marketer must search for relationships between the product or brand and life style groups.

Life style: this Bank of America ad targets achievers.

Personality and Self-Concept

Each person's distinct personality will influence his or her buying behavior. **Personality** is the person's distinguishing psychological characteristics that lead to relatively consistent and lasting responses to his or her own environment. An individual's personality is usually described in terms of such traits as the following:[13]

Achievement	Autonomy	Emotional stability
Adaptability	Change	Order
Affiliation	Defensiveness	Self-confidence
Aggressiveness	Deference	Sociability
Ascendancy	Dominance	

Personality can be useful in analyzing consumer behavior for some product or brand choices. For example, coffee marketers have discovered that heavy coffee drinkers tend to be high on sociability. Thus Maxwell House ads show people relaxing and socializing over a cup of steaming coffee.

Many marketers use a concept related to personality—a person's *self-concept* (also called self-image). All of us have a complex mental picture of ourselves. For example, Jennifer Smith may see herself as being extroverted, creative, and active; she will look for a camera that projects these same qualities. If Nikon promotes its camera as a brand for outgoing and creative people, then its brand image will match Jennifer's self-image, and Nikon will be more likely to make the sale. Marketers try to develop brand images that match the self-image of the target market.

The theory, admittedly, is not that simple. What if Jennifer's *actual self-concept* (how she views herself) differs from her *ideal self-concept* (how she would like to view herself) and from her *others self-concept* (how she thinks others see her). Which self will she try to satisfy when she buys a camera? Some marketers think that buyers' choices will result more from their actual self-concept; others from the ideal self-concept; and still others from the others self-concept. Thus self-concept theory has met with mixed success in predicting consumer responses to brand images.[14]

Psychological Factors

A person's buying choices are also influenced by four major psychological factors—motivation, perception, learning, and beliefs and attitudes.

Motivation

We know that Jennifer Smith became interested in buying a camera. Why? What is she really seeking? What needs is she trying to satisfy?

A person has many needs at any given time. Some needs are *biological*, arising from states of tension such as hunger, thirst, discomfort. Other needs are *psychological*, arising from states of tension such as the need for recognition, esteem, or belonging. Most of these needs will not be strong enough to motivate the person to act at a given point in time. A need becomes a motive when it is aroused to a sufficient level of intensity. A **motive** (or drive) is a need that is sufficiently pressing to direct the person to seek satisfaction of the need.

Psychologists have developed theories of human motivation. Two of the most popular—the theories of Sigmund Freud and Abraham Maslow—have quite different meanings for consumer analysis and marketing.

FREUD'S THEORY OF MOTIVATION. Freud assumes that people are largely unconscious about the real psychological forces shaping their behavior. He sees the person as growing up and repressing many urges. These urges are never eliminated or under perfect control; they emerge in dreams, in slips of the tongue, in neurotic and obsessive behavior, or ultimately in psychoses.

Thus, according to Freud, a person does not fully understand his or her motivation. If Jennifer Smith wants to purchase an expensive camera, she may describe her motive as wanting a hobby or career. At a deeper level, she may be purchasing the camera to impress others with her creative talent. At a still deeper level, she may be buying the camera to feel young and independent again.

When Jennifer looks at a camera, she will react not only to the camera's performance, but also to other cues. The camera's shape, size, weight, material, color, and case can all trigger certain emotions. A rugged-looking camera, for instance, can arouse Jennifer's feelings about being independent, which she can either handle or avoid. In designing a camera, the manufacturer should be aware of the impact of the camera's look and feel and how such elements can trigger emotions that can promote or hinder purchase.

The pioneer of Freudian motivation theory in marketing is Ernest Dichter, who for over two decades has been interpreting buying situations and product choices in terms of underlying unconscious motives. Dichter calls his approach *motivational research.* He and other motivation researchers collect in-depth information from small samples of consumers to uncover the deeper motives for their purchases. They use various *projective techniques* to throw the ego off guard—techniques such as word association, sentence completion, picture interpretation, and role playing.[15] Motivation researchers have reached some interesting and sometimes odd conclusions about what may be in the buyer's mind regarding certain purchases. They have suggested that:

- Consumers resist prunes because they are wrinkled-looking and remind people of sickness and old age.
- Men smoke cigars as an adult version of thumbsucking.
- Ice cream is associated with love and affection.
- People prefer vegetable shortening to animal fats because the latter arouse a sense of guilt over killing animals.
- A woman is very serious when baking a cake because unconsciously she is going through the symbolic act of giving birth.

Despite its sometimes unusual findings, motivation research remains a useful tool for marketers seeking a deeper understanding of consumer behavior.

MASLOW'S THEORY OF MOTIVATION. Abraham Maslow sought to explain why people are driven by particular needs at particular times.[16] Why does one person, for example, spend lots of time and energy on personal safety and another on getting the esteem of others? Maslow's answer is that human needs are arranged in a hierarchy, from the most pressing to the least pressing. Maslow's hierarchy of needs is shown in Figure 5-4. In order of importance, they are *physiological* needs, *safety* needs, *social* needs, *esteem* needs, and *self-actualization* needs. A person will try to satisfy the most important needs first. When the most important need is satisfied, it will stop being a motivator for the present time, and the person will be motivated to satisfy the next most important need.

For example, starving people (need 1) will not take an interest in the latest happenings in the art world (need 5), nor in how they are seen or esteemed by others (needs 3 or 4), nor even in whether they breathe clean air (need 2). But as each important need is satisfied, the next most important need will come into play.

What light does Maslow's theory throw on Jennifer Smith's interest in buying a

FIGURE 5-4
Maslow's hierarchy of needs
Adapted from *Motivation and Personality*, 2nd ed., by Abraham H. Maslow. Copyright © 1970 by Abraham H. Maslow. Reprinted by permission of Harper & Row, Publishers, Inc.

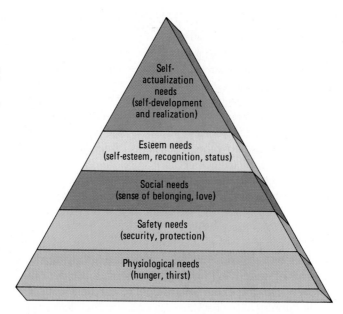

camera? We can guess that Jennifer has satisfied her physiological, safety, and social needs; they do not motivate her interest in cameras. Her camera interest might come from a strong need for more esteem from others. Or it might come from a need for self-actualization; perhaps she wants to be a creative person and express herself through photography.

Perception

A motivated person is ready to act. How the motivated person acts is influenced by his or her perception of the situation. Two people with the same motivation and in the same situation may act quite differently because they perceive the situation differently. Jennifer Smith might consider a fast-talking camera salesperson loud and phony. Another camera buyer might consider the same salesperson intelligent and helpful.

Why do people have different perceptions of the same situation? All of us learn about a stimulus by the flow of information through our five senses: sight, hearing, smell, touch, and taste. However, each of us receives, organizes, and interprets this sensory information in an individual way. **Perception** is the process by which people select, organize, and interpret information to form a meaningful picture of the world.

People can form different perceptions of the same stimulus because of three perceptual processes: selective exposure, selective distortion, and selective retention.

SELECTIVE EXPOSURE. People are exposed to a great number of stimuli every day. For example, the average person may be exposed to over fifteen hundred ads a day. It is impossible for a person to pay attention to all these stimuli; most will be screened out. The real challenge is to explain which stimuli people will notice. Research has shown that people are more likely to notice stimuli that relate to a current need. Jennifer Smith will suddenly notice all kinds of ads about cameras because she wants to buy one. People are also more likely to notice stimuli that they expect. Jennifer Smith is more likely to notice cameras than radios in a camera store, because she did not expect the store to carry radios. Finally, people are more likely to notice stimuli that deviate a lot from the normal. Jennifer Smith will notice

To penetrate consumers' selective perception processes, advertisers have tried such expensive but eye-catching advertising ideas as 3-D pop-ups, musical microchips and stick-on labels.

an ad offering $100 off the list price of a Nikon before noticing one that offers $5 off the list price.

Selective exposure means that marketers have to work especially hard to attract the consumer's attention. Their offer will be lost on most people who are not in the market for the product. Even people who are in the market may not notice the offer unless it stands out from the surrounding sea of other offers.

SELECTIVE DISTORTION. Even stimuli that consumers notice do not always come across in the intended way. Each person tries to fit incoming information into his or her existing mind set. Selective distortion describes the tendency of people to twist information into personal meanings. Jennifer Smith may hear the salesperson mention some good and bad points about a competing camera brand. Since she already has a strong leaning toward Nikon, she is likely to distort the points in order to conclude that Nikon is the better camera. People tend to interpret information in a way that will support what they already believe. Selective distortion means that marketers must try to understand the mind-sets of consumers and how they will affect interpretations of advertising and sales information.

SELECTIVE RETENTION. People will forget much that they learn. They will tend to retain only information that supports their attitudes and beliefs. Because of selective retention, Jennifer is likely to remember good points mentioned about the Nikon and forget good points mentioned about competing cameras. She remembers Nikon's good points because she "rehearses" them more whenever she thinks about choosing a camera.

These three perceptual factors—selective exposure, distortion, and retention—mean that marketers have to work hard to get their messages through. This explains why marketers use so much drama and repetition in sending messages to their market. Interestingly, though marketers worry about whether their offers will be perceived at all, some consumers are worried that they will be affected by advertising messages without even knowing it (see Marketing Highlight 5–3).

Learning

When people act, they learn. **Learning** describes changes in an individual's behavior arising from experience. Most human behavior is learned. Learning theorists say that learning occurs through the interplay of drives, cues, responses, and reinforcement.

We saw that Jennifer Smith has a drive for self-actualization. A *drive* is a strong internal stimulus that calls for action. Her drive becomes a *motive* when it is directed toward a particular *stimulus object*, in this case a camera. Jennifer's response to the idea of buying a camera is conditioned by the surrounding cues. *Cues* are minor stimuli that determine when, where, and how the person responds. Seeing cameras in a shop window, hearing of a special sales price, and being encouraged by her husband are all cues that can influence Jennifer's *response* to the impulse to buy a camera.

Suppose Jennifer buys the camera. If the experience is *rewarding*, the probability is that she will use the camera more and more. Her response to cameras will be *reinforced*. Then the next time she buys a camera, or binoculars, or similar product, the probability is greater that she will by a Nikon. We say that she *generalizes* her response to similar stimuli.

The reverse of generalization is *discrimination*. When Jennifer examines binoculars made by Olympus, she sees that they are lighter and more compact than Nikon's binoculars. Discrimination means that she has learned to recognize differences in sets of products and can adjust her response accordingly.

The practical significance of learning theory for marketers is that they can build up demand for a product by associating it with strong drives, using motivating cues, and providing positive reinforcement. A new company can enter the market by appealing to the same drives as competitors and providing similar cues because buyers are more likely to transfer loyalty to similar brands than to dissimilar ones (generalization). Or it may design its brand to appeal to a different set of drives and offer strong cue inducements to switch (discrimination).

Beliefs and Attitudes

Through acting and learning, people acquire their beliefs and attitudes. These in turn influence their buying behavior. A **belief** is a descriptive thought that a person holds about something. Jennifer Smith may believe that a Nikon takes great pictures, stands up well under hard use, and costs $550. These beliefs may be based on real knowledge, opinion, or faith. They may or may not carry an emotional charge. For example, Jennifer Smith's belief that a Nikon camera is heavy may or may not matter to her decision.

Marketers are very interested in people's beliefs about specific products and services. These beliefs make up product and brand images, and people act on their beliefs. If some of the beliefs are wrong and prevent purchase, the marketer would want to launch a campaign to correct these beliefs.

SUBLIMINAL PERCEPTION: CAN CONSUMERS BE AFFECTED WITHOUT KNOWING IT?

In 1957 the words "Eat popcorn" and "Drink Coca-Cola" were flashed on a screen in a New Jersey movie theater every five seconds for one three-hundredth of a second. The researchers reported that although the audience did not consciously recognize these messages, viewers absorbed them subconsciously and bought 58 percent more popcorn and 18 percent more Coke. Suddenly advertising agencies and consumer protection groups became intensely interested in *subliminal perception*. People voiced fears of being brainwashed, and California and Canada declared the practice illegal. The controversy cooled when scientists failed to replicate these results, but the issue did not die. In 1974 Wilson Bryan Key, in his *Subliminal Seduction*, claimed that consumers were still being manipulated by advertisers in print ads and television commercials.

Subliminal perception has since been studied by many psychologists and consumer researchers. None have been able to show that subliminal messages have any effect on consumer behavior. It appears that subliminal advertising simply doesn't have the power attributed to it by its critics. Most advertisers scoff at the notion of an industry conspiracy to manipulate consumers through "invisible" messages. As one advertising agency executive put it, "We have enough trouble persuading consumers using a series of up-front, thirty-second ads—how could we do it in 1/300th of a second?"

While advertisers may avoid outright subliminal advertising, some critics claim that television advertising employs techniques approaching the subliminal. With more and more viewers reaching for their remote controls to avoid ads by switching channels or by fast-forwarding through VCR tapes, advertisers are using new tricks to grab viewer attention and to affect consumers in ways they may not be aware of. Many ad agencies employ psychologists and neurophysiologists to help develop subtle psychological advertising strategies.

For example, some advertisers purposely try to confuse viewers, throw them off balance, or even make them uncomfortable:

> [They use] film footage that wouldn't pass muster with a junior-high film club. You have to stare at the screen just to figure out what's going on—and

that, of course, is the idea. Take the ads for Wang computers. In these hazy, washed-out spots, people walk partially in and out of the camera frame talking in computer jargon. But the confusion grabs attention. . . . Even people who don't understand a word are riveted to the screen.

Other advertisers use the rapid-fire technique. Images flash by so quickly you can barely register them. Pontiac used such "machine-gun editing" in recent ads—the longest shot lasted one and one-half seconds, the shortest flashed by in one-quarter of a second. The ads scored high in viewer recall.

Some advertisers go after our ears as well as our eyes, taking advantage of the powerful effects some sounds have on human brain waves.

> Advertisers are using sounds to take advantage of the automatic systems built into the brain that force you to stop what you're doing and refocus on the screen . . . you can't ignore these sounds. That's why commercials are starting off with noises ranging from a baby crying (Advil) to a car horn (Hertz) to a factory whistle (Almond Joy). In seeking the right sound . . . advertisers can be downright merciless. . . . [A]ds for Nuprin pain reliever kick off by assaulting viewers with the whine of a dentist's drill . . . to help the viewer recall the type of pain we've all experienced. Hey, thanks.

A few experts are concerned that the new high-tech advertising might even hypnotize consumers, whether consumers know it or not. They suggest that several techniques—rapid scene changes, pulsating music and sounds, repetitive phrases, and flashing logos—might actually start to put some viewers under.

Some critics think that such subtle, hard-to-resist psychological techniques are unfair to consumers, that advertisers can use these techniques to bypass consumers' defenses and affect consumers without their knowing it. The advertisers who use these techniques, however, view them as innovative, creative approaches to advertising.

Sources: See Wilson Bryan Key, *Subliminal Seduction* (New York: NAL, 1974); Timothy E. Moore, "Subliminal Advertising: What You See Is What You Get," *Journal of Marketing,* Spring 1982, pp. 38–47; and Walter Weir, "Another Look at Subliminal 'Facts,' " *Advertising Age,* October 15, 1984, p. 46. Excerpts from David H. Freedman, "Why You Watch Commercials—Whether You Mean To Or Not," *TV Guide,* February 20, 1988, pp. 4–7.

People have attitudes regarding almost everything: religion, politics, clothes, music, food, and so on. An **attitude** is a person's consistently favorable or unfavorable evaluations, feelings, and tendencies toward an object or idea. Attitudes put people into a frame of mind of liking or disliking things, moving toward or away from them. Thus Jennifer Smith may hold such attitudes as "Buy the best," "The Japanese make the best products in the world," and "Creativity and self-expression are among the most important things in life." The Nikon camera therefore fits well into Jennifer's existing attitudes. A company would benefit greatly from researching the various attitudes people have that might bear on its product.

Attitudes lead people to behave consistently toward similar objects. Attitudes economize on energy and thought; people do not have to interpret and react to everything in a fresh way. Attitudes are also very difficult to change. A person's attitudes fit into a pattern, and to change one attitude may require difficult adjustments in many others. Thus a company should usually try to fit its products into existing attitudes, rather than to try to change people's attitudes. There are exceptions, of course, where the great cost of trying to change attitudes may pay off.

> Honda entered the U.S. motorcycle market facing a major decision. It could either sell its motorcycles to a small number of people already interested in motorcycles or try to increase the number interested in motorcycles. The latter would be more expensive because many people had negative attitudes toward motorcycles. They associated motorcycles with black leather jackets, switchblades, and crime. Honda took the second course and launched a major campaign based on the theme "You meet the nicest people on a Honda." Its campaign worked, and many people adopted a new attitude toward motorcycles.

We can now appreciate the many individual characteristics and forces acting on consumer behavior. The person's choice is the result of the complex interplay of cultural, social, personal, and psychological factors. Many of these factors cannot be influenced by the marketer. However, they are useful for identifying interested buyers and shaping products and appeals to better serve their needs.

Attitudes are hard to change, but it can be done. Honda's "You meet the nicest people on a Honda" campaign changed people's attitudes about who rides motorcycles.

■ SUMMARY

Markets have to be understood before marketing strategies can be developed. The consumer market buys goods and services for personal consumption. Consumers vary tremendously in age, income, education, tastes, and other factors. Marketers must understand how consumers transform marketing and other inputs into buying responses. Consumer behavior is influenced by the buyer's characteristics and by the buyer's decision process. Buyer characteristics include four major factors: cultural, social, personal, and psychological.

Culture is the most basic determinant of a person's wants and behavior. It includes the basic values, perceptions, preferences, and behaviors that a person learns from family and other key institutions. Marketers try to track cultural shifts that might suggest new ways to serve consumers. Subcultures are "cultures within cultures" that have distinct values and life styles. Social classes are subcultures whose members have similar social prestige based on occupation, income, education, wealth, and other variables. People with different cultural, subcultural, and social class characteristics have different product and brand preferences. Marketers may want to focus their marketing programs on the special needs of certain groups.

Social factors also influence a buyer's behavior. A person's reference groups—family, friends, social organizations, professional associations—strongly affect product and brand choices. The person's position within each group can be defined in terms of role and status. A buyer chooses products and brands that reflect his or her role and status.

The buyer's age, life-cycle stage, occupation, economic circumstances, life style, personality, and other personal characteristics influence his or her buying decisions. Young consumers have different needs and wants from older consumers; the needs of young married couples differ from those of retirees; consumers with higher incomes buy differently from those who have less to spend. Consumer life styles—the whole pattern of acting and interacting in the world—are also an important influence on buyers' choices.

Finally, consumer buying behavior is influenced by four major psychological factors—motivation, perception, learning, and attitudes. Each of these factors provides a different perspective for understanding the workings of the buyer's "black box."

A person's buying behavior is the result of the complex interplay of all these cultural, social, personal, and psychological factors. Many of these factors cannot be controlled by marketers, but they are useful in identifying and understanding the consumers that marketers are trying to influence.

■ QUESTIONS FOR DISCUSSION

1. What factors could you add to the model of buyer behavior shown in Figure 5-1 to make it a more complete description of consumer behavior?

2. Various wineries have started packaging wine in a new way. A flexible container in a cardboard box keeps several liters of wine fresh indefinitely, and an airtight dispenser allows servings of any amount of wine at any time. Based on your knowledge of cultural, social, personal, and psychological variables influencing consumer behavior, what factors will work for or against the success of this packaging method?

3. Many Americans are of Asian descent, and Asia is currently the primary source of immigrants to the United States. What steps are marketers taking to appeal to this U.S. subculture? What should they be doing?

4. What would each of the following tell you about a person's social class?
   a. Earns income of $30,000 versus $40,000.
   b. Has floors covered with Oriental rugs versus wall-to-wall carpeting.
   c. Shops at Sears versus Bloomingdale's.
   d. Is a college graduate versus high school graduate.
   e. Lives in a condominium versus a suburban house.

5. Ads sponsored by Rockers Against Drunk Driving feature popular recording artists telling listeners of the dangers of drinking and driving. What social factors would you expect to contribute to the success—or failure—of this campaign?

6. In designing the advertising for a soft drink, which would you find more helpful: information about consumer demographics or about consumer life styles? What approach would you use in advertising to Belongers? to Emulators? to I–Am–Mes?

7. One suggestion arising from motivation research is that shaving represents a loss of masculinity to men and that the sting of an aftershave reasserts their manhood. Does this suggestion seem plausible? If yes, how could marketers use this insight in selling men's toiletries?

8. What different levels of Maslow's hierarchy could be appealed to in marketing the following: (a) popcorn, (b) expensive restaurants, (c) the armed forces, (d) a college education?

9. One advertising agency president says, "Perception is reality." What does he mean by this? What psychological processes are represented by this statement?

10. How can an understanding of *attitudes* be used in designing marketing strategies? Give examples.

11. What do these phrases mean to marketers? (a) "If I were going to be a car, I'd be a Porsche." (b) "If my mother were a car, she'd be a Chevrolet." (c) "If my teenage daughter were a car, she'd be a BMW."

■ KEY TERMS

Attitude. A person's consistently favorable or unfavorable evaluations, feelings, and tendencies toward an object or idea.

Belief. A descriptive thought that a person holds about something.

Consumer market. All the individuals and households who buy or acquire goods and services for personal consumption.

Culture. The set of basic values, perceptions, wants, and behaviors learned by a member of society from family and other important institutions.

Learning. Changes in an individual's behavior arising from experience.

Life style. A person's pattern of living as expressed in his or her activities, interests, and opinions.

Motive (or drive). A need that is sufficiently pressing to direct the person to seek satisfaction of the need.

Opinion leaders. People within a reference group who, because of special skills, knowledge, personality, or other characteristics, exert influence on others.

Perception. The process by which people select, organize, and interpret information to form meaningful picture of the world.

Personality. A person's distinguishing psychological characteristics that lead to relatively consistent and lasting responses to his or her own environment.

Reference groups. Groups that have a direct (face-to-face) or indirect influence on the person's attitudes or behavior.

Role. The activities a person is expected to perform according to the people around him or her.

Social classes. Relatively permanent and ordered divisions in a society whose members share similar values, interests, and behaviors.

Status. The general esteem given to a role by society.

Subculture. A group of people with shared value systems based on common life experiences and situations.

■ REFERENCES

1. Excerpts from Peter Schutz and Jack Cook, "Porsche on Nichemanship," *Harvard Business Review,* March-April 1986, pp. 98–106. Copyright © 1986 by the President and Fellows of Harvard College; all rights reserved. Also see Cleveland Horton, "Porsche's Ads Get Racy in '88 with Tie to Indy," *Advertising Age,* November 2, 1987, p. 34; and Mark Maremont, "Europe's Long, Smooth Ride in Luxury Cars Is Over," *Business Week,* March 17, 1988, p. 57.

2. See Leon G. Schiffman and Leslie Lazar Kanuk, *Consumer Behavior*, 3rd ed. (Englewood Cliffs, NJ: Prentice Hall, 1987), pp. 491–503.

3. For more on marketing to Hispanics, blacks, mature consumers, and Asians, see Ed Fitch, "Marketing to Hispanics: Is the Red Carpet Plush Enough?" *Advertising Age,* February 8, 1988, p. S1; Joe Schwartz, "Hispanics in the Eighties," *American Demographics,* January 1988, pp. 43–45; "Marketing to Blacks: Rising Affluence Presents Fertile Market," *Advertising Age,* August 25, 1986, pp. S1-S7; George Sternlieb and James W. Hughes, "Black Households: The $100 Billion Potential," *American Demographics,* April 1988, pp. 35–37; Peter Petre, "Marketers Mine for Gold in the Old," *Fortune,* March 31, 1986, pp. 70–78; David B. Wolfe, "The Ageless Market," *American Demographics,* July 1987, pp. 26–29; and "The Asian Market: Too Good to be True?" *Sales & Marketing Management,* May 1988, pp. 39–42.

4. William O. Bearden and Michael J. Etzel, "Reference Group Influence on Product and Brand Purchase Decisions," *Journal of Consumer Research,* September 1982, p. 185.

5. "Do Real Men Shop?" *American Demographics,* May 1987, p. 14; and Raymond Serafin, "Carmakers Step Up Chase for Women, *Advertising Age,* May 16, 1988, p. 76.

6. For more on family decision making see Schiffman and Kanuk, *Consumer Behavior,* pp. 397–431; Harry L. Davis, "Decision Making Within the Household," *Journal of Consumer Research,* March 1976, pp. 241-60; Rosann L. Spiro, "Persuasion in Family Decision Making," *Journal of Consumer Research*, March 1983, pp. 393–402; and William J. Qualls, "Household Decision Behavior: The Impact of Husbands' and Wives' Sex Role Orientation," *Journal of Consumer Research,* September 1987, pp. 264–79.

7. See Lawrence Lepisto, "A Life Span Perspective of Consumer Behavior," in Elizabeth Hirshman and Morris Holbrook, eds. *Advances in Consumer Research,* Vol. 12 (Provo, Utah: Association for Consumer Research, 1985), p. 47.

8. See William D. Wells, "Psychographics: A Critical Review," *Journal of Marketing Research,* May 1975, pp. 196–213; W. Thomas Anderson and Linda Golden, "Lifestyle and Psychographics: A Critical Review and Recommendations," in Thomas C. Kinnear, ed., *Advances in Consumer Research* (Ann Arbor: Association for Consumer Research, 1984), pp. 405–11; and Bickley Townsend, "Psychographic Glitter and Gold," *American Demographics*, November 1985, pp. 22–29.

9. See Arnold Mitchell, *The Nine American Lifestyles* (New York: Macmillan, 1983).

10. See Schiffman and Kanuk, *Consumer Behavior*, pp. 164–65; and "Emotions Important for Successful Advertising," *Marketing News*, April 12, 1985, p. 18.

11. Kim Foltz, "Wizards of Marketing," *Newsweek*, July 22, 1985, p. 44.

12. For more reading on the pros and cons of using VALS and other life style approaches, see Sonia Yuspeh, "Syndicated Values/Lifestyles Segmentation Schemes: Use Them as Descriptive Tools, Not to Select Targets," *Marketing News*, May 25, 1984, p. 1; Lynn R. Kahle, Sharon E. Beatty, and Pamela Homer, "Alternative Measurement Approaches to Consumer Values: The List of Values (LOV) and Values and Life Styles (VALS)," *Journal of Consumer Research*, December 1986, pp. 405–9; and "Lifestyle Roulette," *American Demographics*, April 1987, pp. 24–25.

13. See Raymond L. Horton, "Some Relationships between Personality and Consumer Decision-Making," *Journal of Marketing Research*, May 1979, pp. 244–45. Also see Harold H. Kassarjian and Mary Jane Sheffet, "Person-ality in Consumer Behavior: An Update," in *Perspectives in Consumer Behavior*, Harold H. Kassarjian and Thomas S. Robertson, eds. (Glenview, IL: Scott Foresman, 1981), pp. 160–80; and Joseph T. Plummer, "How Personality Can Make a Difference," *Marketing News*, March–April 1984, pp. 17–20.

14. For more reading, see Edward L. Grubb and Harrison L. Grathwohl, "Consumer Self-Concept, Symbolism, and Market Behavior: A Theoretical Approach," *Journal of Marketing*, October 1967, pp. 22–27; and M. Joseph Sirgy, "Self-Concept in Consumer Behavior: A Critical Review," *Journal of Consumer Research*, December 1982, pp. 287–300.

15. See Ernest Dichter, *Handbook of Consumer Motivations* (New York: McGraw-Hill, 1964); and Sidney J. Levy, "Dreams, Fairy Tales, Animals, and Cars," *Psychology and Marketing*, Vol. 2, No. 2, Summer 1985, pp. 67–81.

16. Abraham H. Maslow, *Motivation and Personality*, 2nd ed. (New York: Harper & Row, 1970), pp. 80–106.

6 Consumer Markets: Buyer Decision Processes

FOR decades AT&T monopolized the residential telephone market: consumers had to lease whatever telephones the company offered. But in the late 1970s, the Supreme Court opened the way for competition when it ruled that consumers could attach their own phones to AT&T lines. And in the early 1980s, the breakup of AT&T and the invention of cheap, one-piece electronic phones threw the telecommunications industry into competitive chaos. Suddenly, AT&T found itself competing with hundreds of other telephone suppliers in the exploding $1.5 billion residential telephone market. During the next several years, AT&T learned a great deal about consumer buying behavior.

AT&T and its competitors offered hundreds of new phone models meeting every possible consumer want. At one extreme, they offered one-piece electronic phones at prices as low as $7 to $10. At the other extreme, they offered fancy phones selling for several hundred dollars—decorator phones in endless styles and colors, and phones with fancy features such as automatic dialing, last-number redial, cordless operation, mute and hold buttons, and speakers for hands-free conversations.

Despite huge R&D and marketing expenditures, the industry met with disaster. During 1983 and 1984, sales of home telephones boomed, but the companies lost hundreds of millions. By the end of 1984, more than half of all the telephone suppliers were out of the business. AT&T did better than most—but despite a 20 percent market share, the company made little money on its phone sales. Where did AT&T and the others go wrong? In their rush to grab a share of the rapidly growing market, they seriously miscalculated consumer wants and phone buying behavior.

For example, the telephone suppliers assumed that consumers would naturally want to buy rather than lease their phones, and overlooked the need to educate consumers about the benefits of phone ownership. Many consumers were still unaware that they could own their phones or that it made economic sense to buy rather than lease.

Many sellers assumed that consumers would flock to buy cheap, one-piece phones and that the number of phones per home would increase quickly. Though consumers did buy carloads of cheap phones at first, they didn't like the flimsy designs and high failure rates. Demand soon turned back to more traditional and reliable phones. And the average number of phones per household increased only slightly.

The telephone marketers also believed that consumers would buy phones from just about any retailer—or even through catalogs or mail order—if the price was right. But it turned out that buyers wanted to deal with solid retailers who helped them with purchase decisions and backed up the sale. One of the reasons for AT&T's relative success in this market was its recognition that consumers would return to higher-quality phones and retailers after trying cheaper phones from less dependable sources. Thus AT&T developed a solid retail network. In addition to its own 900 phone stores, it sold quality phones through over 10,000 retail outlets including Sears, Penney, K mart, Montgomery Ward, Target, and Ace Hardware.

AT&T, however, erred at the other extreme—it assumed that consumers wanted high-priced phones with fancy features. AT&T offered 215 different models with prices as high as $350. But telephone buyers still wanted good old basic telephones, in traditional styles and colors and at more moderate prices—phones like those they'd been leasing for years. And buyers weren't much interested in fancy "bells and whistles"—in fact, the new features confused many consumers. For these fancy phones, consumers needed more sales help than most retail stores were willing or able to provide. AT&T now has a training program to teach retail salespeople in non-AT&T stores how to demonstrate phone products and answer buyers' questions.

After the shakeout, the telephone market will settle into steady, long-term growth. And most experts agree that demand will shift to fancier phones as consumers grow accustomed to the new technologies. But the shift will involve gradual changes in consumer attitudes. To stay a leader in the more competitive telephone industry, AT&T will have to develop a better understanding of consumers and their telephone buying behavior.[1]

Chapter Objectives   *After reading this chapter, you should be able to:*

1. Identify the different roles people might play in making a buying decision.
2. Discuss how consumer decision making varies with the type of buying decision.
3. Explain the five stages of the buyer decision process.
4. Describe the consumer adoption process for new products.

MARKETERS have to be extremely careful in analyzing consumer behavior. Consumers often turn down what appears to be a winning offer. If they do not vote for a product, the product loses. The new plant and equipment might as well have been built on quicksand. Polaroid found this out when it lost $170 million on its Polarvision instant home movie system. So did Ford when it launched the famous (or infamous) Edsel, losing a cool $350 million in the process. And so did RCA when it swallowed a huge $580 million loss on its SelectaVision videodisc player.

In the previous chapter we looked at all the influences—cultural, social, personal, and psychological—that affect buyers. In this chapter we will look at how consumers make buying decisions. First, we will examine consumer buying roles and the types of decisions consumers face. Then we will look at the main steps in the buyer decision process. Finally we will explore the process by which consumers learn about and buy new products.

CONSUMER BUYING ROLES

The marketer needs to know what people are involved in the buying decision and what role each person plays. For many products, it is fairly easy to identify the decision maker. Men normally choose their own shoes and women choose their own pantyhose. Other products, however, involve a decision-making unit consisting of more than one person. Consider the selection of a family automobile. The suggestion to buy a new car might come from the oldest child. A friend might advise the family on the kind of car to buy. The husband might choose the make. The wife might have a definite opinion regarding the car's style. The husband and wife might then make the final decision jointly. And the wife might end up using the car more than her husband.

Figure 6-1 shows that people might play any of several roles in a buying decision:

- **Initiator:** the person who first suggests or thinks of the idea of buying a particular product or service
- **Influencer:** a person whose advice or views carry some weight in making a final buying decision
- **Decider:** the person who ultimately makes a buying decision or any part of it —whether to buy, what to buy, how to buy, or where to buy
- **Buyer:** the person who makes an actual purchase
- **User:** the person who consumes or uses a product or service

A company needs to identify who occupies these roles because they affect product design and advertising message decisions. If Chevrolet finds that husbands make buying decisions for the family station wagon, it will direct most of its advertising for these models toward husbands. But Chevy ads will include wives, children, and others who might initiate or influence the buying decision. And Chevrolet will design its station wagons with features that meet the needs of all buying decision participants. Knowing the main participants and the roles they play helps the marketer fine-tune the marketing program.

FIGURE 6-1
Consumer buying roles

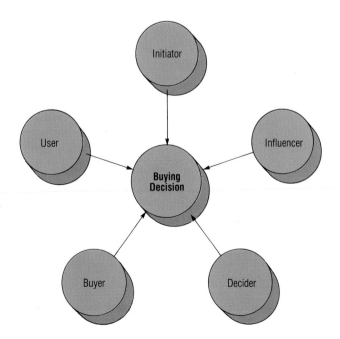

*T*YPES OF BUYING DECISION BEHAVIOR

Consumer decision making varies with the type of buying decision. There are great differences between buying toothpaste, a tennis racket, an expensive camera, and a new car. The more complex decisions are likely to involve more buying participants and more buyer deliberation. Figure 6-2 identifies three types of buying behavior.[2]

Routine Response Behavior

Routine response behavior, the simplest type of buying behavior, occurs when consumers buy low-cost, frequently purchased items. Buyers have very few decisions to make—they know a lot about the product class and major brands available, and they have fairly clear preferences among the brands. They do not always buy the same brand because there may be stockouts, special deals, or a wish for variety. But in general buyers do not give much thought, search, or time to the purchase. The goods in this class are often called *low-involvement goods.* For example, you do not spend a lot of time and effort choosing your laundry detergent or your gas station. You usually just pick one of the brands or places you used last time.

Marketers of products that consumers buy routinely have two tasks. First, they must satisfy current customers by maintaining consistent quality, service, and value. Second, they must try to attract new buyers—break them out of the routine of buying competing products—by introducing new features and using point-of-purchase displays, price specials, and premiums.

Limited Problem Solving

Buying is more complex when buyers confront an unfamiliar brand in a familiar product class. For example, people thinking about buying a new tennis racket may be shown a new brand with an offset handle or one made of boron or another new material. They may ask questions and watch ads to learn more about the new brand. This is described as **limited problem solving** because buyers are fully aware of the product class, but are not familiar with all the brands and their features.

The marketer recognizes that consumers are trying to reduce risk by gathering information. Marketers must design a communication program that will help buyers understand the company's brand and give them confidence in it.

Extensive Problem Solving

Sometimes buyers face complex buying decisions for more expensive, less frequently purchased products in a less familiar product class. For these products, buyers often do not know about available brands or what factors to consider when they evaluate different brands. In these situations, people use **extensive problem solving.** For example, suppose you want to buy an expensive new stereo components system.

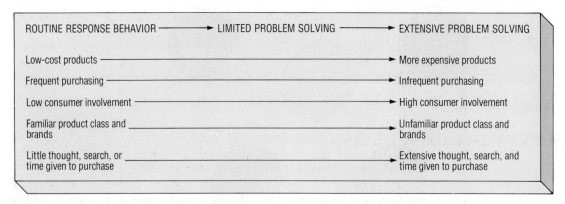

FIGURE 6-2 Types of buying decision behavior

Extensive problem solving: consumers shop different stores, collect information, and compare various brands before buying.

You would probably spend lots of time visiting different stores, collecting information, comparing various brands, and making the final decision.

Marketers of products in this class must understand the information-gathering and evaluation activities of prospective buyers. They need to help buyers learn about important buying criteria and persuade buyers that their brands rate high on important attributes compared with competing products.

STAGES IN THE BUYER DECISION PROCESS

Consumers make many buying decisions every day. Most large companies research consumer buying decisions in great detail. They want to answer questions about what consumers buy, where they buy, how and how much they buy, when they buy, and why they buy (see Marketing Highlight 6–1). Marketers can study consumer

THE WHATS AND WHYS OF CONSUMER BUYING

No one knows better than Mom, right? But does she know how much underwear you own? Jockey International does. Or the number of ice cubes you put in a glass? Coca-Cola knows that one. Or how about which you usually eat first, the broken pretzels in the pack or the whole ones? Try asking Frito-Lay. Big companies know the whats, wheres, hows, and whens of their consumers. They figure out all sorts of things about us we didn't even know ourselves. To marketers, this isn't a trivial pursuit—knowing all about the customer is the cornerstone of effective marketing. Most companies research us in detail and amass mountains of facts.

Coke knows that we put 3.2 ice cubes in a glass, see 69 of its commercials every year, and prefer cans to pop out of vending machines at a temperature of 35 degrees. One million of us drink Coke with breakfast every day. Kodak knows that amateur photographers muff more than two billion pictures every year. This led to the disc camera, which helped elimi-nate almost half of our out-of-focus and overexposed shots and became one of the most successful cameras in Kodak's history.

Each new day brings piles of fresh research reports detailing our buying habits and preferences. Did you know that 38 percent of Americans would rather have a tooth pulled than take their car to a dealership for repairs? We each spend $20 a year on flowers; Arkansas has the lowest consumption of peanut butter in the United States; and if you send a husband and a wife to the store separately to buy beer, there is a 90 percent chance they will return with different brands.

Nothing about our behavior is sacred. Procter & Gamble once conducted a study to find out whether most of us fold or crumple our toilet paper. Abbott Laboratories figured out that one in four of us has "problem" dandruff, and Kimberly Clark, which makes Kleenex, calculated that the average person blows his or her nose 256 times a year.

purchases to find answers to questions about what they buy, where, and how much. But learning about the whys of consumer buying behavior and buying decision process is not so easy—the answers are often locked deep within the consumer's head.

We are now ready to examine the stages buyers pass through to reach a buying decision. We will use the model in Figure 6-3, which shows the consumer as passing through five stages: problem recognition, information search, evaluation of alternatives, purchase decision, and postpurchase behavior. This model emphasizes that the buying process starts long before the actual purchase and continues after the purchase. It encourages the marketer to focus on the entire buying process, rather than just the purchase decision.[3]

This model seems to imply that consumers pass through all five stages with every purchase they make. But in more routine purchases, consumers skip or reverse some of these stages. A woman buying her regular brand of toothpaste would recognize the need and go right to the purchase decision, skipping information search and evaluation. However, we will use the model in Figure 6-3 because it shows all the considerations that arise when a consumer faces a new purchase situation, especially one involving extensive problem solving.

FIGURE 6-3 Buyer decision process

Not that Americans are all that easy to figure out. A few years ago, Campbell Soup gave up trying to learn what we think the ideal-sized meatball is after a series of tests showed us preferring one so big it wouldn't fit in the can.

Hoover hooked up timers and other equipment to vacuum cleaners in people's homes and found out that we spend about 35 minutes each week vacuuming and suck up about eight pounds of dust each year using six bags. Banks know that we write about 24 checks a month, and pharmaceutical companies know that all of us together take 52 million aspirin and 30 million sleeping pills a year. In fact, most everything we swallow is closely monitored by someone. Each year we consume 156 hamburgers, 95 hot dogs, 283 eggs, five pounds of yogurt, nine pounds of cereal, and two pounds of peanut butter. We spend 90 minutes a day preparing our food and 40 minutes a day munching it. We down $650 million of antacid a year to help digest it.

Of all the businesses, the prize for research thoroughness may go to toothpaste makers. Among other things, they know that our favorite toothbrush color is blue and that only 37 percent of us are using one that's more than six months old. About 47 percent of us put water on our brush before we apply the paste, 15 percent of us put water on after the paste, and 24 percent of us do both. Fourteen percent don't wet the brush at all.

So most big marketing companies have answers to all the what, where, when, and how questions about their consumers' buying behavior. Seemingly trivial facts add up quickly and provide important inputs for designing marketing strategies. But to influence consumer behavior, marketers need the answer to one more question. Beyond knowing the whats and wherefores of behavior, they need to know the *whys*—what *causes* our buying behavior? That's a much harder question to answer.

Source: Adapted from John Koten, "You Aren't Paranoid If You Feel Someone Eyes You Constantly," *The Wall Street Journal*, March 29, 1985, pp. 1, 22.

To illustrate this model, we will once again refer to Jennifer Smith and try to understand how she became interested in buying an expensive camera and the stages she went through to make the final brand choice.

Problem Recognition

The buying process starts with **problem recognition**—with the buyer perceiving a problem or need. The buyer senses a difference between his or her actual state and a desired state. The need can be triggered by internal stimuli. One of the person's normal needs—hunger, thirst, sex—rises to a high enough level and becomes a drive. From previous experience, the person has learned how to cope with this drive and is motivated toward products that he or she knows will satisfy this drive.

Or a need can be aroused by an external stimulus. Jennifer Smith passes a bakery and the sight of freshly baked bread stimulates her hunger; she admires a neighbor's new car; or she watches a television commercial for a Jamaican vacation. All of these can lead her to recognize a problem or need. Marketers at this stage need to determine the factors and situations that usually trigger consumer problem recognition. They should research consumers to find out what kinds of needs or problems arose, what brought them about, and how they led to this particular product.

Jennifer Smith might answer that she felt the need for a new hobby. This happened when her busy season at work slowed down, and she thought of cameras after talking to a friend about photography. By gathering such information, the marketer can identify the stimuli that most often trigger interest in the product category and develop marketing programs that capitalize on these stimuli.

Information Search

An aroused consumer may or may not search for more information. If the consumer's drive is strong and a satisfying product is near at hand, the consumer is likely to buy it then. If not, the consumer may simply store the need in memory or undertake an **information search** bearing on the need.

At one level, the consumer may simply have *heightened attention*. Here Jennifer Smith becomes more receptive to information about cameras. She pays attention to camera ads, cameras used by friends, and camera conversations. Or Jennifer may go into *active information search*, where she looks for reading material, phones friends, and gathers product information in other ways. How much search she does will depend upon the strength of her drive, the amount of information she starts with, the ease of obtaining more information, the value she places on additional information, and the satisfaction she gets from searching. Normally the amount of consumer search activity increases as the consumer moves from decisions that involve limited problem solving to those that involve extensive problem solving. The consumer can obtain information from any of several sources. The marketer must know about these sources and the influence each has on buying decisions. Consumer information sources include:

- Personal sources: family, friends, neighbors, acquaintances
- Commercial sources: advertising, salespeople, dealers, packaging, displays
- Public sources: mass media, consumer-rating organizations
- Experiential sources: handling, examining, using the product

The relative influence of these information sources varies with the product and the buyer. Generally the consumer receives the most information about a product from commercial sources, those dominated by the marketer. The most effective sources, however, tend to be personal sources. Each source may perform a different function in influencing the buying decision. Commercial sources normally inform the buyer, but personal sources legitimize and evaluate the purchase for the buyer. For example, physicians normally learn of new drugs from commercial sources, but turn to other doctors for evaluation information.

As a result of gathering information, the consumer increases his or her awareness and knowledge of the available brands and their features. In looking for information, Jennifer Smith found out about the many camera brands available. The information also helped her drop certain brands from consideration. A company must design its marketing mix to make prospects aware of and knowledgeable about its brand. If it fails to do this, the company has lost its opportunity to sell to the customer. The company must also learn which other brands customers consider, so that it knows its competition and can plan its appeals.

The marketer should carefully identify consumers' sources of information and the importance of each source. Consumers should be asked how they first heard about the brand, what information they received, and the importance they place on different information sources. This information is critical in preparing effective communication to target markets.

Evaluation of Alternatives We have seen how the consumer uses information to arrive at a set of final brand choices. Now the question is: How does the consumer choose among alternative brands? The marketer needs to know about **alternative evaluation**—how the consumer uses information to evaluate the options and arrive at brand choices. Unfortunately, there is no simple and single evaluation process used by all consumers, or even by one consumer in all buying situations. There are several decision evaluation processes.

Certain basic concepts will help explain consumer evaluation processes. First, we assume that each consumer sees a product as a bundle of *product attributes*.

Information sources: people usually receive the most information about a product from marketer controlled sources.

For cameras, these attributes include picture quality, ease of use, camera size, price, and other factors. Consumers will vary as to which of these attributes they consider relevant. They will pay the most attention to those attributes connected with their needs. The market for a product can often be segmented according to the attributes that are of primary interest to different customer groups.

Second, the consumer will attach different *degrees of importance* to each attribute. A distinction can be drawn between the importance of an attribute and its salience.[4] *Salient attributes* are those that come to a consumer's mind when he or she is asked to think of a product's characteristics. But these are not necessarily the most important attributes to the consumer. Some of them may be salient because the consumer has just seen an advertisement mentioning them or has had a problem with them, making these attributes "top-of-the-mind." There may also be other attributes that the consumer forgot but whose importance would be recognized if they were mentioned. Marketers should be more concerned with attribute importance than attribute salience.

Third, the consumer is likely to develop a set of *brand beliefs* about where each brand stands on each attribute. The set of beliefs held about a particular brand is known as the **brand image.** The consumer's beliefs may vary from true attributes because of his or her experience and the effect of selective perception, selective distortion, and selective retention.

Fourth, the consumer has a *utility function* for the attributes. The utility function shows how the consumer expects total product satisfaction to vary with alternative levels of each attribute. For example, Jennifer Smith may expect her satisfaction from a camera to increase with better picture quality; to peak with a medium-weight camera as opposed to a very light or very heavy one; to be higher for a 35-mm camera than for a 135-mm camera. If we combine the attribute levels where the utilities are highest, they make up Jennifer's ideal camera. The camera would also be her preferred camera if it were available and affordable.

Fifth, the consumer arrives at attitudes (judgments, preferences) toward the brand alternatives through some *evaluation procedure.* One or more of several evaluation procedures are used, depending on the consumer and the buying decision.

We will illustrate these concepts with Jennifer Smith's camera buying situation. Suppose Jennifer has narrowed her choice set to four cameras A, B, C, and D. Assume that she is primarily interested in four attributes—picture quality, ease of use, camera size, and price. Table 6-1 shows how she believes each brand rates on each attribute. Jennifer believes that brand A (say Nikon) will give her picture quality of 10 on a 10-point scale; is easy to use, 8; has medium size, 6; and is fairly expensive, 4. Similarly, she has beliefs about how the other cameras rate on these attributes. The marketer would like to be able to predict which camera Jennifer will buy.

Clearly, if one camera rated best on all the attributes, we could predict that Jennifer would choose it. But the brands vary in appeal. Some buyers will base their buying decision on only one attribute, and their choices are easy to predict. If Jennifer wants picture quality above everything, she should buy A; if she wants the camera that is easiest to use, she should buy B; if she wants the best camera size, she should buy C; if she wants the lowest-price camera, she should buy D.

Most buyers consider several attributes, but assign different importance to each. If we knew the importance weights Jennifer assigns to the four attributes, we could predict her camera choice more reliably. Suppose Jennifer assigns 40 percent of the importance to the camera's picture quality, 30 percent to ease of use, 20 percent to its size, and 10 percent to its price. To find Jennifer's perceived value for each camera, we can multiply her importance weights by her beliefs about each camera. This gives us the following perceived values:

Camera A = .4(10) + .3(8) + .2(6) + .1(4) = 8.0
Camera B = .4(8) + .3(9) + .2(8) + .1(3) = 7.8
Camera C = .4(6) + .3(8) + .2(10) + .1(5) = 7.3
Camera D = .4(4) + .3(3) + .2(7) + .1(8) = 4.7

We would predict that Jennifer will favor camera A.

This model is called the *expectancy value model* of consumer choice.[5] It is one of several possible models describing how consumers go about evaluating alternatives. Consumers might evaluate a set of alternatives in other ways. For example, Jennifer might decide that she should consider only cameras that satisfy a set of minimum attribute levels. She might decide a camera would have to offer a picture quality greater than 7 *or* ease of use greater than 8. In this case, we would predict that she would choose camera B because only camera B satisfies the minimum requirements. This is called the *conjunctive model* of consumer choice. Or Jennifer might decide that she would settle for a camera that had a picture quality greater

TABLE 6-1
A Consumer's Brand
Beliefs about Cameras

CAMERA	ATTRIBUTE			
	Picture Quality	Ease of Use	Camera Size	Price
A	10	8	6	4
B	8	9	8	3
C	6	8	10	5
D	4	3	7	8

Note: The number 10 represents the highest desirable score on that attribute. In the case of price, a high number means a low cost, which makes the camera more desirable.

than 7 *or* ease of use greater than 8. In this case, A and B both meet the requirements. This is called the *disjunctive model* of consumer choice.

How consumers go about evaluating purchase alternatives depends on the individual consumer and the specific buying situation. In some cases, consumers use careful calculations and logical thinking. At other times, the same consumers do little or no evaluating, instead buying on impulse and relying on intuition. Sometimes consumers make buying decisions on their own; sometimes they turn to friends, consumer guides, salespeople, or even computers for buying advice (see Marketing Highlight 6–2).

Marketers should study buyers to find out how they actually evaluate brand alternatives. If they know what evaluative processes go on, marketers can take steps to influence the buyer's decision. Suppose Jennifer is inclined to buy a Nikon camera because she rates it high on picture quality and ease of use. What strategies might another camera maker, say Minolta, use to influence people like Jennifer? There are several. Minolta could modify its camera so that it delivers better pictures or other features that consumers like Jennifer want. It could try to change buyers' beliefs about how its camera rates on key attributes, especially if consumers currently underestimate the camera's qualities. It could try to change buyers' beliefs about Nikon and other competitors. Finally, it could try to change the list of attributes that buyers consider, or the importance attached to these attributes. For example, it

MARKETING HIGHLIGHT 6–2

THIS COMPUTER GIVES SHOPPERS CUSTOM-MADE ADVICE

Some people break out in a cold sweat when they have to shop. Others get cross-eyed from scanning the ratings in *Consumer Reports*. That consumers are befuddled doesn't surprise Thomas A. Williams. The Rochester Institute of Technology professor of decision sciences says he has been swamped with requests from friends who need help. So Williams is working on a high-tech solution: expert-system programs to help confused consumers shop.

Williams has tried out his computerized advisers for such products as running shoes, washing machines, touring bikes, and cars. The systems grill shoppers about their preferences, personal characteristics, and price ranges. Then they match the data with available products. If you wanted new running shoes, a system would base its recommendation on answers to questions about the anatomy of your feet, the terrain you run on, and how long and how often you run.

Williams is scouting out stores that will let customers try his systems for microcomputers and cameras. He's still not sure shoppers will welcome the electronic adviser. "The typical consumer does not approach a purchasing decision in a logical fashion," he says.

Source: Reprinted from the December 7, 1987, issue of *Business Week* by special permission. © 1987 by McGraw-Hill, Inc.

To rate higher with consumers, Minolta added autofocus, motorized film control, and other features. It took major competitor Canon three years to catch up.

might advertise that all good cameras have about equal picture quality, and that its lighter-weight, lower-priced camera is a better buy for people like Jennifer.

Purchase Decision

In the evaluation stage, the consumer ranks brands and forms purchase intentions. Normally the consumer will buy the most preferred brand, but two factors can come between the purchase intention and the purchase decision. These factors are shown in Figure 6-4.[6]

The first is the *attitudes of others*. Suppose Jennifer Smith's husband feels strongly that Jennifer should buy the lowest-priced camera to keep down expenses. Then the chances of Jennifer's buying the more expensive Nikon will be reduced. How much another person's attitude will affect Jennifer's choice depends on both the strength of the other person's attitudes toward her buying decision and on Jennifer's motivation to comply with the other person's wishes. The more intense the other person's attitudes and the closer the other person is to Jennifer, the more effect the other person will have.

Purchase intention is also influenced by *unexpected situations*. The consumer

FIGURE 6-4
Steps between
evaluation of alternatives
and a purchase decision

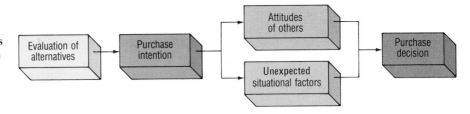

forms a purchase intention based on such factors as expected family income, expected price, and expected benefits from the product. When the consumer is about to act, unexpected situations may arise to change the purchase intention. Jennifer Smith may lose her job, some other purchase may become more urgent, or a friend may report being disappointed in the camera she was about to buy.

Thus preferences and even purchase intentions are not completely reliable predictors of actual purchase choice. They direct purchase behavior but may not fully determine the outcome. Figure 6-5 shows a fairly typical outcome. In a study of one hundred people who stated an intention to buy brand A of an appliance within the next twelve months, only forty-four ended up buying the particular appliance, and only thirty purchased brand A.

A consumer's decision to change, postpone, or avoid a purchase decision is heavily influenced by *perceived risk*.[7] Many purchases involve some risk taking. Consumers cannot be certain about the purchase outcome. This produces anxiety. The amount of perceived risk varies with the amount of money at stake, the amount of purchase uncertainty, and the amount of consumer self-confidence. A consumer takes certain actions to reduce risk, such as avoiding purchase decisions, gathering more information, and looking for national brand names and products with warranties. The marketer must understand the factors that provoke feelings of risk in consumers and provide information and support that will reduce the perceived risk.

Postpurchase Behavior

The marketer's job does not end when the product is bought. After purchasing the product, the consumer will be satisfied or dissatisfied with it. The consumer will also engage in **postpurchase behavior** that is of interest to the marketer. So the marketer's interest in the consumer continues into the postpurchase stage.

Postpurchase Satisfaction

What determines whether the buyer is satisfied or dissatisfied with a purchase? The answer lies in the relationship between the *consumer's expectations* and the product's *perceived performance*.[8] If the product matches expectations, the consumer is satisfied; if it exceeds them, the consumer is highly satisfied; if it falls short, the consumer is dissatisfied.

FIGURE 6-5
Results of purchase
intentions and purchase
decisions

Purchase intention   **Purchase behavior during next 12 months**

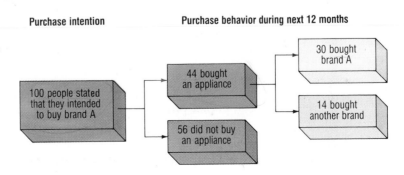

exaggerate ∨ 과장하다

Consumers base their expectations on messages they receive from sellers, friends, and other information sources. If the seller exaggerates the product's performance, consumers will experience *disconfirmed expectations*, which lead to dissatisfaction. The larger the gap between expectations and performance, the greater the consumer's dissatisfaction. This suggests that the seller should make product claims that faithfully represent the product's performance so that buyers are satisfied. Some sellers might even understate performance levels to boost consumers' satisfaction with the product. For example, Boeing sells aircraft worth tens of millions of dollars each—consumer satisfaction is important for repeat purchases and the company's reputation. Boeing's salespeople sell their products with facts and knowledge, not inflated promises. In fact, salespeople tend to be conservative when they estimate their product's potential benefits. They almost always underestimate fuel efficiency—they say it's a five percent savings over current models, and it will turn out to be eight. Customers are delighted with better-than-expected performance; they buy again and tell other potential customers that Boeing lives up to its promises.[9]

Almost all major purchases result in *cognitive dissonance*, or discomfort caused by after-purchase conflict. Consumers are satisfied with the benefits of the chosen brand and glad to avoid the drawbacks of the brands not purchased. On the other hand, every purchase involves compromise, and the drawbacks of the chosen brand, plus the benefits of the brands not purchased, may make consumers feel uneasy about their purchase choice. Thus consumers feel at least some postpurchase dissonance for every major purchase. And they will often take steps after the purchase to reduce dissonance.[10]

Postpurchase Actions

Satisfaction with the product will affect later behavior. A satisfied consumer is more likely to buy the product the next time and will say good things about the product to others. According to marketers, "A satisfied customer is our best advertisement."

A dissatisfied consumer responds differently. Dissatisfied consumers may try to reduce their dissonance by taking any of several actions. They may abandon or return the product, or they may seek information that will confirm its high value. In the case of Jennifer Smith, she may return the camera, or look at Nikon ads that tell of the camera's benefits, or talk with friends who will tell her how much they like her new camera.

Marketers should be aware of the many ways consumers might handle dissatisfaction. Figure 6-6 outlines these ways. Consumers have a choice between taking and not taking any action. If they act, they can take public action or private action. Public actions include complaining to the company, going to a lawyer, or complaining to other groups such as consumer protection agencies that might help the buyer get satisfaction. Or the buyer may simply stop buying the product or warn friends not to buy it. In all these cases, the seller loses something.

Marketers can take steps to minimize consumer postpurchase dissatisfaction and to help customers feel good about their purchase. Automobile companies can send a letter to new car owners congratulating them on having selected a fine car. They can place ads showing satisfied owners driving their new cars. They can obtain customer suggestions for improvements and list the locations of available services. They can write instruction booklets that reduce dissatisfaction. They can send owners a magazine full of articles describing the pleasures of owning the new car. They can send a questionnaire asking about customer satisfaction and then follow up with the dealer and the customer about any noted problem.

Postpurchase communications to buyers have been shown to result in fewer

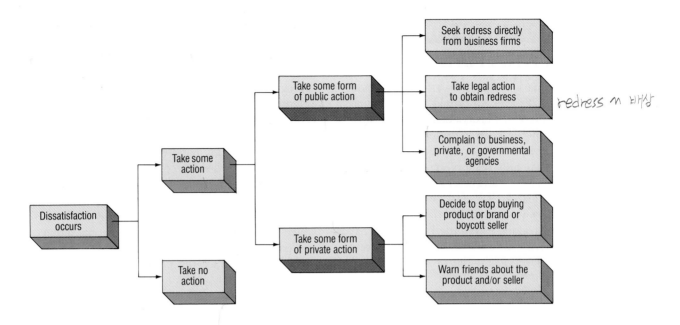

FIGURE 6-6   How customers handle dissatisfaction

Source: Ralph L. Day and E. Laird Landon, Jr., "Toward a Theory of Consumer Complaining Behavior," in *Consumer and Industrial Buying Behavior*, ed. Arch G. Woodside, Jagdish N. Sheth, and Peter D. Bennett (New York: Elsevier North-Holland, 1977), p. 432.

product returns and order cancellations.[11] Paying careful attention to consumer dissatisfactions can help the company to spot and correct problems, resulting in increased postpurchase satisfaction for future buyers (see Marketing Highlight 6–3).

Understanding the consumer's needs and buying process is the foundation of successful marketing. By understanding how buyers go through problem recognition, information search, evaluation of alternatives, the purchase decision, and postpurchase behavior, the marketer can pick up many clues as to how to meet the buyer's needs. By understanding the various participants in the buying process and the major influences on their buying behavior, the marketer can develop an effective marketing program to support an attractive offer to the target market.

*B*UYER DECISION PROCESSES TOWARD NEW PRODUCTS

We have looked at the stages buyers go through in trying to satisfy a need. Buyers may pass quickly or slowly through these stages, and some of the stages may even be reversed. Much depends on the nature of the buyer, the product, and the buying situation.

We will now look at how buyers approach the purchase of new products.[12] We define **new product** as a good, service, or idea that is perceived by some potential customers as new. We define **adoption process** as "the mental process through which an individual passes from first hearing about an innovation to final adoption."[13] We define **adoption** as the decision by an individual to become a regular user of the product.

We are now ready to examine the main generalizations drawn from hundreds of studies of how people accept new ideas.

MARKETING HIGHLIGHT 6–3

CUSTOMERS: P&G'S PIPELINE TO PRODUCT PROBLEMS

One of the first mass marketers to establish a broad service operation, Procter & Gamble Co. is celebrating the 10th anniversary of its 800-number service this year. While it has been a leader in consumer services—it hired its first expert in 1941—its current operation is not as fully computerized as some of the hard-goods makers. P&G first experimented with the phone-line idea in 1971, and by 1979 it began implementing a plan to have an 800 number on every P&G consumer product sold in the U.S.

Last year, P&G received 670,000 mail and phone contacts about its products—the overall figure this year is running 17% ahead of that. And according to G. Gibson Carey, P&G division manager for general advertising, the calls fall into three broad categories: requests for information, complaints, and testimonials.

P&G employs 75 people in its service department, 30 of whom handle calls; the rest answer letters and help collate information for other departments. Phones are manned weekdays from 9:30 A.M. to 7:30 P.M. Employees receive three to five weeks of training. Besides instruction on how to deal with people over the phone, the training includes the history of each product, the company's marketing and advertising

strategy for it, and what happens if it is misused. Telephone representatives have reference manuals and access to technical staff but no computers to help answer questions. Information from P&G customers is tallied by hand and computerized later.

Most callers dial the company with the product package in hand. And every product has a code printed on it identifying the plant, the manufacturing date, and sometimes even the shift and the line on which it was made. Thus, if P&G has supplied defective packages, as happened not long ago with one product, it can trace the problem's source quickly and correct it.

Because of the calls it received on various products, P&G has:

- Included instructions for baking at high altitudes on the Duncan Hines brownies package.
- Added a recipe for making a wedding cake to the information on its white cake mix package.
- Told users what to do if Downy liquid fabric softener accidentally freezes (numerous customers had that problem during a cold spell).

"As a general rule, we don't look at [consumer service] as a source for new product ideas," Carey

---

Stages in the Adoption Process

Consumers go through five stages in the process of adopting a new product:

1. *Awareness*: The consumer becomes aware of the product but lacks information about it.
2. *Interest*: The consumer is stimulated to seek information about the product.
3. *Evaluation*: The consumer considers whether it would make sense to try the product.
4. *Trial*: The consumer tries the product on a small scale to improve his or her estimate of its value.
5. *Adoption*: The consumer decides to make full and regular use of the product.

This suggests that the new-product marketer should think about how to help consumers move through these stages. General Electric might find that many potential customers for its microwave ovens are in the interest stage but do not move to the trial stage because of uncertainty and the large investment. If these same consumers would be willing to use a microwave oven on a trial basis for a small fee, the manufacturer should consider offering a trial-use plan with an option to buy.

Individual Differences in Innovativeness

People differ greatly in their readiness to try new products. In each product area, there are apt to be "consumption pioneers" and early adopters. Some people are the first to adopt new clothing fashions or new appliances. Other individuals adopt

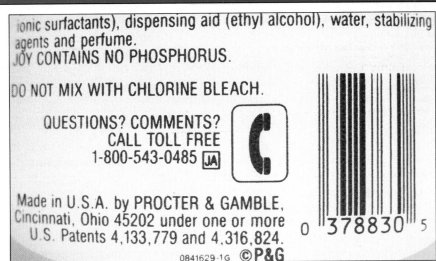

P&G puts an 800 number for customer service on every product it sells in the United States.

concedes. Information from the calls first goes to product-development personnel who track quality control. Each division and top management get a separate report. P&G also surveys customers to determine whether callers were satisfied with the treatment they received.

Carey says the 800-number service is "a distant, early-warning signal" of product problems. Without it, "we wouldn't find out about them for weeks or months." And, he points out: "There's a whole lot of enlightened self-interest in this."

Source: Reprinted from the June 11, 1984, issue of *Business Week* by special permission. © 1984 by McGraw-Hill, Inc.

new products much later. Such individual differences have led to a classification of people into the adopter categories shown in Figure 6-7.

The adoption process is represented as a normal distribution when plotted over time. After a slow start, an increasing number of people adopt the innovation, the number reaches a peak, and then it diminishes as fewer nonadopters remain. Innovators are defined as the first 2.5 percent of the buyers to adopt a new idea; the early adopters are the next 13.5 percent who adopt the new idea; and so forth.

The five adopter groups have differing values. Innovators are venturesome—they are willing to try new ideas at some risk. Early adopters are guided by respect—they are opinion leaders in their community and adopt new ideas early but carefully. The early majority are deliberate—they adopt new ideas before the average person, although they are rarely leaders. The late majority are skeptical—they adopt an innovation only after a majority of people have tried it. Finally, laggards are tradition-bound—they are suspicious of change and adopt the innovation only after it has become somewhat of a tradition itself.

This adopter classification suggests that an innovating firm should research the demographic, psychographic, and media characteristics of innovators and early adopters and direct marketing efforts to them. Identifying early adopters is not always easy. No one has demonstrated the existence of a general personality factor called

deliberate 생각이 깊은
신중한
계획적인

이상이·론은

합의스러운

FIGURE 6-7
Adopter categorization
on the basis of relative
time of adoption
of innovations
Source: Redrawn from Everett M.
Rogers, *Diffusion of
Innovations*, 3rd ed. (New York:
1983), p. 247. Adapted with
permission of Macmillan
Publishing Company, Inc.
Copyright © 1983 by The Free
Press.

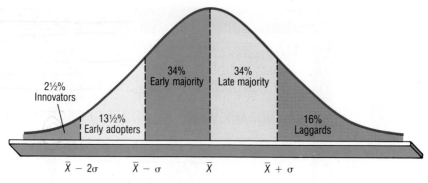

Time of adoption of innovations

innovativeness. Individuals tend to be innovators in certain areas and laggards in others. We can think of a business person who dresses conservatively but who delights in trying new and exotic foods, for example.

The firm wants to identify the characteristics of consumers who are likely to be early adopters of their products. For example, studies show that innovative housewives are usually more outgoing and higher in social status than noninnovative housewives. Home computer innovators are middle-aged, higher in income and education, and tend to be opinion leaders, though they tend to be more rational, more introverted, and less social than later adopters.[14] In general, research has shown that innovators tend to be relatively younger, better educated, and higher in income than later adopters and nonadopters. They are more receptive to unfamiliar things, rely more on their own values and judgment, and are more willing to take risks. They are less brand-loyal and more likely to take advantage of special promotions such as discounts, coupons, and samples.[15]

Role of Personal Influence

Personal influence plays a major role in the adoption of new products. **Personal influence** describes the effect of statements made by one person on another's attitude or probability of purchase. Consumers consult each other for opinions about new products and brands, and the advice of others can strongly influence buying behavior.

Personal influence is more important in some situations and for some individuals than for others. Personal influence is more important in the evaluation stage of the new-product adoption process than in the other stages. It has more influence on later adopters than on early adopters. And it is more important in risky than in safe situations.

Influence of Product Characteristics on Rate of Adoption

The characteristics of the innovation affect its rate of adoption. Some products catch on almost overnight (Frisbees), whereas others take a long time to gain wide acceptance (personal computers). Five characteristics are especially important in influencing an innovation's rate of adoption. We will consider the characteristics in relation to the rate of adoption of personal computers for home use.

The first characteristic is the innovation's *relative advantage*—the degree to which it appears superior to existing products. The greater the perceived relative advantage of using a personal computer, say in preparing income taxes and keeping financial records, the sooner the personal computer will be adopted.

The second characteristic is the innovation's *compatibility*—the degree to which it matches the values and experiences of the people in the community. Personal

Product characteristics affect the rate of adoption—products like home computers take a long time to gain wide acceptance.

computers, for example, are highly compatible with the life styles found in upper-middle-class homes.

The third characteristic is the innovation's *complexity*—the degree to which it is relatively difficult to understand or use. Personal computers are complex and will therefore take a longer than average time to penetrate U.S. homes.

The fourth characteristic is the innovation's *divisibility*—the degree to which it may be tried on a limited basis. To the extent that people can rent personal computers with an option to buy, the product's rate of adoption will increase.

The fifth characteristic is the innovation's *communicability*—the degree to which the results can be observed or described to others. Because personal computers lend themselves to demonstration and description, this will help them diffuse faster in the social system.

Other characteristics influence the rate of adoption, such as initial costs, ongoing costs, risk and uncertainty, scientific credibility, and social approval. The new product marketer has to research all these factors when developing the new product and marketing program.

■ SUMMARY

Before planning its marketing strategy, a company needs to identify its target consumers and the types of decision processes they go through. Although many buying decisions involve only one decision maker, other decisions may involve several participants who play such roles as initiator, influencer, decider, buyer, and user. The marketer's job is to identify the other buying participants, their buying criteria, and their level of influence on the buyer. The marketing program should be designed to appeal to and reach the other key participants as well as the buyer.

The number of buying participants and the amount of buying effort increase with the complexity of the buying situation. There are three types of buying decision behavior: routine response behavior, limited problem solving, and extensive problem solving.

In buying something, the buyer goes through a decision process consisting of problem recognition, information search, evaluation of alternatives, purchase decision, and postpurchase behavior. The marketer's job is to understand the buyer's behavior at each stage and what influences are operating. This understanding allows the marketer to develop a significant and effective marketing program for the target market.

With regard to new products, consumers respond at different rates, depending on the consumer's characteristics and the product's characteristics. Manufacturers try to bring their new products to the attention of potential early adopters, particularly those with opinion leader characteristics.

■ QUESTIONS FOR DISCUSSION

1. What people played the different buying decision roles that led to the choice of the school you are attending?

2. When might the purchase of a low-involvement product lead to limited or extensive problem solving, rather than to routine response behavior? What kinds of high-involvement products might be purchased as a routine response behavior rather than after extensive problem solving? Give examples.

3. Relate the stages of the buyer decision process to your most recent purchase of any kind. Compare these stages with the steps involved in your most recent purchase of a pair of shoes.

4. When you are planning to go to a movie, what information sources do you use in deciding which one to see? Do you use the same sources to help you decide which movie to rent on videotape for watching at home?

5. What factors do you think would be very important to most consumers in deciding where to do their grocery shopping? Using these factors, discuss how the expectancy-value, conjunctive, and disjunctive models of consumer choice could explain a shopper's choice of a supermarket.

6. What kinds of risk are involved in purchasing a lawnmower? Compare these risks with the risks of hiring a service to fertilize your lawn and eliminate weeds and insects. What steps could marketers take to reduce these risks?

7. Why is the postpurchase behavior stage included in the model of the buying process? What relevance does this stage have for marketers?

8. Describe how cents-off coupons, sweepstakes, bonus-size packs, and other forms of sales promotion can help move consumers through the stages of the adoption process. What are the drawbacks, if any, to using these techniques to promote product adoption?

9. Digital audiotape recorders have recently been developed that allow near-perfect fidelity in recording and editing music and in playing prerecorded tapes. When first introduced to the consumer market, these machines cost $2,000 or more, and prerecorded tapes sold for more than $20. How will this innovation's characteristics affect its rate of adoption in the consumer market?

■ KEY TERMS

Adoption The decision by an individual to become a regular user of a product.

Adoption process The mental process through which an individual passes from first hearing about an innovation to final adoption.

Alternative evaluation The stage of the buyer decision process in which the consumer uses information to evaluate alternative brands in the choice set.

Brand image The set of beliefs consumers hold about a particular brand.

Buyer The person who makes an actual purchase.

Decider The person who ultimately makes a buying decision or any part of it—whether to buy, what to buy, how to buy, or where to buy.

Extensive problem solving Buyer behavior in cases where buyers face complex buying decisions for more expensive, less frequently purchased products in an unfamiliar product class. Buyers engage in extensive information search and evaluation.

Influencer A person whose advice or views carry some weight in making a final buying decision.

Information search The stage of the buyer decision process in which the consumer is aroused to search for more information; the consumer may simply have heightened attention or may go into active information search.

Initiator The person who first suggests or thinks of the idea of buying a particular product or service.

Limited problem solving Buying behavior in cases where buyers are aware of the product class but not familiar with all the brands and their features. Buyers engage in limited information search and evaluation.

New product A good, service, or idea that is perceived by some potential customers as new.

Personal influence The effect of statements made by one person on another's attitude or probability of purchase.

Postpurchase behavior The stage of the buyer decision process in which consumers take further action after purchase based on their satisfaction or dissatisfaction.

Problem recognition The first stage of the buyer decision process in which the consumer recognizes a problem or need.

Purchase decision The stage of the buyer decision process in which the consumer actually buys the product.

Routine response behavior Buying behavior in cases where buyers face simple buying decisions for low-cost, low-involvement, frequently purchased items in familiar product classes. Buyers do not give much thought, search, or time to the purchase.

User The person who consumes or uses a product or service.

■ REFERENCES

1. See Brian O'Reilly, "Lessons from the Home Phone Wars," *Fortune*, December 24, 1984, pp. 83–86; and Jules Abend, "Merchandising Home Telephones: Strategies for Grabbing More Market Share," *Stores*, June 1984, pp. 55–60.

2. See John A. Howard and Jagdish N. Sheth, *The Theory of Buyer Behavior* (New York: Wiley, 1969), pp. 27–28.

3. Several models of the consumer buying process have been developed by marketing scholars. The most prominent models are those of Howard and Sheth, *The Theory of Buyer Behavior*; Francesco M. Nicosia, *Consumer Decision Processes* (Englewood Cliffs, NJ: Prentice Hall, 1966); James F. Engel, Roger D. Blackwell, and Paul W. Miniard, *Consumer Behavior,* 5th ed. (New York: Holt, Rinehart & Winston, 1986); and James R. Bettman, *An Information Processing Theory of Consumer Choice* (Reading, MA: Addison-Wesley, 1979).

4. James H. Myers and Mark L. Alpert, "Semantic Confusion in Attitude Research: Salience vs. Importance vs. Determinance," in *Advances in Consumer Research* (Proceedings of the Seventh Annual Conference of the Association for Consumer Research, October 1976), IV, pp. 106–10.

5. This model was developed by Martin Fishbein. See Martin Fishbein and Icek Ajzen, *Belief, Attitude, Intention, and Behavior* (Reading, Mass.: Addison-Wesley, 1975). For a critical review of this model, see Paul W. Miniard and Joel B. Cohen, "An Examination of the Fishbein-Ajzen Behavioral Intentions Model's Concepts and Measures," *Journal of Experimental Social Psychology*, May 1981, pp. 309–99.

6. See Jagdish N. Sheth, "An Investigation of Relationships Among Evaluative Beliefs, Affect, Behavioral Intention, and Behavior," in *Consumer Behavior: Theory and Application*, John U. Farley, John A. Howard, and L. Winston Ring, eds. (Boston: Allyn & Bacon, 1974), pp. 89–114.

7. See Raymond A. Bauer, "Consumer Behavior as Risk Taking," in *Risk Taking and Information Handling in Consumer Behavior*, Donald F. Cox, ed. (Boston: Division of Research, Harvard Business School, 1967); and James W. Taylor, "The Role of Risk in Consumer Behavior," *Journal of Marketing*, April 1974, pp. 54–60.

8. See Priscilla A. LaBarbara and David Mazursky, "A Longitudinal Assessment of Consumer Satisfaction/Dissatisfaction: The Dynamic Aspect of the Cognitive Process," *Journal of Marketing Research*, November 1983, pp. 393–404.

9. See Bill Kelley, "How To Sell Airplanes, Boeing-Style," *Sales and Marketing Management*, December 9, 1985, p. 34.

10. See Leon Festinger, *A Theory of Cognitive Dissonance* (Stanford, CA: Stanford University Press, 1957); and Leon G. Schiffman and Leslie Lazar Kanuk, *Consumer Behavior*, 3rd ed. (Englewood Cliffs, NJ: Prentice Hall, 1987) pp. 304–5.

11. See Mary C. Gilly and Richard W. Hansen, "Consumer Complaint Handling as a Strategic Marketing Tool," *Journal of Consumer Marketing*, Fall, 1985, pp. 5–16; and Thomas Moore, "Would You Buy a Car from This Man?" April 11, 1988, pp. 72–74.

12. The following discussion leans heavily on Everett M. Rogers, *Diffusion of Innovations*, 3rd ed. (New York: Free Press, 1983). Also see Hubert Gatignon and Thomas S. Robertson, "A Propositional Inventory for new Diffusion Research," *Journal of Consumer Research*, March 1985, pp. 849–67.

13. Rogers, *Diffusion of Innovations*.

14. Mary Lee Dickerson and James W. Gentry, "Characteristics of Adopters and Non-Adopters of Home Computers," *Journal of Consumer Research*, September 1983, pp. 225–35.

15. See Schiffman and Kanuk, *Consumer Behavior*, pp. 606–17.

7

Organizational Markets and Organizational Buyer Behavior

GULFSTREAM Aerospace Corporation sells business jets with price tags as high as $16 million to corporate buyers. Locating potential buyers isn't a problem—the organizations that can afford to own and operate

multimillion dollar business aircraft are easily identified. Customers include Exxon, American Express, Seagram, Coca-Cola, General Motors, and many others, including King Fahd of Saudi Arabia. Gulfstream's more difficult problems involve reaching key decision makers, understanding their complex motivations and decision processes, figuring out what factors will be important in their decisions, and designing effective marketing approaches.

Gulfstream Aerospace recognizes the importance of *rational* motives and *objective* factors in buyers' decisions. A company buying a jet will evaluate Gulfstream aircraft on quality and performance, prices, operating costs, and service. And these may *appear* to be the only things that drive the buying decision. But having a superior product isn't enough to land the sale; Gulfstream Aerospace must also

pay attention to the more subtle *human factors* that affect the choice of a jet.

"The purchase process may be initiated by the chief executive officer, a board member (wishing to increase efficiency or security), the company's chief pilot, or through vendor efforts like advertising or a sales visit. The CEO will be central in deciding whether to buy the jet, but he or she will be heavily influenced by the company's pilot, financial officer, and perhaps by the board itself.

"Each party in the buying process has subtle roles and needs. The salesperson who tries to impress, for example, both the CEO with depreciation schedules and the chief pilot with minimum runway statistics will almost certainly not sell a plane if he overlooks the psychological and emotional components of the buying decision. 'For the chief executive,' observes one salesperson, 'you need all the numbers for support, but if you can't find the kid inside the CEO and excite him or her with the raw beauty of the new plane, you'll never sell the equipment. If you sell the excitement, you sell the jet.'

"The chief pilot, as an equipment expert, often has veto power over purchase decisions and may be able to stop the purchase of one or another brand of jet by simply expressing a negative opinion about, say, the plane's bad weather capabilities. In this sense, the pilot not only influences the decision but also serves as an information 'gatekeeper' by advising management on the equipment to select. Though the corporate legal staff will handle the purchase agreement and the purchasing department will acquire the jet, these parties may have little to say about whether or how the plane will be obtained, and which type. The users of the jet—middle and upper management of the buying company, impor-

tant customers, and others—may have at least an indirect role in choosing the equipment.

"The involvement of many people in the purchase decision creates a group dynamic that the selling company must factor into its sales planning. Who makes up the buying group? How will the parties interact? Who will dominate and who submit? What priorities do the individuals have?"

In some ways, selling corporate jets to organizational buyers is like selling cars and kitchen appliances to families. Gulfstream Aerospace asks the same questions as consumer marketers. Who are the buyers, and what are their needs? How do buyers make their buying decisions, and what factors influence these decisions? What marketing program will be most effective? But the answers to these questions are usually different for the organizational buyer. Thus Gulfstream Aerospace faces many of the same challenges as consumer marketers—and some additional ones as well.[1]

Chapter Objectives   *After reading this chapter, you should be able to:*

1. Discuss how organizational markets differ from consumer markets.
2. Identify the major factors that influence organizational buyer behavior.
3. List and define the steps in the industrial buying decision process.
4. Explain how resellers and government buyers make their buying decisions.

IN one way or another most large companies sell to other organizations. Many industrial companies sell *most* of their products to organizations—companies such as Xerox, Du Pont, and countless other large and small firms. Even large consumer products companies do organizational marketing. For example, General Mills makes many familiar products for final consumers—Cheerios, Betty Crocker cake mixes, Gold Medal flour. But to sell these products to final consumers, General Mills must first sell them to the wholesale and retail organizations that serve the consumer market. General Mills also makes products, such as specialty chemicals, that are sold only to other companies.

Organizations make up a vast market. In fact, industrial markets involve many more dollars and items than consumer markets. Figure 7-1 shows the large number of transactions needed to produce and sell a simple pair of shoes. Hide dealers sell to tanners, who sell leather to shoe manufacturers, who sell shoes to wholesalers, who in turn sell shoes to retailers, who finally sell them to consumers. Each party in the chain buys many other goods and services as well. It is easy to see why

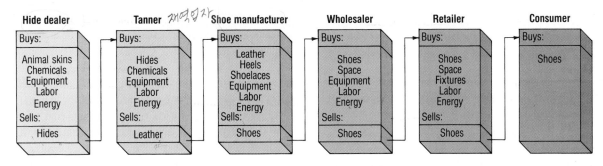

Hide dealer	Tanner 제역업자	Shoe manufacturer	Wholesaler	Retailer	Consumer
Buys:	**Buys:**	**Buys:**	**Buys:**	**Buys:**	**Buys:**
Animal skins Chemicals Equipment Labor Energy	Hides Chemicals Equipment Labor Energy	Leather Heels Shoelaces Equipment Labor Energy	Shoes Space Equipment Labor Energy	Shoes Space Fixtures Labor Energy	Shoes
Sells:	**Sells:**	**Sells:**	**Sells:**	**Sells:**	
Hides	Leather	Shoes	Shoes	Shoes	

FIGURE 7-1 Organizational transactions involved in producing and distributing a pair of shoes

there is more organizational buying than consumer buying—many sets of organizational purchases were made for only one set of consumer purchases.

Organizational buying is "the decision-making process by which formal organizations establish the need for purchased products and services, and identify, evaluate, and choose among alternative brands and suppliers."[2] Companies that sell to other organizations must do their best to understand organizational buyer behavior.

ORGANIZATIONAL MARKETS

Types of Organizational Markets

We will examine three types of organizational markets: the industrial market, the reseller market, and the government market. We identify each briefly here and discuss them in more detail later in the chapter.

The Industrial Market

The **industrial market** consists of all the individuals and organizations that acquire goods and services that enter into the production of other products and services, that are sold, rented, or supplied to others. The industrial market is *huge*: It consists of over 14 million organizations which buy more than $3 *trillion* worth of goods and services each year. (That's more money than most of us can imagine—taped end to end, three trillion one-dollar bills would wrap around the earth over 11,000 times!) Thus, the industrial market is the largest and most diverse organizational market.

The Reseller Market

The **reseller market** consists of all the individuals and organizations that acquire goods for the purpose of reselling or renting them to others at a profit. The reseller market includes over 396,000 wholesaling firms and 1,923,000 retailing firms that combine to purchase over $2 trillion worth of goods and services a year.[3] Resellers purchase goods for resale and goods and services for conducting their operations. In their role as purchasing agents for their own customers, resellers purchase a vast variety of goods for resale—indeed, everything produced except for the few classes of goods that producers sell directly to customers.

The Government Market

The **government market** consists of governmental units—federal, state, and local—that purchase or rent goods and services for carrying out the main functions of government. In 1987, governments purchased an estimated $892 billion dollars worth

How "NutraSweet" It Is!

About 30 years ago, a G. D. Searle researcher discovered aspartame, a miracle substance that tastes like sugar, contains few calories, and is safe to eat or drink. In 1983 the FDA approved the substance, and Searle looked for the best way to market its miracle to commercial food and beverage producers. It came up with a highly effective "branded ingredient" strategy. Instead of just selling aspartame to commercial customers, Searle gave it a brand name—NutraSweet—and launched the kind of consumer marketing campaign you'd expect to see for a laundry soap or soft drink. Searle marketed NutraSweet directly to consumers, even though consumers couldn't directly buy NutraSweet.

Industrial demand for NutraSweet is derived demand—it ultimately comes from consumer demand for products that contain NutraSweet. But before manufacturers would buy the new sweetener and put it in their products, they wanted to be certain that their consumers would accept it. Thus to build commercial demand for NutraSweet, Searle first had to create brand awareness and preference among final consumers. This meant overcoming the public's general mistrust of new sweeteners. People tended to believe the adage that if something tasted too good, it had to be bad for you. Searle needed to prove that, in the case of NutraSweet, this was not true.

Gumballs to the rescue! Searle mailed out thousands of gumballs sweetened with NutraSweet. Included with the gumballs were letters explaining that the new sweetener had few calories, didn't promote tooth decay, and contained nothing artificial. Searle then spent millions on advertising that proclaimed, "Introducing NutraSweet: You can't buy it, but you're going to love it." The ads carried coupons offering free gumballs and other samples.

Mission accomplished. When Coca-Cola, Quaker, Kool-Aid, and other companies began to introduce NutraSweetened products, consumers responded enthusiastically to the new wonder substance. In all sorts of categories—soft drinks, fruit juices, presweetened cereals, frozen deserts, breath mints, and many others—demand increased for products displaying the distinctive red swirl 100 percent NutraSweet logo. NutraSweet became a major selling point for many new brands; it even boosted the sales of entire product categories. For example, within two years of NutraSweet's introduction, following five flat years, sales of powdered soft drinks such as Kool-Aid, Crystal Light, and iced tea mixes had jumped 20 percent. And NutraSweet revolutionized the diet soft drink industry—products containing NutraSweet swept 22 percent of that market.

Monsanto recently acquired Searle and set up a separate division, the NutraSweet Company, to market the successful product. The company now spends over $30 million a year on consumer advertising for NutraSweet, a product consumers can't even buy. But it knows that if it convinces consumers of NutraSweet's merits, they will buy more products that con-

---

of products and services. The federal government accounts for almost 41 percent of the total spent by governments at all levels, making it the nation's largest customer.[4] Federal, state, and local government agencies buy an amazing range of products and services. They buy bombers, sculpture, chalkboards, furniture, toiletries, clothing, fire engines, vehicles, and fuel. Governments represent a tremendous market for any producer or reseller.

Characteristics of Organizational Markets   In some ways, organizational markets are similar to consumer markets—both involve people who assume buying roles and make purchase decisions to satisfy needs. But in many ways, organizational markets differ from consumer markets.[5] The main

The distinctive NutraSweet logo now appears on dozens of familiar brands.

tain the sweetener. If consumers buy more Nutra-Sweetened products, manufacturers will buy more aspartame from the company.

The company's "branded ingredient" strategy has brought sweet success. More than 60 manufacturers now market brands containing NutraSweet, and the list grows daily. The NutraSweet Company rings up more than $600 million worth of NutraSweet sales each year. And when its aspartame patent expires in 1992, though competitors can sell aspartame, they can't use the NutraSweet brand name consumers have learned to look for. How "NutraSweet" it is!

Sources: Based on "How Sweet It Is," *Management Review*, June 1985, p. 8. Also see Michael Hiestand, "Aspartame Ready to Sweeten Four New Categories," *Adweek*, January 5, 1987, p. 6; and Zachary Schiller and James E. Ellis, "NutraSweet Sets Out for Fat-Substitute City," *Business Week*, February 15, 1988, pp. 101–03.

differences are in market structure and demand, the nature of the buying unit, and the types of decisions and the decision process.

Market Structure and Demand

The organizational marketer normally deals with far *fewer, larger buyers* than the consumer marketer. When Goodyear sells replacement tires to consumers, its potential market includes the owners of 100 million American cars currently in use. But Goodyear's fate in the industrial market depends on getting orders from one of only a few large auto makers. Even in large organizational markets, a few buyers normally account for most of the purchasing.

Organizational markets also tend to be more *geographically concentrated* than consumer markets. More than half the nation's industrial buyers are concentrated in seven states: New York, California, Pennsylvania, Illinois, Ohio, New Jersey, and Michigan.

Organizational demand for many industrial products is *derived demand*—it ultimately comes from the demand for consumer goods.[6] General Motors buys steel because consumers buy cars. If consumer demand for cars drops, so will the demand for steel and all the other products used to make cars. Industrial marketers sometimes promote their products directly to final consumers to increase industrial demand (see Marketing Highlight 7–1).

Many organizational markets have *inelastic demand*. Total demand for many industrial products is not much affected by price changes, especially in the short run. A drop in the price of leather will not cause shoe manufacturers to buy much more unless it results in lower shoe prices which increase consumer demand.

Finally, organizational markets have more *fluctuating demand*. The demand for many industrial goods and services tends to change more, and more quickly, than the demand for consumer goods and services. A small percentage increase in consumer demand can cause large increases in industrial demand. Sometimes a rise of only 10 percent in consumer demand can cause as much as a 200 percent rise in industrial demand in the next period.

The Nature of the Buying Unit

As compared with consumer purchases, an organizational purchase often involves more buyers and more *professional purchasing*. Organizational buying is often done by trained purchasing agents who spend their work lives learning how to buy better. The more complex the purchase, the more likely that several persons will participate in the decision-making process. Buying committees made up of technical experts and top management are common in the buying of major goods. This means that organizational marketers must have well-trained salespeople to deal with well-trained buyers.

Types of Decisions and the Decision Process

Organizational buyers usually face *more complex* buying decisions than consumer buyers. Purchases often involve large sums of money, complex technical and economic considerations, and interactions among many people at many levels of the buyer's organization. Because the purchases are more complex, organizational buyers may take longer to make their decisions. A company buying a large computer system may take many months or even more than a year to select a supplier.

The organizational buying process tends to be *more formalized* than the consumer buying process. Large organizational purchases usually call for detailed product specifications, written purchase orders, careful supplier searches, and formal approval. The purchase process may be spelled out in detail in policy manuals.

The Marketer-Customer Relationship

Finally, in the organizational buying process, buyer and seller are often much *more dependent* on each other. Consumer marketers usually stay at a distance from their customers. Organizational marketers may roll up their sleeves and work closely with their customers during all stages of the buying process—from helping customers to define their needs, to finding products and services that meet these needs, to after-sale operation. They often customize their offerings to fit individual customer needs. In the short-run, sales go to suppliers who closely cooperate with the buyer on technical specifications and special delivery requirements. But organizational marketers must also build close *long-run* relationships with customers. In the long- run, sales are kept by companies that build lasting relationships by reliably meeting and anticipating the customer's immediate and future needs.[7]

Other Characteristics of Organizational Markets

DIRECT PURCHASING. Organizational buyers often buy directly from producers rather than through middlemen, especially for items that are technically complex or expensive. For example, Ryder buys thousands of trucks each year in all shapes and sizes. It rents some of these trucks to move-it-yourself customers (the familiar yellow Ryder trucks), leases some to other companies for their truck fleets, and uses the rest in its own freight-hauling businesses. When Ryder buys GMC trucks, it purchases them directly from General Motors rather than from independent GM truck dealers. Similarly, American Airlines buys airplanes directly from Boeing, Kroger buys package goods directly from Procter & Gamble, and the United States government buys personal computers directly from Zenith.

RECIPROCITY. Organizational buyers often select suppliers who also buy from them. An example of reciprocity would be a paper company who buys needed chemicals from a chemical company that in turn buys the company's paper. The Federal Trade Commission and the Justice Department's antitrust division forbid reciprocity if it shuts out competition in an unfair manner. A buyer can still choose

Leasing: American companies lease over $108 billion of equipment each year.

a supplier that it also sells something to, but the buyer should be able to show that it is getting competitive prices, quality, and service from that supplier.[8]

LEASING. Organizational buyers are increasingly leasing equipment instead of buying it outright, American companies lease over $108 billion of equipment each year—everything from printing presses to power plants, helicopters to hay balers, office copiers to offshore drilling rigs. The lessee gains a number of advantages, such as having more available capital, getting the seller's latest products, receiving better servicing, and gaining some tax advantages. The lessor often ends up with a larger net income and the chance to sell to customers who might not have been able to afford outright purchase.[9]

A MODEL OF ORGANIZATIONAL BUYER BEHAVIOR

In trying to understand organizational buyer behavior, marketers must answer some hard questions, What kinds of buying decisions do organizational buyers make? How do they choose among suppliers? Who makes the decisions? What is the organizational buying decision process? What factors affect organizational buying decisions?

At the most basic level, marketers want to know how organizational buyers will respond to various marketing stimuli. A simple model of organizational buyer behavior is shown in Figure 7-2.[10] The figure shows that marketing and other stimuli affect the organization and produce certain buyer responses. The marketing stimuli consist of the four Ps: product, price, place, and promotion. The other stimuli consist of major forces in the environment: economic, technological, political, cultural, and competitive. All these stimuli enter the buying organization and are turned into buyer responses: product or service choice, supplier choice, order quantities, delivery terms and times, service terms, and payment terms. To design good marketing mix strategies, the marketer must understand what happens within the organization to turn the stimuli into purchase responses.

Within the organization, the buying activity consists of two major parts—the buying center (made up of all the people involved in the buying decision) and the buying decision process. The figure shows that the buying center and the buying

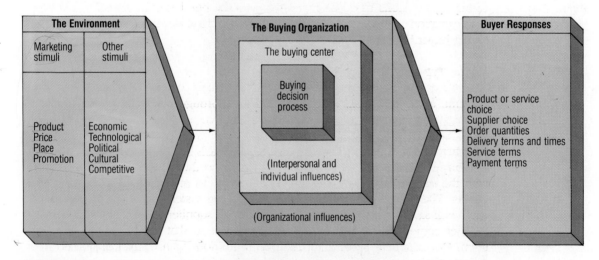

FIGURE 7-2 A model of organizational buyer behavior

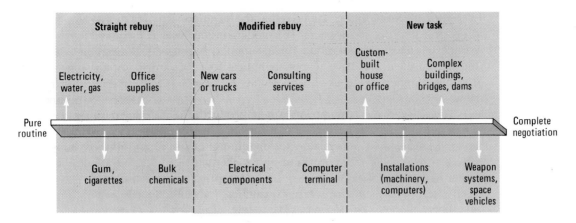

FIGURE 7-3 Three types of industrial buying situations

From *Marketing Principles*, 3rd ed. by Ben M. Enis. Copyright © 1980 Scott, Foresman and Company. Reprinted by permission.

decision process are influenced by internal organizational, interpersonal, and individual factors as well as by external environmental factors.

We will look at the various elements in this organizational buyer behavior model. For now we will focus on the largest and most important organizational market—the industrial market. Later in the chapter we will consider the special characteristics of reseller and government buyer behavior.

*I*NDUSTRIAL BUYER BEHAVIOR

We will examine four questions about industrial buyer behavior: What buying decisions do industrial buyers make? Who participates in the buying process? What are the major influences on buyers? And how do industrial buyers make their buying decisions?

What Buying Decisions Do Industrial Buyers Make?

The industrial buyer faces a whole set of decisions in making a purchase. The number of decisions depends on the type of buying situation. We can identify three types of buying situations based on the newness of the purchase, the amounts and types of information needed, and the number of new purchase alternatives being considered by the buyer.[11]

Major Types of Buying Situations

At one extreme is the straight rebuy, which is a fairly routine decision. At the other extreme is the new task, which may call for thorough research. In the middle is the modified rebuy, which requires some research. For examples, see Figure 7-3.

STRAIGHT REBUY. In a straight rebuy, the buyer reorders something without any modifications. It is usually handled on a routine basis by the purchasing department. The buyer chooses from suppliers on its "list," based on its past buying satisfaction with the various suppliers. The "in" suppliers try to maintain product and service quality. They often propose automatic reordering systems so that the purchasing agent will save reordering time—and not change suppliers. The "out" suppliers try to offer something new or exploit dissatisfaction so that the buyer will consider them. Out suppliers try to get their foot in the door with a small order and then enlarge their purchase share over time.

MODIFIED REBUY. In a modified rebuy, the buyer wants to modify product specifications, prices, terms, or suppliers. The modified rebuy usually involves more decision participants than a straight rebuy. The in-suppliers become concerned about maintaining the business and have to put their best foot forward to protect the account. The out suppliers see it as an opportunity to make a better offer in order to gain some new business.

NEW TASK. A company buying a new product or service for the first time faces a new task. The greater the cost or risk, the larger the number of decision participants and the greater their information seeking. In the new-task situation, the buyer must obtain a great deal of information about alternative products and suppliers. The buyer has to determine product specifications, price limits, delivery terms and times, service terms, payment terms, order quantities, acceptable suppliers, and the selected supplier. Different decision participants influence each decision, and the order in which the decisions are made varies from firm to firm.

The new-task buying situation arises infrequently, but it is very important to marketers because it leads to straight or modified rebuys later on. The new task situation is the marketer's greatest opportunity and challenge. The marketer not only tries to reach as many people with key buying influences as possible, but also provides product information and other related assistance.

The Role of Systems Buying and Selling

Many buyers prefer to buy a whole solution to their problem and not make all the separate decisions involved. Called **systems buying,** it began with government buying of major weapons and communication systems. Instead of buying and putting all the components together, the government would ask for bids from suppliers who would assemble the package or system. The winning supplier would be responsible for buying and assembling the components.

Sellers have increasingly recognized that buyers like to purchase in this way and have adopted the practice of systems selling as a marketing tool.[12] Systems selling has two parts. First, the supplier sells a group of interlocking products. For example, the supplier sells not only glue, but applicators and dryers as well. Second, the supplier sells a system of production, inventory control, distribution, and other services to meet the buyer's need for a smooth-running operation.

Systems selling is a key industrial marketing strategy for winning and holding accounts for large-scale industrial projects, such as dams, steel factories, irrigation systems, pipelines, utilities, even new towns. The contract often goes to the firm that provides the most complete system meeting the customer's needs. Consider the following example: The Indonesian government requested bids to build a cement factory near Jakarta. An American firm's proposal included choosing the site, designing the cement factory, hiring the construction crews, assembling the materials and equipment, and turning the finished factory over to the Indonesian government. A Japanese firm's proposal included all of these services, plus hiring and training workers to run the factory, exporting the cement through their trading companies, and using the cement to build some needed roads and new office buildings in Jakarta. Although the Japanese firm's proposal costs more, it won the contract. Clearly the Japanese viewed the problem not as one of just building a cement factory (the narrow view of systems selling) but of running it in a way that would contribute to the country's economy. They took the broadest view of the customers' needs. This is true systems selling.

Who Participates in the Industrial Buying Process?

Who does the buying of the trillions of dollars worth of goods and services needed by the industrial market? The decision-making unit of a buying organization is called its **buying center,** defined as "all those individuals and groups who participate in the purchasing decision-making process, who share some common goals and the risks arising from the decisions."[13]

The buying center includes all members of the organization who play any of five roles in the purchase decision process.[14]

* **Users:** Members of the organization who will use the product or service. In many cases, users initiate the buying proposal and help define product specifications.
* **Influencers:** People who affect the buying decision. They often help define specifications and also provide information for evaluating alternatives. Technical personnel are particularly important influencers.
* **Buyers:** People with formal authority to select the supplier and arrange terms of purchase. Buyers may help shape product specifications, but they play their major role in selecting vendors and negotiating. In more complex purchases, buyers might include high-level officers participating in the negotiations.
* **Deciders:** people who have formal or informal power to select or approve the final suppliers. In routine buying, the buyers are often the deciders, or at least the approvers.
* **Gatekeepers:** people who control the flow of information to others. For example, purchasing agents often have authority to prevent salespersons from seeing users or deciders. Other gatekeepers include technical personnel and even personal secretaries.

The buying center is not a fixed and formally identified unit within the buying organization. It is a set of buying roles assumed by different persons for different purchases. Within the organization, the size and makeup of the buying center will

This ad recognizes the secretary as a key buying influence.

vary for different products and for different buying situations. For some routine purchases, one person—say a purchasing agent—may assume all the buying center roles and be the only person involved in the buying decision. For more complex purchases, the buying center may include twenty or thirty persons from different levels and departments in the organization. One study of organizational buying showed that the typical industrial equipment purchase involved seven persons from three management levels representing four different departments.[15]

The buying center usually includes some obvious participants who are formally involved in the buying decision—as we saw at the beginning of the chapter, the decision to buy a corporate jet will probably involve the company's chief pilot, a purchasing agent, some legal staff, a member of top management, and others formally charged with the buying decision. It may also involve informal, less obvious participants, some of whom may actually make or strongly affect the buying decision. Sometimes even the people in the buying center are not aware of all the buying participants. For example, the decision about which jet to buy may actually be made by a corporate board member who has an interest in flying and knows a lot about airplanes. This board member may work behind the scenes to sway the decision. Thus many industrial buying decisions result from the complex interactions of ever changing buying center participants.

The buying center concept presents a major marketing challenge. The industrial marketer has to figure out: Who is involved in the decision? What decisions do they affect? What is their relative degree of influence? And what evaluation criteria does each decision participant use? Consider the following example:

> The American Hospital Supply Corporation sells disposable surgical gowns to hospitals. It tries to identify the hospital personnel involved in this buying decision. The decision participants turn out to be (1) the vice-president of purchasing, (2) the operating room administrator, and (3) the surgeons. Each party plays a different role. The vice-president of purchasing analyzes whether the hospital should buy disposable gowns or reusable gowns. If analysis favors disposable gowns, then the operating room administrator compares competing products and prices and makes a choice. This administrator considers the gown's absorbency, antiseptic quality, design, and cost and normally buys the brand that meets requirements at the lowest cost. Finally, surgeons affect the decision later by reporting their satisfaction or dissatisfaction with the brand.

What Are the Major Influences on Industrial Buyers?

Industrial buyers are subject to many influences when they make their buying decisions. Some marketers assume that the major influences are economic. They think buyers will favor the supplier who offers the lowest price, or the best product, or the most service. They concentrate on offering strong economic benefits to buyers. But industrial buyers also respond to personal factors.

> It has not been fashionable lately to talk about relationships in business. We're told that it has to be devoid of emotion. We must be cold, calculating, and impersonal. Don't believe it. Relationships make the world go round. Businesspeople are human and social as well as interested in economics and investments, and salespeople need to appeal to both sides. Purchasers may claim to be motivated by intellect alone, but the professional salesperson knows that they run on both reason and emotion.[16]

Industrial buyers respond to both economic and personal factors. When supplier offers are very similar, industrial buyers have little basis for rational choice. Since they can meet organizational goals with any supplier, buyers can bring in personal factors. Where competing products differ greatly, industrial buyers are more accountable for their choice and pay more attention to economic factors.

The various groups of influences on industrial buyers—environmental, organizational, interpersonal, and individual—are listed in Figure 7-4 and described below.[17]

FIGURE 7-4
Major influences on industrial buying behavior

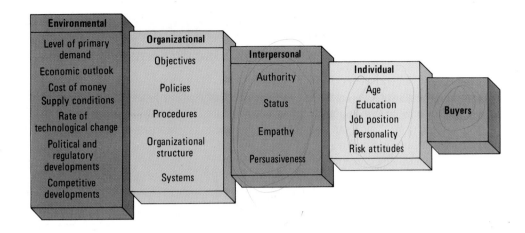

Environmental Factors

Industrial buyers are heavily influenced by factors in the current and expected economic environment, such as the level of primary demand, the economic outlook, and the cost of money. As the economic uncertainty rises, industrial buyers stop making new investments and attempt to reduce their inventories.

An increasingly important environmental factor is shortages in key materials. Many companies are now more willing to buy and hold larger inventories of scarce materials. Industrial buyers are also affected by technological, political, and competitive developments in the environment. The industrial marketer has to watch these factors, determine how they will affect the buyer, and try to turn these problems into opportunities.

Organizational Factors

Each buying organization has its own objectives, policies, procedures, structure, and systems. The industrial marketer has to know these as well as possible. Questions such as these arise: How many people are involved in the buying decision? Who are they? What are their evaluative criteria? What are the company's policies and limits on the buyers? The industrial marketer should be aware of the following organizational trends in the purchasing area.

UPGRADED PURCHASING. Purchasing departments have often occupied a low position in the management hierarchy, even though they often manage more than half of the company's costs. However, many companies have recently upgraded their purchasing departments. Several large corporations have elevated the heads of purchasing to vice-president. Caterpillar and some other companies have combined several functions—such as purchasing, inventory control, production scheduling, and traffic—into a high-level function called *material management*. "New wave" materials managers are actively building new supply sources. Many companies are looking for top talent, hiring MBAs, and offering higher compensation. This means that industrial marketers must also upgrade their salespeople to match the quality of the new buyers.

CENTRALIZED PURCHASING. In companies with many divisions, much purchasing is carried out by the separate divisions because of their differing needs. But recently companies have tried to recentralize some of the purchasing. Headquarters identifies materials purchased by several divisions and considers buying them centrally. Centralized purchasing gives the company more purchasing clout. The individual plants can buy from another source if they can get a better deal, but in general, centralized

MARKETING HIGHLIGHT 7–2

JUST-IN-TIME PRODUCTION CHANGES ORGANIZATIONAL SELLING

Over the past several years, as American business has studied the reasons for Japanese success in world markets, they have learned about and adopted several new manufacturing concepts such as just-in-time (JIT), early supplier involvement, value analysis, quality circles, total quality control, and flexible manufacturing. The adoption of these practices greatly affects how industrial marketers sell to and service their customers.

JIT, in particular, promises to produce significant changes in industrial marketing. Just-in-time means that production materials arrive at the customer's factory at the exact time they are needed for production, rather than being stored in the customer's inventory until used. The goal of JIT is zero inventory with 100 percent quality. It calls for coordination between the production schedules of supplier and customer so that neither has to carry much inventory. Effective use of JIT reduces inventory and lead times and increases quality, productivity, and adaptability to change. In a 1986 survey of 2,000 purchasing executives, 59 percent indicated that their firm used or planned to use JIT. General Motors, through its JIT programs, reduced inventory-related costs from $8 billion to $2 billion.

Industrial marketers need to be aware of the changes that JIT will cause in organizational purchasing practices, and they must learn to exploit the opportunities that JIT will create. The following are the major features and affects of JIT.

Strict Quality Control. Maximum cost savings from JIT are achieved only if the buyer receives pre-inspected goods. JIT buyers thus expect suppliers to have strict quality. The industrial marketer needs to work closely with the customer and meet high quality standards.

Frequent and Reliable Delivery. Daily delivery is often the only way to avoid inventory buildup. Increasingly, customers are setting delivery dates with penalties for not meeting them. Apple even penalizes for early delivery, while Kasle Steel makes around-the-clock deliveries to the General Motors plant in Buick City. Thus, JIT means that industrial marketers must develop reliable transportation arrangements.

Closer Location. Since JIT involves frequent delivery, many industrial marketers have set up locations closer to their large JIT customers. Close locations enable them to deliver smaller shipments more efficiently and reliably. Kasle Steel set up a mill within Buick City to serve the General Motors plant there. Thus, JIT means that an industrial marketer may have to make large commitments to major customers.

---

purchasing produces substantial savings for the company. For the industrial marketer, this development means dealing with fewer and higher-level buyers. Instead of the seller's regional sales forces dealing with separate plants, the seller may use a *national account sales force* to deal with the buyer. For example, at Xerox, over 250 national account managers each handle one to five large national accounts with many scattered locations. The national account managers coordinate the efforts of an entire Xerox team—specialists, analysts, salespeople for individual products—to sell and service important national customers.[18] National account selling is challenging and demands a high-level salesforce and marketing effort.

LONG-TERM CONTRACTS. Industrial buyers are increasingly seeking long-term contracts with suppliers. For example, General Motors wants to buy from fewer suppliers who are willing to locate close to their plants and produce high quality components. Another aspect involves companies supplying *electronic order exchange* systems to their customers. The seller places terminals hooked to its own computers in customers' offices. The customer can order instantly by typing orders directly into the computer. Many hospitals order directly from American Hospital Supply using order-taking terminals in their stockrooms. And many bookstores order from Follett's in this way.[19]

Telecommunication. New communication technologies let suppliers set up computerized purchasing systems that are hooked up to their customers. One large customer even requires that suppliers put their inventory figures and prices in the system. Doing so allows for on-line JIT ordering as the computer looks for the lowest prices for available inventory. Such systems reduce transaction costs but put pressure on industrial marketers to keep prices very competitive.

Single Sourcing. JIT requires that the buyer and seller work closely together to reduce costs. Often, the industrial customer awards a long-term contract to only one trusted supplier. Single sourcing is increasing rapidly under JIT. Thus while General Motors still uses more than 3,500 suppliers, Toyota who has totally adopted JIT, uses fewer than 250.

Value Analysis. The major objectives of JIT are to reduce costs and improve quality, and value analysis is critical to that. To reduce costs of its product, a customer must not only reduce its own costs but also get its suppliers to reduce their costs. Suppliers with a strong value analysis program have a competitive edge because they can contribute to their customers' value analysis program.

Early Supplier Involvement. Industrial buyers are increasingly bringing industrial marketers into the design process. Thus, industrial marketers must employ qualified people who can work with customers' design teams.

Close Relationship. To make JIT successful, the industrial marketer and customer must work closely together to satisfy the customer's needs. The marketer has to customize offerings for the particular industrial customer. In return, the marketer wins the contract for a specific term. Both parties may invest lots of time and money to set up the JIT relationship. Because the costs of changing suppliers are high, industrial customers are very selective in choosing suppliers. Thus industrial marketers must improve their skill in *relationship marketing* as compared to *transaction marketing*. The marketer must try to achieve maximum profits over the entire relationship rather than over each transaction.

Sources: See G.H. Manoochehri, "Suppliers and the Just-In-Time Concept," *Journal of Purchasing and Materials Management*, Winter 1984, pp. 16–21; Somerby Dowst, "Buyers Say VA Is More Important Than Ever, *Purchasing*, June 26, 1986, pp. 64–83; Ernest Raia, "Just-in-time USA," *Purchasing*, February 13, 1986, pp. 48-62; Eric K. Clemons and F. Warren McFarlan, "Telecom: Hook Up or Lose Out," *Harvard Business Review*, July–August 1986, pp. 91–97; and Somerby Dowst and Ernest Raia, "Design Team Signals For More Supplier Involvement," *Purchasing*, March 27, 1986, pp. 76–83.

PURCHASING PERFORMANCE EVALUATION. Some companies are setting up incentive systems to reward purchasing managers for especially good purchasing performance, in much the same way that salespeople receive bonuses for especially good selling performance. These systems will lead purchasing managers to increase their pressure on sellers for the best terms.

JUST-IN-TIME PRODUCTION SYSTEMS. The emergence of just-in-time production systems has had a major impact on organizational purchasing policies. Marketing Highlight 7–2 describes the effects of just-in-time on organizational marketing.

Interpersonal Factors

The buying center usually includes many participants; each affects and is affected by the others. In many cases, the industrial marketer will not know what kinds of group dynamics take place during the buying process. As Bonoma points out:

> Managers do not wear tags that say "decision maker" or "unimportant person." The powerful are often invisible, at least to vendor representatives.[20]

The buying center participant with the highest rank does not always have the most influence. Participants may have influence in the buying decision because they

Industrial buyers respond to more than just economic factors. In this ad the words stress performance but the illustration suggests a smooth, comfortable ride.

control rewards and punishments, because they are well liked, because they have special expertise, or even because they are related by marriage to the company's president. Interpersonal factors are often very subtle. Where possible, industrial marketers try to understand these factors and design strategies that take them into account.

Individual Factors

Each participant in the buying decision process brings in personal motives, perceptions, and preferences. These are affected by age, income, education, professional identification, personality, and attitudes toward risk. Buyers have different buying styles. Some are "computer freaks" who make in-depth analyses of competitive proposals before choosing a supplier. Other buyers are "tough guys" who play off the sellers off one another for the best deal.

Industrial marketers must know their customers and adapt their tactics to environmental, organizational, interpersonal, and individual influences on the buying situation.

How Do Industrial Buyers Make Their Buying Decisions?

We now come to the issue of how industrial buyers move through the purchasing process. Robinson and others identified eight stages of the industrial buying process.[21] They are listed in Table 7-1. The table shows that buyers facing the new task buying situation will go through all the stages of the buying process. Buyers making modified or straight rebuys will skip some of the stages. We will examine these steps for the typical new-task buying situation.

TABLE 7-1
Major Stages of the
Industrial Buying
Process in Relation to
major Buying
Situations

STAGES OF THE BUYING PROCESS	BUYING SITUATIONS		
	New Task	Modified Rebuy	Straight Rebuy
1. Problem recognition	Yes	Maybe	No
2. General need description	Yes	Maybe	No
3. Product specification	Yes	Yes	Yes
4. Supplier search	Yes	Maybe	No
5. Proposal solicitation	Yes	Maybe	No
6. Supplier selection	Yes	Maybe	No
7. Order routine specification	Yes	Maybe	No
8. Performance review	Yes	Yes	Yes

Source: Adapted from Patrick J. Robinson, Charles W. Faris, and Yoram Wind, *Industrial Buying and Creative Marketing* (Boston: Allyn & Bacon, 1967), p. 14.

Problem Recognition

The buying process begins when someone in the company recognizes a problem or need that can be met by acquiring a good or a service. Problem recognition can result from internal or external stimuli. Internally, the company may decide to launch a new product and need new equipment and materials to produce this product. Or a machine breaks down and needs new parts. Some purchased material may turn out to be unsatisfactory and causes the company to search for another supplier. Or a purchasing manager sees a chance to get better prices or quality. Externally, the buyer may get some new ideas at a trade show, or see an ad, or receive a call from a salesperson who offers a better product or a lower price.

General Need Description

Having recognized a need, the buyer next determines the general characteristics and quantity of the needed item. For standard items, this is not much of a problem. For complex items, the buyer will work with others—engineers, users, consultants— to define the item. They will want to rank the importance of reliability, durability, price, and other attributes desired in the item.

The industrial marketer can help the buying company in this phase. Often the buyer is not aware of the value of different product characteristics. An alert marketer can help the buyer define the company's needs.

Product Specification 명세서

The buying organization next develops the item's technical specifications. A value analysis engineering team will be put to work on the problem. **Value analysis** is an approach to cost reduction in which components are carefully studied to determine if they can be redesigned, standardized, or made by cheaper methods of production. Table 7-2 lists the major questions raised in the value analysis. The team will look

TABLE 7-2
Questions Asked in
Value Analysis

1. Does the use of the item contribute value?
2. Is its cost proportionate to its usefulness?
3. Does it need all its features?
4. Is there anything better for its intended use?
5. Can a usable part be made by a lower-cost method?
6. Can a standard product be found that will be usable?
7. Is the product made on proper tooling, considering the quantities that are used?
8. Do material, labor, overhead, and profit total its cost?
9. Will another dependable supplier provide it for less?
10. Is anyone buying it for less?

Source: Albert W. Frey, *Marketing Handbook,* 2nd ed. (New York: Ronald Press, 1965), Sec. 27, p. 21. Copyright © 1985. Reprinted by permission of John Wiley & Sons, Inc.

at the high-cost components in a product—usually 20 percent of the parts account for 80 percent of the costs. The team will decide on the best product characteristics and specify them accordingly. Sellers, too, can use value analysis as a tool for obtaining a new account. By showing a better way to make an object, outside sellers can turn straight rebuy situations into new-task situations in which their company has a chance for business.

Supplier Search

The buyer now tries to find the best vendors. The buyer can look at trade directories, do a computer search, or phone other companies for recommendations. Some of the vendors will not be considered because they are not large enough to supply the needed quantity or because they have a poor reputation for delivery and service. The buyer will end up with a small list of qualified suppliers.

The newer the buying task, and the more complex and costly the item, the greater the amount of time spent in searching for suppliers. The supplier's task is to get listed in major directories and build a good reputation in the marketplace. Salespeople should watch for companies in the process of searching for suppliers and make certain that their firm is considered.

Proposal Solicitation

The buyer will now invite qualified suppliers to submit proposals. Some suppliers will send only a catalog or a salesperson. Where the item is complex or expensive, the buyer will need detailed written proposals from each potential supplier. The buyer will review the suppliers when they make their formal presentations.

Industrial marketers must therefore be skilled in researching, writing, and presenting proposals. Their proposals should be marketing documents, not just technical documents. Their presentations should inspire confidence. They should make their companies stand out from the competition.

Supplier Selection

The members of the buying center now review the proposals and select a supplier(s). They will consider not only the technical competence of the various suppliers, but also their ability to deliver the item on time and provide necessary services. The buying center will often draw up a list of the desired supplier attributes and their relative importance. One survey of purchasing agents listed the following attributes in order of importance:[22]

1. Delivery capability	11. Financial position
2. Quality	12. Attitude toward buyer
3. Price	13. Bidding compliance
4. Repair service	14. Training aids
5. Technical capability	15. Progressive communications
6. Performance history	16. Management and organization
7. Production facilities	17. Packaging capability
8. Aid and advice	18. Moral/legal issues
9. Control systems	19. Geographic location
10. Reputation	20. Labor relations record

The members of the buying center will rate the suppliers against these attributes and identify the most attractive suppliers. They often use a supplier evaluation method similar to the one shown in Table 7-3.

**TABLE 7-3
An Example of Vendor
Analysis**

ATTRIBUTES	RATING SCALE				
	Unacceptable (0)	Poor (1)	Fair (2)	Good (3)	Excellent (4)
Technical and production capabilities					X
Financial strength			X		
Product reliaibility					X
Delivery reliability			X		
Service capability					X

$4 + 2 + 4 + 2 + 4 = 16$

Average score:
$16/5 = 3.2$

Note: This vendor shows up as strong except on two attributes. The purchasing agent has to decide how important the two weaknesses are. The analysis could be redone using importance weights for the five attributes.
Source: Adapted from Richard Hill, Ralph Alexander, and James Cross, *Industrial Marketing*, 4th ed. (Homewood, IL: Irwin, 1975), pp. 101–4.

The importance of various supplier attributes depends on the type of purchase situation the buyer faces.[23] One study of 220 purchasing managers showed that economic criteria were most important in situations involving routine purchases of standard products. Performance criteria became more important in purchases of nonstandard, more complex products. The supplier's ability to adapt to the buyer's changing needs was important for almost all types of purchases.

Buyers may attempt to negotiate with preferred suppliers for better prices and terms before making the final selections. In the end, they may select a single supplier or a few suppliers. Many buyers prefer multiple sources of supply. Then they will not be totally dependent on one supplier in case something goes wrong, and they will be able to compare the prices and performance of several suppliers over time.

Order Routine Specification

The buyer now writes the final order with the chosen supplier(s), listing the technical specifications, quantity needed, expected time of delivery, return policies, warranties, and so on. In the case of MRO (maintenance, repair, and operating) items, buyers are increasingly using *blanket contracts* rather than periodic purchase orders. Writing a new purchase order each time stock is needed is expensive. Nor does the buyer want to write fewer and larger purchase orders because doing so means carrying more inventory.

A blanket contract creates a long-term relationship in which the supplier promises to resupply the buyer as needed at agreed prices for a set time period. The stock is held by the seller; hence the name "stockless purchase plan." The buyer's computer automatically prints out an order to the seller when stock is needed. Blanket contracting leads to more single-source buying and the buying of more items from that single source. This locks the supplier in tighter with the buyer and makes it difficult for other suppliers to break in unless the buyer becomes dissatisfied with prices or service.

Performance Review

In this stage the buyer reviews supplier performance. The buyer may contact users and ask them to rate their satisfaction. The performance review may lead the buyer to continue, modify, or drop the seller. The seller's job is to monitor the same factors used by the buyer to make sure that the seller is giving the expected satisfaction.

We have described the buying stages that would operate in a new-task buying situation. In the modified rebuy or straight rebuy situation, some of these stages would be compressed or bypassed. Each stage represents a narrowing of the number of supplier alternatives. A seller should try to become part of the buyer's buying process in the earliest possible stage.

The eight-stage model provides a simple view of the industrial buying decision process. The actual process is usually much more complex.[24] Each organization buys in its own way, and each buying situation has unique requirements. Different buying center participants may be involved at different stages of the process. Although certain buying process steps usually occur, buyers do not always follow them in the same order, and they may add other steps. Often, buyers repeat certain stages more than once.

RESELLER BUYER BEHAVIOR

In most ways, reseller buyer behavior is like industrial buyer behavior. Reseller organizations have buying centers whose participants interact to make a variety of buying decisions. They have a buying decision process that starts with problem recognition and ends with decisions about which products to buy from which suppliers and under what terms. The buyers are affected by a wide range of environmental, organizational, interpersonal, and individual factors. But there are some important differences between industrial and reseller buying behavior. Resellers differ in the types of buying decisions they make, who participates in the buying decision, and how they make their buying decisions.

What Buying Decisions Do Resellers Make?

Resellers serve as purchasing agents for *their* customers, so they buy products and brands they think will appeal to their customers. They have to decide what product assortment to carry, what vendors to buy from, and what prices and terms to negotiate. The assortment decision is primary, and it positions the reseller in the marketplace. The reseller's assortment strategy will strongly affect its choice of which products to buy and which suppliers to buy from.

Resellers may carry products from only one supplier, or several related products or lines from a few suppliers, or a scrambled assortment of unrelated products from many suppliers. Thus a camera store might carry only Kodak cameras; many brands of cameras; cameras, radios, tape recorders, and stereo equipment; or all these products plus stoves and refrigerators. The reseller's assortment will affect its customer mix, marketing mix, and supplier mix.

Who Participates in the Reseller Buying Process?

Who does the buying for wholesale and retail organizations? The reseller's buying center may include one or many participants assuming different roles. Some will have formal buying responsibility, and some will be behind-the-scenes influencers. In small "mom and pop" firms, the owner usually takes care of buying decisions. In large reseller firms, buying is a specialized function and a full-time job. The buying center and buying process vary for different types of resellers.

Consider supermarkets. In the headquarters of a supermarket chain, specialist buyers have the responsibility for developing brand assortments and listening to new brand presentations made by salespersons. In some chains these buyers have the authority to accept or reject new items. In many chains, however, they are limited

A supermarket chain's buying committee listens to a new product presentation.

to screening "obvious rejects" and "obvious accepts"; otherwise they must bring new items to the chain's buying committee for approval. Even when an item is accepted by a buying committee, chain-store managers may not carry it. Thus producers face a major challenge in trying to get new items into stores. They offer the nation's supermarkets between 150 and 250 new items each week, and store space does not permit more than 10 percent to be accepted.

How Do Resellers Make Their Buying Decisions?

For new items, resellers use roughly the same buying process described for industrial buyers. For standard items, resellers simply reorder goods when the inventory gets low. The orders are placed with the same suppliers as long as their terms, goods, and services are satisfactory. Buyers will try to renegotiate prices if their margins drop due to rising operating costs. In many retail lines, the profit margin is so low (1 to 2 percent on sales in supermarkets, for example) that a sudden drop in demand or rise in operating costs will drive profits into the red.

Resellers consider many factors besides costs when choosing products and suppliers. For example, a panel of supermarket buyers listed the following as important factors when choosing new products for their stores:[25]

- The product's pricing and profit margins
- The product's uniqueness and the strength of the product category
- The seller's intended positioning and marketing plan for the product
- Test market evidence of consumer acceptance of the product
- Advertising and sales promotion support for the product
- The selling company's reputation

Thus sellers stand the best chance when they can report a promising product, show strong evidence of consumer acceptance, present a well-designed advertising and sales promotion plan, and provide strong financial incentives to the retailer.

Sellers are facing increasingly advanced buying on the part of resellers. They need to understand the resellers' changing needs and to develop attractive offers that help resellers serve their customers better. Table 7-4 lists several marketing tools used by sellers to make their offer to resellers more attractive.

TABLE 7-4 **Vendor Marketing Tools Used with Resellers**	*Cooperative advertising*, where the vendor agrees to pay a portion of the reseller's advertising costs for the vendor's product.
	Preticketing, where the vendor places a tag on each product listing its price, manufacturer, size, identification number, and color; these tags help the reseller reorder merchandise as it is being sold.
✓	*Stockless purchasing*, where the vendor carries the inventory and delivers goods to the reseller on short notice.
	Automatic reordering systems, where the vendor supplies forms and computer links for automatic reordering of merchandise by the reseller.
	Advertising aids, such as glossy photos, broadcast scripts.
	Special prices for storewide promotion.
	Return and exchange privileges for the reseller.
	Allowances for merchandise markdowns by the reseller.
	Sponsorship of in-store demonstrations.

GOVERNMENT BUYER BEHAVIOR

The government market offers large opportunities for many companies. Altogether, the federal, state, and local governments contain more than 82,000 buying units. Some companies sell to governments only occasionally or not at all. Others rely on the government market for a large portion of their sales (see Marketing Highlight 7–3).

Government buying and industrial buying are similar in many ways. But there are also differences that must be understood by companies that wish to sell products and services to governments.[26] To succeed in the government market, sellers must locate key decision makers, identify the factors that affect buyer behavior, and understand the buying decision process.

Who Participates in the Government Buying Process?

Who does the buying of the $892 billion of goods and services? Government buying organizations are found at the federal, state, and local levels. The federal level is the largest, and its buying units operate in the civilian and military sectors.

The federal civilian buying establishment consists of seven categories: departments (such as Commerce), administrations (General Services Administration), agencies (Environmental Protection Agency), boards (Railroad Retirement Board), commissions (Federal Communications Commission), the executive office (Bureau of the Budget), and miscellaneous (Tennessee Valley Authority). No single agency buys for all the government's needs, and no single buyer purchases all of any single item of supplies, equipment, or services. Many agencies control a large percentage of their own buying, particularly for industrial products and specialized equipment. At the same time, the General Services Administration plays a major role in centralizing the buying of commonly used items in the civilian section (office furniture and equipment, vehicles, fuels) and in standardizing buying procedures for the other agencies.

Federal military buying is carried out by the Defense Department, largely through the Defense Supply Agency and the army, navy, and air force. The Defense Supply Agency buys and distributes supplies used by all military services in an effort to reduce costly duplication. It operates six supply centers, which specialize in construction, electronics, fuel, personnel support, industrial, and general supplies. The trend has been toward "single managers" for major product classifications. Each service branch buys equipment and supplies in line with its own mission. For example, the Army Department has offices that acquire its own material, vehicles, medical supplies and services, and weapons.

State and local buying agencies include school districts, highway departments, hospitals, housing agencies, and many others. Each has its own buying process that sellers have to master.

The various government agencies may all be potential targets for sellers who wish to sell to this large market. But sellers should study the purchasing patterns of the various agencies. The agencies differ in quality requirements and the amount of marketing effort needed to make a sale. Some agencies buy standardized products whereas others buy mostly customized ones. Sellers should target agencies and buying centers that match their strengths and objectives.[27]

What Are the Major Influences on Government Buyers?

Like consumer and industrial buyers, government buyers are affected by environmental, organizational, interpersonal, and individual factors. A unique thing about government buying is that it is carefully watched by outside publics. One watchdog is Congress, and certain congressmen have made a career out of exposing government waste. Another watchdog is the Bureau of the Budget, which checks on government spending and seeks to improve efficiency. Many private groups also watch government agencies to see how they spend the public's money.

Because spending decisions are subject to public review, government organizations get involved in much paperwork. Elaborate forms must be filled out and signed before purchases are approved. The level of bureaucracy is high, and marketers have to find a way to cut through the red tape.

Noneconomic criteria are playing a growing role in government buying. Government buyers are asked to favor depressed business firms and areas, small-business firms, and business firms that avoid racial, sex, or age discrimination. Sellers need to keep these factors in mind when deciding to go after government business.

How Do Government Buyers Make Their Buying Decisions?

Government buying practices often seem complex and frustrating to suppliers. Suppliers have voiced many complaints about government purchasing procedures. These include too much paperwork, bureaucracy, needless regulations, emphasis on low bid prices, decision-making delays, frequent shifts in buying personnel, and too many policy changes. Yet the ins and outs of selling to the government can be mastered in a short time. The government is generally helpful in providing information about its buying needs and procedures. Government is often as anxious to attract new suppliers as the suppliers are to find customers.

The Small Business Administration prints a booklet entitled *U.S. Government Purchasing, Specifications, and Sales Directory*, which lists thousands of items most frequently purchased by the government, cross-referenced by the agencies most frequently buying them. The Government Printing Office issues the *Commerce Business Daily*, which lists major current purchases, as well as recent contract awards that can provide leads to subcontracting markets. The General Services Administration operates Business Service Centers in several major cities, whose staffs provide a complete education on the way government agencies buy and the steps that suppliers should follow. Various trade magazines and associations provide information on how to reach schools, hospitals, highway departments, and other government agencies.

Government buying procedures fall into two types: the open bid and the negotiated contract. *Open bid buying* means that the government office invites bids from

ZENITH TARGETS THE GOVERNMENT MARKET

In 1979 Zenith entered the already overcrowded microcomputer market. Like IBM, Tandy, AT&T, and several other competitors, Zenith targeted its line of IBM-compatibles at the business and retail markets. But Zenith lacked IBM's marketing muscle; it couldn't sustain the big-budget advertising and marketing campaign needed to challenge big rivals head-on. So in 1981, after limping along for two years, Zenith changed its strategy. It targeted two specialty markets—higher education and the federal government, markets previously overlooked by IBM and the others. By focusing on these segments, Zenith could avoid expensive advertising and costly direct competition.

Cracking the huge government market, however, took lots of effort and investment, patience, and positive thinking. Zenith set up a government salesforce to handle the special needs of the government market. The new salesforce had to learn its way through the complex, convoluted federal government bidding process and how to cut through seemingly endless red tape, bureaucracy, and paperwork. Zenith made its proposals more appealing to cost-conscious government buyers by using the money it saved on adver-

tising to heavily discount its prices. It took Zenith almost two years to land its first government contract, a $29 million order from the Air Force in 1983 for 6,000 microcomputers. Government business began as a trickle, but the trickle soon turned into a flood.

In October 1984, Zenith got a $100 million contract to supply the navy, air force, and marines with "Tempest-grade" microcomputers, machines specially shielded against electronic eavesdropping. In February 1986, Zenith beat out IBM and other large competitors to get the government's largest ever microcomputer order, a $242 million contract for more than 200,000 units. That contract may eventually grow to bring in over $500 million worth of business. Also in 1986, Zenith edged out IBM and Data General to win a $27 million contract from the Internal Revenue Service for 15,000 of the company's acclaimed new "lap-top" models. The company has also won contracts from the U.S. Department of Health and Human Services and several other government agencies. The Army and Air Force Post Exchange Systems (PXs) carry Zenith products, and the company supplies computers to students and faculty at the military, air force, and naval academies. Zenith has even bro-

qualified suppliers for carefully described items, generally awarding a contract to the lowest bidder. The supplier must consider whether it can meet the specifications and accept the terms. For standard items, such as fuel or school supplies, the specifications are not a hurdle. But specifications may be a hurdle for nonstandard items. The government office is usually required to award the contract to the lowest bidder on a winner-take-all basis (the lowest bidder is awarded the entire order). In some cases, allowance is made for the supplier's better product or reputation for completing contracts.

In *negotiated contract buying*, the agency works with one or more companies and negotiates a contract with one of them covering the project and terms. This type of buying occurs primarily with complex projects—those involving major research and development cost and risk or those for which there is little competition. The contract can be reviewed and renegotiated if the supplier's profits seem too high.

Many companies that sell to the government have not been marketing-oriented—for a number of reasons. Total government spending is determined by elected officials rather than by marketing efforts to develop this market. The government buying has emphasized price, making suppliers invest their effort in technology to bring costs down. Where the product's characteristics are carefully specified, product differ-

By focusing on the government market, Zenith established itself as a major contender in the microcomputer market.

now the federal government's largest microcomputer supplier and the world's second-largest producer of IBM-compatibles. Between 1982 and 1986, while most of the microcomputer industry slid downward and many competitors failed, Zenith's yearly computer sales grew by over 550 percent to $548 million. When IBM's sales through retail stores slowed under the onslaught of cheap Asian clones, Zenith was having trouble keeping up with orders from government agencies. By 1987, an estimated one-half of all Zenith's computer sales came from the government market.

By focusing on the government market, Zenith quietly established itself as a major contender in the highly competitive microcomputer market. Now, using its success in the government market as a foundation, Zenith is challenging for a share of the larger retail and business markets.

ken into the state government market, with contracts from the states of Florida, Kansas, and Massachusetts.

Thus Zenith's strategy to target the government market has met with staggering success. Zenith is

Sources: See Thayer C. Taylor, "The PC Fight: Zenith Battles the Heavyweights," *Sales & Marketing Management*, November 1986, pp. 51–55; Kenneth Dreyfack, "Zenith's Side Road to Success in Personal Computers," *Business Week*, December 8, 1986, pp. 100–101; and Frances Seghers and Geoff Lewis, "How Do You Chase a $17 Billion Market? With Everything You've Got," *Business Week*, November 23, 1987, pp. 120–22.

entiation is not a marketing factor. Nor do advertising or personal selling matter much in winning bids on an open bid basis.

More companies are now setting up separate marketing departments for government marketing efforts. J. I. Case, Eastman Kodak, and Goodyear are examples. These companies want to coordinate bids and prepare them more scientifically, to propose projects to meet government needs rather than just respond to government requests, to gather competitive intelligence, and to prepare stronger communications to describe the company's competence.

■ SUMMARY

Organizations make up a vast market. There are three major types of organizational markets—the industrial market, the reseller market, and the government market.

In many ways, organizational markets are like consumer markets, but in other ways they are much different. Organizational markets usually have fewer and larger buyers who are more geographically concentrated. Organizational demand is derived, largely inelastic, and more fluctuating. More buyers are usually involved in the organizational buying decision, and organizational buyers are better trained and more professional than consumer buyers. Organizational purchasing decisions are more complex, and the buying process is more formal.

The *industrial market* includes firms and individuals that buy goods and services in order to produce other goods and services for sale or rental to others. Industrial buyers make decisions that vary with the three types of buying situations—straight rebuys, modified rebuys, and new tasks. The decision-making unit of a buying organization—the buying center—may consist of many persons playing many roles. The industrial marketer needs to know the following: Who are the major participants? In what decisions do they exercise influence? What is their relative degree of influence? And what evaluation criteria does each decision participant use? The industrial marketer also needs to understand the major environmental, organizational, interpersonal, and individual influences on the buying process. The buying process itself consists of eight stages: problem recognition, general need description, product specification, supplier search, proposal solicitation, supplier selection, order routine specification, and performance review. As industrial buyers become more sophisticated, industrial marketers must upgrade their marketing.

The *reseller market* consists of individuals and organizations that acquire and resell goods produced by others. Resellers have to decide on their assortment, suppliers, prices, and terms. In small wholesale and retail organizations, buying may be carried on by one or a few individuals; in large organizations, by an entire purchasing department. With new items, the buyers go through a buying process similar to the one described for industrial buyers; with standard items, the buying process consists of routines for reordering and renegotiating contracts.

The *government market* is a vast one that annually purchases a over trillion dollars of products and services—for defense, education, public welfare, and other public needs. Government buying practices are highly specialized and specified, with open bidding or negotiated contracts characterizing most of the buying. Government buyers operate under the watchful eye of Congress, the Bureau of the Budget, and many private watchdog groups. Hence they tend to fill out more forms, require more signatures, and respond more slowly in placing orders.

■ QUESTIONS FOR DISCUSSION

1. Can your school be considered an industrial market? Is it also an industrial marketer? What are its products, and who are its customers?

2. How are organizational markets and consumer markets similar? How are they different? Do they have more in common in some buying situations than in others?

3. What implications does the geographic concentration of organizational markets have for the marketing efforts of firms selling to organizational buyers?

4. Which of the major types of buying situations are represented by the following? (a) Chrysler's purchase of specialized computers to install in cars to monitor and improve engine performance, (b) Volkswagen's purchase of Bosch spark plugs for its line of Jettas, and (c) Honda's purchase of light bulbs for its new Acura division.

5. If a university decided to introduce *jai alai* as a varsity sport, what elements would a systems seller include in a proposal to start the *jai alai* program and make it succeed? Describe the stages in the buying process for the "purchase" of a complete *jai alai* program.

6. How can an organizational marketer determine who is in the buying center for a particular purchase? Describe how a marketer of dictation equipment could identify the buying center for a law firm's purchase of dictation equipment.

7. Discuss the major environmental factors that would affect the purchase of radar speed detectors by statewide and local police forces.

8. Why do the Federal Trade Commission and the Justice Department discourage reciprocity in organizational buying relationships? In what ways is reciprocity similar to barter, which is an accepted marketing technique? Do electronic order exchange systems have the same effect on competition as reciprocity has?

9. What are the advantages and disadvantages of buying from single suppliers versus multiple suppliers?

10. Why did G. D. Searle promote NutraSweet to the general public, rather than just to industrial buyers? Can this strategy be used successfully with reseller markets, or is it limited to industrial markets?

11. Compare the major buying influences on industrial, reseller, and government buyers.

■ KEY TERMS

Buyers People in an organization's buying center with formal authority to select the supplier and arrange terms of purchase; they may help shape product specifications but play their major role in selecting vendors and negotiating.

Buying center All the individuals and groups who participate in the buying decision process, who share some common goals and the risks arising from the decisions.

Deciders People in an organization's buying center who have formal or informal power to select or approve the final suppliers.

Gatekeepers People in an organization's buying center who control the flow of information to others.

Government market Governmental units—federal, state, and local—that purchase or rent goods and services for carrying out the main functions of government.

Influencers People in an organization's buying center who affect the buying decision; they often help define specifications and also provide information for evaluating alternatives.

Industrial market All the individuals and organizations that acquire goods and services that enter into the production of other products and services that are sold, rented, or supplied to others.

Organizational buying The decision-making process by which formal organizations establish the need for purchased products and services, and identify, evaluate, and choose among alternative brands and suppliers.

Reseller market All the individuals and organizations that acquire goods for the purpose of reselling or renting them to others at a profit.

Systems buying Buying a whole solution to a problem and not making all the separate decisions involved.

Users Members of an organization's buying center who will use a product or service being purchased; users often initiate the buying proposal and help define product specifications.

Value analysis An approach to cost reduction in which components are carefully studied to determine if they can be redesigned, standardized, or made by cheaper methods of production.

■ REFERENCES

1. Excerpts from "Major Sales: Who Really Does the Buying," by Thomas V. Bonoma (May–June 1982). Copyright (c) 1982 by the President and Fellows of Harvard College; all rights reserved. Also see Scott Ticer, "Why Gulfstream's Rivals are Gazing Up in Envy," *Business Week*, February 16, 1987, pp. 66–67.

2. Frederick E. Webster, Jr., and Yoram Wind, *Organizational Buying Behavior* (Englewood Cliffs, NJ: Prentice Hall, 1972), p. 2.

3. See the *1982 Census of Retail Trade* and the *1982 Census of Wholesale Trade*, U.S Department of Commerce, Bureau of the Census, 1985.

4. *Survey of Current Business*, U.S. Department of Commerce, Bureau of Economic Analysis, Vol. 67, No. 4, April 1987.

5. However, for an argument that consumer and organizational marketing do not differ substantially, see Edward F. Fern and James R. Brown, "The Industrial/Consumer Marketing Dichotomy: A Case of Insufficient Justification," *Journal of Marketing*, Fall, 1984, pp. 68–77.

6. See William S. Bishop, John L. Graham, and Michael H. Jones, "Volatility of Derived Demand in Industrial Markets and Its Management Implications," *Journal of Marketing*, Fall 1984, pp. 95–103.

7. See Barbara Bund Jackson, "Build Customer Relationships That Last," *Harvard Business Review*, November–December 1985, pp. 120–28.

8. See Louis W. Stern and Thomas L. Eovaldi, *Legal Aspects of Marketing Strategy* (Englewood Cliffs, NJ: Prentice Hall, 1984), pp. 330–31.

9. See "Leasing Puts Equipment to Work," *Fortune*, November 24, 1986, pp. S1–S24; and "Leasing is on the Move," *Fortune*, June 22, 1987, pp. 127–51.

10. For a discussion of other organizational buyer behavior models, see Raymond L. Horton, *Buyer Behavior: A Decision-Making Approach* (Columbus, OH: Charles E. Merrill, 1984), chap. 16.

11. Patrick J. Robinson, Charles W. Faris, and Yoram Wind, *Industrial Buying Behavior and Creative Marketing* (Boston: Allyn & Bacon, 1967). Also see Erin Anderson, Weyien Chu, and Barton Weitz, "Industrial Purchasing: An Empirical Exploration of the Buyclass Framework," *Journal of Marketing*, July 1987, pp. 71–86.

12. For more on systems selling, see Robert R. Reeder, Edward G. Brierty, and Betty H. Reeder, *Industrial Marketing: Analysis, Planning, and Control* (Englewood Cliffs, NJ: Prentice Hall, 1987), pp. 247–50.

13. Webster and Wind, *Organizational Buying Behavior*, p. 6. For more reading on buying centers, see Bonoma, "Major Sales: Who Really Does the Buying;" and Donald W. Jackson, Jr., Janet E. Keith, and Richard K. Burdick, "Purchasing Agents' Perceptions of Industrial Buying Center Influence: A Situational Approach," *Journal of Marketing*, Fall 1984, pp. 75–83.

14. Webster and Wind, *Organizational Buying Behavior*, pp. 78–80.

15. Wesley J. Johnson and Thomas V. Bonoma, "Purchase Process for Capital Equipment and Services," *Industrial Marketing Management*, 10 (1981), pp. 258–59.

16. Clifton J. Reichard, "Industrial Selling: Beyond Price and Persistence," *Harvard Business Review*, March–April 1985, p. 128.

17. Webster and Wind, *Organizational Buying Behavior*, pp. 33–37.

18. Thayer C. Taylor, "Xerox's Sales Force Learns a New Game," *Sales & Marketing Management*, July 1, 1985, pp. 48–51.

19. See Peter Petre, "How to Keep Customers Happy Captives," *Fortune*, September 2, 1985, pp. 42–46.

20. Bonoma, "Major Sales," p. 114.

21. Robinson, Faris, and Wind, *Industrial Buying*.

22. See William A. Dempsey, "Vendor Selection and the Buying Process," *Industrial Marketing Management*, 7, 1978, pp. 257–67.

23. Donald R. Lehmann and John O'Shaughnessy, "Decision Criteria Used in Buying Different Categories of Products," *Journal of Purchasing and Materials Management*, Spring 1982, pp. 9–14.

24. Wesley J. Johnson and Thomas V. Bonoma, "Purchase Process," p. 261.

25. "Retailers Rate New Products," *Sales & Marketing Management*, November 1986, pp. 75–77.

26. For more reading on similarities and differences, see Jagdish N. Sheth, Robert F. Williams, and Richard M. Hill, "Government and Business Buying: How Similar Are They?" *Journal of Purchasing and Materials Management*, Winter 1983, pp. 7–13.

27. See Warren H. Suss, "How to Sell to Uncle Sam," *Harvard Business Review*, November–December 1984, pp. 136–44.

CASE 3

FAMILY SERVICE, INC.

Introduction

Family Service was established in 1941 as a private nonprofit organization. In 1942, the agency obtained United Way funding for the addition of a school lunch program. Since that time, the agency has undergone a series of name changes in an attempt to reflect changes in service offerings. In 1983, the agency once again operated under the name of Family Service, Inc., and its services included counseling, family life education, and home health care.

During 1983, Ann Marek, director of community affairs, became concerned about the community's lack of knowledge regarding available services. Before embarking on an awareness campaign, however, she felt it necessary first to assess the community's attitudes and perceptions toward Family Service as well as attitudes and perceptions toward other agencies offering similar services.

Ann arranged for a local graduate student in marketing to assist with the project. It was determined that the project would involve a market research survey of the general public with emphasis on home health services, since the home health market was extremely competitive. Ann felt it was important also to survey physicians because many of Family Service's home health clients were referred by their doctors.

General Public Survey

Telephone interviewing yielded 184 completed interviews from a random sample of 400 names drawn from the residence pages of the telephone directory. Respondents were first asked how they would rate the services provided by voluntary organizations in general. Ratings were on a scale of 1 to 5, where 5 was high and 1 was low. The results are shown in Table 1.

Respondents were then asked if they were aware of several specific organizations. Awareness did not mean

TABLE 1   Overall Rating of Voluntary Organizations

RATING	NUMBER
Excellent (5)	38
Good (4)	87
Fair (3)	14
Poor (2)	1
Very poor (1)	1
No rating	43
Mean = 4.13	
Standard deviation = .781	

TABLE 2   Awareness and Ratings of Specific Organizations

ORGANIZATION	NO. AWARE	NO. RATED	MEAN RATING
United Way	160	128	3.70
North Texas Home Health Services	36	23	4.00
Crisis Intervention	118	79	3.84
Family Service	75	48	3.90
Meals on Wheels	170	138	4.59
Parenting Guidance Center	100	69	4.12
Visiting Nurses Association	107	72	4.31
Mental Health/Mental Retardation	154	108	4.11
Home Health Services of Tarrant County	69	41	3.93

knowledge of services, only that they were aware of the organizations' existence. Respondents were then asked to rate (on a scale of 1 to 5) the overall performance of all organizations of which they were aware. The results are shown in Table 2.

The 75 respondents who were aware of Family Service were also asked what they considered to be the most important criterion in selecting a provider of counseling, home health, and educational services. The results are shown in Table 3.

Physician Survey
Telephone interviewing produced 102 completed interviews from a random list of 350 physicians. Each doctor was asked first to rate the efforts of home health organizations in general (scales of 1 to 5). The mean response was 3.82, with 80 no responses.

TABLE 3   Criteria for Selecting Provider of Services

CRITERIA	NO. OF RESPONSES
Quality	5
Accreditation	3
Cost	5
Recommendations*	23
Image/reputation	8
Credentials/knowledge of staff	9
Supportive staff	1
Success rate	2
Needs/benefits	2
Tradition	1
Confidentiality	1
Communication	1
Christian organization	1
Don't know	13

Many respondents specified recommendations from doctors, ministers, school counselors, friends, and relatives.

Physicians were then asked if they were aware of several specific organizations. If aware of an organization, he or she was also asked to rate the performance of that organization. The results are shown in Table 4.

The interviewer noted that several doctors had heard of an organization but did not know enough about it to rate it. Others, however, said they knew of an organization and had actually referred patients to it but were unable to give a rating because they did not know how well the organization had served the patients.

Doctors were also asked to which home health organizations they refer their patients. Of the 102 interviewed physicians, 15 reported that they never refer to home health agencies. Of the remaining 87, 25 could not name any specific agency. Several of these 25 stated that they do not make the actual referral—they prescribe the needed services but the nurse or the hospital discharge planner actually selects the provider.

1. How does the general public view Family Service and the other agencies?

2. What are the marketing implications of Table 3?

3. How do physicians view Family Service and the other agencies?

4. What is the importance of the discrepancy in the number of physicians who were aware of an organization and the number who rated the organization?

5. What are the marketing implications of the 25 doctors who could not name the agency or agencies to which their patients were referred?

6. What recommendations would you make to Family Service?

Source: This case was prepared by Donna Legg, Texas Christian University. Used with permission.

TABLE 4   Awareness of Ratings of Specific Organizations

ORGANIZATION	NO. AWARE	NO. RATED	MEAN RATING
United Way	94	75	3.68
North Texas Home Health Services	52	35	3.86
Crisis Intervention	65	35	4.03
Family Service	50	38	3.71
Meals on Wheels	89	68	4.25
Parenting Guidance Center	50	28	4.00
Visiting Nurses Association	78	61	3.95
Mental/Health/Mental Retardation	91	64	3.63
Home Health Services of Tarrant County	57	41	3.76

FISHER-PRICE TOYS

Dressing toddlers can be a frazzling experience. Executives at Fisher-Price Toys had that point hammered home well to them last year. For four hours they peered through a one-way mirror and eavesdropped as a dozen women in Cleveland complained about their battles with the zippers, buckles, buttons, and snaps on kids' clothing.

"These were combat veterans who had five years experience with two children," says Stephen Muirhead, a manager in Fisher-Price's Diversified-Products Division. "They were talking about things that touch their daily lives very deeply."

Grumpy mothers were just what Fisher-Price hoped to find. The market research convinced the company that with its famous name and a unique design, it could find a niche in the lucrative but increasingly cutthroat children's wear market. This month, the Quaker Oats Co. subsidiary will roll out its first line of preschool playwear, and there isn't a button, zipper, or frill to be found. Nearly all the fasteners are Velcro. "Oshkosh overalls are beautifully designed," says Mr. Muirhead, "but kids being toilet trained need to be Houdini to get out of them."

The Fisher-Price playwear has other features: padded knees and elbows, extra-long shirttails, cuffs that can be unfurled as children grow, and big neck openings to accommodate kids' disproportionately large heads. "Fisher-Price is attacking clothing the way it does everything else," says Ken Wilcox, director of marketing administration at Tonka Corp. "The company identifies an area where kids aren't being served well and then comes up with a nearly indestructable product that's easy to use."

But it won't be an easy jump from toys to playwear. Fisher-Price is trying to break into a splintered industry where style often matters more than durability. "It's very difficult to position yourself on the basis of functionality and performance," says Peter Brown of Kurt Salmon & Associates, a management consulting firm. "Children's wear, blue jeans, and men's underwear are all advertised for their performance characteristics, but it's hard for consumers to see much difference."

And the business is becoming more crowded as other big companies are tempted by what demographers call the "baby-boom echo"—the rising number of births to women of the baby-boom generation. In the past 12 months alone, Gerber Products Co. has acquired three children's clothing companies, including the Buster Brown line. "Incursion of more adult brands into the kids' market is also intensifying the battle on the retail floor," says Terry Jacobs of Walter K. Levy Associates, Inc., retail marketing consultants.

Troubled by sagging sales of jeans to adults, Levi Strauss & Co. will introduce baby Levis next spring. The company will sell blue demin pants and diaper covers for infants, as well as tiny knit shirts proclaiming. "My First Levis." Says Bill Oldenburg, general manager of the youthwear division: "We're trying to develop brand loyalty at an earlier age." (But just in case mothers can't picture their newborns clad in Levis, the company will bring out infantwear under both the new Petite Bijou and Little Levis brand names.)

Levi predicts that by 1990 more than 8 million babies will be crawling about, an increase of 11 percent from 1983. Already, the United States has more moppets under five years—17.8 million—than in any year since 1968. What interests marketers most, though, is the growing percentage of births that are first births. That's when parents and doting grandparents tend to make their largest purchases. Kurt Salmon & Associates currently estimate the preschool clothing market at more than $6 billion a year.

"The outlook is tremendous," says Leo Goulet, president of Gerber. "There are more working mothers who have the money to spend and who are going for better-quality merchandise." The baby-food company expects sales of clothing, furniture, and other nonfood products for kids to double to $450 million in five years.

Working mothers in particular are changing the way children's wear companies design and market products. William Carter Co., for instance, is now selling Swiftly Change suits that contain more snaps to make diapering babies simpler. Fisher-Price found mothers especially interested in clothing that will enable children to dress themselves at an earlier age.

To make its playwear stand out, Fisher-Price is advertising it as "the children's clothing that mothers helped design." The company is also banking heavily on the strong pull of its brand name and its toys, which it says are in 99 percent of the homes where a child under the age of six lives. From now on, all kids featured in toy ads will be dressed in the playwear.

It became apparent rather quickly to Fisher-Price that fashioning playwear is a world apart from building plastic and wooden toys. So the company farmed out manufacturing and distribution to a girls' dressmaker. Fisher-Price retains close control over design and marketing, however, and refuses to license its trademark, as Tonka and the Playskool Division of Milton Bradley Co. have done. Research showed that consumers are fed up with paying a premium for a logo stamped on an otherwise ordinary T-shirt.

Fisher-Price may try to parlay its reputation for durability into kids' underwear and shoes too. "I doubt if we'll ever try to sell party dresses, though," Mr. Muirhead says. "We're not seen as very stylish or avant garde."

1. Assess the research methodology used to help design Fisher-Price playwear. What are the strengths and limitations of the approach. What other research would you recommend and why?

2. Analyze the market opportunity for Fisher-Price children's clothing.

3. Describe the consumer buying process for children's clothing.

4. Discuss the idea of a well-known toy company going into the toddlers clothing business.

5. What do you think about the decision to "farm out" the manufacturing and distribution of playwear?

Source: Ronald Alsop, "Fisher-Price Banks on Name, Design in Foray into Playwear," *The Wall Street Journal* August 2, 1984. Reprinted by permission of *The Wall Street Journal,* © Dow Jones & Company, Inc., 1984. All rights reserved.

CASE 5

LEVI STRAUSS & COMPANY

Levi Strauss & Company has broadened its distribution to include J. C. Penney and Sears, thereby reducing its reliance on jeans specialty chains, jeans boutiques, and upscale department stores. This decision was triggered by a sustained slump in the apparel and retailing industries, a substantial drop in the company's earnings, and the apparent maturing of the market for jeans. Management has found it difficult to make this change and still balance the best interests of its old retailer customers, its new ones (Sears and Penney), and Levi Strauss itself. The company now faces two problems: (1) whether to broaden its distribution even more to include discount and off-price outlets; and (2) deciding what other changes, if any, should be made in its marketing efforts to improve profits on jeans.

The company had experienced several poor years because competition in the jeans market was severe and consumer demand had weakened, especially for designer jeans and the western look. Management decided that broadened distribution would expose Levi's to more potential consumers as well as increase sales to new retailers.

Levi Strauss's plan to sell through mass merchandisers has had an impact on several interest groups. Some of the company's longtime retailers were shocked by the change and the added competition it brought. Independent and chain specialty stores whose businesses were built around Levi's had mixed reactions. Upscale department stores were especially upset by the plan and many, including Macy's, dropped the line. Though the head of one large jeans specialty chain believed that the plan helped both Levi Strauss and its retailers in geographical areas where they were weak, others feared price competition. Sears and, especially, Penney have been promoting their own brands of jeans against Levi's. They and other mass retailers that carry Levi's commonly make price comparisons between their own brands and Levi's in their advertising. It is not clear whether these retailers will want to stock Levi's as traffic builders, image enhancers, or direct contributors to profits. What they decide will be critical to Levi Strauss and its current retailers.

Levi Strauss's management is planning to increase its advertising budget to help retailers. It is also formulating guidelines for determining what types of goods it should sell through Sears and Penney and whether it should shift more of its advertising attention to a few items in its line, such as the button-fly "501" blue jeans, which have sold well.

Earlier the company's Canadian subsidiary had announced the "555," a "limited-edition" style of which only 30,000 to 50,000 pairs would be produced. The "555" retails for a few dollars more than the best-selling nonregistered Levi's, and distribution is exclusively through a Canadian specialty jeans chain, Thrifty's Just Pants. The "555" is a straight-leg jean with a button-fly front and other details similar to the original 1849 Gold Rush blue jeans. Levi's two-horse trademark appears on a leather patch on the rear pocket. A small copper plate carries a five-digit serial number, which is registered in the company's archives when the buyer returns a postage-paid card. Buyers receive a certificate documenting their ownership. A museum director has been quoted as saying that the "555" could in time become a museum piece.

1. Should Levi Strauss expand its distribution of blue jeans to include discount and off-price retailers? What criteria should be used in selecting additional outlets?

2. Should all Levi Strauss products be sold through all the company's outlets?

3. Should the "limited-edition" jeans line be introduced in the United States?

4. What other changes in Levi Strauss's marketing efforts for jeans do you recommend?

5. How will all of the above decisions affect reseller buying decisions in the different reseller segments?

Measuring and Forecasting Demand

IN February 1981, RCA officially introduced its product of the decade—the SelectaVision videodisc player—backed by high hopes, 5,000 retail outlets, and over $22 million in advertising. RCA claimed its research

showed that about 2.4 million people were ready to buy, and modestly forecast first-year sales at 200,000 units. The company set up facilities capable of producing more than 500,000 units a year and predicted it would sell all it could make.

The videodisc player is the visual counterpart of the phonograph. The buyer can hook the player up to a television set, pop in a videodisc, and watch a recent movie, a children's program, a cultural event, or a "how-to" such as Dr. Spock on baby care. The SelectaVision first sold for about $500 and the discs were priced from $15 to $30. RCA was certain it had a winner.

But by the end of the first year, RCA had sold only 65,000 units; by mid-1984, even after a series of drastic price cuts, it had sold a total of only 500,000 units. In April 1984, RCA announced that it was dropping out of the videodisc market and swallow a staggering $580 million loss.

Where did RCA's forecasting go wrong? In part, the people at RCA fell into "better mousetrap" thinking—they got caught up in their own dreams and thought consumers would be as enamored of their

invention as they were. This resulted in overly optimistic forecasts and kept RCA in the videodisc business long after later forecasts soured. Second, RCA based its forecasts on faulty assessments of consumer preferences. The videodisc featured playback only. Owners could not use it to record television programs or take pictures of the family. But SelectaVision's primary competitor—videocassette recorders—*did* offer these features.

RCA counted on consumers buying SelectaVision rather than VCRs because of its lower unit and disc prices (in 1981, VCRs were selling for $600 to $2,000, with tapes costing around $50 to $70). RCA's technological forecasts indicated that VCR unit and tape costs would fall only gradually. The incorrect forecast of future VCR technological improvements and competitive marketing strategies was RCA's third forecasting mistake. By 1984, rapid improvements in technology had dropped VCR prices to under $500. And the rapid growth of the videotape rental market caught RCA by surprise. Videotape rental soon became common—consumers could run to a nearby rental outlet, rent a tape of a favorite movie for $1 to $3, view it once, and return it without having to buy it. This put the software costs of videocassette recorders well below those of the videodisc player. When consumers cast their votes in the marketplace, VCRs became the clear winner. By 1984, Americans had purchased over 8 million VCRs to only 800,000 videodisc players. Fifty percent of all American homes now own a VCR, and many experts predict that 98 percent of all homes will own one by the mid-1990s. Ironically, RCA did forecast this market accurately—it leads the VCR market with a 16 percent market share.

Forecasting the size and growth rate of a new market is always risky. For videodisc players and other new technological products—personal computers, videorecorders, compact disc players—forecasting is even more risky. The marketer must consider possible consumer reactions to the product, competitor responses, future technological developments, environmental consequences, and many other factors. And as RCA and many other companies know only too well, forecasting mistakes can be very costly.[1]

Chapter Objectives   *After reading this chapter, you should be able to:*

1. Define a market and identify the important characteristics of people in a market.
2. Discuss the major methods for estimating current market demand.
3. Explain specific techniques that companies use to forecast future demand.

WHEN a company such as RCA finds an attractive market, it must estimate its current size and future potential carefully. The company can lose a lot of profit by overestimating or underestimating the market. This chapter will present the principles and tools for measuring and forecasting market demand. The next chapter will look at the more qualitative aspects of markets, and at how markets can be further segmented and the most attractive segments selected.

Demand can be measured and forecasted on many levels. Figure 8-1 shows *ninety* different types of demand measurement! Demand can be measured for six different *product levels* (product item, product form, product line, company sales, industry sales, and total sales), five different *space levels* (customer, territory, region, USA, world), and three different *time levels* (short-range, medium range, and long-range).

FIGURE 8-1
Ninety types of demand measurement
(6 × 5 × 3)

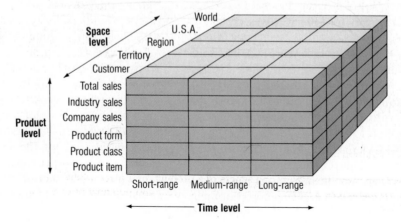

Each type of demand measurement serves a specific purpose. A company might make a short-range forecast of the total demand for a product item to provide a basis for ordering raw materials, planning production, and scheduling short-run financing. Or it might make a long-range forecast of regional demand for its major product line to provide a basis for designing a market expansion strategy.

DEFINING THE MARKET

Market demand measurement calls for a clear understanding of the market involved. The term market has acquired many meanings over the years. In its original meaning, a market is a physical place where buyers and sellers gather to exchange goods and services. Medieval towns had market squares where sellers brought their goods and buyers shopped for goods. Today's buying and selling occurs all over a city in what are called shopping areas rather than markets.

To an economist, a market describes all the buyers and sellers who transact over some good or service. Thus the soft-drink market consists of sellers such as Coca-Cola, Pepsi-Cola, and Seven-Up and all the consumers who buy soft drinks. The economist is interested in the structure, conduct, and performance of each market.

To a marketer, a **market** is the set of all actual and potential buyers of a product. A market is the set of buyers, and an **industry** is the set of sellers. We will adopt this last definition of a market. The size of a market, then, hinges on the number of buyers who might exist for a particular market offer. Those who are in the market for something have three characteristics: *interest, income*, and *access*.

Let us apply these characteristics to the market for motorcycles. We will leave aside companies that purchase motorcycles and concentrate on the consumer market. Honda, Harley-Davidson, and other motorcycle makers must first estimate the number of consumers who have a potential interest in owning a motorcycle. To do this,

The term *market* can mean the buyers and sellers of a product, or a place where they come together. To marketers, a market is the set of all current and potential buyers of a product or service.

they could contact a random sample of consumers and ask the following question: "Do you have a strong interest in owning a motorcycle?" If one person out of ten says yes, we can assume that 10 percent of the total number of consumers would constitute the potential market for motorcycles. The **potential market** is the set of consumers who profess some level of interest in a particular product or service.

Consumer interest alone is not enough to define the motorcycle market. Potential consumers must have enough income to afford the product. They must be able to answer yes to the following question: "Can you afford to buy a motorcycle?" The higher the price, the fewer the number of people who can answer yes to this question. Market size is a function of both interest and income.

Access barriers further reduce motorcycle market size. If motorcycle producers do not distribute their products in certain remote areas because of high shipping costs, potential consumers in those areas are not available as customers. The **available market** is the set of consumers who have interest, income, and access to a particular product or service.

For some market offers, the company may restrict sales to certain groups. A particular state might ban the sale of motorcycles to anyone under 18 years of age. The remaining adults make up the **qualified available market**—the set of consumers who have interest, income, access, and qualifications for the product or service.

The company now has the choice of going after the whole qualified available market or concentrating on certain segments. The **served market** (also called the *target market*) is the part of the qualified available market the company decides to pursue. The company, for example, may decide to concentrate its marketing and distribution efforts on the East Coast. The East Coast becomes its served market.

The company and its competitors will end up selling a certain number of motorcycles in its served market. The **penetrated market** is the set of consumers who have already bought motorcycles.

Figure 8-2 brings all these market concepts together with some hypothetical numbers. The bar on the left of the figure shows the ratio of the potential market—all interested persons—to the total population, here 10 percent. The bar on the right shows several breakdowns of the potential market. The available market—those who have interest, income, and access—is 40 percent of the potential market. The qualified available market—those who can meet the legal requirements—is 20

FIGURE 8-2
Levels of market definition

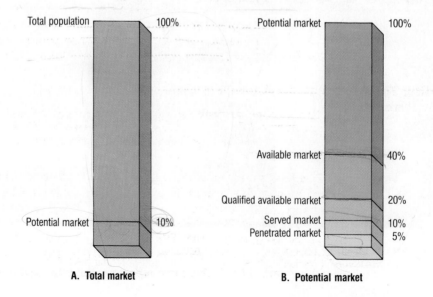

A. Total market

B. Potential market

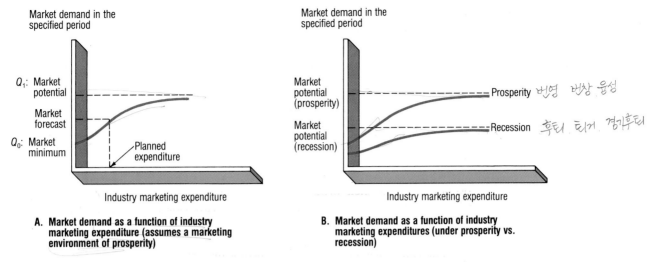

A. **Market demand as a function of industry marketing expenditure (assumes a marketing environment of prosperity)**

B. **Market demand as a function of industry marketing expenditures (under prosperity vs. recession)**

FIGURE 8-3   Market demand

percent of the potential market (or 50 percent of the available market). The company concentrates its efforts on 10 percent of the potential market (or 50 percent of the qualified available market). Finally, the company and its competitors have already penetrated 5 percent of the potential market (or 50 percent of the served market).

These definitions of a market are a useful tool for marketing planning. If the company is not satisfied with current sales, it can consider a number of actions. It can try to attract a larger percentage of buyers from its served market. It can lobby for lower qualifications of potential buyers. It can expand to other available markets. It can lower its price to expand the size of the available market. Or it can try to expand the potential market by increasing its advertising to convert noninterested consumers into interested consumers. This is what Honda did when it ran its successful campaign on the theme, "You meet the nicest people on a Honda."

MEASURING CURRENT MARKET DEMAND

We will now look at practical methods for estimating current market demand. Marketers will want to estimate three different aspects of current market demand—*total market demand*, *area market demand*, and *actual sales and market shares*.

Estimating Total Market Demand

Total market demand is defined as follows:

Total market demand for a product or service is the total volume that would be bought by a defined consumer group in a defined geographic area in a defined time period in a defined marketing environment under a defined level and mix of industry marketing effort.

The most important thing to realize about total market demand is that it is not a fixed number, but a function of the stated conditions. One of these conditions, for example, is the level and mix of industry marketing effort. Another is the state of the environment. The relationship between total market demand and these conditions is shown in Figure 8-3A. The horizontal axis shows different possible levels of industry marketing expenditure in a given time period. The vertical axis shows the resulting demand level. The curve represents the estimated level of market demand

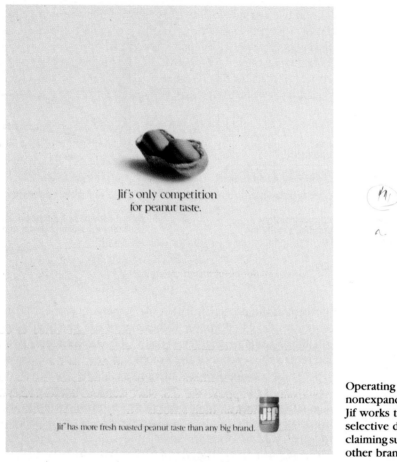

Jif's only competition
for peanut taste.

Jif has more fresh roasted peanut taste than any big brand.

Operating in a mature, nonexpandible market, Jif works to increase selective demand by claiming superiority over other brands.

for varying levels of industry marketing expenditure. Some base sales (called the *market minimum*) would take place without any marketing expenditures. Greater marketing expenditures would yield higher levels of demand, first at an increasing rate, and then at a decreasing rate. Marketing expenditures higher than a certain level would not cause much more demand, suggesting an upper limit to market demand, called the *market potential*. The industry market forecast shows the level of market demand corresponding to the planned level of industry marketing expenditure in the given environment.

The distance between the market minimum and the market potential shows the overall sensitivity of demand to marketing efforts. We can think of two extreme types of markets, the *expandible* and the *nonexpandible*. The size of an expandible market, such as the market for compact disc players, is strongly affected by the level of industry marketing expenditures. In terms of Figure 8-3A, the distance between Q_0 and Q_1 would be fairly large. The size of a nonexpandible market, such as the market for opera, is not much affected by the level of marketing expenditures; the distance between Q_0 and Q_1 would be fairly small. Organizations selling in a nonexpandible market can take **primary demand**—total demand for all brands of a given product on service—as a given. They concentrate their marketing resources on building **selective demand**—demand for their brand of the product or service.

If we assume a different marketing environment, we must estimate a new market demand curve. For example, the market for motorcycles is stronger during prosperity than during recession. The relationship of market demand to the environment is shown in Figure 8-3B. A given level of marketing expenditure will always result in more demand during prosperity than it would during a recession. The main point is that marketers should carefully define the situation for which they are estimating market demand.

Companies have developed various practical methods for estimating total market demand. We will illustrate two here. Suppose RCA wants to estimate the total annual sales of audio cassette tapes. A common way to estimate total market demand is as follows:

$$Q = n \times q \times p \qquad (8-1)$$

where

Q = total market demand
n = number of buyers in the market
q = quantity purchased by an average buyer per year
p = price of an average unit

If there are 100 million buyers of cassette tapes each year, and the average buyer buys six tapes a year, and the average price is $8, then the total market demand for cassette tapes is $4.8 billion (= 100,000,000 × 6 × $8).

A variation on Equation 8–1 is known as the *chain ratio method.* Using this method, the analyst multiplies a base number by a chain of adjusting percentages. For example, suppose the U.S. Navy wants to attract 112,000 new male recruits each year from American high schools. The question is whether this is a reasonable target in relation to the market potential. The navy estimates market potential using the following method:

Total number of male high school graduating students	10,000,000
Percentage who are militarily qualified (no physical, emotional, or mental handicaps)	×.50
Percentage of those qualified who are potentially interested in military service	×.15
Percentage of those qualified and interested in military service who consider the navy the preferred service	×.30

This chain of numbers shows a market potential of 225,000 recruits. Since this exceeds the target number of recruits sought, the U.S. Navy should have little trouble meeting its target if it does a reasonable job of marketing the navy.

Estimating Area Market Demand

Companies face the problem of selecting the best sales territories and allocating their marketing budget optimally among these territories. Therefore they need to estimate the market potential of different territories. Two major methods are available: the *market-buildup method*, which is used primarily by industrial goods firms, and the *market-factor index method*, which is used primarily by consumer goods firms.

Market-Buildup Method

The market-buildup method calls for identifying all the potential buyers in each market and estimating their potential purchases. Suppose a manufacturer of mining instruments developed an instrument for assessing the actual proportion of gold content in gold-bearing ores. The portable instrument can be used in the field to assay gold ore. By using it, miners would not waste their time digging deposits of ore containing too little gold to be commercially profitable. The manufacturer wants to price the instrument at $1,000. It sees each mine as buying one or more instruments, depending on the mine's size. The company wants to determine the market potential for this instrument in each mining state and whether to hire a salesperson to cover that state. It would place a salesperson in each state that has a market potential of over $300,000. The company would like to start by finding the market potential in Colorado.

To estimate the market potential in Colorado, the manufacturer can consult the Standard Industrial Classification (SIC) developed by the U.S. Bureau of the Census. The SIC is the government's coding system that classifies industries for purposes of data collection and reporting according to the product produced or operation performed. All industries fall into the ten major divisions shown in column 1 of Table 8-1.[2] Each major industrial group is assigned to a two-digit code. Mining bears the code numbers 10 to 14. Metal mining has the code number 10 (see column 2). Within metal mining are further breakdowns into three-digit SIC numbers (see column 3). The gold and silver ores category has the code number 104. Finally, gold and silver ores are subdivided into further groups, with four-digit code numbers (see column 4). Thus lode gold has the code number 1042. Our manufacturer is interested in mines that mine lode deposits and placer deposits.

Next the manufacturer can turn to the Census of Mining to determine the number of gold-mining operations in each state, their locations within the state, the number of employees, annual sales, and net worth. Using the data on Colorado, the company prepares the market potential estimate shown in Table 8-2. Column 1 classifies mines into three groups based on the number of employees. Column 2 shows the number of mines in each group. Column 3 shows the potential number of instruments that mines in each size class might buy. Column 4 shows the unit market potential (column 2 times column 3). Finally, column 5 shows the dollar market potential, given that each instrument sells for $1,000. Colorado has a dollar market potential of $370,000, and therefore one salesperson should be hired for Colorado. In the same way, companies in other industries can use the market-buildup method to estimate market potential in specific market areas.

TABLE 8-1
The Standard Industrial Classification (SIC)

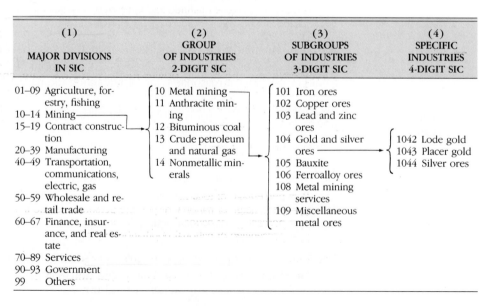

(1) MAJOR DIVISIONS IN SIC	(2) GROUP OF INDUSTRIES 2-DIGIT SIC	(3) SUBGROUPS OF INDUSTRIES 3-DIGIT SIC	(4) SPECIFIC INDUSTRIES 4-DIGIT SIC
01–09 Agriculture, forestry, fishing	10 Metal mining	101 Iron ores	
10–14 Mining	11 Anthracite mining	102 Copper ores	
15–19 Contract construction	12 Bituminous coal	103 Lead and zinc ores	
20–39 Manufacturing	13 Crude petroleum and natural gas	104 Gold and silver ores	1042 Lode gold
40–49 Transportation, communications, electric, gas	14 Nonmetallic minerals	105 Bauxite	1043 Placer gold
50–59 Wholesale and retail trade		106 Ferroalloy ores	1044 Silver ores
60–67 Finance, insurance, and real estate		108 Metal mining services	
70–89 Services		109 Miscellaneous metal ores	
90–93 Government			
99 Others			

SIC	(1) NUMBER OF EMPLOYEES	(2) NUMBER OF MINES	(3) POTENTIAL NUMBER OF INSTRUMENT SALES PER EMPLOYEE SIZE CLASS	(4) UNIT MARKET POTENTIAL (2 × 3)	(5) DOLLAR MARKET POTENTIAL (AT $1,000 PER INSTRUMENT)
1042 (lode deposits)	Under 10	80	1	80	
	10–50	50	2	100	
	Over 50	20	4	80	
		150		260	$260,000
1043 (placer deposits)	Under 10	40	1	40	
	10–50	20	2	40	
	Over 50	10	3	30	
		70		110	110,000
					$370,000

Market-Factor Index Method

Consumer goods companies also have to estimate area market potentials. Consider the following example: A shirt manufacturer was interested in starting a national system of franchised stores to sell T-shirts. Each store would carry several sizes and colors and would print an emblem chosen by the customer on each T-shirt. The customer could choose from hundreds of emblems. The manufacturer estimated that total national potential for T-shirts could reach $200 million annually. It also estimated that a franchise could be profitable in any town where it might sell more than $120,000 a year. It would advertise in the *Wall Street Journal* to attract potential franchisees, examine their business qualifications, and make sure that the town had enough buying potential to justify a store.

The company received an application from a recent graduate of the University of Illinois at Champaign-Urbana. This person wanted to buy a franchise with some inherited money. He had taken some marketing and business courses at the university. The manufacturer wondered whether a store in Champaign, Illinois, could gross enough sales to reward both the franchisee and the manufacturer.

The manufacturer wants to evaluate the market potential for T-shirt sales in Champaign. A common method is to identify market factors that are correlated with area market potential and combine them into a weighted index. An excellent example of this method is called the *buying power index* which is published each year by *Sales and Marketing Management* magazine in its *Survey of Buying Power*.[3] This survey estimates the buying power for each region, state, and metropolitan area of the nation. The buying power index is based on three factors: the area's share of the nation's *disposable personal income*, *retail sales*, and *population*. The buying power index for a specific area is given by

$$B_i = .5y_i + .3r_i + .2p_i \tag{8-2}$$

where

B_i = percentage of total national buying power in area i
y_i = percentage of national disposable personal income in area i
r_i = percentage of national retail sales in area i
p_i = percentage of national population in area i

The three coefficients in the formula reflect the relative weights of the three factors.

The manufacturer looks up Champaign, Illinois, and finds that this market has

A NEW TECHNIQUE FOR REFINING MARKET DEMAND ESTIMATES AND CHOOSING THE BEST MARKET TARGETS

In recent years, several new business information services have arisen to help marketing planners link U.S. Census data with lifestyle patterns to better refine their estimates of market potential down to the zip code level. Among the leading services are PRIZM (by Claritas), Cluster Plus (by Donnelley Marketing Information Services), and Acorn (C.A.C.I., Inc.). These data services can help marketing planners find the best zip-code areas in which to concentrate their marketing efforts. We will look at the PRIZM system as an example.

Using a host of demographic and socioeconomic factors drawn from the U.S. Census data, the PRIZM system has classified all U.S. neighborhood markets into forty clusters, such as "blue blood estates," "money and brains," "furs and station wagons," "shotguns and pickups," and "tobacco roads." The clusters were formed by manipulating such characteristics as education, income, occupation, family life cycle, housing, ethnicity, urbanization, and others. For example, "blue blood estates" neighborhoods are suburban areas populated mostly by white, college-educated, successful managers and professionals. They

include some of America's wealthiest neighborhoods, areas characterized by low household density, highly homogeneous residents, a heavy family orientation, and mostly single-unit housing. On the other hand, the "shotguns and pickups" cluster includes the hundreds of small villages and four-corners towns that dot America's rural areas. Each of the other 38 clusters has a unique combination of characteristics.

Companies can combine these "geodemographic" PRIZM clusters with other data on product and service usage, media usage, and life styles to get a better picture of specific market areas. For example, the "Hispanic mix" cluster prefers high quality dresses, tequila, non-filter cigarettes, and lip gloss. People in this cluster are highly brand-conscious, quality-conscious, and brand loyal. They have a strong family and home orientation. Such information provides a powerful tool for refining demand estimates, selecting target markets, and shaping promotion messages.

Helene Curtis used PRIZM in marketing its Suave shampoo. It found that potential demand is highest in neighborhoods with high concentrations of young

---

.0764 percent of the nation's disposable personal income, .0900 percent of the nation's retail sales, and .0070 percent of the nation's population. The buying power index for Champaign is therefore

$$B = .5(.0764) + .3(.0900) + .2(.0770) = .0806$$

That is, Champaign could account for .0806 percent of the nation's total potential demand for T-shirts. Since the total potential is estimated to be $200 million nationally each year, Champaign's share amounts to $161,200 ($200,000,000 x .000806). Since a successful store sells over $120,000 annually, the manufacturer leans toward selling a franchise to this applicant. The manufacturer needs to make sure that other T-shirt companies are not already operating in the Champaign market and selling some of this volume of T-shirts.

The weights used in the buying power index are somewhat arbitrary. They apply mainly to consumer goods that are neither low-priced staples nor high-priced luxury goods. Other weights can be used. And the manufacturer would want to adjust the market potential for additional factors, such as level of competition in the market, local promotion costs, seasonal changes in demand, and unique local market characteristics. For example, Champaign is a college town with over thirty thousand students, and this might make Champaign even more attractive.

working women. These women responded best to advertising messages that Suave is inexpensive yet would make their hair "look like a million."

An increasing number of manufacturers and retailers are now using geodemographic systems to identify the best clusters and to target their marketing efforts. So are other kinds of organizations. For example, the Seventh Day Adventists recently used clustering techniques to identify the best neighborhoods for recruiting new members.

Source: Kim Foltz, "The Wizards of Marketing," *Newsweek*, July 22, 1985, pp. 42–44; Thomas Moore, "Different Folks, Different Strokes," *Fortune*, September 16, 1985, pp. 65–68; "PRIZM-Guided Retail Plan Yields Dynamic Results," *Direct Marketing*, November 1985, p. 116; "Marketing Firm Slices U.S. Into 240,000 Parts to Spur Clients' Sales," *Wall Street Journal*, November 3, 1986, p. 1; and Leon G. Schiffman and Leslie Lazar Kanuk, *Consumer Behavior*, 3rd Ed. (Englewood Cliffs, NJ: Prentice Hall, 1987), pp. 452–55.

Using services like PRIZM, by Claritas, marketers can refine their estimates of market potential down to the neighborhood level.

Many companies compute additional area demand measures. Marketers can now refine state-by-state and city-by-city measures down to census tracts or zip-code centers. Census tracts are small areas about the size of a neighborhood, and zip-code centers (designed by the U.S. Post Office) are larger areas, often the size of small towns. Information on population size, family income, and other characteristics is available for each type of unit. Marketers can use this data for estimating demand in neighborhoods or other smaller geographic units within large cities. Marketing Highlight 8–1 describes some marketing firms that provide zip code or census information useful for refining market demand estimates and for improved customer targeting.

Estimating Actual Sales and Market Shares

Besides estimating total and area demand, a company will want to know the actual industry sales taking place in its market. Thus it must identify its competitors and estimate their sales.

The industry's trade association will often collect and publish total industry sales, although not listing individual company sales separately. In this way, each company can evaluate its performance against the industry as a whole. Suppose the company's sales are increasing at 5 percent a year and industry sales are increasing at 10 percent. This company is actually losing its relative standing in the industry.

Another way to estimate sales is to buy reports from a marketing research firm that audits total sales and brand sales. For example, the A. C. Nielsen Company audits the retail sales of various product categories in supermarkets and drugstores and sells this information to interested companies. A company can obtain data on total product category sales as well as brand sales. It can compare its performance with that of the total industry or any particular competitor to see whether it is gaining or losing in its relative standing.[4]

FORECASTING FUTURE DEMAND

Having looked at ways to estimate current demand, we will now examine ways to forecast future demand. **Forecasting** is the art of estimating future market demand by anticipating what buyers are likely to do under a given set of conditions. Very few products or services lend themselves to easy forecasting. Those that do generally involve a product with steady sales or sales growth in a stable competitive situation. But most markets do not have stable total and company demand, so good forecasting becomes a key factor in company success. Poor forecasting can lead to overly large inventories, costly price markdowns, or lost sales due to being out of stock. The more unstable the demand, the more the company needs accurate forecasts and elaborate forecasting procedures.

Companies commonly use a three-stage procedure to arrive at a sales forecast. First they make an *environmental forecast*, followed by an *industry forecast*, followed by a *company sales forecast*. The environmental forecast calls for projecting inflation, unemployment, interest rates, consumer spending and saving, business investment, government expenditures, net exports, and other environmental events important to the company. The result is a forecast of gross national product, which is used along with other indicators to forecast industry sales. Then the company prepares its sales forecast by assuming that it will win a certain share of industry sales.

There are several specific techniques companies use to forecast their sales. Many of these techniques are listed in Table 8-3 and described in the following paragraphs.[5] All forecasts are built on one of three information bases: what people say, what people do, or what people have done. The first basis—*what people say*—involves surveying the opinions of buyers or those close to them, such as salespeople or outside experts. It includes three methods: surveys of buyer intentions, composites of salesforce opinions, and expert opinion. Building a forecast on *what people do* involves another method, that of putting the product into a market test to assess buyer response. The final basis—*what people have done*—involves analyzing records of past buying behavior or using time-series analysis or statistical demand analysis.

Survey of Buyers' Intentions

One way to forecast what buyers will do is to ask them directly. This suggests that the forecaster should survey buyers. Surveys are especially valuable if the buyers have clearly formed intentions, will carry them out, and can describe them to interviewers.

TABLE 8-3
Some Common Sales Forecasting Techniques

Surveys of buyers' intentions	Time series analysis
Composite of salesforce opinions	Leading indicators
Expert opinion	Statistical demand analysis
Market-test method	

Several research organizations conduct periodic surveys of consumer buying intentions. These organizations ask questions like the following:

Do you intend to buy an automobile within the next six months?

.00	.10	.20	.30	.40	.50	.60	.70	.80	.90	1.00
No chance		Slight chance		Fair chance		Good chance		Strong chance		For certain

This is called a *purchase probability scale.* In addition, the various surveys ask about the consumer's present and future personal finances and their expectations about the economy. The various bits of information are combined into a *consumer sentiment measure* (Survey Research Center of the University of Michigan) or a *consumer confidence measure* (Sindlinger and Company). Consumer durable goods companies subscribe to these indexes to help them anticipate major shifts in consumer buying intentions so they can adjust their production and marketing plans accordingly.

For *industrial buying*, various agencies carry out intention surveys about plant, equipment, and materials purchases. The two best-known surveys are conducted by the U.S. Department of Commerce and by McGraw-Hill. Most of the estimates have been within 10 percent of the actual outcomes.

Composite of Salesforce Opinions

When buyer interviewing is impractical, the company may base its sales forecasts on information provided by the salesforce. The company typically asks its salespeople to estimate sales by product for their individual territories. It then adds up the individual estimates to arrive at an overall sales forecast.

Few companies use their salesforce's estimates without some adjustments. Sales representatives are biased observers. They may be naturally pessimistic or optimistic, or they may go to one extreme or another because of recent sales setbacks or successes. Furthermore, they are often unaware of larger economic developments and do not know how their company's marketing plans will affect future sales in their territories. They may understate demand so that the company will set a low sales quota. They may not have the time to prepare careful estimates or may not consider it worthwhile.

Assuming these biases can be countered, a number of benefits can be gained by involving the salesforce in forecasting. Salespeople may have better insights into developing trends than any other group. After participating in the forecasting process, the salespeople may have greater confidence in their quotas and more incentive to achieve them. Also, "grassroots" forecasting provides estimates broken down by product, territory, customer, and salesperson.[6]

Expert Opinion

Companies can also obtain forecasts by turning to experts. Experts include dealers, distributors, suppliers, marketing consultants, and trade associations. Thus auto companies survey their dealers periodically for their forecasts of short-term demand. Dealer estimates, however, are subject to the same strengths and weaknesses as salesforce estimates.

Many companies buy economic and industry forecasts from well-known firms such as Data Resources, Wharton Econometric, and Chase Econometric. These forecasting specialists are in a better position than the company to prepare economic forecasts because they have more data available and more forecasting expertise.

Occasionally companies will put together a special group of experts to make a particular kind of forecast. The experts may be asked to exchange views and come up with a group estimate (group discussion method). Or they may be asked to supply their estimates individually, and the analyst combines them into a single

Companies often forecast sales based on salesforce or expert opinions.

estimate (pooling of individual estimates). Or they may supply individual estimates and assumptions that are reviewed by a company analyst, revised, and followed by further rounds of estimation (Delphi method).[7]

Experts can provide good insights upon which to base forecasts, but they can also be wrong (see Marketing Highlight 8–2). Where possible the company should back up experts' opinions with estimates obtained using other methods.

Market-Test Method When buyers do not plan their purchases carefully or are very inconsistent in carrying out their intentions, or when experts are not very good guessers, the company may want to conduct a direct market test. A direct market test is especially useful in forecasting the sales of a new product, or of an established product in a new distribution channel or territory. Market testing is discussed in Chapter 11.

MARKETING HIGHLIGHT 8–2

SOMETIMES "EXPERT OPINION" ISN'T ALL IT SHOULD BE

Before you rely too heavily on expert opinion, you might be interested in learning how some past "experts" came out with their predictions:

- "I think there's a world market for about five computers." Thomas J. Watson, IBM Chairman, 1943.

- "With over 50 foreign cars already on sale here, the Japanese auto industry isn't likely to carve out a big slice of the U.S. market for itself." *Business Week*, 1958.

- "TV won't be able to hold on to any market it captures after the first six months. People will soon get tired of staring at a plywood box every night." Daryl F. Zanuck, head of 20th Century Fox, 1946.

- "By 1980, all power (electric, atomic, solar) is likely to be virtually costless." Henry Luce, founder and publisher of *Time*, *Life*, and *Fortune*, 1956.

- "1930 will be a splendid employment year." U.S. Department of Labor, 1929.

- "My imagination refuses to see any sort of submarine doing anything but suffocating its crew and foundering at sea. H. G. Wells, 1902.

- "Airplanes are interesting toys, but of no military value." France's Marshall Foch, 1911.

Source: Adapted from "Sometimes Expert Opinion Isn't All It Should Be," *Go*, September–October 1985, p. 2.

Time-Series Analysis

Many firms base their forecasts on past sales. They assume that the causes of past sales can be uncovered through statistical analysis. The causal relations can then be used to predict future sales. A time series of a product's past sales can be separated into four major components.

The first component, *trend,* is the long-term, underlying pattern of growth or decline in sales resulting from basic changes in population, capital formation, and technology. It is found by fitting a straight or curved line through past sales.

The second component, *cycle,* captures the medium-term, wavelike movement of sales resulting from changes in general economic and competitive activity. The cyclical component can be useful for medium-range forecasting. Cyclical swings, however, are difficult to predict because they do not occur on a regular basis.

The third component, *season,* refers to a consistent pattern of sales movements within the year. The term "season" describes any recurrent hourly, weekly, monthly, or quarterly sales pattern. The seasonal component may be related to weather factors, holidays, and trade customs. The seasonal pattern provides a norm for forecasting short-range sales.

The fourth component, *erratic events,* includes fads, strikes, snowstorms, earthquakes, riots, fires, and other disturbances. These erratic components are by definition unpredictable and should be removed from past data to see the more normal behavior of sales.

Time-series analysis consists of breaking down the original sales into its trend, cycle, season, and erratic components, then recombining these components to produce the sales forecast. For example, suppose an insurance company sold 12,000 new life insurance policies this year. It would like to predict next year's December sales. The long-term trend shows a 5 percent sales growth rate per year. This information alone suggests sales next year of 12,600 (12,000 × 1.05). However, a business recession is expected next year and will probably result in total sales achieving only 90 percent of the expected trend-adjusted sales. Sales next year will more likely be 11,340 (12,600 × .90). If sales were the same each month, monthly sales would be 945 (11,340/12). However, December is an above-average month for insurance policy sales, with a seasonal index standing at 1.30. Therefore December sales may be as high as 1,228.5 (945 × 1.3). The company expects no erratic events, such as strikes or new insurance regulations. Thus it estimates new policy sales next December at 1,228.5 policies.

Leading Indicators

Many companies try to forecast their sales by finding one or more **leading indicators**—other time series that change in the same direction but in advance of company sales. For example, a plumbing supply company might find that its sales lag the housing starts index by about four months. The housing starts index would then be a useful leading indicator. The National Bureau of Economic Research has identified twelve of the best leading indicators, and their values are published monthly in the *Survey of Current Business.*

Statistical Demand Analysis

Time-series analysis treats past and future sales as a function of time, rather than of any real demand factors. But many real factors affect the sales of any product. **Statistical demand analysis** is a set of statistical procedures used to discover the most important real factors affecting sales and their relative influence. The factors most commonly analyzed are prices, income, population, and promotion.

Statistical demand analysis consists of expressing sales (Q) as a dependent variable and trying to explain sales as a function of a number of independent demand variables $x_1, x_2, \ldots, x_n$. That is:

$$Q = f(x_1, x_2, \ldots, x_n) \qquad (8\text{–}3)$$

Using a technique called multiple-regression analysis, various equation forms can be statistically fitted to the data in the search for the best predicting factors and equation.[8]

For example, a soft-drink company found that the per capita sales of soft drinks by state was well explained by[9]

$$Q = -145.5 + 6.46x_1 - 2.37x_2 \qquad (8\text{–}4)$$

where

x_1 = mean annual temperature of the state (fahrenheit)
x_2 = annual per capita income in the state (in hundreds)

For example, New Jersey had a mean annual temperature of 54 and an annual per capita income of $24 (in hundreds). Using Equation 8–4, we would predict per capita soft-drink consumption in New Jersey to be

$$Q = -145.5 + 6.46(54) - 2.37(24) = 146.6$$

Actual per capita consumption was 143. If the equation predicted this well for other states, it would serve as a useful forecasting tool. Marketing management would predict next year's mean temperature and per capita income for each state and use Equation 8–4 to predict next year's sales.

Statistical demand analysis can be very complex, and the marketer must take care in designing, conducting, and interpreting such analysis. Yet constantly improving computer technology has made statistical demand analysis an increasingly popular approach to forecasting.

■ SUMMARY

To carry out their responsibilities, marketing managers need measures of current and future market size. We define a market as the set of actual and potential consumers of a market offer. Consumers in the market have interest, income, and access to the market offer. The marketer has to distinguish various levels of the market, such as the potential market, available market, qualified available market, served market, and penetrated market.

One task is to estimate current demand. Marketers can estimate total demand through the chain ratio method, which involves multiplying a base number by successive percentages. Area market demand can be estimated by the market-buildup method or the market-factor index method. Estimating actual industry sales requires identifying competitors and using some method of estimating the sales of each. Finally, companies estimate the market shares of competitors to judge their relative performance.

For estimating future demand, the company can use one or a combination of seven possible forecasting methods, based on what consumers say (buyers' intentions surveys, composite of salesforce opinions, expert opinion); what consumers do (market tests); or what consumers have done (time-series analysis, leading indicators, and statistical demand analysis). Which method is best depends on the purpose of the forecast, the type of product, and the availability and reliability of data.

■ QUESTIONS FOR DISCUSSION

1. In market measurement and forecasting, which is the more serious problem: to *overestimate* demand or to *underestimate* it?

2. Big Brothers–Big Sisters of America is a nonprofit organization with 460 affiliates across the country that help children from single-parent households form long-term relationships with adult volunteers. Describe the potential market, available market, and qualified available market for Big Brothers–Big Sisters and its affiliates.

3. List some expandible and nonexpandible markets. Can you think of any markets that have expanded even though they were once considered nonexpandible? What caused the unexpected expansion to occur?

4. People are generally less responsive to marketing efforts during a recession than when the economy is booming. Does this imply that marketers should cut back on their advertising and other marketing efforts during recessions?

5. Hess's, a chain of department stores, is looking for desirable locations for new stores. Which aspect of market demand would Hess's be interested in measuring, and what measuring methods would they use, in

choosing where to locate new stores? What census tract or zip-code information would be relevant?

6. Is the *Sales & Marketing Management* Buying Power Index appropriate for estimating area market potential for breakfast cereals? For compact discs? For telescopes? If not, what factors and weights would be more appropriate?

7. Sales of Izod-Lacoste clothing with the crocodile emblem grew from $15 million in 1969 to $450 million in 1981, but declined so rapidly from their peak that parent company General Mills started looking for buyers for its Izod division in 1985. How could accurate forecasts of sales levels have been made throughout this period?

8. As marketing manager for Cat's Pride cat litter, you notice that sales have jumped 50 percent in the past year, after years of relatively stable sales. How will you forecast sales for the coming year?

9. Identify the trend, cycle, season, and erratic components of alcoholic beverage sales. Are these components the same for beer, wine, and distilled spirits? How does your time-series analysis help you predict future sales of alcoholic beverages?

10. What leading indicators might help you predict sales of diapers? Cars? Hamburgers? Can you describe a general procedure for finding leading indicators of product sales?

■ KEY TERMS

Available market The set of consumers who have interest, income, and access to a particular product or service.
Forecasting The art of estimating future market demand by anticipating what buyers are likely to do under a given set of conditions.
Industry The set of all sellers of a product.
Leading indicators Time series that change in the same direction but in advance of company sales.
Market The set of all actual and potential buyers of a product.
Penetrated market The set of consumers who have already bought a particular product or service.
Potential market The set of consumers who profess some level of interest in a particular product or service.
Primary demand The level of total demand for all brands of a given product or service—for example, the total demand for motorcycles.
Qualified available market The set of consumers who have interest, income, access, and qualifications for a particular product or service.

Selective demand The demand for a given brand of a product or service—for example, the demand for a Honda motorcycle.
Served market (or target market) The part of the qualified available market the company decides to pursue.
Statistical demand analysis A set of statistical procedures used to discover the most important real factors affecting sales and their relative influence; the most commonly analyzed factors are prices, income, population, and promotion.
Time-series analysis Breaking down past sales into the its trend, cycle, season, and erratic components, then recombining these components to produce a sales forecast.
Total market demand The total volume of a product or service that would be bought by a defined consumer group in a defined geographic area in a defined time period in a defined marketing environment under a defined level and mix of industry marketing effort.

■ REFERENCES

1. See "RCA's Slipped Disc," *Fortune*, April 30, 1984, pp. 7–8; "The Anatomy of RCA's Videodisc Failure," *Business Week*, April 23, 1984, pp. 89–90; and Mark Trost, "VCR Sales Explosion Shakes Up Industry," *Advertising Age*, January 9, 1986, p. 14.

2. For some recent changes within these SIC groups, see "The New SIC Codes," *Sales & Marketing Management*, April 25, 1988, p. 8.

3. For more on using this survey, see "The Four Surveys: Putting Them to Work," *Sales and Marketing Management*, July 27, 1987, pp. A8–A30.

4. For a more comprehensive discussion of measuring market demand, see Philip Kotler, *Marketing Management: Analysis, Planning, Implementation, and Control* (Englewood Cliffs, NJ: Prentice Hall, 1988), Chapter 9.

5. For a listing and analysis of these and other forecasting techniques, see David M. Georgoff and Robert G. Murdick, "Manager's Guide to Forecasting," *Harvard Business Review*, January–February 1986, pp. 110–20; and Donald S. Tull and Del I. Hawkins, *Marketing Research: Measurement and Method*, 4th Ed. (New York: Macmillan, 1987), Chapter 15.

6. For more on the salesforce composite method, see Tull and Hawkins, *Marketing Research: Measurement and Method*, pp. 576–78.

7. See Kip D. Cassino, "Delphi Method: A Practical 'Crystal Ball' for Researchers," *Marketing News*, January 6, 1984, Section 2, pp. 10–11.

8. See Tull and Hawkins, *Marketing Research: Measurement and Method*, pp. 603–6.

9. See "The DuPort Company," in *Marketing Research: Text and Cases* (3rd ed.), Harper W. Boyd, Jr., Ralph Westfall, and Stanley Stasch, eds. (Homewood, IL: Irwin, 1977), pp. 498–500.

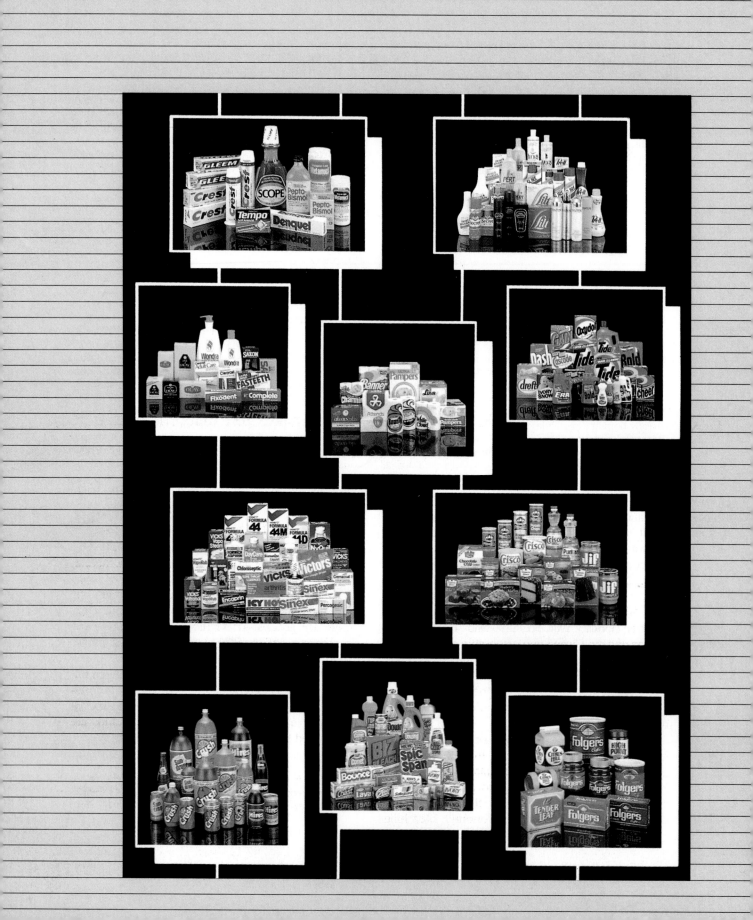

9

Market Segmentation, Targeting, and Positioning

PROCTER & GAMBLE makes ten different brands of laundry detergent—Tide, Cheer, Gain, Dash, Bold 3, Dreft, Ivory Snow, Oxydol, Era, and Solo. It also sells seven brands of hand soap (Zest, Coast, Ivory,

Safeguard, Camay, Kirk's, and Lava), four shampoos (Prell, Head & Shoulders, Ivory, and Pert), four liquid dishwashing detergents (Joy, Ivory, Dawn, and Liquid Cascade), four brands of toothpaste (Crest, Gleam, Complete, and Denquel), and two brands each of deodorant (Secret and Sure), coffee (Folger's and High Point), cooking oil (Crisco and Puritan), fabric softener (Downy and Bounce), floor cleaner (Spic & Span and Mr. Clean), and disposable diapers (Pampers and Luvs). Thus P&G brands compete with one another on the supermarket shelf. But why would P&G introduce several brands in one category instead of concentrating its resources on a single leading brand?

The answer lies in the fact that different people want different mixes of benefits from the products they buy. Take laundry detergents as an example. People use laundry detergents to get their clothes clean. But they also want other things from their detergents—things such as economy, bleaching

power, fabric softening, fresh smell, strength or mildness, and lots of suds. We all want *some* of each of these benefits from our detergent, but we may have different priorities for each benefit. To some people, cleaning and bleaching power are most important; to others, fabric softening is most important; still others want a mild, fresh-scented detergent. Thus, there are groups—or segments—of laundry detergent buyers, and each segment seeks a special combination of benefits.

Procter & Gamble has identified at least ten important laundry detergent segments, and it has developed a different brand designed to meet the special needs of each segment. The ten P&G brands are positioned for different segments, as follows:

- *Tide* is the "extra action," all-purpose detergent for extra-tough laundry jobs. It is a family detergent—"it gets out the dirt kids get into. Tide's in, dirt's out."

- *Cheer* is specially formulated for use in hot, warm, or cold water. It's "all tempa-Cheer."

- *Gain* was originally P&G's "enzyme" detergent but was repositioned as the detergent with a lingering fragrance—"for laundry so clean it's bursting with freshness."

- *Dash* is P&G's concentrated powdered detergent with "three powerful dirt dissolvers." It also makes less suds, so it won't clog "today's automatic washing machines."

- *Bold 3* originally "powered out dirt." Now it's the detergent plus fabric softener. It "cleans, softens, and controls static."

- *Ivory Snow* is "Ninety-nine and forty-four one hundreds percent pure." It's the "mild, gentle soap for diapers and baby clothes."

- *Dreft* is also formulated for baby's diapers and clothes, and it contains borax, nature's natural sweetener.

- *Oxydol* contains bleach. It's for "sparkling whites, a full-power detergent with color-safe bleach."

- *Era* is P&G's concentrated liquid detergent. It contains proteins to clean more stains.

- *Solo* is positioned as a heavy-duty liquid detergent with a fabric softener. "The convenience of a liquid plus a softer wash that doesn't cling."

P&G even offers different versions of a given brand to better meet the preferences of market subgroups. For example, it offers Tide in regular, unscented, and liquid versions, and all of these come in several sizes. By segmenting the market and having several different detergent brands, P&G has an attractive offering for consumers in all important preference groups. All P&G brands combined hold more than a 50 percent share of the laundry detergent market—much more than any single brand could obtain by itself.

Chapter Objectives   *After reading this chapter, you should be able to:*

1. Define market segmentation, market targeting, and market positioning.

2. List and discuss the major bases for segmenting consumer and industrial markets.

3. Explain how companies identify attractive market segments and choose a market-coverage strategy.

4. Tell how companies can position their products for maximum advantage in the marketplace.

MARKETS

Organizations that sell to consumer and industrial markets recognize that they cannot appeal to all buyers in those markets, or at least not to all buyers in the same way. The buyers are too numerous, widely scattered, and varied in needs and buying practices. Different companies will be in better positions to serve certain segments of the market. Each company has to identify the parts of the market that it can serve best. Sellers have not always practiced this philosophy. Their thinking passed through three stages:

- *Mass marketing.* In mass marketing, the seller mass-produces, mass-distributes, and mass-promotes one product to all buyers. At one time Coca-Cola produced only one drink for the whole market, hoping it would appeal to everyone. The argument for mass marketing is that it should lead to the lowest costs and prices and create the largest potential market.

FIGURE 9-1
Steps in market
segmentation, targeting,
and positioning

* *Product-variety marketing.* Here the seller produces two or more products that have different features, styles, quality, and sizes. Later, Coca-Cola produced several soft drinks packaged in different sizes and containers. For example, it offered Coke and Sprite in 12-ounce and 32-ounce bottles and in 12-ounce cans. They were designed to offer variety to buyers rather than appeal to different market segments.

* *Target marketing.* Here the seller identifies market segments, selects one or more of these segments, and develops products and marketing mixes tailored to each segment. For example, Coca-Cola now produces several soft drinks for the sugared-cola segment (Coke, Coca-Cola Classic, and Cherry Coke), the diet segment (Diet Coke and Tab), the no caffeine segment (Caffeine Free Coke), and the non-cola segment (Minute Maid sodas).

Today's companies are moving away from mass marketing and product-variety marketing toward target marketing. Target marketing helps sellers find marketing opportunities better. The sellers can develop the right product for each target market. They can adjust their prices, distribution channels, and advertising to reach the target market efficiently. Instead of scattering their marketing effort ("shotgun" approach), they can focus it on the buyers who have the greatest purchase interest ("rifle" approach).

Target marketing calls for three major steps (Figure 9-1). The first is **market segmentation,** dividing a market into distinct groups of buyers who might call for separate products or marketing mixes. The company identifies different ways to segment the market and develops profiles of the resulting market segments. The second step is **market targeting,** evaluating each segment's attractiveness and selecting one or more of the market segments to enter. The third step is **market positioning,** setting the competitive positioning for the product and a detailed marketing mix. This chapter will describe the principles of market segmentation, market targeting, and market positioning.

MARKET SEGMENTATION

Markets consist of buyers, and buyers differ in one or more ways. They may differ in their wants, resources, locations, buying attitudes, and buying practices. Any of these variables can be used to segment a market.

The General Approach to Segmenting a Market

Figure 9-2A shows a simple market of six buyers. Each buyer is potentially a separate market because of unique needs and wants. Ideally, a seller might design a separate marketing program for each buyer. For example, airplane producers such as Boeing and McDonnell-Douglas face only a few buyers and treat each as a separate market. This complete market segmentation is shown in Figure 9-2B.

Most sellers will not find it worthwhile to "customize" their product to satisfy each specific buyer. Instead, the seller looks for broad classes of buyers who differ in their product needs or buying responses. For example, the seller may find that income groups differ in their wants. In Figure 9-2C, a number (1, 2, or 3) shows

FIGURE 9-2
Different segmentations
of a market

A. No market segmentation   **B. Complete market segmentation**

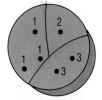

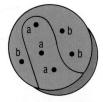

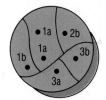

C. Market segmentation by
   income classes 1, 2, and 3

D. Market segmentation by
   age classes a and b

E. Market segmentation
   by income-age class

each buyer's income class. Lines are drawn around buyers in the same income class. Segmentation by income results in three segments.

Or, the seller may find large differences between younger and older buyers. In Figure 9-2D, a letter (*a* or *b*) shows each buyer's age group. Segmentation by age results in two segments, each with three buyers.

Alternatively, income and age may both count heavily in affecting the buyer's behavior toward the product. In this case, the market can be divided into five segments: 1*a*, 1*b*, 2*b*, 3*a*, and 3*b*. Figure 9-2E shows that segment 1*a* contains two buyers and the other segments contain one buyer.

Using more characteristics to segment the market gives the seller finer precision, but at the price of increasing the number of segments and thinning out the populations in each one.

Bases for Segmenting Consumer Markets

There is no single way to segment a market. A marketer has to try different segmentation variables, alone and in combination, hoping to find the best way to view the market structure. Table 9-1 outlines the major variables that might be used in segmenting consumer markets. Here we will look at the major geographic, demographic, psychographic, and behavior variables.

Geographic Segmentation

Geographic segmentation calls for dividing the market into different geographical units such as nations, states, regions, counties, cities, or neighborhoods. The company decides to operate in one or a few geographical areas, or to operate in all areas but pay attention to geographical differences in needs and wants. For example, General Foods' Maxwell House ground coffee is sold nationally but is flavored regionally. People in the West want stronger coffee than people in the East. Campbell makes its nacho cheese soup spicier in Texas and California and sells its spicy Ranchero Beans only in the South and Southwest.

S. C. Johnson & Son practices geographic segmentation for its arsenal of Raid bug killers by emphasizing the right products in the right geographic areas at the right times.

Concerned that its dominant share of the household insecticide market had plateaued just above 40 percent, Johnson figured out where and when different bugs were about

TABLE 9-1
Major Segmentation
Variables for
Consumer Markets

VARIABLE	TYPICAL BREAKDOWNS
Geographic	
Region	Pacific, Mountain, West North Central, West South Central, East North Central, East South Central, South Atlantic, Middle Atlantic, New England
County size	A, B, C, D
City or MSA size	Under 5,000; 5,000–20,000; 20,000–50,000; 50,000–100,000; 100,000–250,000; 250,000–500,000; 500,000–1,000,000; 1,000,000–4,000,000; 4,000,000 or over
Density	Urban, suburban, rural
Climate	Northern, southern
Demographic	
Age	Under 6, 6–11, 12–19, 20–34, 35–49, 50–64, 65+
Sex	Male, female
Family size	1–2, 3–4, 5+
Family life cycle	Young, single; young, married, no children; young, married, youngest child under 6; young, married, youngest child 6 or over; older, married, with children; older, married, no children under 18; older, single; other
Income	Under $10,000; $10,000–$15,000; $15,000–$20,000; $20,000–$30,000; $30,000–$50,000; $50,000 and over
Occupation	Professional and technical; managers, officials, and proprietors; clerical, sales; craftsmen, foremen; operatives; farmers; retired; students; homemakers; unemployed
Education	Grade school or less; some high school; high school graduate; some college; college graduate
Religion	Catholic, Protestant, Jewish, other
Race	White, black, Asian, Hispanic
Nationality	American, British, French, German, Scandinavian, Italian, Latin American, Middle Eastern, Japanese
Psychographic	
Social class	Lower lowers, upper lowers, lower middles, upper middles, lower uppers, upper uppers
Life style	Belongers, achievers, integrateds
Personality	Compulsive, gregarious, authoritarian, ambitious
Behavioristic	
Purchase occasion	Regular occasion, special occasion
Benefits sought	Quality, service, economy
User status	Nonuser, ex-user, potential user, first-time user, regular user
Usage rate	Light user, medium user, heavy user
Loyalty status	None, medium, strong, absolute
Readiness stage	Unaware, aware, informed, interested, desirous, intending to buy
Attitude toward product	Enthusiastic, positive, indifferent, negative, hostile

to start biting, stinging, and otherwise making people's lives miserable. The company promoted cockroach zappers in roach capitals such as Houston and New York and flea sprays in flea-bitten cities like Tampa and Birmingham. Since the program began, . . . Raid has increased its market share in 16 of 18 regions and its overall piece of the $450-million-a-year U.S. insecticide market by five percentage points.[1]

Many companies today are "regionalizing" their marketing programs—localizing their products, advertising, promotion, and sales efforts to fit the needs of individual regions, cities, and even neighborhoods (see Marketing Highlight 9–1).

Demographic Segmentation

Demographic segmentation consists of dividing the market into groups based on demographic variables such as age, sex, family size, family life cycle, income, occupation, education, religion, race, and nationality. Demographic factors are the most popular bases for segmenting customer groups. One reason is that consumer needs, wants, and usage rates often vary closely with demographic variables. Another is that demographic variables are easier to measure than most other types of variables.

REGIONALIZATION—A PASSING FAD OR THE NEW MARKETING ERA?

For most of this century, major consumer products companies have held fast to two mass marketing principles—product standardization and national brand identification. They have marketed the same set of products in about the same way all across the country. But recently, Campbell Soup, Procter & Gamble, General Foods, H. J. Heinz, Frito-Lay, Anheuser-Busch, and others companies are trying a new approach—*regionalization*. Instead of marketing in the same way nationally to all customers, they are tailoring their products, advertising, sales promotions, and personal selling efforts to suit the needs and tastes of specific regions, cities, and even neighborhoods.

Several factors have fueled the move toward regionalization. First, for most products, the American mass market has slowly deteriorated into a profusion of smaller fragments—the baby boomer segment here, the seniors segment there; here the Hispanic market, there the black market; here working women, there single parents; the Sun Belt, the Rust Belt—the list goes on. Today marketers find it very hard to create a single product or program that appeals to all of these diverse groups.

Second, improved information and marketing research technologies have also spurred regionalization. For example, data from retail store scanners allow instant tracking of product sales from store to store, helping companies pinpoint local problems and opportunities that might call for localized marketing actions. A third important factor is the increasing power of retailers. Scanners give retailers mountains of market information, and this information gives them power over manufacturers. Further, competi-

tion has increased dramatically in recent years for the precious shelf space controlled by retailers. The average supermarket now carries over 300,000 stock-keeping units and about ten new products are introduced each day. Retailers are often luke warm about large, national marketing campaigns aimed at masses of consumers. They strongly prefer local programs tied to their own promotion efforts and aimed at consumers in their own cities and neighborhoods. Thus, to keep retailers happy and to get shelf space for their products, manufacturers must now allot more and more of their marketing budgets to local, store-by-store promotions.

Campbell Soup, a pioneer in regionalization, has jumped in with both feet. For starters, Campbell has created many successful regional brands. It sells its spicy Ranchero beans in the Southwest, Creole soup in the South, and red bean soup in Hispanic areas. For Northwesterners, who like their pickles very sour, it created Zesty Pickles. These and other brands appealing to regional tastes add substantially to Campbell's annual sales. But perhaps more significantly, Campbell has reorganized its entire marketing operation to suit its regional strategy. It divided its market into 22 regions, each with new responsibility for planning local marketing programs, and each with its own advertising and promotion budget. The company has allocated 15 to 20 percent of its total marketing budget to support local marketing; this allocation may eventually rise to 50 percent.

Within the regions, Campbell sales managers and salespeople now have the authority to create advertising and promotions geared to local market

Even when market segments are first defined using other bases such as personality or behavior, their demographic characteristics must be known in order to assess the size of the target market and to reach it efficiently.

Here we will show how certain demographic factors have been used in market segmentation.

AGE AND LIFE-CYCLE STAGE. Consumer needs and wants change with age. Some companies offer different products or use different marketing approaches for different age and life-cycle segments. For example, Richardson-Vicks offers four versions of its Life Stage vitamins, each designed for the special needs of specific age segments—chewable Children's Formula for children from 4 to 12 years old; Teens Formula for teenagers; and two adult versions (Men's Formula and Women's Formula). Johnson

needs and conditions. They use local appeals and choose whatever local advertising media work best in their areas, ranging from newspapers and radio to parking meters, shopping carts, and church bulle-

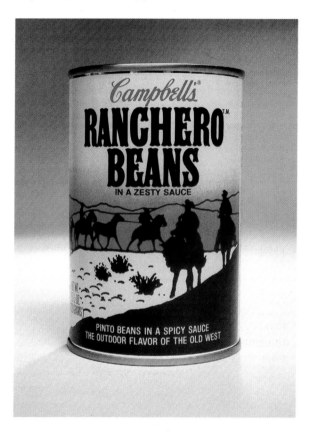

Regionalized marketing: Campbell features spicy Ranchero Beans in the Southwest.

tins. And they work closely with local retailers on displays, coupon offers, price specials, and local promotional events. For example, one sales manager recently offered Campbell's Pork & Beans at a fifty-year-old-price (5 cents) to help a local retailer celebrate its 50th anniversary. Such localized efforts win retailer support and boost consumer sales.

Regionalization offers much promise, but it also presents some problems. Having many different regional products and programs results in higher manufacturing and marketing costs. And letting area sales staff make local marketing decisions causes some problems of quality, logistics, and control. The salespeople will need a lot of training and guidance.

Regionalization is still in its infancy—even Campbell has yet to fully implement the strategy. Some marketers view it as just a fad; they think companies will quickly find that the extra sales gained will not cover the additional costs. But others think that regionalization will revolutionize the way consumer products are marketed. Gone are the days, they say, when a company can effectively mass-market a single product using a single ad campaign all across the country. To these marketers, regionalization signals the start of a new marketing era.

Sources: See Christine Dugas, Mark N. Vamos, Jonathon B. Levine, and Matt Rothmann, "Marketing's New Look," *Business Week*, January 26, 1987, pp. 64–69; Al Urbanski, "Repackaging the Brand Manager," *Sales and Marketing Management*, April 1987, pp. 42–45; Laurie Freeman, "P&G Hops on Regional Trend," *Advertising Age*, April 20, 1987, pp. 1, 96; Joe Schwartz, "The Colorado Kool-Aid Test," *American Demographics*, April 1988, pp. 47–48. and McKinley L. Blackburn and David E. Bloom, "Regional Roulette," *American Demographics*, January 1988, pp. 32–37.

& Johnson developed Affinity Shampoo for women over 40 to help overcome age-related hair changes. McDonald's targets children, teens, adults, and seniors with different ads and media. Its ads to teens feature dance-beat music, adventure, and fast-paced cutting from scene to scene; ads to seniors are soft and sentimental.

Age and life cycle can be tricky variables. For example, Ford used buyers' age in developing the target market for its initial Mustang automobile. The car was designed to appeal to young people who wanted an inexpensive, sporty automobile. But Ford found that the car was being purchased by all age groups. It then realized that its target market was not the physically young but the psychologically young.

SEX. Sex segmentation has long been used in clothing, hairdressing, cosmetics, and magazines. Recently, other marketers have noticed opportunities for sex segmentation. The deodorant market provides a good example. Most deodorant brands are used by men and women alike. Procter and Gamble, however, developed Secret as the brand specially formulated for a woman's chemistry. It packaged and advertised the product to reinforce the female image. The automobile industry has also begun to use sex segmentation extensively.

With the rapid growth in the number of working women and women car owners, most auto makers are now designing marketing strategies to court women buyers. Last year, women spent $30 billion on new cars and influenced the spending of another $60 billion. And they are involved in 81 percent of all new-car purchases. Thus women have evolved as a valued target market for the auto companies. Some manufacturers target women directly. For example, Chevrolet devotes 30 percent of its television advertising budget to advertisements to women. It places large advertising spreads designed especially for women consumers in such magazines as *Cosmopolitan* and *Women's Sport and Fitness*. Chevy also sponsored a nationwide series of career conferences for women. Other companies avoid direct appeals, fearing that women will be offended if they see

Income segmentation: Neiman-Marcus targets affluent consumers.

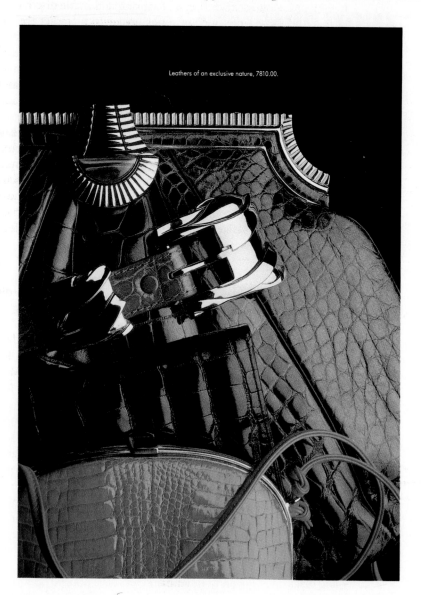

Leathers of an exclusive nature, 7810.00.

advertising directed toward them. It sometimes comes across as condescending. Instead, companies like Toyota, Ford, and Pontiac try to include a realistic balance of men and women in their ads without specific reference to gender.[2]

INCOME. Income segmentation has long been used by the marketers of such products and services as automobiles, boats, clothing, cosmetics, and travel. Many companies target affluent consumers with luxuries and convenience services. Stores like Neiman-Marcus pitch everything from expensive jewelry, fine fashions, and exotic furs to $4 peanut butter and chocolate at $20 a pound.[3]

But not all companies using income segmentation target the affluent. Many companies, such as Family Dollar stores, profitably target low-income consumers. When Family Dollar real estate experts scout locations for new stores, they look for lower-middle-class neighborhoods with people wearing cheap shoes and old cars that drip a lot of oil. The income of a typical Family Dollar customer rarely exceeds $17,000 a year, and the average customer spends only about $6 a trip. Yet the store's low-income strategy made it one of the most profitable discount chains in the country.[4]

At the same time, income does not always predict the customers for a given product. One would think that manual workers would buy Chevrolets and managers would buy Cadillacs. Yet many Chevrolets are bought by managers (often as a second car), and some Cadillacs are bought by manual workers (such as high-paid plumbers and carpenters). Manual workers were among the first purchasers of color television sets; it was cheaper for them to buy these sets than go out to the movies and restaurants.

MULTIVARIATE DEMOGRAPHIC SEGMENTATION. Most companies will segment a market by combining two or more demographic variables. The Charles Home for the Blind (name disguised) serves the needs of blind people for care, psychological counseling, and vocational training. However, because it has limited facilities, it cannot serve all types of blind people. A multiple segmentation of blind people is shown in Figure 9-3, where they are classified by age, sex, and income. The Charles Home has chosen to serve low-income males of working age. It feels that it can do the best job for this group.

Psychographic Segmentation

In **psychographic segmentation**, buyers are divided into different groups based on social class, life style, or personality characteristics. People in the same demographic group can have very different psychographic profiles.

SOCIAL CLASS. We described the seven American social classes in Chapter 5 and showed that social class has a strong affect on preferences in cars, clothes, home furnishings, leisure activities, reading habits, and retailers. Many companies design products or services for specific social classes, building in features that appeal to the target social class.

FIGURE 9-3
Segmentation of blind persons by three demographic variables

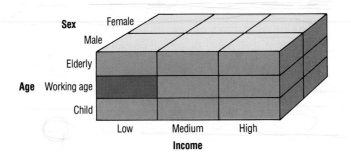

LIFE STYLE. We saw in Chapter 5 that people's interest in various goods is affected by their life styles and that the goods they buy express their life styles. Marketers are increasingly segmenting their markets by consumer life styles. General Foods used life-style analysis to successfully reposition its Sanka decaffeinated coffee. For years, Sanka's market was limited by the product's staid, older image. To turn this situation around, General Foods launched an advertising campaign that positioned Sanka as an ideal beverage for today's healthy, active life styles. The campaign targeted achievers of all ages, using a classic achiever appeal that Sanka "Lets you be your best." Advertising showed people leading adventurous life styles, such as kayaking through rapids.[5]

Redbook magazine also targets a specific life-style segment—women it calls "Redbook Jugglers." The magazine defines the juggler as a 25- to 44-year-old woman who must juggle husband, family, home, and job. According to *Redbook*, this consumer makes an ideal target for marketers of health food and fitness products. She wears out more jogging shoes, swallows more vitamins, drinks more diet soda, and works out more often than other consumer groups.

PERSONALITY. Marketers have also used personality variables to segment markets. They give their products personalities that correspond to consumer personalities. Successful market segmentation strategies based on personality have been used for such products as women's cosmetics, insurance, and liquor. One study identified various drinker-personality types and helped Anheuser-Busch develop messages and media programs to reach them. Another found that blood donors are low in self-esteem, low risk takers, and more concerned about their health; nondonors tend to be the opposite on all these dimensions. This suggests that social agencies should use different marketing approaches for keeping current donors and attracting new ones.[6]

Honda's marketing campaign for its motor scooters provides another good example of personality segmentation.

> Honda appears to target its Spree, Elite, and Aero motor scooters at the hip and trendy 14- to 22-year-old age group. But the company actually designs ads that appeal to a much broader personality group. One ad, for example, shows a delighted child bouncing up and down on his bed while the announcer says, "You've been trying to get there all your life." The ad reminds viewers of the euphoric feelings they got when they broke away from authority and did things their parents told them not to. And it suggests that they can feel that way again riding a Honda scooter. So while Honda seems to be targeting young consumers, the ads appeal to trend setters and independent personalities in all age groups. In fact, over half of Honda's scooter sales are to young professionals and older buyers—fifteen percent are purchased by the over-50 group. Thus, Honda is appealing to the rebellious, independent kid in all of us.[7]

Behavior Segmentation

In **behavior segmentation,** buyers are divided into groups based on their knowledge, attitude, use, or response to a product. Many marketers believe that behavior variables are the best starting point for building market segments.

OCCASIONS. Buyers can be grouped according to occasions when they get the idea, make a purchase, or use a product. For example, air travel is triggered by occasions related to business, vacation, or family. An airline can specialize in serving people who are flying for one of these occasions. Thus frequent-flyer programs appeal to customers who fly a lot on business. Superlow fares to Florida at holiday periods attract family vacation flyers.

Occasion segmentation can help firms build up product usage. For example, orange juice is most often consumed at breakfast. An orange juice company can

Occasion segmentation: Greyhound advertises for the holidays.

promote drinking orange juice at lunch or dinner. Some holidays—Mother's Day and Father's Day for example—were promoted partly to increase the sale of candy, flowers, cards, and other gifts. Recent new occasions promoted by greeting card companies are Secretaries' Day and Grandparents' Day. The Curtis Candy Company promoted the "trick-or-treat" custom at Halloween, with every home ready to give candy to eager little callers knocking at its door.

BENEFITS SOUGHT. A powerful form of segmentation is to group buyers according to the different benefits that they seek from the product. Benefit segmentation requires finding out the major benefits people look for in the product class, the kinds of people who look for each benefit, and the major brands that deliver each benefit. One of the most successful benefit segmentations was conducted in the toothpaste market (see Table 9-2). Research found four benefit segments: those seeking economy, protection, cosmetic, and taste benefits. Each benefit group had special demographic, behavior, and psychographic characteristics. For example, decay prevention seekers had large families, were heavy toothpaste users, and were conservative. Each segment also favored certain brands. Most current brands appeal to one of these segments—Crest tartar control toothpaste stresses protection and appeals to the family segment; Aim looks and tastes good and appeals to children.

Colgate Palmolive used benefit segmentation to reposition its Irish Spring soap. Research showed three deodorant soap benefit segments—men who prefer lightly-scented deodorant soap; women who want a mildly-scented, gentle soap; and a mixed, mostly male segment that wanted a strongly-scented, refreshing soap. The original Irish Spring soap did well with the last segment, but Colgate wanted to

**TABLE 9-2
Benefit Segmentation
of the Toothpaste
Market**

BENEFIT SEGMENTS	DEMO-GRAPHICS	BEHAVIOR	PSYCHO-GRAPHICS	FAVORED BRANDS
Economy (low price)	Men	Heavy users	High autonomy, value oriented	Brands on sale
Medicinal (decay prevention)	Large families	Heavy users	Hypochondriacal, conservative	Crest
Cosmetic (bright teeth)	Teens, young adults	Smokers	High sociability, active	Aqua-Fresh, Ultra Brite
Taste (good tasting)	Children	Spearmint lovers	High self-involvement, hedonistic	Colgate, Aim

Source: Adapted from Russell J. Haley, "Benefit Segmentation: A Decision Oriented Research Tool," *Journal of Marketing*, July 1968, pp. 30–35.

target the larger middle segment. It reformulated the soap and changed its advertising to give the product more of a family appeal.[8]

Thus companies can use benefit segmentation to clarify which benefit segment they are appealing to, its characteristics, and the major competitive brands. They can also search for new benefits and launch a brand that delivers these benefits.[9]

USER STATUS. Many markets can be segmented into nonusers, ex-users, potential users, first-time users, and regular users of a product. High-market-share companies are particularly interested in attracting potential users, whereas smaller firms will try to attract regular users to their brand. Potential users and regular users require different kinds of marketing appeals.

Social marketing agencies pay close attention to user status. Drug rehabilitation agencies sponsor rehabilitation programs to help regular users quit the habit. They sponsor talks by ex-users to discourage young nonusers from trying drugs.

USAGE RATE. Markets can also be segmented into light-, medium-, and heavy-user groups. Heavy users are often a small percentage of the market but account for a high percentage of total buying. Figure 9-4 shows usage rates for some popular consumer products. Product users were divided into two groups—a light-user half and a heavy-user half—according to their buying rates for the specific products. Using beer as an example, the figure shows that 41 percent of the households studied buy beer. But the heavy-user half accounted for 87 percent of the beer consumed, more than seven times as much as the light-user half. Clearly a beer company would prefer to attract one heavy user to its brand over several light users. Most beer companies target the heavy beer drinker, using appeals such as Schaefer's "one beer to have when you're having more than one," or Miller Lite's "tastes great, less filling."

LOYALTY STATUS. A market can also be segmented by consumer loyalty. Consumers can be loyal to brands (Tide), stores (Sears), and companies (Ford). Buyers can be divided into groups according to their degree of loyalty. Some consumers are completely loyal—they buy one brand all the time. Others are somewhat loyal—they are loyal to two or three brands of a given product, or favor one brand but sometimes buy others. Still other buyers show no loyalty to any brand. They want something different each time they buy, or always buy the brand on sale.

Each market is made up of different numbers of each type of buyer. A brand-loyal market is one with a high percentage of buyers showing strong brand loyalty—the toothpaste market and the beer market seem to be fairly high brand-loyal markets. Companies selling in a brand-loyal market have a hard time gaining more market share, and companies trying to enter such a market have a hard time getting in.

FIGURE 9-4
Heavy and light users of common consumer products
Source: See Victor J. Cook and William A. Mindak, "A Search for Constants: The 'Heavy User' Revisited!" *Journal of Consumer Marketing*, Vol. 1, No. 4. (Spring 1984), p. 80.

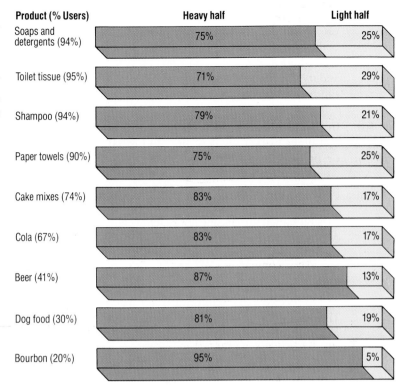

A company can learn a lot by analyzing loyalty patterns in its market. It should study its own loyal customers. Colgate finds that its loyal buyers are more middle class, have larger-size families, and are more health conscious. This pinpoints the target market for Colgate. By studying its less loyal buyers, the company can pinpoint which brands are most competitive with its own. If many Colgate buyers also buy Crest, Colgate can attempt to improve its positioning against Crest, possibly by using direct comparison advertising. By looking at customers who are shifting away from its brand, the company can learn about its marketing weaknesses. As for nonloyals, the company can attract them by putting its brand on sale.

Companies should be aware that what appears to be brand loyalty may actually reflect habit, low price, indifference, or the unavailability of other brands, factors that alert competitors can easily overcome. Thus the concept of brand loyalty must be used carefully.

BUYER READINESS STAGE. At any time, people are in different stages of readiness to buy a product. Some people are unaware of the product; some are aware; some are informed; some are interested; some want the product; and some intend to buy. The relative numbers make a big difference in designing the marketing program. Suppose a health agency wants women to take an annual Pap test to detect cervical cancer. At the beginning, most women are unaware of the Pap test. The marketing effort should go into high-awareness-building advertising using a simple message. If successful, the advertising should then dramatize the benefits of the Pap test and the risks of not taking it, in order to move more women into the stage of desire. Facilities should be readied for handling the large number of women who may be persuaded to take the examination. In general, the marketing program must be adjusted to the changing distribution of buyer readiness.

ATTITUDE. People in a market can be enthusiastic, positive, indifferent, negative, and hostile about a product. Door-to-door workers in a political campaign use the voter's attitude to determine how much time to spend with the voter. They thank enthusiastic voters and remind them to vote; they spend no time trying to change the attitudes of negative and hostile voters. They reinforce those who are positive and try to win the vote of the indifferent voters. In such marketing situations, attitudes can be effective segmentation variables.

Bases for Segmenting Industrial Markets

Industrial markets can be segmented using many of the same variables used in consumer market segmentation. Industrial buyers can be segmented geographically or by benefits sought, user status, usage rate, loyalty status, readiness state, and attitudes. Yet there are also some other variables, as well. Bonoma and Shapiro proposed that companies use the variables shown in Table 9-3 to segment the industrial market. The demographic variables are the most important, followed by operating variables, then purchasing approaches, situational factors, and personal characteristics of buyers.

The table lists major questions that industrial marketers should ask in determining which customers they want to serve. By going after segments instead of the whole market, the company has a much better chance to deliver real value to consumers and to receive maximum rewards for its close attention to segment consumer needs. Thus Goodyear and other tire companies should decide which *industries* they want to serve. Manufacturers seeking original equipment tires vary in their needs. Makers of luxury and high performance cars want higher grade tires than makers of economy models. And the tires needed by aircraft manufacturers must meet much higher safety standards than tires needed by farm tractor manufacturers.

Within the chosen industry, a company can further segment by *customer size* or *geographic location*. The company might set up separate systems for dealing with large or multiple-location customers. For example, Steelcase, a major producer

TABLE 9-3
Major Segmentation Variables for Industrial Markets

Demographic
- *Industry*: which industries that buy this product should we focus on?
- *Company size*: what size companies should we focus on?
- *Location*: what geographical areas should we focus on?

Operating variables
- *Technology*: what customer technologies should we focus on?
- *User/non-user status*: should we focus on heavy, medium, or light users or non-users?
- *Customer capabilities*: should we focus on customers needing many services or few services?

Purchasing approaches
- *Purchasing function organization*: should we focus on companies with highly centralized or decentralized purchasing organizations?
- *Power structure*: should we focus on companies that are engineering-dominated, financially-dominated, or marketing-dominated?
- *Nature of existing relationships*: should we focus on companies with which we already have strong relationships or simply go after the most desirable companies?
- *General purchase policies*: should we focus on companies that prefer leasing? Service contracts? Systems purchases? Sealed bidding?
- *Purchasing criteria*: should we focus on companies that are seeking quality? Service? Price?

Situational factors
- *Urgency*: should we focus on companies that need quick and sudden delivery or service?
- *Specific application*: should we focus on certain applications of our product rather than all applications?
- *Size of order*: should we focus on large or small orders?

Personal characteristics
- *Buyer-seller similarity*: should we focus on companies whose people and values are similar to ours?
- *Attitudes toward risk*: should we focus on risk-taking or risk-avoiding customers?
- *Loyalty*: should we focus on companies that show high loyalty to their suppliers?

Source: Adapted from Thomas V. Bonoma and Benson P. Shapiro, *Segmenting the Industrial Market* (Lexington, Ma.: Lexington Books, 1983).

Industrial segmentation: Steelcase segments by industry, then has separate systems for dealing with large, geographically dispersed customers.

of office furniture, segments customers into ten different industries, including banking, insurance, electronics, and others. Company salespeople work with independent Steelcase dealers to handle smaller, local or regional Steelcase customers in each industry segment. But many national, multiple-location customers, such as Exxon or IBM, have special needs that may reach beyond the scope of individual dealers. So Steelcase uses national accounts managers to help its dealer network handle these large, geographically dispersed accounts.

Within a certain target industry and customer size, the company can segment by *purchase approaches and criteria.* For example, Government laboratories, university laboratories, and industrial laboratories typically differ in their purchase criteria for scientific instruments. Government labs need low prices (because they have difficulty getting funds to buy instruments) and service contracts (because they can easily get money to maintain instruments). University labs want equipment that needs little regular service because they don't have service people on their payrolls. Industrial labs need highly reliable equipment because they cannot afford downtime.

In general, industrial companies do not focus on one segmentation variable but use a combination of many variables. One aluminum company, for instance, used a series of four major variables. It first looked at which *end-use* market to serve: automobile, residential, or beverage containers. Choosing the residential market, it determined the most attractive *product application:* semifinished material, building components, or aluminum mobile homes. Deciding to focus on building components, it next considered the best *customer size* to serve and chose large customers. The company further segmented the large-customer building-components market. It saw customers falling into three *benefit* groups—those who bought on price, those who bought on service, and those who bought on quality. Because the aluminum company had a high-service profile, it decided to concentrate on the service-motivated segment of the market.

Requirements for Effective Segmentation

Clearly, there are many ways to segment a market. But not all segmentations are effective. For example, buyers of table salt could be divided into blond and brunette customers. But hair color does not affect the purchase of salt. Furthermore, if all salt buyers buy the same amount of salt each year, believe all salt is the same, and want to pay the same price, the company would not benefit from segmenting this market.

To be useful, market segments must have the following characteristics:

* *Measurability,* the degree to which the size and purchasing power of the segments can be measured. Certain segmentation variables are difficult to measure. An illustration would be the size of the segment of teenage smokers who smoke primarily to rebel against their parents.
* *Accessibility,* the degree to which the segments can be reached and served. Suppose a perfume company finds that heavy users of its brand are single women who stay out late and socialize a lot. Unless this group lives or shops at certain places and is exposed to certain media, they will be difficult to reach.
* *Substantiality,* the degree to which the segments are large or profitable enough. A segment should be the largest possible homogeneous group worth going after with a tailored marketing program. It would not pay, for example, for an automobile manufacturer to develop cars for persons whose height is less than four feet.
* *Actionability,* the degree to which effective programs can be designed for attracting and serving the segments. A small airline, for example, identified seven market segments, but its staff was too small to develop separate marketing programs for each segment.

MARKET TARGETING

Marketing segmentation reveals the market segment opportunities facing the firm. The firm now has to decide on how many segments to cover and how to identify the best segments.

Market-Coverage Alternatives

The firm can adopt one of three market-coverage strategies, known as undifferentiated marketing, differentiated marketing, and concentrated marketing. These strategies are shown in Figure 9-5 and discussed below.

Undifferentiated Marketing

The firm might decide to ignore market segment differences and go after the whole market with one market offer. This approach is **undifferentiated marketing.** It focuses on what is common in the needs of consumers rather than on what is different. It designs a product and marketing program that appeal to the most buyers. It relies on mass distribution and mass advertising. It aims to give the product a superior image in people's minds. An example of undifferentiated marketing is the Hershey Company's marketing some years ago of only one chocolate candy bar for everyone.

Undifferentiated marketing provides cost economies. The narrow product line keeps down production, inventory, and transportation costs. The undifferentiated advertising program keeps down advertising costs. The absence of segment marketing research and planning lowers the costs of marketing research and product management.

Most modern marketers have strong doubts about this strategy. It is very difficult

FIGURE 9-5
Three alternative
market-coverage
strategies

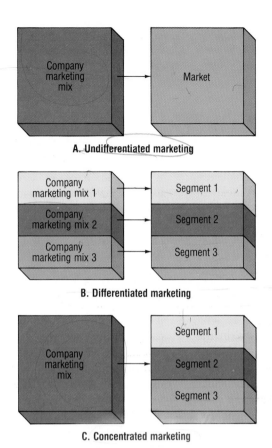

A. Undifferentiated marketing

B. Differentiated marketing

C. Concentrated marketing

to develop a product or brand that will satisfy all consumers. The firms using undifferentiated marketing typically develop an offer aimed at the largest segments in the market. When several firms do this, there is heavy competition in the largest segments and less satisfaction in the smaller ones. The result is that the larger segments may be less profitable because they attract heavy competition. Recognition of this problem has resulted in firms' being more interested in smaller segments of the market.

Differentiated Marketing

The firm may decide to target several market segments and design separate offers to each. This approach is **differentiated marketing.** General Motors tries to produce a car for every "purse, purpose, and personality." By offering product and marketing variations, it hopes for higher sales and a stronger position within each market segment. It hopes that a stronger position in several segments will strengthen consumers' overall identification of the company with the product category. And it hopes for greater repeat purchasing because the firm's offer better matches the customer's desire.

A growing number of firms have adopted differentiated marketing. A&P's segmentation strategy is a good example. A&P uses different food store formats to meet the needs of different customer segments:

> A&P's merchandising strategy attempts to provide a supermarket for every kind of shopper: stark black-and-white Futurestores, with the latest in gourmet departments and electronic services, for exclusive neighborhoods; conventional A&P's . . . for middle class markets; and full-service, warehouse-style Sav-A-Centers, where shoppers have come to expect them.[10]

SAAB FINDS A MARKET NICHE

Is there room for small fry alongside the big fish in the auto industry? Saab thinks so. And so do thousands of consumers. Using a concentrated marketing strategy, Saab has found a profitable niche in the car market.

During World War II Saab made fighter planes. After the war, the company designed a small, inexpensive, fun-to-drive car which had many of the things pilots want from airplanes—aerodynamic design, driver comfort, precise controls, and advanced safety features. The first Saab had many features that did not appear on other cars for another twenty years. Until the late 1970s, Saab was a moderately priced "Swedish Tinkertoy" with annual U.S. sales of about 10,000 cars. Saab buyers were mostly engineers, college professors, and road-rally buffs. Then in the late 1970s, Saab sought a segmentation strategy that would expand sales and profits. It had two major options—the large economy segment or the smaller luxury segment. The major U.S. and Japanese automakers were attacking the economy segment, and Saab had neither the production nor distribution system needed to compete in such a mass market. So management opted to concentrate on the luxury/sports car segment, where it would sell fewer cars but make more profit on each one.

The luxury/sports car segment is small but much less competitive than other car buying segments. And it's a segment that will explode during this decade.

It consists of upscale consumers aged 25 to 44, the fastest-growing age group. This group accounts for some 45 percent of all households. And they are the most affluent, with over 60 percent of these households consisting of two-income families.

The luxury/sport segment is particularly attractive for Saab. The company's strengths fit very well with the market's needs. The segment is small and demands performance and quality. Saab has small capacity, prides itself on the quality, and has a solid reputation for advanced engineering. Upscale buyers in the segment can afford to buy the kind of car Saab makes best.

So beginning in 1979 the company introduced its new Saab 900 Turbo line as "the most intelligent car ever built." It targeted customers who were "willing to pay more for distinctive autos with performance, luxury, styling, and pure image." It backed this position with other things buyers in this segment were looking for. Upscale buyers want creature comforts—the Saab 900 Turbo comes with air conditioning, power brakes, AM/FM stereo cassette player, full instrumentation, power steering, window defoggers, electrically heated seats, and many other features as standard equipment. Sports car buyers want performance information—in the showroom, Saab gives out a 50-page "Engineering Features" book that explains every inch of the car. Affluent buyers want service—salespeople are required to introduce every

---

Differentiated marketing typically creates more total sales than undifferentiated marketing. Procter & Gamble gets a higher total market share with ten brands of laundry detergent than it could with only one. But it also increases the costs of doing business. Modifying a product to meet different market segment requirements usually involves some R&D, engineering, or special tooling costs. It is usually more expensive to produce, say, ten units of ten different products than one hundred units of one product. Developing separate marketing plans for the separate segments requires extra marketing research, forecasting, sales analysis, promotion planning, and reseller management. And trying to reach different market segments with different advertising increases promotion costs. Thus the company must weigh increased sales against increased costs when deciding on a differentiated marketing strategy.

Some firms find that they have *oversegmented* their market and offer too many brands. They would like to manage fewer brands, or have their brands appeal to a broader customer group. Called "countersegmentation" or "broadening the base," they seek a larger volume for each brand.[11] Johnson & Johnson, for example, broadened the target market for its baby shampoo to include adults. And Beecham launched

SAAB'S INNOVATIVE TECHNOLOGY AND ENGINEERING PROWESS START AT AROUND $15,000 AND DON'T STOP UNTIL ABOUT $20 MILLION.

The idea of "shared technology" has a long history at Saab. In fact, the first Saab automobile even shared the technologists themselves, it was designed by aircraft engineers.

This explains why Saab's have always been far better known for their innovativeness than for their slavish adherence to the habits and conventions of the auto industry.

Why long before automakers saw the marketing appeal of the "aero-look," Saab engineers recognized the value of an aerodynamic body and designed the first Saab accordingly.

And why instead of resorting to the automotive world's way of increasing power, (bigger, heavier en-gines), Saab engineers were among the first to employ a turbocharger in a standard production car and were pioneers in the development of 16-valve cylinder head technology.

The litany of innovations found in every Saab, from the $15,000 Saab 900 to the $28,141* Saab 9000 Turbo, also includes significant contributions in the areas of safety and practicality. Saab was one of the earliest proponents of front-wheel drive. (In fact, Saab has never offered anything but.) Saab was also one of the first to combine a hatchback body design with a fold-down rear seat to dramat-ically increase its cargo capacity. And a leader in the development of collapsible,

energy-absorbing steering columns and dual-diagonal braking systems among other things.

And the free exchange of ideas among all the divisions of this aerospace, auto-motive, heavy vehicle and electronics group known as Saab-Scania continues to this day with work in the devel-opment of new, lighter and stronger materials and more sophisticated electronics.

But to experience this technology in a far more moving fashion, we'd sug-gest you visit your nearest Saab dealer. Where the en-tire 1988 model line (minus the supersonic Saab JA-37 Viggen, of course) awaits your inspection.

SAAB
The most intelligent cars ever built.

© 1987 by Saab-Scania of America, Inc. *The Saab 900 Series ranges from $14,985 for the 900 3-door to $29,740 for the 900 Turbo Convertible. The 9000 Series ranges from $23,337 for the 9000S to $28,141 for the 9000 Turbo. Mfg's. sugg. retail prices not including taxes, license, freight, dealer charges or options. Prices subject to change.

Concentrated marketing: Saab focuses on the luxury sports car segment.

Saab buyer to the service manager. Buyers receive mail questionnaires after delivery asking about dealer sales and service performance.

How did the new targeting strategy work? Saab appears to have hit the target. The average buyer of a new Saab is male, age 30 to 40, and well-educated (40 percent have attended graduate school). They are managers and professionals with average household incomes between $50,000 and $80,000. And they are loyal—over 75 percent intend to buy another Saab when the time comes. After the new segmentation strategy began, sales rose steadily. By 1983, the company was selling more than 25,000 Saabs annually in the United States, and demand exceeded supply (some dealers were auctioning Saabs off to the highest bidder). Saab's 42 percent increase in sales was the best in the industry.

This Saab story has a happy ending—it shows how a company with fewer resources can succeed profitably against larger competitors by concentrating on a small, high-quality segment. Saab's competitive strategy is summed up by one Saab executive as follows: "GM is in the business of selling millions of hamburgers. We're just selling a few steaks here and there."

Source: Based on information found in Bernie Whalen, "'Tiny' Saab Drives Up Profits with Market-Niche Strategy, Repositioning," *Marketing News*, March 16, 1984, Sec. 1, pp. 14–16. Used with permission of *Marketing News*, published by the American Marketing Association. Also see "SAAB Hitches Star to Yuppie Market," *Business Week*, November 19, 1984, p. 62.

its AquaFresh toothpaste to attract two benefit segments, those seeking fresh breath and those seeking cavity protection.

Concentrated Marketing

Many firms see a third possibility that is especially appealing when company resources are limited. Instead of going after a small share of a large market, the firm goes after a large share of one or a few submarkets. This approach is **concentrated marketing.** Many examples of concentrated marketing can be found. In computers, Zenith concentrates on the government microcomputer market, Cray focuses on larger, mainframe supercomputers, and Apollo targets the computer work station segment. Oshkosh Truck is the world's largest producer of airport rescue trucks and concrete mixers that unload at the front end. Recycled Paper Products concentrates on the market for alternative greeting cards. And Saab focuses on the luxury sports car market (see Marketing Highlight 9–2).

Through concentrated marketing the firm achieves a strong market position in the segments it serves, owing to its greater knowledge of the segment's needs and the special reputation it acquires. And it enjoys many operating economies because of specialization in production, distribution, and promotion. If the segment is chosen well, the firm can earn a high rate of return on its investment.[12]

At the same time, concentrated marketing involves higher than normal risks. The particular market segment can turn sour. For example, when young women suddenly stopped buying sportswear, it caused Bobbie Brooks's earnings to go deeply into the red. Or larger competitors may decide to enter the same segment. For example, California Cooler's success in the wine cooler segment attracted many large competitors, causing the original owners to sell out to a larger company with more marketing resources. For these reasons, many companies prefer to diversify in several market segments.

Choosing a Market-Coverage Strategy

Many factors need to be considered when choosing a market-coverage strategy. Which strategy is best depends on *company resources*. When the firm's resources are limited, concentrated marketing makes the most sense. The best strategy also depends on the degree of *product homogeneity*. Undifferentiated marketing is more suited for homogeneous products such as grapefruit or steel. Products that can vary in design, such as cameras and automobiles, are more suited to differentiation or concentration. The *product's stage in the life cycle* must also be considered. When a firm introduces a new product, it is practical to launch only one version, and in that case undifferentiated marketing or concentrated marketing makes the most sense. In the mature stage of the product life cycle, differentiated marketing starts making more sense. Another factor is *market homogeneity*. If buyers have the same tastes, buy the same amounts, and react the same way to marketing efforts, undifferentiated marketing is appropriate. Finally, *competitors' marketing strategies* are important. When competitors use active segmentation, undifferentiated marketing can be suicidal. Conversely, when competitors use undifferentiated marketing, a firm can gain by using differentiated or concentrated marketing.

Identifying Attractive Market Segments

Suppose the firm decides on undifferentiated or concentrated marketing. It must now identify the most attractive segments to target. The company first needs to collect data on the various market segments. The data would include current dollar sales, projected sales-growth rates, expected profit margins, strength of competition, and marketing channel needs. Often, the company will want to target segments with large current sales, a high growth rate, a high profit margin, weak competition, and simple marketing channel requirements. Usually no segments will be best in all these areas, and tradeoffs would have to be made. And the largest, fastest-growing segments are not always the most attractive ones for every company. The largest segment is not attractive unless the company has the skills and resources to serve the segment's needs effectively.

After the company assesses the characteristics and requirements of the various segments, it must ask which segments fit its business strengths best. For example, the home computer market is large and very attractive to Zenith Data Systems, but the company has little experience selling computers to consumers and lacks the retail distribution and promotion resources needed to directly challenge IBM and Apple in this segment. On the other hand, Zenith has developed special products and a separate salesforce for the government and higher education market segments. Thus the company focuses on less crowded segments in which it has the necessary business strengths to succeed. It targets the segments in which it has the greatest strategic advantage.

*M*ARKET POSITIONING

Once a company has decided which segments of the market it will enter, it must decide what "positions" it wants to occupy in those segments.

What is Market Positioning?

A **product position** is the way the product is *defined by consumers* on important attributes—the place the product occupies in consumers' minds relative to competing products. Thus Tide is positioned as an all-purpose, family detergent; Era is positioned as a concentrated liquid; Cheer is positioned as the detergent for all temperatures; Hyundai and Subaru are positioned on economy; Mercedes and Cadillac are positioned on luxury; and Porsche and BMW are positioned on performance.[13]

Consumers are overloaded with information about products and services. They cannot reevaluate products every time they make a buying decision. To simplify buying decision making, they organize products into categories—they "position" products, services, and companies in their minds. A product's position is a complex set of consumer perceptions, impressions, and feelings consumers hold for the product compared with competing products. Consumers position products with or without the help of marketers. But marketers do not want to leave their products' positions to chance. They plan positions that will give their products the greatest advantage in selected target markets, and they design marketing mixes to create the planned positions.

Positioning Strategies

The marketer can follow several positioning strategies.[14] It can position its product on specific *product attributes*—Ford Festiva advertises its low price; Saab promotes performance. Or products can be positioned on the needs they fill or the *benefits* they offer—Crest reduces cavities; Aim tastes good. Or products can be positioned according to *usage occasions*. In the summer, Gatorade can be positioned as a beverage for replacing athletes' body fluids; in the winter, it can be positioned as the drink to use when the doctor recommends drinking plenty of liquids. Another approach is to position the product for certain classes of *users*. Johnson & Johnson improved the market share for its baby shampoo from 3 to 14 percent by repositioning the product as one for adults who wash their hair often and need a gentle shampoo.

A product can be positioned directly *against a competitor*. In ads for their personal computers, Compaq and Tandy have directly compared their products with IBM personal computers. In its famous "We're number two, so we try harder" campaign, Avis successfully positioned itself against larger Hertz. A product may also be positioned *away from competitors*—7-Up became the number-three soft drink when it was positioned as the "un-cola," the fresh and thirst-quenching alternative to Coke and Pepsi. Barbasol television ads position the company's shaving cream and other products as "great toiletries for a lot less money."

Finally, the product can be positioned for different *product classes*. For example, some margarines are positioned against butter, others against cooking oils. Camay hand soap is positioned with bath oils rather than with soap. Marketers often use a combination of these positioning strategies. Thus Johnson & Johnson's Affinity shampoo is positioned as a hair conditioner for women over 40 (product class and user). Arm & Hammer baking soda has been positioned as a deodorizer for refrigerators and garbage disposals (product class and usage situation).

Choosing and Implementing a Positioning Strategy

Some firms will find it easy to choose their positioning strategy. A firm that is well-known for quality in other segments, for example, will go for this position in a new segment if there are enough buyers seeking quality. But in many cases, two or more firms will go after the same position. Then each will have to seek further

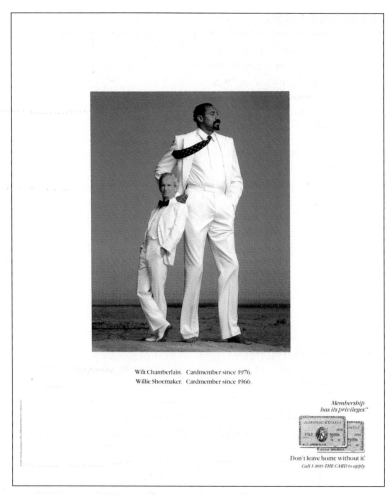

Wilt Chamberlain. Cardmember since 1976.
Willie Shoemaker. Cardmember since 1966.

*Membership
has its privileges.*

Don't leave home without it.
Call 1-800-THE CARD to apply

Positioning away from competitors: American Express positions itself as a card for special people.

differentiation, such as "high quality for a lower cost" or "high quality with more technical service." That is, each firm must build a unique bundle of competitive advantages that appeal to a substantial group within the segment.

The positioning task consists of three steps: identifying a set of possible competitive advantages upon which to build a position, selecting the right competitive advantages, and effectively communicating and delivering the chosen position to the market.

A company differentiates itself from competitors by bundling competitive advantages. It gains **competitive advantage** by offering consumers lower prices than competitors for similar products or by providing more benefits that justify higher prices.[15] Thus the company must do a better job than competitors of keeping costs and prices down, or of developing better products. The company must compare its prices and products to those of competitors and look for possible improvements. To the extent that it can do better than its competitors, it has achieved a competitive advantage.

Not every company will find an abundance of opportunities for gaining competitive advantage. Some companies will find many minor advantages that are easily copied by competitors and therefore highly perishable. The solution for these companies is to continually identify new potential advantages and introduce them one by one to keep the competitors off-balance. These companies do not expect to achieve a major permanent advantage, but rather want to discover many little ones that can be introduced over time to win market share.

Suppose a company is fortunate enough to discover several potential competitive advantages. It must now choose the ones upon which it will build its positioning strategy. Some competitive advantages can be quickly ruled out because they are too slight, too costly to develop, or too inconsistent with the company's profile. Suppose four advantages remain and the company needs a framework for selecting the one that makes the most sense to develop. Table 9-4 shows a systematic way to evaluate several potential competitive advantages and choose the right one.

In the table, the company compares its standing on four attributes—technology, cost, quality, and service—to the standing of its major competitor. Let's assume that both companies stand at 8 on technology (1 = low score, 10 = high score), which means they both have good technology. The company questions whether it can gain much by improving its technology further, especially given the high cost of new technology. The competitor has a better standing on cost (8 instead of 6), which can hurt the company if the market gets more price-sensitive. The company offers higher quality than its competitors (8 instead of 6). Finally both companies offer below-average service.

At first glance, it appears that the company should go after cost or service to improve its market appeal relative to the competitor. However, it must consider other factors. First, how important are improvements in each of these attributes to the target customers? The fourth column shows that cost and service improvements would both be highly important to customers. Next, can the company afford to make the improvements? If so, how fast can it complete them? The fifth column shows that the company could improve service quickly and affordably. But if the firm decided to do this, would the competitor be able to improve its service also? The sixth column shows that the competitor's ability to improve service is low, perhaps because the competitor doesn't believe in service or is strapped for funds. The final column then shows the appropriate actions to take on each attribute. It makes the most sense for the company to invest in improving its service. Service is important to customers; the company can afford to improve its service and do it fast; and the competitor probably can't catch up.

Once it has chosen a position, the company must take concrete steps to communicate and deliver the position to target consumers. All of the company's marketing mix efforts must support the positioning strategy. Positioning the company calls for concrete action, not just talk. Thus if the company decides to build service superiority,

TABLE 9-4 Finding Competitive Advantage

COMPETITIVE ADVANTAGE	COMPANY STANDING (1–10)	COMPETITOR STANDING (1–10)	IMPORTANCE OF IMPROVING STANDING (H-M-L)	AFFORD-ABILITY AND SPEED (H-M-L)	COMPETITOR'S ABILITY TO IMPROVE STANDING (H-M-L)	RECOMMENDED ACTION
Technology	8	8	L	L	M	Hold
Cost	6	8	H	M	M	Watch
Quality	8	6	L	L	H	Watch
Service	4	3	H	H	L	Invest

it should go about quietly hiring and training more service people, find retailers who have a good reputation for service, and develop sales and advertising messages that broadcast its service superiority.

The company's positioning decisions determine who its competitors will be. When setting its positioning strategy, the company should look at its competitive strengths and weaknesses compared to those of competitors, and select a position in which it can attain a strong competitive advantage. We will look more closely at competitive marketing strategies in Chapter 19.

■ SUMMARY

Sellers can take three approaches to a market. Mass marketing is the decision to mass-produce and mass-distribute one product and attempt to attract all kinds of buyers. Product-variety marketing is the decision to produce two or more market offers differentiated in style, features, quality, or sizes, designed to offer variety to the market and to set the seller's products apart from competitor's products. Target marketing is the decision to identify the different groups that make up a market and to develop products and marketing mixes for selected target markets. Sellers today are moving away from mass marketing and product differentiation toward target marketing because the latter is more helpful in spotting market opportunities and developing more effective products and marketing mixes.

The key steps in target marketing are market segmentation, market targeting, and market positioning. Market segmentation is the act of dividing a market into distinct groups of buyers who might merit separate products or marketing mixes. The marketer tries different variables to see which give the best segmentation opportunities. For consumer marketing, the major segmentation variables are geographic, demographic, psychographic, and behavioral. Industrial markets can be segmented by demographics, operating variables, purchasing approaches, situational factors, and buyer characteristics. The effectiveness of the

segmentation analysis depends upon finding segments that are measurable, accessible, substantial, and actionable.

Next, the seller has to target the best market segments. The first decision is how many segments to cover. The seller can ignore segment differences (undifferentiated marketing), develop different market offers for several segments (differentiated marketing), or go after one or a few market segments (concentrated marketing). Much depends on company resources, product and market homogeneity, product life-cycle stage, and competitive marketing strategies. If the company decides to enter one segment, which one should it be? Market segments can be evaluated on their objective attractiveness and on company business strengths needed to succeed in that market segment.

Once a company has decided what segments to enter, it must decide what positions to occupy in these segments. It can position its products on specific product attributes or benefits, according to usage occasion, for certain classes of users, or by product class. They can position against competitors or away from competitors. The positioning task consists of three steps: identifying a set of possible competitive advantages upon which to build a position, selecting the right competitive advantages, and effectively communicating and delivering the chosen position to the market.

■ QUESTIONS FOR DISCUSSION

1. Describe how Ford Motor Company has changed from a mass-marketing company to a target-marketing company. Can you think of other examples of companies whose marketing approaches have evolved over time?

2. What variables are used in segmenting the market for beer? Give examples.

3. If you were a manager of a mass transit company, how would you use benefit segmentation to appeal to different groups of potential riders?

4. Some industrial suppliers make above-average profits by offering service, selection, and reliability—at a premium price. How can these suppliers segment the maket to target customers who are willing to pay more for what the suppliers have to offer?

5. An article in *Advertising Age* reported that baseball fans prefer chocolate ice cream if their favorite team in the 1950s was the Dodgers, vanilla ice cream if

their team was the Yankees, and strawberry or coffee ice cream if they rooted for the Giants. Does this relationship indicate that team preference can be used as a segmentation variable in marketing ice cream?

6. Which is the *most* important characteristic of useful market segments: measurability, accessibility, substantiality, or actionability? Defend your answer.

7. Explain which of these marketers is most likely to use undifferentiated marketing, and why: (a) a retired home-economics teacher who opens a clothing store, (b) an agricultural cooperative that promotes the use of potatoes and onions, (c) a foreign manufacturer that begins exporting automobiles to the United States, and (d) a major television manufacturer that develops a large-screen, wall-hung TV for the consumer market.

8. What roles do product attributes and perceptions of attributes play in positioning a product? Can an attribute

shared by competing brands be used in a successful positioning strategy?

9. A fabric has recently been developed that has the look and feel of cotton but is very stretchable. What segment would you target with casual pants made from this fabric? How would you position these pants?

10. When the Cadillac Cimarron was introduced, Cadillac officials said they would consider the Cimarron a disaster if it sold only to traditional customers, even if they bought every car produced. The Cadillac merchandising director said, "Our salespeople will tell some buyers, 'This car isn't for you.'" Explain this strategy in terms of market segmentation, targeting, and positioning.

■ KEY TERMS

Behavior segmentation Dividing a market into groups based on their knowledge, attitude, use, or response to a product.

Competitive advantage An advantage over competitors gained by offering consumers lower prices than competitors for similar products or by providing more benefits that justify higher prices.

Concentrated marketing A market-coverage strategy in which the company goes after a large share of one or a few submarkets.

Demographic segmentation Dividing the market into groups based on demographic variables such as age, sex, family size, family life cycle, income, occupation, education, religion, race, and nationality.

Differentiated marketing A market-coverage strategy in which a company decides to target several segments and designs separate offers for each.

Geographic segmentation Dividing a market into different geographical units such as nations, states, regions, counties, cities, or neighborhoods.

Market positioning Formulating a competitive positioning for a product and a detailed marketing mix.

Market segmentation dividing a market into distinct groups of buyers who might require separate products or marketing mixes.

Market targeting Evaluating each market segment's attractiveness and selecting one or more segments to enter.

Product position The way the product is defined by consumers on important attributes—the place the product occupies in consumers' minds relative to competing products.

Psychographic segmentation Dividing a market into different groups based on social class, life style, or personality characteristics.

Undifferentiated marketing A market-coverage strategy in which a company goes after the whole market with one market offer.

■ REFERENCES

1. Thomas Moore, "Different Folks, Different Strokes," *Fortune*, September 16, 1985, p. 65; and Michael Oneal, "Attack of the Bug Killers," *Business Week*, May 16, 1988, p. 81.

2. See Jesse Snyder and Raymond Serafin, "Auto Makers Set New Ad Strategy to Reach Women," *Advertising Age*, September 23, 1985, pp. 3, 86.

3. See Pat Grey Thomas, "Marketing to the Affluent," *Advertising Age*, March 16, 1987, p. S-1.

4. Steve Lawrence, "The Green in Blue-Collar Retailing," *Fortune*, May 27, 1985, pp. 74–77.

5. Bickley Townsend, "Psychographic Glitter and Gold," *American Demographics*, November 1985, p. 22.

6. See Shirley Young, "The Dynamics of Measuring Unchange," in *Attitude Research in Transition*, Russell I. Haley, ed. (Chicago: American Marketing Association, 1972), pp. 61–82; Russell L. Ackoff and James R. Emshoff, "Advertising Research at Anheuser-Busch, Inc. (1968–74)," *Sloan Management Review*, Spring 1975, pp. 1–15; and John J. Burnett, "Psychographic and Demographic Characteristics of Blood Donors," *Journal of Consumer Research*, June 1981, pp. 62–66. For a detailed discussion of personality and buyer behavior, see Leon G. Shiffman and Leslie Lazar Kanuk, *Consumer*

Behavior, 3rd Ed. (Englewood Cliffs, NJ: Prentice Hall, 1987), Chapter 4.

7. See Laurie Freeman and Cleveland Horton, "Spree: Honda's Scooters Ride the Cutting Edge," *Advertising Age*, September 5, 1985, pp. 3, 35.

8. See Schiffman and Kanuk, *Consumer Behavior*, p. 48.

9. For more reading on benefit segmentation, see Russell I. Haley, "Benefit Segmentation: Backwards and Forwards," *Journal of Advertising Research*, February–March 1984, pp. 19–25; and Russell I. Haley, "Benefit Segmentation—20 Years Later," *Journal of Consumer Marketing*, 1 (1984), pp. 5–14.

10. Bill Saporito, "Just How Good is the Great A&P?" *Fortune*, March 16, 1987, pp. 92–93.

11. Alan J. Resnik, Peter B. B. Turney, and J. Barry Mason, "Marketers Turn to 'Countersegmentation,'" *Harvard Business Review*, September–October 1979, pp. 100–106.

12. See Stuart Gannes, "The Riches in Market Niches," *Fortune*, April 27, 1987, pp. 227–30.

13. For more reading on positioning, see Yoram Wind, "New Twists for Some Old Tricks," *The Wharton Maga-*

zine, Spring 1980, pp. 34–39; David A. Aaker and J. Gary Shansby, "Positioning Your Product," *Business Horizons*, May–June 1982, pp. 56–62; and Regis McKenna, "Playing for Position," *INC*, April 1985, pp. 92–97.

14. See Wind, "New Twists," p. 36; and Aaker and Shansby, "Positioning Your Product," pp. 57–58.

15. See Michael Porter, *Competitive Advantage* (New York: Free Press, 1985), Chapter 2.

CASE 6

QUAKER OATS COMPANY: GATORADE

The development of a focused positioning for Gatorade, and its continued refinement over time, has allowed Quaker Oats to target core users and identify secondary markets, according to Larry Dykstra, manager of marketing research, Quaker Oats Co., Chicago. Before Quaker acquired the beverage in 1983, Gatorade's previous owner had promoted it by portraying users as competitive athletes, adult men, teens, and caricatures of athletes, said Dykstra.

"When we acquired Gatorade, it was a poorly positioned brand, with a lack of consistent focus," he said. This stood in contrast with the way current users were defined. "There was no message on the uses of this product or under which circumstances and occasions it was supposed to be used."

When Quaker looked at marketing research, he said the company found that Gatorade's main users were men age 19–44, that they understood the product, had a good perception of what it did, and knew when to drink it and how to use it.

Since Gatorade had been developed and marketed primarily in the South, Dykstra said Quaker wanted to find out if there was an opportunity to market the drink in northern areas. An attitudinal piece determined that the target could be expanded geographically. "We felt, based on research, that we could take a narrow, solid positioning of the product that is consistent with southern users and market the product in the North," he said.

Gatorade was positioned for physical activity enthusiasts as a drink that would quench their thirst and replenish the minerals they had lost during exercise better than other beverages did, Dykstra said. Subsequent advertising in 1984 centered around these attributes.

In 1985, he said the company moved away from this core positioning by trying to joke about the product's competitive heritage—a strategy which failed. Those TV ads showed people in different activity situations trying to make sports jokes. A decision was made to go back to narrow positioning in 1986.

"In 1987, we have focused in on our primary target, but there have been refinements," Dykstra said. "We've tried to portray users as accomplished but not professional athletes." Although the drink is perceived as a "serious beverage," he said the ads have added a fun component by showing people enjoying it together. "We tried to show people who didn't alienate customers, but also people they could aspire to be like," Dykstra said.

An effort also was made to portray people's motivations for using the product, he said. A computer graphic that portrays thirst quenching was introduced, which Dykstra said "comes across so strong we've started to change the language."

But being well-focused and consistent in developing the product over time can create other problems, he said. "Because Gatorade is narrowly positioned in terms of users and user occasions, growth opportunities are probably limited. So how can we go about identifying new opportunities?"

The answer, Dykstra said, is to look for opportunities consistent with the product's imagery. "About two years ago, we conducted a large study that included a sample of current users and other possible targets, such as older men and mothers with young children." Quaker also looked in terms of a vertical target, such as whether it should target Gatorade toward runners or basketball players.

"We built a large enough attitudinal study so we could look at people who considered themselves basketball players separate from those who considered themselves to be aerobic athletes," he said. "In the user section, we asked people, 'The next 10 times you're in this specific situation, are you going to use Gatorade?'"

Dykstra also said Quaker felt it could target moms with active children, and found that this group constituted a large market that could be targeted separately. Additionally, the company is attempting to market the product year-round. "We found we were promoting our own seasonality, so we wanted to develop some continuity," he said.

Quaker has most recently started marketing the product to Hispanics. "We felt we could position Gatorade to them because they are a large growing segment, sports is important to them, and their populations are centered in areas where its presence is already well developed," Dykstra said. An ad has been developed for this purpose and is currently being tested.

"We made an effort to do it right and not offend this group," he said. Based on qualitative findings, the TV spot's approach is conservative and narrow, focuses on sports, and includes family members. "We showed it to several focus groups, and made sure the benefits translated." At the same time, Dykstra said, efforts were made to insure that the changes and refinements weren't going to alienate the core users and secondary targets.

1. Define the core and secondary target markets for Gatorade.

2. What did Larry Dykstra mean when he made the following statement: "When we acquired Gatorade, it was a poorly positioned brand, with a lack of consistent focus"?

3. Why did the 1985 advertising strategy fail?

4. Evaluate the pros and cons of the current multisegment targeting strategy.

5. Propose a marketing strategy for penetrating the preteen market.

Source: "Quaker Looks To Expand Market For Gatorade," *Marketing News*, January 4, 1988. Reprinted with permission.

CASE 7

RCA: VIDEO CASSETTE PLAYERS

RCA, a leader in consumer electronics and home entertainment equipment, has a leading position in the sale of video cassette recorder (VCR) hardware and prerecorded VCR tapes. The company must decide whether it should market a video cassette player (VCP) in addition to its VCR line. Several Japanese and Korean companies plan to sell VCPs in the United States for $200 or less.

The VCR is one of the electronic success stories in recent years. Nearly 20 percent of U.S. homes now have one and the number is growing rapidly. But apparently there are some potential buyers who do not want the elaborate recording equipment that comes with the standard VCR. The "play only" market consists of (1) homes with no interest in recording, (2) VCR homes where a second set is wanted for "play only," (3) the rental market retail outlets that sell and rent equipment and tapes for overnight use, and (4) the industrial market for training and related purposes.

A major problem for consumers is incompatible formats. The principal format is VHS, used by RCA. Sony's BetaMax, once the leader is currently losing ground. Now Kodak and others have brought out still another format in smaller-width tape—8mm vs. the conventional ½ inch. The new tape is an effort to develop a system with a camera, which will be better suited for home movies to be shown on a TV screen.

The one-set market consists of those who find the play-and-record machines have more functions than they need. Also included in this market are people who feel the VCR is too expensive, even though the price difference between it and the VCP may be as little as $100.

The second-set market could be huge. Fifty percent of households with color television have at least two color TV sets and VCP owners should follow the same pattern. RCA visualizes less expensive VCP units attached to TVs in bedrooms and children's rooms, in addition to the play-and-record VCR already in the house.

Rental companies constitute a natural market. Rental outlets now buy only about 5 percent of all VCRs sold, but this is a fast-growing market. If present overnight rates of $10 or less continue, a higher profit margin would result from renting the lower-cost VCP. "Eighty percent of our customers don't want the bells and whistles. They just want the playback unit," says William E. Mapes, president of National Video, Inc., a video sales and rental chain based in Portland, Oregon. The chain plans to stock Japanese play-only units selling for $200 or less.

The commercial and industrial market is dominated by laser-type videodisc players made by Magnavox and Pioneer, which are favored despite their considerably higher price because of their higher fidelity and freeze-frame features. However, there may be marginal commercial and industrial uses for a VCP that employs less sophisticated technology and offers lower-quality performance or fewer features.

RCA's SelectaVision videodisc player, which used the CED or tongue-and-groove technology, had limited acceptance in the industrial market relative to the laser-type players. In the consumer market, SelectaVision sales did not meet the company's expectations, so the product was withdrawn and production was permanently stopped after sales of 500,000 players and an investment of over $580 million. The player sold for about $400. Among the reasons given by analysts for the poor sales performance of RCA's videodisc player were its high price relative to its features and functions and the scarcity of good software. Had RCA continued producing its videodisc player, it would have had to compete with the new video cassette player (VCP).

Industry sources say that to obtain sales VCPs will probably have to be priced at least $100 below VCRs, which now sell for as little as $250. VCRs have been aggressively promoted on a price basis. Price comparisons are difficult to make, however, because of the wide range of product features and the variability in reputation and service support of manufacturer and retailers. RCA's experience with videodiscs has caused the company to be cautious about entering the VCP market. When competitors announced their VCP plans, RCA said it had no intentions to market a VCP.

One observer suggested that "in the end, it may well turn out that RCA had the right idea [play-only]—just the wrong product [videodisc]." By introducing a VCP line, RCA might cut into VCR sales.

1. Should RCA market a VCP in addition to its existing line of VCRs?

2. If so, what marketing plan do you recommend for VCPs?

Wear an original.

Charlie

REVLON

If you believe in one
great love as many people do...
then you should wear

Jontue

Wear it and be wonderful.

Jontue by REVLON

10 Designing Products: Products, Brands, Packaging, and Services

EACH year Revlon sells more than $1 billion worth of cosmetics, toiletries, and fragrances to consumers around the world. Its many successful perfume products make Revlon number one in the popular-price segment of the $3 billion fragrance market. In one sense, Revlon's perfumes are no more than careful mixtures of oils and chemicals that have nice scents. But Revlon knows that when it sells perfume, it sells much more than fragrant fluids—it sells what the fragrances will do for the women who use them.

Of course, a perfume's scent contributes to its success or failure. Fragrance marketers agree: "No smell; no sell." Most new aromas are developed by elite "perfumers" at one of 50 or so select "fragrance houses." Perfume is shipped from the fragrance houses in big, ugly oil drums—hardly the stuff of which dreams are made! A $180-an-ounce perfume may cost no more than $3 to produce, but to perfume consumers the product is much more than a few dollars worth of ingredients and a pleasing smell.

Many things beyond the ingredients and scent add to a perfume's allure. In fact, when Revlon designs a new perfume, the scent may be the last element developed. Revlon first researches women's feelings about themselves and their relationships with others. It develops and tests new perfume concepts that match women's changing values, desires, and lifestyles. When Revlon finds a promising new concept, it creates a scent to fit the concept.

Revlon's research in the early 1970s showed that women were feeling more competitive with men and that they were striving to find individual identities. For this new woman of the 1970s, Revlon created Charlie—the first of the "lifestyle" perfumes. Thousands of women adopted Charlie as a bold statement of independence, and it quickly became the world's best-selling perfume.

In the late 1970s, Revlon research showed a shift in women's attitudes—"women had made the equality point, which Charlie addressed. Now women were hungering for an expression of femininity." Revlon subtly shifted Charlie's position away from "lifestyle" and toward "femininity and romance." It also launched a perfume for the woman of the 1980s, Jontue, positioned on a theme of romance.

A perfume's name is an important product attribute. Revlon uses such names as Charlie, Fleurs de Jontue, Ciara, and Scoundrel to create images that support each perfume's positioning. Competitors offer perfumes with such names as Obsession, Poison, Animale, Opium, Joy, White Linen, Youth Dew, and Passion. The names suggest that the perfumes will do more than just make you smell better. Oscar de la Renta's Ruffles perfume *began* as a name, chosen because it created images of whimsy, youth, glamour, and femininity—all well suited to the target market of young, stylish women. A scent was later selected to go with Ruffles' name and positioning.

Revlon must also carefully package its perfumes. To consumers, the bottle and package are the most real symbol of the perfume and its image. Bottles must feel comfortable and be easy to handle, and they must display well in stores. Most importantly, they must support the perfume's concept and image.

So when a woman buys perfume, she buys much, much more than just fragrant fluids. The perfume's image, its promises, its scent, its name and package, the company that makes it, the stores that sell it— all become a part of the total perfume product. When Revlon sells perfume, it sells more than just the tangible product—it sells lifestyle, self-expression, and exclusivity; achievement, success, and status; femininity, romance, passion, and fantasy; memories, hopes, and dreams.[1]

Chapter Objectives   *After reading this chapter, you should be able to:*

1. Define product and the major classifications of consumer and industrial products.
2. Explain why companies use brands and identify the major branding decisions.
3. Describe the roles of product packaging and labeling.
4. Identify the decisions companies must make about services that will accompany their products.
5. Discuss the decisions companies make when developing product lines and mixes.

CLEARLY, perfume is more than just perfume when Revlon sells it. Revlon's success in the rough-and-tumble fragrance world comes from developing an innovative product concept. An effective product concept is the first step in marketing mix planning.

This chapter begins with the question, What is a product? We then look at ways to classify products in consumer and industrial markets and look for links between types of products and marketing strategies. Next, we see that each product involves several decisions beyond basic product design, such as branding, packaging and labeling, and the offering of various customer services. Finally, we move from decisions about individual products to decisions about building product lines and product mixes.

WHAT IS A PRODUCT?

A Kennex tennis racquet, a Supercuts haircut, a Bruce Springsteen concert, a Hawaiian vacation, a GMC truck, Head skis, and a telephone answering service are all products. We define product as follows:

A **product** is anything that can be offered to a market for attention, acquisition, use, or consumption that might satisfy a want or need. It includes physical objects, services, persons, places, organizations, and ideas.[2]

Product planners need to think about the product on three levels. The most basic level is the *core product,* which answers the question, What is the buyer really buying? Every product is really a package of problem-solving services. A woman buying lipstick buys more than lip color. Charles Revson of Revlon, saw this early: "In the factory, we make cosmetics; in the store, we sell hope." Theodore Levitt pointed out that buyers "do not buy quarter-inch drills; they buy quarter-inch holes." And supersalesman Elmer Wheeler would say, "Don't sell the steak—sell the sizzle." Marketers must uncover the needs hiding under every product and *sell benefits,* not *features*. The core product stands at the center of the total product, as illustrated in Figure 10-1.

The product planner has to turn the core product into *a tangible product.* Perfume, computers, and political candidates are all tangible products. Tangible products may have as many as five characteristics: *features, styling*, a *brand name, packaging*, and a *quality level*.

Finally, the product planner may offer additional services and benefits that make up an *augmented product*. IBM's success is partly a result of its skillful augmentation of its actual product, the computer. While its competitors were busy selling computer features to buyers, IBM saw that customers wanted solutions, not hardware. Customers

The Sony Handycam Pro. So advanced, it even freezes water.

What you see here is something you normally don't see. Something that usually goes by in the blink of an eye. But something that's not too quick for the Sony Handycam Pro™ Video 8® camcorder.

The Sony Handycam™ is designed to capture whatever crosses your path. It comes with a high-speed shutter that goes from 1/60 of a second all the way up to 1/2000 with a succession of steps in between. Add to this its noiseless frame-by-frame and slow motion advance and not only can you catch everything but you can play it back with amazing accuracy. Whether it's your daughter chasing her cat or the cat leaping in the air.

Even in light as low as 5 lux, the Sony CCD image sensor for sharper resolution and low-light sensitivity lets you record each scene with beautifully balanced color.

When you put yourself behind the Handycam, you'll realize its lightweight construction gives you incredible flexibility no matter what you're shooting. But its size is very deceiving. Because the Handycam is filled with features you'd expect in camcorders twice its size. Like a Flying Erase™ head, which gives you smooth, noise-free transitions between scenes. And an advanced High Fidelity sound system that picks up even the slightest purr.

But, of course, there are those times when even the Handycam Pro isn't enough. Because, unfortunately, while we usually catch all of the action, we weren't able to catch the vase.

The Sony Handycam Pro. It's everything you want to remember.™

SONY
THE ONE AND ONLY.

Core, tangible, and augmented product: consumers perceive this Sony Camcorder as a complex bundle of tangible and intangible features and services that deliver a core benefit—a convenient, high-quality way to capture important moments.

FIGURE 10-1
Three levels of product

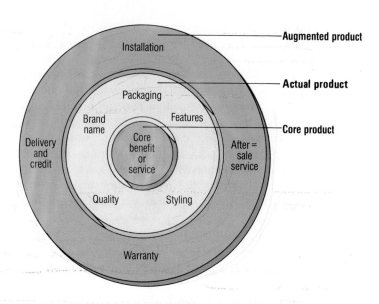

wanted instruction, canned software programs, programming services, quick repairs, and guarantees. IBM sold a system, not just a computer.

Product augmentation leads the marketer to look at the buyer's total consumption system. In this way, the marketer will find many ways to augment its offer and make it more competitive. According to Levitt:

> The *new* competition is not between what companies produce in their factories, but between what they add to their factory output in the form of packaging, services, advertising, customer advice, financing, delivery arrangements, warehousing, and other things that people value.[3]

Thus a product is more than a simple set of tangible features. In fact, some products (a haircut or a doctor's exam) have no tangible features. Consumers see products as complex bundles of benefits that satisfy their needs. When developing products, marketers must first identify the core consumer needs the product will satisfy. They must then design the tangible product and find ways to augment the product to create the bundle of benefits that will best satisfy consumers.

PRODUCT CLASSIFICATIONS

In seeking marketing strategies for individual products, marketers have developed several product classification schemes based on product characteristics.

Durable Goods, Nondurable Goods, and Services

Products can be classified into three groups according to their durability or tangibility.[4]

Nondurable goods are tangible goods normally consumed in one or a few uses. Examples include beer, soap, and salt. Since these goods are consumed fast and purchased often, the marketer wants to make them available in many locations, charge only a small markup, and advertise heavily to induce trial and build preference.

Durable goods are tangible goods that normally survive many uses. Examples include refrigerators, machine tools, and clothing. Durable products normally need more personal selling and service, command a higher margin, and require more seller guarantees.

Services are activities, benefits, or satisfactions that are offered for sale. Examples include haircuts and repairs. Services are intangible, inseparable, variable, and perishable. As a result, they normally require more quality control, supplier credibility, and adaptability. (Because of the growing importance of services in our society, we will look at them more closely in Chapter 22.)

Consumer Goods Classification

Consumer goods are those bought by final consumers for personal consumption. Marketers usually classify these goods based on *consumer shopping habits*. We can distinguish among convenience, shopping, specialty, and unsought goods (see Figure 10-2).[5]

Convenience goods are consumer goods that the customer usually buys frequently, immediately, and with the minimum of comparison and buying effort. Examples include tobacco products, soap, and newspapers.

Convenience goods can be further divided into staples, impulse goods, and emergency goods. *Staples* are goods that consumers buy on a regular basis, such as Heinz ketchup, Crest toothpaste, or Ritz crackers. *Impulse goods* are purchased without any planning or search effort. These goods are normally available in many places because consumers seldom look for them. Thus candy bars and magazines are placed next to checkout counters because shoppers may not have thought of buying them. *Emergency goods* are purchased when a need is urgent—umbrellas during a rainstorm, boots and shovels during the first winter snowstorm. Manufacturers of emergency goods will place them in many outlets to avoid losing the sale when the customer needs these goods.

Shopping goods are consumer goods that the customer, in the process of selection and purchase, usually compares on such bases as suitability, quality, price, and style. Examples include furniture, clothing, used cars, and major appliances.

Shopping goods can be divided into *homogeneous* and *heterogeneous* goods. The buyer sees homogeneous shopping goods as being similar in quality but different enough in price to justify shopping comparisons. The seller has to "talk price" to the buyer. But in shopping for clothing, furniture, and more heterogeneous goods, product features are often more important to the consumer than the price. If the buyer wants a new suit, the cut, fit, and look are likely to be more important than small price differences. The seller of heterogeneous shopping goods must therefore carry a wide assortment to satisfy individual tastes and must have well-trained salespeople to give information and advice to customers.

Specialty goods are consumer goods with unique characteristics or brand identification for which a significant group of buyers is willing to make a special purchase effort. Examples include specific brands and types of fancy goods, cars, stereo components, photographic equipment, and men's suits.

A Mercedes, for example, is a specialty good because buyers are willing to travel a great distance to buy one. Buyers do not compare specialty goods. They only invest time to reach the dealers carrying the wanted products. The dealers do not need convenient locations, but they must let buyers know their locations.

Unsought goods are consumer goods that the consumer does not know about or knows about but does not normally think of buying. New products such as smoke

FIGURE 10-2
Classification of consumer goods

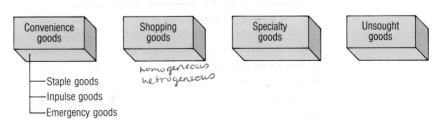

Types of consumer products: convenience, shopping, and specialty goods.

detectors and compact disc players are unsought goods until the consumer is made aware of them through advertising. The classic examples of known but unsought goods are life insurance and encyclopedias.

By their very nature, unsought goods require a lot of advertising, personal selling, and other marketing effort. Some of the most advanced personal selling methods have developed out of the challenge of selling unsought goods.

Industrial Goods Classification

Industrial goods are those bought by individuals and organizations for further processing or for use in conducting a business. Thus the distinction between a consumer good and an industrial good is based on the purpose for which the product is purchased. If a consumer buys a new Snapper lawnmower for use around the home, the lawnmower is a consumer good. If the same consumer buys the same Snapper lawnmower for use in a landscaping business, the lawnmower is an industrial good.

Industrial goods can be classified in terms of how they enter the production process and their cost. There are three groups: materials and parts, capital items, and supplies and services (see Figure 10-3).

Materials and parts are industrial goods that enter the manufacturer's product completely. They fall into two classes: raw materials and manufactured materials and parts.

Raw materials include farm products (wheat, cotton, livestock, fruits and vegetables) and natural products (fish, lumber, crude petroleum, iron ore). Each is marketed somewhat differently. Farm products are supplied by many small producers who turn them over to marketing intermediaries who process and sell them. They are rarely advertised and promoted, but there are some exceptions. From time to time, grower groups will launch campaigns to promote their products—such as potatoes, raisins, oranges, or milk. And some producers even brand their products—as do Sunkist oranges and Chiquita bananas.

Natural products are highly limited in supply. They usually have great bulk and low unit value and require lots of transportation to move them from producer to user. There are fewer and larger producers, who tend to market them directly to industrial users. Because the users depend on these materials, long-term supply contracts are common. The uniformity of natural materials limits demand-creation activity. Price and delivery are the major factors affecting the selection of suppliers.

Manufactured materials and parts include component materials (iron, yarn, cement, wires) and component parts (small motors, tires, castings). Component materials are usually processed further—for example, pig iron is made into steel, and yarn is woven into cloth. The uniform nature of component materials usually means that price and supplier reliability are the most important purchase factors. Component parts enter the finished product completely with no further change in form, as when small motors are put into vacuum cleaners and tires are added on automobiles. Most manufactured materials and parts are sold directly to industrial users. Price and service are the major marketing factors, and branding and advertising tend to be less important than price and service.

Capital items are industrial goods that enter the finished product in part. They include two groups: installations and accessory equipment.

Installations consist of buildings (factories, offices) and fixed equipment (generators, drill presses, computers, elevators). Installations are major purchases. They are usually bought directly from the producer after a long decision period. The producers use top-notch salesforces, which often include sales engineers. The producers have to be willing to design to specification and to supply postsale services. They use advertising, but much less than personal selling.

Accessory equipment includes portable factory equipment and tools (hand tools, lift trucks) and office equipment (typewriters, desks). These products do not become part of the finished product. They simply aid in the production process. They have a shorter life than installations, but a longer life than operating supplies. Most accessory equipment sellers use middlemen because the market is spread out geographically, the buyers are numerous, and the orders are small. Quality, features, price, and service are major factors supplier selection. The salesforce tends to be more important than advertising, although advertising can be used effectively.

Supplies and services are industrial goods that do not enter the finished product at all. *Supplies* include operating supplies (lubricants, coal, typing paper, pencils) and maintenance and repair items (paint, nails, brooms). Supplies are the

FIGURE 10-3
Classification of
industrial goods

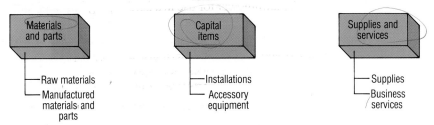

convenience goods of the industrial field because they are usually purchased with a minimum effort or comparison. They are normally marketed through resellers because of the low unit value of the goods and the great number of customers spread out around the country. Price and service are important factors because suppliers are similar and brand preference is not high.

Business services include maintenance and repair services (window cleaning, typewriter repair) and business advisory services (legal, management consulting, advertising). These services are usually supplied under contract. Maintenance services are often provided by small producers, and repair services are often available from the manufacturers of the original equipment. Business advisory services are normally new-task buying situations, and the industrial buyer will choose the supplier on the basis of the supplier's reputation and personnel.

Thus we see that a product's characteristics will have a major affect on marketing strategy. At the same time, marketing strategy will also depend on such factors as the product's stage in the life cycle, the number of competitors, the degree of market segmentation, and the condition of the economy.

BRAND DECISIONS

Consumers view a brand as an important part of the product, and branding can add value to the product. For example, most consumers would perceive a bottle of Chanel No. 5 as a high-quality, expensive perfume. But the same perfume in an unmarked bottle would be viewed as lower in quality even though the fragrance is identical. Thus branding decisions are an important part of product strategy.

First, we should become familiar with the language of branding.[6] A **brand** is a name, term, sign, symbol, or design, or a combination of them, intended to identify the goods or services of one seller or group of sellers and to differentiate them from those of competitors. A **brand name** is that part of a brand that can be vocalized— is utterable. Examples are Avon, Chevrolet, Tide, Disneyland, American Express, UCLA. A **brand mark** is that part of a brand which can be recognized but is not utterable, such as a symbol, design, or distinctive coloring or lettering. Examples are the Pillsbury doughboy, the Metro-Goldwyn-Mayer lion, and the distinctive red K we see on a Kodak film box. A **trademark** is a brand or part of a brand that is given legal protection—it protects the seller's exclusive rights to use the brand name or brand mark. Finally, a **copyright** is the exclusive legal right to reproduce, publish, and sell the matter and form of a literary, musical, or artistic work.

Branding poses difficult decisions to the marketer. The key decisions are shown in Figure 10-4 and discussed below.

Branding Decision
The company must first decide whether it should put a brand name on its product. Historically, most products went unbranded. Producers and middlemen sold their goods directly out of barrels, bins, and cases without supplier identification. Branding's real growth occurred after the Civil War with the growth of national firms and national advertising media. Some of the early brands still survive, such as Borden's Condensed Milk, Quaker Oats, Vaseline, and Ivory Soap.

Branding has grown so strong that today almost everything is branded. Salt is packaged in branded containers, common nuts and bolts are packaged with a distributor's label, and automobile parts—spark plugs, tires, filters—bear brand names that differ from those of the automakers. Even fruits and vegetables are branded—Sunkist oranges, Dole pineapples, and Chiquita bananas command profit margins 10 percent to 60 percent higher than unbranded produce. Campbell is even branding mushrooms.

Campbell . . . has found that consumers like produce with a brand on it and are willing to pay up for it. Campbell's Farm Fresh mushrooms, introduced six years ago, contributed only $65 million to Campbell's 1984 revenues. . . . But the company anticipates that its harvest of mushrooms and other fresh vegetables could ripen into a $1-billion-a-year business by the early 1990s. It has started to test-market premium-priced, branded tomatoes as well as nine vegetable and fruit salads, such as a broccoli and cauliflower mix.[7]

In the late 1970s, there was a return to "no branding" of certain consumer goods. These "generics" are plainly packaged with no manufacturer identification (see Marketing Highlight 10–1). The intent of generics is to bring down the cost to the consumer by saving on packaging and advertising. Though the popularity of generics peaked in the early 1980s, the issue of branding versus no branding is very much alive today.

This issue raises some questions: Why have branding in the first place? Who benefits? How do they benefit? At what cost? Branding helps buyers in many ways. Brand names tell the buyer something about product quality. Buyers who always buy the same brand know that they will get the same quality each time they buy. Brand names also increase the shopper's efficiency. Imagine buyers going into a supermarket and finding thousands of unlabeled products. They would have to touch,

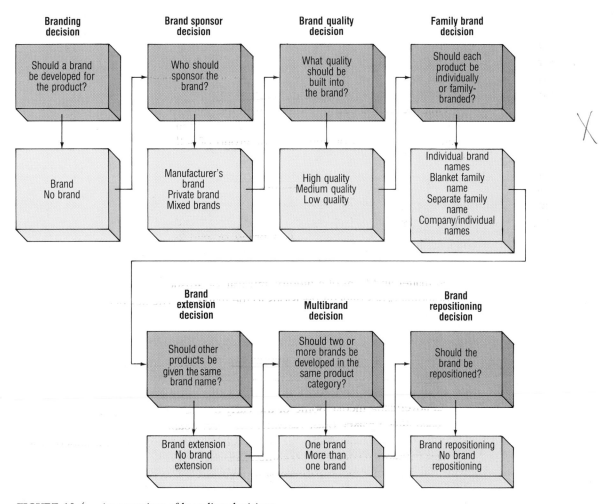

FIGURE 10-4   An overview of branding decisions

GENERICS: THE GROWTH AND DECLINE OF "NO-BRAND, NO-FRILLS" PRODUCTS

In 1978 Jewel Food Stores shocked the grocery world by devoting an entire aisle of valuable shelf space to an assortment of low-priced, no-name products bearing only the black-stenciled labels: TOWELS, SUGAR, CAT FOOD. The age of "generic" products had begun. Generics are unbranded, plainly packaged, less expensive versions of common products such as spaghetti, paper towels, and canned peaches. They offer prices as much as 40 percent lower than national brands. The lower price is made possible by lower-quality ingredients, lower-cost packaging, and lower advertising costs.

Generics took brand-name manufacturers by surprise. By 1982 nearly 80 percent of all supermarkets were selling generics, and consumers could buy no-brand products in three of every four product categories. Fueled by inflation and recession, in just four years generics captured a 2.4 percent share of the grocery business and $2.8 billion in annual sales.

The price savings of generics appeal strongly to consumers, but product quality remains an important factor in consumers' buying decisions. Generics sold better in product areas where consumers care less about quality or see little quality difference between generics and national brands. Areas such as

paper products, frozen foods, peanut butter, canned vegetables, plastic bags, disposable diapers, and dog food were hardest hit by generics. Generics had less success in such areas as health and beauty aids, where consumers were less willing to trade quality for price.

Though generics are probably here to stay, it appears that their popularity peaked in 1982. Since then, the market share for generics has dropped to 1.5 percent of total grocery volume or $1.8 billion in annual sales. This decline resulted partly from an improved economy—prices have stablized and consumers now have more income than they did when generics exploded in the late 1970s and early 1980s. The decline has also resulted from better marketing strategies by brand-name manufacturers. These marketers responded by emphasizing brand image and quality. For example, when threatened by generic pet foods, Ralston-Purina increased its quality rather than reducing its price and targeted pet owners who identified strongly with their pets and cared most about quality. Kraft met the generic threat with advertising showing taste tests in which children preferred the taste of Kraft macaroni and cheese to that of the generic brand.

Another strategy is to cut costs and pass the

taste, and smell many of the products to be sure of their quality before buying. Finally, brand names help call consumers' attention to new products that might benefit them. Brands become the basis upon which a whole story can be built about the new product's special qualities.

Branding also gives the seller several advantages. The brand name makes it easier for the seller to process orders and track down problems. Thus Anheuser-Busch receives an order for a hundred cases of Michelob beer instead of an order for "some of your better beer." The seller's brand name and trademark provide legal protection of unique product features, which would otherwise be copied by competitors. Branding lets the seller attract a loyal and profitable set of customers. Branding helps the seller segment markets—P&G can offer ten detergent brands, not just one general product for all consumers.

Branding also benefits society as a whole. Those favoring branding suggest that branding leads to higher and more consistent product quality. Branding also increases innovation in society by giving producers an incentive to look for new features that can be protected against imitating competitors. Thus branding results in more product variety and choice for consumers. Finally, branding increases shopper efficiency, since it provides much more information about products and where to find them. While branding can be overdone in some cases, it clearly adds value to consumers and society.

savings along to consumers as lower prices and greater values. Or the brand-name manufacturer can introduce lower-quality, lower-priced products that compete head on with generic products. Union Carbide, for example, produced generic garbage bags to compete with its own Glad line. Procter & Gamble introduced its line of Banner paper products. Though this line offered less quality than other P&G brands, it offered greater quality than generics at a competitive price.

The brand-name marketers must continue to convince consumers that their product's higher quality is worth the extra cost. Branded products that offer a large quality difference will not be hurt much by generics. Those most threatened are weak national brands and lower-price store brands that offer little additional quality. Why pay 20 to 40 percent more for a branded item, when its quality is not much different from that of its generic cousin?

Generics peaked in popularity in the early 1980s, but they are probably here to stay.

Sources: See Julie Franz, "Ten Years May Be Generic Lifetime," *Advertising Age*, March 23, 1987, p. 76; Amy Dunkin, "No-Frills Products: 'An Idea Whose Time Has Gone'," *Business Week*, June 17, 1985, pp. 64–65; and Brian F. Harris and Roger A. Strang, "Marketing in an Age of Generics," *Journal of Marketing*, Fall 1985, pp. 70–81.

Brand Sponsor Decision

In deciding to brand a product, the manufacturer has three sponsorship options. The product may be launched as a *manufacturer's brand* (also called a national brand). Or the manufacturer may sell the product to middlemen who put on a *private brand* (also called middleman brand, distributor brand, or dealer brand). Or the manufacturer may sell *some output under its own brand names and some under private labels*. Kellogg's and IBM sell almost all their output under their own manufacturer's brand names. BASF Wyandotte, the world's second-largest antifreeze maker, sells its Alugard antifreeze under about 80 private brands, including K mart, True Value, Pathmark, and Rite Aid. Whirlpool sells products both under its own name and under distributor's names.

Manufacturers' brands have dominated the American scene. Consider such well-known brands as Campbell's soup and Heinz ketchup. While most manufacturers create their own brand names, some of them "rent" well-known brand names by paying a royalty for the use of the name (see Marketing Highlight 10–2). In recent times, however, most large retailers and wholesalers have developed their own brands. The private-label tires of Sears and J.C. Penney are as well known today as the manufacturers' brands of Goodyear and Firestone. Sears has created several names—Diehard batteries, Craftsman tools, Kenmore appliances—that buyers look for and demand. An increasing number of department stores, supermarkets, service stations, clothiers, drugstores, and appliance dealers are launching private labels.

LICENSING BRAND NAMES FOR ROYALTIES

Manufacturers or retailers may take years and spend millions to develop consumer preference for their brands. An alternative is to "rent" names that already hold magic for consumers. Names or symbols previously created by other manufacturers, the names of well-known celebrities, characters introduced in popular movies and books—for a fee, any of these can provide a manufacturer's product with an instant and proven brand name.

Name and character licensing has become a big business in recent years. Retail sales of licensed products jumped from $4 billion in 1977 to over $54 billion in 1987, and experts predict sales of $75 billion by 1990.

Apparel and accessories sellers are the largest users, accounting for about 35 percent of all licensing. Producers and retailers pay sizable royalties to adorn their products with the names of such fashion innova-

tors as Bill Blass, Calvin Klein, Pierre Cardin, Gucci, and Halston, who license their names or initials for everything from blouses to ties and linens to luggage. In recent years, designer labels have become so common that many retailers are discarding them in favor of their own store brands in order to regain exclusivity, pricing freedom, and higher margins. Even less fashionable names can bring astounding success. Coca-Cola clothes by Murjani rang up $100 million in retail sales in just two years. Now other consumer products companies have jumped into corporate fashion licensing—Hershey, Jell-O, Burger King, McDonald's, and others.

Sellers of children's toys, games, food, and other products also make extensive use of name and character licensing. The list of characters attached to children's clothing, toys, school supplies, linens, dolls, lunch boxes, cereals, and other items is almost end-

In the fashion industry, though national brands still dominate, the use of private labels has increased dramatically in recent years. Such manufacturers as Ralph Lauren, Coach, Burberry, and Benetton have opened their own stores that sell only their own labels. Traditional retailers have responded with more private-label goods. For

Familiar brands provide consumer information, recognition, and confidence.

less—from such classics as Disney, Peanuts, Barbie, and Flintstones characters to Cabbage Patch, the Care Bears, and Masters of the Universe; from the venerable Raggedy Ann and Andy to the California Raisin Advisory Board's dancing raisins.

The newest form of licensing is brand-extension licensing—renting a brand name made famous in one category and using it in a related category. Some currently successful examples include Astroturf sport shoes, Louisville Slugger baseball uniforms, Old Spice shaving mugs and razors, Coppertone sunglasses, and Winnebago camping equipment.

Licensed names or characters can add immediate distinction and familiarity to a new product and can set it apart from competitor's products. Customers debating between two similar products will most likely reach for the one with a familiar name on it. In fact, consumers—especially children and their par-

ents—often seek out products that carry their favorite names or characters.

Almost everyone is getting into the licensing act these days, even Harley-Davidson, the motorcycle maker. Over the past 80 years, the Harley-Davidson name has developed a distinct image—some people even tattoo it on their bodies. And Harley-Davidson is now licensing its name for consumer products. One toy manufacturer now markets the Harley-Davidson Big Wheel tricycle, and Harley-Davidson has authorized other products that meet appropriate standards of quality and taste—products ranging from wine coolers, to chocolates, to cologne.

Sources: See Joanne Y. Cleaver, "Licensing: Starring on Marketing Team," *Advertising Age*, June 6, 1985, pp. 15–16; Teresa Carson and Amy Dunkin, "What's in a Name? Millions If It's Leased," *Business Week*, April 8, 1985, pp. 97–98; Patricia Winters and Sara E. Stern, "Burger Warfare Spills Into Clothing for Kids," *Advertising Age*, April 6, 1987; and Lori Kessler, "Licensing: Extensions Leave Brand in New Areas," *Advertising Age*, June 1, 1987, pp. S1–S2.

example, Macy's now has more than 50 in-house labels, and in some categories its private labels account for up to 50 percent of sales. The Limited's private labels—including Forenza and Outback Red—represent 70 percent of the chain's sales.[8]

Private brands are hard to establish and costly to stock and promote. Yet middlemen develop private brands because they can be profitable. Middlemen can often locate manufacturers with excess capacity who will produce the private label at a low cost, resulting in a higher profit margin. Private brands also give middlemen exclusive products that consumers cannot buy from competitors, resulting in greater store traffic and loyalty. For example, if K mart promotes Canon cameras, other stores that sell Canon products will also benefit. Further, if K mart drops the Canon brand, it loses the benefit of its previous promotion for Canon. But if K mart promotes its private brand of Focal cameras, K mart alone benefits from the promotion. And consumer loyalty to the Focal brand becomes loyalty to K mart.

The competition between manufacturers' and middlemen's brands is called the *battle of the brands*. In this battle, middlemen have many advantages. The retailers control scarce shelf space—many manufacturers, especially the newer and smaller ones, cannot get the shelf space needed to introduce products under their own name. Middlemen give better display space to their own brands and make sure they are better stocked. Middlemen's brands are often priced lower than comparable manufacturers' brands, thus appealing to budget-conscious shoppers. And most shoppers know that the private-label products are often made by one of the larger manufacturers anyway. Thus, the dominance of manufacturers' brands has weakened somewhat. Some marketers predict that middlemen's brands will eventually knock out all but the strongest manufacturers' brands.

Manufacturers of national brands get very frustrated. They spend a lot on consumer advertising and promotion to build strong brand preference. Their prices have to be somewhat higher to cover this promotion. At the same time, the large retailers put considerable pressure on them to spend more of their promotional money on trade allowances and deals if they want adequate shelf space. Once manufacturers start giving in, they have less to spend on consumer promotion, and their brand leadership starts slipping. This is the national brand manufacturers' dilemma.[9]

Brand Quality Decision

In developing a brand, the manufacturer has to choose a quality level that will support the brand's position in the target market. Quality is one of the marketer's major positioning tools. Quality stands for the ability of the brand to perform its functions. Quality includes the product's overall durability, reliability, precision, ease of operation and repair, and other valued attributes. Some of these attributes can be measured objectively, but from a marketing point of view, quality should be measured in terms of buyers' perceptions.

To some companies, improving quality means using better quality control to reduce defects that annoy consumers. But strategic quality management means more than this. It means gaining an edge over competitors by offering products that better serve consumers' needs and preferences for quality. As one analyst suggests, "Quality is not simply a problem to be solved; it is a competitive opportunity."[10]

The theme of quality is now attracting stronger interest among consumers and companies. A recent study of 45 fast-growing and profitable companies showed that most of them compete by marketing products that provide more value to consumers rather than ones that cost less.[11] American consumers have been impressed with the product quality found in Japanese automobiles and electronics and in European automobiles, clothing, and food. Many consumers are favoring apparel that lasts and stays in style longer, instead of trendy clothes. They are more interested in fresh and nutritious foods, gourmet items, and cheeses and less interested in soft drinks, sweets, and TV dinners. A number of companies are catering to this growing interest in quality, but much more can be done.

Family Brand Decision

Manufacturers who brand their products face several further choices. There are at least four brand-name strategies:

1. *Individual brand names.* This policy is followed by Procter & Gamble (Tide, Bold, Dash, Cheer, Gain, Oxydol, Solo) and General Mills (Bisquick, Gold Medal, Betty Crocker, Nature Valley, Yoplait).
2. *A blanket family name for all products.* This policy is followed by Heinz and Black & Decker.
3. *Separate family names for all products.* This policy is followed by Sears (Kenmore for appliances, Craftsman for tools, and Homart for major home installations).
4. *Company trade name combined with individual product names.* This policy is followed by Kellogg's (Kellogg's Rice Krispies and Kellogg's Raisin Bran).

What are the advantages of an individual brand-names strategy? A major advantage is that the company does not tie its reputation to the product's acceptance. If the product fails, it does not hurt the company's name.

Using a blanket family name for all products also has some advantages. The cost of introducing the product will be less, because there is no need for heavy advertising to create brand recognition and preference. Furthermore, sales will be strong if the manufacturer's name is good. For example, new soups introduced under the Campbell brand name get instant recognition.

When a company produces very different products, it may not be best to use one blanket family name. Swift & Company uses separate family names for its hams

(Premium) and its fertilizers (Vigoro). Companies will often invent different family brand names for different quality lines within the same product class.

Finally, some manufacturers want to use their company name along with an individual brand name for each product. The company name adds the firm's reputation to the product, while the individual name sets it apart from other company products. Thus *Quaker Oats* in Quaker Oats Cap'n Crunch taps the company's reputation for breakfast cereal and *Cap'n Crunch* sets apart and dramatizes the product.

Brand Extension Decision

A brand extension strategy is any effort to use a successful brand name to launch new or modified products. After Quaker Oats' success with Cap'n Crunch cereal, it used the brand name and cartoon character to launch a line of ice-cream bars, T-shirts, and other products. P&G put its Ivory name on dishwashing detergent, liquid hand soap, and shampoo with excellent results, and it used the strength of the Tide name to launch unscented and liquid laundry detergents. Brand extension saves the manufacturer the high cost of promoting new names and creates instant brand recognition of the new product. At the same time, if the new product fails, it may hurt consumer attitudes toward the other products carrying the same brand name.[12]

Multibrand Decision

In a multibrand strategy, the seller develops two or more brands in the same product category. This marketing practice was pioneered by P&G when it introduced Cheer as a competitor for its already successful Tide. Although Tide's sales dropped slightly, the combined sales of Cheer and Tide were higher. As we have seen, P&G now produces close to a dozen detergent brands.

Manufacturers use multibrand strategies for several reasons. First, they can gain more shelf space, thus increasing the retailer's dependence on their brands. Second, few consumers are so loyal to a brand that they will not try another. The only way to capture the "brand switchers" is to offer several brands. Third, creating new brands develops healthy competition within the manufacturer's organization. Managers of different General Motors brands, for instance, compete to outperform each other. Fourth, a multibrand strategy positions brands on different benefits and appeals, and each brand can attract a separate following.

Companies using a multibrand strategy run the risk of spreading their resources over many marginally profitable brands instead of building a few highly profitable ones. These companies should weed out their weaker brands and carefully screen new brands. Ideally, a company's new brands should take business from competitors' brands, not cannibalize the company's current brands. Or at least the combined profits from the old and new brands should be larger even if some cannibalization occurs.[13]

Brand Repositioning Decision

However well a brand is initially positioned in a market, the company may have to reposition it later. A competitor may launch a brand next to the company's brand and cut into its market share. Or customer wants may shift, leaving the company's brand with less demand. Marketers should consider repositioning existing brands before introducing new ones. In this way they can build on existing brand recognition and consumer loyalty.

Repositioning may require changing both the product and its image. P&G repositioned Bold detergent by adding a fabric-softening ingredient. Arrow added a new line of casual shirts before trying to change its image. Or a brand can be repositioned by changing only the product's image. Ivory Soap was repositioned without product

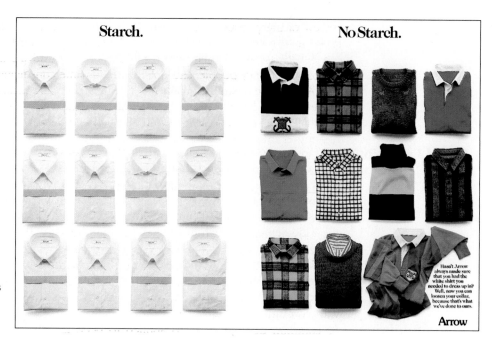

Starch.   **No Starch.**

Hasn't Arrow always made sure that you had the white shirt you needed to dress up in? Well, now you can loosen your collar, because that's what we've done to ours.

Arrow

Product repositioning: long known for its dress shirts, Arrow repositioned by "loosening its collar."

change from a "baby soap" to an "all natural soap" for adults who want healthy-looking skin. Mars launched an advertising offensive to reposition its candy.

> Mars's latest offensive is . . . aimed at convincing consumers that candy is a 'sweet snack,' not fattening, tooth-rotting, pimple-producing junk food. The campaign reached its peak when Mars paid $5 million to have Snickers and M&M's named "the official snack food of the 1984 Olympic Games," and commercials followed in which athletes chomped candy bars as an energy-producing snack. Mars wanted shoppers to think of candy as an alternative to potato chips, pretzels, and cookies—not just as a treat, a reward, or a sin."[14]

Similarly, Kraft repositioned Velveeta from a "cooking cheese" to a "good tasting, natural, and nutritious" snack cheese. The product remained unchanged, but Kraft used new advertising appeals to change consumer perceptions of Velveeta. When repositioning a brand, the marketer must be careful not to drop or confuse current loyal users. When shifting Velveeta's position, Kraft made certain that the product's new position was compatible with its old one. Thus it kept loyal customers while attracting new users.[15]

Selecting a Brand Name

A brand name should be carefully chosen. A good brand name:

> . . . can save millions of dollars over the product's life because it carries its own meaning, describes the product's advantages, is instantly recognized and serves to differentiate the product . . . often millions of dollars are spent to develop a product and to see it just through its first year of public life. That is a lot of cash to bet on haphazard brand name development and vest-pocket testing.[16]

Most large marketing companies have developed a formal brand-name selection process. Finding the best brand name is a difficult task. It begins with a careful

review of the product and its benefits, the target market, and proposed marketing strategies. The company then screens hundreds of potential brand names and selects the best one based on consumer reactions and the advice of company marketing people, ad agency people, and outside brand-name consultants.

Among the desirable qualities for a brand name are these: (1) It should suggest something about the product's benefits and qualities. Examples: Beautyrest, Craftsman, Sunkist, Spic and Span, Zest. (2) It should be easy to pronounce, recognize, and remember. Short names help. Examples: Tide, Crest, Puffs. But longer ones are sometimes effective. Examples: "Gee, Your Hair Smells Terrific" Shampoo, Better Business Bureau. (3) It should be distinctive. Examples: Mustang, Kodak, Exxon. (4) It should translate easily into foreign languages. Before spending $100 million to change its name to Exxon, Standard Oil of New Jersey tested Exxon, Enco, and other names in 54 languages in more than 150 foreign markets. It found that the name Enco referred to a stalled engine when pronounced in Japan.[17] (5) It should be capable of registration and legal protection. A name cannot be registered if it infringes on existing brand names. And brand names that are merely descriptive or suggestive may be unprotectable. For example, the Miller Brewing Company registered the name Lite for its low-calorie beer and invested millions to establish the name with consumers. But the courts later ruled that the terms *lite* and *light* are generic or common descriptive terms applied to beer, and that Miller could not use the Lite name exclusively.[18]

Once chosen, the brand name must be protected. Many firms try to build a brand name that will eventually become identified with the product category. Such brand names as Frigidaire, Kleenex, Levi's, Jello, Scotch Tape, Xerox, and Fiberglas have succeeded in this way. However, their very success may threaten the company's rights to the name. Cellophane, aspirin, nylon, kerosene, escalator, and shredded wheat are now names that any seller can use.[19]

PACKAGING DECISIONS

Many products offered to the market have to be packaged. Some marketers have called packaging a fifth *P*, along with price, product, place, and promotion. Most marketers, however, treat packaging as an element of product strategy.

Packaging is the activities of designing and producing the container or wrapper for a product. The container or wrapper is called the package. The package may include up to three levels of material. The *primary package* is the product's immediate container. The bottle holding Old Spice After-Shave Lotion is the primary package. The *secondary package* is the material that protects the primary package and that is thrown away when the product is about to be used. The cardboard box containing the bottle of after-shave lotion is a secondary package that allows for additional protection and promotion. The *shipping package* is packaging necessary to store, identify, and ship the product. A corrugated box carrying six dozen Old Spice After-Shave Lotions is a shipping package. Finally, *labeling* is part of packaging and consists of printed information appearing on or with the package.

Traditionally, packaging decisions were based mostly on cost and production factors; the primary function of the package was to contain and protect the product. In recent times, however, numerous factors have made packaging an important marketing tool. An increase in self-service means that packages must now perform many

Packaging is an essential part of the product.

An intriguing package is impossible to ignore.

A mysterious bottle in ancient Baghdad was a package nobody could resist. The successful direct marketer needs no less. You can get the same attention with help from Westvaco. Because we'll match you idea for idea.

At Westvaco, your wish is our command. We'll work with you to design and produce the kind of envelope that will arouse interest and get action.

We work with America's leading companies to create the envelopes they need. Then we make them available through any of our 24 locations across the country. Special sizes. Unusual shapes. Windows of all kinds. Envelopes with action devices like labels, pull tabs or punch outs. Envelopes within envelopes. Colorful envelopes. Envelopes that look like leather. Or linen. Or even a genie's bottle.

So let your imagination run wild. Then run your ideas by Westvaco's Creative Engineering Center. We'll find a way to make them real. Call 1-800-628-9265. (In MA, 1-800-332-3836.) Or write Creative Engineering Center,

Westvaco Envelope Division, 2001 Roosevelt Avenue, P.O. Box 3300, Springfield, MA 01101-3300.

Westvaco
Envelope Division

sales tasks—from attracting attention, to describing the product, to making the sale. Rising consumer affluence means that consumers are willing to pay a little more for the convenience, appearance, dependability, and prestige of better packages.[20] Companies are realizing the power of good packaging to create instant consumer recognition of the company or brand. The Campbell Soup Company estimates that the average shopper sees its familiar red and white can 76 times a year, creating the equivalent of $26 million worth of advertising.[21] And innovative packaging can give the company an advantage over competitors. Chesebrough-Ponds increased its overall nail polish sales by 22 percent within six months of introducing its Aziza Polishing Pen. Liquid Tide quickly attained a 10 percent share of the heavy-duty detergent market, partly because of the popularity of its container's innovative drip-proof spout and cap. The first companies to put their fruit drinks in airtight foil and paper cartons (aseptic packages) and toothpastes in pump dispensers attracted many new customers.[22]

In recent years, product safety has also become a major packaging concern. We've all learned to deal with hard-to-open "child-proof" packages. And after the rash of product tampering scares during the 1980s, most drug producers and many food makers are now putting their products in tamper-resistant packages.

Developing a good package for a new product requires many decisions. The first task is to establish the packaging concept. The packaging concept states what the package should *be* or *do* for the product. Should the main functions of the package be to offer product protection, introduce a new dispensing method, suggest certain qualities about the product or the company, or something else? Decisions must be made on specific elements of the package—size, shape, materials, color, text, and brand mark. These various elements must work together to support the product's position and marketing strategy. The package must be consistent with the product's advertising, pricing, distribution, and other marketing strategies.

Companies usually consider several different package designs for a new product. To select the best package, the company must test the various designs to find the one that stands up best under normal use, that dealers find easiest to handle, and that consumers respond to most favorably.

After selecting and introducing the package, the company must check it regularly in the face of changing consumer preferences and advances in technology. In the past, a package design might last for fifteen years before needing changes. In today's rapidly changing environment, most companies must recheck their packaging every two or three years.[23] Keeping a package up to date usually requires only minor but regular changes—changes so subtle that they go unnoticed by most consumers. But some packaging changes involve complex decisions, drastic action, and high cost and risk (see Marketing Highlight 10–3).

Cost remains an important packaging consideration. Developing the packaging for a new product may cost a few hundred thousand dollars and take from a few months to a year. Converting to a new package may cost millions, and implementing a new package design may take several years. Marketers must weigh packaging costs against consumer perceptions of value added by the packaging, and against the role of packaging in helping to attain marketing objectives. In making packaging decisions, the company must also heed growing societal concerns about packaging and make decisions that serve society's interests as well as customer and company objectives (see Marketing Highlight 10–4).

LABELING DECISIONS

Sellers may also design labels for their products. A label may be a simple tag attached to the product or a complex graphic that is part of the package. The label might carry only the brand name or a great deal of information. Even if the seller prefers a simple label, the law may require more information.

Labels perform several functions, and the seller has to decide which ones to use. At the very least, the label *identifies* the product or brand, such as the name Sunkist stamped on oranges. The label might also *grade* the product. Canned peaches, for example, are grade-labeled A, B, and C. The label might *describe* several things about the product—who made it, where it was made, when it was made, its contents, how it is to be used, how to use it safely. and when it should no longer be used. Finally, the label might *promote* the product through its attractive graphics.

Labels of well-known brands seem old-fashioned after a while and need freshening up. The label on Ivory Soap has been redone eighteen times since the 1890s, with gradual changes in the letters. On the other hand, the label on Orange Crush soft drink was substantially changed when its competitors' labels began to picture fresh fruits and pull in more sales. Orange Crush developed a label with new symbols to suggest freshness and much stronger and deeper colors.

There has been a long history of legal concerns about labels. Labels could mislead customers, or fail to describe important ingredients, or fail to include needed safety warnings. As a result, several federal and state laws regulate labeling. The most prominent of these laws is the Fair Packaging and Labeling Act of 1966. Labeling has been affected in recent times by unit pricing (stating the price per unit of standard measure), open dating (stating the expected shelf life of the product), and nutritional labeling (stating the nutritional values in the product). Sellers must make sure their labels contain all the required information.

CANNING CAMPBELL'S CAN

Over the past 87 years, the venerable Campbell Soup Co. has marketed tens of billions of cans of soup adorned with its distinctive red-and-white label and gold medallion. But about a year ago, Campbell management came to the conclusion that the time had finally come to can the can as too expensive, too messy and too inconvenient in this day of fast-acting microwave ovens. Ever since then, the company has been engaged in a multimillion-dollar search for a new container.

For openers, Campbell next winter will begin test-marketing individual portions of soup in a sealed plastic soup bowl, which can be popped into a microwave oven to produce hot soup in a jiffy—with no can to open and no dishes to wash. The company also wants to incorporate into its design the "image of warmth" soup bowls convey, says Frank Terwilliger, Campbell's director of packing. But so far, Campbell hasn't come up with a bowl design whose color and shape it really likes.

The stakes in the search are huge, given Campbell's 80 percent share of the canned-soup market. (It also is the nation's third largest can maker behind American Can Co. and the Continental Group.) To come up with a permanent substitute for the can, Campbell researchers are experimenting with a number of different containers and conducting extensive market research. "We're constantly tracking consumers," says Herbert Baum, Campbell vice president for marketing. "We sit in homes with them. We talk to them in supermarkets."

At this point, Campbell designers are working with an assortment of plastic bags and boxes, all holding 10 ounces of a meatier, "upscale" soup—one with a clearer broth and ingredients of a higher quality than those in the can. The sales pitch on both the plastic bowls and the eventual successor to the tin can will be convenience. "Heat 'n Eat" and "Microready" are among the slogans being considered for the new bowls.

Campbell's move is being hailed by Wall Street analysts. "It's damn hard to open a can of soup, or a can of anything else," says John C. Maxwell of Lehman Brothers, who thinks that the new packaging could help boost overall soup consumption. George Novello of E. F. Hutton says the switch will have a very positive impact on the company's earnings; metals prices have been rising faster than plastics prices and the change should cut Campbell's packaging costs by as much as 15 percent. But achieving that goal will take a lot of time—and a lot of money. Company officials estimate that simply revamping production facilities could cost $100 million or more. Thus, the company estimates it will be five years at least before its soup can takes a final bow.

Campbell's new package prototypes.

Source: "Canning Campbell's Can," *Newsweek*, April 9, 1984, p. 84.

CUSTOMER SERVICE DECISIONS

Customer service is another element of product strategy. A company's offer to the marketplace usually includes some services. Service can be a minor or a major part of the total offer. In fact, the offer can range from a pure tangible good on the one hand to a pure service on the other. In Chapter 22 we discuss services as products

PACKAGING AND PUBLIC POLICY

Packaging is attracting increasing public attention. When making packaging decisions, marketers need to consider the following issues.

Fair Packaging and Labeling

The public is concerned about false and potentially misleading packaging and labeling. The Federal Trade Commission Act of 1914 held that false, misleading, or deceptive labels or packages constitute unfair competition. Consumers are also concerned about confusing package sizes and shapes that make price comparisons difficult. The Fair Packaging and Labeling Act, passed by Congress in 1967, set mandatory labeling requirements, encouraged voluntary industry packaging standards, and allowed federal agencies to set packaging regulations in specific industries. The Food and Drug Administration has required processed-food producers to include nutritional labeling that clearly states the amounts of protein, fat, carbohydrates, and calories contained in products, as well as their vitamin and mineral content as a percentage of the recommended daily allowance. Consumerists have lobbied for additional labeling laws to require open dating (to describe product freshness), unit pricing (to state the product cost in some standard measurement unit), grade labeling (to rate the quality level of certain consumer goods), and percentage labeling (to show the percentage of each important ingredient).

Excessive Cost

Critics have claimed that excessive packaging on some products raises prices. They point to secondary "throwaway" packaging and question its value to the consumer. They note that the package sometimes costs more than the contents; for example, Evian moisturizer consists of five ounces of natural spring water packaged in an aerosol spray selling for $5.50. Marketers respond that they also want to keep packaging costs down but that critics do not understand all the functions of the package.

Scarce Resources

The growing concern over shortages of paper, aluminum, and other materials suggests that industry should try harder to reduce its packaging. For example, the growth of nonreturnable containers has resulted in using many times the resources used with returnable containers. Throwaway containers also waste energy. Some states have passed laws prohibiting or taxing nonreturnable containers.

Pollution

As much as 40 percent of the total solid waste in this country is made up of package material. Many packages end up as broken bottles and bent cans littering the streets and countryside. All of this packaging creates a major problem in solid waste disposal, requiring huge amounts of land, labor, and energy.

Packaging questions such as these have mobilized public interest in new packaging laws. Marketers must be equally concerned. They must try to design fair, economical, and ecological packages for their products.

---

themselves. Here we will discuss services that augment tangible products. Examples include delivery and installation, repair and maintenance, customer information and technical advice, and credit and financing, among many other services. The marketer faces three decisions about customer services: What customer service mix should be offered? What level of service should be offered? And in what forms should the services be provided?

Service Mix Decision The marketer needs to survey customers to find out the main services that might be offered and their importance. The company should at least match competition on services wanted by buyers. But the issue of which services to offer is more subtle than this. A service can be very important to customers and yet not affect supplier selection if all the suppliers offer the service at the same level. Consider the following example:

> The Monsanto Company was seeking a way to improve its customer services mix. Customers were asked to rate Monsanto, Du Pont, and Union Carbide on several attributes. All three companies were seen as offering good delivery and having good salespeople. But none was viewed as giving enough technical service. Monsanto did a study to find out how important technical service is to chemical buyers and found out it was very important. Monsanto then hired and trained more technical people and launched a campaign describing itself as the leader in technical service. This gave Monsanto an advantage in the minds of buyers seeking technical service.

Service Level Decision

Customers not only want certain services, but also want them in the right amount and quality. If bank customers have to stand in long lines or face frowning bank tellers, they might switch to another bank.

Companies need to check on their own and competitors' service levels in relation to customers' expectations. The company can spot service problems in several ways: comparison shopping, customer surveys, suggestion boxes, and complaint systems. This lets the company know how it is doing and helps disappointed customers get satisfaction.

Many companies conduct regular surveys to find out how customers feel about various services. Figure 10-5A shows how customers rated the importance and performance of fourteen elements of an automobile dealer's service department. Consumers rated importance using a four-point scale of "extremely important," "important," "slightly important," and "not important." They rated dealer performance on a four-point scale of "excellent," "good," "fair," and "poor." For example, "Job done right the first time" received average ratings of 3.83 and 2.63, indicating that customers felt it was highly important but was not being performed that well by the dealer.

The ratings of the fourteen service elements are shown graphically in Figure 10-5B. The figure is divided into four sections. Section A shows important service elements that are not being performed well; they include elements 1, 2, and 9. The dealer should concentrate on improving the service department's performance on these elements. Section B shows important service elements that the department is performing well; the dealer's job here is to keep up the good work. Section C shows service elements that are being poorly delivered but do not need any attention because they are not very important. Section D shows that the dealer is performing a minor service element, Sending out maintenance notices, in an excellent manner, a case of possible "overkill." Measuring service elements according to importance and performance tells marketers where to focus their efforts for improvement.

Service Form Decision

Marketers must also decide on the forms in which to offer various services. The first question is, How should each service be priced? For example, consider what Zenith should offer in repair services on its television sets. Zenith has three options. It could offer free repair service for a year with the sale of a set. It could sell a service contract. Or it could decide not to offer repair services at any price, leaving this to television repair specialists.

Another question is, How should the service be delivered? Zenith could provide repair services in several ways. It could hire and train its own service people and locate them across the country. It could arrange with distributors and dealers to provide repair services. Or it could leave it to independent companies to provide repair services.

Attribute number	Attribute description	Average importance rating	Average performance rating
1	Job done right the first time	3.83	2.63
2	Fast action on complaints	3.63	2.73
3	Prompt warranty work	3.60	3.15
4	Able to do any job needed	3.56	3.00
5	Service available when needed	3.41	3.05
6	Courteous and friendly service	3.41	3.29
7	Car ready when promised	3.38	3.03
8	Perform only necessary work	3.37	3.11
9	Low prices on service	3.29	2.00
10	Clean up after service work	3.27	3.02
11	Convenient to home	2.52	2.25
12	Convenient to work	2.43	2.49
13	Courtesy buses and rental cars	2.37	2.35
14	Send out maintenance notices	2.05	3.33

A.

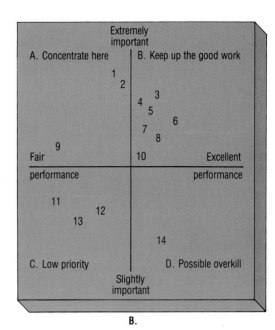

B.

FIGURE 10-5 Importance and performance ratings for automobile dealer's service department

Source: John A. Martilla and John C. James, "Importance Performance Analysis," *Journal of Marketing*, January 1977, pp. 77–79.

For each service, various options exist. The company's decision depends on customer needs and competitors' strategies. Defining customer service needs and shaping competitive service offers are discussed in greater depth in Chapter 22.

The Customer Service Department

Given the importance of customer service as a marketing tool, many companies have set up strong customer service departments to handle complaints and adjustments, credit service, maintenance service, technical service, and consumer information. For example, Whirlpool, Procter & Gamble, and other companies have set up hot lines to handle consumer complaining and requests for information. By keeping records on the types of requests and complaints, the customer service department can press for needed changes in product design, quality control, high-pressure selling, and so on. It costs less to keep the goodwill of existing customers than to attract new customers or woo back lost customers. All these services should be coordinated and used as tools in creating customer satisfaction and loyalty.[24]

PRODUCT LINE DECISIONS

We have looked at product strategy decisions—branding, packaging, and services—for individual products. But product strategy also calls for building a product line. A **product line** is a group of products that are closely related, either because they function in a similar manner, are sold to the same customer groups, are marketed through the same types of outlets, or fall within given price ranges. Thus General Motors produces a line of cars, Revlon produces a line of cosmetics, and IBM produces a line of personal computers.

Product line: "We design each Olympus for a different kind of photographer."

Each product line needs a marketing strategy. Most companies assign a specific person to manage each product line. This person faces a number of tough decisions on product line length and product line featuring.

Product Line Length Decision

Product line managers have to decide on product line length. The line is too short if the manager can increase profits by adding items; the line is too long if the manager can increase profits by dropping items.

Product line length is influenced by company objectives. Companies that want to be positioned as full-line companies or are seeking high market share and market growth will carry longer lines. They are less concerned when some items fail to add to profits. Companies that are keen on high profitability will carry shorter lines consisting of selected items.

Product lines tend to lengthen over time. The product line manager will feel pressure to add new products to use up excess manufacturing capacity. The salesforce and distributors will pressure the manager for a more complete product line to satisfy their customers. The product line manager will want to add items to the product line to increase sales and profits.

However, as the manager adds items, several costs rise: design and engineering costs, inventory carrying costs, manufacturing changeover costs, order processing costs, transportation costs, and promotional costs to introduce new items. Eventually someone calls a halt to the mushrooming product line. Top management may freeze things because of insufficient funds or manufacturing capacity. Or the controller may question the line's profitability and call for a study. The study will probably show a number of money-losing items, and they will be pruned from the line in a major effort to increase profitability. A pattern of uncontrolled product line growth followed by heavy pruning is typical and may repeat itself many times.

The company must plan product line growth carefully. It can systematically increase the length of its product line in two ways: by stretching its line and by filling its line.

Product Line Stretching Decision

Every company's product line covers a certain range of the products offered by the industry as a whole. For example, BMW automobiles are located in the medium to high price range of the automobile market. Toyota focuses on the low to medium price range. Product line stretching occurs when a company lengthens its product line beyond its current range. As shown in Figure 10-6, the company can stretch its line downward, upward, or both ways.

DOWNWARD STRETCH. Many companies initially locate at the high end of the market and later stretch their lines downward. A company may stretch downward for any number of reasons. It may find faster growth taking place at the low end. The company may have first entered the high end to establish a quality image and intended to roll downward. The company may add a low-end product to plug a market hole that would otherwise attract a new competitor. Or it may be attacked at the high end and respond by invading the low end. Beech Aircraft has historically produced expensive private aircraft but recently added less expensive planes to meet a threat from Piper, which began to produce larger planes.

In making a downward stretch, the company faces some risks. The new low-end item might "cannibalize" higher-end items, leaving the company worse off. Or

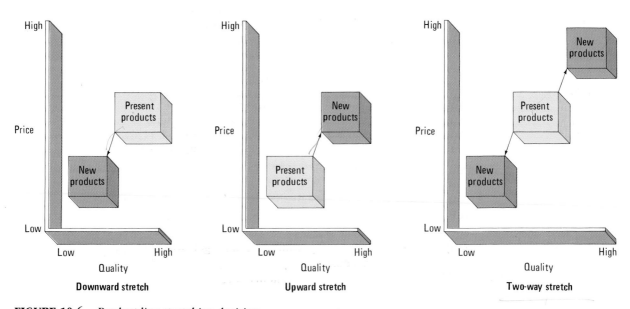

FIGURE 10-6   Product-line stretching decision

the low-end item may provoke competitors to counteract by moving into the higher end. Or the company's dealers may not be willing or able to handle the lower-end products.

One of the great miscalculations of several American companies has been their unwillingness to plug holes in the lower end of their markets. General Motors resisted building smaller cars; Xerox, smaller copying machines; and Harley Davidson, smaller motorcycles. In all these cases, Japanese companies found a major opening and moved in quickly and successfully.

UPWARD STRETCH. Companies at the lower end of the market may want to enter the higher end. They may simply want to position themselves as full-line manufacturers, or they may be attracted to a faster growth rate or higher margins at the higher end. For example, General Electric recently added its Monogram line of high-quality, built-in kitchen appliances targeted at the select few households that earn more than $100,000 a year and live in homes valued at over $400,000. Sometimes companies stretch upward in order to add prestige to their current products, as when Chrysler purchased Lamborghini, maker of exotic, handcrafted sports cars.

An upward stretch decision can be risky. The higher-end competitors not only are well entrenched but may strike back by entering the lower end of the market. Prospective customers may not believe that the newcomer can produce quality products—for example, some experts think that the new association with Chrysler may tarnish Lamborghini's ultraluxury image. Finally, the company's salespeople and distributors may lack the talent and training to serve the higher end of the market—Chrysler's current dealerships would find it hard to sell Lamborghinis.

TWO-WAY STRETCH. Companies in the middle range of the market may decide to stretch their lines in both directions. Sony did this to hold off copycat competitors for its Walkman line of personal tape players. Sony introduced its first Walkman in the middle of the market. As imitative competitors moved in with lower-priced models, Sony stretched downward. At the same time, to add luster to its lower-price models and to attract more affluent consumers, Sony stretched the Walkman line upwards. It now sells more than 100 models ranging from a plain-vanilla play-back-only version for $32 to a high-tech, high-quality $450 version that both plays and records. Using this two-way-stretch strategy, Sony now dominates the personal tape player market with a 30 percent share.[25]

Product Line Filling Decision

A product line can also be lengthened by adding more items within the present range of the line. There are several reasons for product line filling: reaching for extra profits, satisfying dealers, using excess capacity, trying to be the leading full-line company, and plugging holes to keep out competitors. Thus Sony has added solar-powered and waterproof Walkmans and an ultralight model that attaches to a sweatband for joggers, bicyclers, tennis players, and other exercisers.

Line filling is overdone if it results in cannibalization and customer confusion. The company should make sure that new product items are noticeably different from present items.

Product Line Modernization Decision

In some cases, product line length is adequate, but the line needs to be modernized. For example, a company's machine tools may have a 1920s look and lose out to better-styled competitors' lines that are better-styled.

The issue in product line modernization is whether to overhaul the line piecemeal or in one fell swoop. A piecemeal approach allows the company to see how customers and dealers like the new styles before changing the whole line. Piecemeal modernization causes less drain on the company's cash flow. A major disadvantage of piecemeal modernization is that it allows competitors to see changes and start redesigning their own lines.

Product Line Featuring Decision

The product line manager typically selects one or a few items in the line to feature. This is product line featuring. Sometimes managers feature promotional models at the low end of the line to serve as "traffic builders." Thus Sears will announce a special low-priced sewing machine to attract potential buyers. And Rolls Royce announced an economy model selling for only $49,000—in contrast to its high-end model selling for $108,000—to bring people into its showrooms. Once the customers arrive, salespeople may try to get them to buy at the high end of the line.

At other times, managers will feature a high-end item to give the product line "class." Stetson promotes a man's hat selling for $150, which few people buy but which acts to enhance the whole line.

PRODUCT MIX DECISIONS

An organization with several product lines has a product mix. A **product mix** (also called *product assortment*) is the set of all product lines and items that a particular seller offers for sale to buyers.[26] For example, Avon's product mix consists of four major product lines: cosmetics, jewelry, fashions, and household items. Each product line consists of several sublines. Cosmetics breaks down into lipstick, rouge, powder, and so on. Each line and subline has many individual items. All together, Avon's product mix includes 1,300 items. A large supermarket handles as many as 14,000 items; a typical K mart stocks 15,000 items; and General Electric manufactures as many as 250,000 items.

A company's product mix will have certain features: width, length, depth, and consistency. These concepts are illustrated in Table 10-1 in connection with selected Procter & Gamble consumer products.

The *width* of P&G's product mix refers to how many different product lines the company carries. Table 10-1 shows a product mix width of six lines. (In fact, P&G produces many more lines, including mouthwashes, cake mixes, and others.)

TABLE 10-1 Product Mix Width and Product Line Length Shown for Procter & Gamble Products

	DETERGENTS	TOOTHPASTE	BAR SOAP	DEODORANTS	DISPOSABLE DIAPERS	COFFEE
	Ivory Snow	Gleem	Ivory	Secret	Pampers	Folger's
	Dreft	Crest	Camay	Sure	Luvs	Instant Folger's
	Tide		Lava			High Point Instant
	Joy		Kirk's			Folger's Flaked Coffee
	Cheer		Zest			
	Oxydol		Safeguard			
	Dash		Coast			
	Cascade					
	Ivory Liquid					
	Gain					
	Dawn					
	Era					
	Bold 3					
	Liquid Tide					
	Solo					

← Product Mix Width →

Product Line Length ↓

PRODUCT DECISIONS AND PUBLIC POLICY

Marketing managers must heed various laws and regulations when making product decisions. The main areas of product concern are as follows.

Product Additions and Deletions

Under antitrust laws, the government may prevent companies from adding products through acquisition if the effect threatens to lessen competition. Companies dropping products must be aware that they have legal obligations, written or implied, to their suppliers, dealers, and customers who have a stake in the discontinued product.

Patent Protection

The firm must obey the U.S. patent laws when developing new products. A company may not make its product "illegally similar" to another company's established product. An example is Polaroid's successful suit to prevent Kodak from selling an instant picture camera on the grounds that it infringed on Polaroid's instant camera patents.

Product Quality and Safety

Manufacturers must comply with specific laws regarding product quality and safety. The Federal Food, Drug, and Cosmetic Act protects consumers from unsafe and adulterated food, drugs, and cosmetics. Various acts provide for the inspection of sanitary conditions in the meat and poultry processing industries. Safety legislation has been passed to regulate fabrics, chemical substances, automobiles, toys, and drugs and poisons. The Consumer Product Safety Act of 1972 established a Consumer Product Safety Commission, which has the authority to ban or seize potentially hazardous products and set severe penalties for violation of the law. If consumers have been injured by a product that has been defectively de-signed, they can sue manufacturers or dealers. Product liability suits are now occurring at the rate of over one million per year, with individual awards often running in the millions of dollars. This trend has resulted in huge increases in product-liability insurance premiums. For example, Piper Aircraft's insurance bill averages $75,000 for every new plane, more than the cost of producing Piper's smaller planes. The cost of liability insurance for producers of children's car seats rose from $50,000 in 1984 to over $750,000 in 1986. Some companies pass these higher rates along to consumers by raising their prices. Others are forced to discontinue their high-risk product lines.

Product Warranties

Many manufacturers offer written product warranties to convince customers of their product's quality. But these warranties are often limited and written in a language the average consumer does not understand. Too often, consumers learn that they are not entitled to services, repairs, and replacements that seem to be implied. To protect consumers, Congress passed the Magnuson-Moss Warranty Act in 1975. The act requires that full warranties meet certain minimum standards, including repair "within a reasonable time and without charge" or a replacement or full refund if the product does not work "after a reasonable number of attempts" at repair. Otherwise the company must make it clear that it is offering only a limited warranty. The law has led several manufacturers to switch from full to limited warranties and others to drop warranties altogether as a marketing tool.

Sources: See Michael Brody, "When Products Turn," Fortune, March 3, 1986, pp. 20–24; "Marketers Feel Product-Liability Pressure," May 12, 1986, pp. 3, 75; and Louis W. Stern and Thomas L. Eovaldi, Legal Aspects of Marketing Strategy (Englewood Cliffs, NJ: Prentice Hall, 1984), pp. 76–116.

The length of P&G's product mix refers to the total number of items the company carries. In Table 10-1, it is 32. We can also compute the average length of a line at P&G by dividing the total length (here 32) by the number of lines (here 6), or 5.3. The average P&G product line as represented in Table 10-1 consists of 5.3 brands.

The depth of P&G's product mix refers to how many versions are offered of each product in the line. Thus if Crest comes in three sizes and two formulations (regular and mint), Crest has a depth of six. By counting the number of versions within each brand, the average depth of P&G's product mix can be calculated.

The *consistency* of the product mix refers to how closely related the various product lines are in end use, production requirements, distribution channels, or in some other way. P&G's product lines are consistent in that they are consumer goods that go through the same distribution channels. The lines are less consistent insofar as they perform different functions for the buyers.

These four dimensions of the product mix provide the handles for defining the company's product strategy. The company can increase its business in four ways. The company can add new product lines, thus widening its product mix. In this way, its new lines build on the company's reputation in its other lines. Or the company can lengthen its existing product lines to become a more full-line company. Or the company can add more product versions to each product and thus deepen its product mix. Finally, the company can pursue more product line consistency or less, depending upon whether it wants to have a strong reputation in a single field or in several fields.

Thus we see that product strategy is a complex subject calling for decisions on product mix, product line, branding, packaging, and service strategy. These decisions must be made not only with a full understanding of consumer wants and competitors' strategies, but also with increasing attention to the growing public policy affecting product decisions (see Marketing Highlight 10–5).

■ SUMMARY

Product is a complex concept that must be carefully defined. Product strategy calls for making coordinated decisions on product items, product lines, and the product mix.

We can look at each product item offered to customers on three levels. The core product is the essential service the buyer is buying. The tangible product is the features, styling, quality, brand name, and packaging of the product offered for sale. The augmented product is the tangible product plus the various services offered with it, such as warranty, installation, maintenance, and free delivery.

There are several ways to classify products. For example, all products can be classified according to their durability (nondurable goods, durable goods, and services). Consumer goods are usually classified according to consumer shopping habits (convenience, shopping, specialty, and unsought goods). Industrial goods are classified according to their cost and how they enter the production process (materials and parts, capital items, and supplies and services).

Companies have to develop brand policies for their products. They must decide whether to brand at all, whether to do manufacturer or private branding, what quality they should build into the brand, whether to use family brand names or individual brand names, whether to extend the brand name to new products, whether to put out several competing brands, whether to reposition any of the brands, and what the brand name should be.

Products require packaging to create such benefits as protection, economy, convenience, promotion, and product safety. Marketers have to develop a packaging con-

cept and test it to make sure it achieves the desired objectives and is compatible with public policy.

Products also require labeling for identification and possible grading, description, and promotion of the product. U.S. laws require sellers to present certain minimum information on the label to inform and protect consumers.

Companies have to develop customer services that are desired by customers and effective against competitors. The company has to decide on the most important services to offer, the level at which each service should be provided, and the form of each service. The service mix can be coordinated by a customer service department that handles complaints and adjustments, credit, maintenance, technical service, and customer information.

Most companies produce not a single product but a product line. A product line is a group of products related in function, customer purchase needs, or distribution channels. Each product line requires a product strategy. Line stretching raises the question of whether a line should be extended downward, upward, or both ways. Line filling raises the question of whether additional items should be added within the present range of the line. Line modernization raises the question of whether the line needs to be brought up to date. Line featuring raises the question of which items to feature in promoting the line.

Product mix describes the set of product lines and items offered to customers by a particular seller. The product mix can be described by its width, length, depth, and consistency. The four dimensions of the product mix are the tools for developing the company's product strategy.

■ QUESTIONS FOR DISCUSSION

1. What are the core, tangible, and augmented products associated with the college degree you are pursuing?

2. Are restaurants primarily providers of *nondurable goods* or *services* to their customers?

3. In how many retail outlets will each type of consumer good (convenience, shopping, specialty, or unsought) be distributed in a particular geographic area? Illustrate your answer by saying which form of good an umbrella is and describing where umbrellas are sold in your region.

4. Who benefits from the use of brand names? As part of your answer, explain why many people are willing to pay more for branded products than for unbranded products.

5. Compare brand extension by the brand owner with licensing a brand for use by another company. What are the opportunities and risks of each approach?

6. Changing an established brand name can be very expensive and time-consuming. What is the rationale for changing such familiar names as ENCO (ESSO), Bank Americard, and Datsun, to new names—EXXON, VISA, and Nissan? Why do you think these particular new names were chosen?

7. Think of several products you buy regularly, and describe how their packaging or labels could be improved. If you think the packaging change would add to the cost of the product, how much more would you be willing to pay for the improved package?

8. Describe some of the service decisions the following marketers must make: (a) a small clothing store for women, (b) a savings and loan bank, and (c) a supermarket.

9. Relate the concepts of product mix, product line, and product item to one or more hospitals in your area. Do the concepts of upward and downward product-line stretching, or product-mix width and depth, apply to hospitals and other health-care marketers?

10. In recent years, U.S. automakers have tried to reposition many of their brands to the high-quality end of the market. How well have their efforts succeeded? What else could they do to change consumers' perceptions of their cars?

■ KEY TERMS

Brand   A name, term, sign, symbol, or design, or a combination of them, intended to identify the goods or services of one seller or group of sellers and to differentiate them from those of competitors.

Brand mark   That part of a brand that can be recognized but is not utterable, such as a symbol, design, or distinctive coloring or lettering.

Brand name   That part of a brand that can be vocalized—is utterable.

Capital items   Industrial goods that enter the finished product partly, including installations and accessory equipment.

Consumer goods   Goods bought by final consumers for personal consumption.

Convenience goods   Consumer goods that the customer usually buys frequently, immediately, and with the minimum of comparison and buying effort.

Copyright   The exclusive legal right to reproduce, publish, and sell the matter and form of a literary, musical, or artistic work.

Durable goods   Tangible goods that normally survive many uses.

Industrial goods   Goods bought by individuals and organizations for further processing or for use in conducting a business.

Materials and parts   Industrial goods that enter the manufacturer's product completely, including raw materials and manufactured materials and parts.

Nondurable goods   Tangible goods normally consumed in one or a few uses.

Packaging   The activities of designing and producing the container or wrapper for a product.

Product   Anything that can be offered to a market for attention, acquisition, use, or consumption that might satisfy a want or need. It includes physical objects, services, persons, places, organizations, and ideas.

Product line   A group of products that are closely related, either because they function in a similar manner, are sold to the same customer groups, are marketed through the same types of outlets, or fall within given price ranges.

Product mix   The set of all product lines and items that a particular seller offers for sale to buyers. Also called *product assortment.*

Services   Activities, benefits, or satisfactions that are offered for sale.

Shopping goods   Consumer goods that the customer, in the process of selection and purchase, usually compares on such bases as suitability, quality, price, and style.

Specialty goods   Consumer goods with unique characteristics or brand identification for which a significant group of buyers is willing to make a special purchase effort.

Supplies and services   Industrial goods that do not enter the finished product at all.

Trademark   A brand or part of a brand that is given legal protection—it protects the seller's exclusive rights to use the brand name or brand mark.

Unsought goods   Consumer goods that the consumer does not know about or knows about but does not normally think of buying.

■ REFERENCES

1. See Bess Gallanis, "New Strategies Revive the Rose's Fading Bloom," *Advertising Age*, February 27, 1984, pp. M9–M11; "What Lies Behind the Sweet Smell of Success," *Business Week*, February 27, 1984, pp. 139–43; and Pat Sloan, "Making Scents," *Advertising Age*, August 24, 1987, p.3.

2. See *Marketing Definitions: A Glossary of Marketing Terms*, compiled by the Committee on Definitions of the American Marketing Association (Chicago: American Marketing Association, 1960).

3. Theodore Levitt, *The Marketing Mode* (New York: McGraw-Hill, 1969), p. 2.

4. These three definitions can be found in *Marketing Definitions*.

5. The first three definitions can be found in *Marketing Definitions*. For more information on product classifications, see Patrick E. Murphy and Ben M. Enis, "Classifying Products Strategically," *Journal of Marketing*, July 1986, pp. 24–42.

6. The first four definitions can be found in *Marketing Definitions*.

7. Eleanor Johnson Tracy, "Here Come Brand-Name Fruits and Veggies," *Fortune*, February 18, 1985, p. 105.

8. Walter J. Salmon and Karen A. Cmar, "Private Labels are Back in Fashion," *Harvard Business Review*, May–June 1987, pp. 99–106.

9. See Frances Dunne, "Private Labels Are No Secret Anymore," *Advertising Age*, July 25, 1983, p. M30.

10. David A. Garvin, "Competing on Eight Dimensions of Quality," *Harvard Business Review*, November–December 1987, p. 109. Also see Robert Jacobson and David A. Aaker, "The Strategic Role of Product Quality." *Journal of Marketing*, October 1987, pp. 31–44.

11. Tom Peters and Perry Pascarella, "Searching for Excellence: The Winners Deliver on Value," *Industry Week*, April 16, 1984, pp. 61–62.

12. For several more examples, see "Name Game," *Time*, August 31, 1981, pp. 41–42.

13. See Mark B. Traylor, "Cannibalism in Multibrand Firms," *Journal of Business Strategy*, Spring 1986, pp. 69–75.

14. Steve Lawrence, "Bar Wars: Hershey Bites Mars," *Fortune*, July 8, 1985, p. 54.

15. See Bess Gallanis, "Positioning Old Products in New Niches," *Advertising Age*, May 3, 1984, p. M50; and "Marketers Should Consider Restaging Old Brands Before Launching New Ones," *Advertising Age*, December 10, 1982, p.5.

16. Walter Stern, "A Good Name Could Mean a Brand of Fame," *Advertising Age*, January 17, 1983, pp. M53–M54.

17. Stern, "A Good Name," p. M53.

18. Thomas M. S. Hemnes, "How Can You Find a Safe Trademark?" *Harvard Business Review*, March–April 1985, p. 44.

19. For a discussion of legal issues surrounding the use of brand names, see Dorothy Cohen, "Trademark Strategy," *Journal of Marketing*, January 1986, pp. 61–74; and "Trademark Woes: Help Is Coming," *Sales & Marketing Management*, January 1988, p. 84.

20. See Charles A. Moldenhauer, "Packaging Designers Must Be Cognizant of Right Cues if the Consumer Base Is to Expand," *Marketing News*, March 30, 1984, p. 14; and Kate Bertrand, "Convenient and Portable Packaging Pays," *Advertising Age*, February 20, 1986, p. 16.

21. Bill Abrams, "Marketing," *Wall Street Journal*, May 20, 1982, p. 33.

22. See Amy Dunkin, "Want to Wake Up a Tired Old Product? Repackage It," *Business Week*, July 15, 1985, pp. 130–34.

23. Moldenhauer, "Packaging Designers," p. 14.

24. For more examples of how companies have used customer service as a marketing tool, see "Making Service a Potent Marketing Tool," *Business Week*, June 11, 1984, pp. 164–70; Bro Uttal, "Companies That Serve You Best," *Fortune*, December 7, 1987, pp. 98–116; and Bill Kelley, "Five Companies That Do It Right—and Make It Pay," *Sales & Marketing Management*, April 1988, pp. 57–64.

25. See Amy Borrus, "How Sony Keeps the Copycats Scampering," *Business Week*, June 1, 1987, p. 69.

26. This definition can be found in *Marketing Definitions*.

11

Designing Products: New-Product Development and Product Life-Cycle Strategies

THE 3M Company markets more than 60,000 products, ranging from sandpaper, adhesives, and floppy disks to contact lenses, laser optical disks, and heart-lung machines; from coatings that make boat hulls slick to tapes that make anything stick—Scotch Tape, masking tape, super-bonding tape, and even refastening disposable diaper tape. 3M views innovation as its path to growth, and new products as its life blood. The company's long-standing goal is to derive an astonishing 25 percent of each year's sales from products introduced within the previous five years. More astonishing, it usually succeeds! Each year 3M launches more than 200 new products. Its legendary emphasis on innovation has consistently made 3M one of America's most admired companies.

New products don't just happen. 3M works hard to create an environment that supports innovation. It invests 6.5 percent of its annual sales in research and development, almost twice as much as the average company invests. Its "Innovation Task Force" seeks out and destroys corporate bureaucracy that might interfere with new-product progress. Hired consultants help 3M find ways to make employees more inventive.

3M encourages everyone to look for new products. The company's renowned "15 percent rule" allows all employees to spend up to 15 percent of their time "bootlegging"—working on projects of personal interest whether the projects benefit the company or not. When a promising idea comes along,

3M forms a venture team made up of the researcher who developed the idea and volunteers from the manufacturing, sales, marketing, and legal departments. The team nurtures the product and protects it from company bureaucracy. Team members stay with the product until it succeeds or fails, then return to their previous jobs. Some teams have tried three or four times before finally making a success out of an idea. Each year 3M hands out "Golden Step Awards" to venture teams whose new product earned more than $2 million in U.S. sales or $4 million in worldwide sales within three years of introduction.

3M knows that it must try thousands of new product ideas to hit one big jackpot. One well-worn slogan at 3M is, "You have to kiss a lot of frogs to find a prince." "Kissing frogs" often means making mistakes, but 3M accepts blunders and dead ends as a normal part of creativity and innovation. In fact, its philosophy seems to be, "if you aren't making mistakes, you probably aren't doing anything." But as it turns out, "blunders" have turned into some

of 3M's most successful products. Old-timers at 3M love to tell the story about the 3M chemist who accidently spilled a new chemical on her tennis shoes. Some days later, she noticed that the spots hit by the chemical had not gotten dirty. Eureka! The chemical eventually became Scotchgard fabric protector.

And then there's the one about 3M scientist Spencer Silver. Mr. Silver tried to develop a super-strong adhesive; instead he came up with one that didn't stick very well. He sent the apparently useless substance on to other 3M researchers to see if they could find something to do with it. Nothing happened for several years. Then Arthur Fry, another 3M scientist, had a problem—and an idea. As a choir member in a local church, Mr. Fry was having trouble marking places in his hymnal—the little scraps of paper he used kept falling out. He tried dabbing some of Mr. Silver's weak glue on one of the scraps. It stuck nicely and later peeled off without damaging the hymnal. Thus were born 3M's Post-It Notes, a product that now sells almost $100 million a year![1]

Chapter Objectives *After reading this chapter, you should be able to:*

1. List and define the steps in new product development.
2. Explain how companies find and develop new product ideas.
3. Describe the stages of the product life cycle.
4. Discuss how marketing strategy changes during a product's life cycle.

A company has to be good at developing new products. It also has to be good at managing them in the face of changing tastes, technologies, and competition. Every product seems to go through a life cycle—it is born, goes through several phases, and eventually dies as younger products come along that better serve consumer needs.

This product life cycle presents two major challenges. First, because all products eventually decline, the firm must find new products to replace aging ones (the problem of *new product development*). Second, the firm must understand how its products age and adapt its marketing strategies as products pass through life-cycle stages (the problem of *product life-cycle strategies*). We will first look at the problem of finding and developing new products, and then at the problem of managing them successfully over their life cycles.

NEW PRODUCT DEVELOPMENT STRATEGY

Given the rapid changes in tastes, technology, and competition, a company cannot rely only on its existing products. Customers want and expect new and improved products. Competition will do its best to provide them. Every company needs a new product development program. One expert estimates that half of the profits of all U.S. companies come from products that did not even exist ten years ago.[2]

A company can obtain new products in two ways. One is through *acquisition*, by buying a whole company, a patent, or a license to produce someone else's product. The other is through **new product development** in the company's own research and development department. As the costs of developing and introducing major new products have climbed, many large companies decided to acquire existing brands rather than create new ones. Others have saved money by copying competitors' brands or by reviving old brands (see Marketing Highlight 11–1). By "new products"

MARKETING HIGHLIGHT 11–1

GETTING AROUND THE HIGH COSTS AND RISKS OF NEW PRODUCT DEVELOPMENT

The average cost of developing and introducing a major new product from scratch has jumped to well over $100 million. To make things worse, many of these costly new products fail. So companies are now pursuing new product strategies that are less costly and risky than developing completely new brands. We discussed two of these strategies—*licensing* and *brand extensions*—in Chapter 10. Here we describe three other new product strategies—*acquiring new brands*, *developing "me-too" products*, and *reviving old brands*.

Acquiring New Products

Instead of building its own new products from the ground up, a company can buy another company and its established brands. The mid-1980s saw a dramatic flurry of one big consumer company gobbling up another. Procter & Gamble acquired Richardson-Vicks, R. J. Reynolds bought Nabisco, Philip Morris obtained General Foods, Nestle absorbed Carnation, and Beatrice Foods merged with Esmark.

Such acquistions can be tricky—the company must be certain that the acquired products blend well with its current products and that the firm has the skills and resources needed to continue to run the acquired products profitably. Acquisitions can also run into snags with government regulators. For example, even under the Reagan Administration's loose antitrust policy, regulators did not allow Pepsi to acquire 7-Up or Coke to buy up Dr Pepper. Finally,

such acquisitions have high price tags. Philip Morris paid $5.7 billion for General Foods, RJR coughed up $4.9 billion for Nabisco, and Nestle forked over $3 billion for Carnation. Not many companies can afford to buy up market-winning brands.

But despite high initial outlays, buying established brands may be cheaper in the long run than paying the enormous costs of trying to create well-known brand names from scratch. And acquiring proven winners eliminates almost all the risks of new-product failure. Acquisition also provides a quick and easy way to gain access to new markets or strengthen positions in current markets. For example, by acquiring Richardson-Vicks, P&G moved immediately into the health and beauty aids market. It also strengthened its hold in the home remedies segment by getting a medicine cabinet full of such top brands as Vicks VapoRub, Formula 44D Cough Syrup, Sinex, NyQuil, and Clearisil to add to its own Pepto-Bismol and Chloraseptic brands.

Developing "Me-Too" Products

In recent years, many companies have used "me-too" product strategies—introducing imitations of successful competitors' products. Thus Tandy, AT&T, Zenith, and many others produce IBM-compatible personal computers. These "clones" sometimes sell for less than half the price of the IBM models they emulate. Me-too products have also hit the fragrance industry. Several companies now offer smell-alike

---

"knock-offs" (copies) of popular, pricey perfumes at a fraction of the originals' prices. The success of knock-off fragrances has inspired a wave of look-alike designer fashions and imitative versions of prestige cosmetics and hair-care brands. Imitation is now fair play for products ranging from soft drinks and food to mousses and minivans.

Me-too products are often quicker and less expensive to develop—the market leader pioneers the technology and bears most of the product development costs. The imitative products sometimes even give consumers more value than the market-leading originals. The copycat company can build on the leader's design and technology to create an equivalent product at a lower price, or an even better product at the same or a higher price. Me-too products are also less costly and risky to introduce—they enter a proven market already developed by the market leader. Thus IBM invested millions to develop its personal computers and cultivate a market; the clone makers simply rode in on IBM's generous coattails.

A me-too strategy has some drawbacks. The imitating company enters the market late and must battle a successful, firmly entrenched competitor. Some me-too products never take much business from the leader. Others succeed broadly and end up challenging for market leadership. Still others settle into small but profitable niches in the market created by the leader.

Reviving Old Products

Many companies have found "new gold in the old" by reviving once-successful brands that are now dead or dying. Many old and tarnished brand names still hold magic for consumers. Often, simply reviving, reformulating, and repositioning an old brand can give the company a successful "new" product at a fraction of the cost of building new brands.

There are some classic examples of brand revivals. Arm & Hammer Baking Soda sales spurted after it was promoted as a deodorizer for refrigerators, garbage disposals, cars, and kitty litter boxes. Ivory Soap reversed its sales decline in the early 1970s when it was promoted for adult use rather than just for babies. Dannon Yogurt sales rocketed when it was linked to healthy living. In recent years, Warner-Lambert revived Black Jack gum, playing on the nostalgia of its 110-year-old name; Coca-Cola rejuvenated Fresca by adding NutraSweet and real fruit juice; and Campbell expanded the appeal of V8 Juice by tying it to today's fitness craze.

Sometimes a dead product rises again with a new name, as happened with Nestle's New Cookery brand of low-fat, low-sugar, low-salt entrees. Some years ago, Nestle withdrew the product when it failed in test market—the company faulted the times, the product's name, and ordinary packaging. But New Cookery was well-suited to today's health-conscious consumers, and Stouffer, a Nestle company, later revived the line under the Lean Cuisine brand. Lean Cuisine proved a resounding success.

Sources: See "Products of the Year," *Fortune*, December 9, 1985, pp. 106–12; Paul B. Brown, Zachary Schiller, Christine Dugas, and Scott Scredon, "New? Improved? The Brand-Name Mergers," *Business Week*, October 21, 1985, pp. 108–110; Kenneth Dreyfack, "The Big Brands are Back in Style," *Business Week*, January 12, 1987, p. 74; Jeff B. Copeland, Doty Tsiantar, and Linda Buckley, "Perfume Knockoffs: A Scent of Money," *Newsweek*, January 4, 1988; and Arthur Bragg, "Back to the Future," *Sales and Marketing Management*, November 1986, pp. 61–62.

we mean original products, product improvements, product modifications, and new brands that the firm develops through its own research and development efforts. In this chapter, we will concentrate on new product development.

Innovation can be very risky. Ford lost $350 million on its Edsel automobile; RCA lost a staggering $580 million on its SelectaVision videodisc player; Xerox's venture into computers was a disaster; and the Concorde aircraft will never pay back its investment. And here are several other consumer products, launched by sophisticated companies, that failed:

* Red Kettle soup (Campbell)
* Cue toothpaste (Colgate)
* Vim tablet detergent (Lever)
* LA low alcohol beer (Anheuser-Busch)
* PCjr personal computer (IBM)

- Zap Mail electronic mail (Federal Express)
- Polavision instant movies (Polaroid)

One study found that the new product failure rate was 40 percent for consumer products, 20 percent for industrial products, and 18 percent for services. A recent study of 700 consumer and industrial firms found an overall success rate for new products of only 65 percent. Still another source estimates that 80 percent of all new products introduced in the United States fail![3]

Why do so many new products fail? There are several reasons. A high-level executive might push a favorite idea in spite of poor marketing research findings. Or the idea is good, but the market size has been overestimated. Or the actual product has not been designed as well as it should have been. Or it has been incorrectly positioned in the market, priced too high, or advertised poorly. Sometimes the costs of product development are higher than expected, or the competitors fight back harder than expected.

Successful new product development may be even more difficult in the future. Keen competition has lead to increasing market fragmentation—companies must now aim at smaller market segments rather than the mass market, and this means smaller sales and profits for each product. New products must meet growing social and government constraints such as consumer safety and ecological standards. The costs of finding, developing, and launching new products will rise steadily due to rising manufacturing, media, and distribution costs. Many companies cannot afford or cannot raise the funds needed for new product development—they emphasize product modification and imitation rather than true innovation. Even when a new product is successful, rivals are so quick to follow suit that the new product is typically fated for only a short happy life. Thus IBM finds dozens of imitators offering IBM-compatible computers, and Apple finds foreign "knockoffs" (copies) of its computers being sold in the Far East.

So companies face a problem—they must develop new products, but the odds weigh heavily against success. The solution lies in strong new product planning. First, the company can organize effectively for nurturing and handling new products. The most common organizational arrangements are shown in Table 11-1. Then the

TABLE 11-1 **Ways Companies Organize for New Product Development**	1. *Product managers.* Many companies leave new product development to their product managers. In practice, this system has several faults. Product managers are usually so busy managing their product lines that they give little thought to new products other than brand modifications or extensions; they also lack the specific skills and knowledge needed to develop new products.
	2. *New product managers.* General Foods and Johnson & Johnson have new product managers who report to group managers. This position professionalizes the new product function; on the other hand, new product managers tend to think in terms of product modifications and line extensions limited to their product/market.
	3. *New product committees.* Most companies have a high-level management committee charged with reviewing new product proposals. Consisting of representatives from marketing, manufacturing, finance, engineering, and other departments, its function is not development nor coordination so much as reviewing and approving new product plans.
	4. *New product departments.* Large companies often establish a new product department headed by a manager who has substantial authority and access to top management. The department's major responsibilities include generating and screening new ideas, directing and coordinating research and development work, and carrying out field testing and precommercialization work.
	5. *New product venture teams.* Dow, Westinghouse, Monsanto, and General Mills assign major new product development work to venture teams. A *venture team* is a group brought together from various operating departments and charged with bringing a specific product or business into being.

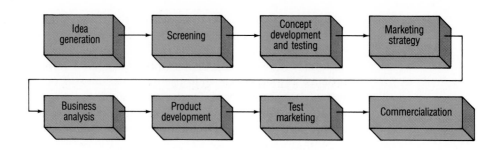

FIGURE 11-1
Major stages in new
product development

```
Idea        →  Screening  →  Concept         →  Marketing
generation                    development        strategy
                              and testing            │
                                                     │
┌────────────────────────────────────────────────────┘
│
Business    →  Product    →  Test        →  Commercialization
analysis       development    marketing
```

company can set up a systematic *new product development process* for finding and growing new products. The major steps in this process are shown in Figure 11-1 and described below.

Idea Generation New product development starts with **idea generation**, the systematic search for new product ideas. A company typically has to generate many ideas in order to find a few good ones. Figure 11-2 shows how many ideas typically survive at each stage of the development process. In 1968 it took fifty-eight new product ideas to yield one good one. In 1981, companies were able to turn one out of seven ideas into a successful new product. The improvement shows that many companies are prescreening and planning more effectively and are investing money only in the best ideas, rather than using a shotgun approach.

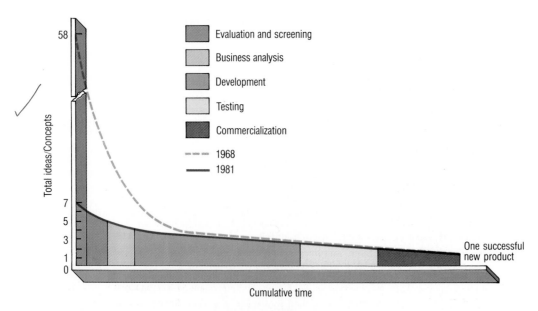

FIGURE 11-2 Decay curve of new product ideas

Source: New Products Management for the 1980s (New York: Booz, Allen & Hamilton, 1982).

The search for new product ideas should be systematic rather than haphazard. Otherwise the company will find many ideas, but most will not be good ones for its type of business. One company spent more than a million dollars for research and development on a new product, only to have top management reject the product because it did not want to get into that type of business.

Top management can avoid such errors by carefully defining its new product development strategy. It should state what products and markets to emphasize. It should state what the company wants from the new products, whether it is high cash flow, market share, or some other objective. It should state the effort to be devoted to developing original products, changing existing products, and imitating competitors' products.

To obtain a flow of new product ideas, the company must tap many idea sources. Major sources of new product ideas include:

* *Internal sources.* One study found that over 55 percent of all new product ideas come from within the company.[4] The company can find new ideas through formal research and development. It can pick the brains of its scientists, engineers, and manufacturing people. Or company executives can brainstorm new product ideas. The company's salespeople are another good source because they are in daily contact with customers.

* *Customers.* Almost 28 percent of all new product ideas come from watching and listening to customers. Consumer needs and wants can be looked at through consumer surveys. The company can analyze customer questions and complaints to find new products that can better solve consumer problems. Company engineers or salespeople can meet with customers to get suggestions. General Electric's Video Products Division has its design engineers talk with final consumers to get ideas for new home electronics products.

Pillsbury's BAKEOFF promotes consumer goodwill and sometimes produces new-product ideas.

National Steel has a product application center where company engineers work with automotive customers to discover customer needs that might require new products.[5] new recipes through its annual Bake-Off—one of Pillsbury's four cake-mix lines and several variations of another came directly from Bake-Off winners' recipes. About one-third of all the software IBM leases for its computers is developed by outside users.[6]

- *Competitors.* About 27 percent of new product ideas come from analyzing competitors' products. The company can watch competitors' ads and other communications to get clues about their new products. Companies buy competing new products, take them apart to see how they work, analyze their sales, and decide whether the company should bring out a new product of its own. For example, when designing its highly successful Taurus, Ford tore down over 50 competing models layer by layer looking for things to copy or improve upon. It copied the Audi's accelerator-pedal "feel," the Toyota Supra fuel gauge, the BMW 528e tire and jack storage system, and 400 other such outstanding features.[7]

- *Distributors and suppliers.* Resellers are close to the market and can pass along information about consumer problems and new product possibilities. Suppliers can tell the company about new concepts, techniques, and materials that can be used to develop new products.

- *Other sources.* Other idea sources include trade magazines, shows, and seminars; government agencies; new product consultants; advertising agencies; marketing research firms; university and commercial laboratories; and inventors.

Idea Screening

The purpose of idea generation is to create a large number of ideas. The purpose of the succeeding stages is to *reduce* the number of ideas. The first idea-reducing stage is **idea screening.** The purpose of screening is to spot good ideas and drop poor ones as soon as possible. Product development costs rise greatly in later stages. The company wants to go ahead only with the product ideas that will turn into profitable products.

Most companies require their executives to write up new product ideas on a standard form that can be reviewed by a new product committee. They describe the product, the target market, and the competition and make some rough estimates of market size, product price, development time and costs, manufacturing costs, and rate of return. They answer the questions: Is this idea good for our particular company? Does it mesh well with the company's objectives and strategies? Do we have the people, skills, and resources to make it succeed?

Many companies have well designed systems for rating and screening new product ideas. Table 11-2 shows a simple rating process for new product ideas. The first column lists factors required for the successful launching of the product in the

TABLE 11-2 Product Idea Rating Process

NEW PRODUCT SUCCESS FACTORS	(A) RELATIVE IMPORTANCE	(B) FIT BETWEEN PRODUCT IDEA AND COMPANY CAPABILITIES											IDEA RATING (A × B)
		.0	.1	.2	.3	.4	.5	.6	.7	.8	.9	1.0	
Company strategy and objectives	.20									X			.160
Marketing skills and experience	.20										X		.180
Financial resources	.15								X				.105
Channels of distribution	.15									X			.120
Production capabilities	.10									X			.080
Research and development	.10								X				.070
Purchasing and supplies	.05						X						.025
Total	1.00												.740*

* Rating scale: .00–.40, poor; .50–.75, fair; .76–1.00 good. Minimum acceptance level: .70

marketplace. In the next column, management rates these factors on their relative importance. Thus management believes that marketing skills and experience are very important (.20) and purchasing and supplies competence is of minor importance (.05). Next, on a scale of .0 to 1.0, management rates how well the new product idea fits the company's profile on each factor. Here management feels that the product idea fits very well with the company's marketing skills and experience (.9) but not too well with its purchasing and supplies capabilities (.5). Finally, management multiplies the importance of each success factor by the rating of fit to obtain an overall rating of the company's ability to launch the product successfully. Thus, if marketing is an important success factor and this product fits the company's marketing skills, this will increase the overall rating of the product idea. In the example, the product idea scored .74, which places it at the high end of the "fair idea" level.

The checklist promotes a more systematic product idea evaluation and basis for discussion—however, it is not designed to make the decision for management.[8]

Concept Development and Testing

Surviving ideas must next be developed into product concepts. It is important to distinguish between a product idea, a product concept, and a product image. A **product idea** is an idea for a possible product that the company can see itself offering to the market. A **product concept** is a detailed version of the idea stated in meaningful consumer terms. A **product image** is the way consumers picture an actual or potential product.

Concept Development

Suppose an car manufacturer figures out how to design an electric car that can go as fast as 60 miles an hour and as far as 80 miles before needing to be recharged. The manufacturer estimates that the electric car's operating costs will be about half of those of a regular car.

This electric car is a product idea. Customers, however, do not buy a product idea; they buy a product concept. The marketer needs to develop this idea into some alternative product concepts, find out how attractive each concept is to customers, and choose the best one.

A prototype of an electric car. This one has a top speed of 60 miles per hour and an in-city driving range of 80 miles.

The following product concepts might be created for the electric car:

- *Concept 1*: An inexpensive subcompact designed as a second family car to be used by the homemaker for short shopping trips. The car is ideal for loading groceries and hauling children, and it is easy to enter.
- *Concept 2*: A medium-cost, medium-size car designed as an all-purpose family car.
- *Concept 3*: A medium-cost sporty compact appealing to young people.
- *Concept 4*: An inexpensive subcompact appealing to conscientious people who want basic transportation, low fuel cost, and low pollution.

Concept Testing

Concept testing calls for testing new product concepts with a group of target consumers. The concepts may be presented through word or picture descriptions. Here, for example, is concept 1:

> An efficient, fun-to-drive, electric-powered subcompact car that seats four. Great for shopping trips and visits to friends. Costs half as much to operate as similar gasoline-driven cars. Goes up to 60 miles an hour and needs to be recharged only every 80 miles. Priced at $8,000.

Consumers are asked to react to each concept with the questions shown in Table 11-3. The answers will help the company decide which concept has the strongest appeal. For example, the last question goes after the consumer's intention-to-buy. Suppose 10 percent of the consumers said they "definitely" would buy the concept 1 car and another 5 percent said "probably." The company would project these figures to the population size of this target group to estimate sales volume. Even then, the estimate would be uncertain because people do not always carry out their stated intentions.[9]

Marketing Strategy Development

Suppose concept 1 for the electric car tests out best. The next step is **marketing strategy development,** designing an initial marketing strategy for introducing this car into the market.

The marketing strategy statement consists of three parts. The first part describes the target market, the planned product positioning, and the sales, market share, and profit goals for the first few years. Thus:

> The target market is households that need a second car for shopping trips, running errands, and visits to friends. The car will be positioned as more economical to buy and operate and more fun to drive than cars now available to this market. The company will aim to sell 200,000 cars in the first year, at a loss of not more than $3 million. The second year will aim for sales of 220,000 cars and a profit of $5 million.

TABLE 11-3
Questions for Electric Car Concept Test

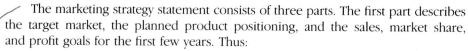

1. Do you understand the concept of an electric car?
2. What do you see as the benefits of an electric car compared with a conventional car?
3. Do you believe the claims about the electric car's performance?
4. Would the electric car meet all your automobile needs?
5. What improvements can you suggest in the car's various features?
6. Would you prefer an electric car to a conventional car? For what uses?
7. What do you think the price of the electric car should be?
8. Who would be involved in your purchase decision for such a car? Who would drive it?
9. Would you buy an electric car? (Definitely, probably, probably not, definitely not)

The second part of the marketing strategy statement outlines the product's planned price, distribution, and marketing budget for the first year:

> The electric car will be offered in three colors and will have optional air-conditioning and power-drive features. It will sell at a retail price of $8,000, with 15 percent off the list price to dealers. Dealers who sell over ten cars per month will get an additional discount of 5 percent on each car sold that month. An advertising budget of $10 million will be split 50:50 between national and local advertising. Advertising will emphasize the car's economy and fun. During the first year, $100,000 will be spent on marketing research to find out who is buying the car and their satisfaction levels.

The third part of the marketing strategy statement describes the planned long-run sales and profit goals and marketing mix strategy over time:

> The company intends to capture a 3 percent long-run share of the total auto market and realize an after-tax return on investment of 15 percent. To achieve this, product quality will start high and be improved over time. Price will be raised in the second and third years if competition permits. The total advertising budget will be raised each year by about 10 percent. Marketing research will be reduced to $60,000 per year after the first year.

Business Analysis Once management has decided on the product concept and marketing strategy, it can evaluate the business attractiveness of the proposal. **Business analysis** involves a review of the sales, costs, and profit projections to find out whether they satisfy the company's objectives. If they do, the product can move to the product development stage.

To estimate sales, the company should look at the sales history of similar products and should survey market opinion. It should estimate minimum and maximum sales to learn the range of risk. Various sales forecasting methods were described in Chapter 8. After preparing the sales forecast, management can estimate the expected costs and profits for the product. The costs are estimated by the R&D, manufacturing, accounting, and finance departments. The planned marketing costs are included in the analysis. The company then uses the sales and costs figures to analyze the new product's financial attractiveness.

Product Development If the product concept passes the business test, it moves into **product development.** Here R&D or engineering develops the product concept into a physical product. Up to now it existed only as a word description, a drawing, or a crude mockup. This step calls for a large jump in investment. It will show whether the product idea can be turned into a workable product.

The R&D department will develop one or more physical versions of the product concept. It hopes to find a prototype that meets the following criteria: (1) Consumers see it as having the key features described in the product concept statement; (2) it performs safely under normal use; (3) it can be produced for the budgeted costs.

Developing a successful prototype can take days, weeks, months, or even years. The prototype must have the required functional features and also convey the intended psychological characteristics. The electric car, for example, should strike consumers as being well built and safe. Management must learn how consumers decide how well built a car is. Some consumers slam the door to hear its "sound." If the car does not have "solid-sounding" doors, consumers may think it is poorly built.

When the prototypes are ready, they must be tested. Functional tests are conducted under laboratory and field conditions to make sure that the product performs safely and effectively. The new car must start well; it must be comfortable; it must be able to go around corners without overturning. Consumer tests are conducted, asking consumers to test-drive the car and rate the car and its attributes.

Test Marketing If the product passes functional and consumer tests, the next step is market testing. **Test marketing** is the stage in which the product and marketing program are tested in more realistic market settings.

Test marketing lets the marketer get experience with marketing the product, find potential problems, and learn where more information is needed before going to the great expense of full introduction. The basic purpose of test marketing is to test the product itself in real market situations. But test marketing also allows the company to test the entire marketing program for the product—the positioning strategy, advertising, distribution, pricing, branding and packaging, and budget levels. The company uses test marketing to learn how consumers and dealers will react to handling, using, and repurchasing the product. Test marketing results can be used to make better sales and profit forecasts.

The amount of test marketing needed varies with each new product. Market testing costs can be enormous, and test marketing takes time during which competitors may gain an advantage. When the costs of developing and introducing the product are low, or when management is already confident that the new product will succeed, the company may do little or no product testing. Minor modifications of current products or copies of successful competitor products might not need testing. For example, Procter & Gamble introduced its Folger's decaffeinated coffee crystals without test marketing, and Pillsbury rolled out Chewy granola bars and chocolate covered Granola Dipps with no standard market testing. But when introducing the new product requires a large investment, or when management is not sure of the product or marketing program, the company may do a lot of test marketing. In fact, some products and marketing programs are tested, then withdrawn, changed, and retested many times over a period of several years before they are finally introduced. The costs of such test markets are high, but they are often small compared with the costs of making a major mistake.

Thus whether or not a company test markets, and the amount of testing it does, depend on the investment cost and risk of introducing the product on the one hand and on the testing costs and time pressures on the other. Test marketing methods vary with the type of product and market situation, and each method has advantages and disadvantages.

When they do use test marketing, consumer-products companies usually choose one of three approaches—standard test markets, controlled test markets, or simulated test markets.

Standard Test Markets

Standard test markets test the new consumer product in situations like those it would face in a full-scale launch. The company finds a small number of representative test cities where the company's salesforce tries to persuade resellers to carry the product and give it good shelf space and promotional support. The company puts on a full advertising and promotion campaign in these markets and uses store audits, consumer and distributor surveys, and other measures to gauge product performance. The results are used to forecast national sales and profits, to discover potential product problems, and to fine-tune the marketing program (see Marketing Highlight 11–2).

Standard test markets have some drawbacks. First, they take a long time to complete—sometimes from one to three years. If it turns out that the testing was unnecessary, the company will have lost many months of sales and profits. Second, extensive standard test markets may be very costly—the average standard test market costs over $3 million, and costs can go much higher. Procter & Gamble spent $15 million developing Duncan Hines ready-to-eat cookies in test market.[10] Finally, standard test markets give competitors a look at the company's new product well before it is introduced nationally. Many competitors will analyze the product and monitor the company's test market results. If the testing goes on too long, competitors will have time to develop defensive strategies and may even beat the company's product to the market. Furthermore, competitors often try to distort test market results by cutting their prices in test cities, increasing their promotion, or even buying up the product being tested. Despite these disadvantages, standard test markets are still the most widely used approach for major market testing. But many companies today are shifting toward quicker and cheaper controlled and simulated test marketing methods.

Controlled Test Markets

Several research firms keep controlled panels of stores that have agreed to carry new products for a fee. The company with the new product specifies the number of stores and geographical locations it wants. The research firm delivers the product to the participating stores and controls shelf location, amount of shelf space, displays and point-of-purchase promotions, and pricing according to specified plans. Sales results are tracked to determine the impact of these factors on demand.

Controlled test marketing systems like Nielsen's ERIM TESTSIGHT and Information Resources Inc's BehaviorScan track individual behavior from the television set to the checkout counter. IRI, for example, keeps a panel of about 3,000 shoppers in eight carefully selected small cities. It uses microcomputers to measure TV viewing in each panel household and can send special commercials to panel member television sets. Panel consumers buy from cooperating stores and show identification cards when making purchases. Detailed electronic scanner information on each consumer's purchases is fed into a central computer, where it is combined with the consumer's demographic and TV viewing information and reported daily. Thus BehaviorScan can provide store-by-store, week-by-week reports on the sales of new products being tested. And because the scanners record the specific purchases of individual consumers, the system can also provide information on repeat purchases and how different types of consumers are reacting to the new product, its advertising, and various other elements of the marketing program.

Controlled test markets take less time than standard test markets (six months to a year) and usually cost less (a year-long BehaviorScan test might cost from $200,000 to $2,000,000). However, some companies are concerned that the limited number of small cities and panel consumers used by the research services may not be representative of their products' markets or target consumers. And, as in standard test markets, controlled test markets allow competitors to get a look at the company's new product.[11]

Simulated Test Markets

Companies also can test new products in a simulated shopping environment. The company or research firm shows a sample of consumers ads and promotions for a variety of products, including the new product being tested. The consumers are given a small amount of money and are invited into a real or laboratory store where they may keep the money or use it to buy items. The company notes how many consumers buy the new product and competing brands. This simulation provides a

A TEST MARKET THAT REALLY MADE A DIFFERENCE

Some test markets do little more than confirm what management already knew. Others prune out the new-product losers—half of all test-marketed consumer products are killed before they reach national distribution. But still other test markets provide highly useful information that can save a promising product or turn an otherwise average product into a blockbuster. Here's a story about a test market that really made a difference.

When they burst onto the market four years ago, Dole Foods' Fruit 'n Juice Bars created a whole new category—fruit-based frozen novelties. The product now rings up $100 million in yearly sales. After that stunning success, Dole worked feverishly to find a follow-up product with the same kind of consumer appeal. It soon came up with Fruit and Cream Bars. Before investing in costly national distribution, Dole decided to run a test market in Orlando, Florida. It chose Orlando for the test market because Fruit 'n Juice was very popular there. Dole began the test market with high expectations—the Fruit and Cream brand manager felt that sales should amount to 70 percent of Fruit 'n Juice sales.

Dole offered Fruit and Cream in three flavors—strawberry, blueberry, and peach—packed four to a box. Packaging mentioned the "100 percent natural" ingredients and showed a bowl of fruit and cream. Dole supported the test market with standard adver-tising and promotion, including television, newspaper, direct mail, point-of-purchase, and coupons to stimulate trial and repeat purchasing. Fruit and Cream ads targeted upscale consumers aged 25 to 54 with kids, centering on the product and its taste and health appeal.

The test market quickly yielded some surprises. It showed that Fruit and Cream had much broader appeal than Dole had expected. The product sold across all novelty ice cream divisions, not just fruit-based. By the end of the third month, it had become the number one brand in the test market area. Focus groups showed that Fruit and Cream buyers saw the product as a real treat and felt they could indulge themselves without too much caloric guilt when they ate it. Consumers indicated that Fruit and Cream's natural ingredients and natural taste made it superior to the competition. Despite dazzling consumer accep-tance and sales performance, however, Dole discov-ered that its television advertising performed poorly—sales didn't jump when the television cam-paign began.

Based on the test market results, Dole made several changes in the Fruit and Cream marketing mix. It redesigned the packaging to greatly increase the size of the "100 percent natural" claim. And a new package picture showed cream being poured over the fruit—a subtle difference, but one that em-

measure of trial and the commercial's effectiveness against competing commercials. Consumers are then asked the reasons for their purchase or nonpurchase. Some weeks later they are interviewed by phone to determine product attitudes, usage, satisfaction, and repurchase intentions. Sophisticated computer models are used to project national sales from results of the simulated test market.

Simulated test markets overcome some of the disadvantages of standard and controlled test markets. They usually cost much less ($35,000 to $75,000) and can be run in eight weeks. And the new product is kept out of competitors' view. Yet, because of their small samples and simulated shopping environments, many marketers do not think that simulated test markets are as accurate or reliable as real-world tests.[12]

Test Marketing Industrial Goods

Industrial marketers use different methods for test marketing their new products. For example, they may conduct *product-use tests*. Here the industrial marketer selects a small group of potential customers who agree to use the new product for a limited time. The manufacturer's technical people watch how these customers use the product.

phasized Fruit and Cream's appetite appeal. Dole created a completely new advertising campaign that focused more heavily on natural taste and created a mellow feeling. The new ads used a Golden Oldie song, *You're Sweet 16, Peaches and Cream*, and emphasized the luxuriant nature of the product. Dole also shortened the test market from one year to six months, raised its estimate of Fruit and Cream sales to 80 percent of Fruit 'n Juice sales, and rushed to get two more flavors (banana and raspberry) ready.

With all the marketing changes, Dole was convinced that Fruit and Cream would take off like a rocket when it went national. But test markets can't predict future market events. Four new competing fruit-based novelty ice cream products came out at the same time as Fruit and Cream—two from Chiquita, one from Jell-O, and one from Minute Maid. The result was a marketer's nightmare. Dole missed all its Fruit and Cream sales projections; so did all the competitors. But Fruit and Cream held on, achieving a 3 percent market share instead of the expected 4 percent. The dust has now settled and Dole expects to hit its original projections this year.

The test market couldn't tell Dole managers erything they needed to know to make Fruit and Cream Bars an unqualified success. It could only show how consumers in a selected market area reacted to the new product and its marketing program. No test market can accurately predict future competitor actions and reactions, economic conditions, changing consumer tastes, and other factors that affect a new product's success. But the people at Dole are still strong believers. According to the Fruit and Cream brand manager, "Without the changes we made as a result of the test market, we would have been hurt much more than we were."

Dole Fruit and Cream Bars: Test marketing really made a difference.

Source: Adapted from Leslie Brennan, "Test Marketing Put to the Test," *Sales and Marketing Management*, March 1987, pp. 65–68.

From this test the manufacturer learns about customer training and servicing requirements. After the test, the marketer asks the customer about purchase intent and other reactions.

New industrial products can also be tested at *trade shows*. These shows draw a large number of buyers who view new products in a few concentrated days. The manufacturer sees how buyers react to various product features and terms, and can assess buyer interest and purchase intentions. The industrial marketer can also test new industrial products in *distributor and dealer display rooms*, where they may stand next to other company products and possibly competitors' products. This method yields preference and pricing information in the normal selling atmosphere for the product.

Finally, some industrial marketers use *standard or controlled test markets* to measure the potential of their new products. They produce a limited supply of the product and give it to the salesforce to sell in a limited number of geographical areas. The company gives the product full advertising, sales promotion, and other marketing support. Such test markets let the company test the product and its marketing program in real market situations.

Commercialization Test marketing gives management the information needed to make a final decision about whether to launch the new product. If the company goes ahead with *commercialization*—introducing and marketing the product—it will face high costs. The company will have to build or rent a manufacturing facility. And it may have to spend, in the case of a new consumer packaged good, between $10 million and $100 million for advertising and sales promotion alone in the first year. For example, McDonald's spent over $5 million dollars *per week* on advertising during the introduction of its McDLT sandwich.

In launching a new product, the company must make four decisions.

When?

The first decision is whether it is the right time to introduce the new product. If the electric car will eat into the sales of the company's other cars, its introduction may be delayed. Or if the electric car can be improved further, the company may wait to launch it next year. Or if the economy is down, the company may want to wait until it improves.

Where?

The company must decide whether to launch the new product in a single location, a region, several regions, the national market, or the international market. Few companies have the confidence, capital, and capacity to launch new products into full national distribution. They will develop a planned market rollout over time. For example, small companies will select an attractive city and put on a blitz campaign to enter the market. They will then enter other cities one at a time. Large companies will introduce their product into a whole region and then move to the next region. Companies with national distribution networks, such as auto companies, often will launch their new models in the national market.

To Whom?

Within the rollout markets, the company must target its distribution and promotion to the best prospect groups. The company has already profiled the prime prospects in earlier test marketing. It must now fine-tune its market identification, looking especially for early adopters, heavy users, and opinion leaders.

How?

The company must develop an action plan for introducing the new product into the selected markets. It must spend the marketing budget on the marketing mix and various other activities. Thus the electric car's launch may be supported by a publicity campaign and then by offers of gifts to draw more people to the showrooms. The company must prepare a separate marketing plan for each new market.

PRODUCT LIFE-CYCLE STRATEGIES

After launching the new product, management wants the product to enjoy a long and happy life. Although it does not expect the product to sell forever, management wants to earn a decent profit to cover all the effort and risk that went into it. Management is aware that each product will have a life cycle, although its exact shape and length are not known in advance.

FIGURE 11-3
Sales and profits over the product's life from inception to demise

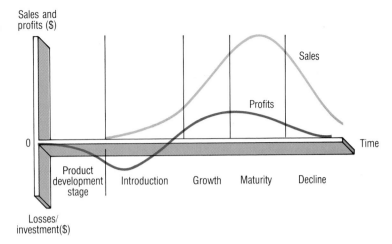

The typical **product life cycle** (PLC) is a curve, as shown in Figure 11-3. It is marked by five distinct stages:

1. *Product development* begins when the company finds and develops a new product idea. During product development, sales are zero and the company's investment costs add up.

2. *Introduction* is a period of slow sales growth as the product is being introduced in the market. Profits are nonexistent in this stage because of the heavy expenses of product introduction.

3. *Growth* is a period of rapid market acceptance and increasing profits.

4. *Maturity* is a period of slowdown in sales growth because the product has achieved acceptance by most of the potential buyers. Profits level off or decline because of increased marketing outlays to defend the product against competition.

5. *Decline* is the period when sales fall off quickly and profits drop.

Some products stay in the maturity stage of the product life cycle for a long, long time: Kikkoman is 358 years old!

FIGURE 11-4
Product life cycles for selected toothpaste brands from 1936 to 1982

Source: "Life Beyond the Life Cycle," *The Nielsen Researcher*, Number 1, 1984, p. 3.

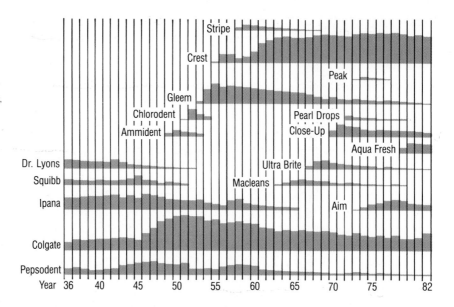

Not all products follow this S-shaped product life cycle curve. Some products are introduced and die quickly. Others stay in the maturity stage for a long, long time. Some enter the decline stage, then are cycled back into the growth stage through strong promotion or repositioning.

The PLC concept can describe a product class (gasoline-powered automobiles), a product form (station wagons), or a brand (Taurus). The PLC concept applies differently in each case. Product classes have the longest life cycles. The sales of many product classes stay in the mature stage for long time. Product forms, on the other hand, tend to have the standard PLC shape. Product forms such as the dial telephone and cream deodorants passed through a regular history of introduction, rapid growth, maturity, and decline. A specific brand's life cycle can change quickly because of changing competitive attacks and responses. The life cycles of several toothpaste brands are shown in Figure 11-4. Most toothpaste brands moved quickly through their life cycles. Only a few major brands remained strong for more than ten years before shopping into decline. The PLC concept can also be applied to what are known as styles, fashions, and fads. Their special life-cycle features are described in Marketing Highlight 11–3.

The PLC concept can be used by marketers as a useful framework for describing how products and markets work. But using the PLC concept for forecasting product performance or for developing marketing strategies presents some practical problems.[13] For example, managers may have trouble identifying a product's current life-cycle stage, when it moves into the next stage, and the factors that affect how the product will move through the stages. In practice, it is very hard to forecast the sales level at each PLC stage, the length of each stage, and the shape of the PLC curve.

Using the PLC concept to develop marketing strategy can be hard because strategy is both a cause and result of the product's life cycle. The product's current PLC position suggests the best marketing strategies, and the resulting marketing strategies affect product performance in later life-cycle stages. Yet when used carefully the PLC concept can help in developing good marketing strategies for different stages of the product life cycle.

We looked at the product development stage of the product life cycle in the

STYLE, FASHION AND FAD CYCLES

In markets where style and fashion influence buying, sales cycles take place, and marketers need to understand and predict them.

A *style* is a basic and distinctive mode of expression. For example, styles appear in homes (colonial, ranch, Cape Cod), clothing (formal, casual), and art (realistic, surrealistic, abstract). Once a style is invented, it may last for generations, coming in and out of vogue. A style has a cycle showing several periods of renewed interest.

A *fashion* is a currently accepted or popular style in a given field. For example, in clothing the "preppie look" of the late seventies gave way to the "loose and layered look" of the mid to late eighties. Fashions pass through four stages. In the *distinctiveness stage*, some consumers take an interest in something new to set themselves apart from other consumers. The product may be custom-made or produced in small quantities by a few producers. In the *copying stage*, other consumers take an interest out of a desire to copy the fashion leaders, and additional manufacturers begin to produce larger quantities of the product. In the *mass fashion stage*, the fashion has become very popular and manufacturers have geared up for mass production. Finally, in the *decline stage*, consumers start moving toward other fashions that are beginning to catch on. Thus fashions tend to grow slowly, remain popular for a while, and decline slowly.

Fads are fashions that come quickly into the public eye, are adopted with great zeal, peak early, and decline very fast. Their acceptance cycle is short, and they tend to attract only a limited following. Fads often have a novel or quirky nature, as when people started buying Rubik's Cubes, Trivial Pursuit games, "pet rocks," or Pound Puppies. Fads appeal to people who are looking for excitement or who want to set themselves apart from others or have something to talk about to others. Fads do not survive for long because they normally do not satisfy a strong need or satisfy it well. It is difficult to predict whether something will only be a fad, and if so, how long it will last—a few days, weeks, or months. The amount of media attention it receives, along with other factors, will help influence its duration.

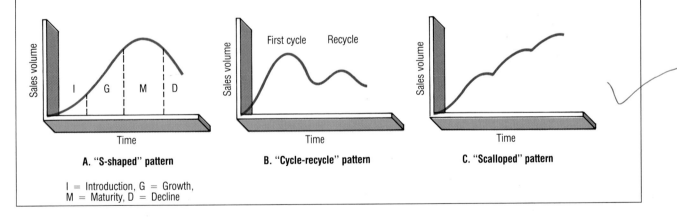

A. "S-shaped" pattern **B. "Cycle-recycle" pattern** **C. "Scalloped" pattern**

I = Introduction, G = Growth,
M = Maturity, D = Decline

first part of the chapter. We now look at strategies for each of the other life-cycle stages.

Introduction Stage   The **introduction stage** starts when the new product is first distributed and made available for purchase. Introduction takes time, and sales growth is apt to be slow. Such well-known products as instant coffee, frozen orange juice, and powdered coffee creamers lingered for many years before they entered a stage of rapid growth.

In this stage, profits are negative or low because of the low sales and high distribution and promotion expenses. Much money is needed to attract distributors and provide them with stocks of the product. Promotion spending is high, in order to inform consumers of the new product and get them to try it.

There are only a few competitors at this stage, and they produce basic versions of the product, since the market is not ready for product refinements. The firms focus their selling on those buyers who are the readiest to buy, usually the higher-income groups. Prices tend to be on the high side because of low output, production problems, and high promotion and other expenses.

Growth Stage   If the new product satisfies the market, it will enter the **growth stage,** and sales will start climbing quickly. The early adopters (buyers) of the product will continue to buy, and later buyers will start following their lead, especially if they hear favorable word-of-mouth. New competitors will enter the market attracted by the opportunities for profit. They will introduce new product features, and this will expand the market. The increase in competitors leads to an increase in the number of distribution outlets, and sales jump just to fill distributor inventories. Prices remain where they are or fall only slightly. Companies keep their promotion spending at the same or a slightly higher level to meet competition and continue educating the market.

Profits increase during the growth stage as promotion costs are spread over a large volume and unit manufacturing costs fall. The firm uses several strategies to sustain rapid market growth as long as possible. It improves product quality and adds new product features and models. It enters new market segments and new distribution channels. It shifts some advertising from building product awareness to building product conviction and purchase, and it lowers prices at the right time to attract more buyers.

The firm in the growth stage faces a tradeoff between high market share and high current profit. By spending a lot of money on product improvement, promotion, and distribution, it can capture a dominant position. But it gives up maximum current profit in the hope of improving profit in the next stage.

Maturity Stage   At some point a product's sales growth will slow down, and the product will enter a **maturity stage.** This maturity stage normally lasts longer than the previous stages, and it poses strong challenges to marketing management. Most products are in the maturity stage of the life cycle, and therefore most of marketing management deals with the mature product.

To sustain growth, Sony keeps adding new features to its Walkman line.

The slowdown in sales growth results in many producers with many products to sell. This overcapacity leads to greater competition. Competitors begin marking down prices, and they increase their advertising and sales promotions. They increase their R&D budgets to find better versions of the product. These steps mean a drop in profit. Some of the weaker competitors start dropping out. The industry eventually contains only well established competitors. Product managers should not simply defend their products. A good offense is the best defense. They should consider changing—modifying—the market, product, and marketing mix.

Market Modification

In using a market modification strategy the company tries to increase the consumption of the current product. It looks for new users and market segments, as when Clinque marketed its new line of skin-care products for men. The manager also looks for ways to increase usage among present customers. Campbell does this by offering recipes and convincing consumers that "soup is good food." Or the company may want to reposition the brand to appeal to a larger or faster-growing segment, as Burger King did when it repositioned as "the best food for fast times."

Product Modification

The product manager can also change product characteristics—such as product quality, features, or style—to attract new users and more usage.

A strategy of *quality improvement* aims at increasing the performance of the product—such as its durability, reliability, speed, or taste. This strategy is effective when the quality can be improved, when buyers believe the claim of improved quality, and when enough buyers want higher quality.

A strategy of *feature improvement* adds new features that expand the product's usefulness, safety, or convenience. Feature improvement has been successfully used by Japanese makers of watches, calculators, copying machines, and consumer electronics. For example, Seiko keeps adding new styles and features to its line of watches.

A strategy of *style improvement* aims to increase the attractiveness of the product. Thus car manufacturers restyle their cars to attract buyers who want a new look. The makers of consumer food and household products introduce new flavors, colors, ingredients, or packages to rejuvenate consumer buying.

Marketing Mix Modification

The product manager can also try to improve sales by changing one or more marketing mix elements. Prices can be cut to attract new users and competitors' customers. A new advertising campaign can be launched. Aggressive sales promotion—trade deals, coupons, gifts, and contests—can be used. The company can move into larger market channels, using mass merchandisers, if these channels are growing. The company can offer new or improved services to the buyers.

Decline Stage   The sales of most product forms and brands eventually dip. The sales decline may be slow, as in the case of oatmeal cereal; or rapid, as for video games. Sales may plunge to zero, or they may drop to a low level where they continue for many years. This is the **decline stage.**

Sales decline for many reasons, including technological advances, shifts in consumer tastes, and increased competition. As sales and profits decline, some firms withdraw from the market. Those remaining may reduce the number of their product offerings. They may drop smaller market segments and marginal trade channels. They may cut the promotion budget and reduce their prices further.

Miller repositioned its High Life brand during the
1970s to move it from maturity or decline
back into the growth stage.

Carrying a weak product can be very costly to the firm, and not just in profit
terms. There are many hidden costs—the weak product may take up too much of
management's time. It often requires frequent price and inventory adjustments. It
requires advertising and salesforce attention that might better be used to make the
"healthy" products more profitable. Its failing reputation can cause customer concerns
about the company and its other products. The biggest cost may well lie in the
future. Keeping weak products delays the search for replacement products, creates
a lopsided product mix, hurts current profits, and weakens the company's foothold
on the future.

For these reasons, companies need to pay more attention to their aging products.
The first task is to identify those products that are in the decline stage by regularly

TABLE 11-4
Product Life Cycle:
Characteristics and
Responses

	INTRODUCTION	GROWTH	MATURITY	DECLINE
Characteristics				
Sales	Low	Fast growth	Slow growth	Decline
Profits	Negligible	Peak levels	Declining	Low or zero
Cash flow	Negative	Moderate	High	Low
Customers	Innovative	Mass market	Mass market	Laggards
Competitors	Few	Growing	Many rivals	Declining number
Responses				
Strategic focus	Expand market	Market penetration	Defend share	Productivity
Marketing expenditures	High	High (declining %)	Falling	Low
Marketing emphasis	Product awareness	Brand preference	Brand loyalty	Selective
Distribution	Patchy	Intensive	Intensive	Selective
Price	High	Lower	Lowest	Rising
Product	Basic	Improved	Differentiated	Unchanged

Source: Peter Doyle, "The Realities of the Product Life Cycle," *Quarterly Review of Marketing*, Summer 1976, p. 5.

reviewing the sales, market shares, cost, and profit trends on each product. For each declining product, management has to decide whether to maintain, harvest, or drop it. Management may decide to maintain its brand without change in the hope that competitors will leave the industry. For example, Procter & Gamble remained in the declining liquid-soap business as others withdrew, and it made good profits. Or management may decide to reposition the brand in hopes of moving it back into the growth stage of the product life cycle. Miller did this with its Miller High Life brand in the 1970s. It changed Miller from an upper-income, "champagne of beers" position to a more middle-American one, and sales grew rapidly. Management may decide to *harvest* the product, which means reducing various costs (plant and equipment, maintenance, R&D, advertising, salesforce) and hoping that sales hold up fairly well for a while. If successful, harvesting will increase the company's profits in the short run. Or management may decide to drop the product from the line. It can sell it to another firm or simply liquidate it at salvage value. If the company plans to find a buyer, it will not want to run down the product through harvesting.[14]

The key characteristics of each stage of the product life cycle are summarized in Table 11-4. The table also lists the marketing responses made by companies in each stage.

■ SUMMARY

Organizations need to develop new products and services. Their current products face limited life spans and must be replaced by newer products. But new products can fail—the risks of innovation are as great as the rewards. The key to successful innovation lies in strong planning and organization, and in a systematic new product development process.

The new product development process consists of eight stages: idea generation, idea screening, concept development and testing, marketing strategy development, business analysis, product development, test marketing, and commercialization. The purpose of each stage is to decide whether the idea should be further developed or dropped.

The company wants to minimize the chances of poor ideas moving forward and of good ideas being rejected.

Each product has a life cycle marked by a changing set of problems and opportunities. The sales of the typical product follows an S-shaped curve made up of five stages. The cycle begins with the product development stage when the company finds and develops a new product idea. The introduction stage is marked by slow growth and low profits as the product is being pushed into distribution. If successful, the product enters a growth stage marked by rapid sales growth and increasing profits. During this stage the company tries to improve the product, enter new market segments and distribution channels, and reduce its price slightly. Then comes a maturity stage in which sales growth slows down and profits stabilize. The company seeks strategies to renew sales growth, including market, product, and marketing mix modification. Finally, the product enters a decline stage where sales and profits fall off. The company's task during this stage is to identify the declining product and decide whether to maintain, harvest, or drop it. In the last case, the product can be sold to another firm or liquidated for salvage value.

■ QUESTIONS FOR DISCUSSION

1. Before videotape cameras for home use became widely available, Polaroid introduced Polavision, a system for making home movies that did not require laboratory processing. Like most other home-movie systems, Polavision film cassettes lasted only a few minutes and did not record sound. Despite the advantage of "instant developing" and heavy promotional expenditures by Polaroid, Polavision never gained wide acceptance. Why do you think Polavision flopped, given Polaroid's previous record of new product successes?

2. If companies can now turn one out of seven new product ideas into successful products, how much time do you think they should spend on idea generation? How many ideas should they generate? List as many new product ideas for McDonald's as you can think of.

3. Less than one-third of new product ideas come from the customer. Does this low percentage conflict with the philosophy of "find a need and fill it" expressed in the marketing concept? At what stage should the customer be brought into the process of product development?

4. What type of test marketing would you recommend for the following products? (a) a deodorant containing baking soda, (b) a headache remedy that is dissolved in water before use, and (c) a mid-calorie cola, sweetened with both sugar and artificial sweetener for fewer calories than regular colas and better taste than diet colas.

5. How are standard test-market cities selected? Describe the characteristics companies should look for in choosing where to test their new products.

6. NutraSweet, the NutraSweet Company's brand name for aspartame, was approved for use in foods in 1981. In 1992, the company's patent expires, and other companies will be able to sell their own brands of aspartame. Describe NutraSweet's life cycle from 1980 to 1999.

7. Before acquiring or imitating a product developed by another organization, a company should consider the product's potential for long-run profitability. How can a company tell products with long life cycles apart from current fads and fashions? What products on the market now do you think are fads or fashions that will soon disappear?

8. What types of promotion are used and how much is spent on promotion at different stages of a product's life cycle? Give examples, and discuss why promotional types and expenditures vary over the product life cycle.

9. Some evidence suggests that consuming oatmeal, and especially oat bran, may be helpful in reducing people's levels of cholesterol. If this evidence is confirmed by further research, what impact could this health benefit have on the life cycle of oat-based products already on the market?

■ KEY TERMS

Business analysis   A review of the sales, costs, and profit projections for a new product to find out whether they satisfy the company's objectives.

Concept testing   Testing new product concepts with a group of target consumers to find out if the concept has strong consumer appeal.

Decline stage   The product life cycle stage in which a product's sales decline.

Growth stage   The product life cycle stage in which sales start climbing quickly.

Idea generation   The systematic search for new product ideas.

Idea screening   Screening new product ideas in order to spot good ideas and drop poor ones as soon as possible.

Introduction stage   The product life cycle stage in which the new product is first distributed and made available for purchase.

Marketing strategy development   Designing an initial marketing strategy for a new product based on the product concept.

Maturity stage   The stage in the product life cycle in which sales growth slows or levels off.

New product development   The development of original products, product improvements, product modifications, and new brands through the firm's own research and development efforts.

Product concept   A detailed version of the new product idea stated in meaningful consumer terms.

Product development   Developing the product concept into a physical product in order to assure that the product idea can be turned into a workable product.

Product idea   An idea for a possible product that the company can see itself offering to the market.

Product image   The way consumers picture an actual or potential product.

Product life cycle (PLC)   The course of a product's

sales and profits over its lifetime. It involves five distinct stages: product development, introduction, growth, maturity, and decline.

Test marketing The stage of new product development in which the product and marketing program are tested in more realistic market settings.

■ REFERENCES

1. See Steven Greenhouse, "An Innovator Gets Down to Business," *The New York Times*, October 12, 1986, Section 3, pp. 1, 8; William Hoffer, "Spurs for Innovation," *Nation's Business*, June 1986, pp. 42–45; and "Keeping the Fires Lit Under the Innovators," *Fortune*, March 20, 1988, p. 45.

2. See "Products of the Year," *Fortune*, December 9, 1985, pp. 106–12.

3. See David S. Hopkins and Earl L. Bailey, "New Product Pressures," *Conference Board Record*, June 1971, pp. 16–24; *New Product Management for the 1980s* (New York: Booz, Allen & Hamilton, 1982); and "Products of the Year," p. 106.

4. See Leigh Lawton and A. Parasuraman, "So You Want Your New Product Planning to Be Productive," *Business Horizons*, December 1980, pp. 29–34.

5. See "Listening to the Voice of the Marketplace," *Business Week*, February 21, 1983, p. 90ff.

6. See Eric vonHipple, "Get New Products from Consumers," *Harvard Business Review*, March–April 1982, pp. 117–22.

7. Russell Mitchell, "How Ford Hit the Bullseye with Taurus," *Business Week*, June 30, 1986, pp. 69–70.

8. For more on idea screening, see Tom W. White, "Use Variety of Internal, External Sources to Gather and Screen New Product Ideas," *Marketing News*, September 16, 1983, Sec. 2, p. 12.

9. For more on product concept testing, see William L. Moore, "Concept Testing," *Journal of Business Research*, 10 (1982), pp. 279–94; and David A. Schwartz, "Concept Testing Can Be Improved—and Here's How," *Marketing News*, January 6, 1984, pp. 22–23.

10. Julie Franz, "Test Marketing: Traveling Through a Maze of Choices," *Advertising Age*, February 13, 1986, p. 11.

11. For more on controlled test markets, see Felix Kessler, "High-Tech Shocks in Ad Research," *Fortune*, July 7, 1986, pp. 58–62.

12. For more on simulated test markets, see Kevin Higgins, "Simulated Test Marketing Winning Acceptance," *Marketing News*, March 1, 1985, pp. 15, 19; and "Test Marketing: New Techniques Restrict the Risk," *Advertising Age*, August 24, 1987, p. 51.

13. See George S. Day, "The Product Life Cycle: Analysis and Applications Issues," *Journal of Marketing*, Fall 1981, pp. 60–67. See also John E. Swan and David R. Rink, "Fitting Market Strategy to Varying Product Life Cycles," *Business Horizons*, January–February 1982, pp. 72–76; and Sak Onkvisit and John J. Shaw, "Competition and Product Management," Can the Product Life Cycle Help?" *Business Horizons*, July–August 1986, pp. 51–62.

14. See Laurence P. Feldman and Albert L. Page, "Harvesting: The Misunderstood Market Exit Strategy," *Journal of Business Strategy*, Spring 1985, pp. 79–85.

CASE 8

HANES CORPORATION: STARBOOKS

The outstanding success of L'eggs pantyhose encouraged Hanes to launch other products using the L'eggs marketing ideas with the hope of duplicating the L'eggs success. The marketing director for new products is working on a plan for marketing high-quality children's paperback books under the name Starbooks. He has called a meeting of his staff to get their ideas and provide a training opportunity.

Starbooks would be aimed at preschool readers, early readers, and readers up to 12 years of age; they would retail at 60 cents to $1.69. The licensing rights to 200 titles from several publishers would be available if it is decided to go ahead. Children's books are sold through book and department stores, direct mail, book clubs, and other retail outlets such as supermarkets and drugstores, each accounting for about 6 percent of total sales. Milwaukee, Rochester, New York, Kansas City, and Salt Lake City are possible test markets.

The marketing director's reasons for focusing on children's books include the following:

- A large market exists ($600 million a year).

- There are many competitors with small market shares. Western Publishing Company's Golden Books are probably the best known.

- Present marketing efforts are not aggressive.

- The trend toward one-store shopping favors supermarkets and large chain drugstores, which already carry children's books.

- Children's books carry a higher percentage gross margin than most items in supermarkets.

- The L'eggs marketing plans seem at least partly suitable for children's books, and the L'eggs direct distribution network is already in place.

The phenomenal success of L'eggs is attributed to the distinctive name and closely related egg-shaped package, which is presented in unique display racks serviced by the company's own salesforce. L'eggs products are sold on a consignment basis, which permits Hanes to control the items offered, size of inventory, and price. The company's computerized information system has made possible effective control of product offerings, inventory, and manufacturing through timely and very accurate knowledge of retail sales. When L'eggs entered the hosiery and pantyhose market, the market was fragmented and little brand advertising was being done.

Follow-up products using the L'eggs strategy have included socks and underwear for men and L'erin cosmetics

for women. None of them achieved the success of L'eggs.

A few days before the staff meeting it was learned that a new marketing plan for Golden Books would soon be launched by Western Publishing Company, a subsidiary of Mattel, Inc., the well-known toy and game marketer. Since Western Publishing has not been innovative or aggressive in the past, the marketing director does not believe its new plan will change the competitive situation very much.

1. What recommendations would you make to the Starbooks marketing director?

CASE 9

CAMPBELL SOUP COMPANY

The Campbell Soup Company, a large diversified branded food company, has been marketing canned soup under its familiar red-and-white label for almost 100 years. It now holds over 80 percent of the U.S. market, with private-label brands supplied by H. J. Heinz a distant second at about 10 percent. Recognizing that environmental and competitive changes may cause a decline in both the size of the canned soup market and the company's share of that market, Campbell's new marketing-minded management is aggressively seeking new market opportunities and new approaches for old product lines. The soup business is of special interest because of its current and historical importance to the company.

Changes in Americans' life styles and other significant environment changes, as well as changes inside the company, present both threats and opportunities. The company is faced with the problem of how to increase the consumption of prepared soup and Campbell's share of the market in an environment vastly different from the one in which the long-time staple product was born and nurtured. A complete rethinking of Campbell's soup marketing is needed.

The short-run problem is how to make canned soup more attractive. Campbell has recently characterized itself as the "well-being" company and promoted its foods as conducive to good health. One advertising campaign presented soup as health insurance. The slogan "Soup is good food" has also been part of the company's advertising. Efforts by Campbell to increase the consumption of soup include promoting it for different occasions (for example, breakfast), other uses (cooking sauces), and creative cookery (mixture of two or more soups). Most of Campbell's soups are condensed and must be diluted. The ready-to-eat chunky soup line was created for people who want to make soup an entire meal.

Also important, because of the development time required, is the phasing in of new forms of soup packaging to make soup more attractive. Among the products being

developed is a microwave soup. The concept being considered is a plastic bowl containing 9.5 ounces of chicken soup with broad egg noodles. It is a shelf-stable product with a plastic overcap that can be slipped off and has a heating time of three minutes. The plastic container is reusable if a person wants to save some of the soup for another time. This will be the first microwavable soup and is said to represent a packaging breakthrough. Also being considered is the instant dry soup market, one in which Lipton is the leader and Campbell has no present position.

Campbell's management believes that the future of food packaging lies in more attractive and more convenient containers, such as plastic, aseptic boxes, and microwavable dishes. It is searching for suitable new packages and a plan to phase them in alongside its familiar canned soup.

The company's director of marketing research says, "The can isn't as user friendly as it used to be." In consumer preference surveys, he continues, canned soup "is being battered and beaten." But the company's director of packaging is quoted in the same source as saying that "deep down everybody feels good about the can. We don't want to muck it up by changing that good solid conservation image." Exchanging a dud for the familiar tin can could be disastrous.

A major objection to the can is inconvenience: It requires using a can opener, mixing with water if the soup is condensed, heating in a pot, and washing the pot.

Another group of objections is centered on health. Younger people, particularly oppose the use of artificial ingredients and preservatives. They also believe that nutrients are lost in the cooking and canning processes. Others contend that the salt content of canned soup is too high. This claim is made by watchdog people of various ages, particularly the elderly, who represent a growing market and generally prefer lighter meals, including soup.

A third major objection to canned soup comes from the rapidly growing segment of U.S. households, now over

40 percent, that use microwave ovens which are not designed for metal containers.

The outstanding advantage of the can is that it allows extended shelf life, but this edge is being eroded by technological advances in plastic. A second advantage is that the rigid tin can protects its contents from physical damage better than almost any other package form.

The technological threat to the can is not immediate. Improved can technology is gradually eliminating the potential health hazard associated with lead in the older soldered seam process. Lighter and less expensive cans are being made. Despite the rapid changes in packaging technology, major food processors, which have a heavy investment in existing technology and are reluctant to switch to tremendously expensive new packaging systems, are holding back on any major moves. The answers to the basic questions of what, where, when, and how to change packaging depend on technical feasibility, economic soundness, and, most importantly, market acceptance.

It is generally held that metal and glass are the best oxygen barriers for packaging. But it is also recognized that the economic attractiveness of plastic will justify some reduction in shelf life, especially when products are "dated" to show shelf life. Present estimates are that the plastic can, which will look very much like the metal can, will be one-third the weight and require half as much energy to produce. Some expect it to be the future workhorse of the food-packaging industry.

Long-term development as seen by one analyst is from cans to semirigid packages, such as aseptics for fruit juices and milk, and then to flexible packages such as films and pouches. Their present use in upscale markets is just the beginning. Eventually, alternative packaging could capture 80 percent or more of the canned soup market. But "the can is going to be around for a long time," according to a Campbell executive. Change is risky when uncertainty is high regarding technological capabilities, economic considerations, and market acceptance.

1. Describe the activities and circumstances involved in the preparation and consumption of soup, considering each of the different forms available in the marketplace, including soup from "scratch." What are the problems and opportunities for improvement of each of these forms from the consumer's point of view?

2. What are your recommendations for increasing the consumption of canned soup and Campbell's share of the market? What are your recommendations with regard to marketing soup in new forms of packaging?

608

609

12 *Pricing Products: Pricing Considerations and Approaches*

A consumer buying a video cassette recorder from Sears faces a bewildering array of models and prices. The recent Sears catalog shows ten different VCR models at six different prices, ranging from $249.99 to $789.99.

The consumer must sort through the catalog descriptions and decide whether the extra features on the more expensive models are worth the extra price.

Consumers may have trouble choosing among the different prices, but Sears probably has more trouble *setting* the prices. Managers at Sears must consider many factors in their complex price-setting process. They first consider the company's overall marketing objectives and the role of price in the marketing mix. Should Sears price to maximize current profits on VCRs or to maximize long-run market share? Should it use a high-price/low-volume strategy or a low-price/high-volume strategy? Sears' overall position as a family department store suggests that it should offer VCR models priced for every family budget.

When setting VCR prices, Sears must also consider costs. These include the costs of making VCRs or buying them from suppliers, and the costs of ship-

ping, storing, stocking, selling, and customer services. Sears must price its VCRs to cover these costs plus a target profit. But costs can be hard to figure out and assign. For example, how much of Sears' general operating and administrative costs should be allocated to each VCR Sears sells? Also, if Sears considers only costs when setting prices, it ignores important demand and competitive factors.

Costs set the floor for prices; consumer demand sets the ceiling. Sears must understand the relationship between price and demand for its VCRs. Consumer-oriented pricing starts with knowing consumer perceptions of each model's value. If Sears charges more than buyers' perceived value, its VCRs will sell poorly. If it charges less, its VCRs will sell very well but will provide less revenue. Sears must find the price that matches buyer value perceptions and maximizes total VCR profit.

Sears must also consider competitors' VCR quality and prices. If Sears VCRs are similar to those of its major competitors, but it charges more, it risks losing sales. If it sets prices much lower than those of comparable products, it will win sales from competitors but lose profit opportunitites.

Thus Sears sets its basic VCR prices on the basis of its costs, demand, and competitors' prices. But setting basic prices is just the beginning. Sears must now adjust these prices to account for different buyers and market situations. For example, consumers vary in how they value different VCR features, so Sears offers many models for different price segments. The basic VHS 105-channel, 14-day/4-program model sells for $249.99. Add direct channel access, and the price jumps to $314.99. Move up to the 120-channel, 1-year/4-program, 3-head model, and you pay $439.99. Add stereo and on-screen programming and you are up to $519.99. Sears best, a VHS 119-channel, 3-head, 1-year/4-program, remote control, stereo VCR with picture-in-picture capability and multichannel visual scan, goes for $789.99. Thus Sears offers a model to fit any consumer preference and pocketbook.

Sears also adjusts its prices for psychological impact. For example, instead of charging $250 for its lowest price model, Sears charges $249.99. This price suggests a bargain, and many consumers will perceive it in the under-$250 rather than the $250-and-over price range. Sears also adjusts prices to meet market conditions and competitor actions. For example, after Christmas it knocked $150 off the price of its best model to clear inventories and promote off-season demand.

Thus when setting prices, Sears must balance costs against demand and competitors' prices. It must constantly adjust prices to account for buyer differences and changing market conditions. And it must do this for each of the thousands of products it sells. Sears pricing strategies can affect its profits and even its survival. In the late 1960s Sears decided to upgrade its merchandise and raise its prices. The higher prices caused many loyal Sears shoppers to shift their buying to K Mart and other lower-priced stores—it took Sears years to overcome the loss.[1]

Chapter Objectives *After reading this chapter, you should be able to:*

1. Discuss how marketing objectives and mix strategy, costs, and other internal company factors affect pricing decisions.
2. List and discuss factors outside the company that affect pricing decisions.
3. Explain how price setting depends on consumer perceptions of price and on the price-demand relationship.
4. Compare the three general pricing approaches.

ALL profit organizations and many nonprofit organizations must set prices on their products or services. Price goes by many names:

Price is all around us. You pay *rent* for your apartment, *tuition* for your education, and a *fee* to your physician or dentist. The airline, railway, taxi, and bus companies charge you a *fare*; the local utilities call their price a *rate*; and the local bank charges you *interest* for the money you borrow. The price for driving your car on Florida's Sunshine Parkway is a *toll*, and the company that insures your car charges you a *premium*. The guest lecturer charges an *honorarium* to tell you about a government official who took a *bribe* to help a shady character steal *dues* collected by a trade association. Clubs or societies to which you belong may make a special *assessment* to pay unusual expenses. Your regular lawyer may ask for a *retainer* to cover her services. The "price" of an executive is a *salary*, the price of a salesperson may be a *commission*, and the price of a worker is a *wage*. Finally, although economists would disagree, many of us feel that *income taxes* are the price we pay for the privilege of making money.[2]

Simply defined, **price** is the amount of money charged for a product or service. More broadly, price is the sum of the values consumers exchange for the benefits of having or using the product or service.

How are prices set? Historically, prices were set by buyers and sellers bargaining with each other. Sellers would ask for a higher price than they expected to get, and buyers would offer less than they expected to pay. Through bargaining, they would arrive at an acceptable price.

Setting one price for all buyers is a fairly modern idea. It was helped along by the development of large-scale retailing at the end of the nineteenth century. F. W. Woolworth, Tiffany and Co., John Wanamaker, J. L. Hudson, and others advertised a "strictly one-price policy" because they carried so many items and had so many employees that bargaining would have been too difficult to control.

Historically, price has been the major factor affecting buyer choice. This fact is still true in poorer nations, among poorer groups, and with commodity products. However, nonprice factors have become more important in buyer choice behavior in recent decades.

Price is the only element in the marketing mix that produces revenue; the other elements represent costs. Further, pricing and price competition have been rated as the number one problem facing marketing executives in the mid-1980s.[3] Yet many companies do not handle pricing well. The most common mistakes are: Pricing is too cost-oriented; price is not revised often enough to reflect market changes; pricing does not take the rest of the marketing mix into account; and price is not varied enough for different product items and market segments.

In this and the next chapter, we will look at the problem of setting prices. This chapter will look at the factors marketers must consider when setting prices and at general pricing approaches. In the next chapter, we will examine pricing strategies for new product pricing, product-mix pricing, initiating and responding to price changes, and adjusting prices for buyer and situational factors.

*F*ACTORS TO CONSIDER WHEN SETTING PRICES

The company's pricing decisions are affected by many internal company factors and by external environmental factors. These factors are shown in Figure 12-1. *Internal factors* include the company's marketing objectives, marketing mix strategy, costs, and organization. *External factors* include the nature of the market and demand, competition, and other environmental factors.

FIGURE 12-1
Factors affecting price decisions

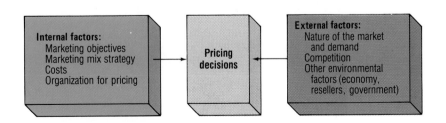

Internal Factors Affecting Pricing Decisions

Marketing Objectives

Before setting price, the company must decide on its strategy for the product. If the company has selected its target market and positioning carefully, then its marketing mix strategy, including price, will be fairly straightforward. For example, if General Motors decides to produce a new sports car to compete with European sports cars in the high-income segment, this position suggests charging a high price. Thus pricing strategy is largely determined by prior decisions on market positioning.

At the same time, the company may pursue additional objectives. The clearer a firm is about its objectives, the easier it is to set price. Examples of common objectives are survival, current profit maximization, market-share maximization, and product quality leadership.

SURVIVAL. Companies set survival as their major objective if troubled by too much capacity, heavy competition, or changing consumer wants. To keep the plant going, companies must set a low price, hoping to increase demand. In such a situation, profits are less important than survival. In recent years, many automobile dealers have resorted to pricing below cost or offering large price rebate programs in order to survive. As long as their prices cover variable costs and some fixed costs, they can stay in business for a while.

CURRENT PROFIT MAXIMIZATION. Many companies want to set a price that will maximize current profits. They estimate what demand and costs will be at different prices and choose the price that will produce the maximum current profit, cash flow, or return on investment. In all cases, the company wants current financial outcomes rather than long-run performance.

MARKET-SHARE LEADERSHIP. Other companies want to obtain the dominant market share. They believe that the company with the largest market share will enjoy the lowest costs and highest long-run profit. To become the market-share leader, they

Sub-Zero charges a premium price for its custom-made refrigerators to attain product-quality leadership.

set prices as low as possible. A variation of this objective is to pursue a specific market-share gain. Say the company wants to increase its market share from 10 percent to 15 percent in one year. It will search for the price and marketing program that will achieve this goal.

PRODUCT QUALITY LEADERSHIP. A company might decide it wants to have the highest quality product on the market. This decision normally calls for charging a high price to cover the high product quality and high cost of R&D. For example, the Sub-Zero Freezer Company seeks product quality leadership. Sub-Zero makes the Rolls-Royce of refrigerators—custom-made, built-in units that look more like hardwood cabinets or pieces of furniture than refrigerators. By offering the highest-quality, Sub-Zero sells over $50 million worth of fancy refrigerators a year, priced at up to $3,000 each.[4]

OTHER OBJECTIVES. The company might use price to attain other more specific objectives. It can set prices low to prevent competition from entering the market or set prices at competitors' levels to stabilize the market. Prices can be set to keep the loyalty and support of resellers, or to avoid government intervention. Prices can be temporarily reduced to create excitement for a product or to draw more customers into a retail store. One product may be priced to help the sales of other products in the company's line. Thus pricing may play an important role in helping to accomplish the company's objectives at many levels.

Marketing Mix Strategy

Price is only one of the marketing mix tools that the company uses to achieve its marketing objectives. Price decisions must be coordinated with product design, distribution, and promotion decisions to form a consistent and effective marketing program. Decisions made for other marketing mix variables may affect pricing decisions. For example, producers who use many resellers and expect these resellers to support and promote their products may have to build larger reseller margins into their prices. Or the decision to develop a high-quality position will mean that the seller must charge a higher price to cover higher costs.

The company often makes its pricing decision first and then bases other marketing mix decisions on the price it wants to charge. For example, Hyundai, Honda, and other makers of low-budget cars discovered a market segment for affordable cars and designed models to sell within the price range that this segment was willing to pay. Here price was a key product positioning factor that defined the product's market, competition, and design. The intended price determined what product features would be offered and what production costs could be incurred.

Thus the marketer must consider the total marketing mix when setting prices. If the product is positioned on nonprice factors, then decisions about quality, promotion, and distribution will strongly affect price. If price is a key positioning factor, then price will strongly affect decisions on the other marketing mix elements. In most cases, the company will consider all the marketing mix decisions together when developing the marketing program.

Costs

Costs set the floor for the price that the company can ask for its product. The company wants to charge a price that covers all its costs for producing, distributing, and selling the product, plus a fair rate of return for its effort and risk. A company's costs may be an important element in its pricing strategy. Many companies work to become the "low-cost producers" in their industries. Companies with lower costs can set lower prices resulting in greater sales and profits (see Marketing Highlight 12–1).

Ford positions its Festiva on price and economy. Jaguar positions on quality and other nonprice factors—its price adds prestige.

FOOD LION'S WINNING LOW-COST, LOW-PRICE STRATEGY

The Food Lion grocery chain began operations in 1957 in a small North Carolina town. At first, despite its heavy use of trading stamps, giveaways, and other marketing gimmicks, Food Lion had trouble drawing shoppers away from older, more established competitors. Ten years later, the company closed nine of its first sixteen stores. Out of desperation, Food Lion slashed storewide prices by 10 percent in its remaining units. The results were startling—sales shot up by 54 percent, profits by 165 percent. The fledgling chain had found its niche and a potent competitive weapon—low prices.

Food Lion aggressively pursued a low-price, low-frills strategy and grew quickly in North Carolina. It's new slogan, LFPINC ("Lowest Food Prices in North Carolina")—featured in advertising, printed on shopping bags, and plastered to the bumpers of thousands of shoppers' cars—became a welcome and familiar sight in cities and towns around the state. In recent years, Food Lion has prospered. Positioned strongly as the low-price leader in most of its markets, the chain now operates almost 500 stores across the Southeast. Food Lion ads confidently claim "extra low everyday prices." And when Food Lion moves into a new town, competitors must generally drop their prices substantially to compete, a fact Food Lion points out in its advertising. When the chain entered Florida recently, its ads boldly asserted, "Food Lion is coming to town, and prices will be coming down!"

Food Lion's price claims are more than empty boasts. In most cases, it really does offer lower prices. Yet the chain remains highly profitable. Food Lion earns an overall net profit margin of 2.57 percent, about twice the industry average. The reason: a total dedication to cost control. The company doggedly pursues even remote opportunities to reduce costs, and its cost-cutting efforts bring big returns. Food Lion pays just $650,000 for each new, no-frills store it builds, much lower than the $1 million competitors

spend for their outlets. It saves on distribution costs by locating stores within 200 miles of one of its three modern distribution warehouses. To streamline and simplify operations, Food Lion stocks fewer brands and sizes than other grocery stores and shuns costly extras such as fresh seafood counters, from-scratch bakeries, and flower shops. And Food Lion is itself a thrifty shopper—it ferrets out wholesaler specials and squeezes suppliers for extra savings.

Food Lion rarely overlooks a chance to economize. It recycles waste heat from refrigeration units to warm its stores and reuses banana crates as bins for cosmetics. It makes $1 million a year selling ground-up bones and fat for fertilizer. Food Lion even economizes on its advertising. The company produces its own ads, using only a few paid actors and Chief Executive Tom E. Smith as advertising spokesman. The average television spot costs only $6,000. And Food Lion saves some $8 million each year by keeping its newspaper ads smaller than those of competitors. As a result, Food Lion's advertising costs amount to one-fourth the industry average. Overall, major competitors spend an average of 21 percent of sales on their total expenses. Food Lion has kept these expenses under 14 percent of sales.

Food Lion's low-cost, low-price strategy has made it the fastest growing and most profitable grocery chain in the nation. Over the last decade, sales have grown an average of 30 percent a year; profits have grown 29 percent annually. Food Lion's 25 percent return on equity last year was best among the thirteen top grocery chains listed in *Business Week's* Top 1000, almost doubling the average return of the other firms. Food Lion's success hinges on a simple strategy—lower costs mean lower prices, and lower prices mean greater sales and profits.

Sources: Richard W. Anderson, "That Roar You Hear Is Food Lion," *Business Week*, August 24, 1987, pp. 65–66; "The Business Week Top 1000," *Business Week*, April 17, 1987, p. 146; and various Food Lion annual reports.

TYPES OF COSTS. A company's costs take two forms, fixed and variable. **Fixed costs** (also known as overhead) are costs that do not vary with production or sales level. Thus a company must pay bills each month for rent, heat, interest, and executive salaries, whatever the company's output. Fixed costs go on no matter what the production level.

Variable costs vary directly with the level of production. Each hand calculator produced by Texas Instruments involves a cost of plastic, wires, packaging, and other inputs. These costs tend to be the same for each unit produced. They are called variable because their total varies with the number of units produced.

Total costs are the sum of the fixed and variable costs for any given level of production. Management wants to charge a price that will at least cover the total costs at a given level of production. The company must watch its costs carefully. If it costs the company more than its competitors to produce and sell a product, the company will have to charge a higher price or make less profit, putting it at a competitive disadvantage.

COSTS AT DIFFERENT LEVELS OF PRODUCTION. To price wisely, management needs to know how its costs vary with different levels of production. For example, suppose Texas Instruments (TI) has built a plant to produce 1,000 hand calculators per day. Figure 12–2A shows the typical short-run average cost (SRAC) curve. It shows that the cost per calculator is high if TI's factory produces only a few per day. But as production moves up to the plant's capacity of 1,000 calculators per day, average cost falls. The reason is that fixed costs are spread over more units, with each unit bearing a smaller fixed cost. TI can try to produce more than 1,000 calculators per day, but average costs will increase because the plant becomes inefficient. Workers have to wait for machines, the machines break down more often, and workers get in each other's way.

If TI believed it could sell 2,000 calculators a day, it should consider building a larger plant. The plant would use more efficient machinery and work arrangements, and the unit cost of producing 2,000 units per day would be less than that of 1,000 units per day, as shown in the long-run average cost (LRAC) curve (Figure 12-2B). In fact, a 3,000-capacity plant would even be more efficient, according to Figure 12-2B. But a 4,000 daily production plant would be less efficient because of increasing diseconomies of scale—too many workers to manage, paperwork slowing things down, and so on. Figure 12-2B shows that a 3,000 daily production plant is the best size to build if demand is strong enough to support this level of production.

COSTS AS A FUNCTION OF PRODUCTION EXPERIENCE. Suppose TI runs a plant that produces 3,000 calculators per day. As TI gains experience in producing hand calculators, it learns how to do it better. Workers learn shortcuts and become more familiar with their equipment. With practice, the work becomes better organized, and TI finds better equipment and production processes. With higher volume, TI becomes more efficient and gains economies of scale. As a result, average cost tends to fall

FIGURE 12-2
Cost per unit at different levels of production per period

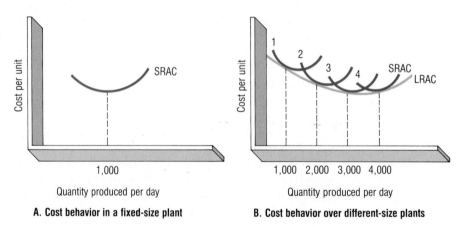

A. Cost behavior in a fixed-size plant

B. Cost behavior over different-size plants

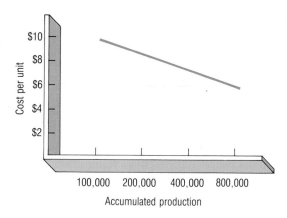

FIGURE 12-3
Cost per unit as a function of accumulated production: the experience curve

Cost ↓ as produce more
— workers more efficient

with accumulated production experience. This relationship is shown in Figure 12-3.[5] Thus the average cost of producing the first 100,000 calculators is $10 per calculator. When the company has produced the first 200,000 calculators, the average cost has fallen to $9. After its accumulated production experience doubles again to 400,000, the average cost decreases to $8. This drop in the average cost with accumulated production experience is called the **experience curve** (or the *learning curve*).

If a downward-sloping experience curve exists, this fact is highly significant for the company. Not only will the company's unit production cost fall, but also it will fall faster if the company makes and sells more during a given time period. However, the market has to stand ready to buy the higher output. And to take advantage of the experience curve, TI must get a large market share early in the product's life cycle. This need suggests the following price strategy: TI should price its calculators low; its sales will then increase, and its costs will decrease through gaining more experience, and then it can lower its prices further.

Some companies have built successful strategies around the experience curve. For example, during the 1980s, Bausch & Lomb has solidified its position in the soft contact lens market by using computerized lens design and steadily expanding its one Soflens plant. As a result, its market share climbed steadily to 65 percent. Yet a single-minded focus on reducing costs and exploiting the experience curve will not always work. Experience curves became somewhat of a fad during the 1970s, and like many fads, the strategy was sometimes misused. Experience curve pricing carries some major risks. The aggressive pricing might give the product a cheap image, as happened when Texas Instruments ran the price of its personal computers down to just $99 compared to competitors' machines selling for over $300. The strategy also assumes that competitors are weak and not willing to fight it out by meeting the company's price cuts. Finally, while the company is building volume under one technology, a competitor may find a lower-cost technology that lets it start at lower prices than the market leader, who still operates on the old experience curve.[6]

Organizational Considerations

Management must decide who within the organization should set prices. Companies handle pricing in a variety of ways. In small companies, prices are often set by top management rather than by the marketing or sales department. In large companies, pricing is typically handled by divisional or product line managers. In industrial markets, salespeople may be allowed to negotiate with customers within certain price ranges. Even in this case, top management sets the pricing objectives and policies and often approves the prices proposed by lower-level management or salespeople.[7] In industries in which pricing is a key factor (aerospace, railroads, oil), companies will often have a pricing department to set prices or help others in setting the best prices. This department reports to the marketing department or top management. Others who have an influence on pricing include sales managers, production managers, finance managers, and accountants.

External Factors Affecting Pricing Decisions

The Market and Demand

Costs set the floor for prices, and the market and demand set the ceiling. Both consumer and industrial buyers balance the price of a product or service against the benefits of owning it. Thus, before setting prices, the marketer must understand the relationship between price and demand for its product.

In this section, we will look at how the price-demand relationship varies for different types of markets and at how buyer perceptions of price affect the pricing decision. Then we will discuss methods for analyzing the price-demand relationship.

PRICING IN DIFFERENT TYPES OF MARKETS. The extent of the seller's pricing freedom varies with different types of markets. Economists recognize four types of markets, each presenting a different pricing challenge.

Under **pure competition,** the market consists of many buyers and sellers trading in a uniform commodity such as wheat, copper, or financial securities. No single buyer or seller has much affect on the going market price. A seller cannot charge more than the going price because buyers can obtain as much as they need at this price. Nor would sellers charge less than the market price because they can sell all they want at the market price. If the price and profits rise, new sellers can easily enter the market. Sellers in these markets do not spend much time on marketing strategy, since the role of marketing research, product development, pricing, advertising, and sales promotion is small as long as the market stays purely competitive.

Under **monopolistic competition,** the market consists of many buyers and sellers who trade over a range of prices rather than a single market price. The reason for the price range is that sellers are able to differentiate their offers to the buyers. Either the physical product can be varied in quality, features, or style, or the accompanying services can be varied. Buyers see differences in sellers' products and will pay different prices. Sellers try to develop differentiated offers for different customer segments and freely use branding, advertising, and personal selling, in addition to price, to set their offers apart from those of others. Most consumer goods industries are monopolistically competitive. For example, H. J. Heinz, Vlassic, and several other national brands of pickles compete with dozens of regional and local brands, all differentiated by price and nonprice factors. Because there are many competitors, each firm is less affected by competitors' marketing strategies than in oligopolistic markets.

Under **oligopolistic competition,** the market consists of a few sellers who are highly sensitive to each other's pricing and marketing strategies. Examples of oligopolistic industries include automobiles, computers, and steel. The product can be homogeneous (steel, aluminum) or heterogeneous (cars, computers). The reason for the few sellers is that it is difficult for new sellers to enter the market. Each seller is alert to competitors' strategies and moves. If a steel company slashes its price by 10 percent, buyers will quickly switch to this supplier. The other steelmakers will have to respond by lowering their prices or increasing their services. An oligopolist is never sure that it will gain anything permanent through a price cut. On the other hand, if the oligopolist raised the price, the competitors might not follow this lead.

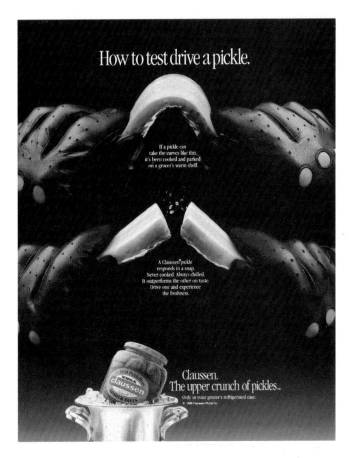

Monopolistic competition: Claussen sets its pickles apart from dozens of other brands using both price and nonprice factors.

The oligopolist would have to retract its price increase or risk losing customers to competitors.

A **pure monopoly** consists of one seller. The seller may be a government monopoly (U.S. Postal Service), a private regulated monopoly (a power company), or a private nonregulated monopoly (Du Pont when it introduced nylon). Pricing is handled differently in each case. A government monopoly can pursue a variety of pricing objectives. It might set a price below cost because the product is important to buyers who cannot afford to pay full cost. Or the price might be set to cover costs or to produce good revenue. Or it might be set quite high to slow down consumption. In a regulated monopoly, the government permits the company to set rates that will yield a "fair return," one that will let the company maintain and expand its plant as needed. Nonregulated monopolies are free to price at the level the market will bear. However, they do not always charge the full price for a number of reasons: desire to penetrate the market faster with a low price, desire not to attract competition, fear of government regulation.

CONSUMER PERCEPTIONS OF PRICE AND VALUE. In the end, the consumer will decide whether a product's price is right. When setting prices, the company must consider consumer perceptions of price and how these perceptions affect consumers' buying decisions. Pricing decisions, like other marketing mix decisions, must be buyer-oriented:

> . . . pricing requires more than technical expertise. It requires creative judgment and a keen awareness of buyers' motivations . . . the key to effective pricing is the same one that opens doors . . . in other marketing functions: a creative awareness of who buyers are, why they buy and how they make their buying decisions. The recognition that buyers differ in these dimensions is as important for effective pricing as it is for effective promotion, distribution, or product development.[8]

When consumers buy a product, they exchange something of value (the price) to get something of value (the benefits of having or using the product). Effective, buyer-oriented pricing involves understanding what value consumers place on the benefits they receive from the product and setting a price that fits this value. The benefits include both actual and perceived benefits. When a consumer buys a meal at a fancy restaurant, it is easy to figure out the value of the meal's ingredients. But it is very hard, even for the consumer, to measure the value of other satisfactions such as taste, a plush environment, relaxation, conversation, and status. And these values will vary for different consumers and for different situations (see Marketing Highlight 12–2). Thus the company will often find it hard to measure the values to evaluate a product's price. If the consumer perceives that the price is greater than the product's value, the consumer will not buy the product.

Marketers must try to look at the consumer's reasons for buying the product, and set price according to consumer perceptions of the product's value. Because consumers vary in the values they assign to different product features, marketers often vary their pricing strategies for different price segments. They offer different sets of product features at different prices. For example, television manufacturers offer small, inexpensive models for consumers who want basic sets and larger, more expensive models loaded with features for consumers who want the extras.

Buyer-oriented pricing means that the marketer cannot design a product and marketing program and then set the price. Good pricing begins with analyzing consumer needs and price perceptions. Price must be considered along with the other marketing mix variables *before* the marketing program is set.[9]

ANALYZING THE PRICE-DEMAND RELATIONSHIP. Each price the company might charge will lead to a different level of demand. The relation between the price charged and the resulting demand level is shown in the familiar **demand curve** in Figure 12-4A. The demand curve shows the number of units the market will buy in a given time period at different prices that might be charged. In the normal case, demand and price are inversely related. That is, the higher the price, the lower the

FIGURE 12-4
Two hypothetical
demand schedules

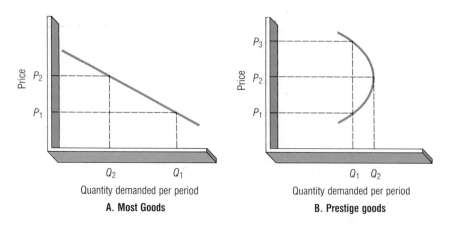

A. Most Goods

B. Prestige goods

WHAT'S A HAMBURGER WORTH?

Is any hamburger worth $4? The answer seems to depend on what consumers you talk to and what they want from their burgers. Most people won't pay more than a dollar and a half, maybe two dollars for a Big Mac or a Whopper with cheese. But there's a growing segment of consumers who seem almost eager to pay as much as $4.00 or $5.00 for a new class of burgers—gourmet burgers—served at restaurants with names like Chili's, Fuddruckers, Flakey Jake's, or J. J. Muggs.

What makes a hamburger worth $4 or more to some consumers? The burgers probably *are* better—bigger and cooked to order from fresh beef. But it's not just the hamburgers that attract customers. The upmarket burger places offer several less tangible benefits that some consumers value highly. They have tables and chairs instead of plastic benches; they sell beer, wine, and cocktails; most provide table service.

The average cost for a hamburger, fries, and a beverage at Fuddruckers runs about $6, compared to about $2.50 at a conventional fast-food restaurant. But when you add up all the values—of the hamburger, the amenities, and the atmosphere—the price of a gourmet burger at Fuddruckers seems more reasonable to some consumers than the lower prices they'd pay at McDonald's or Burger King.

So, who would pay $4 for a hamburger? You'd be surprised just how many people would! Fancyburger restaurants now pull in over $100 million in sales. And even conservative analysts estimate that the market will explode to over $2 to $3 billion annually. Some estimate an eventual $8 billion market for $4 hamburgers.

Source: Based on information from Roger Neal, "Fancyburgers," *Forbes*, June 18, 1984, p. 92.

Fuddruckers and its gourmet burger.

demand. Thus the company would sell less if it raised its price from P_1 to P_2. Consumers with limited budgets will probably buy less of something if its price is too high.

Most demand curves slope downward in either a straight or a curved line as in Figure 12-4A. But for prestige goods, the demand curve sometimes slopes upward, as in Figure 12-4B. A perfume company found that by raising its price from P_1 to P_2, it sold more perfume rather than less. Consumers thought the higher price meant a better or more desirable perfume. However, if the company charges too high a price (P_3), the level of demand will be lower than at P_2.

Most companies try to measure their demand curves. The type of market makes a difference. In a monopoly, the demand curve shows the total market demand resulting from different prices. If the company faces competition, its demand at different prices will depend on whether competitor's prices stay constant or change

FIGURE 12-5

Demand schedule for Quaker State motor oil

Reprinted by permission of the publisher from "Price-Quality Relationships and Price Elasticity Under In-Store Experimentation," by Sidney Bennett and J. B. Wilkinson. Journal of Business Research, *January 1974, pp. 30–34. Copyright 1974 by Elsevier Science Publishing Co.*

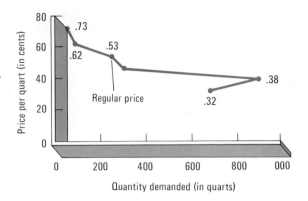

with the company's prices. Here, we will assume that competitor's prices remain constant. Later in this chapter, we will discuss what happens when competitors' prices change. To measure a demand curve requires estimating demand at different prices. Figure 12-5 shows the estimated demand curve for Quaker State Motor oil. Demand rises as the price is lowered from 73 cents to 38 cents, then drops between 38 cents and 32 cents, possibly due to people thinking the oil is too cheap and may damage the car.

In measuring the price-demand relationship, the market researcher must not allow other factors affecting demand to vary. If Quaker State raised its advertising budget when it lowered its price, we would not know how much of the increased demand was due to the lower price and how much to the increased advertising. The same problem arises if a holiday weekend occurs when the lower price is set, because more travel and purchase of motor oil takes place on holidays.

Economists show the impact of nonprice factors on demand through shifts of the demand curve, rather than movements along the demand curve. Suppose the initial demand curve is D_1 in Figure 12-6. The seller is charging P and selling Q_1 units. Now suppose the economy suddenly improves, or the seller doubles its advertising budget. The higher demand is reflected through an upward shift of the demand curve from D_1 to D_2. Without changing the price P, the seller's demand is now Q_2.

PRICE ELASTICITY OF DEMAND. Marketers need to know **price elasticity,** or how responsive demand will be to a change in price. Consider the two demand curves in Figure 12-7. In Figure 12-7A a price increase from P_1 to P_2 leads to a relatively small drop in demand from Q_1 to Q_2. In Figure 12-7B the same price increase leads to a large drop in demand from Q'_1 to Q'_2. If demand hardly changes with a

FIGURE 12-6

Effects of promotion and other nonprice variables on demand shown through shifts of the demand curve

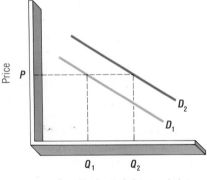

no Δ in price.

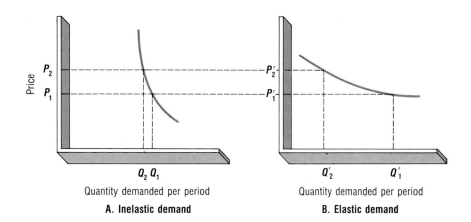

FIGURE 12-7
Inelastic and elastic demand

A. Inelastic demand

B. Elastic demand

Quantity demanded per period

Quantity demanded per period

small change in price, we say the demand is *inelastic*. If demand changes a lot, we say the demand is *elastic*.[10] The price elasticity of demand is given by the following formula:

$$\text{price elasticity of demand} = \frac{\% \text{ change in quantity demanded}}{\% \text{ change in price}}$$

Suppose demand falls by 10 percent when a seller raises its price by 2 percent. Price elasticity of demand is therefore −5 (minus sign confirms the inverse relation between price and demand) and demand is elastic. If demand falls by 2 percent with a 2 percent increase in price, then eleasticity is −1. In this case, the seller's total revenue stays the same: The seller sells fewer items but at a higher price that preserves the same total revenue. If demand falls by 1 percent when price is increased by 2 percent, then elasticity is −½ and demand is inelastic. The less elastic the demand, the more profitable it is for the seller to raise the price.

What determines the price elasticity of demand? Demand is likely to be less elastic under the following conditions: (1) there are few or no substitutes or competitors; (2) buyers do not readily notice the higher price; (3) buyers are slow to change their buying habits and search for lower prices; (4) buyers think the higher prices are justified by quality improvements, normal inflation, and so on.

If demand is elastic rather than inelastic, sellers will consider lowering their price. A lower price will produce more total revenue. This strategy makes sense as long as the extra costs of producing and selling more do not exceed the extra revenue.

Competitors' Prices and Offers

Another external factor affecting the company's pricing decisions is competitors' prices and their possible reactions to the company's pricing moves. A consumer considering buying a Canon camera will evaluate Canon's price and value against the prices and values of comparable products made by Nikon, Minolta, Pentax, and others. Also, the company's pricing strategy may affect the nature of the competition it faces. If Canon follows a high-price, high-margin strategy, it may attract competition. Some competitors may enter the market at the same high price to enjoy the high profit margins. Others may undercut Canon's high price in order to obtain a larger market share. A low-price, low-margin strategy, however, may stop or drive out smaller or less efficient competitors who cannot compete profitably at the lower prices.

The company needs to learn the price and quality of each competitor's offer.

MARKETING HIGHLIGHT 12–3

PRICE DECISIONS AND PUBLIC POLICY

Sellers must understand the law in pricing their products. They must avoid the following practices.

Price Fixing. Sellers must set prices without talking to competitors. Otherwise price collusion is suspected. Price fixing is illegal per se—that is, the government does not accept any excuses for price fixing. The only exception is where price agreements are carried out under the supervision of a government agency, as in many local milk industry agreements, in the regulated transportation industries, and in fruit and vegetable cooperatives.

Resale Price Maintenance. A manufacturer cannot require dealers to charge a specified retail price for its product. However, the seller can propose a manufacturer's suggested retail price to the dealers. The manufacturer cannot refuse to sell to a dealer who takes independent pricing action, nor punish the dealer by shipping late or denying advertising allowances. However, the manufacturer can refuse to sell to a dealer on other grounds presumably not related to the dealer's pricing.

Price Discrimination. The Robinson-Patman Act seeks to ensure that sellers offer the same price terms to a given level of trade. For example, every retailer is entitled to the same price terms whether the retailer is Sears or the local bicycle shop. However, price discrimination is allowed if the seller can prove its costs are different when selling to different retailers; for example, that it costs less per unit to sell a large volume of bicycles to Sears than to sell a few bicycles to a local dealer. Or the seller can discriminate in its pricing if the seller manufactures different qualities of the same product for different retailers. The seller has to prove that these differences exist and that the price differences are proportional. Price differentials may also be used to "meet competition" in "good faith," providing the firm is trying to meet competitors at its own level of competition and that the price discrimination is temporary, localized, and defensive rather than offensive.

Minimum Pricing. A seller is not allowed to sell below cost with the intention of destroying competition. Wholesalers and retailers in over half the states face laws requiring a minimum percentage markup over their cost of merchandise plus transportation. Designed to stop unfair trade practices, these laws attempt to protect small merchants from larger merchants who might sell items below cost to attract customers.

Price Increases. Companies are free to increase their prices to any level except in times of price controls. The major exception to the freedom of pricing is regulated public utilities. Since utilities have monopoly power, their rates are regulated in the public interest. The government has also used its influence from time to time to discourage major industry price hikes during periods of shortages or inflation.

Deceptive Pricing. Deceptive pricing is more common in the sale of consumer goods than business goods, because consumers typically possess less information and buying skill. In 1958, the Automobile Information Disclosure Act required auto manufacturers to affix on auto windshields a statement of the manufacturer's suggested retail price, the prices of optional equipment, and the dealer's transportation charges. In the same year, the FTC issued its Guides Against Deceptive Pricing, warning sellers not to advertise a price reduction unless it is a saving from the usual retail price, not to advertise "factory" or "wholesale" prices unless this is true, not to advertise comparable value prices on imperfect goods, and so forth.

Sources: For more on pricing and public policy, see Thomas T. Nagle, *The Strategy and Tactics of Pricing* (Englewood Cliffs, NJ: Prentice Hall, 1987), pp. 321–37.

Canon might do so in several ways. It can send out comparison shoppers to price and compare Nikon, Minolta, and other competitors' products. It can get competitors price lists and buy competitors' equipment and take it apart. It can ask buyers how they view the price and quality of each competitor's camera.

Once Canon is aware of competitors' price and offers, it can use them as a starting point for its own pricing. If Canon's cameras are similar to Nikon's, it will have to price close to Nikon or lose sales. If Canon's cameras are not as good as Nikon's, the firm will not be able to charge as much. If Canon's products are better than Nikon's, it can charge more. Basically, Canon will use price to position its offer relative to competitors.

Other External Factors

When setting prices, the company must also consider other factors in its external environment. For example, economic conditions can have a strong impact on the outcomes of the firm's pricing strategies. Economic factors such as inflation, boom or recession, and interest rates affect pricing decisions because they effect both the costs of producing a product and consumer perceptions of the product's price and value.

The company must consider what impact its prices will have on other parties in its environment. How will resellers react to various prices. The company should set prices that give resellers a fair profit, encourage their support, and help them to sell the product effectively. The government is another important external influence on pricing decisions. Marketers need to know the laws affecting price and make sure their pricing policies are legal. The major laws affecting price decisions are summarized in Marketing Highlight 12–3.

GENERAL PRICING APPROACHES

The price the company charges will be somewhere between one that is too low to produce a profit and one that is too high to produce any demand. Figure 12-8 summarizes the major considerations in setting price. Product costs set a floor to the price; consumer perceptions of the product's value set the ceiling. The company must consider competitors' prices and other external and internal factors to find the best price between these two extremes.

Companies set prices by selecting a general pricing approach that includes one or more of these sets of factors. We will look at the following approaches: the *cost-based* approach (cost-plus pricing, breakeven analysis, and target profit pricing), the *buyer-based* approach (perceived-value pricing), and the *competition-based* approach (going-rate and sealed-bid pricing).

Cost-Based Pricing

Cost-Plus Pricing

The simplest pricing method is **cost-plus pricing,** which adds a standard markup to the cost of the product. Construction companies, for example, submit job bids by estimating the total project cost and adding a standard markup for profit. Lawyers, accountants, and other professionals typically price by adding a standard markup to their costs. Some sellers tell their customers they will charge cost plus a specified markup; for example, aerospace companies price this way to the government.

FIGURE 12-8
Major considerations in setting price

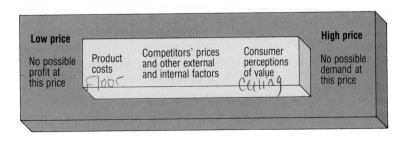

To illustrate markup pricing, suppose a toaster manufacturer had the following costs and expected sales:

Variable cost	$10
Fixed cost	$300,000
Expected unit sales	50,000

Then the manufacturer's cost per toaster is given by:

$$\text{Unit cost} = \text{Variable cost} + \frac{\text{Fixed costs}}{\text{Unit sales}} = \$10 + \frac{\$300,000}{50,000} = \$16$$

Now suppose the manufacturer wants to earn a 20 percent marketup on sales. The manufacturer's markup price is given by:[11]

$$\text{Markup price} = \frac{\text{Unit cost}}{(1 - \text{Desired return on sales})} = \frac{\$16}{1 - .2} = \$20$$

The manufacturer would charge dealers $20 a toaster and make a profit of $4 a unit. The dealers in turn will mark up the toaster. If dealers want to earn 50 percent on sales price, they will mark up the toaster to $40 ($20 + 50% of $40). This number is equivalent to a *markup on cost* of 100 percent ($20/$20).

Markups vary considerably among different goods. Some common markups (on price, not cost) in supermarkets are 9 percent on baby foods, 14 percent on tobacco products, 20 percent on bakery products, 27 percent on dried foods and vegetables, 37 percent on spices and extracts, and 50 percent on greeting cards.[12] But these markups vary a lot around the averages. In the spices and extracts category, for example, markups on retail price range from a low of 19 percent to a high of 56 percent. Markups are generally higher on seasonal items (to cover the risk of not selling), specialty items, slower moving items, items with high storage and handling costs, and items with inelastic demand.

Does using standard markups to set prices make logical sense? Generally, no. Any pricing method that ignores current demand and competition is not likely to lead to the best price. Suppose the toaster manufacturer above charged $20 but sold only 30,000 toasters instead of 50,000. Then the unit cost would have been higher since the fixed costs are spread over fewer units, and the realized percentage markup on sales would have been lower. Markup pricing works only if that price actually brings in the expected level of sales.

Still, markup pricing remains popular for many reasons. First, sellers are more certain about costs than about demand. By tying the price to cost, sellers simplify pricing—they do not have to make frequent adjustments as demand changes. Second, when all firms in the industry use this pricing method, prices tend to be similar and price competition is minimized. Third, many people feel that cost-plus pricing is fairer to both buyers and sellers. Sellers do not take advantage of buyers when buyers' demand becomes great, yet the sellers earn a fair return on their investment.

Breakeven Analysis and Target Profit Pricing

Another cost-oriented pricing approach is **breakeven pricing** or *target profit pricing*. The firm tries to determine the price at which it will break even or make the profit it is seeking. Target pricing is used by General Motors, which prices its automobiles to achieve a 15 to 20 percent profit on its investment. This pricing method is also used by public utilities, which are constrained by government to make a fair return on their investment.

Target pricing uses the concept of a *breakeven chart*. A breakeven chart shows

FIGURE 12-9
Breakeven chart for
determining target price

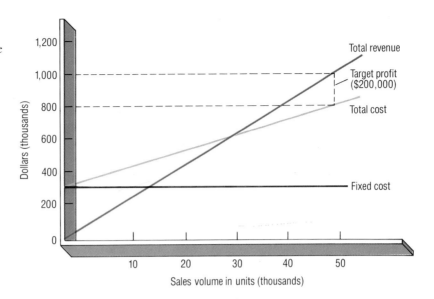

the total cost and total revenue expected at different sales volume levels. Figure 12-9 shows a breakeven chart for the toaster manufacturer discussed above. Fixed costs are $300,000 regardless of sales volume. Variable costs are added to fixed costs to form total costs, which rise with volume. The total revenue curve starts at zero and rises with each unit sold. The slope of the total revenue curve reflects the price of $20 per unit.

The total revenue and total cost curve cross at 30,000 units. This is the *breakeven volume*. At $20, the company must sell at least 30,000 units to break even; that is, for total revenue to cover total cost. Breakeven can be calculated using the following formula:

$$\text{Breakeven volume} = \frac{\text{Fixed cost}}{\text{Price} - \text{Variable cost}} = \frac{\$300,000}{\$20 - \$10} = 30,000$$

If the company wants to make a target profit, it must sell more units at $20 each. Suppose the toaster manufacturer has invested $1,000,000 in the business and wants to set price to earn a 20 percent return, or $200,000. In that case, it must sell at least 50,000 units at $20 each. If the company charges a higher price, it will not need to sell as many toasters to achieve its target return. But the market may not buy even this lower volume at the higher price. Much depends on the price elasticity and competitors' prices.

The manufacturer should consider different prices and estimate breakeven volumes, probable demand, and profits for each. This is done in Table 12-1. The table shows that as price increases, breakeven volume drops (column 2). But as price increases, demand for the toasters also falls off (column 3). At the $14 price, because the manufacturer clears only $4 per toaster ($14 less $10 in variable costs), it must sell a very high volume to break even. Even though the low price attracts many buyers, demand still falls below the high breakeven point, and the manufacturer loses money. At the other extreme, with a $22 price the manufacturer clears $12 per toaster and must sell only 25,000 units to break even. But at this high price, consumers buy too few toasters, and the manufacturer suffers a loss. The table shows that a price of $18 yields the highest profits. Note that none of the prices produces the manufacturer's target profit of $200,000. To achieve this target return, the manufac-

	(1)	(2) UNIT DEMAND NEEDED TO BREAK EVEN	(3) EXPECTED UNIT DEMAND AT GIVEN PRICE	(4) TOTAL REVENUES (1) × (3)	(5) TOTAL COSTS*	(6) PROFIT (4) − (5)
TABLE 12-1 Breakeven Volume and Profits at Different Prices	PRICE					
	$14	75,000	71,000	$ 994,000	$1,100,000	− $32,000
	16	50,000	67,000	1,072,000	970,000	102,000
	18	37,500	60,000	1,080,000	900,000	180,000
	20	30,000	42,000	840,000	720,000	120,000
	22	25,000	23,000	506,000	530,000	−24,000

* Assumes fixed costs of $300,000 and constant unit variable costs of $10.

turer will have to search for ways to lower fixed or variable costs, thus lowering the breakeven point.

Buyer-Based Pricing

An increasing number of companies are basing their prices on the product's perceived value. **Perceived-value pricing** uses buyers' perceptions of value, not the seller's cost, as the key to pricing. The company uses the nonprice variables in the marketing mix to build up perceived value in the buyers' minds. Price is set to match the perceived value.

Consider the various prices different restaurants charge for the same items. A consumer who wants a cup of coffee and a slice of apple pie may pay $1.25 at a drugstore counter, $2.00 at a family restaurant, $3.50 at a hotel coffee shop, $5.00 for hotel room service, and $7.00 at an elegant restaurant. Each succeeding restaurant can charge more because of the value added by the atmosphere.

The company using perceived-value pricing must find out the value in the buyers' minds for different competitive offers. In the last example, consumers could be asked how much they would pay for the same coffee and pie in the different surround-

Perceived value: a less expensive glass would hold water, but some consumers will pay much more for the intangibles.

ings. Sometimes consumers could be asked how much they would pay for each benefit added to the offer. If the seller charges more than the buyers' perceived value, the company's sales will suffer. Many companies overprice their products, and their products sell poorly. Other companies underprice. Their products sell very well, but they produce less revenue than they would if price were raised to the perceived-value level.[13]

Competition-Based Pricing

Going-Rate Pricing

In **going-rate pricing,** the firm bases its price largely on competitors' prices, with less attention paid to its own costs or demand. The firm might charge the same, more, or less than its major competitors. In oligopolistic industries that sell a commodity such as steel, paper, or fertilizer, firms normally charge the same price. The smaller firms "follow the leader." They change their prices when the market leader's prices change, rather than when their own demand or cost changes. Some firms may charge a bit more or less, but they hold the amount of difference constant. Thus minor gasoline retailers usually charge a few cents less than the major oil companies, without letting the difference increase or decrease.

Going-rate pricing is quite popular. Where demand elasticity is hard to measure, firms feel that the going price represents the collective wisdom of the industry concerning the price that will yield a fair return. They also feel that holding to the going price will avoid harmful price wars.

Sealed-Bid Pricing

Competition-based pricing is also used when firms bid for jobs. Using **sealed-bid pricing** the firm bases its price on how it thinks competitors will price rather than solely on its own costs or demand. The firm wants to win the contract, and this requires pricing lower than the other firms.

Yet the firm cannot set its price below a certain level. It cannot price below cost without harming its financial position. On the other hand, the higher it sets its price above its costs, the lower its chance of getting the contract.

The net effect of the two opposite pulls can be described in terms of the *expected profit* of the particular bid (see Table 12-2). Suppose a bid of $9,500 would yield a high chance (say .81) of getting the contract, but only a low profit (say $100). The expected profit with this bid is therefore $81. If the firm bid $11,000, its profit would be $1,600, but its chance of getting the contract might be reduced to .01. The expected profit would be only $16. Thus the company might bid the price that would maximize the expected profit. According to Table 12-2, the best bid would be $10,000, for which the expected profit is $216.

Using expected profit as a basis for setting price makes sense for the large firm that makes many bids. In playing the odds, the firm will make maximum profits in the long run. But a firm that bids only occasionally or needs a particular contract badly will not find the expected-profit approach useful. The approach, for example,

**TABLE 12-2
Effect of Different Bids
on Expected Profit**

COMPANY'S BID	COMPANY'S PROFIT (1)	PROBABILITY OF WINNING WITH THIS BID (ASSUMED) (2)	EXPECTED PROFIT [(1) × (2)]
$ 9,500	$ 100	.81	$ 81
10,000	600	.36	216
10,500	1,100	.09	99
11,000	1,600	.01	16

does not distinguish between a $100,000 profit with a .10 probability and a $12,500 profit with an .80 probability. Yet the firm that wants to keep production going would prefer the second contract to the first.

■ SUMMARY

In spite of the increased role of nonprice factors in the modern marketing process, price remains an important element in the marketing mix. Many internal and external factors influence the company's pricing decisions. Internal factors include the firm's marketing objectives, marketing mix strategy, costs, and organization for pricing.

The pricing strategy is largely determined by the company's target market and positioning objectives. Common pricing objectives include survival, current profit maximization, market-share leadership, and product quality leadership.

Price is only one of the marketing mix tools the company uses to accomplish its objectives, and pricing decisions affect and are affected by product design, distribution, and promotion decisions. Price decisions must be carefully coordinated with the other marketing mix decisions when designing the marketing program.

Costs set the floor for the company's price—the price must cover all the costs of making and selling the product, plus a fair rate of return. Management must decide who within the organization is responsible for setting price. In large companies, some pricing authority may be delegated to lower-level managers and salespeople, but top management usually sets pricing policies and approves proposed prices. Production, finance, and accounting managers also influence pricing.

External factors that influence pricing decisions include the nature of the market and demand, competitors' prices and offers, and other external factors such as the economy, reseller needs, and government actions. The seller's pricing freedom varies with different types of markets. Pricing is especially challenging in markets characterized by monopolistic competition or oligopoly.

In the end, the consumer decides whether the company has set the right price. The consumer weighs the price against the perceived values of using the product—if the price exceeds the sum of the values, consumers will not buy the product. Consumers differ in the values they assign to different product features, and marketers often vary their pricing strategies for different price segments. When assessing the market and demand, the company estimates the demand schedule, which shows the probable quantity purchased per period at alternative price levels. The more inelastic the demand, the higher the company can set its price. Demand and consumer value perceptions set the ceiling for prices.

Consumers compare a product's price to the prices of competitors' products. The company must learn the price and quality of competitors' offers and use them as a starting point for its own pricing.

The company can select one or a combination of three general pricing approaches: the cost-based approach (cost-plus or breakeven analysis and target profit pricing), the buyer-based (perceived-value) approach, and the competition-based (going-rate or sealed-bid pricing) approach.

■ QUESTIONS FOR DISCUSSION

1. Products that have high levels of energy consumption, provide few servings per container, require frequent maintenance, and so on, may *cost* much more than products selling for a higher *price*. How can an awareness of a product's costs to the consumer help marketers in pricing and promoting their products?

2. What kinds of firms might have a marketing objective of survival, profit maximization, market-share leadership, or product-quality leadership? Give examples.

3. Which type of production cost is more relevant in setting the price of a product—fixed costs or variable costs? Does your answer depend on whether you are focusing on short-term versus long-term profits?

4. What are the major factors influencing the setting of prices in the four market types discussed in the chapter—pure competition, monopolistic competition, oligopolistic competition, and pure monopoly? Give examples of these market types, and describe prices of products available in each.

5. From a social perspective, is monopolistic competition—and the power that it gives marketers over the prices they charge—good or bad for the consumer? How would our marketing system change if monopolistic competition were somehow made illegal?

6. In a supermarket, which will have a larger price elasticity of demand, hamburger or steak? If the demand for steak is elastic, would raising the price of steak increase or decrease revenues from steak sales? What would be the effect on profits of an increase in the price of steaks?

7. In test markets, Procter & Gamble has replaced 16-ounce packages of regular Folgers coffee with 13-ounce "fast roast" packages. More efficient processing allows Procter & Gamble to use fewer green coffee beans per can, with no impact on flavor or the number of servings per package. What approach should Procter & Gamble use in setting the test market price for the reformulated Folgers coffee?

8. You have inherited an automatic car wash where annual fixed costs are $100,000 and variable costs are $0.50 per car washed. An establishment a block away charges $0.75 for soap and water for self-service car washing.

How much should you charge per car wash? What would be the break-even volume at that price?

9. Sales of Fleischmann's gin *increased* when prices were raised 22 percent over a two-year period. What does this tell you about the demand curve and the elasticity of demand for Fleischmann's gin? What implications does this have for using perceived-value pricing in marketing alcoholic beverages?

10. Columnist Dave Barry jokes that federal law requires this message under the sticker price of new cars: "WARNING TO STUPID PEOPLE: DO NOT PAY THIS AMOUNT." Why is the sticker price often higher than the actual selling price of a car? Why is it sometimes lower? How do car dealers set the actual prices of the cars they sell?

■ KEY TERMS

Breakeven pricing Setting price to break even on the costs of making and marketing a product or to make the deisred profit. Also called target profit pricing.

Cost-plus pricing Adding a standard markup to the cost of a product.

Demand curve A curve that shows the number of units the market will buy in a given time period at different prices that might be charged.

Experience curve The drop in the average per-unit production cost that comes with accumulated production experience. Also called the *learning curve*.

Fixed costs Costs that do not vary with production or sales level. Also called *overhead*.

Going-rate pricing Setting price based largely on following competitors' prices rather than on company costs or demand.

Monopolistic competition A market in which many buyers and sellers trade over a range of prices rather than a single market price.

Oligopolistic competition A market in which there are a few sellers who are highly sensitive to each other's pricing and marketing strategies.

Perceived-value pricing Setting price based on buyers' perceptions of value rather than on the seller's cost.

Price The amount of money charged for a product or service, or the sum of the values consumers exchange for the benefits of having or using the product or service.

Price elasticity A measure of the sensitivity of demand to changes in price.

Pure competition A market in which many buyers and sellers trade in a uniform commodity; no single buyer or seller has much affect on the going market price.

Pure monopoly A market in which there is a single seller—it may be a government monopoly, a private regulated monopoly, or a private nonregulated monopoly.

Sealed-bid pricing Setting price based on how the firm thinks competitors will price rather than solely on its own costs or demand; used when a company bids for jobs.

Total costs The sum of the fixed and variable costs for any given level of production.

Variable costs Costs that vary directly with the level of production.

■ REFERENCES

1. Based on information from Sears catalogs and other sources.

2. See David J. Schwartz, *Marketing Today: A Basic Approach*, 3rd ed. (New York: Harcourt Brace Jovanovich, 1981), pp. 270–73.

3. See "Segmentation Strategies Create New Pressure among Marketers," *Marketing News*, March 28, 1986, p. 1.

4. Kathleen Deveny, "Sub-Zero Isn't Trembling Over a Little Competition," *Business Week*, March 3, 1986, p. 118.

5. Here accumulated production is drawn on a semi-log scale so that equal distances represent the same percentage increase in output.

6. For more on experience curve strategies, see Pankaj Ghemawat, "Building Strategy on the Experience Curve," *Harvard Business Review*, March–April 1985, pp. 143–49; and George S. Day and David B. Montgomery, "Diagnosing the Experience Curve," *Journal of Marketing*, Spring 1983, pp. 44–58.

7. See P. Ronald Stephenson, William L. Cron, and Gary L. Frazier, "Delegating Pricing Authority to the Sales Force: The Effects on Sales and Profit Performance," *Journal of Marketing*, Spring 1979, pp. 21–28.

8. Thomas T. Nagle, "Pricing as Creative Marketing," *Business Horizons*, July–August 1983, p. 19.

9. See Thomas T. Nagle, *The Strategy and Tactics of Pricing* (Englewood Cliffs, NJ: Prentice Hall, 1987), pp. 1–9.

10. It should be noted that price elasticity is not the same at all price levels along a typical demand curve. Thus demand elasticity is usually measured within a *relevant range* of prices. See Nagle, *The Strategy and Tactics of Pricing*, pp. 76–80.

11. The arithmetic of markups and margins is discussed in Appendix 1, "Marketing Arithmetic."

12. "Supermarket 1984 Sales Manual," *Progressive Grocer*, July 1984.

13. For more on value-based pricing, see John L. Forbis and Nitin T. Mehta, "Value-Based Strategies for Industrial Products," *Business Horizons*, May–June 1981, pp. 32–42; and Ely S. Lurin, "Make Sure Product's Price Reflects Its True Value," *Marketing News*, May 8, 1987, p. 8.

13 Pricing Products: Pricing Stategies

CATERPILLAR INC., the world's leading maker of heavy construction and mining equipment, has been locked in a long price war with Japanese challenger Komatsu Ltd. In this bloody battle, both companies are using price to buy long-run market share, even if it means lower profits or even losses in the short-run.

For over 50 years, Caterpillar has dominated the U.S. and world markets for giant construction equipment. It built its 40 percent market share by emphasizing high product quality, dependable after-sale service, and a strong dealer body. It used a premium pricing strategy—making high profit margins by convincing buyers that Cat's higher quality and trouble-free operation provided greater value and justified a higher price.

But all this began to change when Komatsu entered the market. The Japanese firm started cautiously in the United States with only a few products. It realized the importance of nonprice factors in the buyer's purchase decision. Like Caterpillar, Komatsu stressed high quality, and it expanded slowly to allow its parts and service capacity to keep up with sales. But Komatsu's major weapon for taking share from Caterpillar was price. A strong dollar and lower manufacturing costs allowed Komatsu to cut prices ruthlessly—its initial prices were as much as 40 percent lower than Caterpillar's. On a giant dump truck sold by Cat for $500,000, that could mean a savings of up to $200,000! Riding its strong price advantage, Komatsu grabbed a 17 percent market share by 1986.

Caterpillar fought back to protect its number one market position, and the price war was on. To support lower prices, Cat reduced its workforce by a third and slashed costs by 22 percent. It vowed to meet Komatsu's prices and in some cases even initiated price cutting. With heavy discounting by both companies, manufacturer's list prices became meaningless. For example, a bulldozer that listed for $140,000 regularly sold for $110,000. In the battle for market share, all competitors lost out on profits. Lesser companies such as International Harvester (Navistar) and Clark Equipment were driven to the brink of ruin. Caterpillar lost $1 billion in less than five years and Komatsu, even with its cost advantages, saw its profits decline by 30 percent.

By 1988, thanks to a falling dollar and its cost-cutting programs, Caterpillar had managed to regain a quarter of Komatsu's U.S. market share. And the long and damaging price war may be coming to an end. With a weaker dollar eating into Komatsu's price advantage, the challenger recently raised its prices 5 to 10 percent. Though fierce price competition continues, Komatsu may be signaling that it wants an end to the fighting and a return to peaceful coexistence and better profits for both companies. It hopes that Caterpillar will respond by raising its prices too. Says the president of Komatsu America, "If they don't meet our price increase, I'll have to think of some kind of countermeasure to ensure the survival of Komatsu and our distributors. It all depends on how much our market share declines."[1]

Chapter Objectives *After reading this chapter, you should be able to:*

1. Describe the major strategies for pricing new products.
2. Discuss how companies find a set of prices that maximizes the profits from the total product mix.
3. Explain how companies adjust their prices to take into account different types of customers and situations.
4. Tell why companies decide to change their prices.

IN this chapter, we will look at pricing dynamics. A company does not set a single price but, rather, a pricing structure that covers different items in its line. This pricing structure changes over time as products move through their life cycles. The company adjusts product prices to reflect changing costs and demand and to account for variations in buyers and situations. As the competitive environment changes, the company at times considers initiating price changes and at other times responds to them. This chapter will examine the major dynamic pricing strategies available to management. We will look at *new product pricing strategies* for products in the introductory stage of the product life cycle; *product-mix pricing strategies* for related products in the product mix; *price-adjustment strategies* that account for customer differences and changing situations; and *strategies for initiating and responding to price changes.*[2]

NEW PRODUCT PRICING STRATEGIES

Pricing strategies usually change as the product passes through the product life cycle. The introductory stage is especially challenging. We will look at the differences between pricing a real product innovation that is patent-protected and pricing a product that imitates existing products.

Pricing an Innovative Product

Companies bringing out a new patent-protected innovative product can choose between *market-skimming* pricing and *market penetration pricing.*

Market-Skimming Pricing
Many companies that invent new products set high prices initially to "skim" maximum revenue from the segments willing to pay the high price. This strategy is called **market-skimming pricing.** Polaroid is a prime user of market skimming. On its

The Polaroid Spectra System.

A total photographic system designed for those who appreciate the difference between a snapshot and a photograph.

Like a 35mm, the Spectra camera has a precise autofocus system. It's linked to our exclusive Quintic lens. Its surface is molded to a tolerance of 20 millionths of an inch for sharp images with virtually no optical distortion.

The Spectra camera's full information viewfinder gives you a digital readout of your subject's distance from the camera and tells you when conditions are right for taking a picture.

The camera's sophisticated light-metering system (dual silicon photo-diodes) measures light you can't even see. But you definitely see the results: truer skin tones and more evenly exposed pictures.

The quick recharge flash (as quick as 1/10th of a second) automatically blends just the right amount of daylight and flash.

Helping eliminate the shadows that may have marred your pictures in the past.

The Spectra camera also has a built-in film advance. Just like many 35mm's.

Which leads us right to something the Spectra System has that no 35mm camera has.

The Spectra Instant Film. 18 micro-thin layers of advanced chemistry which produce the finest, most brilliant instant pictures you've ever seen.

Larger, rectangular pictures with brighter, truer, more accurate colors and with more background detail than ever before.

Pictures so sharp and so incredibly lifelike that we guarantee them. In writing. For the complete picture just call us, toll-free, at 1-800-343-5000.

Of course, like a 35mm system, you'll find a whole series of optional Spectra accessories to help you get the most out of your picture taking. Interchangeable filters, a wireless remote control, a collapsible tripod, even a custom designed camera bag to hold it all.

But there's more to the Spectra System than just taking great pictures.

How much more? Up to 8″x10″ more, to be exact.

Using the latest in laser and computer technology, we have developed a new copy system that produces high-quality borderless prints and enlargements of your favorite Spectra photographs.

In all, you'll find that the Polaroid Spectra System is really quite extraordinary. And happily, so are the photographs you'll take with it.

PolaroidSpectraSystem

—WE TAKE YOUR PICTURES SERIOUSLY—

SPECTRA. THE POLAROID CAMERA THAT THINKS IT'S A 35MM.

Market skimming: Polaroid introduced its Spectra at a high price, then brought out lower-priced versions to draw in new segments.

original instant camera, it found the highest price it could charge given the benefits of its new product over other products customers might buy. Polaroid set a price that made it just worthwhile for some segments of the market to adopt the new camera. After the initial sales slowed down, it lowered the price to draw in the next price-sensitive layer of customers. Polaroid used the same approach with its new Spectra camera. It introduced the Spectra at about twice the price of its previous entry in the field. After about a year, it began bringing out simpler, lower-priced versions to draw in new segments. In this way, Polaroid skimmed a maximum amount of revenue from the various segments of the market.[3]

Market skimming makes sense only under certain conditions. The product's quality and image should support the higher price, and enough buyers must want the product at that price. The costs of producing a small volume cannot be so high that they cancel the advantage of charging more. And competitors should not be able to easily enter the market and undercut the high price.

Market Penetration Pricing

Other companies use **market penetration pricing**—setting a low price on their innovative product, hoping to attract a large number of buyers and win a large market share. Texas Instruments (TI) is a prime user of this market penetration pricing. TI will build a large plant, sets its price as low as possible, win a large market share, experience falling costs, and cut its price further as costs fall. Warehouse

FIGURE 13-1
Nine marketing
mix strategies on
price/quality

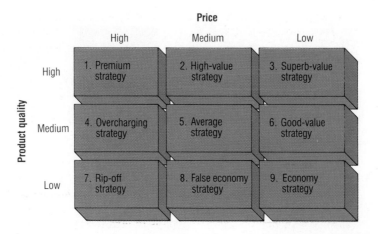

stores and discount retailers also use penetration pricing. They charge low prices to attract high volume; the high volume results in lower costs which in turn let the discounter keep prices low.

Several conditions favor setting a low price. The market must be highly price-sensitive so that a low price produces more market growth. Production and distribution costs must fall as sales volume increases. And the low price must help to keep out the competition.

Pricing an Imitative New Product

A company that plans to develop an imitative new product faces a product-positioning problem. It must decide where to position the product on quality and price. Figure 13-1 shows nine possible price-quality strategies. If the existing market leader has taken box 1 by producing the premium product and charging the highest price, the newcomer might prefer to use one of the other strategies. The newcomer could design a high-quality product and charge a medium price (box 2), design an average-quality product and charge an average price (box 5), and so on. The newcomer must consider the size and growth rate of the market in each box and the competitors it would face.

PRODUCT-MIX PRICING STRATEGIES

The strategy for setting a price on a product is different when the product is part of a product mix. In this case, the firm looks for a set of prices that maximize the profits on the total product mix. Pricing is difficult because the various products have related demand and costs and face different degrees of competition. We will look at four product-mix pricing situations.

Product-Line Pricing

Companies usually develop lines rather than single products. For example, Panasonic offers five different color video sound cameras, ranging from a simple one weighing 4.6 pounds to a complex one weighing 6.3 pounds that includes automatic focusing, fade control, and two-speed zoom lens. Each successive camera in the line offers more features. Management must decide on the price steps to set between the various cameras.

The price steps should take into account cost differences between the cameras, customer evaluations of the different features, and competitors' prices. If the price difference between two successive cameras is small, buyers will buy the more advanced camera, which will increase company profits if the cost difference is smaller than the price difference. If the price difference is large, customers will buy the less advanced cameras.

In many industries, sellers use well-established price points for the products in their line. Thus men's clothing stores might carry men's suits at three price levels: $180, $250, and $340. The customers will associate low-, average-, and high-quality suits with the three price points. Even if the three prices are raised a little, men will normally buy suits at their preferred price point. The seller's task is to establish perceived quality differences that support the price differences.

Optional Product Pricing

Many companies offer to sell optional or accessory products along with their main product. A car buyer can order electric windows, defoggers, and cruise control. Pricing these options is a sticky problem. Automobile companies have to decide which items to build into the base price and which ones to offer as options. General Motors' normal pricing strategy is to advertise a stripped-down model for $9,000 to pull people into showrooms and devote most of the showroom space to showing loaded cars at $11,000 or $12,000. The economy model is stripped of so many comforts and conveniences that most buyers reject it. When GM launched its new front-wheel drive J-cars in the early 1980s, it took a cue from the Japanese automakers and included in the sticker price many useful items previously sold only as options. Now the advertised price represented a well-equipped car. Unfortunately, however, the price was high and many car shoppers balked.

Captive Product Pricing

Companies in some industries make products that must be used with the main product. Examples of captive products are razor blades, camera film, and computer software. Producers of the main products (razors, cameras, computers) often price them low and set high markups on the supplies. Thus Polaroid prices its cameras

Product-line pricing: Snapper sells a lawn mower for every pocketbook.

low because it makes its money on selling film. Those camera makers who do not sell film have to price their cameras higher in order to make the same overall profit.

In the case of services, this strategy is called *two-part pricing*. The price of the service is broken into a fixed fee plus variable usage rate. Thus a telephone company charges a monthly rate plus charges for calls above some minimum number. Amusement parks charge admission plus fees for food, the midway, and rides over a minimum number. The service firm must decide how much to charge for the basic service and how much for the variable usage. The fixed amount should be low enough to induce usage of the service. Then profit can be made on the variable usage fees.

By-Product Pricing

In producing processed meats, petroleum products, chemicals, and other products, there are often by-products. The pricing of the main product will be affected. If the by-products have no value and getting rid of them is costly, the manufacturer will seek a market for these by-products and should accept any price that covers more than the cost of storing and delivering them. Thus the seller can reduce the main product's price to make it more competitive.

Product-Bundle Pricing

Sellers often combine several of their products and offer the set at a reduced price. Thus theaters and sports teams sell season tickets at less than the cost of buying tickets individually; hotels sell specially priced packages that include room, meals, and entertainment; and automobile companies sell attractively priced options packages. Price bundling can promote the sales of products consumers might not otherwise buy, but the combined price must be low enough to get them to buy the bundle.[4]

Product-bundle pricing: Hyatt offers a specially priced package.

PRICE-ADJUSTMENT STRATEGIES

Companies adjust their basic prices to account for various customer differences and changing situations. We will look at the following adjustment strategies: discount pricing and allowances, discriminatory pricing, psychological pricing, promotional pricing, and geographical pricing.

Discount Pricing and Allowances

Most companies will adjust their basic price to reward customers for certain acts, such as early payment of bills, volume purchases, and buying off season. These price adjustments—called discounts and allowances—are described below.

Cash Discounts

A **cash discount** is a price reduction to buyers who pay their bills promptly. A typical example is "2/10, net 30," which means that payment is due within thirty days, but the buyer can deduct 2 percent if the bill is paid within ten days. The discount must be granted to all buyers meeting these terms. Such discounts are customary in many industries and help to improve the seller's cash situation and reduce credit collection costs and bad debts.

Quantity Discounts

A **quantity discount** is a price reduction to buyers who buy large volumes. A typical example is "$10 per unit for less than 100 units; $9 per unit for 100 or more units." By law, quantity discounts must be offered to all customers and must not exceed the seller's cost savings associated with selling large quantities. These savings include lower expenses for selling, inventory, and transportation. Discounts provide an incentive to the customer to buy more from a given seller rather than to from many sources.

Functional Discounts

A **functional discount** (also called a *trade discount*) is offered by the seller to trade channel members—retailers and wholesalers—who perform certain functions such as selling, storing, and recordkeeping. Manufacturers may offer different functional discounts to different trade channels because of the varying services they perform, but manufacturers must offer the same functional discounts within each trade channel.

Seasonal Discounts

A **seasonal discount** is a price reduction to buyers who buy merchandise or services out of season. Seasonal discounts allow the seller to keep production steady during the year. For example, ski manufacturers offer seasonal discounts to retailers in the spring and summer to encourage early ordering. Hotels, motels, and airlines offer seasonal discounts in their slower selling periods.

Allowances

Allowances are other types of reductions from the list price. For example, **trade-in allowances** are price reductions given for turning in an old item when buying a new one. Trade-in allowances are most common in the automobile industry and are also given for some other durable goods. **Promotional allowances** are payments or price reductions to reward dealers for participating in advertising and sales-support programs.

Discriminatory Pricing

Companies will often adjust their basic prices to allow for differences in customers, products, and locations. In **discriminatory pricing,** the company sells a product or service at two or more prices, where the difference in prices is not based on differences in costs. Discriminatory pricing takes several forms:

- *Customer-segment pricing.* Here different customers pay different prices for the same product or service. For example, museums will charge a lower admission for students and senior citizens.

- *Product-form pricing.* Here different versions of the product are priced differently but not according to differences in their costs. SCM Corporation prices its most expensive Proctor-Silex fabric iron at $54.95, which is five dollars more than its next most expensive iron. The top model has a light that signals when the iron is ready to use. Yet the extra feature costs less than one dollar to make.

- *Location pricing.* Here different locations are priced differently even though the cost of offering each location is the same. A theatre varies its seat prices because of audience preferences for certain locations. Colleges charge higher tuition for out-of-state students.

- *Time pricing.* Here prices are varied seasonally, by the day, and even by the hour. Public utilities vary their prices to commercial users by time of day and weekend versus weekday. The telephone company offers lower "off-peak" charges, and resorts give seasonal discounts.

For discriminatory pricing to be an effective strategy for the company, certain conditions must exist. The market must be segmentable and the segments must show different degrees of demand. Members of the segment paying the lower price should not be able to turn around and resell the product to the segment paying

Discriminatory pricing: AT&T offers lower prices to those who make calls at "offpeak" times.

the higher price. Competitors should not be able to undersell the firm in the segment being charged the higher price. The cost of segmenting and watching the market should not exceed the extra revenue obtained from the price difference. The practice should not lead to customer resentment and ill will. Finally, the discriminatory pricing must be legal.

With the current deregulation taking place in certain industries, such as airlines and trucking, companies in these industries have used more discriminatory pricing. Consider the pricing used by airlines. The passengers on a plane bound from Raleigh to Los Angeles may pay as many as eleven different round-trip fares for the same flight! Those who check carefully benefit from the intense competition among different carriers flying this route. The ten fares are: first class, $1,512; first class—night, $1,064; first class—night, child, $851; first class—youth, $1,208; coach, $1,014; coach—night, $816; coach—night, child, $810; Super-Saver (nonrefundable fare), $238; Super-Saver (25 percent cancellation penalty), $368; and military personnel, $498.

Psychological Pricing

Price says something about the product. For example, many consumers use price to judge quality. A $100 bottle of perfume may contain only $3 worth of scent, but people are willing to pay $100 because the high price seems to indicate something special.

In using **psychological pricing,** sellers consider the psychology of prices and not simply the economics. A study of the relationship between price and quality perceptions of cars found that higher-priced cars were perceived to possess higher quality.[5] And higher quality cars were perceived to be higher priced than they actually were. Another study showed that consumers refused to buy a certain new car wax until its initial very low price was more than doubled. Consumers could not judge quality before buying the wax, and the initial low price signaled a cheap product. When consumers can judge the quality of a product by examining it or through previous experience with it, price is little used as an indicator of quality. But when consumers cannot judge quality because they lack information or expertise, price becomes an important quality signal (see Marketing Highlight 13–1).[6]

Another aspect of psychological pricing is reference prices. Buyers carry a reference price in their minds when they look at a particular product. The reference price might be formed by noting current prices, remembering past prices, or analyzing the buying context. Sellers can influence or use these consumers' reference prices when setting price. For example, a company could display its product next to more expensive ones to imply that it belongs in the same class. Department stores often sell women's clothing in separate departments differentiated by price; clothing found in the more expensive department is assumed to be of better quality. Companies can also influence consumers' reference prices by stating higher manufacturer's suggested prices, or by noting that the product was priced much higher originally, or by pointing to a competitor's high price.

Even small differences in price can suggest product differences to consumers. Consider a stereo priced at $300 compared to one priced at $299.95. The actual price difference is only 5 cents, but the psychological difference can be much greater. For example, some consumers will see the $299.95 as a price in the $200 range rather than in the $300 range. The $299.95 will more likely be seen as a bargain price, and the $300 price suggests more quality. Some psychologists even argue that each digit has symbolic and visual qualities that should be considered in pricing. Thus 8 is round and even and creates a soothing effect, and 7 is angular and creates a jarring effect.

MARKETING HIGHLIGHT 13–1

HOW PRICE SIGNALS PRODUCT QUALITY

Heublein produces Smirnoff, America's leading brand of vodka. Some years ago, Smirnoff was attacked by another brand, Wolfschmidt, priced at one dollar less a bottle and claiming to have the same quality. Concerned that customers might switch to Wolfschmidt, Heublein considered several possible counter-strategies. It could lower Smirnoff's price by one dollar to hold on to market share; it could hold Smirnoff's price but increase advertising and promotion expenditures; or it could hold Smirnoff's price and let its market share fall. All three strategies would lead to lower profits, and it seemed that Heublein faced a no-win situation.

At this point Heublein's marketers thought of a fourth strategy—and it was brilliant. Heublein raised the price of Smirnoff by one dollar! The company then introduced a new brand, Relska, to compete with Wolfschmidt. And it introduced another brand, Popov, priced lower than Wolfschmidt. This product-line pricing strategy positioned Smirnoff as the elite brand and Wolfschmidt as an ordinary brand. Heublein's clever strategy produced a large increase in its overall profits.

The irony is that Heublein's three brands are pretty much the same in taste and manufacturing costs. Heublein has learned that a product's price signals its quality. Using price as a signal, Heublein sells about the same product at three different quality positions.

Promotional Pricing

With **promotional pricing**, companies will temporarily price their products below the list price, and sometimes even below cost, to increase sales. Promotional pricing takes several forms. Supermarkets and department stores will price a few products as *loss leaders* to attract customers to the store in the hope that they will buy other items at normal markups. Sellers will use *special-event pricing* in certain seasons to draw in more customers. Thus linens are promotionally priced every January to attract shopping-weary customers into the stores. Manufacturers will sometimes offer *cash rebates* to consumers who buy the product from dealers within a specified time. The manufacturer sends the rebate directly to the customer. Rebates have recently been popular with automakers and with durable goods and small appliance producers. Some manufacturers offer *low-interest financing, longer warranties, or free maintenance* to reduce the consumer's "price." This strategy has been a favorite of the auto industry recently. Or, the seller may simply offer *discounts* from normal prices to increase sales and reduce inventories.

Geographical Pricing

The company must decide how to price its products to customers located in different parts of the country. Should the company charge higher prices to distant customers to cover the higher shipping costs and thereby risk losing their business? Or should the company charge the same to all customers regardless of location? We will look at five geographical pricing strategies for the following hypothetical situation:

> The Peerless Paper Company is located in Atlanta, Georgia, and sells paper products to customers all over the United States. The cost of freight is high and affects customers' decisions about their paper suppliers. Peerless wants to design a geographical pricing policy. It is trying to determine how to price a $100 order to three specific customers: customer A (Atlanta); customer B (Bloomington, Indiana); and customer C (Compton, California).

FOB Origin Pricing

Peerless can ask each customer to pay the shipping cost from the Atlanta factory to the customer's location. All three customers would pay the same factory price of

$100, with customer A paying, say, $10 for shipping, customer B paying $15, and customer C paying $25. Called **FOB origin pricing,** it means that the goods are placed free on board a carrier, at which point the title and responsibility pass to the customer, who pays the freight from the factory to the destination.

Supporters of FOB pricing feel that this is the fairest way to assess freight charges, because each customer picks up its own cost. The disadvantage, however, is that Peerless will be a high-cost firm to distant customers. If Peerless's main competitor is in California, this competitor would outsell Peerless in California. In fact, the competitor would outsell Peerless in most of the West, and Peerless would dominate the East. A vertical line could be drawn on a map connecting the cities where the two companies' price plus freight would just be equal. Peerless would have the price advantage east of this line, and its competitor would have the price advantage west of this line.

Uniform Delivered Pricing

Uniform delivered pricing is the exact opposite of FOB pricing. Here the company charges the same price plus freight to all customers regardless of their location. The freight charge is set at the average freight cost. Suppose this is $15. Uniform delivered pricing therefore results in a high charge to the Atlanta customer (who pays $15 freight instead of $10) and a lower charge to the Compton customer (who pays $15 instead of $25). The Atlanta customer would prefer to buy paper from another local paper company that uses FOB origin pricing. On the other hand, Peerless has a better chance to win the California customer. Other advantages are that uniform delivered pricing is fairly easy to administer and lets the firm advertise its price nationally.

Zone Pricing

Zone pricing falls between FOB origin pricing and uniform delivered pricing. The company sets up two or more zones. All customers within a zone pay the same total price, and this price is higher in the more distant zones. Peerless might set up an East zone and charge $10 freight to all customers in this zone; a Midwest zone and charge $15; and a West zone and charge $25. In this way, the customers within a given price zone receive no price advantage from the company. A customer in Atlanta and Boston pay the same total price to Peerless. The complaint, however, is that the Atlanta customer is paying part of the Boston customer's freight cost. In addition, a customer just on the west side of the line dividing the East and Midwest pays much more than one just on the east side of the line, although they may be within a few miles of each other.

Basing-Point Pricing

Basing-point pricing allows the seller to select some city as a basing point and charge all customers the freight cost from that city to the customer location, regardless of the city from which the goods are actually shipped. For example, Peerless might set Chicago as the basing point and charge all customers $100 plus the freight from Chicago to their location. This means that an Atlanta customer pays the freight cost from Chicago to Atlanta even though the goods may be shipped from Atlanta. Using a basing-point location other than the factory raises the total price to customers near the factory and lowers the total price to customers far from the factory.

If all the sellers used the same basing-point city, delivered prices would be the same for all customers, and price competition would be eliminated. Such industries as sugar, cement, steel, and automobiles used basing-point pricing for years, but this method is less popular today. Some companies set up multiple basing points to create more flexibility; they quoted freight charges from the basing-point city nearest to the customer.

Freight Absorption Pricing

The seller who is anxious to do business with a certain customer or geographical area might use **freight absorption pricing.** This strategy involves absorbing all or part of the actual freight charges in order to get the business. The seller might reason that if it can get more business, its average costs will fall and more than compensate for the extra freight cost. Freight absorption pricing is used for market penetration and also to hold on to increasingly competitive markets.

PRICE CHANGES

Initiating Price Changes

After developing their price structures and strategies, companies will face occasions when they will want to cut or raise prices.

Initiating Price Cuts

Several situations may lead a firm to consider cutting its price. One situation is excess capacity. Here the firm needs more business and cannot get it through increased sales effort, product improvement, or other measures. In the late 1970s many companies dropped "follow-the-leader pricing" and turned to "aggressive pricing" to boost their sales. But as the airline, construction equipment, and other industries have learned in recent years, cutting prices in an industry loaded with excess capacity may lead to price wars as competitors try to hold on to market share.

Another situation that may lead to price cuts is falling market share in the face of strong price competition. Several American industries—automobiles, consumer electronics, cameras, watches, and steel—have been losing market share to Japanese competitors whose high-quality products carry lower prices than American products. Zenith, General Motors, and other American companies have resorted to more aggressive pricing action. General Motors, for example, cut its subcompact car prices by 10 percent on the West Coast, where Japanese competition is strongest.

Companies will also cut prices in a drive to dominate the market through lower costs. Either the company starts with lower costs than its competitors, or it cuts prices in the hope of gaining market share that will lead to falling costs through larger volume. For example, Bausch and Lomb used an aggressive low-cost, low-price strategy to become the leader in the competitive soft-contact-lens market (see Marketing Highlight 13–2).

Initiating Price Increases

Many companies have had to raise prices in recent years. They do so knowing that the price increases are likely to be resented by customers, dealers, and the company's own salesforce. Yet a successful price increase can greatly increase profits. For example, if the company's profit margin is 3 percent of sales, a 1 percent price increase will increase profits by 33 percent if sales volume is unaffected.

A major situation leading to price increases is rising costs, which squeeze profit margins and lead companies to regular rounds of price increases. Companies often raise their prices by more than the cost increase in anticipation of further inflation. Because of rising costs, companies do not want to make long-run price agreements with customers—they fear that cost increases will eat up their profit margins. Another

BAUSCH AND LOMB'S HARDBALL PRICING

Bausch and Lomb was the first company to develop and sell soft contact lenses. For many years after introducing these lenses in the early 1970s, B&L held 100 percent of the market. But in the late 1970s, as a dozen competitors entered the soft-lens market, Bausch and Lomb was quickly losing its market share dominance. To make matters worse, the company was late in developing extended-wear lenses—thinner soft lenses that can be worn for up to a month at a time without taking them out. B&L's overall share dropped under 50 percent by the early 1980s, largely because it had no share of the fast-growing extended-ware-lens segment.

Bausch finally brought out its own brand of extended-wear lenses in 1983, two years after competitors' entries. To overcome its late start, B&L used all of its considerable marketing strength and a tough marketing strategy. At the heart of this strategy was aggressive, low pricing. *Business Week* described Bausch's "hardball pricing" and competitors' reactions:

> [Bausch and Lomb's] entry price of $20 was 50% or more below the industry norm for extended-wear lenses. . . . [Competitor] CooperVision hit back in March with a new, top-quality lens it offered for about $15 wholesale. Bausch retaliated in April by lowering all its prices even further. Now its high-water model wholesales for $10 to $15, while its basic low-water lens lists at $8 to $13 depending on volume, and a new daily-wear lens has been introduced at a low price of $7 to $12.

Thus, shortly after entering the market, Bausch was selling its high-quality lenses for only 20 to 30 percent of competitors' previous prices. The company's aggressive initial pricing, and its quick reactions to competitors' price thrusts paid off well.

> Within a month, B&L's sales staff had supplies of the new lenses in more than 90% of the 12,000 professional eye-care outlets in the U.S. that sell contact

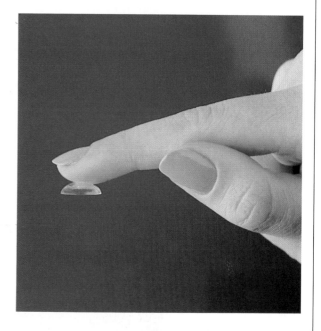

Bausch and Lomb created the soft contact lens market, then used "hardball pricing" to hold off competitors.

lenses. Within four months, Bausch captured 37% of the [extended-wear lens] market and was the No. 1 marketer.

Bausch and Lomb's low price resulted in large sales volume, which in turn lowered unit production costs, allowing still lower prices. Bausch is now firmly positioned as the industry's lost-cost, low-price producer, and its competitors face some tough decisions. Bausch and Lomb's low prices have caused an industry shakeout as competitors race to figure out how to respond. Those that cannot find a good answer will have to drop out of the running.

Sources: Excerpts from "Bausch and Lomb: Hardball Pricing Helps It To Regain Its Grip in Contact Lenses," *Business Week*, July 16, 1984, pp. 78–80. Also see Lois Therrien, "Bausch & Lomb is Correcting Its Vision of Research," *Business Week*, March 30, 1987, p. 91.

factor leading to price increases is overdemand. When a company cannot supply all its customers' needs, it can raise its prices, ration products to customers, or both.

Companies can increase their prices in a number of ways to keep up with rising costs.[7] Prices can be raised almost invisibly by dropping discounts and adding higher-priced units to the line. Or prices can be pushed up openly. In passing price increases on to customers, the company should avoid the image of price gouger. The price increases should be supported with a company communication program telling customers why prices are being increased. The company salesforce should help customers find ways to economize.

Where possible, the company consider ways to <u>meet higher costs</u> or demand <u>without raising prices.</u> For example, it can shrink the product instead of raising the price, as candy bar manufacturers often do. Or it can substitute less expensive ingredients. It can remove product features, packaging, or services. Or it can "unbundle" its products and services, removing and separately pricing elements that were formerly part of the offer. IBM, for example, now offers training as a separately priced service. Many restaurants have shifted from dinner pricing to a la carte pricing.

Buyer Reactions to Price Changes

Whether the price is raised or lowered, the action will affect buyers, competitors, distributors, and suppliers, and it may interest government as well.

Customers do not always put a straightforward interpretation on price changes. They may view a price cut in several ways. For example, what would you think if IBM were to suddenly cut its personal computer prices in half? You might think the computers are about to be replaced by a later model, or that they have some fault and are not selling well. You might think that IBM is in financial trouble and

Buyer reactions to price changes: what would you think if the price of Joy was suddenly cut in half?

may not stay in the business to supply future parts. Or you might believe that quality has been reduced, or that the price will come down even further, and it will pay to wait.

A price increase, which would normally lower sales, may carry some positive meanings to the buyers. What would you think if IBM raised the price of its most recently introduced personal computer model? You might think that the item is very "hot" and may be unobtainable unless you buy it soon. Or you might think the computer is an unusually good value, or that IBM is greedy and charging what the traffic will bear.

Competitor Reactions to Price Changes

A firm considering a price change has to be concerned about the reactions of competitors as well as customers. For example, if the firm raises prices but major competitors do not follow, it may lose business to the lower-priced competitors. Or if the firm lowers its prices and competitors react by lowering their prices even further, a costly price war may result. Competitors are very likely to react when the number of firms is small, the product is uniform, and the buyers are well informed.

How can the firm figure out the likely reactions of its competitors? Assume that the firm faces one large competitor. If the competitor reacts in a set way to price changes, the reaction can be anticipated. But if the competitor treats each price change as a fresh challenge and reacts according to its self-interest, the company will have to figure out what makes up the competitor's self-interest at the time.

The problem is complex because the competitor can interpret a company price cut in many ways. It might think that the company is trying to steal the market, or that the company is doing poorly and is trying to boost its sales, or that the company wants the whole industry to cut prices in order to increase total demand.

When there are several competitors, the company must guess each competitor's likely reaction. If all competitors behave alike, this amounts to analyzing only a typical competitor. If the competitors do not behave alike because of differences in size, market shares, or policies, then separate analyses are necessary. If some competitors will match the price change, there is good reason to expect that the rest will also match it.

Responding to Price Changes

Here we reverse the question and ask how a firm should respond to a price change by a competitor. Should it follow suit or maintain its current prices? The firm needs to consider several issues. Why did the competitor change the price? Is it to steal the market, to use excess capacity, to meet changing cost conditions, or to lead an industry-wide price change? Does the competitor plan to make the price change temporary or permanent? What will happen to the company's market share and profits if it does not respond? Are other companies going to respond? And what are the competitor's and other firms' responses likely to be to each possible reaction?

Besides these issues, the company must make a broader analysis. The company has to consider the product's stage in the life cycle, its importance in the company's product mix, the intentions and resources of the competitor, the price and value sensitivity of the market, the behavior of costs with volume, and the company's other opportunities.

The company cannot always make an extended analysis of its alternatives at the time of a price change. The competitor may have spent much time preparing this decision, but the company may have to react within hours or days. About the only way to cut down reaction time is to plan ahead for possible competitor's price

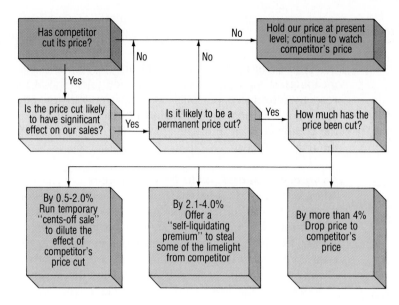

FIGURE 13-2
Price reaction program for meeting a competitor's price cut
Source: Redrawn with permission from a working paper by Raymond J. Trapp, Northwestern University, 1964.

changes and possible responses. Figure 13-2 shows a company's price reaction program for meeting a competitor's possible price cut. Reaction programs for meeting price changes are most often used in industries where price changes occur often and where it is important to react quickly. Examples can be found in the meatpacking, lumber, and oil industries.

■ SUMMARY

Pricing is a dynamic process. Companies design a pricing structure that covers all their products, change it over time, and adjust it to account for different customers and situations.

Pricing strategies usually change as a product passes through its life cycle. In pricing innovative new products, the company can follow a skimming policy by setting prices high initially to "skim" the maximum amount of revenue from various segments of the market. Or it can use penetration pricing by setting a low initial price to win a large market share. The company can decide on one of nine price-quality strategies for introducing an imitative product.

When the product is part of a product mix, the firm searches for a set of prices that will maximize the profits from the total mix. The company decides on the price zones for items in its product line and on the pricing of optional products, captive products, and by-products, and product bundles.

Companies apply a variety of price-adjustment strategies to account for differences in consumer segments and situations. One is discount pricing and allowances, in which the company establishes cash discounts, quantity discounts, functional discounts, seasonal discounts, and allowances. A second is discriminatory pricing, in which the company

sets different prices for different customers, product forms, places, or times. A third is psychological pricing, in which the company adjusts the price to better communicate a product's intended position. A fourth is promotional pricing, in which the company decides on loss-leader pricing, special-event pricing, and psychological discounting. A fifth is geographical pricing, in which the company decides how to price to distant customers, choosing from such alternatives as FOB pricing, uniform delivered pricing, zone pricing, basing-point pricing, and freight absorption pricing.

When a firm considers initiating a price change, it must also consider customers' and competitors' reactions. Customers' reactions are influenced by the meaning customers see in the price change. Competitors' reactions flow from a set reaction policy or a fresh analysis of each situation. The firm initiating the price change must also anticipate the probable reactions of suppliers, middlemen, and government.

The firm that faces a price change initiated by a competitor must try to understand the competitor's intent and the likely duration of the change. If swiftness of reaction is desirable, the firm should preplan its reactions to different possible price actions by competitors.

QUESTIONS FOR DISCUSSION

1. Describe which strategy—market skimming or market penetration—these companies use in pricing their products: (a) McDonald's (fast food), (b) Curtis Mathes (television and other home electronics), and (c) Bic Corporation (pens, lighters, shavers, and related products). Are these companies using the right pricing approaches? Would another approach be better? Why or why not?

2. GE has developed a revolutionary light bulb that lasts five times longer than ordinary bulbs and uses only one-third as much electricity. GE is considering a price of $10 for the bulb, which would save consumers $20 in lower electric bills over the bulb's life. Do you think the bulb will be successful at this price? What approach should GE take in marketing this innovation?

3. What types of discount pricing tactics might Head Skis use in dealing with the retail outlets that carry its products?

4. Discuss the different pricing strategies used by movie theaters. What market segments are these different strategies designed to appeal to?

5. A clothing store sells men's suits at three price levels—$180, $250, and $340. If shoppers use these price points as reference prices in comparing different suits, what would be the effect of adding a new line of suits at a different price point? If the new line cost $280, would you expect sales of the $250 suits to increase, decrease, or stay the same?

6. A garden supply company located in New York uses catalogs to sell seeds, bulbs, shrubs, and even trees to gardeners in every part of the country. What geographical pricing strategy should this company use for maximum profits?

7. Decreases in the price of cocoa resulting from sudden increases in worldwide supply have lowered production costs for chocolate products. What impact will this cost reduction have on pricing strategies for chocolate? What approach to cutting prices is appropriate if manufacturers expect the cost of cocoa to go back up next year?

8. If McDonald's announced a new price for Big Macs of only 99 cents, how would you expect competing hamburger chains to react? Would they react the same way if the price decrease were for Chicken McNuggets rather than Big Macs? Why or why not?

9. Armco, a major sheet-metal producer, has developed a process for galvanizing steel sheets so that they can be painted—something not previously possible. These sheets could be used in car-body parts to prevent rust. What factors should Armco consider in setting a price for this new product?

KEY TERMS

Basing-point pricing A geographic pricing strategy in which the seller designates some city as a basing point and charges all customers the freight cost from that city to the customer location, regardless of the city from which the goods are actually shipped.

Cash discount A price reduction to buyers who pay their bills promptly.

Discriminatory pricing Selling a product or service at two or more prices, where the difference in prices is not based on differences in costs.

FOB origin pricing A geographic pricing strategy in which goods are placed free on board a carrier, and the customer pays the freight from the factory to the destination.

Freight absorption pricing A geographic pricing strategy in which the company absorbs all or part of the actual freight charges in order to get the business.

Functional discount A price reduction offered by the seller to trade channel members who perform certain functions such as selling, storing, and recordkeeping.

Market penetration pricing Setting a low price for a new product in order to attract a large number of buyers and a large market share.

Market-skimming pricing Setting a high price for a new product to skim maximum revenue from the segments willing to pay the high price; the company makes fewer but more profitable sales.

Promotional allowance A payment or price reduction to reward dealers for participating in advertising and sales-support programs.

Promotional pricing Temporarily pricing products below the list price, and sometimes even below cost, to increase short-run sales.

Psychological pricing A pricing approach that considers the psychology of prices and not simply the economics—the price is used to say something about the product.

Quantity discount A price reduction to buyers who buy large volumes.

Seasonal discount A price reduction to buyers who buy merchandise or services out of season.

Trade-in allowance A price reduction given for turning in an old item when buying a new one.

Uniform delivered pricing A geographic pricing strategy in which the company charges the same price plus freight to all customers regardless of their location.

Zone pricing A geographic pricing strategy in which the company sets up two or more zones, all customers within a zone pay the same total price, and this price is higher in the more distant zones.

■ REFERENCES

1. See Bill Kelley, "Komatsu in Cat Fight," *Sales and Marketing Management*, April 1986, pp. 50–53; Jack Willoughby, "Decision Time in Peoria," *Forbes*, January 27, 1986, p. 36; Kathleen Deveny, "Caterpillar is Betting Big on Pint-Size Machines," *Business Week*, December 25, 1985, p. 41; and Kevin Kelly, "A Weekend Komatsu Tries to Come Back Swinging," *Business Week*, February 22, 1988, p. 48.

2. For a comprehensive description and comparison of various pricing strategies, see Gerald J. Tellis, "Beyond the Many Faces of Price: An Integration of Pricing Strategies," *Journal of Marketing*, October 1986, pp. 146–60.

3. See James E. Ellis, "Spectra's Instant Success Gives Polaroid a Shot in the Arm," *Business Week*, November 3, 1986, pp. 32–34; and Thomas T. Nagle, *The Strategy and Tactics of Pricing* (Englewood Cliffs, NJ: Prentice Hall, 1987), pp. 116–17.

4. See Tellis, "Beyond the Many Faces of Price," p. 155; and Nagle, *The Strategy and Tactics of Pricing*, pp. 170–72.

5. Gary M. Erickson and Johny K. Johansson, "The Role of Price in Multi-Attribute Product Evaluations," *Journal of Consumer Research*, September 1985, pp. 195–99.

6. See Nagle, *The Strategy and Tactics of Pricing*, pp. 66–8; and Tellis, "The Many Faces of Price," pp. 152–53.

7. Norman H. Fuss, Jr., "How to Raise Prices—Judiciously—to Meet Today's Conditions," *Harvard Business Review*, May–June 1975, p. 10; and Mary Louise Hatten, "Don't Get Caught with Your Prices Down," *Business Horizons*, March–April 1982, pp. 23–28.

CASE 10

TEXAS INSTRUMENTS, INC.: SPEAKING LEARNING-AID PRODUCTS

Texas Instuments, Inc. has changed its drive into consumer markets in the past few years by discontinuing its digital watch and home computer lines and introducing several new products. The company is at the point where it must decide what strategies and action programs it should use to ensure successful participation in the market for small electronic learning-aid products. A major question is pricing strategy. In the past, TI used a low-price, high-volume strategy for its digital watches and hand-held calculators.

Texas Instruments has a number of learning-aid products (LAPs) already on the market or being considered for introduction. Several hand-held LAPs teach spelling (Spelling B and Speak and Spell), reading (Speak and Read), and math (Speak and Math). The Magic Wand Speaking Reader helps children to teach themselves to read by sliding a hand-held wand across a bar-code strip printed under the words in special books. VOCAID is designed to provide capabilities for the voiceless by emitting synthesized vocal expressions when keys on its keyboard are pressed. Additional modules and matching keyboard templates to expand VOCAID's capability will be available.

LAPs. Although the LAPs differ significantly in both form and function from earlier TI consumer products (calculators, personal computers, and watches) and are in the introductory and growth stages of the product life cycle, the marketing strategy used to date is virtually identical to that used earlier for the company's more mature products. The LAPs' educational value suggests that they could be marketed to schools as a supplementary learning aid, but only a limited effort has been made to develop either the educational or the home entertainment market. As with any new-product introduction, TI is faced with assessing market potential and familiarizing potential customers with a previously unheard-of product. These problems are particularly acute in this case because the products were developed as a result of technological innovation rather than in response to expressed consumer needs.

The learning aids began in 1972 with TI, along with such firms as Bowmar, National Semiconductor, and Commodore, packaged inexpensive calculators with game books. TI's Little Professor and Dataman machines went further by preprogramming specific math problems within each machine's memory. Spelling B and Speak & Spell were introduced next. Speak & Spell uses TI's voice synthesizer technology. It contains 230 of the most commonly misspelled words in order of difficulty. It asks you to spell a word that it clearly pronounces, say *treasure*. When you finish spelling, you press a button, and if you were right, it says, "That is correct, now spell [the next word]." If you misspelled *treasure*, it says, "Wrong, try again," and you have another chance. If you miss again, the unit says. "The correct spelling is T-R-E-A-S-U-R-E." The unit also automatically displays the number of right and wrong answers at the end of a block of ten words. Speak & Spell can be used as a pronunciation guide and as the basis for a number of games, and it will accept additional small memory modules that raise the spelling difficulty. The new technology holds enormous potential, since voice-command control will eventually be an important aspect of life. The speech synthesis chip, which has gained such wide attention for Speak & Spell, is a far more advanced (and compact) version of the circuit and chip systems that have been used for almost two decades in commercial and industrial "talking machines," such as those in banking and telephone systems.

The high levels of consumer interest and user involvement along with the company's leading technological position, suggest that a well-planned line of voice-synthesized learning aids should be actively marketed year round. This would be in contrast to TI's past efforts, which have involved year-end promotion of two or three items.

The Magic Wand. Texas Instruments developed an educational tool that brings the teaching of reading into the electronics age. By combining two new technologies and building on its Speak & Spell learning aid, TI produced what it calls the Magic Wand Speaking Reader. With it, preschool children can help teach themselves to read by sliding a hand-held "wand" across a strip of bars printed under the words in special books.

The plastic wand, about the size of a fat pen, uses a tiny beam of infrared light to decode vocal instructions contained in the bar-code strips. It operates much as checkout scanners in supermarkets decode product-identification data from the bar codes printed on grocery items. But TI's wand costs about a fourth as much as other systems on the market. The Magic Wand is said to be the first of a family of learning aids and portable computing products that will use bar-code storage. A list price of $120 is being considered for the battery-operated device.

The Magic Wand may prove to be the key to low-cost electronic publishing because it requires no change in the printing techniques and equipment now in use. TI plans to encourage publishing houses to turn out their own books. Publishers will supply the text, and TI, using a computerized "bar-code factory," will translate the words into bars and spaces that the Magic Wand can read. Mattel's Western Publishing Company, which produces the Golden Books, is using a similar approach in developing a talking reader.

VOCAID. TI has designed a device that will give the voiceless speech capabilities. VOCAID consists of a keyboard with each key identified by a word or expression. When the appropriate keys are depressed, the VOCAID emits a synthesized voice expression of the selected message. Additional modules and matching keyboard templates will be available for separate purchase to expand VOCAID's capability. There is some uncertainty as to what retail prices TI should suggest for the VOCAID hardware and the additional cartridges and templates. Should the company price the items according to their value to the buyer rather than base prices on cost? It remains to be seen how potential user/buyers can be identified and how the value to user/buyers can be determined.

Other Products. Several future uses have been proposed for voice synthesis chips, including foreign language education and electronic games. An example is the electronic dictionary, already being offered by at least two firms. It can translate as many as 1,500 English words and phrases into a foreign language, such as French, German, Spanish, Russian, or Japanese. Languages can be changed by switching modules available at $25 to $50 each. Models made by Lexicon and Craig are pocket-size and sell for about $200.

TI's Consumer Products Group's direct salesforce sells LAPs as well as calculators to major retail chains. Smaller stores either place their orders directly with TI or purchase through distributors. In a recent year, advertising amounted to about $1 million for learning-aid products and was confined to the four weeks following Thanksgiving. The chief advertising medium used was television, with very heavy exposure. The company also placed some ads in trade magazines, but this program was not extensive. Cooperative advertising was offered to retailers, with a specified percentage of total purchase available to dealers for co-op advertising purposes.

TI achieved its dominant position in hand-held calculators and digital watches by using a low-margin, high-volume strategy. Relatively low prices were set on a few models expecting that large production volumes and greater experience in manufacturing and marketing would result in lower costs. This, in turn, permitted still lower prices, with the result that TI gained dominant market share and, for a while, healthy profits.

So far, the company has failed to duplicate this strategy in its learning-aid product line. On numerous occasions Speak & Spell has been in short supply. The retail price for Speak & Spell has varied a lot by year and by type of retail outlet, ranging from less than $40 to over $60. This price variation has raised the question of whether the company's low price, high volume pricing strategy, basic to the nonconsumer business, is appropriate for the consumer-oriented aid products.

1. For the learning-aid products line, should Texas Instruments employ the low-price strategy it used for digital watches and hand-held calculators and computers?

2. Should Magic Wand be marketed along with learning-aid products? Why or why not?

3. What recommendations would you give TI management concerning the pricing of VOCAID? How should it be marketed?

CASE 11

LOCTITE CORPORATION

Loctite is a highly profitable and rapidly growing manufacturer and marketer of adhesives, sealants, and related specialty chemicals, with annual sales of almost $200 million. The company's growth has been in the "wonder glues," specifically in the anaerobic type, which cures quickly in absence of air, and the "crazy glues" (cyanoacrylates), which cure instantly upon exposure to the moisture that is present in trace amounts on surfaces to be bonded. In the industrial market, this product sells for over $60 per pound, each pound containing roughly 30,000 drops that are gener-

TABLE 1
Marketing Strategy Before and After Field Testing

	BEFORE	AFTER
Market target	Design engineers[1]	Maintenance workers[2]
Product	Thin liquid	Gel
Package	Bottle (red)	Tube (silver)
Name	RC 601	Quick Metal
Price	Cost based	Value based
Promotion	Technical description[3]	"Keeps machines running until parts arrive"
Sales effort	Routine	Special promotions and incentives at all levels
Sales results		700% increase after changes

[1] Reluctant to try unproven products.
[2] Able to buy anything anywhere needed to make machine operate.
[3] Nonmigrating thoxotropic anaerobic gel.

ally applied a few drops at a time. Consumer packages are much smaller, containing about one-tenth of an ounce, and sell for up to $2 per tube, or about $20 or more per ounce.

The company's phenomenal success in the industrial market has attracted competitors, including some large and aggressive ones, such as the 3M Company. Competitive anaerobic and cyanoacrylate products are being marketed in most countries where Loctite conducts business. The company has patent protection for its anaerobics in the United States and in a number of foreign countries. Nearly all competitive anaerobic sealants and adhesives are sold at prices lower than Loctite's. Although the company has selectively reduced prices to meet competition from time to time, it believes that its technical service and attention to customer needs will enable it to maintain its market position without significant price reductions.

Loctite plans to intensify its "application engineering" approach, which helped it overtake Eastman Kodak in the more competitive "crazy glue" market. This approach casts well-trained technical service personnel as customer problem solvers using Loctite's products, often especially formulated for the customer's application. The company has three principal user markets for its products: the industrial market, the consumer market, and the automotive aftermarket. Loctite's Industrial Products Group makes approximately 60 percent of sales through independent distributors, some of which sell adhesives and sealants made by other companies. The remaining 40 percent of sales are made directly to end users. The company maintains close and continued contact with its distributors and major end users in order to provide technical assistance and support for the use

of its products. In the United States and Canada, sales are made through approximately 120 technically trained district managers and sales engineers, as well as through approximately 2,800 independent industrial distributors.

Hoping to improve profitability, Loctite decided to try consumer goods marketing techniques in marketing RC 601, a puttylike adhesive for repairing worn machine parts. After going into the field to determine what potential customers wanted and studying the product from the customers' point of view, the company made certain changes in its marketing effort. The before-and-after contrast is shown in Table 1.

The Industrial Products Division faces the problem of pricing three new products. The details are as follows.

- *Bond-a-matic*. This is an instant glue applicator for assembly lines and is targeted at small- and medium-sized manufacturers that put a lot of parts together. The product avoids "adhesive clog," a common and costly problem. The company is so confident of Bond-a-matic's performance that it will mail a demonstration kit for a thirty-day free trial. The product should be priced low enough so that it can be bought by production managers without getting approval for a capital expenditure.

- *Quick Repair Kits*. This includes an assortment of materials to make quick minor repairs requiring fast-curing adhesives or sealants to keep equipment running and minimize waste of materials in small shops and factories. The kit includes a pair of Vise-Grip pliers as a premium.

TABLE 2
Product Costs

	BOND-A-MATIC	QUICK REPAIR KIT	QUICK-METAL
LOCTITE:			
Cost to make	$27.00	$ 6.25	$1.50
All other costs	23.00	5.75	3.50
Total cost per unit	$50.00	$12.00	$5.00
DISTRIBUTOR:			

Usual gross margin on this type of product is 33⅓% of selling price.

• *Quick-Metal*. This is a puttylike adhesive for temporary repair of worn metal bearings and other machine parts. Quick-Metal gets equipment ready to run in one hour compared with twelve hours for "metalizers," the most commonly used alternative method. Loctite claims that the product can save the user up to $4,000 in time and labor. It is packaged in 50 cc tubes.

All of these products are to be sold through the Industrial Products Division's distributors. In determining the sug-gested price to be charged by the distributors for each product, assume the costs shown in Table 2.

1. What factors should be considered by Loctite in deter-mining the suggested price its distributors would charge their customers?

2. What price would you recommend that Loctite suggest its distributors charge for each product?

3. How would you use the problem-solving marketing ap-proach when selling through distributors and retailers?

14 *Placing Products: Distribution Channels and Physical Distribution*

SINCE its founding in 1979, Esprit de Corp has grown with a vengeance, parlaying its colorful, breezy fashions into an $800 million worldwide fashion empire. Now the funky fashion marketer is shifting its attention

from developing new fashions to pursuing a new and potentially pivotal retailing thrust. Esprit is changing its distibution channels—it is decreasing reliance on its traditional department store channels and building a network of franchised and company-owned retail stores.

Esprit began as a fashion design company. To build initial sales for its new and unknown lines, it relied heavily on the marketing clout and merchandising savvy of department stores. But now that Esprit has grown large, with strong consumer recognition and preference, it is seeking new channels—and for good reasons. First, department stores are growing only slowly, while specialty stores are gaining strength. By opening its own specialty stores, Esprit believes it can strengthen its retail presence while

cashing in on retail profits. But perhaps more important, Esprit wants more control over point-of-sale marketing efforts for its products. Department stores have been boosting their margins by cutting back on their sales staffs and merchandising-display money. Thus they often give the Esprit line less sales and merchandising support than the company thinks it needs. And department stores are known for cramming many competing lines together so that each one loses its individuality. Also, department stores tend to deal erratically with vendors, "cherry picking" the vendor's collection and taking merchandising liberties that could potentially kill the line. By opening its own outlets, Esprit can make its sales pitch directly to customers, and it can better control the way its wares are displayed and merchandised.

Esprit's new channel strategy has two major thrusts. First, Esprit is revamping its department store channel by pruning out weaker retailers, cutting its customer list from a high of 2,400 department stores to less than 1,000. And Esprit now exerts more merchandising control over stores that carry the line. It dictates strict rules on how to arrange its goods on the floor, how to present the logo and advertise the Esprit name, and how much of each collection a retailer must buy to remain an active account. It also offers no "markdown money," an unwritten convention in which vendors offset the store's costs of inventory clearances. Department stores grumble, but they put up with such restrictive policies because of the Esprit's market strength. "I'll never drop the Esprit line unless their sales fall," says one major department store buyer. But in the same breath she adds, "I hate working with Esprit. They're the most difficult vendor in the market."

The second major thrust of Esprit's new channel strategy is its gutsy and dramatic move into retailing. Esprit opened its first store in 1980, a factory outlet across from its San Francisco headquarters. Three years later, it opened a dramatic fashion "superstore" in West Hollywood, the fashion ghetto of Los Angeles. This huge store with sparse shelving, few racks and fixtures, and an uncluttered floor allows Esprit to experiment with its belief that most retailers cram too much merchandise on a floor. Esprit has since opened a New Orleans superstore, and it has two more under construction in Dallas and Washington. In all, Esprit plans to open as many as 30 new company-owned superstores. In addition, it expects to sponsor many times that number of franchised stores.

Esprit's aggressive new channel strategy is loaded with risk. First, the company's current success stems from its fashion design and manufacturing prowess; it may not have the skills and resources needed to repeat this success in the highly competitive retailing field. But the greatest danger is that Esprit might alienate its major department stores clients. By opening its own stores, Esprit competes directly with the department stores for retail business. And by laying down tough restrictions, the company risks driving off some of its best department store customers. Esprit can get away with this strong independent stance as long as its lines stay hot. But if demand wavers, such actions could come back to haunt the company. For now, since Esprit has only a relatively small number of stores, large retail customers don't seem to feel threatened. And Esprit believes that opening its own stores will strengthen the line's exposure and reputation, thereby reinforcing department store business rather than harming it. Anything that helps the Esprit image only helps department store business, the company argues.

Implementing the new channel strategy will take a long time—at least ten years. And it will cost a lot—each new store runs more than $10 million. But Esprit management thinks it's worth the effort, money, and risk. The new channel strategy places control over Esprit's fate more squarely where it belongs—in the hands of the company's managers. As Doug Tompkins, Esprit's founder and president, puts it, "Retailers do well as merchants, buying and selling, and for that we give them a lot of credit. But . . . who's going to do the best job with our product? Nobody will do it better than us."[1]

Chapter Objectives *After reading this chapter, you should be able to:*

1. Explain why companies use distribution channels and the functions these channels perform.

2. Discuss how channel members interact and how they organize to do the work of the channel.

3. Identify the major distribution channel alternatives open to a company.

4. Tell how companies select, motivate, and evaluate channel members.

5. Discuss the issues firms face when setting up physical distribution systems.

DECISIONS about how to distribute products and services to consumers are among the most important facing management. These marketing channel decisions directly affect every other marketing decision. The company's pricing depends on whether it uses mass merchandisers or high quality specialty stores. The firm's salesforce and advertising decisions depend upon how much persuasion, training, and motivation the dealers need. Whether a company develops or acquires certain new products may depend on how well the products fit the abilities and capacity of channel members.

Companies often pay too little attention to their distribution channels, sometimes with damaging results. For example, automobile companies have lost large shares of the parts and service business to NAPA, Midas, Goodyear, and other firms because they resist making needed changes in their dealer franchise networks. On the other hand, many companies have used imaginative distribution systems to gain a substantial competitive advantage. Federal Express' imaginative and formidable distribution system made it the industry leader in the small-package delivery industry. And American Hospital Supply gained a strong advantage over its competition by linking up its distribution system directly to hospitals through a sophisticated data processing system.[2]

Distribution channel decisions often involve long-term commitments to other firms. A furniture manufacturer can quickly and easily change its advertising, prices, or promotion programs. It can scrap old product designs and introduce new ones as market tastes demand. But when it sets up a distribution channel through contracts with independent dealers, it cannot easily replace this channel with company-owned branches if conditions change. Therefore management must design its channels carefully, with an eye on tomorrow's likely selling environment as well as today's.

In this chapter we will examine four major distribution channel questions: What is the nature of distribution channels? How do channel firms interact and organize to do the work of the channel? What problems to companies face in designing and managing their channels? And what role does physical distribution play in attracting and satisfying customers? In the next chapter we will look at distribution channel issues from the viewpoint of retailers and wholesalers.

*T*HE NATURE OF DISTRIBUTION CHANNELS

Most producers use middlemen to bring their products to market. They try to forge a distribution channel.

> A **distribution channel** is the set of firms and individuals that take title, or assist in transferring title, to a good or service as it moves from the producer to the final consumer or industrial user.

Why Are Middlemen Used? Why do producers give some of the selling job to middlemen? Doing so means giving up some control over how and to whom the products are sold. But producers gain certain advantages from using middlemen. These advantages are described below.

Many producers lack the financial resources to carry out direct marketing. For example, General Motors sells its automobiles through thousands of independent franchise dealers. Even General Motors would be hard pressed to raise the cash to buy out its dealers.

Direct marketing would require many producers to become middlemen for the products of other producers in order to achieve mass-distribution economies. For example, the Wrigley Company would not find it practical to set up small retail

From the Coca-Cola Company, to the bottler, to the retailer, to the consumer—channel members must all work together to make Coke successful.

gum shops around the country or to sell gum door to door or by mail order. It would have to sell gum along with many other small products and would end up in the drugstore and foodstore business. Wrigley finds it easier to work through a network of privately owned distributors.

Even producers who can afford to set up their own channels can often earn a greater return by increasing their investment in their main business. If a company earns a 20 percent rate of return on manufacturing and foresees only a 10 percent return on retailing, it will not want to do its own retailing.

The use of middlemen largely boils down to their greater efficiency in making goods available to target markets. Through their contacts, experience, specialization, and scale of operation, middlemen usually offer the firm more than it can achieve on its own.

Figure 14-1 shows one way that using middlemen can provide economies. Part A shows three manufacturers each using direct marketing to reach three customers. This requires nine different contacts. Part B shows the three manufacturers working through one distributor, who contacts the three customers. This system requires only six contacts. In this way, middlemen reduce the amount of work that must be done.

From the economic system's point of view, the role of middlemen is to transform the assortment of products made by producers into the assortments wanted by consumers. Producers make narrow assortments of products in large quantities. But consumers want broad assortments of products in small quantities. In the distribution channels, middlemen buy the large quantities of many producers and break them down into the smaller quantities and broader assortments wanted by consumers. Thus, middlemen play an important role in matching supply and demand.

Distribution Channel Functions

A distribution channel moves goods from producers to consumers. It overcomes the major time, place, and possession gaps that separate goods and services from those who would use them. Members of the marketing channel perform many key functions:

- *Research*—gathering of information needed for planning and aiding exchange.
- *Promotion*—developing and spreading persuasive communications about the offer.
- *Contact*—finding and communicating with prospective buyers.
- *Matching*—shaping and fitting the offer to the buyer's needs. Matching includes such activities as manufacturing, grading, assembling, and packaging.
- *Negotiation*—reaching an agreement on price and other terms of the offer so that ownership or possession can be transferred.
- *Physical distribution*—transporting and storing of goods.
- *Financing*—acquiring and using funds to cover the costs of the channel work.
- *Risk taking*—assuming the risks in connection with carrying out the channel work.

The first five functions help to complete transactions; the last three help fulfill the completed transactions.

The question is not *whether* these functions need to be performed—they must be—but rather *who* is to perform them. All the functions have three things in common—they use up scarce resources, they can often be performed better through specialization, and they can be shifted among channel members. To the extent that the manufacturer performs them, its costs go up and its prices have to be higher. When some functions are shifted to middlemen, the producer's costs and prices are lower, but the middlemen must add a charge to cover their work. In dividing up the work of the channel, the various functions should be assigned to the channel members who can perform them most efficiently and effectively to provide satisfactory assortments of goods to target consumers.

FIGURE 14-1
How a distributor reduces the number of channel transactions

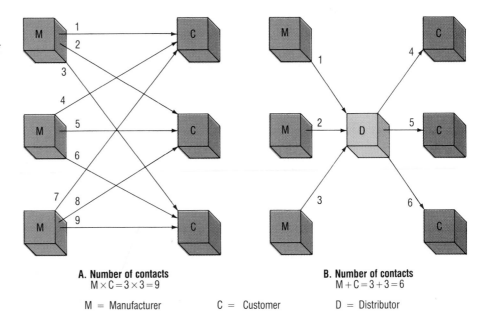

A. Number of contacts
$M \times C = 3 \times 3 = 9$

M = Manufacturer   C = Customer

B. Number of contacts
$M + C = 3 + 3 = 6$

D = Distributor

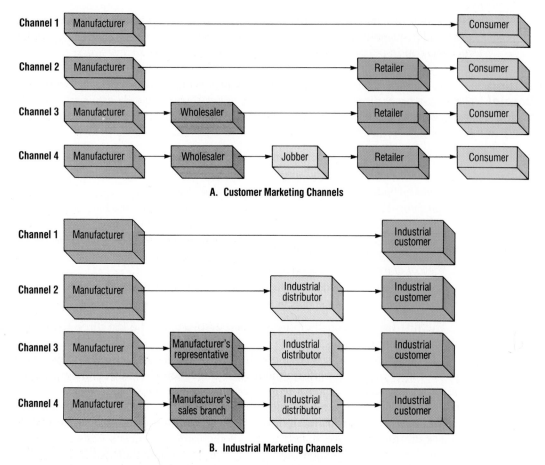

FIGURE 14-2   Consumer and industrial marketing channels

Number of Channel Levels

Distribution channels can be described by the number of channel levels. Each middleman that performs some work in bringing the product and its ownership closer to the final buyer is a *channel level*. Since the producer and the final consumer both perform some work, they are part of every channel. We will use the number of *channel levels* to indicate the *length* of a channel. Figure 14-2A shows several consumer distribution channels of different lengths.

Channel 1, called a *direct marketing channel*, has no intermediary levels. It consists of a manufacturer selling directly to consumers. For example, Avon and World Book Encyclopedia sell their products door-to-door; Franklin Mint sells collectible objects through mail order; and Singer sells its sewing machines through its own stores. Channel 2 contains one middleman level. In consumer markets this is typically a retailer. For example, large retailers such as Sears and K Mart sell televisions, cameras, tires, furniture, major appliances, and many other products that they buy directly from manufacturers. Channel 3 contains two middleman levels. In consumer markets they are typically a wholesaler and a retailer. This channel is often used by small manufacturers of food, drug, hardware, and other products. Channel 4 contains three middlemen levels. For example, in the meatpacking industry jobbers usually come between wholesalers and retailers. The jobber buys from wholesalers and sells to smaller retailers, who generally are not served by the large wholesalers.

Distribution channels with more levels are sometimes found, but less often. From the producer's point of view, the greater the number of levels, the less control the producer has. And the more levels, the greater the channel's complexity.

Figure 14-2B shows some common industrial distribution channels. The industrial goods producer can use its own sales force to sell directly to industrial customers (Channel 1). Or it can sell to industrial distributors who in turn sell to the industrial customers (Channel 2). Or it can sell through manufacturer's representatives (Channel 3) or its own sales branches (Channel 4) to industrial customers, or use them to sell through industrial distributors.

All of the institutions in the distribution channel are connected by several types of flows. These include the *physical product flow* and *title flow* as products and their ownership move from the manufacturer through resellers and on to customers. Other flows include a *payment flow* from customers paying their bills through banks and other financial institutions, and an *information flow* from channel members exchanging information. Finally, a *promotion flow* involves flows of influence (advertising, personal selling, sales promotion, and public relations) between various channel institutions. These flows can make even channels with only one or a few levels very complex.

Channels in the Service Sector

The concept of distribution channels is not limited to the distribution of physical goods. Producers of services and ideas also face the problem of making their output *available* to target populations. They develop "educational distribution systems" and "health delivery systems." They must figure out agencies and locations for reaching a widely spread population:

> Hospitals must be located in geographic space to serve the people with complete medical care, and we must build schools close to the children who have to learn. Fire stations must be located to give rapid access to potential conflagrations, and voting booths must be placed so that people can cast their ballots without expending unreasonable amounts of time, effort, or money to reach the polling stations. Many of our states face the problem of locating branch campuses to serve a burgeoning and increasingly well educated population. In the cities we must create and locate playgrounds for the children. Many overpopulated countries must assign birth control clinics to reach the people with contraceptive and family planning information.[3]

Distribution channels also are used in "person" marketing. Before 1940, professional comedians could reach audiences through vaudeville houses, special events, nightclubs, radio, movies, carnivals, and theaters. In the 1950s television became a strong channel and vaudeville disappeared. More recently, the comedian's channels have grown to include promotional events, product endorsements, cable television, and videotapes. Politicians also must find cost-effective channels—mass media, rallies, coffee hours—for distributing their messages to voters.[4] We will discuss person marketing in more depth in Chapter 22.

CHANNEL BEHAVIOR AND ORGANIZATION

Distribution channels are more than simple collections of firms tied together by various flows. They are complex behavioral systems in which people and companies interact to accomplish individual, company, and channel goals. Some channel systems consist of only informal interactions among loosely organized firms; others consist of formal interactions guided by strong organizational structures. And channel systems are not static—new types of middlemen surface and whole new channel systems evolve. Here we will look at channel behavior and at how members organize to do the work of the channel.

Channel Behavior   A distribution channel is made up of unlike firms that have banded together for their common good. Each channel member is dependent on the other channel members. A Ford dealer depends on the Ford Motor Company to design cars that meet consumer needs and to advertise them nationally to the public. In turn, Ford depends on the dealer to attract consumers, persuade them to buy Ford cars, and service these cars after the sale. The Ford dealer also depends on other dealers to provide good sales and service that will uphold the reputation of Ford and its dealer body. In fact, the success of individual Ford dealers will depend on how well the entire Ford distribution channel competes with the channels of other auto manufacturers.

Each channel member plays a role in the channel and specializes in performing one or more functions. For example, IBM's role is to produce personal computers that consumers will like and to create demand through national advertising. Computerland's role is to display these computers in convenient locations, answer the buyers' questions, close sales, and provide service. The channel will be most effective when each member is assigned the tasks it can do best.

Ideally, because the success of individual channel members depends on overall channel success, all channel firms should work smoothly together. They should understand and accept their roles, coordinate their goals and activities with those of other channel members, and cooperate to attain overall channel goals. Manufacturers, wholesalers, and retailers should work together to produce greater profits than they could obtain individually. By cooperating, they can more effectively sense, serve, and satisfy the target market.

But individual channel members rarely take such a broad view. They are usually more concerned with their own short-run goals and their dealings with firms next to them in the channel. Cooperating to achieve overall channel goals sometimes means giving up individual company goals. Though channel members are dependent on one another, they often act alone in their own short-run best interests. They often disagree on the roles each should play—on who should do what and for what rewards. Such disagreements over goals and roles generate *channel conflict*.

Horizontal conflict is conflict between firms at the same level of the channel. Some Ford dealers in Chicago complain about other dealers in the city stealing sales from them by being too aggressive in their pricing and advertising or by selling outside their assigned territories. Some Pizza Inn franchisees complain about other Pizza Inn franchisees cheating on ingredients, giving poor service, and hurting the overall Pizza Inn image.

Vertical conflict is even more common and refers to conflicts between different levels of the same channel. For example, General Motors came into conflict with its dealers some years ago when trying to enforce policies on service, pricing, and advertising. And Coca-Cola came into conflict with its bottlers who agreed to bottle Dr Pepper. McCulloch caused conflict when it decided to bypass its wholesale distributors and sell its chain saws directly to large retailers such as J.C. Penney and K mart, which then competed directly with its smaller retailers.

Some conflict in the channel takes the form of healthy competition. This competition can be good for the channel—without it, the channel could become passive and noninnovative. But sometimes conflict can damage the channel. Here is an example:

When retail druggists were pressing manufacturers to maintain retail prices on their brands . . . Lever Brothers found it difficult to control the pricing behavior of "pine board" (cut rate) drug stores relative to Pepsodent, the best-selling brand of toothpaste at the time. In retaliation, the druggists removed the brand from their shelves, thereby forcing consumers to request packages each time they wanted to replenish their household supplies. Surely this was a pathological move in a conflict situation, for in the process of "hurting" Lever Brothers, the druggists hurt themselves by foregoing sales volume and by inconveniencing their customers. The entire system suffered as a result of the boycott.[5]

For the channel as a whole to perform well, each channel member's role must be specified, and channel conflict must be managed. Cooperation, assigning roles, and conflict management in the channel are attained through strong channel leadership. The channel will perform better if it contains a firm, agency, or mechanism that has the power to assign roles and manage conflict. Traditionally, distribution channels have lacked the needed leadership. In recent years, however, new types of channel organizations have appeared that provide stronger leadership and improved performance. We will look now at these organizations.[6]

Channel Organization

Historically, distribution channels have been loose collections of independently owned and managed companies, each showing little concern for overall channel performance. These *conventional distribution channels* have lacked strong leadership and have been troubled by damaging conflict and poor performance.

Growth of Vertical Marketing Systems

In recent years, one of the biggest channel developments has been the *vertical marketing systems* that have emerged to challenge conventional marketing channels. Generally they provide stronger leadership and improved performance. Figure 14-3 contrasts the two types of channel arrangements.

A **conventional distribution channel** consists of independent producer(s), wholesaler(s), and retailer(s). Each is a separate business seeking to maximize its own profits, even at the expense of profits for the system as a whole. No channel member has much control over the other members, and there are no formal means for assigning roles and resolving channel conflict.

A **vertical marketing system (VMS)**, by contrast, consists of the producer(s), wholesaler(s), and retailer(s) acting as a unified system. Either one channel member owns the others, or has contracts with them, or has so much power that they will cooperate.[7] The VMS can be dominated by the producer, wholesaler, or retailer. Vertical marketing systems came into being to control channel behavior and manage channel conflict. They achieve economies through size, bargaining power, and elimina-

FIGURE 14-3
Comparison of conventional marketing channel with vertical marketing system

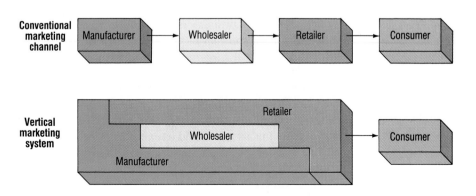

FIGURE 14-4
Major types of vertical marketing systems

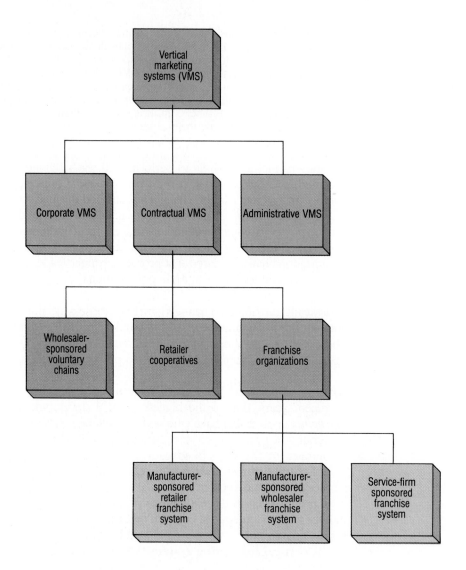

tion of duplicated services. VMSs have become dominant in consumer marketing, serving as much as 70 percent of the total market.

We will now look at the three major types of VMSs shown in Figure 14-4. Each type uses a different means for setting up leadership and power in the channel. In a *corporate VMS*, coordination and conflict management are attained through common ownership at different levels of the channel. In a *contractual VMS*, they are attained through contractual agreements among channel members. In an *administered VMS*, leadership is assumed by one or a few dominant channel members.

CORPORATE VMS. A **corporate VMS** combines successive stages of production and distribution under single ownership. For example, Sears obtains over 50 percent of the goods it sells from companies that it partly or wholly owns. Sherwin-Williams makes paint but also owns and operates 2,000 retail outlets. Giant Food Stores operates and ice-making facility, a soft-drink bottling operation, an ice-cream making plant, and a bakery that supplies Giant stores with everything from bagels to birthday cakes.[8] And Gallo, the world's largest wine maker, does much more than simply turn grapes into wine.

> The [Gallo] brothers own Fairbanks Trucking Company, one of the largest intrastate truckers in California. Its 200 semis and 500 trailers are constantly hauling wine out of Modesto and raw materials back in—including . . . lime from Gallo's quarry east of Sacramento. Alone among wine producers, Gallo makes bottles—two million a day—and its Midcal Aluminum Co. spews out screw tops as fast as the bottles are filled. Most of the country's 1,300 or so wineries concentrate on production to the neglect of marketing. Gallo, by contrast, participates in every aspect of selling short of whispering in the ear of each imbiber. The company owns its distributors in about a dozen markets and probably would buy many . . . more . . . if the laws in most states did not prohibit doing so.[9]

In such corporate systems, cooperation and conflict management are handled through regular organizational channels.

CONTRACTUAL VMS. A **contractual VMS** consists of independent firms at different levels of production and distribution who join together through contracts to obtain more economies or sales impact than they could achieve alone. Contractual VMSs have expanded rapidly in recent years. There are three types of contractual VMSs: wholesaler-sponsored voluntary chains, retailer cooperatives, and franchise organizations.

Wholesaler-sponsored voluntary chains are systems in which wholesalers organize voluntary chains of independent retailers to help them compete with large chain organizations. The wholesaler develops a program in which independent retailers standardize their selling practices and achieve buying economies that let the group compete effectively with chain organizations. Examples include the Independent Grocers Alliance (IGA), Western Auto, and Sentry Hardwares.

Retailer cooperatives are systems in which retailers organize a new, jointly owned business to carry on wholesaling and possibly production. Members buy most of their goods through the retailer co-op and plan their advertising jointly. Profits are passed back to members in proportion to their purchases. Nonmember retailers may also buy through the co-op but do not share in the profits. Examples include Certified Grocers, Associated Grocers, and True Value Hardware.

In *Franchise organizations*, a channel member called a franchiser might link several stages in the production-distribution process. Franchising has been the fastest-growing retailing form in recent years. Franchised businesses now account for about one-third of retail sales in the U.S. and may account for one-half by the year 2000.[10] Almost every kind of business has been franchised, from motels and fast food restaurants to dentists and dating services, from wedding consultants and maid services to funeral homes and tub and tile refinishers. Although the basic idea is an old one, some forms of franchising are quite new. There are three forms of franchises.

The first form is the *manufacturer-sponsored retailer franchise system*, as found in the automobile industry. Ford, for example, licenses dealers to sell its cars—the dealers are independent businesspeople who agree to meet various conditions of sales and service.

The second type of franchise is the *manufacturer-sponsored wholesaler franchise system*, as found in the soft-drink industry. Coca-Cola, for example, licenses bottlers (wholesalers) in various markets who buy its syrup concentrate and then carbonate, bottle, and sell it to retailers in local markets.

The third franchise form is the *service-firm-sponsored retailer franchise system*. Here a service firm organizes a whole system for bringing its service to consumers. Examples are found in the auto rental business (Hertz, Avis), fast-food service business (McDonald's, Burger King), and motel business (Holiday Inn, Ramada Inn).

The fact that most consumers cannot tell the difference between contractual and corporate VMSs shows how successful the contractual organizations have been in competing with corporate chains. The various contractual VMSs are discussed more in Chapter 15.

ADMINISTERED VMS. An **administered VMS** coordinates successive stages of production and distribution, not through common ownership or contractual ties, but through the size and power of one of the parties. Manufacturers of a top brand can obtain strong trade cooperation and support from resellers. Thus Procter & Gamble, Kraft, and Campbell Soup can command unusual cooperation from resellers regarding displays, shelf space, promotions, and price policies.

Growth of Horizontal Marketing Systems

Another channel development is **horizontal marketing systems,** in which two or more nonrelated companies at one channel level join together to follow a new marketing opportunity. By working together the companies can combine their capital, production capabilities, or marketing resources and strengths to accomplish more than either company could accomplish working alone. Called *symbiotic marketing,*[11] the companies may work with each other on a temporary or permanent basis, or they may create a separate company. Here are some examples:

> Pillsbury lacked the resources to market its new line of refrigerated dough products because they required special refrigerated display cases. So it set up an arrangement with Kraft in which Pillsbury makes and advertises its refrigerated dough products while Kraft uses its expertise to sell and distribute these products to the stores.

> The Lamar Savings Bank of Texas arranged to locate its savings offices and automated teller machines in Safeway stores. Lamar gained quicker market entry at a low cost and Safeway was able to offer in-store banking convenience to its customers.

> Beecham Products and Johnson & Johnson have jointly sponsored combined sales promotions of the former's Aqua-Fresh toothpaste and the latter's Reach toothbrush.

> General Motors and Procter & Gamble teamed up for a car-giveaway contest—consumers finding special plastic keys in Crest, Tide, and other P&G products could win a new Chevrolet Beretta, Corsica, or pickup truck.[12]

> Sears and McDonald's joined forces to market the McKids line of "Fun clothes for small fries." McDonald's franchisees and Sears stores will work together to develop local promotion programs.[13]

Such symbiotic marketing arrangements have increased dramatically in recent years, and the end is nowhere in sight.

Growth of Multichannel Marketing Systems

In the past, many companies used a single channel to sell to a single market or market segment. Today, with the proliferation of customer segments and channel possibilities, more and more companies have adopted dual distribution or multichannel distribution. Such *multimarketing* occurs when a single firm sets up two or more marketing channels to reach one or more customers segments.[14] Here are some examples:

> General Electric sells large home appliances through independent retailers (department stores, discount houses, catalog houses) and also directly to large housing-tract builders, thus competing to some extent with its retailers.

> IBM quickly put its new personal computers into 2,500 stores by using a multichannel approach. It opened its own IBM Product Centers (which it later sold); signed contracts with Sears, Computerland, and an assortment of independent computer stores; enlisted

Just where did we get the idea kids' clothes could be more fun?

We were having lunch at our favorite restaurant, just minding our own business, when these cute little characters popped right out of nowhere.

"Put some real fun back into children's clothes," they giggled. "And maybe we'll let you call 'em McKids."

Seemed like a good idea to us.

So back at Sears headquarters, we called the whole gang together. "Only the very brightest colors!" we said. "Only the most comfortable fabrics!" we urged. "Only the most exciting designs!" we insisted.

Well, what happened next surprised even us.

Almost overnight, the most fabulous children's clothes started appearing. The cutest sportswear for little girls. Fun pants with real suspenders for little boys. Really terrific pajamas for toddlers, complete with little feet.

Not to mention the most delightful sweaters and socks and shoes and jackets and bottoms and tops and . . . .

To make it brief, we went back to our favorite restaurant and showed everything to our little friends. (Pictured right.)

And they liked these new clothes so much they said we could call 'em McKids.

And now you can see the whole amazing collection—in sizes for infants, toddlers, girls 4 to 6x, and boys 4 to 7—at any one of our Sears children's departments across the country. At amazingly reasonable prices, we might add.

We're kinda excited about the whole thing.

And once you see McKids, we think you'll understand why.

McKIDS
Exclusively at Sears

Horizontal marketing systems: Sears and McDonald's team up to sell McKids, "Fun clothes for small fries."

office product dealers; and sold through resellers who adapted the machines and software for special applications. IBM also sold its computers to colleges at heavy discounts, causing complaints from its other retailers.

McDonald's sells through a network of independent franchisees but owns about half of its outlets. The wholly-owned restaurants compete to some extent with those owned by McDonald's franchisees.

The multimarketer gains volume with each new channel but also risks offending existing channels. Existing channels can cry "unfair competition" and threaten to drop the multimarketer unless it limits the competition or repays them in some way.

In some cases, the multimarketer's channels are all under its own ownership and control. For example, J. C. Penney operates department stores, mass-merchandising stores, and specialty stores, each offering different product assortments to different market segments. Here there is no conflict with outside channels, but the marketer might face internal conflict over how much financial support each channel deserves.

CHANNEL DESIGN DECISIONS

We will now look at several channel decision problems facing manufacturers. In designing marketing channels, manufacturers have to struggle between what is ideal and what is available. A new firm usually starts by selling in a limited market area. Since it has limited capital, it usually uses only a few existing middlemen in each market—a few manufacturers sales agents, a few wholesalers, some existing retailers, a few trucking companies, and a few warehouses. Deciding on the best channels might not be a problem. The problem might be to convince one or a few good middlemen to handle the line.

If the new firm is successful, it might branch out to new markets. Again, the manufacturer will tend to work through the existing middlemen, although doing so might mean using different types of marketing channels in different areas. In the smaller markets the firm might sell directly to retailers; in the larger markets it might sell through distributors. In one part of the country it might grant exclusive franchises because the merchants normally work this way; in another, it might sell through all outlets willing to handle the merchandise. The manufacturer's channel system thus evolves to meet local opportunities and conditions.

Designing a channel system calls for analyzing consumer service needs, setting the channel objectives and constraints, identifying the major channel alternatives, and evaluating them.

Analyzing Consumer Service Needs

Designing the distribution channel starts with finding out what services consumers in various target segments want from the channel. Channel services fall into five categories:[15]

* *Lot size*. Do consumers want to buy one unit or many? The smaller the lot size, the greater the level of service provided by the channel.
* *Market decentralization*. Do consumers want to buy from nearby locations, or will they buy from more distant centralized locations by traveling, phoning, or buying through the mail? The more decentralized the channel, the greater the service it provides.
* *Waiting time*. Do consumers want immediate delivery, or are they willing to wait? Faster delivery means greater service from the channel.
* *Product variety*. Do consumers value breadth of assortment, or do they prefer specialization? The greater the assortment provided by the channel, the higher the service level.
* *Service backup*. Do consumers want many add-on services (delivery, credit, repairs, installation), or will they obtain these services elsewhere? More add-on services mean a higher level of channel service.

Consider the distribution channel service needs of personal computer buyers:

The delivery or service might include such things as demonstration of the product before the sale or provision of long-term warranties and flexible financing. After the sale, there might be training programs for using the equipment and a program to install and repair it. Customers might appreciate "loaners" while their equipment is being repaired or technical advice over a telephone hot line.[16]

Thus to design an effective channel, the designer must know the service levels desired by consumers. But providing all the desired services may not be feasible or practical. The company and channel members may not have the resources or skills needed to provide all the desired services. And providing higher levels of service means higher costs for the channel and higher prices for consumers. The company must balance consumer service needs against the feasibility and costs of meeting these needs and against customer price preferences. The success of discount stores shows that consumers are often willing to accept lower service levels if they mean lower prices.

Setting the Channel Objectives and Constraints

The channel objectives should be stated in terms of the desired service level of target consumers. Usually, the company can identify several segments demanding different levels of channel service. Effective channel planning means that the company should decide which segments to serve and the best channels to use in each case.

In each segment, the company wants to minimize the total channel cost of delivering the desired service level.

Thus, channel objectives should be consumer oriented. But each company's channel objectives are constrained by the nature of its products, company policies, middlemen, competitors, and the environment.

Channel design is greatly affected by *product characteristics*. For example, perishable products require more direct marketing because of the dangers caused by delays and too much handling. Bulky products, such as building materials or soft drinks, require channels that minimize the shipping distance and the amount of handling. Products needing installation or service are usually sold and maintained by the company or its franchised dealers.

Company characteristics also play an important role in channel selection. The company's size determines the size of its markets and its ability to get desired dealers. Its financial resources affect which marketing functions it can handle and which to give to middlemen. The wider the company's product mix, the better the company can deal with customers directly; the greater the depth of its product mix, the more it will favor exclusive or selective distribution. And the company's marketing strategy will affect channel design. A policy of speedy customer delivery affects the functions the producer wants middlemen to perform, the number of outlets, and the choice of transportation methods.

Middlemen characteristics influence channel design. The company must find middlemen who are willing and able to perform the needed tasks. In general, middlemen differ in their abilities to handle promotion, customer contact, storage, and credit. For example, manufacturer's representatives, who are hired by several different firms, can contact customers at a low cost per customer because several clients share the total cost. But the selling effort behind the product is less intense than if the company's own salesforce did the selling.

When designing its channels, the company will want to consider *competitors' channels*. It may want to compete in or near the same outlets that carry competitors' products. Thus food companies want their brands to be displayed next to competing brands, and Burger King wants to locate near McDonald's. In other industries, produc-

Product characteristics affect channel decisions: fresh flowers must be delivered quickly with a minimum of handling.

ers may avoid the channels used by competitors. Avon decided not to compete with other cosmetics makers for scarce positions in retail stores and instead set up a profitable door-to-door selling operation.

Finally, *environmental factors* such as economic conditions and legal constraints affect channel design decisions. For example, in a depressed economy, producers want to distribute their goods in the most economical way, using shorter channels and dropping unneeded services that add to the final price of the goods. Legal regulations prevent channel arrangements that "may tend to substantially lessen competition or tend to create a monopoly."

Identifying the Major Alternatives

Suppose a company has defined its target market and desired positioning. It should next identify its major channel alternatives in terms of types of middlemen, number of middlemen, and the responsibilities of each channel member.

Types of Middlemen

The firm should identify the types of middlemen available to carry on its channel work. Consider the following example. A manufacturer of test equipment developed an audio device that detects poor mechanical connections in any machine with moving parts. The company executives felt that this product would have a market in all industries where electric, combustion, or steam engines were made or used. This meant such industries as aviation, automobile, railroad, food canning, construction, and oil. The company's salesforce was small, and the problem was how best to reach these different industries. The following channel alternatives came out of management discussion:

- *Company salesforce*. Expand the company's direct salesforce. Assign salespeople to territories and have them contact all prospects in the area. Or develop separate company salesforces for the different industries.
- *Manufacturer's agency*. Hire manufacturer's agencies in different regions or industries to sell the new test equipment.
- *Industrial distributors*. Find distributors in the different regions or industries who will buy and carry the new line. Give them exclusive distribution, good margins, product training, and promotional support.

Companies should also search for more innovative new distribution channels. For example, when the Conn Organ Company decided to merchandise organs through department and discount stores, the company's organs drew more attention than they had ever enjoyed in small music stores. A daring new channel was found when the Book-of-the Month Club decided to market books through the mail. Other sellers followed soon after, with Record-of-the Month clubs, Candy-of-the Month clubs, and dozens of others. L'eggs became the world's leading hosiery product when it was distributed through food and drug stores rather than department stores and women's specialty stores.

Sometimes a company has to develop a channel other than the one it prefers because of the difficulty or cost of using the preferred channel. The decision sometimes turns out extremely well. For example, the U.S. Time Company first tried to sell its inexpensive Timex watches through regular jewelry stores. But most jewelry stores refused to carry them. The company then managed to get its watches into mass-merchandise outlets. This turned out to be a wise decision because of the rapid growth of mass merchandising.

Number of Middlemen

Companies must decide on the number of middlemen to use at each level. Three strategies are available.

INTENSIVE DISTRIBUTION. Producers of convenience goods typically seek **intensive distribution**—that is, stocking their product in as many outlets as possible. These goods must be available where and when consumers want them. For example, toothpaste, candy, and other similar items are sold in millions of outlets to provide maximum brand exposure and consumer convenience.

EXCLUSIVE DISTRIBUTION. Some producers purposely limit the number of middlemen handling their products. The extreme form of this is **exclusive distribution,** in which a limited number of dealers are given the exclusive right to distribute the company's products in their territories. It often goes with *exclusive dealing*, where the manufacturer requires these dealers not to carry competing lines. Exclusive distribution is often found in the distribution of new automobiles and prestige women's apparel brands. By granting exclusive distribution, the manufacturer hopes for stronger distributor selling support and more control over middlemen's prices, promotion,

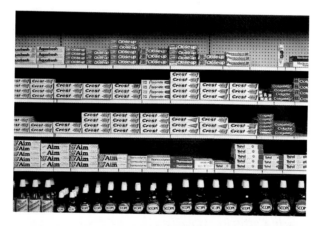

Convenience goods, such as toothpaste, are sold through every available outlet. Prestige goods, such as furs, are sold exclusively through a limited number of stores.

credit, and services. Exclusive distribution often enhances the product's image and allows higher markups.

SELECTIVE DISTRIBUTION. Between intensive and exclusive distribution is **selective distribution**—the use of more than one but less than all the middlemen who are willing to carry a company's products. The company does not have to spread its efforts over many outlets, including many marginal ones. It can develop a good working relationship with the selected middlemen and expect a better-than-average selling effort. Selective distribution lets the producer gain good market coverage with more control and less cost than intensive distribution. Most television, furniture, and small appliance brands are distributed selectively.

Responsibilities of Channel Members

The producer and middlemen must agree on the terms and responsibilities of each channel member. They must agree on price policies, the conditions of sale, the territorial rights, and the specific services to be performed by each party. The producer must set up a list price and a fair set of discounts for middlemen. It must define each middleman's territory and be careful where it places new resellers. Mutual services and responsibilities must be carefully spelled out, especially in franchise and exclusive distribution channels. For example, the McDonald's Company provides franchisees promotional support, a recordkeeping system, training, and general management assistance. In turn, franchisees must meet company standards for physical facilities, cooperate with new promotion programs, provide requested information, and buy specified food products.

Evaluating the Major Channel Alternatives

Suppose a company has identified several channel alternatives and wants to select the one that will best satisfy the its long-run objectives. The firm must evaluate each alternative against economic, control, and adaptive criteria. Consider the following situation: A Memphis furniture manufacturer wants to sell its line through retailers on the West Coast. The manufacturer is trying to decide between two alternatives.

1. It could hire ten new sales representatives who would operate out of a sales office in San Francisco. They would receive a base salary plus a commission on their sales.
2. It could use a San Francisco manufacturer's sales agency that has extensive contacts with retailers. The agency has thirty salespeople who would receive a commission based on their sales.

Economic Criteria

Each channel alternative will produce a different level of sales and costs. The first step is to figure out what sales would be produced by a company salesforce compared to a sales agency. Most marketing managers believe that a company salesforce will sell more. Company salespeople sell only the company's products and are better trained to handle them. They sell more aggressively because their future depends on the company. And they are more successful because customers prefer to deal directly with the company.

On the other hand, the sales agency could possibly sell more than a company salesforce. First, the sales agency has thirty salespeople, not just ten. Second, the agency salesforce may be just as aggressive as a direct salesforce, depending on how much commission the line offers in relation to other lines carried. Third, some customers prefer dealing with agents who represent several manufacturers rather than with salespeople from one company. Fourth, the agency has many existing contacts, whereas a company salesforce would have to build them from scratch.

The next step is to estimate the costs of selling different volumes through each

FIGURE 14-5
Breakeven cost chart for the choice between a company salesforce and a manufacturer's sales agency.

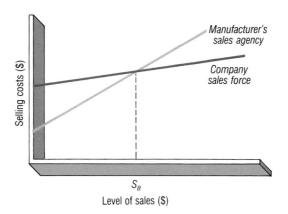

channel. The costs are shown in Figure 14-5. The fixed costs of using a sales agency are lower than those of setting up a company sales office. But costs rise faster through a sales agency because sales agents get a larger commission than company salespeople. There is one sales level (S_B) at which selling costs are the same for the two channels. The company would prefer to use the sales agency at any sales volume below S_B, and the company sales branch at any volume higher than S_B. In general, sales agents tend to be used by smaller firms, or by larger firms in smaller territories where the sales volume is too low to warrant a company salesforce.

Control Criteria

Next evaluation must be broadened to consider control issues with the two channels. Using a sales agency poses more of a control problem. A sales agency is an independent business firm interested in maximizing its profits. The agent may concentrate on the customers who buy the largest volume of goods from their entire mix of client companies rather than those most interested in a particular company's goods. And the agency's salesforce may not master the technical details of the company's product or handle its promotional materials effectively.

Adaptive Criteria

Each channel involves some long-term commitment and loss of flexibility. A company using a sales agency may have to offer a five-year contract. During this period, other means of selling, such as a company salesforce, may become more effective, but the company cannot drop the sales agency. To be considered, a channel involving a long commitment should be greatly superior on economic or control grounds.

CHANNEL MANAGEMENT DECISIONS

Once the company has reviewed its channel alternatives and decided on the best channel design, it must implement and manage the chosen channel. Channel management calls for selecting and motivating individual middlemen and evaluating their performance over time.

Selecting Channel Members

Producers vary in their ability to attract qualified middlemen. Some producers have no trouble signing up middlemen. For example, IBM has no trouble attracting retailers to sell its personal computers. In fact, it has to turn down many would-be resellers.

In some cases, the promise of exclusive or selective distribution for a desirable product will draw enough applicants.

At the other extreme are producers who have to work hard to line up enough qualified middlemen. When Polaroid started, it could not get photography stores to carry its new cameras and had to go to mass-merchandising outlets. Small food producers often find it hard to get grocery stores to carry their products.

When selecting middlemen, the company should determine what characteristics distinguish the better middlemen. It will want to evaluate the middlemen's years in business, other lines carried, growth and profit record, profitability, cooperativeness, and reputation. If the middlemen are sales agents, the company will want to evaluate the number and character of other lines carried and the size and quality of the salesforce. If the middleman is a retail store that wants exclusive or selective distribution, the company will want to evaluate the store's customers, location, and future growth potential.

Motivating Channel Members

Once selected, middlemen must be continuously motivated to do their best. The company must sell not only *through* the middlemen, but *to* them. Most producers see the problem as finding ways to gain middlemen's cooperation.[17] They use the carrot-and-stick approach. They offer such positive motivators as higher margins, special deals, premiums, cooperative advertising allowances, display allowances, and sales contests. At times they will use negative motivators such as threatening to reduce margins, slow down delivery, or end the relationship. The weakness of this approach is that the producer has not really studied the needs, problems, strengths, and weaknesses of the distributors.

More sophisticated companies try to forge a long-term partnership with their distributors. The manufacturer develops a clear sense of what it wants from its distributors and what its distributors can expect. The manufacturer seeks an agreement from its distributors on their roles and responsibilities, and rewards them accordingly.

Distribution programming is the most advanced arrangement. This involves building a planned, professionally managed, vertical marketing system that meets

Frigidaire informs and motivates its retailers at a dealer sales meeting.

the needs of both the manufacturer and the distributors.[18] The manufacturer sets up a department in the marketing area called *distributor relations planning*, and its job is to identify the distributors' needs and build up programs to help each distributor market the product. This department and the distributors jointly plan the merchandising goals, inventory levels, merchandising strategies, sales training, and advertising and promotion plans. The aim is to convince distributors that they make their money by being part of an advanced vertical marketing system.

Evaluating Channel Members

The producer must regularly check middlemen's performance against such standards as reaching sales quotas, average inventory levels, customer delivery time, treatment of damaged and lost goods, cooperation in company promotion and training programs, and services to the customer.

The producer typically sets sales quotas for the middlemen. After each period, the producer might circulate a list showing the sales performance of each middleman. This list should motivate middlemen at the bottom to do better and middlemen at the top to keep up their performance. Each middleman's sales performance can be compared with performance in the last period. The average percentage improvement for the group can be used as a norm.

A company may periodically "requalify" its middlemen and prune out the weaker ones. For example, when IBM introduced its new Personal System/2 computers, it reevaluated its dealers and allowed only the best ones to carry the new models. Each IBM dealer had to turn in a business plan, send a sales and service employee to IBM training classes, and meet new sales quotas. Only about two-thirds of IBM's 2,200 dealers qualified to carry the PS/2 models.[19]

Manufacturers need to be sensitive to their dealers. Those who treat their dealers lightly risk not only losing their support, but also causing some legal actions. Marketing Highlight 14–1 describes various rights and duties of manufacturers and their channel members.

PHYSICAL DISTRIBUTION DECISIONS

We are now ready to look at physical distribution—how companies store, handle, and move goods so that they will be available to customers at the right time and place. Customers are heavily affected by the seller's physical distribution system. Here we will consider the nature, objectives, systems, and organizational aspects of physical distribution.

Nature of Physical Distribution

The main elements of the physical distribution mix are shown in Figure 14-6. **Physical distribution** involves planning, implementing, and controlling the physical flow of materials and final goods from points of origin to points of use to meet the needs of customers at a profit. The major physical distribution cost is transportation, followed by inventory carrying, warehousing, and order processing/customer service.

Management has become concerned about the total cost of physical distribution, and experts believe that large savings can be gained in the physical distribution area. Poor physical distribution decisions result in high costs. Even large companies sometimes make too little use of modern decision tools for coordinating inventory levels, transportation modes, and plant, warehouse, and store locations. For example, at least part of the blame for Sears' slow sales growth and sinking earnings over the past several years goes to its antiquated and costly distribution system. Outmoded

DISTRIBUTION DECISIONS AND PUBLIC POLICY

For the most part, manufacturers are free under the law to develop whatever channel arrangements suit them. In fact, the law affecting channels seeks to make sure that manufacturers are not prevented from using channels as the result of the exclusionary tactics of others. But this places them under obligation to proceed cautiously in their own possible use of exclusionary tactics. Most of the law is concerned with mutual rights and duties of the manufacturer and channel members once they have formed a relationship.

Exclusive Dealing. Many manufacturers and wholesalers like to develop exclusive channels for their products. The policy is called *exclusive distribution* when the seller enfranchises only certain outlets to carry its products. It is called *exclusive dealing* when the seller requires these outlets not to handle competitors' products. Both parties draw benefits from exclusive dealing, the seller achieving more dependable outlets without having to invest capital in them, and the distributors gaining a steady source of supply and seller support. However, the result is that other manufacturers are excluded from selling to these dealers. This has brought exclusive dealing contracts under the purview of the Clayton Act. They are legal as long as they do not substantially lessen competition, or tend to create a monopoly, and both partners enter into the agreement voluntarily.

Exclusive Territorial Distributorships. Exclusive dealing often includes exclusive territorial agreements. The seller may agree not to sell to other distributors in the area, or the buyer may agree to confine sales to its own territory. The first practice is fairly normal under franchise systems as a way to increase dealer enthusiasm and investment in the area. A seller is under no legal compulsion to sell through more outlets than it wishes. The second practice, where the manufacturer tries to restrain each dealer to sell only in its own territory, has become a major legal issue.

Tying Agreements. Manufacturers of a strongly demanded brand occasionally sell it to dealers on condition that the dealers take some or all of the rest of the line. This practice is called *full-line forcing*. Such tying arrangements are not illegal per se, but they do run afoul of the Clayton Act if they tend to lessen competition substantially. Buyers are being prevented from freely choosing among competing suppliers of these other brands.

Dealers' Rights. Sellers are free to select their dealers, but their right to terminate dealerships is somewhat qualified. In general, sellers can drop dealers "for cause." But they cannot drop dealers, for example, if the dealers refuse to cooperate in a dubious legal arrangement, such as exclusive dealing or tying agreements.

---

multistory warehouses and non-automated equipment have made Sears much less efficient than its competitors. Distribution costs amount to 8 percent of sales at Sears compared to less than 3 percent at close competitors K mart and Wal-Mart.[20]

Physical distribution is not only a cost but also a potent tool in demand creation. Companies can attract more customers by giving better service or lower prices through better physical distribution. Companies lose customers when they fail to supply goods on time. In the summer of 1976 Kodak launched its national advertising campaign for its new instant camera before it had delivered enough cameras to the stores. When customers found that it was not available, many bought a Polaroid instead.

The Physical Distribution Objective   Many companies state their objective as getting the right goods to the right places at the right time for the least cost. Unfortunately, no physical distribution system can both maximize customer service and minimize distribution costs. Maximum customer service implies large inventories, the best transportation, and many ware-

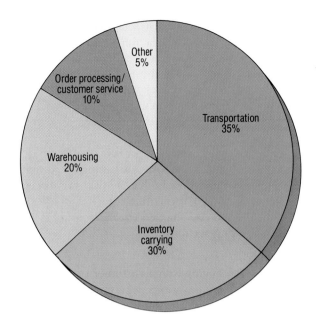

houses, all of which raise distribution cost. Minimum distribution cost implies cheap transportation, low inventories and few warehouses, all of which lower a firm's customer service capabilities.

The company cannot simply let each physical distribution manager keep down his or her costs. Physical distribution costs interact, often in an inverse way:

• The traffic manager favors rail shipment over air shipment whenever possible. Rail shipment reduces the company's freight bill. But because the railroads are slower, this mode ties up working capital longer, delays customer payment, and may cause customers to buy from competitors offering faster service.

• The shipping department uses cheap containers to minimize shipping costs. The containers lead to a high rate of damaged goods in transit and customer ill will.

• The inventory manager favors low inventories to reduce inventory cost. However, low inventories increase stockouts, back orders, paperwork, special production runs, and high-cost fast-freight shipments.

Because physical distribution activities involve strong tradeoffs, decisions must be made on a total system basis. The starting point for designing the system is to study what customers want and what competitors are offering. Customers want several things from suppliers: on-time delivery, large enough inventories, ability to meet emergency needs, careful handling of merchandise, good after-sale service, and willingness to take back or quickly replace defective goods. The company has to research the importance of these services to customers. For example, service repair time is very important to buyers of copying equipment. So Xerox developed a service system that can usually put a disabled machine anywhere in the United States back into operation within hours after receiving a service request.

The company must look at competitors' service standards in setting its own. It will normally want to offer at least the same level of service as competitors. But the objective is to maximize profits, not sales. The company has to look at the costs of providing higher levels of service. Some companies offer less service and charge a lower price. Other companies offer more service than competitors and charge a high price to cover their higher costs.

The company ultimately must set physical distribution objectives to guide its planning. For example, Coca-Cola wants "to put Coke within an arm's length of desire." Companies go further and define standards for each service factor. One appliance manufacturer has set the following service standards: to deliver at least 95 percent of the dealer's orders within seven days of order receipt, to fill the dealer's order with 99 percent accuracy, to answer dealer questions on order status within three hours, and to ensure that damage to merchandise in transit does not exceed 1 percent.

Given a set of objectives, the company is ready to design a physical distribution system that will minimize the cost of attaining these objectives. The major decision issues are: How should orders be handled (*order processing*)? Where should stocks be located (*warehousing*)? How much stock should be kept on hand (*inventory*)? And how should goods be shipped (*transportation*)? We will look at each of these topics in the following sections.

Order Processing

Physical distribution begins with a customer order. The order department prepares invoices and sends them to various departments. Items out of stock are back-ordered. Shipped items are accompanied by shipping and billing documents with copies going to various departments.

The company and customers benefit when these steps are carried out quickly and accurately. Ideally, salespeople send in their orders daily, often using online computers. The order department processes these orders quickly, and the warehouse sends the goods out on time. Bills go out as soon as possible. The computer is often used to speed up the order-shipping-billing cycle. For example, General Electric operates a computer-based system which, upon receipt of a customer's order, checks the customer's credit standing and whether and where the items are in stock. The computer issues an order to ship, bills the customer, updates the inventory records, sends a production order for new stock, and relays the message back to the salesperson that the customer's order is on its way, all in less than fifteen seconds.

Warehousing

Every company has to store its goods while they wait to be sold. A storage function is needed because production and consumption cycles rarely match. For example, many agricultural commodities are produced seasonally, but demand is continuous. Snapper, Toro, and other lawnmower makers must produce all year long and store up their product for the heavy spring and summer buying season. The storage function overcomes differences in needed quantities and timing.

The company must decide on the best number of stocking locations. More stocking locations mean that goods can be delivered to customers more quickly. However, total warehousing costs increase as more stocking locations are added. In making the decision about number of stocking locations, the company must balance the level of customer service against distribution costs.

Some company stock is kept at or near the plant, and the rest is located in warehouses around the country. The company might own private warehouses and rent space in public warehouses. Companies have more control in owned warehouses, but they tie up their capital and are less flexible if desired locations change. Public warehouses, on the other hand, charge for the rented space and provide additional services (at a cost) for inspecting goods, packaging them, shipping them, and invoicing them. In using public warehouses, companies have a wide choice of locations and warehouse types.

This Xerox automated warehouse is a high-rise storage facility which uses robots for automatic storage and retrieval.

Companies use storage warehouses and distribution centers. Storage warehouses store goods for moderate to long periods of time until they are needed. **Distribution centers** are geared toward moving goods rather than just storing them. They are large and highly automated warehouses designed to receive goods from various plants and suppliers, take orders, fill them efficiently, and deliver goods to customers as quickly as possible. For example, Wal-Mart Stores, a regional discount chain, operates four distribution centers. One center covers 400,000 square feet on a 93-acre site. The shipping department loads fifty to sixty trucks daily, delivering merchandise on a twice-weekly basis to its retail outlets. This system is less expensive than supplying each retail outlet directly from each plant.

Warehousing facilities and equipment technology have improved greatly in recent years. Older multistoried warehouses with slow elevators and outdated materials-handling methods are facing competition from newer single-storied *automated warehouses* with advanced materials-handling systems under the control of a central computer. In these automated warehouses, only a few employees are necessary. The computer reads orders and directs lift trucks electric hoists, or robots to gather goods, move them to loading docks, and issue invoices. These warehouses have reduced worker injuries, labor costs, theft, and breakage and have improved inventory control.

Inventory   Inventory levels also affect customer satisfaction. Marketers would like their companies to carry enough stock to fill all customer orders right away. However, it costs too much for a company to carry this much inventory. Inventory costs increase at an increasing rate as the customer service level approaches 100 percent. Management would need to know whether sales and profits would increase enough to justify larger inventories.

Inventory decisions involve knowing when to order, and how much to order. In deciding when to order, the company balances the risks of running out of stock against the costs of carrying too much stock. In deciding how much to order, the company needs to balance order-processing costs against inventory carrying costs.

TABLE 14-1
Characteristics of
Major Transportation
Modes

TRANSPORTATION MODE	INTERCITY CARGO VOLUME* (%)			TYPICAL PRODUCTS SHIPPED
	1965	1975	1985	
Rail	709 (43.3%)	759 (36.7%)	898 (37.2%)	Farm products, minerals, sand, chemicals, automobiles
Truck	359 (21.9)	454 (22.0)	600 (24.9)	Clothing, food, books, computers, paper goods
Water	262 (16.0)	342 (16.6)	348 (14.4)	Oil, grain, sand, gravel, metallic ores, coal
Pipeline	306 (18.7)	507 (24.5)	562 (23.3)	Oil, coal, chemicals
Air	1.9 (0.12)	3.7 (0.19)	6.4 (0.26)	Technical instruments, perishable products, documents

* In billions of cargo ton-miles
Source: Statistical Abstract of the United States, 1986 and 1987.

Larger average order size means fewer orders and lower order-processing costs, but it also means larger inventory-carrying costs.

Transportation

Marketers need to take an interest in their company's transportation decisions. The choice of transportation carriers affects the pricing of the products, delivery performance, and the condition of the goods when they arrive, all of which will affect customer satisfaction.

In shipping goods to its warehouses, dealers, and customers, the company can choose among five transportation modes: rail, truck, water, pipeline, and air. Each transportation mode's characteristics are summarized in Table 14-1 and discussed in the following paragraphs.

Rail

Railroad use declined until the mid-1970s, but railroads nevertheless remain the nation's largest carrier, accounting for 37 percent of total cargo moved. Railroads are one of the most cost-effective modes for shipping large amounts of bulk products—coal, sand, minerals, farm and forest products—over long distances. Railroads have recently begun to increase their customer services. They have designed new equipment to handle special categories of goods, provided flatcars for carrying truck trailers by rail (piggyback), and provided in-transit services such as diversion of shipped goods to other destinations en route and processing of goods en route.

Truck

Trucks have steadily increased their share of transportation and now account for 25 percent of total cargo. They account for the largest portion of transportation within cities as opposed to between cities. Each year trucks travel over 140 billion miles—equal to nearly 300,000 round trips to the moon.[21] Trucks are highly flexible in their routing and time schedules. They can move goods door to door, saving shippers the need to transfer goods from truck to rail and back again at a loss of time and risk of theft or damage. Trucks are efficient for short hauls of high-value merchandise. Their rates are competitive with railway rates in many cases, and trucks can usually offer faster service.

Combining modes of transportation through containerization (clockwise): piggyback, fishyback, airtruck, and trainship.

Water

A large amount of goods moves by ships and barges on coastal and inland waterways. The cost of water transportation is very low for shipping bulky, low-value, nonperishable products such as sand, coal, grain, oil, and metallic ores. On the other hand, water transportation is the slowest transportation mode and is sometimes affected by the weather.

Pipeline

Pipelines are a specialized means of shipping petroleum, coal, and chemicals from sources to markets. Pipeline shipment of petroleum products costs less than rail shipment but more than water shipment. Most pipelines are used by their owners to ship their own products.

Air

Air carriers transport less than 1 percent of the nation's goods but are becoming more important as a transportation mode. Although air freight rates are much higher than rail or truck rates, air freight is ideal where speed is needed or distant markets

**TABLE 14-2
Rankings of
Transportation Modes
(1 = Highest Rank)**

	SPEED (door-to-door delivery time)	DEPENDABILITY (meeting schedules on time)	CAPABILITY (ability to handle various products)	AVAILABILITY (no. of geographic points served)	COST (per ton-mile)
Rail	3	4	2	2	3
Water	4	5	1	4	1
Truck	2	2	3	1	4
Pipeline	5	1	5	5	2
Air	1	3	4	3	5

Source: See Carl M. Guelzo, *Introduction to Logistics Management* (Englewood Cliffs, NJ: Prentice Hall, 1986), p. 46.

have to be reached. Among the most frequently airfreighted products are perishables (fresh fish, cut flowers) and high-value, low bulk items (technical instruments, jewelry). Companies find that air freight reduces inventory levels, number of warehouses, and costs of packaging

Choosing Transportation Modes

Until the late 1970s, routes, rates, and service in the transportation industry were heavily regulated by the federal government. Today, most of these regulations have been eased. Deregulation has caused rapid and substantial changes. Railroads, ships and barges, trucks, airlines, and pipeline companies are now much more competitive, flexible, and responsive to the needs of their customers. These changes have resulted in better services and lower prices for shippers. But the changes also mean that marketers must do better transportation planning if they want to take full advantage of new opportunities in the changing transportation environment.[22]

In choosing a transportation mode for a product, shippers consider as many as five criteria. Table 14-2 ranks the various modes on these criteria. Thus if a shipper needs speed, air and truck are the prime choices. If the goal is low cost, then water or pipeline might be best. Trucks appear to offer the most advantages, explaining their growing share.

Shippers are increasingly combining two or more modes of transportation, thanks to **containerization.** Containerization consists of putting goods in boxes or trailers that are easy to transfer between two transportation modes. A number of terms have evolved to describe various "multimode" transportation systems.[23] *Piggyback* describes the use of rail and trucks; *fishyback*, water and trucks; *trainship*, water and rail; and *airtruck*, air and trucks. Each combination offers advantages to the shipper. For example, piggyback is cheaper than trucking alone and yet provides flexibility and convenience.

Organizational Responsibility for Physical Distribution

We see that decisions on warehousing, inventory, and transportation require much coordination. A growing number of companies have set up a permanent committee made up of managers responsible for different physical distribution activities. This committee meets often to set policies for improving overall distribution efficiency. Some companies have a vice-president of physical distribution, who reports to the marketing vice-president or manufacturing vice-president, or even to the president. The location of the physical distribution department within the company is a secondary concern. The important thing is that the company coordinate its physical distribution and marketing activities in order to create high market satisfaction at a reasonable cost.

■ SUMMARY

Distribution channel decisions are among the most complex and challenging decisions facing the firm. Each channel system creates a different level of sales and costs. Once a distribution channel has been chosen, the firm must usually stick with it for a long time. The chosen channel will strongly affect and be affected by the other elements in the marketing mix.

Each firm needs to identify alternative ways to reach the market. They vary from direct selling to using one, two, three, or more intermediary channel levels. The organizations making up the marketing channel are connected by physical product, title, payment, information, and promotion flows. Marketing channels face continuous and sometimes dramatic change. Three of the most important trends are the growth of vertical, horizontal, and multichannel marketing systems. These trends affect channel cooperation, conflict, and competition.

Channel design begins with assessing customer channel service needs and company channel objectives and constraints. The company then identifies the major channel alternatives in terms of the types and number of middlemen, and the responsibilities of channel members. Each channel alternative has to be evaluated according to economic, control, and adaptive criteria.

Channel management calls for selecting qualified middlemen and motivating them. Individual channel members must be evaluated regularly against their own past sales and other channel members' sales.

Just as the marketing concept is receiving increased recognition, more business firms are paying attention to the physical distribution concept. Physical distribution is an area of potentially high cost savings and improved customer satisfaction. When order processors, warehouse planners, inventory managers, and transportation managers make decisions, they affect each other's costs and ability to handle demand. The physical distribution concept calls for treating all these decisions within a unified framework. The task is to design physical distribution systems that minimize the total cost of providing a desired level of customer services.

■ QUESTIONS FOR DISCUSSION

1. The Book-of-the-Month Club has been successfully marketing books by mail for over 50 years. Why do book publishers use this middleman, rather than selling directly to consumers themselves? How has the BOMC survived competition from B. Dalton, Waldenbooks, and other large booksellers?

2. How many channel levels are commonly used by these companies? Why do they use this number of levels, rather than more or fewer? (a) Dean Witter, (b) Sears, (c) American Tobacco Co.

3. What organizations are needed to conduct the flows of products, payment, information, and promotion from the manufacturer to the customer? Are these organizations considered to be part of the distribution channel? Why or why not?

4. How are the channels of distribution used for services similar to the channels used for physical goods? How are they different? Illustrate your answer by describing typical channels for candy bars and insurance.

5. A channel of distribution will function more effectively if it has a leader to assign tasks to members and to manage conflict. How is the leader chosen? How much power must the leader have to get other members to work for the overall good of the channel, rather than just for their own good?

6. Why is franchising such a fast-growing form of retail organization? What advantages and disadvantages does it have compared to other types of vertical marketing systems?

7. Why have symbiotic marketing arrangements become more common in recent years? What other opportunities for these arrangements can you suggest? Identify several pairs of companies and describe how a symbiotic marketing program would help both companies in each pair.

8. Describe the channel service needs of (a) consumers buying a computer for home use, (b) retailers buying computers to resell to individual consumers, and (c) purchasing agents buying computers for company use. What channels would a computer manufacturer design to satisfy these different service needs?

9. Which distribution strategies—intensive, selective, or exclusive—are used for the following products, and why? (a) Piaget watches, (b) Hyundai automobiles, (c) Snickers candy bars.

10. Discuss the economic, control, and adaptive criteria that Esprit appears to use in evaluating its channel alternatives. Do other clothing marketers appear to use the same criteria? Why or why not?

11. How do physical distribution decisions differ from channel decisions? Compare Sears' physical distribution system with its channels of distribution to illustrate your answer.

12. How can computers be used to facilitate physical distribution? How can they affect the development and operation of channels of distribution?

■ KEY TERMS

Administered VMS   A vertical marketing system that co-ordinates successive stages of production and distribution, not through common ownership or contractual ties, but through the size and power of one of the parties.

Containerization   Putting goods in boxes or trailers that are easy to transfer between two transportation modes. They are used in "multimode" systems commonly referred to as piggyback, fishyback, trainship, and airtruck.

Contractual VMS   A vertical marketing system in which independent firms at different levels of production and distribution join together through contracts to obtain more economies or sales impact than they could achieve alone.

Conventional distribution channel   A channel consisting of independent producer(s), wholesaler(s), and re-tailer(s), each a separate business seeking to maximize its own profits, even at the expense of profits for the system as a whole.

Corporate VMS   A vertical marketing system that combines successive stages of production and distribution under single ownership; channel leadership is established through common ownership.

Distribution center   A large and highly automated warehouse designed to receive goods from various plants and suppliers, take orders, fill them efficiently, and deliver goods to customers as quickly as possible.

Distribution channel   The set of firms and individuals that take title, or assist in transferring title, to a good or service as it moves from the producer to the final consumer or industrial user.

Exclusive distribution   Giving a limited number of dealers the exclusive right to distribute a company's products in their territories.

Horizontal marketing system   A channel arrangement in which two or more nonrelated companies at one level join together to follow a new marketing opportunity.

Intensive distribution   Stocking a product in as many outlets as possible.

Physical distribution   Planning, implementing, and controlling the physical flow of materials and final goods from points of origin to points of use to meet the needs of customers at a profit.

Selective distribution   The use of more than one but less than all the middlemen who are willing to carry a company's products.

Vertical marketing system (VMS)   A distribution channel structure in which the producer(s), wholesaler(s), and retailer(s) act as a unified system; either one channel member owns the others, or has contracts with them, or has so much power that they all cooperate.

■ REFERENCES

1. Portions adapted from Cleveland Horton, "Esprit to Skirt Retail Clients by Setting Up Its Own Stores," *Advertising Age*, January 26, 1987, pp. 12, 65.

2. See Louis W. Stern and Frederick D. Sturdivant, "Customer-Driven Distribution Systems," *Harvard Business Review*, July–August 1987, p. 34.

3. Ronald Abler, John S. Adams, and Peter Gould, *Spatial Organizations: The Geographer's View of the World* (Englewood Cliffs, NJ: Prentice Hall, 1971), pp. 531–32.

4. See Irving Rein, Philip Kotler, and Martin Stoller, *High Visibility* (New York: Dodd, Mead, Inc., 1987).

5. Louis W. Stern and Adel I. El-Ansary, *Marketing Channels*, 2nd Edition, (Englewood Cliffs, NJ: Prentice Hall, 1982), pp. 291–92.

6. For an excellent summary of channel conflict and power, see Stern and El-Ansary, *Marketing Channels*, Chs. 6 and 7.

7. See Bert C. McCammon, Jr., "Perspectives for Distribution Programming," in *Vertical Marketing Systems*, Louis P. Bucklin, ed. (Glenview, IL: Scott Foresman, 1970), pp. 32–51.

8. Janet Myers, "Giant Stocks Up on Service, Vertical Integration," *Advertising Age*, April 28, 1986, *Advertising Age*, p. S4.

9. Jaclyn Fierman, "How Gallo Crushes the Competition," *Fortune*, September 1, 1986, p. 27.

10. Faye Rice, "How to Succeed at Cloning a Small Business," *Fortune*, October 28, 1985, p. 60; and Laura Zinn, "Want to Buy a Franchise? Look Before You Leap," *Business Week*, May 23, 1988. pp. 186–87.

11. See Lee Adler, "Symbiotic Marketing," *Harvard Business Review*, November–December 1966, pp. 59–71; and P. "Rajan" Varadarajan and Daniel Rajaratnam, "Symbiotic Marketing Revisited," *Journal of Marketing*, January 1986, pp. 7–17.

12. See Ronald Grover and Dean Foust, "Joint TV Commercials: It's Two, Two, Two Ads in One," *Business Week*, July 6, 1987, p. 27.

13. See Laurie Freeman, "McKids Grow Up: Adult Clothing May Join Sears' Kids' Line," *Advertising Age*, June 1, 1987, p. 82.

14. See Robert E. Weigand, "Fit Products and Channels to Your Markets," *Harvard Business Review*, January–February 1977, pp. 95–105.

15. See Stern and Sturdivant, "Customer-Driven Distribution Systems," p. 35.

16. Ibid., p. 35.

17. See Bert Rosenbloom, *Marketing Channels: A Manage-*

ment View (Hinsdale, IL: Dryden Press, 1978), pp. 192–203.

18. See McCammon, "Perspectives for Distribution Programming," p. 43; and James A. Narus and James C. Anderson, "Turn Your Industrial Distributors into Partners," *Harvard Business Review*, March–April 1986, pp. 66–71.

19. See Katherine M. Hafner, "Computer Retailers: Things Have Gone from Worse to Bad," *Business Week*, June 8, 1987, p. 104.

20. Michael Oneal, "Can Sears Get Sexier but Keep the Common Touch?" *Business Week*, July 6, 1987, p. 93.

21. See "Trucking," *Fortune*, November 22, 1987, p. 148.

22. See Lewis M. Schneider, "New Era in Transportation Strategy," *Harvard Business Review*, March–April 1985, pp. 118–26.

23. For more discussion, see Norman E. Hutchinson, *An Integrated Approach to Logistics Management* (Englewood Cliffs, NJ: Prentice Hall, 1987), p. 69.

This is a home furnishings store?

IKEA (👁 🔑 ah!)

15 Placing Products: Retailing and Wholesaling

WHEN Scandinavian furniture giant IKEA (pronounced eye-KEY-ah) opened its first U.S. store in 1985, it caused quite a stir. On opening day, people flocked to the suburban Philadelphia store in droves, from as far away as Washington, D.C. Traffic on the nearby turnpike backed up for six miles, and at one point the store was so tightly packed with customers that management ordered the doors closed until the crowds thinned out. In the first week, the IKEA store packed in 150,000 people who bought over $1 million worth of furniture. And when the dust had settled, the store was still averaging 50,000 customers a week.

IKEA is one of a new breed of retailers called "category killers." They get their name from their marketing strategy: carry a huge selection of merchandise in a single product category at such good prices that you destroy the competition. Category killers are now striking in a wide range of industries, including furniture, toys, records, sporting goods, housewares, and consumer electronics.

IKEA stores are about three football fields in size. Each store stocks more than 6,000 items—all furnishings and housewares, ranging from coffee mugs to leather sofas to kitchen cabinets. IKEA sells Scandinavian design "knock-down" furniture—each item reduces to a flat-pack kit and has to be assembled at home. Consumers browse through the store's comfortable display area, where signs and stickers on each item note its price, how it's made, assembly instructions, how different pieces complement one another, and where the item is located in the adjacent warehouse. Customers wrestle desired items from warehouse stacks, haul their choices away on large trollies, and pay at giant-sized check-out counters. The store provides a reasonably-priced restaurant for hungry shoppers and a supervised children's play area for weary parents. But best of all, IKEA has low prices. The store operates on the philosophy of providing a wide variety of well-designed home furnishings at prices that the majority of people can afford.

The first category killer, Toys 'R' Us, appeared in the late 1950s, but other retailers have just recently adopted the idea. Unlike warehouse clubs and other "off-price" retailers, which offer the lowest prices but few choices within a category, the category killers offer an exhaustive selection in one line. Toys 'R' Us stocks 18,000 different toy items in football field-size stores. Huge Sportmart stores stock 100,000 sporting goods items including 70 types of sleeping bags, 265 styles of athletic socks, 12,000 pairs of shoes, and 15,000 fishing lures. Tower Records stores carry up to 75,000 titles, 25 times more than the average competitor. And Branden's, the housewares and home furnishings category killer, offers a choice of 30 different coffee pots, 25 irons, 100 patterns of bed sheets, and 800 kitchen gadgets. With such large assortments, the category killers generate big sales, often allowing them to charge prices as low as those of their discount competitors.

The category killers face a few problems. IKEA has encountered occasional difficulty managing its huge inventory, sometimes overpromising or inconveniencing customers. The company's expansive stores require large investments and huge markets in order to succeed. And some customers find that they want more personal service than IKEA gives, or that the savings are not worth the work required to find products in the huge store, haul them out, and assemble them at home. Despite such problems, IKEA has prospered beyond its founders' dreams. It now has 89 stores in 19 countries racking up over $1 billion a year in sales. It recently opened a second U.S. store in the Washington, D.C., suburbs and will soon have a third in Baltimore. In all, IKEA plans to open 60 stores around the country during the next 25 years.

Most retailing experts predict great success for stores like IKEA. One analyst, Wallace Epperson, Jr., "estimates IKEA will win at least a 15 percent share of any market it enters and will expand the market as it does so. If Mr. Epperson is any indication, IKEA's prospects are good. Touring IKEA in his professional capacity, Mr. Epperson couldn't resist the store. 'I spent $400,' he says. 'It's incredible.'"[1]

Chapter Objectives *After reading this chapter, you should be able to:*

1. Discuss the roles of retailers and wholesalers in the distribution channel.
2. Describe the major types of retailers and give examples of each.
3. Identify the major types of wholesalers and give examples of each.
4. Discuss the marketing decisions facing retailers and wholesalers.

THIS chapter looks at retailing and wholesaling. In the first section we look at retailing's nature and importance, major types of store and nonstore retailers, decisions retailers make, and the future of retailing. In the second section, we discuss the same topics for wholesalers.

RETAILING

What is retailing? We all know that Sears and K mart are retailers, but so are the Avon representative, the local Holiday Inn, and a doctor seeing patients. We define retailing as follows:

Retailing is all activities involved in selling goods or services directly to final consumers for their personal, nonbusiness use.

Many institutions—manufacturers, wholesalers, retailers—do retailing. But most retailing is done by **retailers,** businesses whose sales come primarily from retailing.

And most retailing is done in retail stores, but in recent years nonstore retailing—selling by mail, telephone, door-to-door, vending machines, electronically—has grown explosively.

Retailing is a major industry. Retail stores outnumber manufacturers and wholesalers by more than seven to one and are the third largest source of the nation's jobs. Some retailers are true giants—Sears and K mart are among the world's largest businesses. At the other extreme are "mom and pop" stores, important because they are everywhere and offer consumers more convenience and personal service than retailing giants do. Because store retailing accounts for most of the retail business, we will discuss it first. Then we will look at nonstore retailing.

STORE RETAILING

Retail stores come in all shapes and sizes, and new retail types keep emerging. They can be classified by one or more of several characteristics: amount of service, product line sold, relative prices, control of outlets, and type of store cluster. These classifications and the corresponding retailer types are shown in Table 15-1 and discussed below.

Amount of Service
Different products need different amounts of service, and customers' service preferences vary. Table 15-2 shows three levels of service and the types of retailers that use them.

Self-service retailing in this country grew rapidly in the Great Depression of the 1930s. Customers were willing to carry out their own "locate-compare-select" process to save money. Today self-service is the basis of all discount operations and is typically used by sellers of convenience goods and nationally branded, fast-moving shopping goods.

Limited-service retailers such as Sears or J.C. Penney provide more sales assistance because they carry more shopping goods for which customers need more information. They also offer additional services such as credit and merchandise return not usually offered by low-service stores. Their increased operating costs result in higher prices.

In *full-service retailing*, found in specialty stores and first-class department stores, salespeople assist customers in every phase of the shopping process. Full-service stores usually carry more specialty goods and slower-moving items such as cameras, jewelry, and fashions, for which customers like to be "waited on." They provide more liberal returns policies, various credit plans, free delivery, home servicing, and extras such as lounges and restaurants. More services result in much higher operating costs, which are passed along to customers as higher prices.

TABLE 15-1
Different Ways to Classify Retail Outlets

AMOUNT SERVICE	PRODUCT LINE SOLD	RELATIVE PRICE EMPHASIS	CONTROL OF OUTLETS	TYPE OF STORE CLUSTER
Self-service	Specialty store	Discount store	Corporate chain	Central business district
Limited service	Department store	Off-price retailers	Voluntary chain and retailer cooperative	Regional shopping center
Full service	Supermarket	Catalog show-room	Consumer cooperative	Community shopping center
	Convenience store		Franchise organization	Neighborhood shopping center
	Combination store, superstore, and hypermarket		Merchandising conglomerate	
	Service business			

DECREASING SERVICES ←		→ INCREASING SERVICES
Self-service	**Limited service**	**Full service**
Attributes		
Very few services	Small variety of services	Wide variety of services
Price appeal	Shopping goods	Fashion merchandise
Staple goods		Specialty merchandise
Convenience goods		
Examples		
Warehouse retailing	Door-to-door sales	Specialty stores
Grocery stores	Department stores	Department stores
Discount retailing	Telephone sales	
Variety stores	Variety stores	
Mail-order retailing		
Automatic vending		

Source: Adapted from Larry D. Redinbaugh, *Retailing Management: A Planning Approach* (New York: McGraw-Hill, 1976), p. 12.

Product Line Sold

Retailers can be classified by the length and breadth of their product assortments. Among the most important types are the specialty store, department store, supermarket, convenience store, and superstore.

Specialty Store

A **specialty store** carries a narrow product line with a deep assortment within that line. Examples include stores selling sporting goods, furniture, books, electronics, flowers, or toys. Specialty stores can be further classified by the narrowness of their product lines. A clothing store is a *single-line store*, a men's clothing store is a *limited-line store*, and a men's custom shirt store is a *superspecialty store*.

Today, specialty stores are flourishing for several reasons. The increasing use of market segmentation, market targeting, and product specialization has resulted in a greater need for stores that focus on specific products and segments. And because of changing consumer life styles and the increasing number of two-income households, many consumers have greater incomes but less time to spend shopping. They are attracted to specialty stores which provide high quality products, nearby locations, good store hours, excellent service, and quick entry and exit. The shopping center

Specialty stores focus on specific products and segments.

boom has also contributed to the recent growth of specialty stores, which occupy 60 to 70 percent of the total shopping center space.

Department Store

A **department store** carries a wide variety of product lines—typically clothing, home furnishings, and household goods. Each line is operated as a separate department managed by specialist buyers or merchandisers. Examples of well-known department stores include Bloomingdale's (New York), Marshall Field (Chicago), and Filene's (Boston). *Specialty department stores*, can also be found. Examples are Saks Fifth Avenue and I. Magnin, which carry only clothing, shoes, cosmetics, luggage, and gift items.

The first department stores were housed in impressive buildings in fashionable central locations and sold the concept of "shopping for enjoyment." They grew rapidly through the first half of the century. But after World War II, they began to lose ground to a growing list of other types of retailers, including discount stores, specialty store chains, and "off-price" retailers. And the heavy traffic, poor parking, and general decaying of central cities, where many department stores still have their biggest investments, have made downtown shopping less appealing. As a result, many department stores have closed or merged with others.

Department stores are today waging a "comeback war." Most have opened suburban stores, and many have added "bargain basements" to meet the discount threat. Still others have remodeled their stores or set up "boutiques" that compete with specialty stores. Many are trying mail order and telephone selling. To reduce costs, some department stores are cutting back on employees, services, and product lines, but this strategy may remove their major appeals—assortment and service. Overall, department stores need to find better ways to increase their falling profits.

In recent years, many large department stores have been joining rather than fighting the competition by diversifying into discount and specialty stores. Dayton-Hudson, for example, operates Target (discount stores), Mervyn's (lower-price clothing), B. Dalton (books), and many other discount and specialty chains. Its Dayton's, Hudson's, and other department stores now account for less than 20 percent of total corporate sales.[2]

Supermarket

Supermarkets are large, low-cost, low-margin, high-volume, self-service stores that carry a wide variety of food, laundry, and household products. Most U.S. supermarket stores are owned by supermarket chains like Safeway, Kroger, A&P, Winn-Dixie, and Jewel. Chains account for almost 70 percent of all supermarket sales.[3]

The first supermarkets introduced the concepts of self-service, customer turnstiles, and checkout counters. Supermarket growth took off in the 1930s for several reasons. The Great Depression made consumers more price conscious, and mass automobile ownership reduced the need for small neighborhood stores. An increase in brand preselling through advertising reduced the need for salesclerks. Finally, stores selling grocery, meat, produce, and household goods in a single place allowed one-stop shopping and pulled consumers from farther away, giving supermarkets the volume needed to offset their lower margins.

Most supermarkets today are facing slow sales growth because of a proliferation of stores, slower population growth, and the appearance of innovative competitors such as convenience stores, discount food stores, and superstores. They have also been hit hard by the rapid growth of out-of-home eating. Thus, supermarkets are looking for new ways to build their sales. Most chains now operate fewer but larger stores and carry a larger variety of items. They practice "scrambled merchandising," carrying many nonfood items—beauty aids, housewares, toys, prescriptions, appliances, videocassettes, sporting goods, garden supplies—hoping to find high-margin lines to improve profits.

Supermarkets are also improving their facilities and services to attract more customers. Typical improvements are better locations, flashier decor, longer store hours, check cashing, delivery, and even childcare centers. Although consumers have always expected supermarkets to offer good prices, convenient locations, and speedy checkout, today's more affluent and sophisticated food buyer wants more. Many supermarkets are "moving upscale" with the market:

> Retailers are adding drama and sizzle to their operations with such amenities as full-service seafood departments, "from-scratch" bakeries, gourmet prepared foods and catering departments, specialty foods, and in-store restaurants complete with sushi bars, jazz pianists, and wine stewards.[4]

Finally, to attract more customers, large supermarket chains are starting to customize their stores for individual neighborhoods. They are tailoring store size, product assortments, prices, and promotions to the economic and ethnic needs of local markets.

Convenience Store

Convenience stores are small stores that carry a limited line of high-turnover convenience goods. Examples include 7-Eleven, Circle K, and Open Pantry. These stores locate near residential areas and remain open long hours and seven days a week. Convenience stores must charge high prices to make up for higher operating costs and lower sales volume. But they satisfy an important consumer need. Consumers use convenience stores for "fill-in" purchases at off hours or when time is short, and they are willing to pay for the convenience. The number of convenience stores increased from about 2,000 in 1957 to about 43,000, with sales of $20 billion, in 1984.[5]

Superstore, Combination Store, and Hypermarket

These three types of stores are larger than the conventional supermarket. **Superstores** are almost twice the size of regular supermarkets and carry a large assortment of routinely purchased food and nonfood items. They offer such services as laundry, dry cleaning, shoe repair, check cashing, bill paying, and bargain lunch counters. Because of their wider assortment, superstore prices are 5 to 6 percent higher than those of conventional supermarkets. Many leading chains are moving toward superstores. Examples include Safeway's Pak 'N Pay and Pathmark Super Centers. Kroger has opened nothing but superstores since 1972, and almost 80 percent of Safeway's new stores over the past several years have been superstores. In 1975, superstores accounted for only about 3 percent of total food store sales, but by 1986 they took in over 26 percent of the business.[6]

Combination stores are combined food and drug stores. They average about one and one half football fields in size—about twice the size of superstores. Examples are A&P's Family Mart and Kroger-Sav-On. Combination stores take in less than 5 percent of the business done by food stores.

Hypermarkets are even bigger than combination stores, ranging in size up to about *six* football fields. The hypermarket combines supermarket, discount, and warehouse retailing. It carries more than routinely purchased goods, also selling furniture, appliances, clothing, and many other things. The hypermarket offers discount prices

Hypermarkets: huge stores that combine supermarket, discount, and warehouse retailing.

and operates like a warehouse. Products in wire "baskets" are stacked high on metal racks; forklifts move through aisles during selling hours to restock shelves. Customers select items from bulk displays, and the store gives discounts to customers who carry their own heavy appliances and furniture out of the store. Examples include Bigg's in Cincinnati, Ralph's Giant Stores in Southern California, and Carrefour USA in Philadelphia. While hypermarkets have grown quickly in Europe, American chains have proceeded more slowly. But this concept now appears to be catching on in the United States, with major retailers such as Wal-Mart and K mart now opening these giant stores. Industry experts estimate that 150 U. S. hypermarkets will be in operation by 1990.

Service Business

For some businesses, the "product line" is actually a service. Service retailers include hotels and motels, banks, airlines, colleges, hospitals, movie theaters, tennis clubs, bowling alleys, restaurants, repair services, barber and beauty shops, and dry cleaners. Service retailers in the United States are growing faster than product retailers, and each service industry has its own retailing drama. Banks look for new ways to distribute their services, including automatic tellers, direct deposit, and telephone banking. Health organizations are changing the ways consumers get and pay for health services. The amusement industry has spawned Disney World and other theme parks. H&R Block has built a franchise network to help consumers pay as little as possible to Uncle Sam.

Relative Prices   Retailers can also be classified by their prices. Most retailers charge regular prices and offer normal quality goods and customer service. Some offer higher-quality goods and service at higher prices—Gucci's justifies its high prices by saying, "You will remember the goods long after the prices are forgotten." Discount stores run lower-cost, lower-service operations and sell goods for lower prices. Here we will look at discount stores, "off-price" retailers, and catalog showrooms.

Discount Store

A **discount store** sells standard merchandise at lower prices by accepting lower margins and selling higher volume. The use of occasional discounts or specials does not make a discount store. A true discount store *regularly* sells its merchandise at lower prices, offering mostly national brands, not inferior goods. The early discount stores cut expenses by operating in warehouse-like facilities in low-rent but heavily traveled districts. They slashed prices, advertised widely, and carried a reasonable width and depth of products.

In recent years, facing intense competition from other discounters and department stores, many discount retailers have traded up. They have improved decor, added new lines and services, and opened suburban branches—leading to higher costs and prices. And as some department stores have cut their prices to compete with discounters, the distinction between many discount and department stores has blurred. As a result, several major discount stores folded in the 1970s because they lost their price advantage. And many department store retailers have upgraded their stores and services to set themselves apart from the improved discounters.

Off-Price Retailers

When the major discount stores traded up, a new wave of **off-price retailers** moved in to fill the low-price, high-volume gap. Ordinary discounters buy at regular wholesale prices and accept lower margins to keep their prices down. Off-price retailers, on the other hand, buy at less than regular wholesale prices and charge consumers less-than-retail. They tend to carry a changing and unstable collection of higher quality merchandise, often leftover goods, overruns, and irregulars obtained at reduced prices from manufacturers or other retailers. Off-price retailers have made the biggest inroads in apparel, accessories, and footwear; it is expected that they will grab a 20 to 25 percent share of all clothing sales by the end of the decade. But off-price retailers can be found in all areas, from no-frills banking and discount brokerages to food stores and electronics (see Marketing Highlight 15–1).

There are three main types of off-price retailers. *Factory outlets* are owned and operated by manufacturers. They usually carry one line—normally the manufacturer's surplus, discontinued, or irregular goods. Examples are The Burlington Coat Factory Warehouse, Manhattan's Brand Name Fashion Outlet, and the well-known factory outlets of Levi Strauss, Carter's, and Ship 'n Shore. The outlets sometimes group together in *factory outlet malls*, where dozens of outlet stores offer prices as much as 50 percent below retail on a wide range of items. The number of factory outlet malls grew from less than 60 in 1980 to over 370 in 1986.[7]

Independent off-price retailers are owned and run by entrepreneurs or are divisions of larger retail corporations. Though many off-price operations are run by smaller independents, most of the large off-price retailer operations are owned by bigger retail chains. Examples include Loehmann's (operated by Associated Dry Goods, owner of Lord & Taylor), Designer Depot (K mart), Filene's Basement (Federated Department Stores), and T. J. Maxx (Zayre).

Warehouse clubs (or wholesale clubs) sell a limited selection of brand-name grocery items, appliances, apparel, and a hodgepodge of other goods at deep discounts to members who pay a $25 to $50 annual membership fee. Examples are the Price Club, Sam's Wholesale Club, BJ's Wholesale Club, and Pace Membership Warehouse. These wholesale clubs operate in huge, low-overhead facilities and offer few frills:

> The stores are drafty when the weather is cold and stuffy when it is hot. Customers have to find dollies and grappling hooks and then wrestle refrigerators, desks, and other heavy items into the checkout line themselves, There are no home deliveries. Credit cards are not accepted, and shoppers even pay a membership fee for the privilege of spending their money. But no one seems to mind. . . . These huge stores offer rock-bottom prices on everything from dishwashers and stoves to canned goods and TV dinners. . . . they typically sell merchandise at 20 percent to 40 percent below supermarket and discount-store prices.[8]

OFF-PRICE RETAILING AT 47TH STREET PHOTO

On the surface, 47th Street Photo doesn't look like much of a retailing operation. Its main store is a small, dingy affair located above Kaplan's Delicatessen on New York's West 47th Street. Its second store, a small computer outlet located a few blocks away, is only slightly more attractive. But beneath the surface, 47th Street Photo represents the state of the art in off-price retailing—selling quality, branded merchandise at large discounts. In business for only fifteen years, 47th Street's two tiny stores annually sell more than $100 million worth of electronics products, and its sales are growing at 25 percent a year.

47th Street Photo is typical of the new discounters that emerged at retailing's low end to fill the gap created when more mature discount institutions began to trade up their merchandise, services, and prices. 47th Street maintains a low-cost, low-margin, high-volume philosophy. It carries a huge inventory of over 25,000 fast-moving, branded electronics products—including such items as cameras and camera equipment (only 30 percent of its business), personal computers, calculators, typewriters, telephones, answering machines, and videotape machines. It keeps its costs down through low-cost, no-frills facilities, efficient operations, and smart buying. Then it offers customers the lowest prices and turns its inventory quickly.

47th Street Photo's customers endure more abrupt treatment and enjoy fewer services than they would at plusher speciality stores. Like a well-run restaurant, 47th Street gets 'em in, feeds 'em, and gets 'em out. Customers line up at the sale counter to be waited on by efficient but curt salespeople who prefer that customers know what they want before coming in. In-store product inspections and comparisons are discouraged, and salespeople offer little information or assistance.

But the price is right! 47th Street Photo regularly monitors competitor prices to be certain that its own prices support its "lowest-price" position. Price examples: Suggested retail price of the Canon PC-20 copier, $1,295; at 47th Street Photo, it's $880. Macy's offers a Brother typewriter for $400, and on a recent Sunday it's out of stock. At 47th Street the same model is $289 and, of course, in stock.

Half of 47th Street Photo's sales come from mail-order and telephone customers. Its 224-page catalog, toll-free numbers, and packed ads in the *New York Times*, *Wall Street Journal*, and several other business and special interest magazines make New York's "only dopes pay retail" shopping style available to the rest of the country. Over the years, 47th Street has built a solid reputation for trustworthiness. A price is a price, no bait-and-switch, no haggling or hidden prices.

So on the surface, 47th Street Photo doesn't look like much of a retailing operation. But behind its low-overhead exterior is a gutsy, finely tuned merchandising machine.

Source: Adapted from John Merwin, "The Source," *Forbes*, April 9, 1984, pp. 74–78.

47th Street Photo doesn't look like much, but it's a finely tuned merchandising machine.

Off-price retailing blossomed during the early 1980s, and competition has stiffened in recent years as more and more off-price retailers enter the market. But the growth of off-price retailing has slowed a bit recently because of an upswing in the economy and more effective counter-strategies by department stores and regular discounters. Still, off-price retailing remains a vital and growing force in modern retailing.[9]

Catalog Showroom

A **catalog showroom** sells a wide selection of high-markup, fast-moving, brand-name goods at discount prices. These include jewelry, power tools, cameras, luggage, small appliances, toys, and sporting goods. Catalog showrooms make their money by cutting costs and margins to provide low prices that will attract a higher volume of sales. The catalog showroom industry is led by companies such as Best Products and Service Merchandise.

Emerging in the late 1960s, catalog showrooms became one of retailing's hottest new forms. By the mid-1980s, they accounted for about 5 percent of the total retail market.[10] But catalog showrooms have been struggling in recent years to hold their share of the retail market. Department stores and discount retailers now run regular sales that match showroom prices. And off-price retailers consistently beat catalog prices. As a result, many showroom chains are broadening their lines, doing more advertising, renovating their stores, and adding services such as film processing in order to attract more business.

Control of Outlets

About 80 percent of all retail stores are independents, and they account for two-thirds of all retail sales. Here we will look at several other forms of ownership—the corporate chain, voluntary chain and retailer cooperative, consumer cooperative, franchise organization, and merchandising conglomerate.

Corporate Chain

The chain store is one of the most important retail developments of this century. **Chain stores** are two or more outlets that are commonly owned and controlled, have central buying and merchandising, and sell similar lines of merchandise. Common ownership and control sets corporate chains apart from voluntary chains and franchise operations. Central buying and merchandising means that headquarters largely decides on the chain's product assortment, places orders to get quantity discounts, sends goods to individual units, and sets pricing, promotion, and other policies for the units. The fact that corporate chains sell similar lines of goods sets them apart from merchandising conglomerates, which combine several chains under common ownership.

Corporate chains appear in all types of retailing—in supermarket, discount, variety, specialty, and department stores. They are strongest in department stores, variety stores, food stores, drug stores, shoe stores, and women's apparel stores. Corporate chains gain many advantages over independents. Their size allows them to buy in large quantities at lower prices. They can afford to hire corporate-level specialists to deal with such areas as pricing, promotion, merchandising, inventory control, and sales forecasting. And chains gain promotional economies because their advertising costs are spread over many stores and a large sales volume.

Voluntary Chain and Retailer Cooperative

The great success of corporate chains caused many independents to band together in one of two forms of contractual associations. One is the *voluntary chain*—a wholesaler-sponsored group of independent retailers that engage in group buying and common merchandising. Examples include the Independent Grocers Alliance (IGA), Sentry Hardwares, and Western Auto. The other is the *retailer cooperative*— a group of independent retailers that band together and set up a jointly owned central wholesale operation and conduct joint merchandising and promotion efforts. Examples include Associated Grocers and True Value Hardware. These organizations give independents the buying and promotion economies they need to meet the prices of corporate chains.

Consumer Cooperative

A **consumer cooperative** is a retail firm owned by its customers. Residents of a community may start a consumer co-op when they feel local retailers are charging too high prices or providing poor product assortment or quality. The members contribute money to open their own store, and they vote on its policies and elect managers. The store may set low prices or give members dividends based on their purchase levels. Although there are a few thousand cooperatives in the United States, they have never become an important retailing force.

Franchise Organization

A **franchise** is a contractual association between a manufacturer, wholesaler, or service organization (the franchiser) and independent businesspeople (franchisees) who buy the right to own and operate one or more units in the franchise system. The main difference between a franchise and other contractual systems (voluntary chains and retail cooperatives) is that franchise systems are normally based on some unique product or service; on a method of doing business; or on a trade name, goodwill, or patent that the franchiser has developed. Franchising has been prominent in fast foods, motels, gas stations, video stores, health and fitness centers, auto rentals, hair cutting, real estate, travel agencies, and dozens of other product and service areas.

The compensation the franchiser receives may include an initial fee, a royalty on sales, lease fees for equipment, and a share of the profits. McDonald's franchisees may pay $500,000 in initial start-up costs for a franchise. Then McDonald's charges a 3.5 percent service fee and a rental charge of 8.5 percent of the franchisee's volume. It also requires franchisees to go to Hamburger University for three weeks to learn how to manage the business.

The franchiser usually requires that the franchised "product" be used or sold in a certain way. McDonald's once required that all franchisees' equipment and many supplies be obtained from McDonald's or authorized suppliers. But this type of requirement was challenged, and a federal court ruled that it must be dropped from franchising contracts. Franchisees can buy from whatever sources they wish, as long as they meet strict quality standards.

Merchandising Conglomerate

Merchandising conglomerates are corporations that combine several different retailing forms under central ownership and that share some distribution and management functions. Examples include Allied Stores, Dayton-Hudson, J. C. Penney, and F. W. Woolworth. For example, F. W. Woolworth, in addition to its variety stores, operates 28 specialty chains, including Kinney Shoe Stores, Afterthoughts (costume jewelry and handbags), Face Fantasies (budget cosmetics), Herald Square Stationers, Frame Scene, Foot Locker (sports shoes), and Kids Mart.[11] Diversified retailing is likely to increase through the 1990s.

Type of Store Cluster

Most stores today cluster together to increase their customer pulling power and to give consumers the convenience of one-stop shopping. The main types of store clusters are the central business district and the shopping center.

Central Business District

Central business districts were the main form of retail cluster until the 1950s. Every large city and town had a central business district with department stores, specialty stores, banks, and movie theaters. When people began to move to the suburbs, these central business districts, with their traffic, parking, and crime problems, began to lose business. Downtown merchants opened branches in suburban shopping centers, and the decline of the central business districts continued. Only recently have the cities joined with merchants to try to revive downtown shopping areas by building malls and underground parking. Some central business districts have made a comeback; others remain in a slow and possibly irreversible decline.

Shopping Center

A **shopping center** is a group of retail businesses planned, developed, owned, and managed as a unit. Shopping centers can be classified by the numbers and types of stores they contain and by the nature of the trade area they serve.

A *regional shopping center* is the largest and most dramatic of the shopping centers. A regional shopping center is like a mini-downtown. It contains from 40 to 100 stores and pulls customers from a wide area. Larger regional malls often have several department stores and a wide variety of specialty stores on several shopping levels. Many have added new types of retailers over the years—dentists, optometrists, health clubs, and even branch libraries. Most newer malls are enclosed to provide comfortable shopping in any weather.

A regional shopping center is like a mini-downtown.

A *community shopping center* contains 15 to 50 retail stores. The center normally contains a primary store, usually a branch of a department or variety store, and a supermarket, specialty stores, convenience goods stores, professional offices, and sometimes a bank. Most shopping centers are *neighborhood shopping centers* that contain 5 to 15 stores. They are close and convenient for consumers. They usually contain a supermarket and several service stores—a dry cleaner, self-service laundry, drugstore, barber or beauty shop, a hardware, or other stores often located in an unplanned strip.

All shopping centers combined now account for about one-third of all retail sales, but they may be reaching their saturation point. Many areas contain too many malls; sales per square foot are dropping, and vacancy rates are climbing. Some malls have gone out of business. The current trend is toward smaller malls located in medium-size and smaller cities in fast-growing areas such as the Southwest.

*N*ONSTORE RETAILING

Although most goods and services are sold through stores, nonstore retailing has been growing much faster than store retailing. Nonstore retailing now accounts for more than 14 percent of all consumer purchases, and it may account for a third of all sales by the end of the century.[12] Here we will examine three types of nonstore retailing: *direct marketing*, *direct selling*, and *automatic vending*.

Direct Marketing

Direct marketing uses various advertising media to interact directly with consumers, generally calling for the consumer to make a direct response.[13] We will now look at four major forms of direct marketing.

Direct Mail and Catalog Marketing

Direct mail marketers send single mailings that include letters, glossy ads, samples, foldouts, and other "salespeople on wings" to prospects on their mailing lists. The mailing lists are developed from customer lists or obtained from mailing-list houses that can provide lists of names fitting almost any description—the superwealthy, mobile home owners, veterinarians, pet owners, or about anything else.

A recent study showed that direct mail and catalogs accounted for 48 percent of all direct response offers that lead to orders (compared with telephone at 7 percent, circulars at 7 percent, and magazines and newspapers, each at 6 percent).[14] Direct mail is increasingly popular because it permits high target market selectivity, can be personalized, is flexible, and allows easy measurement of results. While the cost-per-thousand people reached is higher than with mass media such as television or magazines, the people reached are much better prospects. Over 35 percent of Americans have responded to direct-mail ads, and the number is growing. Direct mail has proved very successful in promoting books, magazine subscriptions, and insurance and is increasingly being used to sell novelty and gift items, clothing, gourmet foods, and industrial products. Direct mail is also used heavily by charities, which raised over $35 billion in 1986 and accounted for about 25 percent of all direct mail revenues.[15]

Mail-order catalog marketers mail catalogs to a select list of customers and make catalogs available on their premises. This approach is used by huge general merchandise mail-order houses—such as Sears, J. C. Penney, and Spiegel—carrying a full line of merchandise. But the day of the huge general merchandise catalogs may be coming to an end. Recently, the giants have been challenged by thousands

Almost 12 billion catalogs are mailed out each year; the average household receives 50 catalogs annually.

of specialty catalogs with more sharply focused audiences. These smaller catalog retailers have successfully filled highly specialized market niches.

Consumers can buy just about anything from a catalog. Over 11.8 billion copies of more than 8,500 different catalogs are mailed out annually, and the average household receives at least 50 catalogs a year.[16] Hanover House sends out 22 different catalogs selling everything from shoes to decorative lawn birds. Sharper Image sells $2,400 jet-propelled surf boards. The Banana Republic Travel and Safari Clothing Company features all you would need while hiking in the Sahara. The list of specialty catalogers is almost endless. Recently, specialty department stores such as Neiman-Marcus, Bloomingdale's, and Saks Fifth Avenue have begun sending catalogs to cultivate an upper-middle-class market for high-priced, often exotic, merchandise. Several major corporations have also developed or acquired mail-order divisions. For example, Avon now issues ten women's fashions catalogs along with catalogs for children's and men's clothes. Hershey and other food companies are investigating catalog opportunities.

Most consumers enjoy receiving catalogs and will sometimes even pay to get them. Many catalog marketers are now even selling their catalogs at book stores and magazine stands. Some companies are also experimenting with videotape catalogs. Royal Silk sells a 35-minute video catalog to its catalog customers for $5.95 and plans to market them to video stores. The tape contains a polished presentation of Royal Silk products, tells customers how to care for silk, and provides ordering information.[17]

Telemarketing
Telemarketing has become a major direct marketing tool. In 1986, marketers spent an estimated $41 billion in telephone charges to help sell their products and services.[18] Telemarketing blossomed in the late 1960s with the introduction of inward and

outward Wide Area Telephone Service (WATS). With IN WATS, marketers can use toll-free 800-numbers to receive orders from television and radio ads, direct mail, or catalogs. With OUT WATS, they can use the phone to sell directly to consumers and businesses.

During January 1982, more than 700 people dialed an 800-number every minute in response to television commercials. The average household receives 19 telephone sales calls each year and makes 16 calls to place orders. Some telemarketing systems are fully automated. For example, automatic dialing and recorded message players (ADRMPs) self-dial numbers, play a voice-activated advertising message, and take orders from interested customers on an answering-machine device or by forwarding the call to an operator. Telemarketing is used in business marketing as well as consumer marketing. For example, Raleigh Bicycles used telemarketing to reduce the amount of personal selling needed for contacting its dealers. In the first year, salesforce travel costs were reduced by 50 percent, and sales in a single quarter were up 34 percent.

Television Marketing

Television is used in two different ways to market products directly to consumers. The first is through *direct-response advertising*. Direct marketers air television spots, often 60 or 120 seconds long, that persuasively describe a product and give customers a toll-free number for ordering. Direct-response advertising works well for magazines, books, small appliances, records and tapes, collectibles, and many other products. Some successful direct-response ads run for years and become classics. Dial Media's ads for Ginsu knives ran for seven years and sold almost three million sets of knives worth over $40 million in sales; its Armourcote cookware ads generated more than twice that much in sales.[19]

Home shopping channels, another form of television direct marketing, are programs or entire channels dedicated to selling goods and services. The largest is the Home Shopping Network (HSN). With HSN, viewers tune in the Home Shopping Club, which broadcasts 24 hours a day. The program's hosts offer bargain prices on

Television marketing: The Home Shopping Network reaches more than 40 million homes.

general merchandise ranging from jewelry, lamps, collectible dolls, and clothing to power tools and consumer electronics—usually obtained by HSN at closeout and liquidation prices. The show is upbeat, with the hosts honking horns, blowing whistles, and praising viewers for their good taste. Viewers call an 800-number to order merchandise. At the other end, 400 operators handle more than 1,200 incoming lines, entering orders directly into their computer terminals. Orders are shipped within 48 hours.

Sales through this medium grew from $450 million in 1986 to $2 billion in 1987, and they are expected to reach $7.2 billion by 1992. HSN alone reaches more than 15 million cable TV homes and another 26 million UHF broadcast channel homes. More than half of all U.S. homes have access to HSN or one of a dozen other home shopping channels such as Cable Value Network, Value Club of America, Home Shopping Mall, or TelShop. Most major retailers are now looking into the home shopping industry—Sears has joined with the QVC Network to sell Sears products on a home shopping program. And K mart, J. C. Penney, and Spiegel are investigating similar arrangements. Some experts contend that TV home shopping is just a fad, but most think it is here to stay.[20]

Electronic Shopping

The major form of electronic shopping is *videotex*. Videotex is a two-way system that links consumers with the seller's computer data banks by cable or telephone lines. The videotex service makes up a computerized catalog of products offered by producers, retailers, banks, travel organizations, and others. Consumers use an ordinary television set that has a special keyboard device and is connected to the system by two-way cable. Or they hook into the system by telephone using a home computer. They sort through the catalog, compare products and prices, and place orders. A consumer wanting to buy a new compact disk player could request a list of all CD brands in the computerized catalog, compare the brands, and order one using a charge card—all without leaving home.

Videotex is still a new idea—it accounts for less than one percent of all direct marketing sales. In recent years, several large videotex systems have failed because of too few subscribers or too little use. One such system called Gateway offered in-home shopping services and much more. Through Gateway, consumers could order goods from local and national retailers; do their banking through direct links with local banks' computer centers; see the contents of the *Los Angeles Times* the evening before the paper was printed; book airline, hotel, and car rental reservations; look at the text of an entire encyclopedia; take college courses; buy tickets to concerts and sporting events; play games, quizzes, and contests; get tips on plumbing repair, first aid, physical fitness, home decorating, and hundreds of other topics; and send messages and video greeting cards to one another. Though Gateway failed, other large companies are investing in even more promising systems. IBM and Sears are jointly forming a system called Trintex, and Chemical Bank, Bank of America, Time, and AT&T are forming one called Covidea. The acceptance of such electronic systems will grow as more consumers acquire cable television and personal computers and as consumers discover the wonders of electronic shopping.[21]

Direct Selling   **Door-to-door retailing**, which started centuries ago with roving peddlers, has grown into a huge industry. More than 600 companies sell either door-to-door, office-to-office, or at home-sales parties. The pioneers in door-to-door selling are the Fuller Brush Company, vacuum cleaner companies like Electrolux, and book-selling companies like World Book and Southwestern. The image of door-to-door selling improved greatly when Avon entered the industry with its Avon representative—the homemaker's friend and beauty consultant. And Tupperware and Mary Kay Cosmetics helped to popularize home-sales parties, in which several friends and neighbors attend a party in someone's home where products are demonstrated and sold.

The advantages of door-to-door selling are consumer convenience and personal attention. But the high costs of hiring, training, paying, and motivating the salesforce result in higher prices. Though some door-to-door companies are still thriving, door-to-door selling has a somewhat uncertain future. The increase in the number of single-person and working-couple households decreases the chances of finding a buyer at home. Home-party companies are having trouble finding nonworking women who want to sell products part-time. And with the recent advances in interactive direct marketing technology, the door-to-door salesperson may well be replaced in the future by the household telephone, television, or home computer.[22]

Automatic Vending

Automatic vending is not new—in 215 B.C. Egyptians could buy sacrificial water from coin-operated devices. But this method of selling soared after World War II. Today's automatic vending uses space-age and computer technology to sell a wide variety of convenience and impulse goods—cigarettes, beverages, candy, newspapers, foods and snacks, hosiery, cosmetics, paperback books, records and tapes, T-shirts, insurance policies, and even shoeshines and fishing worms. Vending machines are found everywhere, in factories, offices, lobbies, retail stores, gasoline stations, airports, and train and bus terminals. Automatic teller machines provide bank customers with checking, savings, withdrawals, and funds-transfer services. As compared with store retailing, vending machines offer consumers 24-hour selling, self-service, and less damaged goods. But automatic vending is a more costly channel, and prices of vended goods are often 15 to 20 percent higher. Customers must also put up with aggravating machine breakdowns, out-of-stocks, and the fact that merchandise cannot be returned.

RETAILER MARKETING DECISIONS

We will now look at the major marketing decisions retailers must make about their target markets, product assortment and services, price, promotion, and place.

Target Market Decision

Retailers must first define the target market and decide how they will be positioned in the target market. The retailer's positioning guides all other marketing decisions. Product assortment, services, pricing, advertising, store decor, and other decisions must all support the retailer's position in its market segment.

Too many retailers fail to define their target markets and positions clearly. They try to have "something for everyone" and end up satisfying no market well. Even large department stores like Sears must define their major target markets so that they can design effective strategies for serving these markets. Some retailers have defined their target markets quite well. Here's a prime example:

> Leslie H. Wexner borrowed $5,000 in 1963 to create The Limited which started as a single store targeted to young, fashion conscious, moderately affluent women. All aspects of the store—clothing assortment, fixtures, music, colors, personnel—were orchestrated to match this target consumer. Wexner continued to open more stores but a decade later his original customers had aged out of the "young" group. To catch the new "youngs," he started the Limited Express. Over the years, he began or acquired other targeted store chains, including Lane Bryant, Victoria's Secrets, Lerner's, and others. The Limited now operates 2,400 stores in seven different market segments with yearly sales of $2.4 billion.

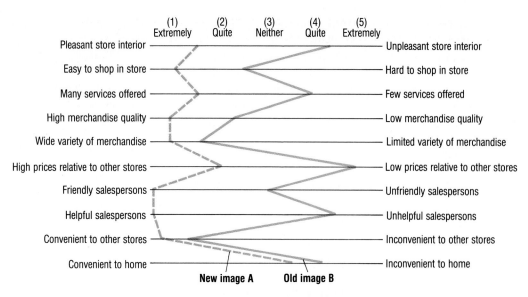

	(1) Extremely	(2) Quite	(3) Neither	(4) Quite	(5) Extremely	
Pleasant store interior						Unpleasant store interior
Easy to shop in store						Hard to shop in store
Many services offered						Few services offered
High merchandise quality						Low merchandise quality
Wide variety of merchandise						Limited variety of merchandise
High prices relative to other stores						Low prices relative to other stores
Friendly salespersons						Unfriendly salespersons
Helpful salespersons						Unhelpful salespersons
Convenient to other stores						Inconvenient to other stores
Convenient to home						Inconvenient to home

New image A　　**Old image B**

FIGURE 15-1　A comparison between the old and the new image of a store seeking to appeal to a class market

Source: Adapted from David W. Cravens, Gerald E. Hills, and Robert B. Woodruff, *Marketing Decision Making: Concepts and Strategy* (Homewood, IL: Irwin, 1976), p. 234.

A retailer should do periodic marketing research to check that the company is satisfying its target customers. Consider a store that wants to attract wealthy consumers, but whose store image is shown by the red line in Figure 15-1. The store does not currently appeal to its target market; it must change its target market or redesign itself into a "classier" store. Suppose the store now upgrades its products, services, and salespeople and raises its prices. Some time later, a second customer survey reveals the image shown by the blue line in Figure 15-1. The store has now achieved a position that matches its target market choice.

Product Assortment and Services Decision

Retailers have to decide on three major product variables: product assortment, services mix, and store atmosphere.

The retailer's *product assortment* must match what target shoppers expect. In fact, assortment becomes a key element in the competitive battle with other retailers. The retailer has to decide on product assortment *width* and *depth*. Thus a restaurant can offer a narrow and shallow assortment (small lunch counter), a narrow and deep assortment (delicatessen), a wide and shallow assortment (cafeteria), or a wide and deep assortment (large restaurant). Another product assortment element is the *quality* of the goods. The customer is interested not only in the range of choice, but also in the quality of the products.

No matter what the store's product assortment and quality level, there will always be competitors with similar assortments and quality. Thus, the retailer must search for ways to *differentiate* itself from similar competitors. It can use any of several product differentiation strategies. It can offer merchandise that no other competitor carries—its own private brands or national brands on which it holds exclusives. Thus The Limited designs most of the clothes carried by its store, and Saks gets exclusive rights to carry a well-known designer's labels. Or the retailer can feature blockbuster merchandising events—Bloomingdale's is known for running spectacular shows featuring goods from a certain country, such as India or China. Or the retailer can offer surprise merchandise, as when Loehmann's offers surprise assortments of

TABLE 15-3
Typical Retail Services

PRIMARY SERVICES		SUPPLEMENTAL SERVICES
Alterations	Baby strollers	Packaging and gift wrapping
Complaint handling	Bill payment	Product locator
Convenient store hours	Bridal registries	Restaurants or snack counters
Credit	Check cashing	Shopping consultants
Delivery	Children's play rooms	Shopping information
Fitting rooms	Demonstrations	Shows, displays, and exhibits
Installation and assembly	Layaway	Special ordering
Merchandise returns and adjustments	Lost and found	Wheelchairs
Parking	Personal shopping	
Rest rooms	Package checkrooms	
Service and repair		
Telephone ordering		

distress goods, overstocks, and closeouts. The retailer can differentiate itself by offering a highly targeted product assortment—Lane Bryant carries goods for larger women; Brookstone offers an unusual assortment of gadgets in what amounts to an adult toy store.

Retailers also must decide on the *services mix* to offer customers. The old "mom and pop" grocery stores offered home delivery, credit, and conversation, services that today's supermarkets have dropped. The services mix is one of the key tools of nonprice competition for setting one store apart from another. Table 15-3 lists some of the major services full-service retailers can offer.

The *store's atmosphere* is a third element in its product arsenal. Every store has a physical layout that makes moving around hard or easy. Every store has a "feel"; one store is dirty, another is charming, a third is plush, a fourth is somber. The store must have a planned atmosphere that suits the target market and moves

Store atmospheres: Chanel's (left) and Bergdorf Goodman (right) create very different store atmospheres to match their different target markets.

customers to buy. A bank should be quiet, solid, and peaceful, and a nightclub should be bright, loud, and vibrating. Increasingly, retailers are working to create shopping environments that match their target markets. Chains like the Banana Republic and Laura Ashley are turning their stores into theaters that transport customers into unusual, exciting shopping environments. Even conservative Sears divides the clothing areas within each store into six distinct "shops," each with its own selling environment designed to meet the tastes of individual segments.[23]

Price Decision The retailer's prices are a key positioning factor and must be decided in relation to the target market, the product and service assortment, and competition. All retailers would like to charge high markups and achieve high volumes, but usually the two do not go together. Most retailers seek either high markups on lower volume (most specialty stores) or low markups on higher volume (mass merchandisers and discount stores). Thus Bijan's on Rodeo Drive in Beverly Hills prices men's suits starting at $1,000 and shoes at $400—it sells a low volume but makes a lot of profit on each sale. At the other extreme, T. J. Maxx sells brand-name clothing at discount prices, settling for a lower margin on each sale but selling a much higher volume.

Retailers must also pay attention to pricing tactics. Most retailers will put low prices on some items to serve as traffic builders or loss leaders. They will run store-wide sales on some occasions. They will plan markdowns on slower-moving merchandise. For example, shoe retailers expect to sell 50 percent of their shoes at the normal 60 percent markup, 25 percent at a 40 percent markup, and the remaining 25 percent at cost.

Promotion Decision Retailers use the normal promotion tools—advertising, personal selling, sales promotion, and publicity—to reach consumers. They advertise in newspapers, magazines, radio, and television. The advertising may be supported by circulars and direct mail pieces. Personal selling requires careful training of salespeople in how to greet customers, meet their needs, and handle their complaints. Sales promotion may include in-store demonstrations, trading stamps, contests, and visiting celebrities. Publicity is always available to retailers who have something interesting to say.

Place Decision Retailers often say that there are three critical factors in retailing success: location, location, and location. The retailer's location is key to its ability to attract customers. And the costs of building or leasing facilities have a major impact on the retailer's profits. Thus site location decisions are among the most important the retailer makes. Small retailers may have to settle for whatever locations they can find or afford. Large retailers usually employ specialists who select locations using advanced site-location methods.[24]

*T*HE FUTURE OF RETAILING

Several trends will affect the future of retailing. The slowdown in population and economic growth means that retailers will no longer have sales and profit growth through natural expansion in current and new markets. Growth will have to come from increasing shares of current markets. But greater competition and new types of retailers will make it harder to improve market shares. Consumer demographics, life styles, and shopping patterns are changing rapidly. To be successful, retailers will have to choose target segments carefully and position themselves strongly.

Quickly rising costs will make more efficient operation and smarter buying essential to successful retailing. Thus retail technology is growing in importance as a competitive tool. Progressive retailers are using computers to produce better forecasts, control inventory costs, order electronically from suppliers, communicate between stores, and even sell to consumers within stores. They are adopting checkout scanning systems, in-store television, on-line transaction processing, and electronic funds transfer.

Many retailing innovations are partially explained by the *wheel of retailing* concept.[25] According to this concept, many new types of retailing forms begin as low-margin, low-price, low-status operations. They challenge established retailers that have become "fat" over the years by letting their costs and margins increase. The new retailers' success leads them to upgrade their facilities and offer more services. This raises their costs and forces them to increase their prices. Eventually, the new retailers become like the conventional retailers they replaced. The cycle begins again when still newer types of retailers evolve with lower costs and prices (see Marketing Highlight 15–2). The wheel of retailing concept seems to explain

MARKETING HIGHLIGHT 15–2

THE WHEEL OF RETAILING TURNS AT K MART

Over the past two decades, K mart has been the model for discount department stores and has held unswervingly to the principles of discount merchandising. But like many other discount retailers in recent years, K mart has moved away from the formula that made it the number two retailer in the country behind Sears. K mart is trading up and away from its no-frills, low-price strategy toward an upscale philosophy emphasizing quality and value rather than low prices. With this new strategy, K mart hopes to get more business from the increasing numbers of more affluent consumers, consumers who currently shop at K mart only to "cherry-pick" sales items.

To establish the new image, K mart is making gradual but sweeping changes in its merchandise assortment and store facilities. Its broadened and upgraded product assortment will include more well-known national brands and higher-quality store brands. More store space will be devoted to fashions, sporting goods, electronics, and other higher-margin goods. K mart advertising will feature fewer sales, more branded products, and more "life style" appeals.

K mart is spending a whopping $2.2 billion to modernize and upgrade its more than 2,000 stores. The plain fixtures and long rows of pipe racks are being replaced. Store space is being modularized into special departments—a Kitchen Korner, home electronics center, nutrition center, hardcover books section, and others—to provide a more pleasing shopping environment for more discriminating shoppers.

Thus, the wheel of retailing turns at K mart. The new, upgraded K mart stores will more closely resemble Sears' or Penney's stores than discount stores. The new strategy could be risky—while K mart attempts to woo more upscale consumers, other discounters will emerge and try to lure away the core of price-conscious, lower-scale consumers that made K mart so successful in the first place.

But K mart understands the wheel of retailing and has taken steps to assure that it won't be displaced at the bottom of the retailing ladder. At the same time that it is upgrading its K mart stores, the company is also moving into off-price and other new forms of discount retailing to pick up the low-end business that might be lost under the new upscale strategy. In recent years, K mart has developed or acquired a number of discount specialty chains—Designer Depot (designer label clothing at large discounts), Garment Rack (lower-quality clothing), Accent (quality gifts and housewares at discount prices), Bishop Buffets and Furr's Cafeterias (inexpensive food), Builders Square (do-it-yourself hardware), Pay Less Drug Stores, and other businesses that combine for 15 percent of total company sales. And the company is considering additional discount operations in such areas as toys, sporting goods, jewelry, and books. Rather than falling victim to the wheel of retailing, K mart appears to be using it to advantage.

Sources: See Russell Mitchell, "K mart Spruces Up the Bargain Basement," *Business Week*, September 8, 1986, pp. 45–48; Patricia Strnad, "Big Idea Links K mart, Jordache," *Advertising Age*, March 2, 1987, p. 58; and Patricia Strnad, "K mart Dangles Lure for Affluent Shoppers," *Advertising Age*, August 24, 1987. p. 12.

the initial success and later troubles of department stores, supermarkets, and discount stores and the recent success of off-price retailers.

New retail forms will continue to emerge to meet new consumer needs and new situations. But the life cycle of new retail forms is getting shorter. Department stores took about 100 years to reach the mature stage of the life cycle; more recent forms reach maturity in about 10 years. Retailers can no longer sit back with a successful formula. To remain successful, they must keep adapting.

WHOLESALING

Wholesaling includes all activities involved in selling goods and services to those buying for resale or business use. A retail bakery does wholesaling when it sells pastry to the local hotel. But we will call **wholesalers** firms engaged *primarily* in wholesaling activity.

Wholesalers differ from retailers in several ways. First, because they deal mostly with business customers rather than final consumers, wholesalers pay less attention to promotion, atmosphere, and location. Second, wholesalers usually cover larger trade areas and have larger transactions than retailers. Third, wholesalers face different legal regulations and taxes.

Wholesalers buy mostly from producers and sell mostly to retailers, industrial consumers, and other wholesalers. But why are wholesalers used at all? For example, why would a producer use wholesalers rather than selling directly to retailers or consumers? The answer is that wholesalers are often better at performing one or more of the following channel functions:

- *Selling and promoting*. Wholesalers' salesforces help manufacturers reach many small customers at a low cost. The wholesaler has more contacts and is often more trusted by the buyer than the distant manufacturer.
- *Buying and assortment building*. Wholesalers can select items and build assortments needed by their customers, thus saving the consumers much work.
- *Bulk-breaking*. Wholesalers save their customers money by buying in carload lots and breaking bulk (breaking large lots into smaller quantities).
- *Warehousing*. Wholesalers hold inventories, thereby reducing the inventory costs and risks of suppliers and customers.
- *Transportation*. Wholesalers can provide quicker delivery to buyers because they are closer than the producers.
- *Financing*. Wholesalers finance their customers by giving credit, and they finance their suppliers by ordering early and paying bills on time.
- *Risk bearing*. Wholesalers absorb risk by taking title and bearing the cost of theft, damage, spoilage, and obsolescence.
- *Market information*. Wholesalers give information to suppliers and customers about competitors, new products, and price developments.
- *Management services and advice*. Wholesalers often help retailers to train their salesclerks, improve store layouts and displays, and set up accounting and inventory control systems.

TYPES OF WHOLESALERS

Wholesalers fall into three major groups (see Table 15-4): merchant wholesalers, brokers and agents, and manufacturers' sales branches and offices. We will now look at each of these groups of wholesalers.

TABLE 15-4
Classification of
Wholesalers

MERCHANT WHOLESALERS	BROKERS AND AGENTS	MANUFACTURERS' AND RETAILERS' BRANCHES AND OFFICES
Full-service wholesalers	Brokers	Sales branches and offices
Wholesale merchants	Agents	Purchasing offices
Industrial distributors		
Limited-service wholesalers		
Cash-and-carry wholesalers		
Truck wholesalers		
Drop shippers		
Rack jobbers		
Producers' cooperatives		
Mail order wholesalers		

Merchant Wholesalers

Merchant wholesalers are independently owned businesses that take title to the products they handle. They are the largest single group of wholesalers, accounting for about 58 percent of all wholesaling. Merchant wholesalers include two broad types: full-service wholesalers and limited-service wholesalers.

Full-Service Wholesalers

Full-service wholesalers provide a full set of services such as carrying stock, using a salesforce, offering credit, making deliveries, and providing management assistance. They are either wholesale merchants or industrial distributors.

Wholesale merchants sell mostly to retailers and provide a full range of services. They vary in the width of their product line. Some carry several lines of goods to meet the needs of both general merchandise retailers and single-line retailers. Others carry one or two lines of goods in a greater depth of assortment. Examples are hardware wholesalers, drug wholesalers, and clothing wholesalers. Some specialty wholesalers carry only part of a line in great depth. Examples are health food wholesalers, seafood wholesalers, and automotive parts wholesalers. They offer customers deeper choice and greater product knowledge.

Industrial distributors are merchant wholesalers who sell to producers rather than to retailers. They provide inventory, credit, delivery, and other services. They may carry a broad range of merchandise, a general line, or a specialty line.

Limited-Service Wholesalers

Limited-service wholesalers offer fewer services to their suppliers and customers. There are several types of limited-service wholesalers.

Cash-and-carry wholesalers have a limited line of fast-moving goods, sell to small retailers for cash, and normally do not deliver. A small fish store retailer, for example, normally drives at dawn to a cash-and-carry fish wholesaler and buys several crates of fish, pays on the spot, and drives the merchandise back to the store and unloads it.

Truck wholesalers (also called truck jobbers) perform a selling and delivery function. They carry a limited line of goods (such as milk, bread, snack foods), which they sell for cash as they make their rounds of supermarkets, small groceries, hospitals, restaurants, factory cafeterias, and hotels.

Drop shippers operate in bulk industries such as coal, lumber, and heavy equipment. They do not carry inventory or handle the product. Once an order is received, they find a producer who ships the goods directly to the customer. The drop shipper takes title and risk from the time the order is accepted to the time it is delivered

A typical Fleming Companies, Inc., wholesale food distribution center. The average Fleming warehouse contains 500,000 square feet of floor space (with 30-foot high ceilings), carries 16,000 different food items, and serves 150-200 retailers within a 500-mile radius.

to the customer. Because drop shippers do not carry inventory, their costs are lower and they can pass on some savings to customers.

Rack jobbers serve grocery and drug retailers, mostly in the area of nonfood items. These retailers do not want to order and maintain displays of hundreds of nonfood items. The rack jobbers send delivery trucks to stores, and the delivery person sets up racks of toys, paperbacks, hardware items, health and beauty aids, or other items. They price the goods, keep them fresh, and set up and keep inventory records. Rack jobbers sell on consignment, which means that they retain title to the goods and bill the retailers only for the goods sold to consumers. Thus they provide such services as delivery, shelving, inventory, and financing. They do little promotion because they carry many branded items that are highly advertised.

Producers' cooperatives, owned by farmer-members, assemble farm produce to sell in local markets. Their profits are divided among members at the end of the year. They often try to improve product quality and promote a co-op brand name, such as Sun Maid raisins, Sunkist oranges, or Diamond walnuts.

Mail-order wholesalers send catalogs to retail, industrial, and institutional customers offering jewelry, cosmetics, special foods, and other small items. Their main customers are businesses in small outlying areas. They have no salesforce to call on customers. The orders are filled and sent by mail, truck, or other means.

Brokers and Agents

Brokers and agents differ from merchant wholesalers in two ways: They do not take title to goods, and they perform only a few functions. Their main function is to aid in buying and selling, and for this they earn a commission on the selling price. Like merchant wholesalers, they generally specialize by product line or customer types. They account for 11 percent of the total wholesale volume.

Brokers

A **broker** brings buyers and sellers together and assists in negotiation. Brokers are paid by the party that hired them. They do not carry inventory, get involved in financing, or assume risk. The most familiar examples are food brokers, real estate brokers, insurance brokers, and security brokers.

Agents

Agents represent buyers or sellers on a more permanent basis. There are several types. *Manufacturers' agents* (also called manufacturers' representatives) are the most numerous type. They represent two or more manufacturers of related lines. They have a formal agreement with each manufacturer covering prices, territories, order-handling procedures, delivery and warranties, and commission rates. They know each manufacturer's product line and use their wide contacts to sell the products. Manufacturers' agents are used in such lines as apparel, furniture, and electrical goods. Most manufacturers' agents are small businesses, with only a few employees who are skilled salespeople. They are hired by small producers who cannot afford to maintain their own field salesforces and by large producers who want to open new territories or sell in areas that cannot support a full-time salesperson.

Selling agents contract to sell a producer's entire output. The manufacturer either is not interested in the doing the selling or feels unqualified. The selling agent serves as a sales department and has much influence over prices, terms, and conditions of sale. The selling agent normally has no territory limits. Selling agents are found in such product areas as textiles, industrial machinery and equipment, coal and coke, chemicals, and metals.

Purchasing agents generally have a long-term relationship with buyers. They make purchases for buyers, and often receive, inspect, warehouse, and ship goods to the buyers. One type consists of *resident buyers* in major apparel markets, who look for apparel lines that can be carried by small retailers located in small cities. They know a lot and provide helpful market information to clients as well as obtain the best goods and prices available.

Commission merchants (or houses) are agents that take physical possession of products and negotiate sales. They are not normally used on a long-term basis. They are used most often in agricultural marketing by farmers who do not want to sell their own output and do not belong to cooperatives. The commission merchant would take a truckload of farm products to a central market, sell it for the best price, deduct a commission and expenses, and pay the balance to the farmer.

Manufacturers' Sales Branches and Offices

The third major type of wholesaling is that done in **manufacturers' sales branches and offices** by sellers or buyers themselves, rather than through independent wholesalers. Manufacturers' offices and sales branches account for about 31 percent of all wholesale volume. Manufacturers often set up their own sales branches and offices to improve inventory control, selling, and promotion. *Sales branches* carry inventory and are found in such industries as lumber and automotive equipment and parts. *Sales offices* do not carry inventory and are most often found in dry goods and notions industries. Many retailers set up *purchasing offices* in major market centers such as New York and Chicago. These purchasing offices perform a role similar to that of brokers or agents, but are part of the buyer's organization.

WHOLESALER MARKETING DECISIONS

Wholesalers also make decisions about target markets, product assortments and services, pricing, promotion, and place.

Target Market Decision

Wholesalers, like retailers, need to define their target markets and not try to serve everyone. They can choose a target group by size of customer (only large retailers), type of customer (convenience food stores only), need for service (customers who need credit), or other factors. Within the target group, they can identify the more profitable customers and design stronger offers and build better relationships with them. They can propose automatic reordering systems, set up management training and advising systems, or even sponsor a voluntary chain. They can discourage less profitable customers by requiring larger orders or adding charges to smaller ones.

Product Assortment and Services Decision

The wholesaler's "product" is its assortment. Wholesalers are under great pressure to carry a full line and stock enough for immediate delivery. But this can damage profits. Wholesalers today are cutting down on the number of lines they carry, choosing to carry only the more profitable ones. Wholesalers are also rethinking which services count most in building strong customer relationships and which should be dropped or charged for. The key is to find the mix of services most valued by their target customers.

Pricing Decision

Wholesalers usually mark up the cost of goods by a standard percentage, say 20 percent. Expenses may run 17 percent of the gross margin, leaving a profit margin of 3 percent. In grocery wholesaling the average profit margin is often less than 2 percent. Wholesalers are now trying new pricing approaches. They may cut their margin on some lines in order to win important new customers. They will ask suppliers for a special price break when they can turn it into an increase in the supplier's sales.

Promotion Decision

Most wholesalers are not promotion-minded. Their use of trade advertising, sales promotion, publicity, and personal selling is largely scattered and unplanned. Many are behind the times in personal selling—they still see selling as a single salesperson talking to a single customer instead of a team effort to sell, build, and service major accounts. And wholesalers also need to adopt some of the nonpersonal promotion techniques used by retailers. They need to develop an overall promotion strategy and to make greater use of supplier promotion materials and programs.

Place Decision

Wholesalers typically locate in low-rent, low-tax areas and put little money into their physical setting and offices. Their materials-handling and order-processing systems are often out of date. To meet rising costs, large and progressive wholesalers are turning to the automated warehouse and on-line ordering systems. Orders are fed from the retailer's system directly into the wholesaler's computer, and the items are picked up by mechanical devices and automatically taken to the shipping platform where they are assembled. Many wholesalers are turning to computers to carry out accounting, billing, inventory control, and forecasting. Progressive wholesalers are adapting their services to the needs of target customers and finding cost-reducing methods of doing business.

*T*RENDS IN WHOLESALING

Manufacturers always have the option to bypass wholesalers or to replace an inefficient wholesaler with a more dynamic one. Manufacturers' voice several major complaints against wholesalers. They often complain that wholesalers charge too much for their services but do not aggressively promote the manufacturer's product line, acting more like order takers. Or they do not carry enough inventory and therefore fail to fill customers' orders fast enough. Or they do not supply the manufacturer with up-to-date market and competitive information.[26]

Progressive wholesalers, on the other hand, change their ways to meet the needs of their suppliers and target customers. They recognize that in the long run their only reason for existence comes from increasing the efficiency and effectiveness of the entire marketing channel. To achieve this aim they must constantly improve their services and reduce their costs.

Foremost-McKesson, a large drug wholesaler, provides an example of progressive wholesaling. To survive, it had to remain more cost effective than manufacturers' sales branches. To do this, the company automated 72 of its warehouses, set up direct computer links with 32 drug manufacturers, designed a computerized accounts-receivable program for pharmacists, and provided drug stores with computer terminals for ordering inventories. Thus Foremost-McKesson delivered better value to both manufacturers and customers.

One study predicts several developments in the wholesaling industry.[27] Wholesaling companies will grow larger, primarily through acquisition, merger, and geographic expansion. Geographic expansion will require distributors to learn how to compete effectively over wider and more diverse areas. Wholesalers will be helped in this by the increased use of computerized and automated systems; by 1990, over three-fourths of the wholesalers will use on-line order systems.

The distinction between large retailers and large wholesalers continues to blur. Many retailers now operate formats such as wholesale clubs and hypermarkets that perform many wholesale functions. In return, many large wholesalers are setting

Drug wholesaler Foremost-McKesson improved efficiency by setting up direct computer links with manufacturers and retail pharmacies.

up their own retailing operations. Super Valu, Fleming, and Wettrau, all leading wholesalers, now operate their own retail outlets.

Wholesalers will continue to increase the services they provide to retailers— retail pricing, co-op advertising, marketing and management information reports, accounting services, and others. Rising costs on the one hand and the demand for increased services on the other will put the squeeze on wholesaler profits. Wholesalers who do not find efficient ways to deliver value to their customers will soon drop by the wayside.

■ SUMMARY

Retailing and wholesaling consist of many organizations bringing goods and services from the point of production to the point of use. Retailing includes all the activities involved in selling goods or services directly to final consumers for their personal, nonbusiness use. Retailers can be classified as store retailers and nonstore retailers. Store retailers can be further classified by the amount of service they provide (self-service, limited service, or full service); product line sold (specialty stores, department stores, supermarkets, convenience stores, superstores, combination stores, hypermarkets, and service businesses); relative prices (discount stores, off-price retailers, and catalog showrooms); control of outlets (corporate chains, voluntary chains and retailer cooperatives, consumer cooperatives, franchise organizations, and merchandising conglomerates); and type of store cluster (central business districts and shopping centers).

Nonstore retailing is growing faster than store retailing. It consists of direct marketing (direct mail and catalog retailing, telemarketing, television marketing, and electronic shopping), door-to-door selling, and automatic vending.

Retailers make decisions on their target market, product assortment and services, pricing, promotion, and place. In the future, new types of retailers will emerge and retail competition will grow. More efficient operation and smarter buying will be essential to retailer success. Retailers will need to choose target segments carefully and position themselves strongly.

Wholesaling includes all the activities involved in selling goods or services to those who are buying for the purpose of resale or for business use. Wholesalers perform many functions, including selling and promoting, buying and assortment building, bulk-breaking, warehousing, transporting, financing, risk bearing, supplying market information, and providing management services and advice. Wholesalers fall into three groups. Merchant wholesalers take possession of the goods. They include full-service wholesalers (wholesale merchants, industrial distributors) and limited-service wholesalers (cash-and-carry wholesalers, truck wholesalers, drop shippers, rack jobbers, producers' cooperatives, and mail-order wholesalers). Agents and brokers do not take possession of the goods but are paid a commission for aiding buying and selling. Manufacturers' branches and offices are wholesaling operations conducted by nonwholesalers to bypass the wholesalers. Wholesaling is holding its own in the economy. Progressive wholesalers are adapting their services to the needs of target customers and are seeking cost-reducing methods of doing business.

■ QUESTIONS FOR DISCUSSION

1. Quality of service is becoming more important to many consumers than such factors as price or convenience. If this trend continues, what impact will it have on full-service retailers? Will it affect self-service and limited-service retailers? Why or why not?

2. Compare the length and breadth of the product assortments of specialty stores, convenience stores, supermarkets, and "category killers." Which would do more to increase a convenience store's sales—an increase in length or an increase in breadth? What effect would an increase in length or breadth have on the profits of a 7-Eleven store?

3. Off-price retailers provide tough price competition to other retailers. Will large retailers' growing power in channels of distribution affect manufacturers' willingness to sell to off-price retailers at below-regular wholesale rates? What policy should Procter & Gamble have toward selling to off-price retailers? Should Levi Strauss have the same policy?

4. Postal rate hikes make it more expensive to send consumers direct mail, catalogs, and purchased products. What effects would you expect a rate hike to have on direct mail and catalog marketing?

5. In two of its San Diego outlets, Montgomery Ward opened "Law Stores" that offered customers one-shot legal consultations for only $10. These stores connected customers with lawyers at a central office, who answered questions over the telephone. Discuss the retailer marketing decisions Montgomery Ward made for the Law Store.

6. Which retailing innovations can be explained by the wheel of retailing concept? Which innovations cannot be explained by this concept? Do you think retailing operations will continue to evolve as described by the wheel of retailing?

7. A typical "country store" in a farming community sells a variety of food and nonfood items—staples, hardware, snacks, and so on. What kinds of wholesalers do the owners of such stores use to obtain the items they sell? Are these the same suppliers that a supermarket uses?

8. What advantages would a manufacturers' agent offer to a small producer of lawn and garden tools? What advantages would a selling agent offer? What factors would determine which type of agent the producer would choose?

9. Are there any fundamental differences between retailers, wholesalers, and manufacturers in the types of marketing decisions they make? Give examples of the similarities or differences in the marketing decisions made by the three groups.

10. Why has the promotion area of marketing strategy traditionally been weak for wholesalers? How can wholesalers use promotion to improve their competitive positions?

11. The distinction between large retailers and large wholesalers is becoming blurred. Which strategy do you think will be more common: retailers dealing directly with manufacturers rather than through wholesalers, or wholesalers setting up their own retailing operations to sell to consumers? What factors will contribute to these trends?

■ KEY TERMS

Agent   A wholesaler who represents buyers or sellers on a more permanent basis, performs only a few functions, and does not take title to goods.

Automatic vending   Selling through vending machines.

Broker   A wholesaler who does not take title to goods and whose function is to bring buyers and sellers together and assist in negotiation.

Catalog showroom   A retail operation that sells a wide selection of high-markup, fast-moving, brand-name goods at discount prices.

Chain stores   Two or more outlets that are commonly owned and controlled, have central buying and merchandising, and sell similar lines of merchandise.

Consumer cooperative   A retail firm that is owned by its customers.

Convenience store   A small store, located near a residential area, open long hours seven days a week, and carrying a limited line of high-turnover convenience goods.

Department store   A retail organization that carries a wide variety of product lines—typically clothing, home furnishings, and household goods; each line is operated as a separate department managed by specialist buyers or merchandisers.

Direct marketing   Using various advertising media to interact directly with consumers, generally calling for the consumer to make a direct response.

Discount store   A retail institution that sells standard merchandise at lower prices by accepting lower margins and selling higher volume.

Door-to-door retailing   Selling door-to-door, office-to-office, or at home sales parties.

Franchise   A contractual association between a manufacturer, wholesaler, or service organization (a franchiser) and independent businesspeople (franchisees) who buy the right to own and operate one or more units in the franchise system.

Manufacturers' sales branches and offices   The wholesaling operations of the sellers or buyers who do their own wholesaling rather than use independent wholesalers.

Merchandising conglomerates   Corporations that combine several different retailing forms under central ownership and that share some distribution and management functions.

Merchant wholesaler   An independently owned business that takes title to the products it handles.

Off-price retailers   Retailers who buy at less than regular wholesale prices and sell at less than retail, usually carrying a changing and unstable collection of higher quality merchandise, often leftover goods, overruns, and irregulars obtained from manufacturers at reduced prices. They include factory outlets, independents, and warehouse clubs.

Retailers   Businesses whose sales come *primarily* from retailing.

Retailing   All activities involved in selling goods or services directly to final consumers for their personal, nonbusiness use.

Shopping center   A group of retail businesses planned, developed, owned, and managed as a unit.

Specialty store   A retail outlet that carries a narrow product line with a deep assortment within that line.

Supermarkets   Large, low-cost, low-margin, high-volume, self-service stores that carry a wide variety of food, laundry, and household products.

Superstore   A store almost twice the size of a regular supermarket that carries a large assortment of routinely purchased food and nonfood items, and offers such services as laundry, dry cleaning, shoe repair, check cashing, bill paying, and bargain lunch counters.

Wholesalers   Firms engaged *primarily* in wholesaling activity.

Wholesaling   All activities involved in selling goods and services to those buying for resale or business use.

■ REFERENCES

1. The quote is from Steve Weiner, "With Big Selection and Low Prices, 'Category Killer' Stores Are a Hit," *The Wall Street Journal*, June 17, 1986, p. 33. Also see Eleanor Johnson Tracy, "Shopping Swedish-Style Comes to the U.S.," *Fortune*, January 20, 1986, p. 63; Carolyn Pfaff, "IKEA: The Supermarket of Furniture Stores," *Adweek*, May 5, 1986, pp. MM26–28; and Bill Kelley, "The New Wave from Europe," *Sales & Marketing Management*, November 1987, pp. 45–50.

2. For more on department stores, see Arthur Bragg, "Will Department Stores Survive?" *Sales and Marketing Management*, April 1986, pp. 60–64; and Anthony Ramirez, "Department Stores Shape Up," *Fortune*, September 1, 1986, pp. 50–52.

3. Julie Liesse Erickson, "Supermarket Chains Work to Fill Tall Order," *Advertising Age*, April 28, 1986, pp. S1–S2.

4. Denise Frenner, "From Piano to Sushi Bars, Grocers Jazz Up Service," *Advertising Age*, May 4, 1987, p. S1.

5. See H. R. Janes, "Reaching Out for the Shopper: Retail Formats are Changing," *The Nielsen Researcher*, Number 3, 1985, p. 9.

6. See Mary McCabe English, "Competition Gains Ground," *Advertising Age*, April 18, 1985, p. 17; and Cynthia Valentino, "In a Fragmented Market, Grocers Cover Niches," *Advertising Age*, May 4, 1987, p. S8.

7. See Lois Therrien and Amy Dunkin, "The Wholesale Success of Factory Outlet Malls," *Business Week*, February 3, 1986, pp. 92–94.

8. Amy Dunkin, Todd Mason, Lois Therrien, and Teresa Carson, "Boom Times in a Bargain Hunter's Paradise," *Business Week*, March 11, 1985, p. 116. Also see Bill Saporito, "The Mad Rush to Join the Warehouse Club," *Fortune*, January 6, 1986, pp. 59–61.

9. See Jack G. Kaikati, "Don't Discount Off-Price Retailers," *Harvard Business Review*, May–June 1985, pp. 85–92; and "Off-Pricers Grab Growing Retail Market Share," *Marketing News*, March 13, 1987, pp. 9, 14.

10. See Kimberly Carpenter, "Catalog Showrooms Revamp to Keep Their Identity," *Business Week*, June 10, 1985, pp. 117, 120.

11. See Amy Dunkin, "How They're Knocking the Rust Off Two Old Chains," *Business Week*, September 8, 1986, pp. 44–48.

12. See Richard Green, "A Boutique in Your Living Room," *Forbes*, May 7, 1984, pp. 86–94.

13. For more detail, see "Direct Marketing—What Is It?" *Direct Marketing*, August 1988, p. 30.

14. See Eileen Norris, "Alternative Media Try to Get Their Feet in the Door," *Advertising Age*, October 17, 1985, p. 15.

15. Arnold Fishman, "The 1986 Mail Order Guide," *Direct Marketing*, July 1987, p. 40.

16. Janice Steinberg, "Cacophony of Catalogs Fill all Niches," *Advertising Age*, October 26, 1987, p. S2.

17. See Elaine Santoro, "Royal Silk Shines," *Direct Marketing*, April 1987, p. 53; and "Direct Marketing: Emerging Technologies on the Horizon, *Advertising Age*, January 18, 1988, p. S-1.

18. Rudy Oetting, "Telephone Marketing: Where We've Been and Where We Should Be Going," *Direct Marketing*, February 1987, p. 98.

19. Jim Auchmute, "But Wait There's More!" *Advertising Age*, October 17, 1985, p. 18.

20. See Mark Ivey, Mary J. Pitzer, Kenneth Drayfack, and Mark N. Vamos, "Home Shopping: Is It a Revolution in Retailing or Just a Fad?" *Business Week*, December 15, 1986, pp. 62–69; Arthur Bragg, "TV's Shopping Shows: Your Next Move?" *Sales & Marketing Management*, October 1987, pp. 85–89; and Mary J. Pitzer, "A Bargain Basement Where the TV Reception Is Great," *Business Week*, May 30, 1988, p. 79.

21. See Catherine L. Harris, Anne R. Field, Scott Ticer, and Scott Scredon, "Two Videotex Heavyweights Quit—$80 Million Lighter," *Business Week*, March 31, 1986, pp. 31–32; Cleveland Horton, "Big Advertisers Link to Videotex Venture," *Advertising Age*, June 15, 1987, p. 72; and Laura Loro, "Videotex Ventures," *Advertising Age*, May 9, 1988, p. 78S.

22. See Bill Saporito, "A Door-to-Door Bell Ringer," *Fortune*, December 10, 1984, pp. 83–88.

23. See Jennet Conant, Janet Huck, and Maggie Malone, "Beautiful Ways to Shop," *Newsweek*, November 10, 1986, pp. 88–90; and Michael Oneal, "Can Sears Get Sexier But Keep the Common Touch?" *Business Week*, July 6, 1987, pp. 93–96.

24. For more on retail site location, see Lewis A. Spaulding, "Beating the Bushes for New Store Locations," *Stores*, October 1980, pp. 30–35; R. L. Davies and D. S. Rogers, eds., *Store Location and Store Assessment Research* (New York: John Wiley & Sons, 1984); and Avijit Ghosh and C. Samuel Craig, "An Approach to Determining Optimal Locations for New Services," *Journal of Marketing Research*, November 1986, pp. 354–62.

25. See Malcolm P. McNair, "Significant Trends and Developments in the Postwar Period," in *Competitive Distribution in a Free, High-Level Economy and Its Implications for the University*, A. B. Smith, ed. (Pittsburgh: University of Pittsburgh Press, 1958), pp. 1–25; and Malcolm P. McNair and Eleanor G. May, "The Next Revolution of the Retailing Wheel," *Harvard Business Review*, September–October 1978, pp. 81–91.

26. See James A. Narus and James C. Anderson, "Contributing as a Distributor to Partnerships with Manufacturers," *Business Horizons*, September–October, 1987.

27. See Arthur Andersen & Co., *Future Trends in Wholesale Distribution: A Time of Opportunity* (Washington, D.C.: Distribution Research and Education Foundation, 1982), pp. 96–101. Also see Madhav Kacker, "Wholesaling Ignored Despite Modernization," *Marketing News*, February 14, 1986, p. 35.

CASE 12

HOLLY FARMS

Holly Farms Corporation thought it had created the Cadillac of poultry with its roasted chicken.

The fully cooked bird seemed just the ticket for today's busy consumers: a modern, more convenient alternative to raw chicken. It scored big in a year of test marketing.

The company began phasing in national distribution of the product last fall. But it fared so dismally that the planned expansion into more markets was halted so Holly Farms could reconsider its marketing strategy.

One analyst, Bonnie Rivers of Salomon Brothers, Inc., cites the blunder as a major reason she recently slashed her estimate for Holly Farms' profit for the year ending May 31 by 22%, to $2.25 a share from $2.90. Higher feed and persistently low chicken prices also contributed to the lower profit projection, she says. In fiscal 1987, the Memphis, Tennessee-based poultry and food concern earned $71.7 million, or $4.31 a share, on revenue of $1.42 billion.

"Losing a Lot of Business"

Company executives acknowledge that the roasted-chicken product will hurt fiscal 1988 earnings, but they won't make any projections. "We're just losing a lot of business," says John Creel, Holly Farms' senior director of sales and marketing. Grocers are buying far less of the product than Holly Farms had hoped, he says, because they believe it doesn't last long enough on the shelf. Until this problem is solved, Holly Farms decided not to expand distribution of its roasted chicken, now available in about 50% of the nationwide market.

Holly Farms' experience is a classic example of how a food company can stumble in launching a product. While the extensive test marketing identified strong consumer support for the product—22% of Atlanta women surveyed said they had tried it, and of those, 90% said they would buy it again—the company failed to detect the concerns and resistance of its front-line customer, the grocer.

Several grocers concur that the problem isn't with the roasted chicken itself. Ray Heatherington, meat merchandising manager for Safeway Stores, Inc.'s Northern California division, calls the product—which comes in Cajun, barbecue, and original flavors—"outstanding." But his stores dropped it after several weeks, because of the short shelf life.

Holly Farms says the chicken's quality lasts for a good 18 days. So to be safe, it marks the last sale date as 14 days after the chicken is roasted. But it can take as long as nine days to get the chicken to stores from the North Carolina plant, on which Holly Farms spent $20 million just for handling the roasted-chicken product. That doesn't give grocers much lead time. To avoid being stuck with an outdated backlog, many are waiting until they run out before reordering.

In the case of raw chicken, shelf life isn't a factor because the product's high volume means it is sold in the first few days after delivery and grocers know from experience how much to stock.

"A Hard Sell"

A general suspicion of new products also has probably hurt the effort. "It's a hard sell to get into the supermarket, particularly if you've got a new product that the consumers and retailers haven't seen before," says Joe Scheringer, an editor at *Grocery Marketing* magazine. The meat department is probably the most resistant to change, he adds.

Some competitors believe Holly Farms didn't do enough preliminary groundwork with retailers. Holly Farms acknowledges it probably didn't go far enough to tailor its marketing program to each supermarket chain or spend sufficient time educating meat managers.

But it plans to mend fences soon. Hoping to lengthen the shelf life by five to 10 days, Holly Farms is developing a new system to pack chickens. To shorten delivery time, the company is considering giving the product its own distribution system, instead of delivering it along with raw poultry.

Holly Farms also plans to shift a hefty portion of its marketing budget out of television and radio and into the grocery store in the form of promotions, coupons, consumer demonstrations, and contests for meat managers. Nearly two-thirds of Holly Farms' roughly $14 million in a half year's marketing expenditures for the product went to media advertising; that proportion is being lowered to about one-half, the company said.

High Hopes for a Blockbuster

Holly Farms still believes the roasted-chicken product will be a blockbuster. So does Salomon Brothers' Ms. Rivers, who says, "I definitely agree with what they're doing and why they're doing it."

At least one competitor is reserving judgment: Tyson Foods, Inc., of Springdale, Arkansas, which is test marketing a similar chicken product in Indianapolis, says it has no immediate plans to broaden distribution, in part because of Holly Farms' experience.

1. Identify and briefly discuss the changes needed in Holly Farms' marketing strategy for roasted chicken.

2. What could Holly Farms have done prior to introducing roasted chicken to avoid its marketing blunder?

3. What lesson can we learn from Holly Farms about the relationship between test market results and marketing success or failure?

Source: Arthur Buckler, "Holly Farms' Marketing Error: The Chicken That Laid An Egg," *The Wall Street Journal*, February 9, 1988. Reprinted by permission of *The Wall Street Journal*, © Dow Jones & Company, Inc., 1988. All rights reserved.

CASE 13

COMP-U-CARD INTERNATIONAL

Comp-U-Card was acquired in 1976 by Walter A. Forbes, with the thought that consumers would soon be shopping from their living rooms, using TV sets tied to two-way cable systems to examine merchandise and order it from factories. The idea was to make Comp-U-Card the next Sears by hooking into the system a central computer that would hold all sorts of items and handle ordering and billing automatically. But most consumers lacked the necessary equipment and even those with the equipment showed little inclination to use it. The conversion of people to electronic shopping is taking longer than originally expected. Comp-U-Card now offers Comp-U-Store, a much less sophisticated approach. The company lost almost $14 million in its first six years before showing a profit of $31,000, but it is said to be the largest shopping club for bargain hunters in the country.

The Comp-U-Store service currently being promoted by Comp-U-Card is described in the following excerpts from promotional material, with brand names omitted.

Introducing the Electronic Shopping Mall

Let me show you how easy it is to shop the Comp-U-Store way. Suppose you want to shop for a XXX VCR Model #2700. Here's how you do it:

You call Comp-U-Store's toll-free number, anytime between 8 A.M. and 11 P.M. E.S.T., Monday-Friday, 9 A.M.–7 P.M. Saturdays; and 12 A.M.–5 P.M. Sundays.

Tell your shopping consultant you'd like a price quote on a XXX Video Cassette Recorder Model #2700.

You will be quoted the lowest available price (Comp-U-Store's prices are updated every day). And that's the total cost, delivered to your home. There's nothing extra to pay.

You can charge the item to your new SUPER CARD over the phone (remember, your SUPER CARD carries an instant line of credit).

Or you can just shop. You don't have to buy from Comp-U-Store if you don't want to. But you still save time and money by asking Comp-U-Store for the latest, and the lowest, prices from all over the country.

Just think of Comp-U-Store as your own electronic shopping mall: where your fingers do the walking!

Here's the Secret of Comp-U-Store's Low Prices

Comp-U-Store is not like a regular store. They carry no stock (the suppliers do that) so there is no money tied up in inventory. Nor do they have retail expenses like high-rent locations or expensive advertising campaigns.

Because Comp-U-Store gives you a direct link to suppliers, you typically may save up to 40% (sometimes more!) off the manufacturer's suggested list price. (That includes delivery. Remember, Comp-U-Store's price is the TOTAL price—delivered to your home.)

Compare that to some retail markups of 100%!

With Comp-U-Store It's as if You're the Only Person in the Store

Call Comp-U-Store and you talk one-on-one with a shopping consultant, committed to your total satisfaction. There is no other customer to push ahead of you. Instead you have your consultant's full attention . . . to give you prices . . . to arrange delivery to your home. Or, if you prefer, directly to the homes of your friends or business associates.

For an annual membership fee of $25 people get access to a service that lists some 60,000 brand-name products that may be ordered, paid for by credit card, and delivered to their door, usually by United Parcel Service. The company now has about 700,000 members who bought $20 million of merchandise in a recent year. Orders are expected to double in the near future.

The recent rapid growth of Comp-U-Store is attributed to the heavy promotional efforts of the Super Visa Credit Card sponsor, Bank One (based in Columbus, Ohio), and Comp-U-Store itself. Direct mailings offering the service, along with free Visa cards, have been sent to more than 22 million middle-class households.

Comp-U-Card's management is confident that electronic shopping is imminent. They believe that people are value conscious and don't like to go shopping nearly as much as retailers think. They have been testing this idea by putting shopping machines (kiosks equipped with videodisc players) in dime stores and drugstores in the Midwest and Southeast, where customers can punch up demonstrations of merchandise they want and use the Comp-U-Card service to check prices and place orders.

R. R. Donnelly & Sons, the largest commercial printer in the United States, is marketing the Electronistore to retailers for in-store use. In the Electronistore, which is a computer-shopping terminal or an electronic kiosk, products are displayed in color and information is provided through a touch-control system. Payment is made by credit card and the merchandise is shipped to an address designated by the customer. Retailers see these shopping machines as an opportunity to cut costs and as an intermediate step in the development of electronic shopping through home terminals.

1. Discuss the pros and cons of electronic shopping from the perspective of the consumer, the retailer, and the manufacturer.

2. Why has electronic shopping not become popular as quickly as Walter Forbes predicted?

3. What channel functions does Comp-U-Store perform? What channel functions does it not perform?

4. Is Comp-U-Store a retailer, a wholesaler, or both?

5. Describe the target market for Comp-U-Store. What people are most likely to use it? What people are least likely to use it?

6. Are some types of products more suitable than others for electronic shopping? Discuss.

16 *Promoting Products: Communication and Promotion Strategy*

MOST Quaker Oats brands have become staples in American pantries. Quaker dominates the hot cereal market with a whopping 67 percent share, and its Aunt Jemima brand is tops in frozen breakfast products and

pancake mixes. Quaker captures 25 percent of the huge pet food market (Gravy Train, Gainesburgers, Cycle, Ken-L Ration, Kibbles 'n Bits). And it's the number four ready-to-eat cereal producer (Cap'n Crunch, Life, Oh!s, 100% Natural). Other leading Quaker brands include Gatorade, Van Camp's Pork and Beans, Granola Bars, and Rice-A-Roni. In all, brands with leading market shares account for over 60 percent of Quaker's nearly $4 billion in yearly sales.

A company the size of Quaker has lots to say to its many publics and several promotion tools with which to communicate. Hundreds of Quaker employees work in advertising, personal selling, sales promotion, and publicity units around the company. A half dozen large advertising and public relations agencies aim carefully planned communications to consumers, retailers, the media, stockholders, employees, and other publics.

As consumers we know most about Quaker's

advertising—Quaker bombards us each year with almost $250 million worth of advertising, telling us about its brands and persuading us to buy them. Quaker also spends heavily on consumer sales promotions such as coupons, premiums, and sweepstakes to coax us further. You may remember the "Treasure Hunt" promotion in which Quaker gave away $5 million in silver and gold coins randomly inserted in Ken-L Ration packages. Or the "Where's the Cap'n?" promotion—Quaker removed the picture of Cap'n Horatio Crunch from the front of its cereal boxes, then provided clues to his location on the back. Consumers who used the clues to find the Cap'n could win cash prizes. The 14-week promotion cost Quaker $18 million but increased sales by 50 percent. Consumer advertising and sales promotions work directly to create consumer demand, and this demand "pulls" Quaker products through the channel.

But consumer advertising and sales promotions

account for only a small portion of Quaker's total promotion mix. The company spends many times as much on behind-the-scenes promotion activities that "push" its products toward consumers. Personal selling and trade promotions are major weapons in Quaker's battle for retailer support. The main objective is shelf space in over 300,000 supermarkets, convenience stores, and corner grocers across the country. Quaker's army of salespeople court retailers with strong service, trade allowances, attractive displays, and other trade promotions. They urge retailers to give Quaker products more and better shelf space and to run ads featuring Quaker brands. These "push-promotion" activities work closely with "pull-promotion" efforts to build sales and market share. The pull activities persuade consumers to look for Quaker brands; the push activities assure that Quaker products are available, easy to find, and effectively merchandised when consumers start looking.

In addition to advertising, sales promotion, and personal selling, Quaker communicates through publicity and public relations. The company's publicity department and public relations agency place newsworthy information about Quaker and its products in the news media. They prepare annual reports to communicate with investor and financial publics and hold press conferences to communicate with the media publics. Quaker sponsors many public relations activities to promote the company as a good citizen. For example, the Quaker Oats Foundation donates millions of dollars in cash and products each year to worthy causes, matches employee donations to non-profit organizations, donates food to needy people, and supports a network of centers providing therapy for families with handicapped children.

Quaker owes much of its success to its quality products which appeal strongly to millions of consumers around the world. But success also depends on Quaker's skill in telling its publics about the company and its products. All of Quaker's promotion tools—advertising, personal selling, sales promotion, and public relations—must blend harmoniously into an effective communication program to tell the Quaker story.[1]

Chapter Objectives   *After reading this chapter, you should be able to:*

1. Name and define the four tools of the promotion mix.
2. Discuss the elements of the marketing communication process.
3. Explain the methods for setting the promotion budget.
4. Discuss the factors that affect the design of the promotion mix.

MODERN marketing calls for more than developing a good product, pricing it attractively, and making it available to target customers. Companies must also communicate with their customers. What is communicated, however, should not be left to chance.

To communicate well, companies hire advertising agencies to develop effective ads; sales promotion specialists to design sales incentive programs; and public relations firms to develop the corporate image. They train their salespeople to be friendly, helpful, and persuasive. For most companies the question is not whether to communicate, but how much to spend and in what ways.

A modern company manages a complex marketing communications system (see Figure 16-1). The company communicates with its middlemen, consumers, and various publics. Its middlemen communicate with their consumers and publics. Consumers have word-of-mouth communication with each other and with other publics. Meanwhile each group provides feedback (dotted lines) to every other group.

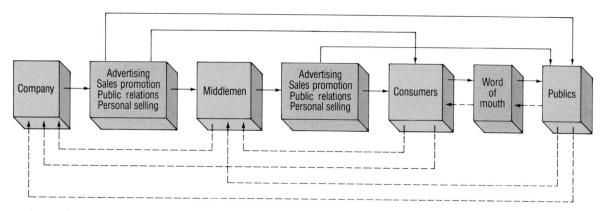

FIGURE 16-1 The marketing communications system

The marketing communications mix (also called the promotion mix) consists of four major tools:

Advertising: Any paid form of nonpersonal presentation and promotion of ideas, goods, or services by an identified sponsor.

Sales promotion: Short-term incentives to encourage purchase or sales of a product or service.

Public relations: Building good relations with the company's various publics by obtaining favorable publicity, building up a good "corporate image," and handling or heading off unfavorable rumors, stories, and events.

Personal selling: Oral presentation in a conversation with one or more prospective purchasers for the purpose of making sales.[2]

Within the categories are specific tools such as sales presentations, point-of-purchase displays, specialty advertising, trade shows, fairs, demonstrations, catalogs, literature, press kits, posters, contests, premiums, coupons, and trading stamps. At the same time, communication goes beyond these specific tools. The product's design, its price, the package shape and color, and the salesperson's manner all communicate something to buyers. The whole marketing mix, not just the promotion mix, must be coordinated for greatest communication impact.

This chapter looks at two questions: What are the major steps in developing effective marketing communication? How should the promotion budget and mix be determined? Chapter 17 will look at mass communication tools—advertising, sales promotion, and public relations. Chapter 18 will look at the salesforce as a communication and promotion tool.

STEPS IN DEVELOPING EFFECTIVE COMMUNICATION

Marketers need to understand how communication works. Communication involves the nine elements shown in Figure 16-2. Two elements are the major parties in a communication—*sender* and *receiver*. Another two are the major communication tools—*message* and *media*. Four are major communication functions—*encoding*,

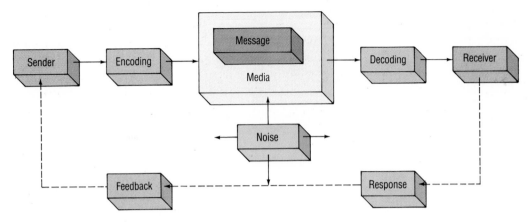

FIGURE 16-2   Elements in the communication process

decoding, response, and *feedback.* The last element is *noise* in the system. These elements are defined below and applied to a McDonald's television ad:

- *Sender*: The party sending the message to another party—McDonald's.
- *Encoding*: The process of putting thought into symbolic form—McDonald's advertising agency assembles words and illustrations into an advertisement that will convey the intended message.
- *Message*: The set of symbols that the sender transmits—the actual McDonald's advertisement.
- *Media*: The communication channels through which the message moves from sender to receiver—in this case, television and the specific television programs McDonald's selects.
- *Decoding*: The process by which the receiver assigns meaning to the symbols encoded by the sender—a consumer watches the ad and interprets the words and illustrations it contains.
- *Receiver*: The party receiving the message sent by another party—the consumer who watches the McDonald's ad.
- *Response*: The reactions of the receiver after being exposed to the message—any of hundreds of other possible responses, such as the consumer likes McDonald's better, is more likely to eat at McDonald's next time he or she eats fast food, or does nothing.
- *Feedback*: The part of the receiver's response communicated back to the sender—McDonald's research shows that consumers like and remember the ad, consumers write or call McDonald's praising or criticizing the ad or McDonald's products, and others.
- *Noise*: The unplanned static or distortion during the communication process that results in the receiver's getting a different message than the sender sent—for example, the consumer is distracted by family members while watching the ad or has poor TV reception.

The model points out the key factors in good communication. McDonald's must know what audiences it wants to reach and what responses it wants consumers to make. It must be good at creating messages that take into account how the target audience interprets messages. It must send the message through media that reach the target audience. And it must develop feedback channels in order to know the audience's response to the message.

Thus the marketing communicator must take the following steps: (1) identify the target audience, (2) determine the response sought, (3) choose a message, (4) choose the media, (5) select the message source, and (6) collect feedback.

Identifying the Target Audience

A marketing communicator must start with a clear target audience in mind. The audience may be potential buyers, current users, deciders, or influencers; it may be individuals, groups, special publics, or the general public. The target audience will heavily affect the communicator's decisions on *what* will be said, *how* it will be said, *when* it will be said, *where* it will be said, and *who* is to say it.

Determining the Response Sought

Once the target audience has been defined, the marketing communicator must decide what response is sought. Of course, the final response desired in most cases is purchase. But purchase is the result of a long process of consumer decision making. The marketing communicator needs to know where the target audience now stands and to what state it needs to be moved.

The target audience may be in any of six **buyer readiness states**—awareness, knowledge, liking, preference, conviction, or purchase. These states are shown in Figure 16-3 and discussed below.

Awareness

The communicator must first know how aware the target audience is of the product or organization. The audience may be unaware of it, know only its name, or know one or a few things about it. If most of the target audience is unaware, the communicator tries to build awareness, perhaps just name recognition. This can be done with simple messages repeating the name. Even then, building awareness takes time. Suppose a small Iowa college called Pottsville seeks applicants from Nebraska but has no name recognition in Nebraska. And suppose there are 30,000 high school seniors in Nebraska who may potentially be interested in Pottsville College. The college might set the objective of making 70 percent of these students aware of Pottsville's name within one year.

Knowledge

The target audience might have company or product awareness, but not know much more. Pottsville may want its target audience to know that it is a private four-year college in eastern Iowa with excellent programs in English and the language arts. Pottsville College needs to learn how many people in the target audience have little, some, and much knowledge about Pottsville. The college may decide to build up product knowledge as its first communication objective.

Liking

If the target audience knows about the product, how do audience members feel about it? We can develop a scale covering degrees of liking—dislike very much, dislike somewhat, indifferent, like somewhat, like very much. If the audience looks unfavorably on Pottsville College, the communicator has to find out why and then develop a communications campaign to build up favorable feelings. If the unfavorable view is based on real problems of the college, then communications will not do the job. Pottsville would have to fix its problems and then communicate its quality. Good public relations call for "good deeds followed by good words."

FIGURE 16-3
Buyer readiness states

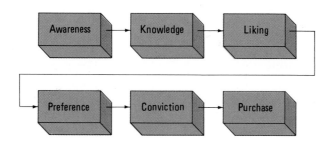

Preference

The target audience might like the product, but not prefer it to others. In this case, the communicator will try to build consumer preference. The communicator will promote the product's quality, value, performance, and other features. The communicator can check on the campaign's success by measuring the audience's preferences again after the campaign. If Pottsville College finds that many high school seniors like Pottsville but choose to attend other colleges, it will have to identify areas where its offerings are better than those of competing colleges. Then it must promote these advantages to build preference among prospective students.

Conviction

A target audience might prefer the product but not develop a conviction about buying it. Thus some high school seniors may prefer Pottsville, but may not be sure they want to go to college. The communicator's job is to build conviction that going to college is the right thing to do.

Purchase

Some members of the target audience might have conviction, but not quite get around to making the purchase. They may wait for more information or plan to act later. The communicator must lead these consumers to take the final step. This might include offering the product at a low price, offering a premium, or letting consumers try it on a limited basis. Thus Pottsville might invite selected high school students to visit the campus and attend some classes. Or it might offer scholarships to deserving students.

The buyer readiness states are important to the marketing communicator. Buyers normally pass through these stages on their way to purchase. The communicator's task is to identify the stage most consumers are in and develop a communication campaign that will move them to the next stage.

Choosing a Message

Having defined the desired audience response, the communicator moves to developing an effective message. Ideally, the message should get *Attention*, hold *Interest*, arouse *Desire*, and obtain *Action* (known as the AIDA model). In practice, few messages take the consumer all the way from awareness to purchase, but the AIDA framework suggests the desirable qualities.

In putting together the message, the marketing communicator must solve three problems: what to say (*message content*), how to say it logically (*message structure*), and how to say it symbolically (*message format*).

Message Content

The communicator has to figure out an appeal or theme that will produce the desired response. There are three types of appeals. **Rational appeals** relate to the audience's self-interest. They show that the product will produce the desired benefits. Examples would be messages showing a product's quality, economy, value, or performance. Thus, in ads for its Excel car, Hyundai offers "Cars that make sense," stressing low price, operating economy, and sensible features. When pitching computer systems to business users, IBM salespeople talk about quality, performance, reliability, and improved productivity.

Emotional appeals attempt to stir up negative or positive emotions that will motivate purchase. These include fear, guilt, and shame appeals that get people to do things they should (brush their teeth, buy new tires) or stop doing things they should not do (smoke, drink too much, overeat). For example, a recent Crest ad invoked mild fear when it claimed, "There are some things you just can't afford to

A mild fear appeal: "When you get a cavity, there's no second chance."

gamble with" (cavities). So did Michelin tire ads which featured cute babies and suggested, "Because so much is riding on your tires." Communicators also use positive emotional appeals such as love, humor, pride, and joy. Thus AT&T's long-running ad theme, "Reach out and touch someone," stirs a bundle of strong emotions.

Moral appeals are directed to the audience's sense of what is right and proper. They are often used to urge people to support social causes such as a cleaner environment, better race relations, equal rights for women, and aid to the needy. An example is the March of Dimes appeal: "God made you whole. Give to help those He didn't." Moral appeals are less often used for everyday products than for social causes.

Message Structure
The communicator has to decide on three message structure issues. The first is whether to draw a conclusion or leave it to the audience. Early research showed that drawing a conclusion was usually more effective. More recent research, however, suggests that in many cases the advertiser is better off asking questions and letting buyers come to their own conclusions. The second message structure issue is whether to present a one-sided or two-sided argument. Usually a one-sided argument is more effective in sales presentations, except when the audiences are highly educated and negatively disposed. The third message structure issue is whether to present the strongest arguments first or last. Presenting them first gets strong attention, but may lead to an anticlimactic ending.[3]

Message Format
The communicator must use a strong format for the message. In a print ad, the communicator has to decide on the headline, copy, illustration, and color. To attract attention, advertisers can use novelty and contrast, eye-catching pictures and headlines,

distinctive formats, message size and position, and color, shape, and movement. If the message is to be carried over the radio, the communicator has to choose words, sounds, and voices. The "sound" of an announcer promoting a used car has to be different from one promoting quality furniture. If the message is to be carried on television or in person, then all these elements, plus body language, have to be planned. Presenters have to watch facial expressions, gestures, dress, posture, and hair style.

If the message is carried on the product or its package, the communicator has to watch texture, scent, color, size, and shape. For example, color plays a major communication role in food preferences. When consumers sampled four cups of coffee that had been placed next to brown, blue, red, and yellow containers (unknown to the consumers, all the coffee was identical) 75 percent felt that the coffee next to the brown container tasted too strong; nearly 85 percent judged the coffee next to the red container to be the richest; nearly everyone felt that the coffee next to the blue container was mild; and the coffee next to the yellow container was judged as weak. Thus, if the coffee company wants to communicate that its coffee is rich, it would use a red container, along with label copy about the coffee's rich taste.

Choosing Media The communicator must now select channels of communication. There are two broad types of communication channels—personal and nonpersonal.

Personal Communication Channels

In **personal communication channels,** two or more people communicate directly with each other. They might communicate face to face, person to audience, over the telephone, or even through the mail. Personal communication channels are effective because they allow for personal addressing and feedback.

Most marketers use personal communication channels—for example, they have company salespeople contact buyers in the target market. But other communicators may also reach buyers about the product. These others might include independent experts making statements to target buyers—consumer advocates, consumer buying guides, and others. Or they might be neighbors, friends, family members, and associates talking to target buyers. This last channel, known as *word-of-mouth influence*, has considerable effect in many product areas. Personal influence carries great weight for products that are expensive or risky, or for products that are highly visible. Buyers of automobiles and major appliances often go beyond mass-media sources to seek the opinions of knowledgeable people.

Companies can take several steps to put personal influence channels to work for them. They can devote extra effort to selling their products to well-known people or companies, who will in turn influence others to buy. They can create opinion leaders—people whose opinions are sought by others—by supplying certain people with the product on attractive terms. Companies can work through community members such as disc jockeys, class presidents, and presidents of local organizations. Also, they can use influential people in their advertisements or develop advertising that has high "conversation value."

Nonpersonal Communication Channels

Nonpersonal communication channels are media that carry messages without personal contact or feedback. They include mass and selective media, atmospheres, and events. **Mass and selective media** consist of print media (newspapers, magazines, direct mail), electronic media (radio, television), and display media (billboards, signs, posters). Mass media are aimed at large, often unsegmented audiences; selective media are aimed at smaller, selected audiences. **Atmospheres** are designed environments that create or reinforce the buyer's leanings toward buying the product. Thus lawyers' offices and banks are designed to communicate confidence and other things that might be valued by the clients. **Events** are designed occurrences that communicate messages to target audiences. Public relations departments arrange press conferences, grand openings, public tours, and other events to communicate with specific audiences.

Nonpersonal communication affects buyers directly. In addition, using mass media often affects buyers indirectly by causing more personal communication. Mass communications affect attitudes and behavior through a two-step flow-of-communication process: "Ideas often flow from radio and print to opinion leaders and from these to the less active sections of the population."[4] This two-step flow means the effect of mass media may not be as direct, powerful, and automatic as supposed. Rather, opinion leaders step between the mass media and their audiences. The opinion leaders are more exposed to mass media, and they carry messages to people who are less exposed to media.

The two-step flow concept challenges the notion that people's buying is affected by a "trickle-down" of opinions and information from higher social classes. Since people mostly interact with others in their own social class, they pick up their fashion and other ideas from people like themselves who are opinion leaders. The two-step flow concept also suggests that mass communicators should direct their messages directly to opinion leaders, letting them carry the message to others. Thus pharmaceutical firms, like Burroughs-Wellcome and others, first try to promote their new drugs to the most influential doctors.

Selecting the Message Source

A message's impact on the audience is affected by how the audience views the sender. Messages delivered by highly credible sources are more persuasive. For example, pharmaceutical companies want doctors to tell about their products' benefits because doctors are very credible. Marketers also hire well-known actors and athletes to deliver their messages. Such famous people are used because they enhance an audience's attention to the message and retention of it. Bill Cosby speaks for Jell-O, Michael J. Fox tells us about Pepsi, basketball star Michael Jordan soars for Nike, and the entire cast from the old MASH television program gushes over IBM personal computers.

But what factors make a source credible? The three factors most often found are expertise, trustworthiness, and likability. *Expertise* is the degree to which the communicator appears to have the authority needed to back the claim. Doctors, scientists, and professors rank high on expertise in their fields. *Trustworthiness* is related to how objective and honest the source appears to be. Friends are trusted more than salespeople. *Likability* is how attractive the source is to the audience; people like sources who are open, humorous, and natural. The most highly credible source would be a person who scored high on all three factors—expertise, trustworthiness, and likability.

Collecting Feedback

After sending the message, the communicator must research its effect on the target audience. This involves asking the target audience whether they remember the message, how many times they saw it, what points they recall, how they felt about the message, and their past and present attitudes toward the product and company. The communicator would also like to measure behavior resulting from the message, such as how many people bought the product and talked to others about it.

Figure 16-4 shows an example of feedback measurement. Looking at brand A, we find that 80 percent of the total market is aware of brand A, 60 percent of those who are aware have tried it, and only 20 percent of those who have tried it are satisfied. These results suggest that the communication program is creating awareness, but that the product fails to give consumers what they expect. The company should try to improve the product and stay with the successful communication program. On the other hand, only 40 percent of the total market is aware of brand B, only 30 percent of those aware have tried it, but 80 percent of those who have tried it are satisfied. In this case, the communication program needs to be stronger to take advantage of the brand's power to obtain satisfaction.

SETTING THE TOTAL PROMOTION BUDGET AND MIX

We have looked at the steps in planning and sending communications to a target audience. But how does the company decide on (1) the total promotion budget and (2) its division among the major promotional tools to create the promotion mix? We will now look at these questions.

Setting the Total Promotion Budget

One of the hardest marketing decisions facing companies is how much to spend on promotion. John Wanamaker, the department store magnate, said: "I know that half of my advertising is wasted, but I don't know which half. I spent $2 million for advertising, and I don't know if that is half enough or twice too much."

Thus it is not surprising that industries and companies vary widely in how much they spend on promotion. Promotion spending may be 20 to 30 percent of sales in the cosmetics industry and only 5 to 10 percent in the industrial machinery industry. Even within a given industry, low- and high-spending companies can be found.

Celebrities impart some of their own likability and trustworthiness to the products they endorse.

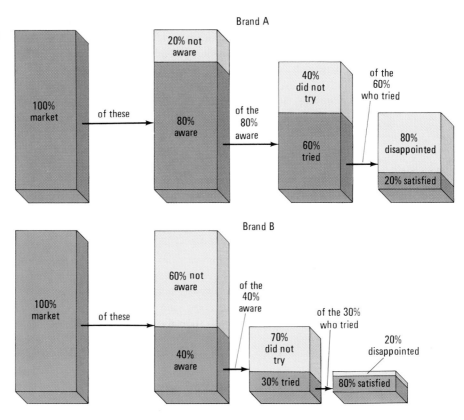

FIGURE 16-4
Current consumer states
for two brands

How do companies decide on their promotion budget? We will look at four common methods used to set the total budget for advertising.[5]

Affordable Method

Many companies use the **affordable method.** They set the promotion budget at what they think the company can afford. One executive explained this method as follows: "Why it's simple. First, I go upstairs to the controller and ask how much they can afford to give this year. He says a million and a half. Later, the boss comes to me and asks how much we should spend and I say 'Oh, about a million and a half.' "[6]

This method of setting budgets completely ignores the effect of promotion on sales volume. It leads to an uncertain annual promotion budget, which makes long-range market planning difficult. The affordable method can result in overspending on advertising, but it more often results in underspending.

Percentage-of-Sales Method

Many companies use the **percentage-of-sales method,** setting their promotion budget at a certain percentage of current or forecasted sales. Or they budget a percentage of the sales price. Automobile companies usually budget a fixed percentage for promotion based on the planned car price. Oil companies set the budget at some fraction of a cent for each gallon of gasoline sold under their label.

A number of advantages are claimed for the percentage-of-sales method. Using the method means that promotion spending is likely to vary with what the company can "afford." It also helps management to think about the relationship between promotion spending, selling price, and profit per unit. Finally, it supposedly creates competitive stability because competing firms tend to spend about the same percent of their sales on promotion.

In spite of these claimed advantages, the percentage-of-sales method has little to justify it. It uses poor logic in viewing sales as the *cause* of promotion rather than as the *result*. The budget is based on availability of funds rather than on opportunities. It prevents the increased spending sometimes needed to turn around falling sales. Because the budget varies with year-to-year sales, long-range planning is difficult. Finally, the method does not provide any basis for choosing the specific percentage, except what has been done in the past or what competitors are doing.

Competitive-Parity Method

Some companies use the **competitive-parity method,** setting their promotion budgets to match competitors' outlays. They watch competitors' advertising or get industry promotion spending estimates from publications or trade associations, and then set their budgets based on the industry average.

Two arguments support this method. One is that competitors' budgets represent the collective wisdom of the industry. The other is that spending what competitors do helps prevent promotion wars. Neither argument is valid. There are no grounds for believing that the competition has a better idea of what a company should be spending on promotion than the company itself does. Companies differ greatly, and each has its own special promotion needs. And there is no evidence that budgets based on competitive parity prevent promotion wars.

Objective-and-Task Method

The most logical budget setting method is the **objective-and-task method.** Using it, marketers develop their promotion budget by (1) defining specific objectives, (2) determining the tasks that must be performed to achieve these objectives, and (3) estimating the costs of performing these tasks. The sum of these costs is the proposed promotion budget.

The objective-and-task method makes management spell out its assumptions about the relationship between dollars spent and promotion results. But it is the most difficult method. It is often hard to figure out which specific tasks will achieve specific objectives. For example, suppose Sony wants 95 percent target market awareness for its new Walkman-size personal videocassette player during the six-month introductory period. What specific advertising messages and media schedules would Sony need to attain this objective? How much would these messages and media schedules cost? Sony management has to think about such questions even though they are hard to answer. With the objective-and-task method, the company sets its promotion budget based on what it wants to accomplish with promotion.

The overall answer to how large the promotion budget should be depends on where the company's products are in their life cycles, how much they differ from competing products, whether they are routinely sought out by consumers or have to be "sold," and other factors.

Setting the Promotion Mix   The **promotion mix** is the specific mix of advertising, personal selling, sales promotion, and public relations a company uses to pursue its advertising and marketing objectives. Companies within the same industry differ a lot in how they design their promotion mixes. Avon spends most of its promotion funds on personal selling and catalog marketing (its advertising is only 1.5 percent of sales), whereas Revlon spends heavily on consumer advertising (about 8 percent of sales). Electrolux sells 75 percent of its vacuum cleaners door-to-door, whereas Hoover relies more on advertising. Thus a company can achieve a given sales level with various mixes of advertising, personal selling, sales promotion, and public relations.

Companies are always looking for ways to improve promotion by replacing one promotion tool with a more economical one. Many companies have replaced a portion of their field sales activity with telephone sales and direct mail. Other companies have increased their sales promotion spending in relation to advertising to gain quicker sales.

Designing the promotion mix is even more complex when one tool must be used to promote another. Thus when McDonald's decides to run Million Dollar Sweepstakes in its fast-food outlets (a sales promotion), it has to run ads to inform the public. When General Mills uses a consumer advertising and sales promotion campaign to back a new cereal, its salesforce must promote this campaign to the resellers to win their support.

Many factors influence the marketer's choice of promotion tools. We will now look at these factors.

Nature of Each Promotion Tool

Each promotion tool—advertising, personal selling, sales promotion, and public relations—has unique characteristics and costs. Marketers need to understand these characteristics in selecting the tools.

ADVERTISING. Because of the many forms and uses of advertising, it is hard to generalize about its unique qualities as a part of the promotion mix. Yet several qualities can be noted. Advertising's public nature suggests that the advertised product is standard and legitimate. Because many people see ads for the product, buyers know that purchasing the product will be publicly understood and accepted. Advertising lets the seller repeat a message many times, and it lets the buyer receive and compare the messages of various competitors. Large-scale advertising by a seller says something positive about the seller's size, popularity, and success.

Advertising is also very expressive, letting the company dramatize its products through the artful use of print, sound, and color. On the one hand, advertising can be used to build up a long-term image for a product (such as Coca-Cola ads), and on the other it can be used to trigger quick sales (as when Sears advertises a weekend sale). Advertising can reach masses of geographically spread out buyers at a low cost per exposure.

Advertising also has some shortcomings. Though it reaches many people quickly, advertising is impersonal and cannot be as persuasive as a company salesperson. The audience does not feel that it has to pay attention or respond. Advertising is able to carry on only a one-way communication with the audience. And advertising can be very costly. Some forms, such as newspaper and radio advertising, can be done on a small budget; but other forms, such as network TV advertising, require a very large budget.

PERSONAL SELLING. Personal selling is the most effective tool at certain stages of the buying process, particularly in building up buyers' preference, conviction, and action. The reason is that personal selling, as compared with advertising, has several unique qualities. Personal selling involves personal interaction between two or more people, so each person can observe the other's needs and characteristics up close and make quick adjustments. Personal selling lets all kinds of relationships spring up, ranging from a matter-of-fact selling relationship to a deep personal friendship. The effective salesperson keeps the customer's interests at heart in order to build a long-run relationship. And with personal selling, the buyer feels a greater need to listen and respond, even if the response is a polite "no thank you."

With personal selling, the customer feels a greater need to listen and respond, even if the response is a polite "no thank you."

These unique qualities come at a cost. A salesforce requires a longer-term commitment than advertising—advertising can be turned on and off, but salesforce size is harder to change. And personal selling is the company's most expensive promotion tool, costing industrial companies an average of $179 per sales call in 1986.[7] American firms spend up to three times as much on personal selling as they do on advertising.

SALES PROMOTION. Sales promotion includes a wide assortment of tools—coupons, contests, cents-off deals, premiums, and others—and these tools have many unique qualities. They attract consumer attention and provide information that may lead the consumer to buy the product. They offer strong incentives to purchase by providing inducements or contributions that give value to consumers. And sales promotions invite and reward quick response. Where advertising says "buy our product," sales promotion says "buy it now."

Companies use sales promotion tools to create a stronger and quicker response. Sales promotion can be used to dramatize product offers and to boost sagging sales. Sales promotion effects are usually short-lived, however, and are not effective in building long-run brand preference.

PUBLIC RELATIONS. Public relations offers several unique qualities. It is very believable—news stories, features, and events seem more real and believable to readers

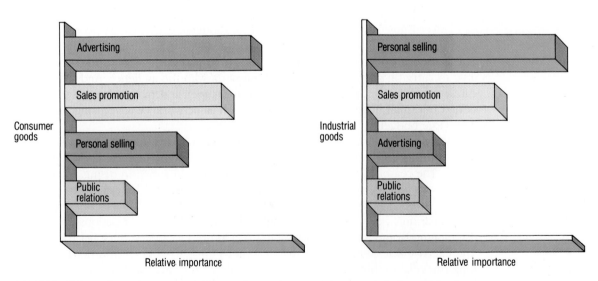

FIGURE 16-5   Relative importance of promotion tools in consumer versus industrial markets

than do ads. Public relations can reach many prospects who avoid salespeople and advertisements—the message gets to the buyers as news rather than as a sales-directed communication. And like advertising, public relations can dramatize a company or product.

Marketers tend to underuse public relations or use it as an afterthought. Yet a well-thought-out public relations campaign used with other promotion mix elements can be very effective and much less costly.

Factors in Setting the Promotion Mix

Companies consider many factors when developing their promotion mixes. We look at these factors below.

TYPE OF PRODUCT AND MARKET. The importance of the different promotion tools varies between consumer and industrial markets. The differences are shown in Figure 16-5. Consumer goods companies usually put more of their funds in advertising, followed by sales promotion, personal selling, and then public relations. Industrial goods companies put most of their funds in personal selling, followed by sales promotion, advertising, and public relations. In general, personal selling is more

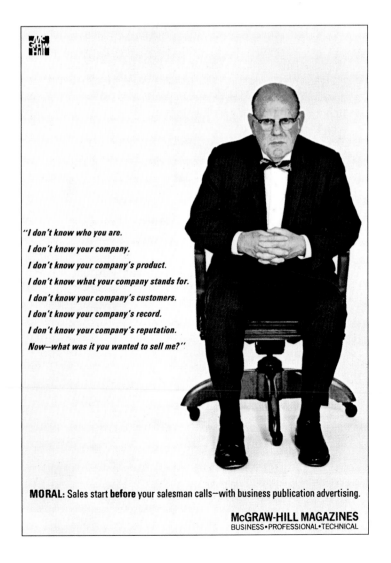

"I don't know who you are.
I don't know your company.
I don't know your company's product.
I don't know what your company stands for.
I don't know your company's customers.
I don't know your company's record.
I don't know your company's reputation.
Now—what was it you wanted to sell me?"

MORAL: Sales start **before** your salesman calls—with business publication advertising.

McGRAW-HILL MAGAZINES
BUSINESS•PROFESSIONAL•TECHNICAL

Advertising can play a dramatic role in industrial marketing as shown in this classic McGraw-Hill ad.

heavily used with expensive and risky goods and in markets with fewer and larger sellers.

Although advertising is less important than sales calls in industrial markets, it still plays an important role. Advertising can build product awareness and knowledge, develop sales leads, and reassure buyers.

Similarly, personal selling can add a lot to consumer goods marketing efforts. It is simply not the case that "salespeople put products on shelves and advertising takes them off." Well-trained consumer goods salespeople can sign up more dealers to carry a particular brand, convince them to give the brand more shelf space, urge them to use displays, and sign them up for special promotions.

PUSH VERSUS PULL STRATEGY. The promotion mix is heavily affected by whether the company chooses a push or a pull strategy. The two strategies are contrasted in Figure 16-6. A **push strategy** calls for using the salesforce and trade promotion to push a product through the channels. The producer promotes the product to wholesalers, the wholesalers promote the product to retailers, and the retailers promote the product to consumers.[8] A **pull strategy** calls for spending a lot of money on advertising and consumer promotion to build up consumer demand. If the strategy is effective, consumers will demand the product from their retailers, who will demand it from wholesalers, who will in turn demand it from producers.

Some small industrial goods companies use only push strategies; some direct marketing companies use only pull. Most large companies use some combination of push and pull. For example, Procter & Gamble uses mass-media advertising to pull its products and a large salesforce and trade promotions to push its products through the channels. In recent years, consumer goods companies have been decreasing the pull portions of their promotion mixes in favor of more push (see Marketing Highlight 16–1).

BUYER READINESS STAGE. Promotion tools vary in their effects at different stages of buyer readiness. Advertising, along with public relations, plays the major role in the awareness and knowledge stages, more important than that played by "cold calls" from salespeople. Customer liking, preference, and conviction are more affected by personal selling, followed closely by advertising. Finally, closing the sale is mostly done with sales calls and sales promotion. Clearly, personal selling, given its high costs, should focus on the later stages of the customer's buying process.

PRODUCT LIFE-CYCLE STAGE. The effects of different promotion tools vary with stages of the product life cycle. In the introduction stage, advertising and public relations are good for producing high awareness, and sales promotion is useful in promoting early trial. Personal selling must be used to get the trade to carry the product. In the growth stage, advertising and public relations continue to be powerful, and sales promotion can be reduced because fewer incentives are needed. In the mature stage, sales promotion again becomes important relative to advertising.

FIGURE 16-6
Push versus pull strategy

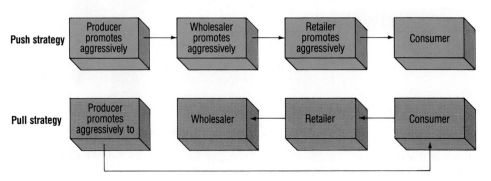

CONSUMER GOODS COMPANIES ARE GETTING "PUSHY"

Consumer package goods companies like Procter & Gamble, General Foods, Quaker, Campbell, and Gillette grew into giants by using mostly pull promotion strategies. They used massive doses of national advertising to differentiate their products, build market share, and maintain customer loyalty. But during the past two decades, these companies have gotten more "pushy," deemphasizing national advertising and funneling more of their promotion budgets into personal selling and sales promotions. Trade promotions (trade allowances, displays, co-op advertising) now account for 37 percent of total consumer product company marketing expenditures; consumer promotions (coupons, cents-off deals, premiums) account for another 29 percent. That leaves only 34 percent of total marketing expenditures for media advertising, down from 42 percent just eight years ago.

Why are these companies shifting so heavily toward push strategies? One reason is that mass media campaigns are more expensive and less effective these days. Network television costs have risen sharply while audiences have fallen off, making national advertising less cost-effective. Companies are increasingly segmenting their markets and tailoring their marketing efforts more narrowly, making national advertising less suitable than localized retailer promotions. And in these days of brand extensions and me-too products, companies sometimes have trouble finding meaningful product differences to feature in advertising. So they differentiate their products through price reductions, premium offers, coupons, and other push techniques.

Another factor speeding the shift is the greater strength of retailers. Today's retailers are larger and have more access to product sales and profit information. They now have the power to demand and get what they want—and what they want is more push. National advertising bypasses them on its way to the masses, but push promotion benefits them directly. Consumer promotions give retailers an immediate sales boost, and cash from trade allowances pads retailer profits. Thus producers often must use push just to obtain good shelf space and advertising support from important retailers.

Many marketers are concerned that the reckless use of push will lead to fierce price competition and a never-ending spiral of price slashing and deal making. This will mean lower margins, and companies will have less to invest in the research and development, packaging, and advertising needed to improve products and maintain long-run consumer preference and loyalty. If used improperly, the company can mortgage a brand's future for short-term gains.

Yet push strategies are very important in package goods marketing, where success often depends more on retailer support than on the producer's advertising. And if well designed, push strategies can help rather than hinder in building a long-run consumer franchise. The company needs to blend both push and pull elements into an integrated promotion program that meets immediate consumer and retailer needs as well as long-run company strategic needs.

Sources: See Richard Edel, "No End in Sight to Promotion's Upward Spiral," *Advertising Age*, March 23, 1987, pp. S1–S4; Alvin A. Achenbaum and F. Kent Mitchel, "Pulling Away From Push Marketing," *Harvard Business Review*, May–June 1987, pp. 38–40; Thomas F. Schuster, "A Breeze in the Face," *Harvard Business Review*, November–December 1987, pp. 36–45; and Len Strawzewski, "Promotional Carnival Gets Serious," *Advertising Age*, May 2, 1988, pp. 51–2.

Buyers know the brands, and advertising is needed only to remind them of the product. In the decline stage, advertising is kept at a reminder level, public relations is dropped, and salespeople give the product only a little attention. Sales promotion, however, might continue strong.[9]

Responsibility for Marketing Communications Planning

Members of the marketing department often have different views on how to split the promotion budget. The sales manager would rather hire two or three more salespeople than spend $150,000 on a single television commercial. The public relations manager feels that he or she can do wonders with some money shifted from advertising to public relations.

In the past, companies left these decisions to different people. No one person was responsible for thinking through the roles of the various promotion tools and coordinating the promotion mix. Today, companies are moving toward appointing a marketing communications director who is responsible for all of the company's marketing communications. This director develops policies for using the different promotion tools, keeps track of all promotion spending by product, tool, and results, and coordinates the promotion mix activities when major campaigns take place.

■ SUMMARY

Promotion is one of the four major elements of the company's marketing mix. The main promotion tools—advertising, sales promotion, public relations, and personal selling—work together to achieve the company's communication objectives.

In preparing marketing communications, the communicator has to understand the nine elements of any communication process: sender, receiver, encoding, decoding, message, media, response, feedback, and noise. The communicator's first task is to identify the target audience and its characteristics. Next, the communicator has to define the response sought, whether it be awareness, knowledge, liking, preference, conviction, or purchase. Then a message should be constructed containing an effective content, structure, and format. Media must be selected, both for personal communication and nonpersonal communication. The message must be delivered by a credible source—someone who is an expert, trustworthy, and likable. Finally,

the communicator must collect feedback by watching how much of the market becomes aware, tries the product, and is satisfied in the process.

The company has to decide how much to spend for promotion. The most popular approaches are to spend what the company can afford, use a percentage of sales, base promotion on competitors' spending, or base it on an analysis and costing of the communication objectives and tasks.

The company has to split the promotion budget among the major tools to create the promotion mix. Companies are guided by the characteristics of each promotion tool, the type of product and market, whether the company needs a push or a pull strategy, the buyer's readiness stage, and the product life-cycle stage. The different promotion activities require strong coordination for maximum impact.

■ QUESTIONS FOR DISCUSSION

1. Which form of marketing communications does each of the following represent? (a) a U2 T-shirt sold at a concert, (b) a *Rolling Stone* interview with Bruce Springsteen arranged by his manager, (c) a scalper auctioning tickets at a Michael Jackson concert, and (d) a record store selling Prince albums for $2 off the week his latest movie opens.

2. The Department of Defense spends two-thirds of the U.S. government's advertising budget. Describe how advertising is used along with sales promotion, public relations, and personal selling to obtain recruits for the armed services.

3. Relate the six buyer-readiness states to (a) a product you bought on impulse at a grocery store, (b) your feelings about purchasing Coke, Coke Classic, and Pepsi, and (c) your choice of a scholastic major.

4. Long-distance services have tried to attract customers with emotional appeals ("AT&T—Reach out and touch someone") and with rational appeals ("If your long distance bills are too much, call MCI"). Which approach do you think is more effective? Why?

5. Bill Cosby has appeared in ads for such products and companies as Jell-O, Coke, Texas Instruments, and E. F. Hutton. Is he a credible source for *all* these companies,

or does his credibility vary? Is he chosen for his credibility as a spokesperson or for some other characteristics?

6. How can an organization get feedback on the effects of its communication efforts? Describe how (a) the March of Dimes, (b) McGraw-Hill, and (c) Procter & Gamble can get feedback on the results of their communications.

7. When a decline in oil prices caused economic troubles in Texas and nearby states, Houston-based National Convenience Stores temporarily stopped advertising to cut costs. Which budgeting approach does this strategy represent? Would you have recommended another approach to setting the promotional budget for this chain of stores? Why?

8. Why do some industrial marketers advertise on national television, when their target audience is only a fraction of the people receiving their message? List some nonconsumer-oriented commercials you have seen on TV, and describe what the marketer was trying to accomplish with them.

9. Does the decision to use a push or a pull strategy depend on the number of levels in the channel of distribution? What other factors are involved in the push versus pull decision?

■ KEY TERMS

Advertising Any paid form of nonpersonal presentation and promotion of ideas, goods, or services by an identified sponsor.

Affordable method Setting the promotion budget at what management thinks the company can afford.

Atmospheres Designed environments that create or reinforce the buyer's leanings toward buying a product.

Buyer readiness states The stages consumers normally pass through on their way to purchase, including awareness, knowledge, liking, preference, conviction, or purchase.

Competitive-parity method Setting the promotion budget to match competitors' outlays.

Emotional appeals Message appeals that attempt to stir up negative or positive emotions that will motivate purchase; examples include fear, guilt, shame, love, humor, pride, and joy appeals.

Events Designed occurrences that communicate messages to target audiences, such as news conferences, grand openings, or others.

Mass and selective media Print media (newspapers, magazines, direct mail), electronic media (radio, television), and display media (billboards, signs, posters) aimed at large, unsegmented audiences (mass media) or at selected audiences (selective media).

Moral appeals Message appeals that are directed to the audience's sense of what is right and proper.

Nonpersonal communication channels Media that carry messages without personal contact or feedback, including mass and selective media, atmospheres, and events.

Objective-and-task method Developing the promotion budget by (1) defining specific objectives, (2) determining the tasks that must be performed to achieve these objectives, and (3) estimating the costs of performing these tasks; the sum of these costs is the proposed promotion budget.

Percentage-of-sales method Setting the promotion budget at a certain percentage of current or forecasted sales, or as a percentage of the sales price.

Personal communication channels Channels through which two or more people communicate directly with each other, including face to face, person to audience, over the telephone, or through the mail.

Personal selling Oral presentation in a conversation with one or more prospective purchasers for the purpose of making sales.

Promotion mix The specific mix of advertising, personal selling, sales promotion, and public relations a company uses to pursue its advertising and marketing objectives.

Public relations Building good relations with the company's various publics by obtaining favorable publicity, building up a good "corporate image," and handling or heading off unfavorable rumors, stories, and events.

Pull strategy A promotion strategy that calls for spending a lot on advertising and consumer promotion to build up consumer demand; if the strategy is successful, consumers will demand the product from their retailers, who will demand it from wholesalers, who will in turn demand it from producers.

Push strategy A promotion strategy that calls for using the salesforce and trade promotion to push the product through the channels; the producer promotes the product to wholesalers, the wholesalers promote to retailers, and the retailers promote to consumers.

Rational appeals Message appeals that relate to the audience's self-interest and show that the product will produce the claimed benefits; examples include appeals of product quality, economy, value, or performance.

Sales promotion Short-term incentives to encourage purchase or sales of a product or service.

■ REFERENCES

1. See Kenneth Dreyfack, "Quaker is Feeling Its Oats Again," *Business Week*, September 22, 1986, pp. 80–81; "Quaker Oats Co.," *Advertising Age*, September 4, 1986, p. 144–45; Richard Edel, "No End in Sight for Promotion's Upward Spiral," *Advertising Age*, March 23, 1987, p. S2; and Julie Liesse Erickson, "Quaker Fortifies Oatmeal Position," *Advertising Age*, January 11, 1988, p. 54.

2. These definitions, except for *sales promotion*, are from *Marketing Definitions: A Glossary of Marketing Terms* (Chicago: American Marketing Association, 1960).

3. For more on message content and structure, see Leon G. Schiffman and Leslie Lazar Kanuk, *Consumer Behavior*, 3rd ed. (Englewood Cliffs, NJ: Prentice-Hall, 1987), pp. 347–53.

4. P. F. Lazarsfeld, B. Berelson, and H. Gaudet, *The People's Choice*, 2nd ed. (New York: Columbia University Press, 1948), p. 151. Also see Schiffman and Kanuk, *Consumer Behavior*, pp. 571–72.

5. For a more comprehensive discussion on setting promotion budgets, see Michael L. Rothschild, *Advertising* (Lexington, MA: D. C. Heath, 1987), Ch. 20.

6. Quoted in Daniel Seligman, "How Much for Advertising?" *Fortune*, December 1956, p. 123.

7. See Richard Kern, "From a Reporter to a Source: A New Survey of Selling Costs," *Sales & Marketing Management*, February 16, 1987, p. 12.

8. For more on push strategies, see Michael Levy, John Webster, and Roger Kerin, "Formulating Push Marketing Strategies: A Method and Application," *Journal of Marketing*, Winter 1983, pp. 25–34; and Alvin A. Achenbaum and F. Kent Mitchel, "Pulling Away from Push Marketing," *Harvard Business Review*, May–June 1987, pp. 38–40.

9. For more on advertising and the product life cycle, see John E. Swan and David R. Rink, "Fitting Market Strategy to Product Life Cycles," *Business Horizons*, January–February 1982, pp. 60–67.

17 Promoting Products: Advertising, Sales Promotion, and Public Relations

THE California raisin producers had a problem. Raisin production was booming—in fact, output was almost doubling annual sales. But consumer sales were dropping at a rate of one or two percent a month. Research

by the California Raisin Advisory Board showed that consumers knew a lot about the natural health benefits of the dark wrinkly fruit, but they found it emotionally boring. To most consumers, raisins were dull, uninteresting, and, worst of all, wimpy.

So the Advisory Board handed its advertising agency, Foote, Cone & Belding, an improbable advertising challenge—make raisins hip! The agency responded with an equally improbable advertising campaign. The first ad featured a conga line of sneaker-shod raisins, singing and dancing to the 1960s hit "I Heard It Through the Grapevine." The ad quickly became the hottest 30 seconds on television, and the imaginative dancing raisins campaign has become an award-winning classic.

The plump and personable raisin characters spring to life through a new technique called Claymation. An ad is first filmed using live actors, then anima-

tors carefully sculpt purple, potato-sized clay figures to imitate the actors' expressions and movements. Using stop-action photography and making gradual changes in the clay figures—24 for each second of film—the animators create live action. It takes many months of tedious work to film a single 30-second ad. During the months of filming, the clay figures get droopy and dirty, so the animators sculpt a drawer full of fresh backups for each character.

The process isn't cheap. The Advisory Board paid more than $200,000 for the first ad, plus another $120,000 for music rights. And it budgeted $7 million for the first six months of television time. But the investment paid off—the campaign was both well-liked and effective. Following the first ad, consumers clamored for more, swamping the Advisory Board and ad agency with enthusiastic fan mail. Halloween parties that year were overrun with raisin look-alikes in black tights and plastic garbage bags. The infectious little raisin critters easily beat out the Pillsbury Doughboy, Tony the Tiger, the Keebler Elves, and other classic personalities in consumer voting for their favorite animated characters. The California Raisin Board reacted with new ads, point-of-purchase displays featuring the raisin stars, a national contest to name the three lead raisins, a music album, television specials, and licensing agreements that will have the hip raisins dancing on everything from T-shirts and bed sheets to lunch boxes and watches.

Raisins are now cool and sales are surging, with increases of 5 to 6 percent a month since the campaign began. The editors of *Advertising Age* chose Foote, Cone & Belding as their advertising agency of the year and the dancing raisins ad as the year's top 30-second spot.[1]

Chapter Objectives   *After reading this chapter, you should be able to:*

1. Define the roles of advertising, sales promotion, and public relations in the promotion mix.
2. Describe the major decisions made in developing an advertising program.
3. Discuss how sales promotion campaigns are developed and implemented.
4. Explain how companies use public relations to communicate with their publics.

COMPANIES must do more than make good products—they must inform consumers of product benefits and carefully position products in consumers' minds. To do this they must skillfully use the mass-promotion tools of advertising, sales promotion, and public relations. We examine these tools in this chapter.

ADVERTISING

We define advertising as follows:

Advertising is any paid form of nonpersonal presentation and promotion of ideas, goods, or services by an identified sponsor.

In 1987, advertising ran up a bill of over $109 billion. The spenders included not only business firms, but museums, professionals, and social organizations that advertise their causes to various target publics. In fact, the twenty-ninth largest advertising spender is a nonprofit organization—the U.S. government.

The top one hundred national advertisers account for over one-fourth of all advertising.[2] Table 17-1 lists the top ten advertisers in 1986. Procter & Gamble is the leader with $1.4 billion, or 12.2 percent of its total U.S. sales. The other major spenders are found in the auto, food, retailing, and tobacco industries. Advertising as a percentage of sales is low in the auto industry and high in food, drugs, toiletries, and cosmetics, followed by gum, candy, and soaps. Companies spending the largest percentages of their sales on advertising were Warner-Lambert (32 percent) and Noxell (30 percent).

Advertising dollars go into many media: magazines and newspapers, radio and television, outdoor, direct mail, and others. And advertising has many uses: to build an organization's image, build a brand, announce a sale, or support an idea or cause.

Advertising's roots can be traced back to early history (see Marketing Highlight 17–1). Although advertising is mostly used by private enterprise, it is used in all

RANK	COMPANY	TOTAL U.S. ADVERTISING (millions)	TOTAL U.S. SALES (millions)	ADVERTISING AS A PERCENT OF SALES
1	Procter & Gamble	$1,435	$11,805	12.2%
2	Philip Morris	1,364	17,568	7.8
3	Sears	1,004	44,281*	2.3
4	RJR Nabisco	935	15,978	5.9
5	General Motors	839	91,343	0.9
6	Ford	649	50,034	1.3
7	Anheuser-Busch	644	8,402*	7.7
8	McDonald's	592	3,077	19.2
9	K mart	590	23,812*	2.5
10	PepsiCo	581	8,065	7.2

* Worldwide sales—U.S. sales not available.

Source: Reprinted with permission from September 24, 1987, issue of *Advertising Age.* Copyright 1987, Crain Communications, Inc.

MARKETING HIGHLIGHT 17–1

HISTORICAL MILESTONES IN ADVERTISING

Advertising goes back to the very beginnings of recorded history. Archaeologists working in the countries around the Mediterranean Sea have dug up signs announcing various events and offers. The Romans painted walls to announce gladiator fights, and the Phoenicians painted pictures promoting their wares on large rocks along parade routes. A Pompeii wall painting praised a politician and asked for the people's votes.

Another early form of advertising was the town crier. During the Golden Age in Greece, town criers announced the sale of slaves, cattle, and other goods. An early "singing commercial" went as follows: "For eyes that are shining, for cheeks like the dawn/For beauty that lasts after girlhood is gone/For prices in reason, the woman who knows/Will buy her cosmetics of Aesclyptos."

Another early advertising form was the mark that tradespeople placed on their goods such as pottery. As the person's reputation spread by word of mouth, buyers began to look for his special mark, just as trademarks and brand names are used today. Over 1000 years ago in Europe, Osnabrück linen was carefully controlled for quality and commanded a price 20 percent higher than unbranded Westphalian linens. As production became more centralized and markets became more distant, the mark became more important.

The turning point in the history of advertising came in the year 1450 when Gutenberg invented the printing press. Advertisers no longer had to produce extra copies of a sign by hand. The first printed advertisement in the English language appeared in 1478.

In 1622, advertising got a big boost with the launching of the first English newspaper, *The Weekly Newes.* Later Addison and Steele published the *Tatler* and became supporters of advertising. Addison gave this advice to copy writers: "The great art in writing advertising is the finding out the proper method to catch the reader, without which a good thing may pass unobserved, or be lost among commissions of bankrupts." The September 14, 1710, issue of the *Tatler* contained ads for razor strops, patent medicine, and other consumer products.

Advertising had its greatest growth in the United States. Ben Franklin has been called the father of American advertising because his *Gazette*, first published in 1729, had the largest circulation and advertising volume of any paper in colonial America. Several factors led to America's becoming the cradle of advertising. First, American industry led in mass production, which created surpluses and the need to convince consumers to buy more. Second, the development of a fine network of waterways, highways, and roads allowed the transportation of goods and advertising media to the countryside. Third, the establishment in 1813 of compulsory public education increased literacy and the growth of newspapers and magazines. The invention of radio and, later, television created two more amazing media for the spread of advertising.

HOW DOES AN ADVERTISING AGENCY WORK?

Madison Avenue is a familiar name to most Americans. It's an avenue in New York City where some major advertising agency headquarters are located. But most of the nation's ten thousand agencies are found outside New York, and almost every city has at least one agency, even if it's a one-person shop. Some ad agencies are huge—the largest U.S. agency, Young & Rubicam, has annual billings of over $4 billion.

Advertising agencies were started in the mid-to-late 1800s by salespeople and brokers who worked for the media and received a commission for selling advertising space to companies. As time passed, the salespeople began to help customers prepare their ads. Eventually they formed agencies and grew closer to the advertisers than to the media. These agencies offered more and more advertising and marketing services to their clients.

Even companies with strong advertising departments use advertising agencies. Agencies employ specialists who often can perform advertising tasks better than the company's staff. Agencies also bring an out-side point of view to solving the company's problems, along with lots of experience from working with different clients and situations. Agencies are paid partly from media discounts and often cost the firm very little. And since the firm can drop its agency at any time, an agency works hard do a good job.

Advertising agencies usually have four departments: *creative*, which develops and produces ads; *media*, which selects media and places ads; *research*, which studies audience characteristics and wants; and *business*, which handles the agency's business activities. Each account is supervised by an account executive, and people in each department are assigned to work on one or more accounts.

Agencies often attract new business through their reputation or size. Generally, however, a client invites a few agencies to make a presentation for its business and then selects one of them.

Ad agencies have traditionally been paid through commissions and some fees. Under this system, the agency receives 15 percent of the media cost as a

---

the countries of the world, including socialist countries. Advertising is a good way to inform and persuade, whether the purpose is to sell Coca-Cola all over the world or to get consumers in a developing nation to drink milk or use birth control.

Organizations handle advertising in different ways. In small companies, advertising might be handled by someone in the sales department. Large companies set up advertising departments, whose job is to set the advertising budget, work with the ad agency, and handle direct mail advertising, dealer displays, and other advertising not done by the agency. Most large companies use an outside advertising agency because it offers several advantages (see Marketing Highlight 17–2).

MAJOR DECISIONS IN ADVERTISING

Marketing management must make five important decisions in developing an advertising program. These decisions are listed in Figure 17-1 and discussed below.

Setting Objectives   The first step in developing an advertising program is to set the advertising objectives. These objectives are based on past decisions about the target market, positioning, and marketing mix. The marketing positioning and mix strategy defines the job that advertising must do in the total marketing program.

Many communication and sales objectives can be set for advertising. Colley lists fifty-two possible advertising objectives in his well-known *Defining Advertising Goals for Measured Advertising Results*.[3] He outlines a method called DAGMAR (after the book's title) for turning advertising objectives into specific measurable goals.

rebate. Suppose the agency buys $60,000 of magazine space for a client. The magazine bills the advertising agency for $51,000 ($60,000 less 15 percent), and the agency bills the client for $60,000, keeping the $9,000 commission. If the client bought space directly from the magazine, it would have paid $60,000 because these commissions are paid only to recognized advertising agencies.

Both advertisers and agencies have become more and more unhappy with the commission system. Larger advertisers complain that they pay more for the same services received by smaller ones simply because they place more advertising. Advertisers also believe that the commission system drives agencies away from low-cost media and short advertising campaigns. Agencies are unhappy because they perform extra services for an account without getting any more pay. The trend is toward paying either a straight fee or a combination commission and fee. Today, only about 40 percent of companies still pay their agencies on a commission-only basis.

Another trend is also hitting the advertising agency business. In recent years, as growth in advertising spending has slowed, many agencies have tried to keep growing by gobbling up other agencies, creating huge agency holding companies. The largest of these agency "supergroups," Saatchi & Saatchi PLC, includes several large agencies—Saatchi & Saatchi Compton, Ted Bates Worldwide, DFS Dorland Worldwide, and others—with combined billings exceeding $11.3 billion. Many agencies have also sought growth by diversifying into related marketing services. These new "superagencies" offer a complete list of integrated marketing and promotion services under one roof, including advertising, sales promotion, direct marketing, and public relations.

Sources: See "U.S. Advertising Agency Profiles," a special issue of *Advertising Age*, March 30, 1988; Christine Dugas, "How Adversity Is Reshaping Madison Avenue," *Business Week*, September 15, 1986, pp. 142–50; and Anthony Ramirez, "Do Your Ads Need a Superagency?" *Fortune*, April 27, 1987, pp. 84–89.

An **advertising goal** is a specific communication task to be accomplished with a specific *target* audience in a specific period of *time*. DAGMAR outlines an approach to measuring whether advertising goals have been achieved.

Advertising objectives can be classified as to whether their aim is to inform, persuade, or remind. Table 17-2 lists examples of these objectives. *Informative advertising* is used heavily when introducing a new product category, where the objective

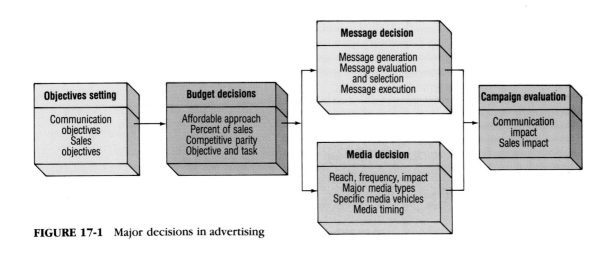

FIGURE 17-1 Major decisions in advertising

TABLE 17-2
Possible Advertising Objectives

To inform	
Telling the market about a new product	Describing available services
Suggesting new uses for a product	Correcting false impressions
Informing the market of a price change	Reducing consumers' fears
Explaining how the product works	Building a company image
To persuade:	
Building brand preference	Persuading customer to purchase now
Encouraging switching to your brand	Persuading customer to receive a sales call
Changing customer's perception of product attributes	
To remind:	
Maintaining its top-of-mind awareness	Keeping it in their minds during off-seasons
Reminding them where to buy it	Reminding consumers that the product may be needed in the near future

is to build primary demand. Thus the producers of compact disk players must first inform consumers of the sound and convenience benefits of CDs.

Persuasive advertising becomes more important as competition increases, and where a company's objective is to build selective demand. For example, when compact disk players are established and accepted, Sony will try to persuade consumers that its brand offers the best quality for the money. It will try to build a "very best" position for Sony CDs in the consumer's mind.

Some persuasive advertising has become **comparison advertising,** which compares one brand directly or indirectly to one or more other brands. In its classic comparison campaign, Avis positioned itself against market-leading Hertz by claiming, "We're number two, but we try harder." Procter & Gamble positioned Scope against Listerine, claiming that minty-fresh Scope "fights bad breath and doesn't give medicine breath." Comparison advertising has been used for such products as computers, deodorants, toothpastes, automobiles, wines, and pain relievers.

Reminder advertising is important for mature products, to keep the consumer thinking about the product. Expensive Coca-Cola ads on television are designed to remind people about Coca-Cola, not to inform or persuade them.

Budget Decision   After determining advertising objectives, the company can next set its advertising budget for each product. The role of advertising is to affect demand for a product. The company wants to spend the amount needed to achieve the sales goal. Four commonly used methods for setting the advertising budget—affordable, percentage-of-sales, competitive-parity, and objective-and-task—were discussed in Chapter 16. Here we will describe some specific factors that should be considered when setting the advertising budget:[4]

* *Stage in the product life cycle.* New products typically need large advertising budgets to build awareness and to gain consumer trial. Mature brands usually require lower budgets as a ratio to sales.

* *Market share.* High market share brands usually need more advertising spending as a percent of sales than low-share brands. To build the market or to take share from competitors requires larger advertising spending than simply maintaining current share.

* *Competition and clutter.* In a market with many competitors and high advertising spending, a brand must advertise more heavily to be heard above the noise in the market.

Comparison advertising: Here Budget Gourmet compares itself directly to competitor Lean Cuisine.

- *Advertising frequency.* When many repetitions are needed to put across the brand's message to consumers, the advertising budget must be larger.
- *Product differentiation.* A brand that closely resembles other brands in its product class (cigarettes, beer, soft drinks) requires heavy advertising to differentiate it. When the product differs substantially from competitors, advertising can be used to point out the differences to consumers.

Companies such as Du Pont and Anheuser-Busch often run experiments as part of their advertising budgeting process. They spend more in some territories and less in others, then compare results to those in control territories to measure sales gains or losses. In fact, Anheuser-Busch recently began testing a new ultrapremium beer, named Anheuser, with no advertising at all to see what would happen. No mainstream beer is likely to survive without advertising, but the company wants to see if this specialty beer can make it on word-of-mouth alone. In fact, the lack of advertising might even add to the beer's allure. If the new brand succeeds without advertising support, Anheuser-Busch will probably take a careful look at the over $500 million it spends each year advertising its other products.[5]

Message Decision   A large advertising budget does not guarantee a successful advertising campaign. Two advertisers can spend the same amount on advertising yet have very different results. Studies have shown that creative advertising messages can be more important to advertising success than the number of dollars spent. No matter how big the budget, advertising can succeed only if commercials gain attention and communicate well. The budget must be invested in effective advertising messages.

Good advertising messages are especially important in today's costly and cluttered advertising environment. Take the situation facing network television advertisers. They typically pay $100,000 to $200,000 for thirty seconds of advertising time during a popular prime-time TV program—even more if it's an especially popular program such as the Cosby Show ($380,000 per spot) or the Super Bowl ($550,000!). Then their ads are sandwiched in with a clutter of some sixty other commercials, announcements, and network promotions per hour. And this clutter will increase as advertisers make greater use of 15-second commercials.

But wait, things get worse! Until recently, television viewers were pretty much a captive audience for advertisers. Viewers had only a few channels to choose from. Those who found the energy to get up and change channels during boring commercial breaks usually found only more of the same on the other channels. But with the growth in cable TV, VCRs, and remote control units, today's viewers have many more options. They can avoid boring ads by watching commercial-free cable channels. They can "zap" commercials by pushing the fast-forward button during taped programs. With remote control, they can instantly turn off the sound during a commercial or "zip" around the channel to see what else is on. Advertisers take such "zipping" and "zapping" seriously. One expert predicts that by the year 2000, 60 percent of all TV viewers may be tuning out commercials.[6]

Thus, just to gain and hold attention, today's advertising messages must be better planned, more imaginative, more entertaining, and more rewarding to consumers. Creative strategy will play an increasingly important role in advertising success. Advertisers go through three steps to develop a creative strategy: message generation, message evaluation and selection, and message execution.

Message Generation

Creative people have different ways to find advertising message ideas. Many creative people start by talking to consumers, dealers, experts, and competitors. Others try to imagine consumers using the product and figure out the benefits consumers seek when buying and using it. Generally, advertisers create many possible messages, only a few of which will be used.

Message Evaluation and Selection

The advertiser must evaluate the possible messages. The appeals used in messages should have three characteristics. First, they should be *meaningful,* pointing out benefits that will make the product more desirable or interesting to consumers. Second, the appeals should be *distinctive*—they should tell how the product is better than competing brands. Finally, the appeals must be *believable.* It may be hard to make message appeals believable; many consumers doubt the truth of advertising in general. One study found that, on average, consumers rate advertising messages as only "somewhat unbelievable."[7]

Advertisers should evaluate their advertising messages on the above factors. For example, The March of Dimes searched for an advertising theme to raise money for its fight against birth defects.[8] Twenty possible messages came out of a brainstorming session. A group of young parents were asked to rate each message for interest, distinctiveness, and believability, giving up to 100 points for each. For example, "Five hundred thousand unborn babies die each year from birth defects" scored 70, 60, and 80 on interest, distinctiveness, and believability, while "Your next baby could be born with a birth defect" scored 58, 50, and 70. The first message was rated higher than the second and was used in advertising.

Message execution styles: The National Dairy Board shows how milk contributes to a healthy, natural life style. 9-Lives created Morris the 9-Lives Cat as a personality symbol.

Message Execution

The message's impact depends not only on what is said but also on how it is said. The advertiser has to put the message across in a way that wins the target market's attention and interest.

The advertiser usually begins with a *copy strategy statement* describing the objective, content, support, and tone of the desired ad. Here is such a statement for a Pillsbury product called 1869 Brand Biscuits:

> The objective of the advertising is to convince biscuit users that now they can buy a canned biscuit that's as good as homemade—Pillsbury's 1869 Brand Biscuits. The content of the advertising will emphasize that the biscuits look like homemade biscuits, have the same texture as homemade, and taste like homemade biscuits. Support for the "good as homemade" promise will be twofold: (1) 1869 Brand Biscuits are made from a special kind of flour (soft wheat flour) used to make homemade biscuits but never before used in making canned biscuits, and (2) the use of traditional American biscuit recipes. The tone of the advertising will be a news announcement, tempered by a warm, reflective mood coming from a look back at traditional American baking quality.

Creative people must now find a style, tone, words, and format for executing the message. Any message can be presented in different *execution styles,* such as:

1. *Slice-of-life.* This style shows one or more people using the product in a normal setting. A family seated at the dinner table might talk about a new biscuit brand.

NEVER A DULL MOMENT.

Schick* blades don't get dull before their time. So you get close, clean comfortable shaves—shave after shave.
Try the convenient Schick Plus disposable razor. Or Ultrex Plus cartridges, both with a lubricating "comfort" strip.

© 1988 Warner-Lambert Co.

In this award-winning ad, the illustation, headline, and copy work closely together to deliver the message.

2. *Life style.* This style shows how a product fits in with a life style. National Dairy Board ads show women exercising and talks about how milk adds to a healthy, active life style.

3. *Fantasy.* This style creates a fantasy around the product or its use. Revlon's first ad for Jontue showed a barefoot woman in a chiffon dress, coming out of an old French barn, crossing a meadow, meeting a handsome young man on a white horse, and riding away with him.

4. *Mood or image.* This style builds a mood or image around the product, such as beauty, love, or serenity. No claim is made about the product except through suggestion. Many coffee ads create moods.

5. *Musical.* This style shows one or more people or cartoon characters singing a song about the product. Many soft drink ads have used this format.

6. *Personality symbol.* This style creates a character that represents the product. The character might be *animated* (Green Giant, Cap'n Crunch, Garfield the Cat) or real (Marlboro man, Morris the 9-Lives Cat).

7. *Technical expertise.* This style shows the company's expertise in making the product. Thus Hills Brothers shows one of its buyers carefully selecting the coffee beans, and Gallo tells about its many years of wine-making.

8. *Scientific evidence.* This style presents survey or scientific evidence that the brand is better or better liked than one or more other brands. For years, Crest toothpaste has used scientific evidence to convince buyers that Crest is better than other brands at fighting cavities.

9. *Testimonial evidence.* This style features a highly believable or likable source endorsing the product. It could be a celebrity like Bill Cosby (Jell-O and Kodak) or ordinary people saying how much they like the product.

The advertiser must also choose a *tone* for the ad. Procter & Gamble always uses a positive tone: Its ads say something very positive about the product. P&G avoids humor that might take attention away from the message. On the other hand, ads for Bud Light beer use humor and poke fun at people who order "just any light."

Memorable and attention-getting *words* must be found. The themes listed below on the left would have had much less impact without the creative phrasing on the right:[9]

THEME	CREATIVE COPY
• 7-up is not a cola.	• "The Uncola."
• Let us drive you in our bus instead of driving your car.	• "Take the bus, and leave the driving to us" (Greyhound).
• If you drink a beer, Schaefer is a good beer to drink.	• "The one to have when you're having more than one."
• We don't rent as many cars, so we have to do more for our customers.	• "We're number 2, so we try harder" (Avis).
• Hanes socks last longer than less expensive ones.	• "Buy cheap socks and you'll pay through the toes."
• Nike shoes will help you jump higher and play better basketball.	• "Parachute not included."

Format elements will make a difference in an ad's impact as well as its cost. A small change in the way an ad is designed can make a big difference in its effect. A number of studies of print advertisements report that the *illustration, headline,* and *copy* are important. The illustration is the first thing the reader notices, and it must be strong enough to draw attention. Then the headline must effectively entice the right people to read the copy. The copy itself must be simple but strong and convincing. Even then, a really outstanding ad will be noted by less than 50 percent of the exposed audience; about 30 percent of the exposed audience might recall the main point of the headline; about 25 percent might remember the advertiser's name; and less than 10 percent will have read most of the body copy. Ordinary ads, unfortunately, would not achieve even these results.

Media Decision

The advertiser next chooses advertising media to carry the advertising message. The steps are (1) deciding on reach, frequency, and impact; (2) choosing among major media types; (3) selecting specific media vehicles; and (4) deciding on media timing.

Deciding on Reach, Frequency, and Impact

To select media, the advertiser must decide what reach and frequency are needed to achieve the advertising objectives. **Reach** is a measure of the percentage of people in the target market who are exposed to the ad campaign during the given period of time. For example, the advertiser might try to reach 70 percent of the target market during the first year. **Frequency** is a measure of how many times the average person in the target market is exposed to the message. For example, the advertiser might want an average exposure frequency of three. The advertiser must also decide what *impact* the exposure should have. Messages on television may have more impact than messages on radio because television uses sight and sound, not just sound. The same message in one magazine (say, *Newsweek*) may be more believable than in another (say, *Police Gazette*).

Now suppose the advertiser's product might appeal to a market of one million consumers. The goal is to reach 700,000 consumers (70 percent of 1,000,000). Since

TABLE 17-3 Profiles of Major Media Types

MEDIUM	VOLUME IN BILLIONS	PERCENTAGE	EXAMPLE OF COST	ADVANTAGES	LIMITATIONS
Newspapers	$ 29.4	26.8%	$29,800 for one page, weekday *Chicago Tribune*	Flexibility; timeliness; good local market coverage; broad acceptance; high believability	Short life; poor reproduction quality; small "pass along" audience
Television	23.9	21.8	$1,500 for thirty seconds of prime time in Chicago	Combines sight, sound, and motion; appealing to the senses; high attention; high reach	High absolute cost; high clutter; fleeting exposure; less audience selectivity
Direct mail	19.1	17.4	$1,520 for the names and addresses of 40,000 veterinarians	Audience selectivity; flexibility; no ad competition within the same medium; personalization	Relatively high cost; "junk mail" image
Radio	7.2	6.6	$700 for one minute of drive time (during commuting hours, A.M. and P.M.) in Chicago	Mass use; high geographic and demographic selectivity; low cost	Audio presentation only; lower attention than television; non-standardized rate structures; fleeting exposure
Magazines	5.6	5.1	$84,390 for one page, four-color, in *Newsweek*	High geographic and demographic selectivity; credibility and prestige; high-quality reproduction; long life; good pass-along readership	Long ad purchase lead time; some waste circulation; no guarantee of position
Outdoor	1.0	0.9	$25,500 per month for seventy-one billboards in metropolitan Chicago	Flexibility, high repeat exposure; low cost; low competition	No audience selectivity; creative limitations
Other	23.4	21.4			
Total	109.6	100.0%			

Source: Columns 2 and 3 are from *Advertising Age,* June 3, 1988, p. 64. Printed with permission. Copyright © 1988, Crain Communications, Inc.

the average consumer will receive three exposures, 2,100,000 exposures (700,000 × 3) must be bought. Of the advertiser wants exposures of 1.5 impact (assuming 1.0 impact is the average) a rated number of exposures of 3,150,000 (2,100,000 × 1.5) must be bought. If a thousand exposures with this impact cost $10, the advertising budget will have to be $31,500 (3,150 × $10). In general, the more reach, frequency, and impact the advertiser seeks, the higher the advertising budget will have to be.

Choosing Among Major Media Types

The media planner has to know the reach, frequency, and impact of each of the major media types. The major advertising media are summarized in Table 17-3. The major media types, in order of their advertising volume, are newspapers, television, direct mail, radio, magazines, and outdoor. Each medium has its advantages and limitations.

Media planners consider many factors when making their media choices. The *media habits of target consumers* will affect media choice—for example, radio and television are the best media for reaching teenagers. So will the *nature of the product.*

Dresses are best shown in color magazines, and Polaroid cameras are best demonstrated on television. Different *types of messages* may require different media. A message announcing a major sale tomorrow will require radio or newspapers; a message with a lot of technical data might require magazines or mailings. *Cost* is also a major factor in media choice. Television is very expensive, whereas newspaper advertising costs much less. What counts is the cost per thousand exposures rather than the total cost.

Ideas about media impact and cost must be reexamined regularly. For a long time, television and magazines have enjoyed dominant positions in the media mixes of national advertisers, and other media were often neglected. In recent years, however, the costs and clutter of these media have gone up, audiences have dropped as competition has increased, and marketers are adopting strategies beamed at narrower segments. As a result, TV and magazine advertising revenues have leveled off or declined. Advertisers are increasingly turning to alternative media ranging from cable TV and outdoor advertising to parking meters and shopping carts (see Marketing Highlight 17–3). Thus advertisers must periodically review the different media to determine their best buys.

Given these and other media characteristics, the media planner must decide how much of each media type to buy. For example, in launching its new biscuit, Pillsbury might decide to spend $3 million on daytime network television, $2 million on women's magazines, and $1 million on daily newspapers in twenty major markets.

Selecting Specific Media Vehicles

The media planner now chooses the best media vehicles—specific media within each general media type. For example, television vehicles include "The Bill Cosby Show," "Sixty Minutes," and the "CBS Evening News." Magazine vehicles include *Newsweek, People, Sports Illustrated*, and *Reader's Digest*. If advertising is to be placed in magazines, the media planner looks up the circulation figures and the costs of different ad sizes, color options, ad positions, and frequencies for various specific magazines. The planner evaluates each magazine on such factors as credibility, status, reproduction quality, editorial focus, and lead time. The media planner decides which vehicles give the best reach, frequency, and impact for the money.

Media planners compute the cost per thousand people reached by a vehicle. If a full-page, four-color advertisement in *Newsweek* costs $84,000 and *Newsweek's* readership is 3 million people, the cost of reaching each one thousand people is $28. The same advertisement in *Business Week* may cost $30,000 but reach only 775,000 persons, at a cost per thousand of $39. The media planner would rank each magazine by cost per thousand and favor those magazines with the lower cost per thousand.

The media planner must also consider the costs of producing ads for each medium. Newspaper ads may cost very little to produce; flashy television ads may cost millions. On average, advertisers must pay $114,000 to produce a single 30-second television commercial. Timex paid a million dollars to make one 30-second ad for its Atlantis 100 sports watch, and Apple Computer recently spent $6 million to produce eleven spots.[10] The media planner must think about production costs when considering each medium.

The media planner must adjust these initial cost measures in several ways. First, the measures should be adjusted for audience quality. For a baby lotion advertisement, *New Parents* magazine would have a high exposure value; *Gentlemen's Quarterly* would have a low exposure value. Second, the exposure value should be adjusted for audience attention. Readers of *Vogue*, for example, pay more attention to ads

ADVERTISERS SEEK ALTERNATIVE MEDIA

As network television costs soar and audiences shrink, many advertisers are looking for new ways to reach consumers. And the move toward regionalized strategies, focused more narrowly on specific consumer groups, has also fueled the search for alternative media to replace or supplement network television. Advertisers are shifting larger portions of their budgets to media that cost less and target more effectively.

Two media benefiting most from the shift are outdoor advertising and cable television. Billboards

have undergone a resurgence in recent years. Gone are the ugly eyesores of the past; in their place we see cleverly designed, colorful attention-grabbers. Outdoor advertising provides an excellent way to reach important local consumer segments. For example, Anheuser-Busch sells its Budweiser, Busch, and Bud Lite beers on billboards in black and Hispanic neighborhoods.

Cable television is also booming. Today almost 50 percent of all U.S. households subscribe to cable,

Marketers have discovered a dazzling array of "alternative media."

and cable TV advertising revenues exceed $2.5 billion a year. Cable systems allow narrow programming formats such as all sports, all news, nutrition programs, arts programs, and others that target select groups. Advertisers can take advantage to this "narrowcasting" to rifle in on special market segments, rather than using the shotgun approach offered by network broadcasting.

Cable TV and outdoor advertising seem to make good sense. But increasingly, ads are popping up in far less likely places. In their efforts to find less costly and more highly targeted ways to reach consumers, advertisers have discovered a dazzling collection of "alternative media." As consumers, we're used to seeing ads on television, in magazines and newspapers, on the radio, and along the roadways. But these days, no matter where you go or what you do, you will probably run into some new form of advertising.

Tiny billboards attached to shopping carts and ads on grocery bags urge you to treat yourself to Jell-O Pudding Pops or Pampers disposable diapers. Signs atop parking meters hawk everything from Minolta cameras to Recipe dog food. You escape to the ballpark, only to find billboard-size video screens running Budweiser ads while a blimp with an elec-tronic message board circles lazily overhead. You pay to see a movie at your local theater, but first you see a two-minute science fiction fantasy that turns out to be an ad for General Electric portable stereo boxes. Then the movie is full of not-so-subtle promotional plugs for Pepsi, Alka-Seltzer, MasterCard, Fritos, or one of a dozen other products. Boats cruise along public beaches flashing advertising messages for Sundown Sunscreen or Gatorade to sunbathers. Even your church bulletin carries ads for Campbell's Soup.

Some of these alternative media seem a bit far-fetched, and they sometimes irritate consumers. But for many marketers, these media can save money and provide a way to hit selected consumers where they live, shop, work, and play. Of course, this may leave you wondering if there are any commercial-free havens remaining for ad-weary consumers. The back seat of a taxi, perhaps, or stalls in a public restroom? Forget it! Both have already been invaded by innovative marketers.

Sources: See Kim Foltz, "Ads Popping Up All Over," *Newsweek*, August 12, 1985, pp. 50–51; Christine Dugas, "'Ad Space' Now Has a Whole New Meaning," *Business Week*, July 29, 1985, p. 52; and Kenneth R. Hey, "We Are Experiencing Network Difficulties," *American Demographics*, October 1987, pp. 38–42.

than readers of *Newsweek*. Third, the exposure value should be adjusted for the medium's editorial quality—*Time* and *Reader's Digest* are more believable and prestigious than the *National Enquirer*.

Media planners increasingly use more sophisticated measures of media effectiveness and employ them in mathematical models for arriving at the best media mix. Many advertising agencies use computer programs to select the initial media, then make further improvements based on subjective factors not included in the model.[11]

Deciding on Media Timing

The advertiser has to decide how to schedule the advertising over the course of the year. Suppose sales of a product peak in December and drop off in March. The firm can vary its advertising to follow the seasonal pattern, to oppose the seasonal pattern, or to be the same all year. Most firms do seasonal advertising. Even here, the firm has to decide whether its advertising should come before or during seasonal sales.

The advertiser also has to choose the pattern of the ads. **Continuity** means scheduling ads evenly within a given period. **Pulsing** means scheduling ads unevenly over the time period. Thus fifty-two ads could be scheduled at one per week during the year, or pulsed in several bursts. Those who favor pulsing feel that the audience will learn the message more completely with pulsing and that money can be saved. Anheuser-Busch's research found that Budweiser could drop advertising in a given market with no harm to sales for at least a year and a half. Then the company could use a six-month burst of advertising and regain the past sales growth rate. This led Budweiser to adopt a pulsing strategy.[12]

Advertising Evaluation

The advertising program should regularly evaluate the communication and sales effects of advertising.

Measuring the Communication Effect

Measuring the communication effect tells whether an ad is communicating well. Called **copy testing,** it can be done before or after an ad is printed or broadcast. There are three major methods of advertising *pretesting*. The first is through *direct rating*, where the advertiser exposes a consumer panel to alternative ads and asks them to rate the ads. These direct ratings indicate how well the ads get attention and how they affect consumers. Although an imperfect measure of an ad's actual impact, a high rating indicates a potentially more effective ad. In *portfolio tests*, consumers view or listen to a portfolio of advertisements, taking as much time as they need. They then are asked to recall all the ads and their content, aided or unaided by the interviewer. Their recall level indicates the ability of an ad to stand out and its message to be understood and remembered. *Laboratory tests* use equipment to measure consumers' physiological reactions to an ad—heartbeat, blood pressure, pupil dilation, perspiration. These tests measure an ad's attention-getting power but reveal little about its impact on beliefs, attitudes, or intentions.

There are two popular methods of *posttesting* ads. Using *recall tests*, the advertiser asks people who have been exposed to magazines or television programs to recall everything they can about the advertisers and products they saw. Recall scores indicate the ad's power to be noticed and retained. In *recognition tests*, the researcher asks readers of a given issue of, say, a magazine to point out what they recognize as having seen before. Recognition scores can be used to assess the ad's impact in different market segments and to compare the company's ads with competitors' ads.

ADVERTISING DECISIONS AND PUBLIC POLICY

By law, companies must avoid deception or discrimination in their use of advertising. Here are the major issues:

False Advertising. Advertisers must not make false claims, such as stating that a product cures something that it does not cure. Advertisers must avoid false demonstrations, such as using sand-covered plexiglass instead of sandpaper in a commercial to demonstrate that a razor blade can shave sandpaper.

Deceptive Advertising. Advertisers must not create ads that have the capacity to deceive, even though no one may be deceived. A floor wax cannot be advertised as giving six months' protection unless it does so under typical conditions, and a diet bread cannot be advertised as having fewer calories simply because its slices are thinner. The problem is to tell the difference between deception and "puffery," with puffery being acceptable.

Bait-and-switch Advertising. Sellers should not attract buyers on false pretenses. For example, the seller advertises a $79 sewing machine. When consumers try to buy the advertised machine, the seller refuses to sell it, downplays its features, shows a faulty one, or promises unreasonable delivery dates, trying to switch the buyer to a more expensive machine.

Promotional Allowances and Services. Companies must make promotional allowances and services available to all customers on proportionately equal terms.

Sources: See Kim Foltz, "Ads Popping Up All Over," *Newsweek*, August 12, 1985, pp. 50–51; Christine Dugas, "'Ad Space' Now Has a Whole New Meaning," *Business Week*, July 29, 1985, p. 52; and Kenneth R. Hey, "We Are Experiencing Network Difficulties," *American Demographics*, October 1987, pp. 38–42.

Measuring the Sales Effect

What sales are caused by an ad that increases brand awareness by 20 percent and brand preference by 10 percent? The sales effect of advertising is often harder to measure than the communication effect. Sales are affected by many factors besides advertising, such as product features, price, and availability.

One way to measure the sales effect of advertising is to compare past sales with past advertising expenditures. Another way is through experiments. Du Pont was one of the first companies to use advertising experiments.[13] Du Pont's paint department divided fifty-six sales territories into high, average, and low market share territories. In one-third of the group, Du Pont spent the normal amount for advertising; in another third, two and one-half times the normal amount; and in the remaining third, four times the normal amount. At the end of the experiment, Du Pont estimated how many extra sales had been created by higher levels of advertising expenditure. Du Pont found that higher advertising spending increased sales at a diminishing rate, and that the sales increase was weaker in Du Pont's high market share territories.

To spend a large advertising budget wisely, advertisers must define their advertising objectives; make careful budget, message, and media decisions; and evaluate advertising's results. Advertising also draws much public attention, because of its power to affect life styles and opinions. Advertising faces substantial regulation to ensure that it performs responsibly (see Marketing Highlight 17–4).[14]

SALES PROMOTION

Advertising is joined by two other mass-promotion tools—sales promotion and public relations.

Sales promotion consists of short-term incentives to encourage purchase or sales of a product or service.

Sales promotion includes a wide variety of promotion tools designed to stimulate earlier or stronger market response. It includes **consumer promotion**—samples, coupons, rebates, prices-off, premiums, patronage rewards, displays, and contests and sweepstakes; **trade promotion**—discounts, allowances, free goods, cooperative advertising, push money, and conventions and trade shows; and **salesforce promotion**—bonuses, contests, sales rallies.

Sales promotion tools are used by most organizations, including manufacturers, distributors, retailers, trade associations, and nonprofit institutions. (For example, churches sponsor bingo games, theater parties, and raffles; museums offer group rates, special exhibits, and discounts to students and seniors.) Estimates of annual sales promotion spending run as high as $100 billion, and this spending has increased rapidly in recent years.[15] A few decades ago, the ratio of advertising to sales promotion spending was about 60/40. Today, in many consumer packaged goods companies, the picture is reversed, with sales promotion often accounting for 60 or 70 percent of all marketing expenditures.

There is a danger, however, in letting advertising take a back seat to sales promotion. When a brand is price promoted too much of the time, the consumer begins to think of it as a cheap brand or will buy it only on sale. And though sales promotions bring faster sales results than advertising, most marketers feel promotions do not build long-term consumer preference and loyalty, as does advertising. Promotions usually build short-term volume which is not maintained.

Some sales promotion tools are "consumer franchise building"—they promote the product's positioning and include a selling message along with the deal. These promotions build long-run consumer demand rather than temporary brand switching. They include samples, coupons when they include a selling message, and premiums when they are related to the product. Sales promotion tools that are usually not consumer franchise building include cents-off deals, consumer premiums not related to a product, contests and sweepstakes, refund offers, and trade allowances. If properly designed, however, every sales promotion tool has consumer franchise building potential. Sellers should always try to use franchise-building promotions because they have longer-lasting effects.[16]

Sales promotions are usually used together with advertising or personal selling. Consumer promotions must usually be advertised and can add excitement and pulling power to ads. Trade and salesforce promotions support the firm's personal selling process.

In using sales promotion, a company must set objectives; select the tools; develop the program; pretest, implement, and control it; and evaluate the results.

Sales promotion objectives vary widely. Sellers may use consumer promotions to increase short-term sales or to help build long-term market share. The objective may be to entice consumers to try a new product, lure consumers away from competitors' products, get consumers to "load up" on a mature product, or hold and reward loyal customers. Objectives for trade promotions include getting the retailer to carry new items and more inventory, getting them to advertise the product and give it more shelf space, and getting them to buy ahead. For the *salesforce*, objectives include getting more salesforce support for current or new products or getting salespeople to sign up new accounts.

Selecting Sales Promotion Tools

Many tools can be used to accomplish the sales promotion objectives. The promotion planner should consider the type of market, sales promotion objectives, the competition, and the costs and effectiveness of each tool. The main consumer and trade promotion tools are described below.

Consumer Promotion Tools

The main consumer promotion tools include samples, coupons, cash refunds, price packs, premiums, patronage rewards, point-of-purchase displays and demonstrations, and contests, sweepstakes, and games.

Samples are offers of a trial amount of a product to consumers. Some samples are free; for others the company charges a small amount to offset the cost. The sample might be delivered door to door, sent in the mail, handed out in a store, attached to another product, or featured in an ad. Sampling is the most effective but most expensive way to introduce a new product. For example, Lever Brothers had so much confidence in its new Surf detergent that it spent $43 million to distribute free samples to four out of five American households.

Coupons are certificates that give buyers a saving when they purchase a product. Over 200 billion coupons are distributed each year, with a total face value of over $55 billion. Consumers redeem about 7.3 billion of these coupons, saving almost

Companies send out over 200 billion coupons each year and spend hundreds of millions of dollars on samples.

$3 billion on their shopping bills.[17] Coupons can be mailed, included with other products, or placed in ads. Several package goods companies are experimenting with point-of-sale coupon dispensing machines and computerized printers that automatically print out coupons at the cash register when certain products pass over the scanner. Coupons can stimulate sales of a mature brand and promote early trial of a new brand.

Cash refund offers (or rebates) are like coupons except that the price reduction occurs after the purchase rather than at the retail outlet. The consumer sends a "proof of purchase" to the manufacturer who then "refunds" part of the purchase price by mail. Cash refunds have been used for major products such as automobiles as well as for small appliances and packaged goods.

Price packs (also called cents-off deals) offer consumers savings off the regular price of a product. The reduced prices are marked by the producer directly on label or package. Price packs can be single packages sold at a reduced price (such as two for the price of one), or two related products banded together (such as a toothbrush and toothpaste). Price packs are very effective—even more so than coupons—in stimulating short-term sales.

Premiums are goods offered free or at a low cost as an incentive to buy a product. In its "Treasure Hunt" promotion, for example, Quaker Oats inserted $5 million dollars of gold and silver coins in Ken-L Ration dog food packages. In its recent premium promotion, Cutty Sark scotch offered a brass tray with the purchase of one bottle of Cutty and a desk lamp with the purchase of two bottles. A premium may come inside (in-pack) or outside (on-pack) the package. The package itself, if reusable (such as a decorative tin), may serve as a premium. Premiums are sometimes mailed to consumers who send in a proof of purchase, such as a box top. A self-liquidating premium is an item sold below its normal retail price to consumers who request it. Manufacturers now offer consumers all kinds of premiums bearing the company's name: Budweiser fans can order T-shirts, hot-air balloons, and hundreds of other items with Bud's name on them.

Patronage rewards are cash or other awards for regular use of a certain company's products or services. For example, airlines offer "frequent flyer plans," awarding points for miles traveled that can be turned in for free airline trips. Marriott Hotels adopted an "honored guest" plan that awards points for users of their hotels. Trading stamps are also patronage rewards in that customers receive stamps when buying from certain merchants and can redeem them for goods at redemption centers or through mail order catalogs.

Point-of-purchase (POP) *displays and demonstrations* take place at the point of purchase or sale. An example is a five-foot-high cardboard display of Cap'n Crunch next to Cap'n Crunch cereal boxes. Unfortunately, many retailers do not like to handle the hundreds of displays, signs, and posters they receive from manufacturers each year. Manufacturers have responded by offering better POP materials, tying them in with television or print messages, and offering to set them up. A good example is the award-winning Pepsi "tipping can" display. From an ordinary display of Pepsi six-packs along the supermarket aisle, a mechanically rigged six-pack begins to tip forward, grabbing the attention of passing shoppers who think the six-pack is falling. A sign on the tipping six-pack reminds shoppers, "Don't forget the Pepsi!" In test market stores, the display helped get more trade support and greatly increased Pepsi sales.

Contests, sweepstakes, and games give consumers the chance to win something—such as cash, trips, or goods—by luck or through extra effort. A contest calls for consumers to submit an entry—a jingle, guess, or suggestion—to be judged by a

Pepsi's tipping can and tipping bottle displays grab shopper attention.

panel that will select the best entries. A *sweepstakes* calls for consumers to submit their names for a drawing. A *game* presents consumers with something every time they buy—bingo numbers, missing letters—that may or may not help them win a prize. A sales contest urges dealers or the salesforce to increase their efforts, with prizes going to the top performers.

Trade Promotion Tools

More sales promotion dollars are directed to retailers and wholesalers (55 percent) than to consumers (45 percent).[18] Trade promotion can persuade the retailers or wholesalers to carry a brand, give it shelf space, promote it in their advertising, and push it to consumers. Shelf space is so scarce these days that manufacturers often have to offer price-offs, allowances, buy-back guarantees, or free goods to get on the shelf, and once there, to stay on the shelf. In fact, the trade has grown to depend on promotion money from the manufacturers. For example, the promotion money grocery stores receive from packaged goods manufacturers equals three times as much as their entire reported profits. Were this money withdrawn, grocers would have to greatly increase their prices. No single manufacturer could stop offering trade allowances without losing channel support.

Manufacturers use several trade promotion tools. Many of the tools used for consumer promotions—contests, premiums, displays—can also be used as trade promotions. Or the manufacturer may offer a straight *discount* off the list price on each case purchased during a stated period of time (also called a price-off, off-invoice, or off-list). The offer encourages dealers to buy in quantity or to carry a new item. Dealers can use the discount for immediate profit, for advertising, or for price reductions to their customers.

Manufacturers may offer an *allowance* (usually so much off per case) in return for the retailer's agreement to feature the manufacturer's products in some way. An advertising allowance compensates retailers for advertising the product. A display allowance compensates them for using special displays.

Manufacturers may offer *free goods*, which are extra cases of merchandise, to middlemen who buy a certain quantity or who feature a certain flavor or size. They may offer *push money*, cash or gifts to dealers or their salesforce to push the manufacturer's goods. Manufacturers may give retailers free *specialty advertising items* that carry the company's name, such as pens, pencils, calendars, paperweights, matchbooks, memo pads, ashtrays, and yardsticks.

Companies and trade associations organize *conventions and trade shows* to promote their products. Firms selling to the industry show their products at the trade show. Over 5,600 trade shows take place every year, drawing approximately 80 million people. The vendors get many benefits, such as finding new sales leads, contacting customers, introducing new products, meeting new customers, and selling more to present customers.

Developing the Sales Promotion Program

The marketer must make some other decisions in order to define the full sales promotion program. The marketer must decide on the *size of the incentive*. A certain minimum incentive is necessary if the promotion is to succeed. Up to a point, a larger incentive will produce more sales response. Some of the large firms who sell consumer packaged goods have a sales promotion manager who studies past promotions and recommends incentive levels to brand managers.

The marketer must also set *conditions for participation*. Incentives might be offered to everyone or to select groups. A premium might be offered only to those who turn in boxtops. Sweepstakes might not be offered in certain states, or to families of company personnel, or to persons under a certain age.

The marketer must decide how to *promote and distribute the promotion* program. A fifty-cents-off coupon could be given out in a package, at the store, by mail, or in an advertisement. Each distribution method involves a different level of reach and cost. The *length of the promotion* is also important. If the sales promotion period is too short, many prospects will not be able to take advantage of it, since they may not be buying during that time. If the promotion runs too long, the deal will lose some of its "act now" force. Brand managers need to set calendar dates for the promotions. The dates will be used by production, sales, and distribution. Some unplanned promotions may also be needed, requiring cooperation on short notice.

Finally, the marketer has to decide on the *sales promotion budget*. It can be developed in two ways. The marketer can choose the promotions and estimate their total cost. The more common way is to use a percentage of the total budget for sales promotion. One study found three major problems in how companies budget for sales promotion. First, they do not consider cost effectiveness. Second, instead of spending to achieve objectives, they simply extend last year's spending, take a percentage of expected sales, or use the "affordable approach." Finally, advertising and sales promotion budgets are too often prepared separately.[19]

Pretesting Sales promotion tools should be pretested when possible to find out if they are appropriate and of the right incentive size. Yet few promotions are ever tested ahead of time. Consumer sales promotions can be quickly and inexpensively pretested. Consumers can be asked to rate or rank different possible promotions, or the promotions can be tried on a limited basis in selected geographic areas.

Implementing Companies should have implementation plans for each promotion, covering lead time and sell-off time. Lead time is the time necessary to prepare the program before launching it. Sell-off time begins with the launch and ends when the promotion ends.

Evaluating the Results Evaluation is very important, yet few companies evaluate their sales promotion programs or evaluate them only superficially. Manufacturers can use one of many evaluation methods. The most common method is to compare sales before, during, and after a promotion. Suppose a company has a 6 percent market share before the promotion, which jumps to 10 percent during the promotion, falls to 5 percent right after, and rises to 7 percent later on. The promotion seems to have attracted new triers and more buying from current customers. After the promotion, sales fell as consumers used up their inventories. The long-run rise to 7 percent means that the company gained some new users. If the brand's share returned to the old level, then the promotion changed only the timing of demand rather than the total demand.

Consumer research would show the kinds of people who responded to the promotion and what they did after the promotion. Surveys can provide information on how many consumers recall the promotion, what they thought of it, how many took advantage of it, and how it affected their buying. Sales promotions can also be evaluated through experiments that vary such factors as incentive value, length, and distribution method.

Clearly, sales promotion plays an important role in the total promotion mix. To use it well, the marketer must define the sales promotion objectives, select the best tools, design the sales promotion program, pretest it, implement it, and evaluate the results. Marketing Highlight 17–5 describes some award-winning sales promotion campaigns.[20]

PUBLIC RELATIONS

Another major mass promotion tool is public relations.

> **Public relations** involves building good relations with the company's various publics by obtaining favorable publicity, building up a good "corporate image," and handling or heading off unfavorable rumors, stories, and events.

The old name for marketing public relations was **publicity,** which was seen as activities to promote a company or its products by planting news about it in media not paid for by the sponsor. Public relations is a much broader concept that includes publicity and many other activities. Public relations departments use many different tools:[21]

- *Press relations*: Placing newsworthy information into the news media to attract attention to a person, product, or service.
- *Product publicity*: Publicizing specific products.
- *Corporate communications*: Creating internal and external communications to promote understanding of the firm or institution.
- *Lobbying*: Dealing with legislators and government officials to promote or defeat legislation and regulation.
- *Counseling*: Advising management about public issues and company positions and image.

 Public relations is used to promote products, people, places, ideas, activities, organizations, and even nations. Trade associations have used public relations to rebuild interest in declining commodities such as eggs, milk, apples, and potatoes.

MARKETING HIGHLIGHT 17–5

AWARD-WINNING SALES PROMOTIONS

Each year American companies bombard consumers with thousands upon thousands of assorted sales promotions. Some fizzle badly, never meeting their objectives; others yield blockbuster returns. Here are examples of some award-winning sales promotions.

Quaker's "Where's the Cap'n" Contest

In this contest for kids, Quaker removed the likeness of Cap'n Crunch from the front of its cereal boxes and offered cash rewards totaling a million dollars to children who could find him. Clues to the Cap'n's whereabouts were provided inside the box, along with a free detective kit. Quaker supported the contest with large amounts of advertising during children's network television programming and in children's magazines. Coupons were distributed to parents offering discounts on boxes of Cap'n Crunch cereal. The promotion's objective: to turn around the brand's declining sales and market share. It accomplished this objective—and more. The contest became a major media event. Though it cost Quaker $18 million, brand awareness rose quickly, and Cap'n Crunch sales increased by a dramatic 50 percent!

9-Lives "Free Health Exam for Your Cat" Offer

In this unusual premium promotion, Star-Kist Foods teamed with the American Animal Hospital Association to offer cat owners a free $15 cat physical in exchange for proofs of purchase from 9-Lives cat food products. The 1,500 AAHA members donated their services to get cat owners into the habit of regular pet checkups. Star-Kist supported the premium offer with 63 million coupons and with trade discounts to boost retailer support. The promotion cost about $600,000 (excluding media). Consumers redeemed coupons at a rate 40 percent higher than normal, and Star-Kist gave out more than 50,000 free exam certificates. During the promotion, 9-Lives canned products achieved their highest share of the market in two years.

"The Red Baron Fly-In" Promotion

Red Baron Pizza Service used an imaginative combination of special events, couponing, and charitable activities to boost sales of its frozen pizza. The company re-created World War I flying ace Baron Manfred von Richtofen—complete with traditional flying gear and open-cockpit Stearman biplanes—as its company spokesperson. Red Baron pilots barnstormed thirteen markets, showed the plane, did stunts, gave out coupons, and invited consumers to "come fly with the Red Baron." The company donated $500 to a local youth organization in each market and urged consumers to match the gift. Trade promotions and local tie-in promotions boosted retailer support. The total budget: about $1 million. The results: For the four-week period during and after the fly-ins, unit sales in the thirteen markets jumped an average of 100 percent. In the 90 days following the fly-in, sales in some markets increased as much as 400 percent.

Source: See William A. Robinson, "The Best Promotions of 1983," *Advertising Age*, May 31, 1984, pp. 10–12; and William A. Robinson, "1985 Best Promotions of the Year," *Advertising Age*, May 5, 1986, pp. S10–S11. For other examples, see "A Gallery of Best Sales Promotions," *Advertising Age*, February 23, 1987, pp. 49–50.

The great "Cabbage Patch Panic."

New York City's image turned around when its "I Love New York" campaign took root, bringing millions more tourists to the city. Johnson & Johnson's masterly use of public relations played a major role in saving Tylenol from extinction after its product tampering scare. Lee Iaccoca's speeches and autobiography helped create a new winning image for Chrysler. Nations have used public relations to attract more tourists, foreign investment, and international support.

Public relations can have a strong impact on public awareness at a much lower cost than advertising. The company does not pay for the space or time in the media. It pays for a staff to develop and circulate stories and manage events. If the company develops an interesting story, it could be picked up by several different media, having the same effect as advertising that would cost millions of dollars. And it would have more credibility than advertising. Public relations's results can sometimes be spectacular. Consider the case of Cabbage Patch dolls:

> Public relations played a major role in making Coleco's Cabbage Patch dolls an overnight sensation. The dolls were formally introduced at a Boston press conference where local school children performed a mass adoption ceremony for the press. Thanks to Coleco's public relations machine, child psychologists publicly endorsed the Cabbage Patch Kids, and Dr. Joyce Brothers and other newspaper columnists proclaimed that the Kids were healthy playthings. Major women's magazines featured the dolls as ideal Christmas gifts, and after a 5-minute feature on the "Today" show, the Kids made the complete talk-show circuit. Marketers of other products used the hard-to-get Cabbage Patch dolls as premiums, and retailers used them to lure customers into their stores. The word spread, and every child just *had* to have one. The dolls were quickly sold out, and the great "Cabbage Patch Panic" began.

Public relations is often described as a marketing stepchild because of its limited and scattered use. The public relations department is usually located at corporate headquarters. Its staff is so busy dealing with various publics—stockholders, employees, legislators, city officials—that public relations to support product marketing objectives may be ignored. And marketing managers and public relations practitioners do not always talk the same language. Marketing managers tend to be much more bottom-line oriented, primarily interested in how advertising promotion, and public relations affect sales and profits. Many public relations practitioners see their job as simply communicating. But this difference is changing. Companies now want their public relations departments to manage all of their activities with a view toward marketing the company and improving the bottom line. Some companies are setting up special units called *marketing public relations* to directly support corporate and product promotion and image making. In a recent survey of marketing managers, three-fourths reported that their companies use marketing public relations. They found it particularly effective in building brand awareness and knowledge for both new and established products. In several cases, it proved more cost-effective than advertising.[22]

Major Public Relations Tools

Public relations professionals have several tools at their disposal. One of the major tools is *news*. PR professionals find or create favorable news about the company and its products or people. Sometimes news stories occur naturally, or sometimes the PR person can suggest events or activities that would create news. *Speeches* can also create product and company publicity. Iaccoca's charismatic talks to large audiences have helped to sell Chrysler cars to consumers and stock to investors. Increasingly, company executives must field questions from the media or give talks at trade associations or sales meetings, and these can build or hurt the company's image. Another PR tool is *special events*, including news conferences, seminars, exhibits, competitions, anniversaries, and grand openings, that will reach and interest the target publics.

Public relations people also prepare *written materials* to reach and influence their target markets. These materials include annual reports, brochures, articles, and company newsletters and magazines. *Audio-visual materials* such as films, slides-and-sound programs, and video and audio cassettes are used increasingly as communication tools. *Corporate identity materials* can also help to create a corporate identity that the public immediately recognizes. Logos, stationery, brochures, signs, business forms, business cards, buildings, uniforms, and company cars and trucks—all become marketing tools when they are attractive, distinctive, and memorable.

Companies can also improve public goodwill by contributing money and time to *public service activities*. For example, in 1987 Procter & Gamble and Publishers' Clearing House held a joint promotion to aid the Special Olympics. The Publishers' Clearing House mailing included product coupons, and Procter & Gamble donated to the Special Olympics ten cents for each coupon redeemed. In another example, B. Dalton Booksellers earmarked $3 million over a four year period toward the fight against illiteracy.

Major Public Relations Decisions

In considering when and how to use product public relations, management should set PR objectives, choose the PR messages and vehicles, implement the PR plan, and evaluate the results.

Setting Public Relations Objectives

The first task is to set objectives for public relations. Some years ago, the Wine Growers of California hired a public relations firm to develop a program to support

Attractive, distinctive, memorable company logos become strong marketing tools, as they are for these PepsiCo companies.

two major marketing objectives: Convince Americans that wine drinking is a pleasant part of good living, and improve the image and market share of California wines among all wines. The following public relations objectives were set: Develop magazine stories about wine and get them placed in top magazines (such as *Time*, and *House Beautiful*) and in newspapers (food columns and feature sections); develop stories about wine's many health values and direct them to the medical profession; and develop specific publicity for the young adult market, college market, governmental bodies, and various ethnic communities. These objectives were turned into specific goals so that final results could be evaluated.

Choosing Public Relations Messages and Vehicles

The organization next finds interesting stories to tell about the product. Suppose a little known college wants more public recognition. It will search for possible stories. Do any faculty members have unusual backgrounds, or are any working on unusual projects? Are any interesting new courses being taught or any interesting events taking place on campus? Usually this search will uncover hundreds of stories that can be fed to the press. The stories chosen should reflect the image this college wants.

If there are not enough stories, the college could sponsor newsworthy events. Here the organization creates news rather than finding it. Ideas might include hosting major academic conventions, inviting well-known speakers, and holding news conferences. Each event creates many stories for many different audiences.

Event creation is very important in publicizing fundraising drives for nonprofit organizations. Fundraisers have developed a large set of special events such as art exhibits, auctions, benefit evenings, bingo games, book sales, cake sales, contests, dances, dinners, fairs, fashion shows, phonothons, rummage sales, tours, and walka-thons. No sooner is one type of event created, such as a walkathon, than competitors create new versions such as readathons, bikeathons, and jogathons.

Implementing the Public Relations Plan

Implementing public relations requires care. Take the matter of placing stories in the media. A great story is easy to place—but most stories are not great, and they may not get past busy editors. One of the main assets of publicists is their personal relationships with media editors. Publicists are often ex-journalists who know many media editors and know what they want. Publicists look at media editors as a market to satisfy so that these editors will continue to use their stories.

Evaluating Public Relations Results

Public relation's contribution is difficult to measure because it is used with other promotion tools and its impact is indirect. If it is used before the other tools come into action, its contribution is easier to evaluate.

The easiest measure of publicity effectiveness is the number of exposures in the media. Publicists give the client a clippings book showing all the media that carried news about the product and a summary such as the following:

> Media coverage included 3,500 column inches of news and photographs in 350 publications with a combined circulation of 79.4 million; 2,500 minutes of air time on 290 radio stations and an estimated audience of 65 million; and 660 minutes of air time on 160 television stations with an estimated audience of 91 million. If this time and space had been purchased at advertising rates, it would have amounted to $1,047,000. [23]

This exposure measure is not very satisfying. It does not tell how many people actually read or heard the message, and what they thought afterward. It does not give information on the net audience reached, since the media overlap in readership and viewership.

A better measure is the change in product awareness, knowledge, and attitude resulting from the publicity campaign. Determining the change requires measuring the before-and-after levels of these measures. The Potato Board learned, for example, that the number of people who agreed with the statement "Potatoes are rich in vitamins and minerals" went from 36 percent before its public relations campaign to 67 percent after the campaign. That change represented a large increase in product knowledge.

Sales and profit impact, if obtainable is the best measure of public relations effort. For example, 9-Lives sales increased 43 percent at the end of a major "Morris the Cat" publicity campaign. However, advertising and sales promotion had been stepped up, and their contribution has also to be considered.

■ SUMMARY

Three major tools of mass-promotion are advertising, sales promotion, and public relations. They are mass-marketing tools as opposed to personal selling, which targets specific buyers.

Advertising—the use of paid media by a seller to inform, persuade, and remind about its products or organi-zation—is a strong promotion tool. American marketers

spend over $100 billion each year on advertising, and it takes many forms and has many uses. Advertising decision making is a five-step process consisting of setting objectives, budget decision, message decision, media decision, and evaluation. Advertisers should set clear goals as to whether the advertising is supposed to inform, persuade, or remind buyers. The advertising budget can be based on what is affordable, a percentage of sales, competitors' spending, or objectives and tasks. The message decision calls for designing messages, evaluating them, and executing them effectively. The media decision calls for defining reach, frequency, and impact goals; choosing major media types; selecting media vehicles; and scheduling the media. Finally, evaluation calls for evaluating the communication and sales effects of advertising before, during, and after the advertising is placed.

Sales promotion covers a wide variety of short-term incentive tools—coupons, premiums, contests, buying allowances—designed to stimulate consumers, the trade, and the company's own salesforce. Sales promotion spending has been growing faster than advertising spending in recent years. Sales promotion calls for setting sales promotion objectives; selecting tools; developing, pretesting, and implementing the sales promotion program; and evaluating results.

Public relations—which involve gaining favorable publicity and creating a favorable company image—is the least used of the major promotion tools, although it has great potential for building awareness and preference. Public relations involves setting PR objectives; choosing PR messages and vehicles; implementing the PR plan; and evaluating PR results.

■ QUESTIONS FOR DISCUSSION

1. In 1712, England's Tory government reacted to criticisms in newspapers by taxing periodicals and periodical advertising. The taxes reduced both the amount of criticism and the volume of advertising. Would an advertising tax have the same effect on advertising levels today? Describe the impact an advertising tax would have on advertisers, consumers, the media, and the economy.

2. Is it feasible for an advertising agency to work for two competing clients at the same time. What should a company do if its agency merges with another agency that works for a competing company? How much competition between accounts handled by an agency is "too much" competition?

3. According to advertising expert Steuart Henderson Britt, good advertising objectives spell out the intended audience, the advertising message, the desired effects, and the criteria for determining whether the effects were achieved (for example, not just "increase product awareness," but "increase product awareness 20%"). Why should these components be part of the advertising objective? List several effects, or goals, an advertiser might want a campaign to achieve.

4. What advantages and disadvantages does comparison advertising have to both advertisers and consumers? Which has more to gain from using comparison advertising—the leading brand in a market or a lesser brand? Why?

5. Describe several ads that you think are particularly effective and compare them with other ads that you think are ineffective. How would you improve the less effective ads? Which is more important to the effective-ness of an advertisement—what you say, or how you say it?

6. What factors call for more *frequency* in an advertising media schedule? What factors call for more *reach*? In a year-long campaign, how could you increase both frequency and reach without increasing your advertising expenditures?

7. An ad for Almost Home cookies states that, except for homemade cookies, they are the "moistest, chewiest, most perfectly baked cookies the world has ever tasted." If you think some other brand of cookies is moister or chewier, is the Almost Home claim false? Do any government or media organizations regulate this type of claim? Why or why not?

8. Compare the costs to the marketer of the various consumer promotion tools. Which promotions are most effective in getting consumers to try a product? Which are most effective in building loyalty to a product? Why do the different promotions have different effects?

9. Why are many companies spending more on sales promotion than on advertising? Why is more spent on trade promotion than on consumer promotions? Is heavy spending on sales promotion a good strategy for long-term profits?

10. The Graduate School of Business Administration at the University of North Carolina at Chapel Hill has announced plans to hire a public relations firm. What objectives might this or another business school set for a public relations campaign? What PR tools could be used to achieve these objectives? How could the results of the campaign be measured?

■ KEY TERMS

Advertising Any paid form of nonpersonal presentation and promotion of ideas, goods, or services by an identified sponsor.

Advertising goal A specific communication task to be accomplished with a specific target audience in a specific period of time.

Comparison advertising Advertising that compares one brand directly or indirectly to one or more other brands.

Consumer promotion Sales promotion designed to stimulate consumer purchasing, including samples, coupons, rebates, prices-off, premiums, patronage rewards, displays, and contests and sweepstakes.

Continuity Scheduling ads evenly within a given period.

Copy testing Measuring the communication effect of an advertisement before or after it is printed or broadcast.

Frequency The number of times the average person in the target market is exposed to an advertising message during a given period.

Public relations Building good relations with the company's various publics by obtaining favorable publicity, building up a good "corporate image," and handling or heading off unfavorable rumors, stories, and events. Major PR tools include press relations, product publicity, corporate communications, lobbying, and counseling.

Publicity Activities to promote a company or its products by planting news about it in media not paid for by the sponsor.

Pulsing Scheduling ads unevenly in bursts over a time period.

Reach The percentage of people in the target market exposed to an ad campaign during the given period.

Sales promotion Short-term incentives to encourage purchase or sales of a product or service.

Salesforce promotion Sales promotion designed to motivate the salesforce and make salesforce selling efforts more effective, including bonuses, contests, and sales rallies.

Trade promotion Sales promotion designed to gain reseller support and to improve reseller selling efforts, including discounts, allowances, free goods, cooperative advertising, push money, and conventions and trade shows.

■ REFERENCES

1. See Alice Z. Cuneo, "FCB Creativity Bears Fruit," *Advertising Age*, July 6, 1987, p. 25; Joan O'C. Hamilton, "You've Come a Long Way, Gumby," *Business Week*, December 8, 1986, p. 74; "Product Characters Raisin' Awareness," *Advertising Age*, June 1, 1987, p. S12; and Alice Z. Cuneo, "Hot Raisins: It's Licensed Products That Bring Big Bucks," *Advertising Age*, May 16, 1988, p. 30.

2. Statistical information in this section on advertising's size and composition draws on the September 24, 1987 special issue of *Advertising Age* on the hundred leading national advertisers.

3. Russel H. Colley, *Defining Advertising Goals for Measured Advertising Results* (New York: Association for National Advertisers, 1961). For a more complete discussion of DAGMAR, see Michael L. Rothschild, *Advertising* (Lexington, Mass.: D. C. Heath, 1987), pp. 142–55.

4. See Donald E. Schultz, Dennis Martin, and William P. Brown, *Strategic Advertising Campaigns* (Chicago: Crain Books, 1984), pp. 192–97.

5. See Scott Hume, "Anheuser Beer Arrives Without Ads," *Advertising Age*, July 6, 1987, p. 2.

6. Christine Dugas, "And Now, A Whittier Word from Our Sponsors," *Business Week*, March 24, 1986, p. 90. Also see Felix Kessler, "In Search of Zap-Proof Commercials," *Fortune*, January 21, 1985, pp. 68–70; and Dennis Kneale, "'Zapping' of TV Ads Appears Pervasive," *Wall Street Journal*, April 25, 1988, p. 29.

7. See "Ad Quality Good, Believability Low," *Advertising Age*, May 31, 1984, p. 3.

8. See William A. Mindak and H. Malcolm Bybee, "Marketing's Application to Fund Raising," *Journal of Marketing*, July 1971, pp. 13–18.

9. See L. Greenland, "Is This the Era of Positioning?" *Advertising Age*, May 19, 1972.

10. James P. Forkan, "Spot Production Costs Drop 4%," *Advertising Age*, October 26, 1987, p. 46; Christine Dugas, "And Now, a Wittier Word from Our Sponsor," *Business Week*, March 24, 1986, p. 91; and Cleveland Horton, "Why Apple Downloads," *Advertising Age*, May 4, 1987, p. 28.

11. See Roland T. Rust, *Advertising Media Models: A Practical Guide* (Lexington, MA: Lexington Books, 1986).

12. Philip H. Dougherty, "Bud 'Pulses' the Market," *New York Times*, February 18, 1975, p. 40.

13. See Robert D. Buzzell, "E. I. Du Pont de Nemours & Co.: Measurement of Effects of Advertising," in his *Mathematical Models and Marketing Management* (Boston: Division of Research, Graduate School of Business Administration, Harvard University, 1964), pp. 157–79.

14. For more on the legal aspects of advertising and sales promotion, see Louis W. Stern and Thomas L. Eovaldi, *Legal Aspects of Marketing Strategy* (Englewood Cliffs, NJ: Prentice Hall, 1984), Chaps. 7 and 8.

15. Len Strawzewski, "Promotion 'Carnival' Gets Serious," *Advertising Age*, May 2, 1988, pp. S1–2.

16. See Roger Strang, Robert M. Prentice, and Alden G. Clayton, *The Relationship Between Advertising and Promotion in Brand Strategy* (Cambridge, MA: Marketing Science Institute, 1975), Chap. 5; and P. Rajan Varadarajan, "Cooperative Sales Promotion: An Idea Whose Time Has Come," *Journal of Consumer Marketing*, Winter 1986, pp. 15–33.

17. See Nancy Zeldis, "Targeted Coupons Hit Nonusers," *Advertising Age*, April 27, 1987, p. S26.

18. See Felix Kessler, "The Costly Coupon Craze," *Fortune*, June 9, 1986, p. 83.

19. Roger A. Strang, "Sales Promotion—Fast Growth, Faulty Management," *Harvard Business Review*, July–August 1976, p. 119.

20. For more on sales promotion, see Don E. Schultz and William A. Robinson, *Sales Promotion Management* (Chicago: Crain Books, 1982); John Keon and Judy Bayer, "An Expert Approach to Sales Promotion Management," *Journal of Advertising Research*, June–July 1986, pp. 19–26; and Kenneth G. Hardy, "Key Success Factors for Manufacturer's Sales Promotions in Package Goods, *Journal of Marketing*, July 1986, pp. 13–23.

21. Adapted from Scott M. Cutlip, Allen H. Center, and Glen M. Brown, *Effective Public Relations*, 6th ed. (Englewood Cliffs, NJ: Prentice Hall, 1985), pp. 7–17.

22. Tom Duncan, *A Study of How Manufacturers and Service Companies Perceive and Use Marketing Public Relations* (Muncie, Ind.: Ball State University, December 1985).

23. Arthur M. Merims, "Marketing's Stepchild: Product Publicity," *Harvard Business Review*, November–December 1972, pp. 111–12.

18 *Promoting Products: Personal Selling and Sales Management*

November 7:	United Airlines announces it will buy one hundred and ten Boeing 737s and six 747s.	*Price*:	$3.1 billion
October 22:	Northwest Airlines announces it will buy ten 747s and ten 757s.	*Price*:	$2 billion
October 9:	International Lease Finance announces it will buy two 737s.	*Price*:	$50 million
October 8:	USAir announces it will buy two 737s.	*Price*:	$50 million
October 2:	Western Airlines announces it will buy twelve 737s.	*Price*:	$250 million
October 1:	Republic Airlines announces it will buy six 757s.	*Price*:	$240 million

Not a bad couple of weeks' work! But you might expect that from a company with a 60 percent share of the commercial airplane market, a company whose average order size is $34.9 million, and a company whose dedication to making a sale has been called obsessive. The company is Boeing, the $16.3 billion aerospace giant. In a field where big sales aren't often big news, Boeing got everyone's attention when, during just six weeks, it received orders worth $6.23 billion (the sales listed above plus others).

Most of the responsibility for marketing Boeing's commercial aircraft falls on the shoulders of the company's salesforce. In some ways, selling airplanes differs from selling other industrial products. There are only about 55 potential customers nationwide; there are only three major competitors (Boeing, McDonnell-Douglas, and Airbus); and the high-tech product is especially complex and challenging. But in many other ways, selling commercial aircraft is like selling any other industrial product. The salespeople determine needs, demonstrate how their product fulfills needs, try to close the sale, and follow up after the sale.

In order to determine needs, Boeing salespeople

become experts on the airlines they are responsible for, much like Wall Street analysts. They find out where each airline wants to grow, when it wants to replace planes, and its financial situation. Then the salespeople find ways to fulfill these customer needs. They run Boeing and competing planes through computer systems, simulating the airline's routes, cost per seat, and other factors to show that their planes are most efficient. And, more than likely, they'll bring in financial, planning, and technical people to answer any questions.

Then the negotiations begin. Deals are cut, discounts made, training programs offered; sometimes the top executives from the airline and Boeing are brought in to close the deal. The selling process is nerve-rackingly slow—it can take two or three years from the day the salesperson makes the first presentation to the day the sale is announced. And after getting the order, salespeople must keep in touch almost constantly to monitor the account's equipment needs and to make certain the customer stays satisfied. Success depends on building solid long-term relationships with customers based on performance and trust. According to one analyst, Boeing's salespeople "are the vehicle by which information is collected and contacts are made so all other things can take place."

The Boeing salesforce is made up of experienced salespeople who use a conservative, straightforward sales approach. They are smooth and knowledgeable, and they like to sell on facts and logic rather than hype and promises. In fact, they tend to understate rather than overstate product benefits. For example, one writer notes that "they'll always underestimate fuel efficiency. They'll say it's a five percent savings, and it'll be eight." Thus, a customer thinking about making a $2 billion purchase can be certain that after the sale Boeing products will live up to expectations.

Boeing salespeople have a head start on the competition. They have a broad mix of excellent products to sell, and Boeing's size and reputation help them get the orders. The salespeople are proud to be selling Boeing aircraft, and this pride creates an attitude of success. The sales attitude at Boeing is perhaps best summed up by the company's director of marketing communications: "The popular saying is that Boeing is the Mercedes of the airline industry. We think that's backward. We like to think that Mercedes is the Boeing of the auto industry."[1]

Chapter Objectives *After reading this chapter, you should be able to:*

1. Discuss the role of a company's salespeople.
2. Identify the seven major salesforce management decisions.
3. Explain how companies set salesforce objectives and strategy.
4. Tell how companies recruit, select, and train salespeople.
5. Describe how companies supervise salespeople and evaluate their effectiveness.

ROBERT LOUIS STEVENSON noted that "everyone lives by selling something." Salesforces are found in nonprofit as well as profit organizations. College recruiters are the college's salesforce for attracting students. Churches use membership committees to attract new members. The U.S. Agricultural Extension Service sends agricultural specialists to sell farmers on using new farming methods. Hospitals and museums use fundraisers to contact donors and raise money from them.

The people who do the selling are called by many names: salespeople, sales representatives, account executives, sales consultants, sales engineers, field representatives, agents, district managers, and marketing representatives. Selling is one of the oldest professions in the world (see Marketing Highlight 18–1).

There are many stereotypes of salespeople. "Salesman" may bring to mind the image of Arthur Miller's pitiable Willy Loman in *Death of a Salesman* or Meredith

MILESTONES IN THE HISTORY OF SELLING AND SALESMANSHIP

Selling goes back to the dawn of history. Paul Hermann described a Bronze Age traveling salesman's sample case: ". . . a solid wooden box, 26 inches in length, containing in specially hollowed compartments various types of axes, sword blades, buttons, etc." Early sellers and traders were not held in high esteem. The Roman word for salesman meant "cheater," and Mercury, the god of cunning and barter, was regarded as the patron deity of merchants and traders.

The buying and selling of commodities flourished over the centuries and centered in market towns. Traveling peddlers carried goods to the homes of prospective customers who were unable to get to the market towns.

The first salesmen in the United States were Yankee peddlers (pack peddlers), who carried clothing, spices, household wares, and notions in backpacks from East Coast manufacturing centers to settlers in the western frontier regions. The pack peddlers also traded with the Indians, exchanging knives, beads, and ornaments for furs. Many traders came to be viewed as shrewd, unprincipled tricksters who would not think twice about putting sand in the sugar, dust in the pepper, and chicory in the coffee. They often sold colored sugar water as "medicine" guaranteed to cure all possible ills.

In the early 1800s, some of the peddlers began to use horse-drawn wagons and to stock heavier goods, such as furniture, clocks, dishes, weapons, and ammunition. Some of these wagon peddlers settled in frontier villages and opened the first general stores and trading posts.

The larger retailers traveled once or twice a year to the nearest major city to replenish their stock. Eventually, wholesalers and manufacturers hired greeters, or drummers, who would seek out and invite retailers to visit the displays of their employers. The drummers would meet incoming trains and ships to beat their competitors. In time, the drummers traveled to their customers' places of business. Prior to 1860, there were fewer than 1,000 traveling salesmen, many of whom were credit investigators who also took orders for goods. By 1870, there were 7,000; by 1880, 28,000; and by 1900, 93,000 traveling salesmen.

Modern selling and sales management techniques were refined by John Henry Patterson (1844–1922), widely regarded as the father of modern salesmanship. Patterson ran the National Cash Register Company (NCR). He asked his best salesmen to demonstrate their sales approaches to the other salesmen. The best sales approach was printed in a "Sales Primer" and distributed to all NCR salesmen to be followed to the letter. This was the beginning of the canned sales approach. In addition, Patterson assigned his salesmen exclusive territories and sales quotas to stretch their effort. He held frequent sales meetings that served as both sales training sessions and social gatherings. He sent his salesmen regular communications on how to sell. One of the young men trained by Patterson was Thomas J. Watson, who later founded IBM. Patterson showed other companies the way to turn a salesforce into an effective tool for building sales and profits.

Willson's cigar-smoking, back-slapping, joke-telling Harold Hill in *The Music Man*. Salespeople are typically pictured as loving to be sociable—although many salespeople actually dislike it. They are blamed for forcing goods on people—although buyers often search out salespeople.

Actually the term **salesperson** covers a wide range of positions, whose differences are often greater than their similarities. Here's one popular classification of sales positions:

- Positions in which the salesperson's job is largely to deliver the product, such as milk, bread, fuel, oil.
- Positions in which the salesperson is largely an *inside order taker*, such as the department store salesperson standing behind the counter, or an *outside order taker* such as the packing house, soap, or spice salesperson.

The term "salesperson" covers a wide range of positions, from selling in a retail store to the engineering salesperson who consults with client companies.

- Positions in which the salesperson is not expected or permitted to take an order but only *builds goodwill or educates buyers*—the distiller's "missionary salesperson" or the "detailer" for a pharmaceutical company.
- Positions in which the major emphasis is on *technical knowledge*—the engineering salesperson who is mostly a consultant to client companies.
- Positions that demand the *creative sale of tangible products*, like appliances, encyclopedias, houses, or technical equipment; or of *intangibles* such as insurance, advertising services, or education.[2]

This list ranges from the least to the most creative types of selling. The jobs at the top of the list call for servicing accounts and taking orders, and the last ones call for hunting down buyers and getting them to buy. We will focus on the more creative types of selling and on the process of building and managing an effective salesforce. We define salesforce management as follows:

> **Salesforce management** is the analysis, planning, implementation and control of salesforce activities. It includes setting salesforce objectives; designing salesforce strategy; and recruiting, selecting, training, supervising, and evaluating the firm's salespeople.

The major salesforce management decisions are shown in Figure 18-1 and discussed in the following sections.

SETTING SALESFORCE OBJECTIVES

Companies set different objectives for their salesforces. IBM's salespeople are to "sell, install, and upgrade" customer computer equipment; AT&T salespeople should "develop, sell, and protect" accounts. Salespeople usually perform one or more of many tasks for their companies. They find and develop new customers and communi-

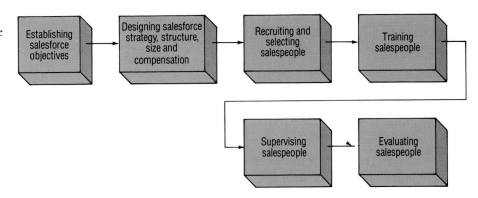

FIGURE 18-1
Major steps in salesforce management

Establishing salesforce objectives → Designing salesforce strategy, structure, size and compensation → Recruiting and selecting salespeople → Training salespeople → Supervising salespeople → Evaluating salespeople

cate information about the company's products and services. They sell products by approaching customers, presenting their products, answering objections, and closing sales with customers. Salespeople provide services to customers, carry out market research and intelligence work, and fill out sales call reports.

Some companies are very specific about their salesforce objectives and activities. One company advises its salespeople to spend 80 percent of their time with current customers and 20 percent with prospects and 85 percent of their time on current products and 15 percent on new products. The company believes that if norms are not set, salespeople tend to spend most of their time selling current products to current accounts and neglect new products and new prospects.

As companies increase their market orientation, their salesforces need to become more market-oriented. The old view is that salespeople should worry about sales and the company should worry about profit. The newer view is that salespeople should know how to produce customer satisfaction and company profit. They should know how to look at sales data, measure market potential, gather market intelligence, and develop marketing strategies and plans. Salespeople need marketing analysis skills, especially at higher levels of sales management. A market-oriented rather than a sales-oriented salesforce will be more effective in the long run.

*D*ESIGNING SALESFORCE STRATEGY

Once the company has set its salesforce objectives, it is ready to face questions of salesforce strategy, structure, size, and compensation.

Salesforce Strategy
The company will be competing with other firms to get orders from customers. It must base its strategy on an understanding of the customer buying process. The company can use one or more of several sales approaches to contacting customers. A salesperson can talk to a prospect or customer in person or over the phone. Or the salesperson can make a sales presentation to a buying group. A sales team (such as a company executive, a salesperson, and a sales engineer) can make a sales presentation to a buying group. In *conference selling*, a salesperson brings resource people from the company to meet with one or more buyers to discuss problems and opportunities. In *seminar selling*, a company team conducts an educational seminar for technical people in a customer company about state-of-the-art developments.

Thus the salesperson often acts as an "account manager" who arranges contacts between people in the buying and selling companies. Selling calls for teamwork, since salespeople need help from others in the company. These others include top management, especially when major sales are at stake; technical people who provide technical information to customers; customer-service representatives who provide installation, maintenance, and other services to customers; and office staff such as sales analysts, order processors, and secretaries.

Salesforce Structure

The company must also decide on how to structure its salesforce. This decision is simple if the company sells one product line to one industry with customers in many locations; here the company would use a *territorial salesforce structure*. If the company sells many products to many types of customers, it might need a *product salesforce structure* or *customer salesforce structure*. These three structures are discussed below.

Territorial Salesforce Structure

In a **territorial salesforce structure,** each salesperson is given an exclusive territory in which to sell the company's full line. This salesforce structure is the simplest sales organization and has many advantages. It clearly defines the salesperson's job, and because only one salesperson works the territory, she or he gets all the credit or blame for territory sales. The territorial structure also increases the salesperson's desire to build local business and personal ties. These ties improve the salesperson's selling effectiveness and personal life. Finally, travel expenses are relatively small, since each salesperson travels within a small geographical area.

Territorial sales organization is often supported by a many levels of sales management positions. For example, Campbell Soup recently changed from a product salesforce structure to a territorial one, in which each salesperson is responsible for selling all Campbell Soup products. Starting at the bottom of the organization, sales merchandisers report to sales representatives, who report to retail supervisors, who report to directors of retail sales operations, who in turn report to one of 22 regional sales managers. The regional sales managers are headed by one of four general sales managers (West, Central, South, and East), who report to a vice president and general sales manager.[3]

Product Salesforce Structure

Salespeople must know their products, especially when the products are numerous, unrelated, and complex. This need, together with the trend toward product management, led many companies to the **product salesforce structure** in which the salesforce sells along product lines. For example, some college textbook publishers divide their salesforce into groups that sell humanities and social science books, business and professional books, or physical science books.

The product structure, however, can lead to problems if many of the company's products are bought by the same customers. For example, the American Hospital Supply Corporation has several product divisions, each with its own salesforce. It is possible that several AHS salespeople could call on the same hospital on the same day. This means that they travel over the same routes, and each waits to see the customer's purchasing agents. These extra costs must be compared to the benefits of better product knowledge and attention to individual products.

Customer Salesforce Structure

Companies often use a **customer salesforce structure** in which they structure the salesforce along customer lines. Separate salesforces may be set up for different industries, for serving current customers versus finding new ones, and for major versus regular accounts. Xerox, for example, classifies its customers into four major groups, each served by a different Xerox salesforce. The top group consists of large national accounts with multiple and scattered locations; these customers are handled by 250 to 300 *national account managers*. Next are major accounts that are not national in scope but that may have several locations within a region; these are handled by one of Xerox's 1,000 or so *major account managers*. The third customer group consists of standard commercial accounts with potential of $5,000 to $10,000; they are served by *account representatives*. All other customers are handled by *marketing representatives*.[4]

The biggest advantage of customer specialization is that each salesforce can know more about specific customer needs. It can also reduce total salesforce costs. At one time a pump manufacturer used highly trained sales engineers to sell to all its customers—to manufacturers who needed highly technical assistance and to wholesalers who did not. Later the company split its salesforce and used lower-paid, less technical salespeople to deal with the wholesalers. This change reduced salesforce costs without reducing customer service.

The major disadvantage of a customer structure arises when customers are scattered across the country. Such geographical disbursement means a great deal of travel by each of the company's salesforces.

Salesforce Size

Once the company has set its strategy and structure, it is ready to consider salesforce size. Salespeople are one of the company's most productive—and most expensive—assets. Increasing their number will increase both sales and costs.

Many companies use the *workload approach* to establish salesforce size. Under this approach, the company groups accounts into different size classes, then figures out how many salespeople are needed to call on them the desired number of times. The company might think as follows: Suppose we have 1,000 Type A accounts and 2,000 Type B accounts in the nation. Type A accounts require 36 calls a year and Type B accounts 12 calls a year. This means the company needs a salesforce that can make 60,000 calls a year—the salesforce's *workload* [$(1{,}000 \times 36) + (2{,}000 \times 12) = 36{,}000 + 24{,}000 = 60{,}000$]. Suppose our average salesperson last year made 1,000 calls a year. The company needs 60 salespeople ($60{,}000 \div 1{,}000$).

Salesforce Compensation

To attract the needed salespeople, the company has to have an attractive compensation plan. These plans vary a lot by industry and by company within the same industry. The level of compensation must be close to the "going rate" for the type of sales job and skills needed. For example, the average earnings of an experienced, middle-level salesperson in 1987 amounted to $36,500.[5] To pay less than the going rate will attract too few quality salespeople; to pay more is unnecessary.

Compensation is made up of several elements—a fixed amount, a variable amount, expenses, and fringe benefits. The fixed amount, which might be salary or a drawing account, gives the salesperson some stable income. The variable amount, which might be commissions, a bonus, or profit sharing, rewards the salesperson for greater effort. Expense allowances let the salespeople undertake needed and desirable selling efforts. And fringe benefits, such as paid vacations, sickness or accident benefits, pensions, and life insurance, provide job security and satisfaction. Management must decide what mix of these compensation elements makes the most sense for each sales job.

Fixed and variable compensation give rise to four basic types of compensation plans—straight salary, straight commission, salary plus bonus, and salary plus commissions. A recent study of salesforce compensation plans showed that about 5 percent paid straight salary, 3 percent paid straight commission, 46 percent paid salary plus bonus, and 46 percent paid salary plus commission.[6]

RECRUITING AND SELECTING SALESPEOPLE

Having set the strategy, structure, size, and compensation for the salesforce, the company now must set up systems for recruiting and selecting, training, supervising, and evaluating salespeople.

Importance of Careful Selection

At the heart of successful salesforce operation is the selection of good salespeople. The performance levels of an average and a top salesperson can be quite different. In a typical salesforce, the top 30 percent of the salespeople might bring in 60 percent of the sales. Careful salesperson selection can greatly increase overall salesforce performance.

Beyond the differences in sales performance, poor selection results in costly turnover. One study found an average annual salesforce turnover rate for all industries of almost 20 percent. The costs of high turnover can be great. When a salesperson quits, the costs of finding and training a new salesperson plus the costs of lost sales can run as high as $50,000 to $75,000. And a salesforce with a lot of new people is less productive.[7]

What Makes a Good Salesperson

Selecting salespeople would not be a problem if the company knew what traits to look for. If good salespeople are outgoing, aggressive, and energetic, these characteristics could be checked in applicants. But many successful salespeople are also bashful, mild mannered, and very relaxed. Successful salespeople include men and women who are tall and short, who speak well and speak poorly, who dress well and who dress shabbily.

Still, the search continues for the magic list of traits that spells sure-fire sales ability. Many lists have been drawn up. One survey suggests that good salespeople have lots of enthusiasm, persistence, initiative, self-confidence, and job commitment. They are committed to sales as a way of life and have a strong customer orientation.[8] Charles Garfield found that good salespeople are goal-directed risk takers who identify strongly with their customers (see Marketing Highlight 18–2).

How can a company find out what traits salespeople in its industry should have? The job duties suggest some of the traits to look for. Is there a lot of paper work? Does the job call for much travel? Will the salesperson face a lot of rejections? The successful salesperson should be suited to these duties. The company should also look at the characteristics of its most successful salespeople for clues on needed traits.

Recruiting Procedures

After management has decided on the needed traits, it must recruit. The personnel department looks for applicants by getting names from current salespeople, using employment agencies, placing job ads, and contacting college students. Companies have sometimes found it hard to sell college students on selling. Many students think that selling is a job and not a profession, that salespeople must be deceitful to be effective, and that there is too much insecurity and travel in selling. Some women believe that selling is a man's career. To counter these objections, recruiters talk about high starting salaries, income growth, and the fact that more than one-fourth of the presidents of large U.S. corporations started out in marketing and

WHAT MAKES A SUPERSALESPERSON?

Charles Garfield, clinical professor of psychology at the University of California, San Francisco School of Medicine, claims his twenty-year analysis of more than 1,500 superachievers in every field of endeavor is the longest running to date. *Peak Performance— Mental Training Techniques of the World's Greatest Athletes*, the first book Garfield wrote about his findings, was published June 1. Although he says it will be followed shortly by a book on business which will cover supersalespeople, many companies (such as IBM, which took 3,000) have ordered the current book for their salesforces. Garfield says that the complexity and speed of change in today's business world means that to be a peak performer in sales requires greater mastery of different fields than to be one in science, sports, or the arts. The following are the most common characteristics he has found in peak sales performance.

- Supersalespeople are always taking risks and making innovations. Unlike most people, they stay out of the "comfort zone" and try to surpass their previous levels of performance.
- Supersalespeople have a powerful sense of mission and set the short-, intermediate-, and long-term goals necessary to fulfill that mission. Their personal goals

are always higher than the sales quotas set by their managers. Supersalespeople also work well with managers, especially if the managers also are interested in peak performance.

- Supersalespeople are more interested in solving problems than in placing blame or bluffing their way out of situations. Because they view themselves as professionals in training, they are always upgrading their skills.
- Supersalespeople see themselves as partners with their customers, and as team players rather than adversaries. Peak performers believe their task is to communicate with people, while mediocre salespeople psychologically change their customers into objects and talk about the number of calls and closes they made as if it had nothing to do with human beings.
- Supersalespeople take each rejection as information they can learn from, whereas mediocre salespeople personalize rejection.
- The most surprising finding is that, like peak performers in sports and the arts, supersalespeople use mental rehearsal. Before every sale they review it in their mind's eye, from shaking the customer's hand when they walk in to discussing the customer's problems and asking for the order.

Source: "What Makes a Supersalesperson?" *Sales and Marketing Management*, August 13, 1984, p. 86.

---

sales. They point out that more than 21 percent of the people selling manufactured products are women (see Marketing Highlight 18–3).

Selecting Salespeople Recruiting will attract many applicants, and the company must select the best ones. The selection procedure can vary from a single informal interview to lengthy testing and interviewing. Many companies give formal tests to sales applicants. The tests typically measure sales aptitude, analytical and organizational skills, personality traits, and other characteristics. Test scores provide only one piece of information in a set that includes personal characteristics, references, past employment history, and interviewer reactions. But test results are weighted heavily by such companies as IBM, Prudential, Procter & Gamble, and Gillette. Gillette claims that tests have reduced turnover by 42 percent and have correlated well with the later performance of new salespeople.

TRAINING SALESPEOPLE

Many companies used to send their new salespeople into the field almost right away after hiring them. They would be given samples, order books, and general instructions ("sell west of the Mississippi"). Training programs were luxuries. To

ON THE JOB WITH A SUCCESSFUL XEROX SALESWOMAN

The word "salesman" is beginning to have an archaic ring. The entry of women into what was once a male bastion has been swift and dramatic. More than 21 percent of people selling manufactured products are women, vs. 7 percent a decade ago. And women are making special strides selling high-tech equipment. At Xerox, for example, they are 39 percent of the salesforce.

Nancy Reck decided that sales offered the best opportunity when she and her husband, Miles, moved from Jacksonville, Florida, to Chapel Hill, North Carolina, 3½ years ago so he could work on a doctorate. They were holding down five jobs between them to make ends meet when Nancy, 30, found what she had been looking for: a single job that paid enough to support both of them. Sales, says the former schoolteacher, "is a field where compensation is related to performance. You write your own ticket."

Reck signed up with Xerox as a sales representative and quickly made her mark. In each of the last three years, she has qualified for the President's Club, which means she exceeded all of her sales goals, an honor won by only one of every five members of the sales force last year. Her income, which she won't discuss, is probably about $50,000 a year.

A native of tiny Seaboard, North Carolina, Reck earned her spurs on the "low volume" beat, selling Xerox copiers and electronic typewriters door to door to small businesses in 17 counties in her home state. Recently she was promoted to a new job that is a stepping stone to management.

Reck worried she would have to develop an artificial personality to succeed in sales. Instead she found she could just be herself: "I treat every cus-

Nancy Reck doing business despite the weather.

tomer as if he were my father, my brother, or my best friend.

Source: "On the Job With a Successful Xerox Saleswoman," *Fortune*, April 30, 1984, p. 102 © 1984 Time Inc. All rights reserved.

many companies, a training program meant spending a lot for instructors, materials, and space; paying a person who was not yet selling; and losing sales opportunities because he or she was not in the field.

Today's new salespeople may spend a few weeks to many months in training. The median training period is seventeen weeks in industrial products companies, and nineteen in consumer products companies.[9] At IBM, new salespeople are not on their own for two years! And IBM expects its salespeople to spend 15 percent of their time each year in additional training.

The training programs have several goals. Salespeople need to know and identify with the company, so most companies spend the first part of the training program

Companies spend hundreds of millions of dollars to train their salespeople in the art of selling.

describing the company's history and objectives, its organization, its financial structure and facilities, and its chief products and markets. Salespeople need to know the company's products, so sales trainees are shown how products are produced and how they work in various uses. Salespeople need to know customers' and competitors' characteristics. The training program teaches them about competitors' strategies and about different types of customers and their needs, buying motives, and buying habits. Salespeople need to know how to make effective presentations. They get training in the principles of salesmanship, and the company outlines the major sales arguments for each product. Finally, salespeople need to understand field procedures and responsibilities. They learn how to divide time between active and potential accounts and how to use the expense account, prepare reports, and route communications effectively.

Principles of Salesmanship

One of the major objectives of training programs is to teach salespeople the art of selling. Companies spend hundreds of millions of dollars on seminars, books, cassettes, and other materials. Almost a million copies of books on selling are purchased every year, with such tantalizing titles as *How to Outsell the Born Salesman*, *How to Sell Anything to Anybody*, *The Power of Enthusiastic Selling*, *How Power Selling Brought Me Success in 6 Hours*, *Where Do You Go from No. 1?*, *and 1000 Ways Salespeople Can Increase Their Sales*. One of the most lasting books on selling is Dale Carnegie's *How to Win Friends and Influence People*.

All of the training approaches try to convert a salesperson from being a passive order taker to being an active order getter. Order takers assume that customers know their own needs, that they would resent any attempt at influence, and that they prefer salespeople who are polite and reserved. An example of an order taker would be a salesperson who calls on a dozen customers each day, simply asking if the customer needs anything.

There are two approaches to training salespeople to be order getters—a sales-oriented approach and a customer-oriented approach. The sales-oriented approach trains the salesperson in high-pressure selling techniques, such as those sometimes used in selling encyclopedias or automobiles. The techniques include overstating the product's merits, criticizing competing products, using a slick canned presentation, selling yourself, and offering some concession to get the order on the spot. This form of selling assumes that customers will not buy except under pressure; that they are influenced by a slick presentation; and that they will not be sorry after signing the order, or if they are, that it doesn't matter.

The customer-oriented approach, the one most often used in today's professional selling, trains salespeople in customer problem solving. The salesperson learns how to identify customer needs and find good solutions. This approach assumes that customer needs provide sales opportunities, that customers appreciate good suggestions, and that customers will be loyal to salespeople who have their long-term interests at heart. In one survey, purchasing agents described these qualities as the ones they most disliked in salespeople: pushy, arrogant, unreliable, too talkative, fails to ask about needs. The qualities they valued most included reliability and credibility, integrity, innovativeness in solving problems, and product knowledge.[10] The problem solver salesperson fits better with the marketing concept than the hard seller or order taker.

Most training programs view the **selling process** as consisting of several steps that the salesperson must master. These steps are shown in Figure 18-2 and discussed below.[11]

Prospecting and Qualifying

The first step in the selling process is to identify prospects. The salesperson must approach many prospects to get a few sales. In one segment of the insurance industry, for example, only one out of nine prospects becomes a customer. In the computer business, 125 phone calls result in 25 interviews leading to 5 demonstrations and 1 sale.[12] Although the company supplies leads, salespeople need skill in finding their own leads. Salespeople can obtain leads many ways. They can ask current customers for the names of prospects. They can build referral sources, such as suppliers, dealers, noncompeting salespeople, and bankers. They can join organizations to which prospects belong, or engage in speaking and writing activities that will draw attention. They can search for names in newspapers or directories and use the telephone and mail to track down leads. Or they can drop in unannounced on various offices (cold calling).

Salespeople need to know how to qualify leads, that is, how to identify the good ones and screen out the poor ones. Prospects can be qualified by looking at their financial ability, volume of business, special needs, location, and possibilities for growth.

FIGURE 18-2
Major steps in effective selling

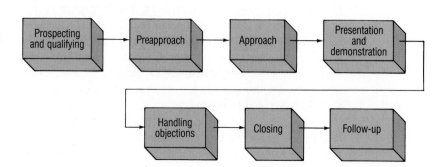

Preapproach

Before calling on a prospect, the salesperson should learn as much as possible about it (what it needs, who is involved in the buying) and its buyers (their characteristics and buying styles). The salesperson can consult standard sources (*Moody's, Standard and Poor's, Dun and Bradstreet*), acquaintances, and others to learn about the company. The salesperson should set *call objectives*, which might be to qualify the prospect, or gather information, or to make an immediate sale. Another task is to decide on the best approach, which might be a personal visit, a phone call, or a letter. The best timing should be thought out because many prospects are busy at certain times. Finally, the salesperson should give thought to an overall sales strategy for the account.

Approach

The salesperson should know how to meet and greet the buyer to get the relationship off to a good start. This involves the salesperson's appearance, the opening lines, and the follow-up remarks. The salesperson should wear clothes similar to what the buyer wears; show courtesy and attention to the buyer; and avoid distracting mannerisms, such as pacing the floor or staring at the customer. The opening lines should be positive, such as "Mr. Jones, I am Chris Smith from the Alltech Company. My company and I appreciate your willingness to see me. I will do my best to make this visit profitable and worthwhile for you and your company." This might be followed by some key questions to learn more about the customer's needs or the showing of a display or sample to attract the buyer's attention and curiosity.

Presentation and Demonstration

The salesperson now tells the product "story" to the buyer, showing how the product will make or save money. The salesperson describes the product features but concentrates on presenting customer benefits.

Companies use three styles of sales presentation. The oldest is the *canned approach*, which is a memorized or scripted talk covering the main points. An encyclopedia salesperson might describe the encyclopedia as "a once-in-a-lifetime buying opportunity" and focus on some beautiful four-color pages of sports pictures, hoping to trigger desire for the encyclopedia. Scripted presentations are often very effective in telephone selling. A properly prepared and rehearsed script sounds natural and moves the salesperson smoothly through the presentation. With electronic scripting,

In the sales presentation, the salesperson tells the product story to buyers.

computers can lead the salesperson through a sequence of selling messages tailored on the spot to the prospect's responses.[13]

The *formula approach* of sales presentation first identifies the buyer's needs and buying style. The salesperson draws the buyer into a discussion that reveals the buyer's needs and attitudes. Then the salesperson moves into a formula presentation that shows how the product will satisfy that buyer's needs. It is not canned but follows a general plan.

The *need-satisfaction approach* starts with a search for the customer's real needs by getting the customer to do most of the talking. This approach calls for good listening and problem-solving skills. One marketing director describes the approach this way:

> [High-performing salespeople] make it a point to understand customer needs and goals before they pull anything out of their product bag. . . . Such salespeople spend the time needed to get an in-depth knowledge of the customer's business, asking questions that will lead to solutions our systems can address.[14]

Any style of sales presentation can be improved with demonstration aids such as booklets, flip charts, slides, videotapes or videodiscs, and product samples. If buyers can see or handle the product, they will better remember its features and benefits.

Handling Objections

Customers almost always have objections during the presentation or when asked to place an order. The problem can be logical or psychological. And objections are often unspoken. To handle these objections, the salesperson uses a positive approach, seeks out hidden objections, asks the buyer to clarify any objections, takes the objections as an opportunity to provide more information to the buyer, and turns the objections into reasons for buying. The salesperson needs training in the skills of handling objections.

Closing

The salesperson now tries to "close" the sale. Some salespeople do not get to this stage or do not handle it well. They lack confidence, or feel guilty about asking for the order, or do not recognize the right moment to close the sale. Salespeople need to know how to recognize closing signals from the buyer, including physical actions, comments, and questions. For example, the customer may sit forward and nod approvingly or ask about prices and credit terms. Salespeople can use one of several closing techniques. They can ask for the order, review the points of agreement, offer to help write up the order, ask whether the buyer wants this model or that one, get the buyer to make minor choices such as the color or size, or indicate that the buyer will lose out if the order is not placed now. The salesperson may offer the buyer special reasons to close, such as a lower price or an extra quantity at no charge.

Follow-Up

This last step is necessary if the salesperson wants to ensure customer satisfaction and repeat business. Right after closing, the salesperson should complete any details on delivery time, purchase terms, and other matters. The salesperson should schedule a follow-up call when the initial order is received to make sure there is proper installation, instruction, and servicing. This visit would show any problems, assure the buyer of the salesperson's interest, and reduce any buyer concerns that might have arisen.

SUPERVISING SALESPEOPLE

New salespeople need more than a territory, compensation, and training—they need supervision. Through supervision, the company directs and motivates the salesforce to do a better job.

Directing Salespeople
Companies vary in how closely they supervise their salespeople. Salespeople who are paid mostly on commission and who are expected to hunt down their own prospects are generally left on their own. Those who are salaried and must cover assigned accounts usually are more closely supervised.

Developing Customer Targets and Call Norms

Most companies classify customers into A, B, and C accounts, based on the account's sales volume, profit potential, and growth potential. They set the desired number of calls per period on each account class. Thus A accounts may receive nine calls a year; B, six calls; and C, three calls. The call norms depend upon competitive call norms and profits expected from the account.

Developing Prospect Targets and Call Norms

Companies often specify how much time their salesforce should spend prospecting for new accounts. Spector Freight wants its salespeople to spend 25 percent of their time prospecting and to stop calling on a prospect after three unsuccessful calls. Companies set up prospecting standards for several reasons. If left alone, many salespeople will spend most of their time with current customers. Current customers are better-known quantities. Salespeople can depend upon them for some business, whereas a prospect may never deliver any business. Unless salespeople are rewarded for opening new accounts, they may avoid new account development. Some companies rely on a special salesforce to open new accounts.

Using Sales Time Efficiently

Salespeople need to know how to use their time efficiently. One tool is the annual call schedule showing which customers and prospects to call on in which months, and which activities to carry out. The activities include taking part in trade shows, attending sales meetings, and carrying out marketing research. The other tool is time-and-duty analysis. In addition to time spent selling, the salesperson spends

Many companies are computerizing their salesforces to make salespeople more efficient and effective.

time traveling, waiting, eating and taking breaks, and doing administrative chores. On average, actual selling time accounts for only 25 percent of total working time![15] If selling time could be raised from 25 to 30 percent, this would be a 20 percent increase in the time spent selling. Companies are always looking for ways to save time—using phones instead of traveling, simplifying recordkeeping forms, finding better call and routing plans, and supplying more and better customer information.

Advances in technological equipment—desk-top and lap-top computers, videocassette recorders, videodiscs, automatic dialers, teleconferencing—have allowed dramatic breakthroughs in improving sales force productivity. Salespeople have truly gone "electronic." One expert predicts that by 1991, 28 percent of all salespeople will use personal computers (PCs) on the job. Salespeople use computers to profile customers and prospects, analyze and forecast sales, enter orders, check inventories and order status, prepare sales and expense reports, process correspondence, and carry out many other activities. In a recent survey, salesforces using PCs reported an average 43 percent productivity gain.[16]

To reduce time demands on their *outside salesforces*, many companies have increased the size of their *inside salesforces*. One survey of 135 electronics distributors found that an average of 57 percent of the salesforce members were inside salespeople.[17] Managers gave as reasons the rising costs of outside sales calls and the growing use of computers and innovative telecommunications equipment. These managers think the proportion of inside salesforce members will reach two-thirds by 1990.

Inside salespeople include three types. *Technical support people* provide technical information and answers to customers' questions. *Sales assistants* provide clerical backup for the outside salespeople. They call ahead and confirm appointments, conduct credit checks, follow up on deliveries, and answer customers' questions when outside salespeople cannot be reached. *Telemarketers* use the phone to find new leads, qualify prospects, and sell to them (see Marketing Highlight 18–4). A telemarketer can call up to 50 customers a day compared to the 4 that an outside salesperson can see. The inside salesforce frees the outside salespeople to spend more time selling to major accounts and finding major new prospects.

Motivating Salespeople

Some salespeople will do their best without any special urging from management. To them, selling is the most fascinating job in the world. They are ambitious self-starters. But the selling job often involves frustration. Salespeople usually work alone, and they are sometimes away from home. They may face aggressive, competing salespeople and difficult customers. They sometimes do not have the authority to do what is needed to win a sale, and they may lose large orders they have worked hard to obtain. Thus salespeople often need special encouragement to work at their best level. Management can boost salesforce morale and performance through its organizational climate, sales quotas, and positive incentives.

Organizational Climate

Organizational climate describes the feeling that the salespeople have about their opportunities, value, and rewards for a good performance within the company. Some companies treat salespeople as if they are not very important. Other companies treat their salespeople as the prime movers and allow unlimited opportunity for income and promotion. The company's attitude toward its salespeople affects their behavior. If they are held in low esteem, there is much turnover and poor performance. If they are held in high esteem, there is little turnover and high performance.

Treatment from the salesperson's immediate superior is important. A good sales

TELEMARKETING: A PHONE CAN BE BETTER THAN A FACE

Selling face-to-face is by far the best way to achieve personal rapport with a prospect, right? Wrong, says LeRoy Benham, president of Climax Portable Machine Tools. By combining telemarketing and computers, a small company can save money and lavish the kind of attention on buyers that will amaze them.

True, such a strategy depends on what your market is and your stake in it, but few would argue with Benham's track record. At a time when most U.S. machine tool manufacturers have been in a deep depression, he has carved out a niche for the portable cutting tools he sells. This year, sales will rise 20 percent to $5 million. And company profits will climb more than 20 percent for the third year in a row since Climax began phasing out its distributor network and switched to telephone selling.

Under the old system, sales engineers spent one-third of their time on the road, training distributor salespeople and accompanying them on calls. "They'd make about four contacts a day," says Benham. "They found they actually got more information from the prospects when they were back here setting up travel appointments by phone." Now, each of the five sales engineers on Benham's telemarketing team calls about 30 prospects a day, following up on leads gener-ated by ads and direct mail. It takes about five calls to close a sale, and the sales engineers update a computer file on prospects each time they speak to them, noting their degree of commitment, require-ments, next-call date, and personal comments.

"If someone mentions he's going on a fishing trip, our sales engineer enters that in the computer and uses it to personalize the next phone call," says Benham, noting that's just one way to build good relations. Another: The first mailing to a prospect includes the sales engineer's business card with his picture on it.

It takes more than friendliness to sell $15,000 machine tools (special orders may run $200,000) over the phone, of course, but Benham has proof that personality pays. When customers were asked in a survey, "Do you see the sales engineer often enough?" the response was overwhelmingly positive. Obviously many people didn't realize that the only contact they'd had with Climax had been on the phone.

Source: Adapted from "A Phone Is Better Than a Face," *Sales and Marketing Management*, October 1987, p. 29.

---

manager keeps in touch with the salesforce through letters and phone calls, visits in the field, and evaluation sessions in the home office. At different times the sales manager acts as the salesperson's boss, companion, coach, and confessor.

Sales Quotas

Many companies set quotas for their salespeople stating the dollar amount they should sell during the year and how that should be divided among the company's product. Compensation is often related to how well salespeople meet their quotas.

Sales quotas are set when developing the annual marketing plan. The company first decides on a sales forecast that is reasonably achievable. Based on this forecast, management plans production, workforce size, and financial needs. It then sets sales quotas for its regions and territories. Sales quotas are set higher than the sales forecast to stretch sales managers and salespeople to their best effort. If they fail to make their quotas, the company may still make its sales forecast.

Each area sales manager divides the area's quota among the area's salespeople. There are three schools of thought on quota setting. One group sets quotas higher than what most salespeople will achieve but still makes them attainable. This group believes that high quotas spur extra effort. Another group sets quotas that a majority of the sales force can achieve, believing the salesforce will accept the quotas as

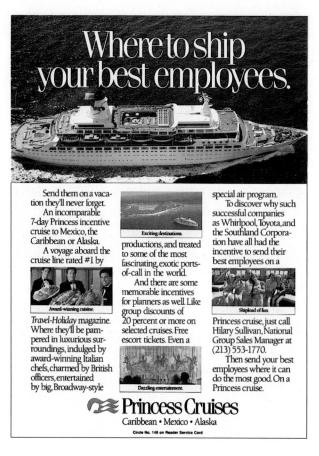

Salesforce incentives: some companies award trips as incentives for outstanding sales performance.

fair, attain them, and gain confidence. The final group thinks that individual differences among salespeople warrant high quotas for some, modest quotas for others. They believe that people react differently and that quotas should be based on individual factors.

Positive Incentives

Companies use several incentives to increase salesforce effort. Sales meetings provide a social occasion, a break from routine, a chance to meet and talk with "company brass," and a chance to air feelings and to identify with a larger group. They sometimes are also a forum for introducing new products to the salesforce. Companies also sponsor sales contests to spur the salesforce to make a selling effort above what would normally be expected. Other incentives include honors, merchandise and cash awards, trips, and profit-sharing plans.

*E*VALUATING SALESPEOPLE

We have described how management communicates what the salespeople should be doing and motivates them to do it. But this requires good feedback. And good feedback means getting regular information from salespeople to evaluate their performance.

Sources of Information

Management gets information about its salespeople in several ways. The most important source is sales reports. Additional information comes from personal observation, customers' letters and complaints, customer surveys, and talks with other salespeople.

Sales reports are divided into plans for future activities and writeups of completed activities. The best example of the first is the work plan, which salespeople submit a week or month in advance. The plan describes intended calls and routing. This report leads the salesforce to plan and schedule activities, informs management of their whereabouts, and provides a basis for comparing plans and performance. Salespeople can be evaluated on their ability to "plan their work and work their plan." Sometimes, sales managers contact individual salespeople after receiving their plans to suggest improvements.

Companies are beginning to require their salespeople to draft an annual territory marketing plan in which they outline their plans for building new accounts and increasing sales from existing accounts. The formats vary greatly—some ask for general ideas on territory development and others ask for detailed sales and profit estimates. This type of report casts salespeople into the role of marketing managers and profit centers. Their managers study these plans, make suggestions, and use them to develop sales quotas.

Salespeople write up their completed activities on call reports. Call reports keep sales management informed of the salesperson's activities, show what is happening with each customer's account, and provide information that might be useful in later calls. Salespeople also turn in expense reports for which they are partly or wholly repaid. Some companies also ask for reports on new business, reports on lost business, and reports on local business and economic conditions.

These reports supply the raw data from which sales management can evaluate salesforce performance. Are salespeople making too few calls per day? Are they spending too much time per call? Are they spending too much money on entertainment? Are they closing enough orders per hundred calls? Are they finding enough new customers and holding on to the old customers?

Formal Evaluation of Performance

Using salesforce reports and other information, sales management evaluates members of the salesforce. Formal evaluation produces three benefits. First, management must have and communicate clear standards for judging performance. Second, management must gather well-rounded information about each salesperson. And third, salespeople know they will have to sit down one morning with the sales manager and explain their performance.

Comparing Salespeople's Performance

One type of evaluation is to compare and rank the sales performance of the different salespeople. Such comparisons, however, can be misleading. Salespeople may perform differently because of differences in factors such as territory potential, workload, level of competition, and company promotion effort. Further, sales are not usually the best indicator of achievement. Management should be more interested in how much each salesperson contributes to net profits. And this requires looking at each salesperson's sales mix and sales expenses.

Comparing Current Sales With Past Sales

A second type of evaluation is to compare a salesperson's current performance with past performance. Such a comparison should directly indicate the person's progress. An example is shown in Table 18-1.

The sales manager can learn many things about Chris Smith from this table.

TABLE 18-1
Evaluating
Salespeople's
Performance

	TERRITORY: MIDLAND		SALESPERSON: CHRIS SMITH	
	1985	1986	1987	1988
1. Net sales product A	$251,300	$253,200	$270,000	$263,100
2. Net sales product B	$423,200	$439,200	$553,900	$561,900
3. Net sales total	$674,500	$692,400	$823,900	$825,000
4. Percent of quota product A	95.6	92.0	88.0	84.7
5. Percent of quota product B	120.4	122.3	134.9	130.8
6. Gross profits product A	$ 50,260	$ 50,640	$ 54,000	$ 52,620
7. Gross profits product B	$ 42,320	$ 43,920	$ 53,390	$ 56,190
8. Gross profits total	$ 92,580	$ 94,560	$109,390	$108,810
9. Sales expense	$ 10,200	$ 11,100	$ 11,600	$ 13,200
10. Sales expense to total sales (%)	1.5	1.6	1.4	1.6
11. Number of calls	1,675	1,700	1,680	1,660
12. Cost per call	$ 6.09	$ 6.53	$ 6.90	$ 7.95
13. Average number of customers	320	324	328	334
14. Number of new customers	13	14	15	20
15. Number of lost customers	8	10	11	14
16. Average sales per customer	$ 2,108	$ 2,137	$ 2,512	$ 2,470
17. Average gross profit per customer	$ 289	$ 292	$ 334	$ 326

Smith's total sales increased every year (line 3). This does not necessarily mean that Smith is doing a better job. The product breakdown shows that Smith has been able to push the sales of product B further than those of product A (lines 1 and 2). According to the quotas for the two products (lines 4 and 5), the success in increasing product B sales may be at the expense of product A sales. According to gross profits (lines 6 and 7), the company earns twice as much gross profit (as a ratio to sales) on A as it does on B. Smith may be pushing the higher-volume, lower-margin product at the expense of the more profitable product. Although Smith increased total sales by $1,100 between 1987 and 1988 (line 3), the gross profits on those total sales actually decreased by $580 (line 8).

Sales expense (line 9) shows a steady increase, although total expense as a percentage of total sales seems to be under control (line 10). The upward trend in Smith's total dollar expenses does not seem to be explained by any increase in the number of calls (line 11), although it may be related to his success in acquiring new customers (line 14). However, there is a possibility that in prospecting for new customers, Smith is neglecting present customers, as indicated by an upward trend in the annual number of lost customers (line 15).

The last two lines in the table show the level and trend in Smith's sales and gross profits per customer. These figures become more meaningful when they are compared with overall company averages. If Chris Smith's average gross profit per customer is lower than the company's average, Chris may be concentrating on the wrong customers or may not be spending enough time with each customer. Looking back at the annual number of calls (line 11), Smith may be making fewer calls than the average salesperson. If distances in the territory are not much different, this may mean that Smith is not putting in a full workday, is poor at planning routing or minimizing waiting time, or spends too much time with certain accounts.

PERSONAL SELLING AND PUBLIC POLICY

Sales representatives must follow the rules of "fair competition" in trying to obtain orders. Certain activities are illegal or heavily regulated. Sales representatives are to refrain from offering bribes to buyers, purchasing agents, or other influence sources. It is illegal to produce technical or trade secrets of competitors through espionage or bribery. They must not disparage competitors or their products by suggesting things that are not true. They must not sell used items as new or mislead the customer about the buying advantages. They must inform customers of their rights, such as the seventy-two-hour "cooling-off" period in which customers can return the merchandise and receive their money back. They must not discriminate against buyers on the basis of their race, sex, or creed.

Source: For more on the legal aspects of personal selling, see Louis W. Stern and Thomas L. Eovaldi, *Legal Aspects of Marketing Policy* (Englewood Cliffs, N.J.: Prentice-Hall, Inc., 1984), pp. 447–550.

Qualitative Evaluation of Salespeople

A qualitive evaluation usually looks at the salesperson's knowledge of the company, products, customers, competitors, territory, and tasks. Personal traits can be rated, such as general manner, appearance, speech, and temperament. The sales manager can also review any problems in motivation or compliance. The sales manager should check to make sure that the salesperson knows the law (see Marketing Highlight 18–5). Each company must decide what would be most useful to know. It should communicate these criteria to the salespeople so that they understand how performance is evaluated and can make an effort to improve it.

■ SUMMARY

Most companies use salespeople, and many companies assign them the key role in the marketing mix. The high cost of the salesforce calls for an effective sales management process consisting of six steps: setting salesforce objectives; designing salesforce strategy, structure, size, and compensation; recruiting and selecting; training; supervising; and evaluating.

As an element of the marketing mix, the salesforce is very effective in achieving certain marketing objectives and carrying on certain activities such as prospecting, communicating, selling and servicing, and information gathering. Under the marketing concept, the salesforce needs skills in marketing analysis and planning in addition to the traditional selling skills.

Once the salesforce objectives have been set, strategy answers the questions of what type of selling would be most effective (solo selling, team selling) what type of salesforce structure would work best (territorial, product, or customer structured), how large the salesforce should be, and how the salesforce should be compensated in terms of salary, commission, bonus, expenses, and fringe benefits.

Salespeople must be recruited and selected carefully to hold down the high costs of hiring the wrong people. Training programs familiarize new salespeople with the company's history, its products and policies, the characteristics of the market and competitors, and the art of selling. The art of selling involves a seven-step sales process: prospecting and qualifying, preapproach, approach, presentation and demonstration, handling objections, closing, and follow-up. Salespeople need supervision and continuous encouragement because they must make many decisions and face many frustrations. Periodically, the company must evaluate their performance to help them do a better job.

■ QUESTIONS FOR DISCUSSION

1. Media representatives sell advertising space or time for newspapers, radio stations, and other advertising media. How creative is this type of selling? What objectives would a radio station have for its salesforce?

2. Describe the advantages each of the different salesforce structures would have for Unisys (the world's second-largest manufacturer of computers and related office equipment). Which structure do you think is most appropriate for Unisys? Why?

3. How does the size of the salesforce relate to a company's spending on other forms of promotion? Choose a company and describe the tradeoffs it would consider in deciding to spend more on advertising versus hiring more salespeople.

4. Why do so many salesforce compensation plans combine salary with bonus or commission? What are the advantages and disadvantages of using bonuses, rather than commissions, as incentives?

5. What two personal characteristics do you think are most likely to lead to an individual's success as a sales representative? What kinds of tests could be used to detect these characteristics in an applicant for a selling job? Are there any risks to using these kinds of tests to select salespeople?

6. Many people feel they do not have the ability to be a successful salesperson. What role does training play in helping someone develop selling ability? Does the potential impact of sales training vary with the level of creativity required in the selling task?

7. How would you apply the different steps in the selling process in a summer job as an encyclopedia salesperson? Would these steps be the same or different in

working after graduation as a marketing representative for Xerox?

8. What kinds of companies would find it worthwhile to have an inside salesforce? What companies could not use an inside salesforce? What major factors determine whether or not an inside salesforce is appropriate for a company?

9. The surest way to become a salesforce manager is to be an outstanding salesperson. What are the advantages and disadvantages of promoting top salespeople to management positions? Why might an outstanding salesperson refuse to be promoted?

10. Several salespeople you supervise expect very positive evaluations because they sold at least 20 percent more than their quotas during the past year. What other factors must you consider before you can write their evaluations? What might lead you to write an unfavorable evaluation of one or more of these salespeople?

11. Good salespeople are familiar with their competitors' products as well as their own. What would you do if your company expected you to sell a product that you thought was inferior to the competition's? Discuss the ethical considerations involved in choosing your course of action.

■ KEY TERMS

Customer salesforce structure A salesforce organization under which salespeople specialize in selling only to certain customers or industries.

Product salesforce structure A salesforce organization under which salespeople specialize in selling only a portion of the company's products or lines.

Salesforce management The analysis, planning, implementation and control of salesforce activities. It includes setting salesforce objectives; designing salesforce strategy; and recruiting, selecting, training, supervising, and evaluating the firm's salespeople.

Salesperson An individual acting for a company who performs one or more of the following activities: prospecting, communicating, servicing, and information gathering.

Selling process The steps that the salesperson follows when selling, which include prospecting and qualifying, preapproach, approach, presentation and demonstration, handling objections, closing, and follow-up.

Territorial salesforce structure A salesforce organization that assigns each salesperson to an exclusive geographic territory in which the salesperson carries the company's full line.

■ REFERENCES

1. Adapted from Bill Kelley, "How to Sell Airplanes, Boeing-Style," *Sales and Marketing Management,* December 9, 1985, pp. 32–34. Also see Katherine M. Hafner, "Bright Smiles, Sweaty Palms," *Business Week,* February 1, 1988, pp. 22–23.

2. See Robert N. McMurry, "The Mystique of Super-Salesmanship," *Harvard Business Review,* March–April 1961, p. 114. For a comparison of several classifications, see William C. Moncrief III, "Selling Activity and Sales Position Taxonomies for Industrial Salesforces," *Journal of Marketing Research,* August 1986, pp. 261–70.

3. See Rayna Skolnik, "Campbell Stirs Up Its Salesforce," *Sales and Marketing Management,* April 1986, pp. 56–58.

4. See Thayer C. Taylor, "Xerox's Sales Force Learns a New Game," *Sales and Marketing Management,* July

1, 1986, pp. 48–51; and Thayer C. Taylor, "Xerox's Makeover," *Sales and Marketing Management,* June 1987, p. 68.

5. "1988 Survey of Selling Costs," *Sales and Marketing Management,* February 22, 1988, p. 37.

6. "Survey of Selling Costs: 1987," *Sales & Marketing Management,* February 16, 1987, p. 55. Also see "Finding the Best Compensation Plan," *Sales and Marketing Management,* August 1986, pp. 46–49.

7. George H. Lucas, Jr., A. Parasuraman, Robert A. Davis, and Ben M. Enis, "An Empirical Study of Salesforce Turnover," *Journal of Marketing,* July 1987, pp. 34–59.

8. Thayer C. Taylor, "Anatomy of a Star Salesperson," *Sales and Marketing Management,* May 1986, pp. 49–51.

9. "Survey of Selling Costs: 1987," p. 62.

10. "PAs Examine the People Who Sell to Them," *Sales and Marketing Management*, November 11, 1985, pp. 38–41.

11. Some of the following discussion is based on W. J. E. Crissy, William H. Cunningham, and Isabella C. M. Cunningham, *Selling: The Personal Force in Marketing* (New York: Wiley, 1977), pp. 119–29.

12. Vincent L. Zirpoli, "You Can't 'Control' the Prospect, So Manage the Presale Activities to Increase Performance," *Marketing News*, March 16, 1984, p. 1.

13. See Richard L. Bencin, "What's My Line?" *Sales and Marketing Management*, June 1987, pp. 94–101.

14. Thayer C. Taylor, "Anatomy of a Star Salesperson," p. 50.

15. "Are Salespeople Gaining More Selling Time?" *Sales and Marketing Management*, July 1986, p. 29.

16. Thayer C. Taylor, "Computers in Sales and Marketing: S&MM's Survey Results," *Sales and Marketing Management*, May 1987, pp. 50–53.

17. James A. Narus and James C. Anderson, "Industrial Distributor Selling: The Roles of Outside and Inside Sales," *Industrial Marketing Management*, Vol. 15, 1986, pp. 55–62.

CASE 14

THE PILLSBURY COMPANY: TOTINO'S PIZZA

Totino's, a Minneapolis-based frozen pizza company, was acquired by the Pillsbury Company in 1975 when Totino's annual sales growth rate was 20 percent. Within two years, Totino's revolutionary crisp-crust technology had been developed and the company was ready to put into action an aggressive marketing plan designed to make it the leader in consumer frozen pizza. The key aspects of the plan were product improvement, aggressive promotional efforts, and coverage of the three basic segments of the market: high, medium, and low price.

The plan was successful, and within three years Totino's was the leading brand of frozen pizza in the United States despite new competitive entries sponsored by General Mills (Saluto), H. J. Heinz (La Pizzeria), Nestlé (Stouffer's), Quaker Oats (Celeste), and more vigorous competition from over 100 smaller regional firms.

In 1984, Pillsbury introduced a frozen pizza designed exclusively to be prepared in microwave ovens. This product was brought out under the Pillsbury Microwave brand name, which includes other microwavable products like pancakes and popcorn.

Jeno's, Inc., the former leader in the frozen pizza market, sought to regain leadership by trying to overcome Totino's crisp-crust and distinctive package advantages. Jeno's followed Totino's by two years in introducing its "Crisp and Tasty Crust." The package for its "regular" size (about 10 ounces) could be confused with Totino's package for the same size. After legal action, Jeno's changed its packaging design. In the early 1980s, Jeno's increased its market share through acquisition of Chef Saluto from General Mills and two regional brands, John's and Gino's, but still remained in second place.

In general, the food industry trend is toward more upscale and healthful food products. Perhaps because there are more women in the workforce consumers are demanding higher-quality, more nutritious foods and are willing to pay for them. Within the pizza industry, the products coming the closest to answering these needs are the Delivered Store Door (DSD) brands and Deli pizzas, made fresh on the premises of some large supermarkets. Totino's My Classic Pizza competes in this higher-priced segment.

Advertising expenditures for the industry amount to about 2 percent of sales, among the lowest for food products and a level usually associated with commodity-type products. On the other hand, a considerable amount is spent at the retail level in the form of display, advertising, and other types of allowances such as sales incentives. Consumers are also offered incentives, usually promotional price specials and coupons. Hardly a week goes by without some special promotion for items in the frozen pizza case.

Retailers prefer profit-producing brands. With limited freezer cabinet space, they favor the seller who spends the most on advertising and promotion, especially trade allowances, which directly improve profitability. On the other hand, Totino's and other manufacturers recognize that such allowances and most types of sales promotion are only short-term sales stimulators and build little consumer loyalty. Totino's management wants to spend its advertising and promotional dollars effectively to build customer loyalty—that is, a strong consumer franchise. Yet competitors, especially marginal manufacturers, spend for immediate sales stimulation.

In view of the new competitive situation and changing consumer life styles, Totino's management must now reconsider its marketing objectives and activities, especially with regard to advertising and promotion.

Additional Industry Information

1. While frozen pizza represents about 30 percent of all pizza consumed, over 70 percent of all pizza, including pizzeria pizza, is eaten at home.

2. Frozen pizza is growing in dollar volume, but more slowly than other frozen prepared foods.

3. Regional taste differences are wide, and the variety makes it difficult for fast-food chains to customize, which makes it easier for small regional pizza chains

to survive. Pizza is more fragmented and less chain-dominated than the hamburger segment of the fast-food chain business. Regional taste differences were also a reason why, until recently, the frozen pizza industry was highly fragmented—with no strong national brands.

4. The popularity of pizza crosses market segments. *Chain Institutions Magazine* found that in a recent year over 48 percent of the service operations surveyed reported that pizza is a "good seller" when it is on the menu. They included full-service restaurants, fast-food restaurants, hotels/motels, hospitals, nursing homes, schools, colleges/universities, and employee feeding facilities.

5. A number of large food processors are in the frozen pizza business, including Pillsbury (Totino's Fox De Luxe, Pillsbury Microwave) Quaker Oats (Celeste), Nestle's (Stouffer), and American Home Products (Chef-Boy-Ar-Dee). The major independents include Jeno's (Jeno's, Mr. P's, John's, Gino's, Chef Saluto), United Products (La Pizzeria), Tony's (Tony's, Red Baron), and Tombstone (Tombstone). Pillsbury holds a 30 percent share of the frozen pizza market and Jeno's a 25 percent share. No other competitor holds more than 8 percent.

6. Totino's pizza is distributed in virtually all geographic areas. Totino's has a very strong brand position, especially in the regular (Party Pizza) segment, in many

areas. However, in some markets local brands or strongly entrenched brands of major consumer goods companies have the dominant market share.

7. Trade deals are a major marketing tool for the industry. They are designed to encourage low-price promotions by the retailer to the consumer. The warfare for market share keeps prices low and cuts potentially high margins. In the trade, it is said that no one is making a lot of money yet from frozen pizzas. *"There isn't space in the cabinet for everybody and you go with the guys who are spending money* (advertising and promotional dollars)," stated a food retailer.

8. Until the introduction of Pillsbury's Microwave Pizza (a single serve size), microwave ovens produced an undesirably limp crust. Pillsbury's product uses technologically advanced packaging which includes a cooking device that allows the crust to stay crisp. Because of the costliness of this packaging, it would not make sense to use it on large-size pizzas or on those purchased by conventional oven users.

9. Some retailers indicate that deli/refrigerated pizza sales have caused a sizable increase in total pizza volume. It appears that deli/refrigerated pizza is a high impulse purchase item.

What recommendations would you give Totino's management concerning the marketing of the product, particularly advertising and sales promotion?

CASE 15

NOXELL CORPORATION

A company that has made millions from the skin game now has a new wrinkle. Noxell Corporation, producer of Noxema creams and the Cover Girl line of makeup for younger women, is cashing in on the aging of the population. The company has introduced its Clarion line of cosmetics for Cover Girl's older sister, the woman who is over 30 and has sensitive skin. And in an enormously successful marketing ploy, Clarion is using an in-store computer that helps customers select the most becoming shades of makeup. Computers have long lent that touch of "science" to the expensive lines sold in department stores, but Clarion is the first mass distributor of medium-priced brands to marry makeup and the microchip.

The erasable, programmable 16-bit computer works like a cash machine. A customer punches in the color of her eyes and hair and the type and the color of her skin. The machine immediately displays the base, blushers, eye shadows, and lipsticks she should dab on. Clarion's computer has been a hit with customers, giving them confidence that they are selecting colors that enhance their looks and capitalizing on the color analysis trend popularized in the book *Color Me Beautiful.*

In the crowded cosmetics firmament, where higher-priced brands like Coty and Charles of the Ritz are fading

fast, Noxell glows like the skin of the pretty models who adorn its ads. Its Cover Girl line helped the company overtake Revlon and Maybelline last year as the leader of the industry's $2.6-billion-a-year mass-market segment. Mass-market cosmetics are sold in grocery, drug, and discount stores. In the past several years, Noxell's sales have risen about 14% annually, to $439 million, and profits have been growing at an average 17% rate, to $37 million.

Introduced in September, the Clarion line rang up a remarkable $25 million in sales in the last quarter of 1986, and security analysts reckon the total will climb to $70 million this year. While the makeup is designed for women who are a bit more mature and for those who are often allergic to the ingredients in many cosmetics, the real reaction has come from Wall Street. "Clarion has the biggest potential of any new brand that we have seen in the cosmetics business in more than a decade," says security analyst Brenda Lee Landry of Morgan Stanley. She expects that in two or three years, Clarion will boost Noxell's share of the mass-market cosmetics business from the current 21% to as much as 30%.

Clever marketing has been the foundation of Noxell's success ever since 1914, when George Bunting whipped up the first batch of Dr. Bunting's Sunburn Remedy in his Baltimore pharmacy. Soon a customer who tried a free sample exclaimed that it had "knocked my eczema." and Bunting promptly renamed his concoction Noxema. Advertising and promotion helped him cultivate an image for it as a multipurpose cream to soothe tired feet at the end of the day, soften chapped hands, and take the sting out of kitchen burns. In one early ad, a nurse called the "Angel of Mercy" extolled the product's many medical uses. Seventy-three years later it is still the country's top-selling sunburn remedy and medicated facial cleanser, and Noxema shave cream is also cleaning up.

Today, under the third generation of the Bunting family and located in suburban Hunt Valley, Maryland, Noxell hasn't changed its formula much. The company still produces high-quality, moderately priced products that it sells for a third to half the price of department store cosmetics. It advertises heavily, using easily recognized, fresh-faced superstar models like Carol Alt, Christie Brinkley, Jennifer O'Neill, and Cheryl Tiegs. Tiegs has been the Cover Girl for an astonishing 19 years, and O'Neill began her relationship with Noxell 23 years ago. Noxell allots 20% of sales to advertising, consistently outspending Revlon and Maybelline.

"Unlike some of its schizophrenic competitors, Noxell scores well on every part of the marketing equation," says analyst Nancy Hall of Smith Barney. When Maybelline recently changed the color of its packaging from yellow to blue, Hall notes, it did not make a complete changeover in the stores. Some of the packaging on the racks was blue, some was yellow, and customers were confused. "Noxell doesn't do things like that," says Hall. Display is sufficiently important to Noxell that the company since 1980 has been producing its own modular, translucent black racks to showcase its cosmetics. The fixtures are so eye-catching that many retailers order them to display all the cosmetic lines.

When launching Clarion, the company dusted off the basic plan that was devised 25 years earlier for Cover Girl's debut. In 1980, having thoroughly researched the market to determine the need for a reasonably priced makeup line for sensitive skin, Noxell called in its advertising agency, SSC&B. The assignment: Build an image around a new group of products designed for the growing group of women beyond 30.

Over the years Noxell had tried to crack the older market by bringing out such Cover Girl line extensions as Moisture Wear and Replenishing makeup and allowing its models Tiegs and O'Neill to age gracefully. The formula never worked. Cover Girl had been all too successful in appealing to consumers in their teens and twenties, and older women did not feel comfortable using products with such a youthful image.

Meanwhile industrial designers were busy working on the computer. The brand managers who conceived of it realized that customers would get no sales help in self-service drug stores and supermarkets. Women would be on their own, trying to figure out what colors they should

buy and reluctant to try products they weren't sure would work best with their skin tone and hair color. The computer would be a surrogate salesperson, advising the customer on what she should wear.

Last fall, five years after its development began, Clarion hit the market with a thunderous $20-million TV ad campaign. Fans of "Cosby," "Moonlighting," and "Dynasty" heard the pitch: "Clarion is beautiful makeup with a sensitive touch." It was delivered by an almost clinical female voice while an attractive brunette model stroked on makeup.

Not all of Noxell's adventures in the skin trade have been as successful as Clarion and Cover Girl. In 1974 Raintree, a moisturizing lotion, arrived in drugstores bolstered by an ad campaign that showed a model on horseback riding through a desert. "The ad didn't make sense because a parched desert did not relate to moisturizing your face," recalls industry consultant Allan Mottus. Not surprisingly, Raintree sales dried up.

Now that Noxell has finally found a winner in the over-30 market, it is working on a product specifically for aging skin. Treatments for aging skin are the new frontier in the millenniums-old cosmetics trade, and they are growing faster than any other part of it. But the Food and Drug Administration has warned manufacturers about claiming their products have any effect on the aging process. So far all of the action is at the top end of the market, where the price tags are a jaw-sagging $60 to $100 an ounce. Noxell hopes to have a product by 1988 that it can sell for around $7 a bottle, or about 10% of the cost of the high-priced spreads.

Chairman George Bunting, 48, a low-key, friendly man who roars around northern Maryland on his 1,000-cc silver BMW motorcycle in his leisure time, dismisses the prospect of entering the haughty, upscale cosmetic market. Noxell's skin treatment products will continue to be moderately priced and distributed to drug and grocery chains. Why spend money on commissions to outside salespeople or leases for counter space, which companies must do to merchandise cosmetics in department stores? Completely at home in the mass market, Bunting says firmly, "We've studied the top end, but we don't feel we know it."

1. Why are Wall Street analysts so optimistic about Clarion's potential?

2. What is the role of in-store computers in the marketing strategy for Clarion?

3. Discuss the pros and cons of the Clarion target market strategy.

4. Discuss the overall marketing strategy designed for Clarion.

Source: Faye Rice, "Making Millions On Women Over 30," *Fortune*, May 25, 1987. Reprinted with permission.

19 Competitor Analysis and Competitive Marketing Strategies

YOU'VE probably never heard of Vernor's ginger ale. And if you tried it, you might not even think it tastes like ginger ale. Vernor's is "aged in oak," the company boasts, and "deliciously different." The caramel-colored soft drink is sweeter and smoother than other ginger ales you've tasted. But to many people in Detroit who grew up with Vernor's, there's nothing quite like it. They drink it morning, noon, and night; summer and winter; cold and hot; from the bottle and at the soda fountain counter. They like the way the bubbles tickle their noses. And they'll say you haven't lived until you've tasted a Vernor's float. To many, Vernor's even has some minor medicinal qualities—they use warm Vernor's to settle a child's upset stomach or to soothe a sore throat. To most Detroit adults, the familiar green and yellow packaging brings back many pleasant childhood memories.

The soft-drink industry is headed by two giants—Coca-Cola leads with a 40 percent market share; Pepsi challenges strongly with about 30 percent. Coke and Pepsi are the main combatants in the "soft-drink wars." They wage constant and pitched battles for retail shelf space. Their weapons include a steady stream of new products, heavy price discounts, an army of distributor salespeople, and large advertising and promotion budgets.

A few "second-tier" brands—Dr Pepper, 7-Up, and Royal Crown—combined 20 percent or so of the market challenge Coke and Pepsi in the cola segments. When Coke and Pepsi battle for shelf space, these second-tier brands often get squeezed. Coke and Pepsi set the ground rules, and if the smaller brands don't follow along, they risk being pushed out or gobbled up. In fact, Pepsi recently tried to acquire 7-Up, and Coke moved to buy Dr Pepper, but the federal government prevented these acquisitions on antitrust grounds.

A group of specialty brands with small but loyal followings fight for what's left of the market. While large in number, each holds a tiny market share, usually less than one percent of the market. Vernor's falls into this "all others" group, along with A&W root beer, Shasta sodas, Squirt, Faygo, Soho Natural Soda, Yoo-hoo, Dr Brown's Cream Soda, A. J. Canfield's Diet Chocolate Fudge Soda, and a dozen others. Whereas Dr Pepper and 7-Up get squeezed in the soft-drink wars, these small fry risk being crushed.

When you compare Vernor's to Coca-Cola, for example, you wonder how Vernor's survives. Coca-Cola spends more than $200 million a year advertising its soft drinks; Vernor's spends less than $1 million. Coke offers a long list of brands and versions—Coke, Coke Classic, Cherry Coke, Diet Coke, Caffeine-Free Coke, Diet Cherry Coke, Caffeine-Free Diet Coke, Sprite, Tab, Mello Yello, Minute Maid soda, and others; Vernor's sells only two versions—original and diet. Coke's large distributor salesforce sways retailers with huge discounts and promotion allowances; Vernor's has only a small marketing budget and carries little clout with retailers. When you visit your local supermarket, if you're lucky enough to find Vernor's, it's usually tucked away on the bottom shelf with other specialty beverages. Even in Detroit, Vernor's stronghold, stores usually give Vernor's only a few shelf-facings, compared with 50 or 100 facings for the many Coca-Cola brands.

Yet Vernor's does more than survive—it thrives! How? Instead of going head-to-head with the bigger companies, Vernor's niches in the market. It concentrates on serving the special needs of loyal Vernor's drinkers. Vernor's knows that it could never seriously challenge Coca-Cola for a large share of the soft-drink market. But it also knows that Coca-Cola could never create another Vernor's ginger ale, at least not in the minds of Vernor's drinkers. As long as Vernor's keeps these special customers happy, it can capture a small but profitable share of the market. And "small" in this market is nothing to sneeze at— a one-percent market share equals $380 million in retail sales! Thus, through smart niching, Vernor's prospers in the shadows of the soft-drink giants.[1]

Chapter Objectives *After reading this chapter, you should be able to:*

1. Explain the importance of developing competitive marketing strategies that position the company against competitors and give it the strongest possible competitive advantage.

2. Identify the steps companies go through in analyzing competitors.

3. Discuss the competitive strategies that market leaders use to expand the market and to protect and expand their market share.

4. Describe the strategies market challengers and followers use to increase their market share and profits.

5. Discuss how market nichers find and develop profitable corners of the market.

UNDERSTANDING consumers is not enough today. In the fast-growth environment of the 1960s, companies could ignore their competitors because most markets were growing. But in the turbulent 1970s and flat 1980s, companies realized that sales gains would have to come from wresting market share away from competitors. As a result, today's companies are starting to pay as much attention to tracking their competitors as to understanding target consumers.

Under the marketing concept, companies succeed by designing offers that satisfy target consumer needs better than competitors' offers. Thus marketing strategies must consider not only the needs of target consumers, but also the strategies of competitors. The first step is **competitor analysis,** the process of identifying key competitors; assessing their objectives, strengths and weaknesses, strategies, and reaction patterns; and selecting which competitors to attack or to avoid. The second step is developing **competitive strategies** that strongly position the company against competitors and that give the company the strongest possible competitive advantage.

COMPETITOR ANALYSIS

To plan effective competitive marketing strategies, the company needs to find out all it can about its competitors. Through its competitive intelligence systems, it must constantly compare its products, prices, channels, and promotion with those of close competitors. In this way the company can find areas of potential competitive advantage and disadvantage. And it can launch more precise attacks on its competitors as well as prepare stronger defenses against attacks.

But what do companies need to know about their competitors? They want to know: Who are our competitors? What are their objectives? What are their strategies? What are their strengths and weaknesses? What are their reaction patterns? Which competitors should be attacked, and which should be avoided? The major steps in analyzing competitors are shown in Figure 19-1 and discussed below.

Identifying the Company's Competitors

Normally, it would seem a simple task for a company to identify its competitors. Coca-Cola knows that Pepsi-Cola is its major competitor; and General Motors knows that it competes with Ford. At the most obvious level, a company can define its competitors as other companies offering a similar product and services to the same customers at similar prices. Thus Buick might see Ford as a major competitor, but not Mercedes or Hyundai.

But companies actually face a much broader range of competitors. More broadly, the company can define competitors as all firms making the same product or class of products. Here Buick would see itself as competing against all other automobile makers. Even more broadly, competitors might include all companies making products that supply the same service. Here Buick would see itself competing against not only other automobile manufacturers but also against the makers of motorcycles, bicycles, and trucks. Finally, and still more broadly, competitors might include all companies that compete for the same consumer dollars. Here Buick would see itself competing with companies that sell major consumer durables, foreign vacations, new homes, or major home repairs.

The Industry Point of View

Many companies identify their competitors from the *industry* point of view. An **industry** is a group of firms that offer a product or class of products that are close substitutes for each other. We talk about the auto industry, the oil industry, the pharmaceutical industry, or the beverage industry. In a given industry, if the price of one product rises, it causes the demand for another product to rise. In the beverage industry, for example, an increase in the price of coffee leads people to switch to tea or lemonade or soft drinks. Thus coffee, tea, lemonade, and soft drinks are substitutes, even though they are physically different products. A company must strive to under-

FIGURE 19-1
Steps in analyzing competitors

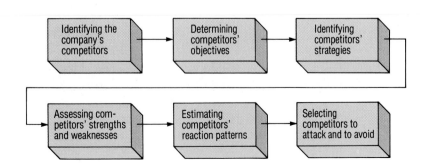

stand the competitive pattern in its industry if it hopes to be an effective "player" in that industry.

The Market Point of View

Instead of identifying competitors from the industry point of view, the company can take a market point of view. Here it defines competitors as companies that are trying to satisfy the same customer need or serve the same customer group. From an industry point of view, Coca-Cola might see its competition as Pepsi, Dr Pepper, 7-Up, and other soft drink manufacturers. From a market point of view, however, the customer really wants "thirst quenching." This need can be satisfied by iced tea, fruit juice, bottled water, or many other fluids. Similarly, Crayola might define its competitors as other makers of crayons and children's drawing supplies. But from a market point of view, it would include as competitors all firms making recreational products for the children's market. In general, the market concept of competition opens the company's eyes to a broader set of actual and potential competitors, and it leads to better long-run market planning.

The key to identifying competitors is to link industry and market analysis by mapping out product/market segments. Figure 19-2 shows the product/market segments in the toothpaste market by product types and customer age groups. We see that P&G (with several versions of Crest and Gleem) and Colgate-Palmolive (with Colgate) occupy six of the segments. Lever Brothers (Aim), Beecham (Aqua Fresh), and Topol each occupy two segments. If Topol wanted to enter other segments, it would need to estimate the market size of each segment, the market shares of the current competitors, and their current capabilities, objectives, and strategies. Clearly each product/market segment would pose different competitive problems and opportunities.

Determining Competitors' Objectives

Having identified the main competitors, marketing management now asks: What is each competitor seeking in the marketplace? What drives each competitor's behavior?

The marketer might at first assume that all competitors will simply strive to maximize their profits and choose their actions accordingly. But companies differ in the weights they put on short–term versus long–term profits. And some competitors might be oriented toward "satisficing" rather than "maximizing" profits: They have target profit goals and are satisfied in achieving them, even if more profits could have been produced by other strategies.

Thus marketers must look beyond competitors' profit goals. Each competitor

FIGURE 19-2
Product/market segments for toothpaste
Source: William A. Cohen. *Winning on the Marketing Front* (New York: John Wiley & Sons, 1986), p. 63.

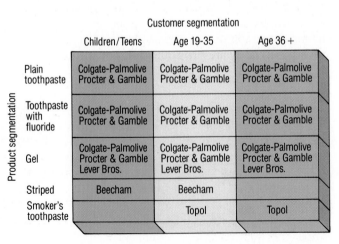

Product/market segments: Procter & Gamble targets various versions of Crest at many different product/market segments, including children. Topol targets smokers and others who want a "stain-free smile."

has a mix of objectives with different weights. The company wants to know the relative weights that a competitor places on current profitability, market share growth, cash flow, technological leadership, service leadership, and others. Knowing a competitor's weighted mix of objectives reveals whether the competitor is satisfied with its current situation, and how it might react to different competitive actions. For example, a company that pursues low cost leadership will react much more strongly to a competitor's cost-reducing manufacturing breakthrough than to the same competitor's advertising increase. A company must also monitor its competitors' objectives for attacking various product/market segments. There might be an opportunity if the company finds that a competitor has discovered a new segment. If it finds that competitors plan new moves into segments now served by the company, it will be forewarned and, hopefully, forearmed.

Identifying Competitors' Strategies

The more closely one firm's strategy resembles another firm's strategy, the more the firms compete. In most industries, the competitors can be sorted into groups that pursue different strategies. A **strategic group** is a group of firms in an industry following the same or a similar strategy. For example, in the major appliance industry, General Electric, Whirlpool, and Sears all belong to the same strategic group. Each markets a full line of medium-price appliances. Maytag and KitchenAid, on the other hand, belong to a different strategic group. They market a narrow line of high quality appliances and charge a premium price.

Some important insights emerge from strategic group identification. First, some strategic groups are harder to enter than others. A small company that is new to an industry might find it easiest to enter the strategic group that requires the least investment and reputation. A stronger and more established company, however, might be able to break into more difficult and competitive strategic groups. Second, when a company chooses to enter a specific strategic group, it selects the members of that group as its key competitors. If a company enters the group containing General Electric, Whirlpool, and Sears, it can succeed only if it develops some strategic advantages over these large competitors.

Although competition is most intense within a strategic group, there is also rivalry between groups. First, some of the strategic groups may appeal to overlapping customer segments. For example, no matter what their strategy, all major appliance marketers will go after the apartment and home builders segment. Second, the customers may not see much difference in the offers of different groups—they may see little difference in quality between Whirlpool and Maytag. Finally, members of one strategic group might expand into new strategy segments. Thus General Electric now offers a premium-quality, premium-price line of kitchen appliances to compete with KitchenAid.

The company needs to look at all of the dimensions that identify strategic groups within the industry. It needs to know each competitor's product quality, features,

Expanding into a new strategy segment: General Electric offers a premium-quality, premium-price line of kitchen appliances.

and mix; customer services; pricing policy; distribution coverage; salesforce strategy; and advertising and sales promotion programs. And it must study the details of each competitor's R&D, manufacturing, purchasing, financial, and other strategies.

Assessing Competitors' Strengths and Weaknesses

Can the various competitors carry out their strategies and reach their goals? This depends on each competitor's resources and capabilities. Marketers need to accurately identify each competitor's strengths and weaknesses.

As a first step, a company gathers key data on each competitor's business over the last few years. It wants to know about competitors' goals, strategies, and performance. Admittedly, some of this information will be hard to collect. For example, industrial goods companies find it hard to estimate competitors' market shares because they do not have the same syndicated data services that are available to consumer packaged goods companies. Still, any information they can find will help them form a better estimate of each competitor's strengths and weaknesses.

Companies normally learn about their competitors' strengths and weaknesses through secondary data, personal experience, and hearsay. But they can also increase their knowledge by conducting primary marketing research with customers, suppliers, and dealers. They can carry out a **customer value analysis,** asking customers what benefits they value and how they rate the company versus competitors on important attributes (see Marketing Highlight 19–1). This information shows which competitors are open to attack and in what ways. It also points out areas in which the company is vulnerable to competitors' actions.

In searching for competitors' weaknesses, the company should try to identify any assumptions they make about their businesses and the market that are no longer valid. For example, some companies believe they produce the best quality in the industry, when they in fact no longer do. Many companies are victims of rules of thumb such as "customers prefer full line companies," "the salesforce is the only important marketing tool," or "customers value service more than price." If a competitor is operating on a major wrong assumption, the company can take advantage of it.

Estimating Competitors' Reaction Patterns

A competitor's objectives, strategies, and strengths and weaknesses go a long way toward explaining its likely actions and its reactions to company moves such as a price cut, a promotion increase, or a new product introduction. In addition, each competitor has a certain philosophy of doing business, a certain internal culture and guiding beliefs. Marketing managers need a deep understanding of a given competitor's mentality if they want to anticipate how the competitor will act or react.

Each competitor reacts differently. Some do not react quickly or strongly to a competitor's move. They may feel their customers are loyal; they may be slow in noticing the move; they may lack the funds to react. Some competitors react to only certain types of assaults and not others. They might always respond strongly to price cuts in order to signal that these will never succeed; but they might not respond at all to advertising increases, believing these to be less threatening. Other competitors react swiftly and strongly to any assault. Thus P&G does not let a new detergent come easily into the market. Many firms avoid direct competition with P&G and look for easier prey, knowing that P&G will fight fiercely if challenged. Finally, some competitors show no predictable reaction pattern. They might or might not react on a given occasion, and there is no way to foresee what they will do based on their economics, history, or anything else.

CUSTOMER VALUE ANALYSIS: THE KEY TO COMPETITIVE ADVANTAGE

In analyzing competitors and searching for competitive advantage, one of the most important marketing tools is *customer value analysis*. The aim of a customer value analysis is to determine what benefits target customers value and how they rate the relative value of various competitors' offers. The major steps in customer value analysis are described below.

1. *Identify the major attributes that customers value.* Various people in the company may have different ideas about what customers value. Thus the company's marketing researchers must ask customers themselves what features and performance levels they look for in choosing a product or seller. Different customers will mention different features and benefits. If the list gets too long, the researcher can remove overlapping attributes. Still, the final list of things that customers value may run as high as ten or twenty items.

2. *Assess the importance of different attributes.* Here customers are asked to rate or rank the importance of the different factors. If the customers differ very much in their ratings, they should be grouped into different customer segments.

3. *Assess the company's and competitors' performance on different customer values against their rated importance.* Next customers are asked where they rate each competitor's performance on each attribute. Ideally, the company's own performance will be high on the attributes the customers value most and low on the attributes which customers value least. Two

pieces of bad news would be: (a) the company's performance ranks high on some minor attributes—a case of "overkill"; and (b) the company's performance ranks low on some major attributes—a case of "underkill." The company must also look at how each competitor ranks on the important attributes.

4. *Examine how customers in a specific segment rate the company's performance against a specific major competitor on an attribute-by-attribute basis.* The key to gaining competitive advantage is to take each customer segment and examine how the company's offer compares to that of its major competitor. If the company's offer exceeds the competitor's offer on all important attributes, the company can charge a higher price and earn higher profits, or it can charge the same price and gain more market share. But if the company is seen as performing at a lower level than its major competitor on some important attributes, it must invest in strengthening those attributes or finding other important attributes where it can build a lead on the competitor.

5. *Monitor customer values over time.* Although customer values are fairly stable in the short run, they will probably change as competing technologies and features appear and as customers face different economic climates. A company that assumes that customer values will remain stable flirts with danger. The company must periodically review customer values and competitors' standings if it wants to remain strategically effective.

In some industries, competitors live in relative harmony; in others, they fight constantly. Knowing how key competitors react gives the company clues on how best to attack competitors or how best to defend the company's current positions.

Selecting Competitors to Attack and to Avoid

Management has already largely determined its major competitors through prior decisions on customer targets, distribution channels, and marketing mix strategy. These decisions define the strategic group to which the company belongs. Management must now decide which competitors to compete against most vigorously. The company can focus its attack on one of several classes of competitors.

Strong or Weak Competitors

Most companies prefer to aim their shots at their weak competitors. Doing so requires fewer resources and time. But in the process, the firm may gain little. The argument could be made that the firm should also compete with strong competitors in order to sharpen its abilities. Furthermore, even strong competitors have some weaknesses, and succeeding against them often provides greater returns.

Close or Distant Competitors

Most companies will compete with those competitors who resemble them the most. Thus Chevrolet competes more against Ford than against Jaguar. At the same time, the company may want to avoid trying to "destroy" a close competitor. Here is an example of a questionable "victory":

> Bausch and Lomb in the late 1970s moved aggressively against other soft lens manufacturers with great success. However this led one after another competitor to sell out to larger firms such as Revlon, Johnson & Johnson, and Schering-Plough, with the result that Bausch and Lomb now faced much larger competitors.[2]

In this case, the company's success in hurting its closest rival brought in tougher competitors.

"Well-Behaved" or "Disruptive" Competitors

A company really needs and benefits from competitors. The existence of competitors results in several strategic benefits. Competitors may help increase total demand. They share the costs of market and product development and help to legitimize new technology. They may serve less attractive segments or lead to more product differentiation. Finally, they lower the antitrust risk and improve bargaining power versus labor or regulators.

However, a company may not view all of its competitors as beneficial. An industry often contains "well-behaved" competitors and "disruptive" competitors.[3] Well-behaved competitors play by the rules of the industry. They favor a stable and healthy industry, set prices in a reasonable relation to costs, motivate others to lower costs or improve differentiation, and accept a reasonable level of market share and profits. Disruptive competitors, on the other hand, break the rules: they try to buy share rather than earn it, take large risks, invest in overcapacity, and in general shake up the industry. For example, IBM views Cray Research as a well-behaved competitor because it plays by the rules, sticks to its supercomputer segment, and does not attack IBM's core markets. But IBM views Fujitsu as a disruptive competitor because it attacks IBM in its core markets with subsidized prices and little differentiation. A company might be smart to support well-behaved competitors, aiming its attacks at disruptive competitors.

"Well-behaved" companies often try to shape an industry into one that consists only of well-behaved competitors. Through careful licensing, selective retaliation, and other means, they try to limit the industry to competitors that behave rationally and harmoniously, follow the rules, try to earn share rather than buy it, and differentiate somewhat to compete less directly.

Designing the Competitive Intelligence System

We have described the main types of information that company decision makers need to know about their competitors. This information must be collected, interpreted, distributed, and used. While the cost in money and time of gathering competitive intelligence is high, the cost of not gathering it is higher. Yet the company must design its competitive intelligence system in a cost-effective way.

The competitive intelligence system first identifies the vital types of competitive information and the best sources of this information. Then the system continuously collects information from the field (salesforce, channels, suppliers, market research firms, trade associations) and from published data (government publications, speeches, articles). Next the system checks the information for validity and reliability, interprets it, and organizes it in an appropriate way. Finally, it sends key information to relevant decision makers and responds to inquiries from managers about competitors.

With this system, company managers will receive timely information about competitors in the form of phone calls, bulletins, newsletters, and reports. In addition, managers can contact the system when they need an interpretation of a competitor's sudden move, or when they want to know a competitor's weaknesses and strengths, or how a competitor will respond to a planned company move.

Smaller companies that cannot afford to set up a formal competitive intelligence office can assign specific executives to watch specific competitors. Thus a manager who used to work for a competitor might follow closely all developments connected with that competitor; he or she would be the "in-house" expert on that competitor. Any manager needing to know the thinking of a given competitor could contact the assigned in-house expert.

COMPETITIVE STRATEGIES

Having identified and evaluated the major competitors, the company must now design broad competitive marketing strategies that will best position its offer against competitors' offers in the minds of consumers. These strategies will give the company or its product the strongest possible competitive advantage.[4] But what broad marketing strategies might the company use? Which ones are best for a particular company or for the company's different divisions and products?

No one strategy is best for all companies. Each company must determine what makes the most sense given its position in the industry and its objectives, opportunities, and resources. Even within a company, different strategies may be required for different businesses or products. For example, Johnson & Johnson uses one marketing strategy for its leading brands in stable consumer markets and a different marketing strategy for its new high-tech health care businesses and products. We will now look at broad competitive marketing strategies that companies can use.

Competitive Positions

Firms competing in a given target market will, at any point in time, differ in their objectives and resources. Some firms will be large, others small. Some will have great resources, others will be strapped for funds. Some will be old and established, others new and fresh. Some will strive for rapid market share growth, others for long-term profits. And the firms will occupy different competitive positions in the target market.

Michael Porter suggests four basic competitive positioning strategies that companies can follow—three winning strategies and one losing one.[5]

- *Overall cost leadership*. Here the company works hard to achieve the lowest costs of production and distribution so that it can price lower than its competitors and win a large market share. Texas Instruments is a leading practitioner of this strategy.
- *Differentiation*. Here the company concentrates on creating a highly differentiated product line and marketing program so that it comes across as the class leader in the industry. Most customers would prefer to own this brand if its price is not too high. IBM and Caterpillar follow this strategy in computers and heavy construction equipment, respectively.
- *Focus*. Here the company focuses its effort on serving a few market segments well rather than going after the whole market. Thus glass-maker AFG Industries focuses on users of tempered and colored glass—it makes 70 percent of the glass for microwave oven doors and 75 percent of the glass for shower doors and patio table tops.[6]

Companies that pursue a clear strategy—one of the above—are likely to perform well. The firm that carries off that strategy best will make the most profits. But firms that do not pursue a clear strategy—*a middle-of-the-road strategy*—do the worst. Chrysler and International Harvester both came upon difficult times because neither stood out as the lowest in cost, highest in perceived value, or best in serving some market segment. Middle-of-the-roaders try to be good on all strategic counts but end up being not very good at anything.

We will adopt a different classification of competitive positions, based on the role firms play in the target market—that of leading, challenging, following, or niching. Suppose that an industry contains the firms shown in Figure 19-3. Forty percent of the market is in the hands of the **market leader,** the firm with the largest market share. Another 30 percent is in the hands of a **market challenger,** a runner-up that is fighting hard to increase its market share. Another 20 percent is in the hands of a **market follower,** another runner-up that wants to hold its share without rocking the boat. The remaining 10 percent is in the hands of **market nichers,** firms, like Vernor's ginger ale, that serve small segments not being pursued by larger firms.

We will now look at specific marketing strategies that are available to market leaders, challengers, followers, and nichers. In the sections that follow, you should remember that the classifications of competitive positions often do not apply to a whole company, but only to its position in a specific industry. For example, large and diversified companies such as IBM, Sears, or General Mills—or their individual businesses, divisions, or products—might be leaders in some markets and nichers in others. For example, IBM leads in the overall personal computer market and in the business segment, but it challenges Apple in the educational segment. Such companies often use different strategies for different business units, depending on the competitive situations of each.

Market-Leader Strategies

Most industries contain an acknowledged market leader. This firm has the largest market share, and it usually leads the other firms in price changes, new product introductions, distribution coverage, and promotion spending. The leader may or may not be admired or respected, but other firms concede its dominance. The leader is a focal point for competitors, a company to challenge, imitate, or avoid. Some of the best-known market leaders are General Motors (autos), Kodak (photography), IBM (computers), Procter & Gamble (consumer packaged goods), Caterpillar (earth-moving equipment), Coca-Cola (soft drinks), Sears (retailing), McDonald's (fast food), and Gillette (razor blades).

A leading firm's life is not easy. It must maintain a constant watch. Other firms keep challenging its strengths or trying to take advantage of its weaknesses. The market leader can easily miss a turn in the market and plunge into second or third place. A product innovation may come along and hurt the leader—as when Tylenol's nonaspirin painkiller took the lead from Bayer Aspirin, or when P&G's Tide, the first synthetic laundry detergent, beat out Lever Brothers' leading brands. Or the leading firm might grow fat and slow, losing out against new and peppier rivals. For example, Xerox's share of the world copier market fell from over 80 percent to less than 35 percent in just five years when Japanese producers challenged with cheaper and more reliable copiers.

FIGURE 19-3
Hypothetical market structure

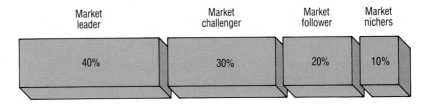

Market leader	Market challenger	Market follower	Market nichers
40%	30%	20%	10%

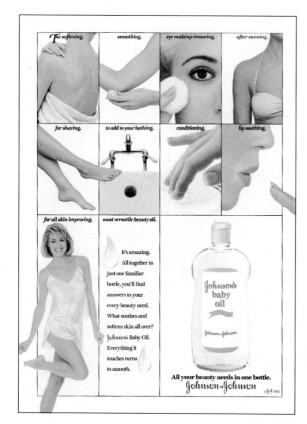

Expanding the total market: Johnson & Johnson develops new users (adults); Arm & Hammer promotes new uses.

Leading firms want to remain number one. Doing so calls for action on three fronts. First, the firm must find ways to expand total demand. Second, the firm must protect its current market share through good defensive and offensive actions. Third, the firm can try to expand its market share further, even if market size remains constant.

Expanding the Total Market

The leading firm normally gains the most when the total market expands. If Americans do more picture-taking, Kodak stands to gain the most because it sells more than 80 percent of this country's film. If Kodak can convince more Americans to take pictures, or to take pictures on more occasions, or to take more pictures on each occasion, it will benefit greatly. In general, the market leader should look for new users, new uses, and more usage of its products.

NEW USERS. Every product class can attract buyers who are still unaware of the product, or who are resisting it because of its price or its lack of certain features. A seller can usually find new users in many places. For example, Revlon might find new perfume users in its current markets by convincing women who do not use perfume to try it. Or it might find users in new demographic segments, say by convincing men to start using perfume. Or it might expand into new geographic segments, perhaps by selling its perfume in other countries.

Johnson's Baby Shampoo provides a classic example of developing new users. When the baby boom had passed and the birth rate slowed down, the company grew concerned about future sales growth. But J&J's marketers noticed that other family members sometimes used the baby shampoo for their own hair. Management developed an advertising campaign aimed at adults. In a short time, Johnson's Baby Shampoo became a leading brand in the total shampoo market.

NEW USES. The marketer can expand markets by discovering and promoting new uses for the product. Du Pont's nylon provides a classic example of new-use expansion. Every time nylon became a mature product, some new use was discovered. Nylon was first used as a fiber for parachutes; then for women's stockings; later as a major material in shirts and blouses; and still later in automobile tires, upholstery, and carpeting. Another example of new-use expansion is Arm & Hammer baking soda. Its sales had flattened after 125 years. Then the company discovered that consumers were using baking soda as a refrigerator deodorizer. It launched a heavy advertising and publicity campaign focusing on this use and persuaded consumers in half of America's homes to place an open box of baking soda in their refrigerators and to replace it every few months.

MORE USAGE. A third market expansion strategy is to convince people to use the product more often, or to use more per occasion. Campbell advertises that "Soup is Good Food" to encourage people to eat soup more often. Procter & Gamble advises users that its Head and Shoulders shampoo is more effective with two applications instead of one per shampoo.

Some years ago, the Michelin Tire Company found a creative way to increase usage per occasion. It wanted French car owners to drive more miles per year, resulting in more tire replacement. Michelin began rating French restaurants on a three-star system. It reported that many of the best restaurants were in the south of France, leading many Parisians to take weekend drives south. Michelin also published guidebooks with maps and sights along the way to further entice travel.

Protecting Market Share

While trying to expand total market size, the leading firm must also constantly protect its current business against competitor attacks. Coca-Cola must constantly guard against Pepsi-Cola; Gillette against Bic; Kodak against Fuji; McDonald's against Burger King; General Motors against Ford.

What can the market leader do to protect its position? First, it must prevent or fix weaknesses that provide opportunities for competitors. It must keep its costs down and its prices in line with the value the customers see in the brand. The leader must "plug holes" so that competitors do not jump in. But the best defense is a good offense, and the best response is *continuous innovation*. The leader refuses to be content with the way things are and leads the industry in new products, customer services, distribution effectiveness, and cost cutting. It keeps increasing its competitive effectiveness and value to customers. It takes the offensive, sets the pace, and exploits competitors' weaknesses (see Marketing Highlight 19–2).

Increased competition in recent years has sparked management's interest in models of military warfare.[7] Leader companies have been advised to protect their market positions with competitive strategies patterned after successful military defense strategies. Six defense strategies that a market leader can use are shown in Figure 19-4 and described below.[8]

POSITION DEFENSE. The most basic defense is a position defense in which a company builds fortifications around its current position. But simply defending one's current position or products rarely works. Henry Ford tried it with his Model-T and brought an enviably healthy Ford Motor Company to the brink of financial ruin. Even such lasting brands as Coca-Cola and Bayer Aspirin cannot be relied upon to supply all

MARKETING HIGHLIGHT 19–2

PROCTER & GAMBLE LEADS WITH INNOVATION

P&G has always invested heavily to find innovative products that solve consumer problems. This constant innovation has made P&G the leader in the American consumer package goods industry. P&G markets the leading brand in 21 of the 40 product categories in which it competes. P&G spent years developing a toothpaste that would effectively reduce tooth decay. When introduced, Crest soon passed up less effective brands, and with constant improvement, it remained the leading toothpaste for over thirty years. P&G looked at the shampoo market and found that consumers wanted dandruff control, but no brand provided it. Years of research produced Head and Shoulders, an instant market leader. Then P&G looked at the paper products business. It found that new parents wanted relief from handling and washing diapers. Again P&G found an innovative solution—Pampers—an affordable disposable paper diaper, which immediately won market leadership. Thus innovative marketing took P&G to the top in consumer products.

Yet in the early 1980s, P&G appeared to let up some on its pressure to innovate. And more innovative competitors quickly challenged P&G's leadership in several product areas, especially toothpaste and disposable diapers.

P&G's Crest toothpaste was hard hit. In 1983, Minnetonka innovated with Check-Up, the first plaque-fighting toothpaste packaged in a pump container. And Lever Brothers and Beecham introduced gels, clear and better tasting forms of toothpaste that appeal strongly to children. While P&G lagged behind on these innovations, its major competitor, Colgate, surged ahead. Colgate poured money into research and development and beat P&G to the market by many months with the pump, gels, and a plaque-fighting formula. Colgate soon grabbed 50 percent of the pump segment and boosted its overall share of the $1 billion toothpaste market from 18 percent in 1979 to 28 percent by the end of 1984. During the last six months of 1984, Crest's share plunged from 36 percent to 30 percent.

Procter & Gamble took a similar beating in the disposable diaper market. Its Pampers brand created the disposables category, and for years P&G's Pampers and Luvs brands dominated with a combined share exceeding 75 percent. But in 1984, while P&G coasted, Kimberly-Clark came out with Huggies, an innovative brand with greater absorbency, a contour shape, and refastenable tapes. By mid-1985, P&G found itself following rather than leading this market. Its overall share fell to 46 percent, and Pampers slid to second place behind Huggies. In 1985, P&G suffered its first income decline in 33 years.

P&G was down, but far from out. It struck back hard with innovations in both product areas. In late 1985, P&G introduced a superior pump and extended its line to include gels. And it did the challengers one better by introducing Crest Tartar Control Formula paste and gel in pumps and tubes. P&G also spent over $500 million to create a new generation of Pampers and an improved Luvs. Competitors were left scrambling to match P&G's new Ultra Pampers, a super-thin, super-absorbent disposable diaper.

Procter & Gamble's surge of fresh innovation produced amazing results. In less than six months, Crest's share of the toothpaste market jumped to 38 percent; Colgate's fell to 22 percent. P&G's share of the disposable diaper market climbed quickly to 60 percent, and Pampers regained a comfortable market share lead.

Thus the weapon P&G first used to reach the top was used by its competitors to threaten P&G's leadership, and used again by P&G to regain the lost ground. The weapon was innovation. The message is a simple one—to stay ahead, P&G must continue to lead.

Sources: See Nancy Giges and Laurie Freeman, "Wounded Tiger? Trail of Mistakes Mars P&G Record," *Advertising Age*, July 29, 1985, pp. 1, 50–51; Faye Rice, "The King of Suds Reigns Again," *Fortune*, August 4, 1986, pp. 130–34; and Laurie Freeman, "Toothpastes Polish Up New Ads," *Advertising Age*, January 25, 1988, p. 30.

FIGURE 19-4
Defense strategies

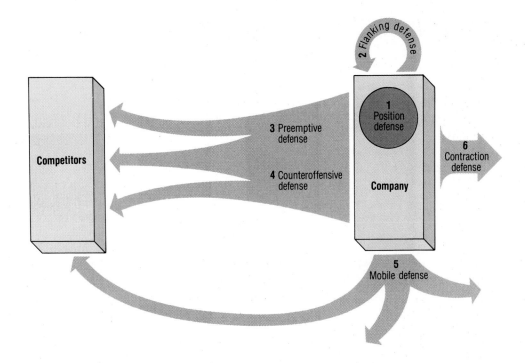

future growth and profitability for their companies. These brands must be improved and adapted to changing conditions, and new brands must be developed. Coca-Cola today, in spite of producing over a third of America's soft drinks, is aggressively extending its beverage lines and has diversified into desalinization equipment and plastics.

FLANKING DEFENSE. When guarding its overall position, the market leader must watch its weaker flanks closely. Smart competitors will normally attack the company's weaknesses. Thus the Japanese successfully entered the small car market because U.S. automakers left a gaping hole in that submarket. Using a flanking defense, the company carefully checks its flanks and protects the more vulnerable ones.

PREEMPTIVE DEFENSE. The leader can launch a more aggressive preemptive defense, striking competitors before they can move against the company. A preemptive defense assumes that an ounce of prevention is worth a pound of cure. Thus Sony innovates continuously with its Walkman line, bringing out newer and better models before its competitors can.

COUNTEROFFENSIVE DEFENSE. When a market leader is attacked despite its flanking or preemptive efforts, it can launch a counteroffensive defense. When Fuji attacked Kodak in the U.S. film market, Kodak counterattacked by dramatically increasing its promotion and introducing several innovative new film products. When attacked by UPS's low-price claims, Federal Express counterattacked by slashing its prices. Sometimes companies hold off for a while before countering. This may seem a dangerous game of "wait and see," but there are often good reasons for not barreling in. By waiting, the company can more fully understand the competitor's offense, and perhaps find a gap through which a successful counteroffensive can be launched.

MOBILE DEFENSE. A mobile defense involves more than aggressively defending a current market position. The leader stretches to new markets that can serve as future bases for defense and offense. Through *market broadening*, the company shifts its focus from the current product to the broader underlying consumer need. For example, Armstrong Cork redefined its focus from "floor covering" to "decorative room

When Fuji attacked, Kodak counterattacked with innovative new films and more promotion.

covering" (including walls and ceilings) and expanded into related businesses that were balanced for growth and defense. *Market diversification* into unrelated industries is the other alternative for generating "strategic depth." When U.S. tobacco companies like R. J. Reynolds and Philip Morris faced growing curbs on cigarette smoking, they moved quickly into new industries such as consumer food products and beer.

CONTRACTION DEFENSE. Large companies sometimes find they can no longer defend all of their positions. Their resources are spread too thin, and competitors are nibbling away on several fronts. The best action then appears to be a contraction defense (or strategic withdrawal). The company gives up weaker positions and concentrates its resources on stronger ones. During the 1970s, many companies diversified wildly and spread themselves too thin. In the slow-growth 1980s, ITT, Gulf & Western, Georgia Pacific, General Mills, Kraft, Quaker, and dozens of other companies pruned their portfolios to concentrate resources on products and businesses in their core industries. These companies now serve fewer markets but serve them much better.

Expanding Market Share
Market leaders can also grow by increasing their market shares further. Many studies have found that profitability rises with increasing market share.[9] Businesses with very large relative market shares averaged substantially higher returns on investment. Because of these findings, many companies have sought expanded market shares to improve profitability. General Electric, for example, declared that it wants to be at least number one or two in each of its markets or else get out. GE shed its computer, air-conditioning, and small appliances and television businesses because it could not achieve top-dog position in these industries.

Other studies have found that many industries contain one or a few highly profitable large firms, several profitable and more focused firms, and a large number of medium-sized firms with poorer profit performance.

> The large firms . . . tend to address the entire market, achieving cost advantages and high market share by realizing economies of scale. The small competitors reap high profits by focusing on some narrower segment of the business and by developing specialized approaches to production, marketing, and distribution for that segment. Ironically, the medium-sized competitors . . . often show the poorest profit performance. Trapped in a strategic "No Man's Land," they are too large to reap the benefits of more focused competition, yet too small to benefit from the economies of scale that their larger competitors enjoy.[10]

Thus it appears that profitability increases as a business gains share relative to competitors in its *served market*. For example, Mercedes holds only a small share of the total car market, but it earns high profit because it is a high-share company in its luxury car segment. And it has achieved this high share in its served market because it does other things right, such as producing high quality, giving good service, and holding down its costs.

Companies must not think, however, that gaining increased market share will automatically improve profitability. Much depends on their strategy for gaining increased share. We see many high-share companies with low profitability, and many low-share companies with high profitability. The cost of buying higher market share may far exceed the returns. Higher shares tend to produce higher profits only when (1) unit costs fall with increased market share or (2) when the company offers a superior-quality product and charges a premium price that more than covers the cost of offering higher quality.

Market-Challenger Strategies

Firms that are second, third, or lower in an industry are sometimes quite large, such as Colgate, Ford, K mart, Avis, Westinghouse, Miller, and Pepsi-Cola. These runner-up firms can adopt one of two competitive strategies. They can attack the leader and other competitors in an aggressive bid for more market share (be market challengers). Or they can play along with competitors and not rock the boat (be market followers). We will now look at competitive strategies for market challengers.

Defining the Strategic Objective and Competitor

A market challenger must first define its strategic objective. Most market challengers seek to increase their profitability by increasing their market shares. But the strategic objective chosen depends on who the competitor is. In most cases, the company can choose which competitors it will challenge.

The challenger can attack the market leader, a high-risk but potentially high-gain strategy which makes good sense if the leader is not serving the market well. To succeed with such an attack, a company must have some sustainable competitive advantage over the leader—a cost advantage leading to lower prices, or the ability to provide better value at a premium price. In the construction equipment industry, Komatsu successfully challenged Caterpillar by offering the same quality at much lower prices. And P&G grabbed a big share of the toilet-tissue market by offering a softer and more absorbent product than the one offered by market leader Scott. When attacking the leader, a challenger must also find a way to minimize the leader's retaliation. Otherwise its gains may be short lived.[11]

The challenger can avoid the leader and instead attack firms its own size or smaller local and regional firms. Many of these firms are underfinanced and may not be serving their customers well. Several of the major beer companies grew to their present size not by attacking large competitors, but by gobbling up small local or regional competitors. For example, G. Heileman Brewing Company expanded to become the nation's fourth-largest brewer by acquiring and melding such regional brands as Old Style, Colt 45, Carling Black Label, Rainier, Blatz, C. Schmidt, Lone Star, and Tuborg.

Thus the challenger's strategic objective depends on which competitor it chooses to attack. If the company goes after the market leader, its objective may be to wrest a certain market share. Bic knows that it cannot topple Gillette in the razor market—it simply wants a larger share. Or the challenger's goal might be to take over market leadership. IBM entered the personal computer market late, as a challenger, but quickly became the market leader. If the company goes after a small local company, its objective may be to put that company out of business. The important point remains: The company must choose its opponents carefully and have a clearly defined and attainable objective.

Choosing an Attack Strategy

How can the market challenger best attack the chosen competitor and achieve its strategic objectives? Five possible attack strategies are shown in Figure 19-5 and discussed below.

FRONTAL ATTACK. In a full frontal attack, the challenger matches the competitor's product, advertising, price, and distribution efforts. It attacks the competitor's strengths rather than its weaknesses. The outcome depends on who has the greater strength and endurance. Even great size and strength may not be enough to successfully challenge a firmly entrenched and resourceful competitor.

Unilever is the world's largest packaged goods company. It has twice the worldwide sales of Procter & Gamble and five times the sales of Colgate-Palmolive. Yet its American subsidiary, Lever Brothers, trails P&G by a wide margin in the United States. Lever recently

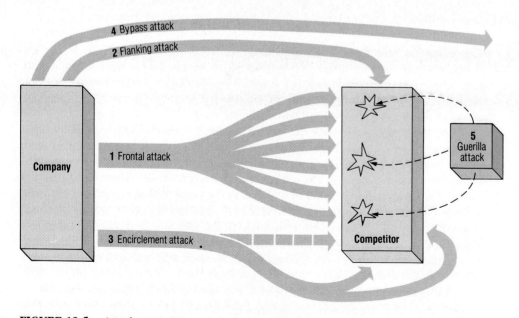

FIGURE 19-5 Attack strategies

Unilever launched a frontal attack against P&G with Surf, Sunlight, and Snuggle.

launched a full frontal assault against P&G in the detergent market. Lever's Wisk was already the leading liquid detergent. In quick succession, it added a barrage of new products—Sunlight dishwashing detergent, Snuggle fabric softener, Surf laundry powder—and backed them with aggressive promotion and distribution efforts. But P&G spent heavily to defend its brands and held on to most of its business. And it counterattacked with Liquid Tide, which came from nowhere in just 17 months to run neck-and-neck with Wisk. Lever did gain market share, but most of it came from smaller competitors.[12]

If the market challenger has fewer resources than the competitor, a frontal attack makes little sense. GE and Xerox learned this the hard way when they launched frontal attacks on IBM, overlooking its superior defensive position.

FLANKING ATTACK. Rather than attacking head on, the challenger can launch a flanking attack. The competitor often concentrates its resources to protect its strongest positions, but it usually has some weaker flanks. By attacking these weak spots, the challenger can concentrate its strength against the competitor's weakness. Flank attacks make good sense when the company has fewer resources than the competitor. For example, PepsiCo flanked Coca-Cola when it created Slice, a soft drink with real fruit juice added. Coke's lemon-lime drink, Sprite, contained no fruit juice. Slice quickly replaced Sprite as the No. 2 lemon-lime drink behind 7-Up in most markets.

Another flanking strategy is to find gaps that are not being filled by the industry's products, fill them, and develop them into strong segments. German and Japanese automakers chose not to compete with American automakers by producing large, flashy, gas-guzzling automobiles. Instead they recognized an unserved consumer segment that wanted small, fuel-efficient cars and moved to fill this hole. To their satisfaction and Detroit's surprise, the segment grew to be a large part of the market.

ENCIRCLEMENT ATTACK. An encirclement attack involves attacking from all directions, so that the competitor must protect its front, sides, and rear at the same time. The encirclement strategy makes sense when the challenger has superior resources and believes that it can quickly break the competitor's hold on the market. An example is Seiko's attack on the watch market. For several years, Seiko has been gaining distribution in every major watch outlet and overwhelming competitors with its variety of constantly changing models. In the United States it offers some four hundred models, but its marketing clout is backed by the twenty-three hundred models it makes and sells worldwide.

BYPASS ATTACK. A bypass attack is an indirect strategy. The challenger bypasses the competitor and targets easier markets. The bypass can involve diversifying into unrelated products, moving into new geographic markets, or leapfrogging into new technologies to replace existing products. Technological leapfrogging is a bypass strategy used often in high-technology industries. Instead of copying the competitor's product and mounting a costly frontal attack, the challenger patiently develops the next technology. When satisfied with its superiority, it launches an attack where it has an advantage. Thus Minolta toppled Canon from the lead in the 35mm SLR camera market when it introduced its technologically advanced autofocusing Maxxum camera. Canon's market share dropped toward 20 percent while Minolta's zoomed past 30 percent. It took Canon three years to introduce a matching technology.[13]

GUERRILLA ATTACK. A guerrilla attack is another option available to market challengers, especially smaller or poorly financed ones. The challenger makes small, periodic attacks to harass and demoralize the competitor, hoping eventually to establish permanent footholds. It might use selective price cuts, executive raids, intense promotional outbursts, or assorted legal actions. The key is to focus the attack narrowly. For example, Diamond Crystal salt had less than a 5 percent share of the national salt market compared with Morton's 50 percent. In no way could it compete broadly with Morton. So Diamond focused its attack against Morton in its own core regional market and launched an aggressive marketing compaign. It managed to build a three-to-one lead over Morton in this territory. Normally, guerrilla actions are taken by smaller firms against larger ones. But continuous guerrilla campaigns can be expensive, and they must eventually be followed up by a stronger attack if the challenger wishes to "beat" the competitor. Thus guerrilla campaigns are not necessarily cheap.

Market-Follower Strategies

Not all runner-up companies will challenge the market leader. The effort to draw away the leader's customers is never taken lightly by the leader. If the challenger's lure is lower prices, improved service, or additional product features, the leader can quickly match these to diffuse the attack. The leader probably has more staying power in an all-out battle. A hard fight might leave both firms worse off, and this means the challenger must think twice before attacking. Thus many firms prefer to follow rather than attack the leader.

In some industries—such as steel, fertilizers, and chemicals—opportunities for differentiation are low, service quality is often comparable, and price sensitivity runs high. Price wars can erupt at any time. Companies in these industries avoid short-run grabs for market share because that strategy only provokes retaliation. Most firms decide against stealing each other's customers. Instead they present similar offers to buyers, usually by copying the leader. Market shares show a high stability.

Yet market followers are not without strategies. A market follower must know how to hold current customers and win a fair share of new ones. Each follower tries to bring distinctive advantages to its target market—location, services, financing. The follower is a major target of attack by challengers. Therefore the market follower must keep its manufacturing costs low and its product quality and services high. It must also enter new markets as they open up. Following is not the same as being passive or a carbon copy of the leader. The follower has to define a growth path, but one that does not create competitive retaliation.

A company may *follow closely*, emulating the leader in as many areas as possible. A close follower almost appears to be a challenger, but no direct conflict occurs. Some close followers may even put very little into stimulating the market, hoping to live off the market leader's investments. Or a company may *follow at a distance*. The follower maintains some differentiation but follows the leader in major market and product innovations, general price levels, and distribution. This follower is quite acceptable to the market leader, who sees little interference and likes having the follower around to help avoid charges of market monopoly. The distant follower may achieve growth by acquiring smaller firms in the industry. Market followers, although they have lower market shares than the leader, may be as profitable or even more profitable.

Market-Nicher Strategies Almost every industry includes smaller firms that specialize in serving market niches that the majors overlook or ignore. Market niching is of interest not only to small companies, but also to smaller divisions of larger companies that are not able to achieve major standing in that industry. These firms try to find one or more market niches that are safe and profitable. An ideal market niche is big enough to be profitable and has growth potential. It is one that the firm can serve effectively. Perhaps most importantly, the niche is of little interest to major competitors. And the firm can build the skills and customer goodwill to defend itself against an attacking major competitor as the niche grows and becomes more attractive.

The key idea in "nichemanship" is specialization. The firm has to specialize along market, customer, product, or marketing mix lines. Here are several specialist roles open to a market nicher:

- *End-use specialist*. The firm specializes in serving one type of end-use customer. For example, a law firm can specialize in the criminal, civil, or business law markets.
- *Vertical-level specialist*. The firm specializes at some level of the production-distribution cycle. For example, a copper firm may concentrate on producing raw copper, copper components, or finished copper products.
- *Customer-size specialist*. The firm concentrates on selling to either small, medium, or large customers. Many nichers specialize in serving small customers who are neglected by the majors.
- *Specific-customer specialist*. The firm limits its selling to one or a few major customers. Many firms sell their entire output to a single company, such as Sears or General Motors.
- *Geographic specialist*. The firm sells only in a certain locality, region, or area of the world.
- *Product or feature specialist*. The firm specializes in producing a certain product, product line, or product feature. Within the laboratory equipment industry are firms that produce only microscopes, or even more narrowly, only lenses for microscopes.
- *Quality-price specialist*. The firm operates at the low or high end of the market. For example, Hewlett-Packard specializes in the high-quality, high-price end of the hand-calculator market.
- *Service specialist*. The firm offers one or more services not available from other firms. An example is a bank that takes loan requests over the phone and hand delivers the money to the customer.

Niching carries a major risk in that the market niche may dry up or be attacked. That is the reason many companies practice *multiple niching*. By developing two or more niches, the company increases its chances for survival. Even some large firms prefer a multiple-niche strategy to serving the total market. One large law firm has developed a national reputation in the three areas of mergers and acquisitions, bankruptcies, and prospectus development, and does little else.

A recent study of highly successful midsize companies found that, in almost all cases, these companies niched within a larger market rather than going after the whole market.[14] An example is A. T. Cross, which niches in the high-price pen and pencil market. It makes the famous gold writing instruments that every executive owns or wants to own. By concentrating in the high-price niche, Cross has enjoyed great sales growth and profit. Of course, the study found other features shared by the successful smaller companies—offering high value, charging a premium price, and strong corporate cultures and vision. The main point is that low-share firms can be profitable too, and smart niching is one of the main reasons.

*B*ALANCING CUSTOMER AND COMPETITOR ORIENTATIONS

We have stressed the importance of a company watching its competitors closely. Whether a company is a market leader, challenger, follower, or nicher, it must find the competitive marketing strategy that positions it most effectively against its competitors. And it must continually adapt its strategies to the fast-changing competitive environment.

A question now arises: Can the company spend too much time and energy tracking competitors, damaging its customer orientation? The answer is yes! A company can become so competitor-centered that it loses its even more important customer focus. A **competitor-centered company** is one whose moves are mainly based on competitors' actions and reactions. The company spends most of its time tracking competitors' moves and market shares and trying to find strategies to counter them.

This mode of strategy planning has some pluses and minuses. On the positive side, the company develops a fighter orientation. It trains its marketers to be on a constant alert, watching for weaknesses in their own position, and watching for competitors' weaknesses. On the negative side, the company becomes too reactive. Rather than carrying out its own consistent customer-oriented strategy, it bases its moves on competitors' moves. As a result, it does not move in a planned direction toward a goal. It does not know where it will end up, since so much depends on what the competitors do.

A **customer-centered company**, in contrast, focuses more on customer developments in designing its marketing strategies. Clearly, the customer-centered company is in a better position to identify new opportunities and set a strategy that makes long-run sense. By watching customer needs evolve, it can decide what customer groups and what emerging needs are the most important to serve, given its resources and objectives.

In practice, today's companies must be **market-centered companies**, watching both their customers and their competitors. They must not let competitor watching blind them to customer focusing. Figure 19-6 shows four orientations through which companies typically evolve. In the first stage, companies are product-oriented, paying little attention to either cusomters or competitors. In the second stage, they become customer-oriented and start to pay attention to customers. In the third stage, when they begin to pay attention to competitors, they become competitor-oriented. Today companies need to be market-oriented, paying balanced attention to both customer and competitors.

FIGURE 19-6
Evolving company
orientations

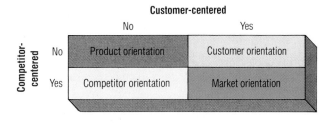

Q10 is useful for summarizing and applying the material in this chapter.

■ SUMMARY

In order to prepare an effective marketing strategy, a company must consider its competitors as well as its actual and potential customers. It must continuously analyze its competitors and develop competitive marketing strategies that effectively position it against competitors and give it the strongest possible competitive advantage.

Competitor analysis first involves identifying the company's major competitors, using both an industry-based and a market-based analysis. The company then gathers information on competitors' objectives, strategies, strengths and weaknesses, and reaction patterns. With this information in hand, it can select competitors to attack or to avoid. Competitive intelligence must be collected, interpreted, and distributed continuously. Company marketing managers should be able to obtain full and reliable information about any competitor affecting their decisions.

Which competitive marketing strategy makes the most sense depends on the company's industry position and its objectives, opportunities, and resources. The company's competitive marketing strategy depends on whether it is a market leader, challenger, follower, or nicher.

A market leader faces three challenges: expanding the total market, protecting market share, and expanding market share. The market leader is interested in finding ways to expand the total market because it will benefit most from any increased sales. To expand market size, the leader looks for new users of the product, new uses, and more usage. To protect its existing market share, the market leader has several defenses: position defense, flanking defense, preemptive defense, counteroffensive defense,

mobile defense, and contraction defense. The most sophisticated leaders cover themselves by doing everything right, leaving no openings for competitive attack. Leaders can also try to increase their market shares. This makes sense if profitability increases at higher market-share levels.

A market challenger is a firm that aggressively tries to expand its market share by attacking the leader, other runner-up firms, or smaller firms in the industry. The challenger can choose from a variety of attack strategies, including a frontal attack, flanking attack, encirclement attack, bypass attack, and guerrilla attack.

A market follower is a runner-up firm that chooses not to rock the boat, usually out of fear that it stands to lose more than it might gain. The follower is not without a strategy, however, and seeks to use its particular skills to gain market growth. Some followers enjoy a higher rate of return than the leaders in their industry.

A market nicher is a smaller firm that serves some part of the market that is not likely to attract the larger firms. Market nichers often become specialists in some end use, vertical level, customer size, specific customer, geographic area, product or product feature, quality-price or service.

A competitive orientation is important in today's markets, but companies should not overdo their focus on competitors. Companies are more likely to be hurt by missing emerging consumer needs and by new competitors than by existing competitors. Companies that balance consumer and competitor considerations are practicing a true market orientation.

■ QUESTIONS FOR DISCUSSION

1. Erol's is a chain of videotape rental stores with outlets in Washington, D.C., and other eastern cities. Who are its competitors? What product/market segments do Erol's and its competitors serve?

2. What different strategic groups can you identify in the automobile industry? Which groups compete with which other groups? Be sure to consider foreign manufacturers as well as domestic manufacturers.

3. Do a customer value analysis for Levi Strauss. Compare Levi's strengths and weaknesses with those of its competitors.

4. "Well-behaved" companies prefer well-behaved competition. Should it make any difference to consumers whether competition is "well-behaved" or "disruptive"? Why or why not?

5. Hewlett-Packard, a market leader in the high-priced end of the calculator market, has found itself in a squeeze between aggressively promoted portable computers and less expensive calculators with increasingly sophisticated features. What market leader strategy would you recommend for Hewlett-Packard? Why?

6. How could Morton Salt expand the total market for table salt? Discuss the role sales promotion would play in getting new users, communicating new uses, or increasing usage of table salt.

7. After the initial success of California Cooler, over one hundred wine coolers were introduced in the United States. What strategies did Bartles & Jaymes and Seagram's use to overtake California Cooler? What defensive strategy could California Cooler have used to maintain its leadership?

8. Many medium-sized firms are in an unprofitable middle ground between very large firms and smaller, more focused firms. Discuss how medium-sized firms could use market nicher strategies to improve their profitability.

9. Which will have more impact on a market-centered company's strategies—competitors or customers? Will the company do more research on customers or on competitors, or will research expenditures be balanced?

10. A small firm has developed a desktop copier using advanced technology for better—and more economical—performance. Suggest a strategy for this firm to use in entering the photocopying market. Justify your recommendation.

■ KEY TERMS

Competitive strategies Strategies that strongly position the company against competitors and that give the company the strongest possible strategic advantage.

Competitor analysis The process of identifying key competitors; assessing their objectives, strategies, strengths and weaknesses, and reaction patterns; and selecting which competitors to attack or to avoid.

Competitor-centered company A company whose moves are mainly based on competitors' actions and reactions; it spends most of its time tracking competitors' moves and market shares and trying to find strategies to counter them.

Customer-centered company A company that focuses on customer developments in designing its marketing strategies.

Customer value analysis Analysis conducted to determine what benefits target customers value and how they rate the relative value of various competitors' offers.

Industry A group of firms that offer a product or class of products that are close substitutes for each other.

Market-centered company A company that pays balanced attention to both customers and competitors in designing its marketing strategies.

Market challenger A runner-up firm in an industry that is fighting hard to increase its market share.

Market follower A runner-up firm in an industry that wants to hold its market share without rocking the boat.

Market leader The firm in an industry with the largest market share; it usually leads other firms in price changes, new product introductions, distribution coverage, and promotion spending.

Market nichers Firms in an industry that serve small segments that the larger firms overlook or ignore.

Strategic group A group of firms in an industry following the same or a similar strategy.

■ REFERENCES

1. See Betsy Bauer, "Giants Loom Larger Over Pint-Sized Soft-Drink Firms," *USA Today*, May 27, 1986, p. 5B; and Jennifer Lawrence and Patricia Strnad, "A & W Spices Up Lineup," *Advertising Age*, August 31, 1987, p. 27.

2. See Michael E. Porter, *Competitive Advantage* (New York: The Free Press, 1985), pp. 226–27.

3. Ibid, Chapter 6. Porter calls these "good" competitors and "bad" competitors.

4. See Michael E. Porter, *Competitive Advantage*; Pankaj Ghemawat, "Sustainable Advantage," *Harvard Business Review*, September–October 1986, pp. 53–58; and Michael E. Porter, "From Competitive Advantage to Corporate Strategy," *Harvard Business Review*, May–June 1987, pp. 43–59.

5. Michael E. Porter, *Competitive Strategy: Techniques for Analyzing Industries and Competitors* (New York: Free Press, 1980), Ch. 2.

6. Stuart Gannes, "The Riches in Market Niches," *Fortune*, April 27, 1987, p. 228.

7. See Al Ries and Jack Trout, *Marketing Warfare* (New York: McGraw-Hill, 1986); and Gerald A. Michaelson, *Winning the Marketing War* (Lanham, MD: Madison Books, 1987).

8. These six defense strategies and the five attack strategies described later in the chapter are from Philip Kotler and Ravi Singh, "Marketing Warfare in the 1980s," *Journal of Business Strategy*, Winter 1981, pp. 30–41.

9. See Robert D. Buzzell, Bradley T. Gale, and Ralph G. M. Sultan, "Market Share—the Key to Profitability," *Harvard Business Review*, January–February 1975, pp. 97–106; and Ben Branch, "The Laws of the Marketplace and ROI Dynamics," *Financial Management*, Summer 1980, pp. 58–65. Others suggest that the relationship between market share and profits has been exagger-

ated. See Carolyn Y. Woo and Arnold C. Cooper, "Market-Share Leadership—Not Always So Good," *Harvard Business Review*, January–February 1984, pp. 2–4; and Robert Jacobson and David A. Aaker, "Is Market Share All It's Cracked Up to Be?" *Journal of Marketing*, Fall 1985, pp. 11–22.

10. See John D. C. Roach, "From Strategic Planning to Strategic Performance: Closing the Achievement Gap," *Outlook*, (New York: Booz, Allen & Hamilton), Spring 1981, p. 21. Michael Porter makes the same point in his *Competitive Strategy* (New York: The Free Press, 1980).

11. See Michael E. Porter, "How to Attack the Industry Leader," *Fortune*, April 19, 1985, pp. 153–66.

12. See Andrew C. Brown, "Unilever Fights Back in the U.S.," *Fortune*, May 26, 1986, pp. 32–38.

13. See Otis Port, "Canon Finally Challenges Minolta's Mighty Maxxum," March 2, 1987, pp. 89–90.

14. Donald K. Clifford and Richard E. Cavanagh, *The Winning Performance: How America's High- and Midsize-Growth Companies Succeed* (New York: Bantam Books, 1985).

20 *Planning, Implementing, and Controlling Marketing Programs*

DURING the 1970s, IBM became stodgy and bureaucratic. The highly structured and tradition-bound IBM organization was having trouble competing against smaller, more flexible competitors in fast-changing, high-growth segments. Thus when IBM decided in the early 1980s to enter the personal computer market, industry analysts were skeptical. The strategy was sound enough—to carry the IBM name and reputation for quality and service into the fastest-growing segment of the computer market. But with personal computers, the company would be selling a very different product, to very different customers, with very different competition. Could large and ponderous IBM successfully *plan* for and *implement* a new strategy so different from previous strategies? Despite its great size and power, few expected IBM to have much of an immediate impact against more nimble competitors in the personal computer market.

But the introduction of the IBM PC became a classic story of smart marketing planning and innovative implementation. IBM pulled some big surprises, swept aside traditional methods, and broke many long-held rules. It set up a "special operating unit" called the Entry Systems Division (ESD) with complete responsibility for the IBM PC. This independent "company within a company" developed a culture and operating style similar to those of its smaller competitors. Free of close IBM control, ESD ignored traditions and did many "non-IBM-like" things. For example:

- IBM had *always* built its computers from the ground up, using only IBM electronic components. But to get the PC to the market more quickly, ESD made it from readily available components bought from outside suppliers.

- IBM had *always* carefully guarded its computer designs and developed its own software. Not so for the PC! To increase acceptance and sales, ESD published the PC's technical specifications to show how the machine was built. This made it easier for outside companies to design PC-compatible software. The resulting wealth of available software made the PC even more attractive to consumers. IBM machines soon became the industry standard for software producers.

- IBM had *always* sold its products directly through its own salesforce. But for the PC, ESD used a network of independent retailers, including such large ones as Sears and Computerland.

- Until the late 1970s, IBM had *always* been slow but sure in making product and price changes. But ESD spent millions to build modern production facilities that could turn out PCs at low cost, then used aggressive pricing to keep competitors off balance.

Thus to plan and implement its strategy to enter the personal computer market, IBM made several tradition-shattering changes in its structure, operations, and tactics. And the new approach paid off. The IBM PC went from initial planning to market in just 13 months. In less then three years, IBM claimed a 40 percent market share (60 to 70 percent in the company segment). Though using available parts and publishing designs later made it easier for copycat competitors to crank out IBM imitations, without these moves IBM would not likely have gotten to market so quickly or penetrated so deeply. And when IBM introduced its next generation System/2 personal computers in 1987, even with a dozen low-priced "clones" on the market, the venerable old IBM PC still held a 30 percent market share, compared with only 7 percent shares for nearest competitors Apple and Compaq.

The Entry Systems Division, which began as a 12-person team, has grown into a 10,000-employee division. IBM is now blending ESD into the rest of the $50 billion company. But the new approach worked so well that IBM has set up more than a dozen more special business units to develop products for software, robotics, high-tech health care, and other fast-growing markets.[1]

Chapter Objectives   *After reading this chapter, you should be able to:*

1. Identify the sections of a marketing plan and what each section contains.
2. Discuss why companies have trouble implementing marketing plans and programs.
3. Describe the elements of the marketing implementation process.
4. List and compare four ways of organizing the marketing department.
5. Explain three ways in which companies control their marketing activities.

IN this chapter, we will look more closely to each marketing management function—analysis, planning, implementation, and control. Figure 20-1 shows the relationship between these marketing activities. The company first develops overall strategic plans. These companywide strategic plans are then translated into marketing and other plans for each division, product, and brand.

Through implementation, the company turns the strategic and marketing plans into actions that will achieve the company's strategic objectives. Marketing plans are implemented by people in the marketing organization working with others inside and outside the company. Control consists of measuring and evaluating the results of marketing plans and activities, then taking corrective action to make sure objectives are being reached. Marketing analysis provides information and evaluations needed for all of the other marketing management activities.

We will discuss planning first to review all the factors that marketers must consider when designing marketing programs. But discussing it first does not mean that planning always comes first or that planning ends before marketers move on to the other activities. Figure 20-1 shows that planning and the other activities are

FIGURE 20-1
The relationship between analysis, planning, implementation, and control

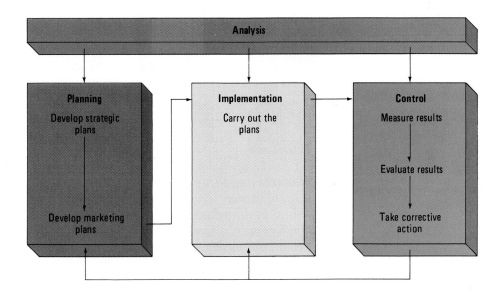

closely related. Marketers must plan their analysis, implementation, and control activities; analysis provides inputs for planning, implementation, and control; control provides feedback for future planning and implementation.

In Chapters 4 and 8 we examined many of the tools used in marketing analysis. In this chapter we will discuss marketing planning and how plans are implemented and controlled by people in the marketing department.

MARKETING PLANNING

The strategic plan defines the company's overall mission and objectives. Within each business unit, functional plans must be prepared—including marketing plans. If the business unit consists of different product and customer segments, plans might be written for each. Marketing plans might include product plans, brand plans, or market plans.

The Components of a Marketing Plan

How does a marketing plan look? Our discussion will focus on product or brand plans. A product or brand plan should contain the following sections: executive summary, current marketing situation, threats and opportunities, objectives and issues, marketing strategies, action programs, budgets, and controls (see Figure 20-2).

Executive Summary

The marketing plan should open with a short summary of the main goals and recommendations to be presented in the plan. Here is a short example:

> The 1989 Marketing Plan outlines an approach to attaining a significant increase in company sales and profits over the preceding year. The sales target is $80 million, a planned 20 percent sales gain. We think this increase is attainable because of the improved economic, competitive, and distribution picture. The target operating margin is $8 million, a 25 percent increase over last year. To achieve these goals, the sales promotion budget will be $1.6 million, or 2 percent of projected sales. The advertising budget will be $2.4 million, or 3 percent of projected sales. . . . [More detail follows.]

The executive summary helps top management to quickly find the major points of the plan. A table of contents should follow the executive summary.

FIGURE 20-2
Components of a
marketing plan

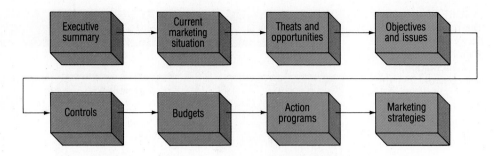

Current Marketing Situation

The first major section of the plan describes the target market and the company's position in it. In this section, the planner provides information about the market, product performance, competition, and distribution. It includes a *market description* which defines the market, including major market segments. The planner shows market size in total and by segment for several past years, then reviews customer needs and factors in the marketing environment that may affect customer purchasing. Next the *product review* shows sales, prices, and gross margins of the major products in the product line. A section on *competition* identifies major competitors and each of their strategies for product quality, pricing, distribution, and promotion. It also shows the market shares held by the company and each competitor. Finally, a section on *distribution* describes recent sales trends and developments in the major distribution channels.

Threats and Opportunities

This section requires the manager to look ahead for major threats and opportunities that the product might face. The purpose is to make the manager anticipate important developments that can have an impact on the firm. Managers should list as many threats and opportunities as they can imagine. Suppose the manager at a cigarette company comes up with the following list:

1. Congress is considering a new law that every cigarette package include a skull and crossbones on the front with the warning: "Scientific evidence shows that daily smoking shortens a person's life by an average of seven years."

2. An increasing number of public places are prohibiting smoking or are setting up separate sections for smokers and nonsmokers.

3. A new insect is attacking tobacco-growing areas, leading to the possibility of smaller crops in the future and larger price increases if some means cannot be found to control it.

4. The company's research lab is close to finding a way to turn lettuce into an enjoyable but harmless tobacco.

5. Cigarette smoking is rapidly increasing in foreign markets, especially in developing nations.

The first three items are *threats*. Not all threats call for the same attention or concern; the manager should assess how likely to occur each threat is and how much harm it would cause. The manager should then focus on the most probable and harmful threats and prepare plans in advance to meet them.

The last two items in the list are marketing opportunities. A **company marketing opportunity** is an attractive arena for marketing action in which the company would enjoy a competitive advantage.

The manager should assess each opportunity according to its potential attractiveness and the company's probability of success. Figure 20-3 shows that the company should pursue only the opportunities that fit its objectives and resources. Every

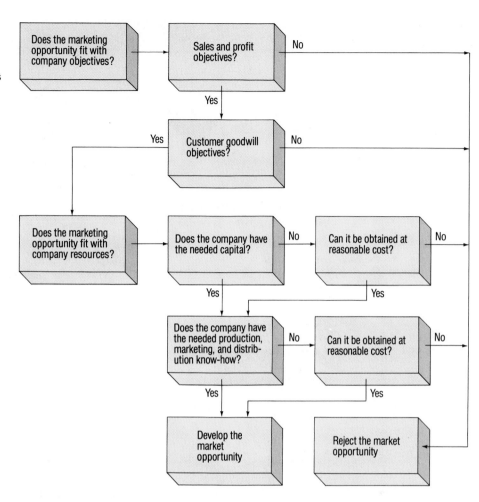

FIGURE 20-3
Evaluating a company marketing opportunity in terms of company objectives and resources

Boxes in flowchart:

Does the marketing opportunity fit with company objectives? → Sales and profit objectives? → No

Yes ↓

Customer goodwill objectives? → No

Yes ↓

Does the marketing opportunity fit with company resources? → Does the company have the needed capital? → No → Can it be obtained at reasonable cost? → No

Yes ↓

Does the company have the needed production, marketing, and distribution know-how? → No → Can it be obtained at reasonable cost? → No

Yes

Develop the market opportunity

Reject the market opportunity

company has objectives based on its business mission. And each opportunity requires that the company have certain amounts of capital and know-how. Companies can rarely find ideal opportunities that exactly fit their objectives and resources. Developing opportunities involves risks. When evaluating opportunities, the manager must decide whether the expected returns justify this risk.

Objectives and Issues

Having studied the product's threats and opportunities, the manager can now set objectives and consider issues that will affect them. The objectives should be stated as goals the company would like to reach during the plan's term. For example, the manager might want to achieve a 15 percent market share, a 20 percent pretax profit on sales, and a 25 percent pretax profit on investment. Suppose the current market share is only 10 percent. This situation poses a key issue: How can market share be increased? The manager will want to consider the major issues involved in trying to increase market share.

Marketing Strategies

In this section, the manager outlines the broad marketing strategy or "game plan" for attaining the objectives. **Marketing strategy** is the marketing logic by which the business unit hopes to achieve its marketing objectives. It consists of specific strategies for target markets, the marketing mix, and the marketing budget.

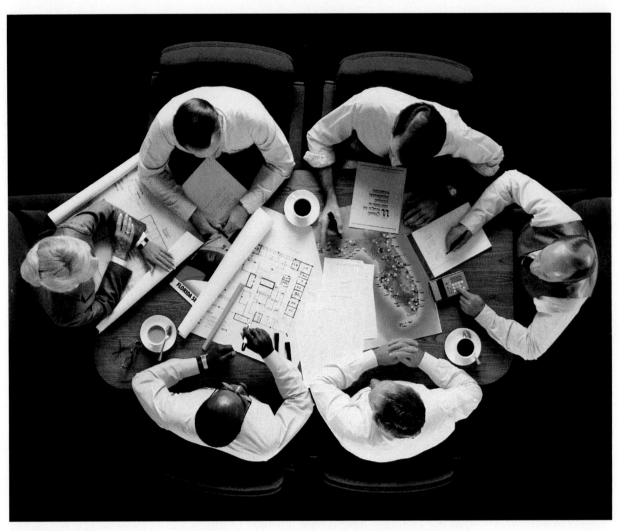

Marketers must continually plan their analysis, implementation, and control activities.

Marketing strategy should spell out the market segments on which the company will focus. These segments differ in their needs and wants, responses to marketing, and profitability. The company would be smart to put its effort and energy into those market segments it can best serve from a competitive point of view. It should develop a marketing strategy for each targeted segment. The manager should outline specific strategies for such marketing mix elements as new products, field sales, advertising, sales promotion, prices, and distribution. The manager should explain how each strategy responds to the threats, opportunities, and key issues spelled out earlier in the plan.

Action Programs

The marketing strategies are next turned into specific action programs that answer the following questions: *What* will be done? *When* will it be done? *Who* is responsible for doing it? *How much* will it cost? For example, the manager may want to step up sales promotion as a key strategy for winning market share. A sales promotion action plan should be drawn up that outlines special offers and their dates, trade shows entered, new point-of-purchase displays, and other promotions. The action plan shows when activities will be started, reviewed, and completed.

Budgets

The manager should also spell out the marketing budget that will be needed to carry out its strategies and programs. The manager knows that higher budgets will produce more sales but is looking for the marketing budget that will produce the best profit picture.

The detailed action plan allows the manager to make a supporting budget that is essentially a projected profit and loss statement. On the revenue side, it shows the forecasted number of units that would be sold and the average net price. On the expense side, it shows the cost of production, physical distribution, and marketing. The difference is the projected profit. Higher management will review the budget and approve or modify it. Once approved, the budget is the basis for materials buying, production scheduling, manpower planning, and marketing operations.

Controls

The last section of the plan outlines the controls that will be used to monitor progress. Typically, goals and budgets are spelled out for each month or quarter. This means that higher management can review the results each period and spot businesses or products that are not meeting their goals. The managers of these businesses and products have to explain the problems and what corrective actions they will take.

Developing the Marketing Budget

We will now look at how marketing managers construct a marketing budget to attain a given level of sales and profits. We will first examine a common budget-setting approach, then describe some improvements.

Target Profit Planning

Suppose Jason Gray, the ketchup product manager at Heinz, has to prepare his annual marketing plan. He will probably follow the procedure shown in Table 20-1 called *target profit planning*.

Jason Gray first estimates the total household market for ketchup for the coming year. To make this estimate, he applies the recent market growth rate (6 percent) to the current year's market size (23.6 million cases). This calculation forecasts a market size of 25 million cases for next year. Jason assumes that Heinz's current 28 percent market share will continue and forecasts next year's sales at 7 million cases.

Next, based on expected increases in labor and material costs, Jason sets next years' distributor price at $4.45 per case and calculates that sales revenue will be $31.15 million. He then estimates next year's variable costs at $2.75 per case. The contribution margin to cover fixed costs, profits, and marketing is $11.9 million. Suppose the company charges this brand with a fixed cost of $1 per case, or $7 million. Subtracting the fixed costs leaves a contribution margin to cover profits and marketing of $4.9 million.

Jason now enters the target profit goal. Suppose higher management will be satisfied with a profit level of $1.9 million, a 10 percent increase over this year's profit. Jason then subtracts the target profit from what remains of the contribution margin, leaving $3 million available for marketing.

Finally, Jason allocates the marketing budget to some of the marketing mix elements, such as advertising, sales promotion, and marketing research. Jason decides that this year's split should use the same proportions as last year's. He spends two-thirds of the money on advertising, almost one-third on sales promotion, and the remainder on marketing research.

TABLE 20-1
Target Profit Plan

1. *Forecast of total market* This year's total market (23,600,000 cases) × recent growth rate (6%)	25,000,000 cases
2. *Forecast of market share*	28%
3. *Forecast of sales volume* [(1) × (2)]	7,000,000 cases
4. *Price to distributor*	$4.45 per case
5. *Estimate of sales revenue* [(3) × (4)]	$31,150,000
6. *Estimate of variable costs* Tomatoes and spices ($0.50) + bottles and caps ($1.00) + labor ($1.10) + physical distribution ($0.15)	$2.75 per case
7. *Estimate of contribution margin to cover fixed costs, profits, and marketing* {[(14) − (6)] × (3)}	$11,900,000
8. *Estimate of fixed costs* Fixed charge $1 per case × 7 million cases	$7,000,000
9. *Estimate of contribution margin to cover profits and marketing* [(7) − (8)]	$4,900,000
10. *Estimate of target profit goal*	$1,900,000
11. *Amount available for marketing* [(9) − (10)]	$3,000,000
12. *Split of the marketing budget* Advertising Sales promotion Marketing research	 $2,000,000 $ 900,000 $ 100,000

Although this method produces a workable budget, Jason could make improvements. He could estimate market size and share by examining past trends and considering changes in the marketing environment that would lead to a different demand forecast. Rather than assuming he would continue last year's marketing strategy, Jason could have considered one or several alternative strategies and their potential impact on sales, profits, and the budget. Jason set price mainly to cover expected costs but could have used a more market-oriented method, which might have resulted in a more competitive price and higher sales. Jason allocated the budget to the marketing mix using "more-of-the-same" thinking but should have considered each marketing element's potential contribution given this year's marketing objectives and the product's current situation. Finally, Jason's plan and budget seek only satisfactory profits. Instead, Jason could look for a plan that optimizes profits.

Profit Optimization Planning

We will now consider how to find the optimal profit plan. To optimize profits, the manager must first identify the relationship between sales and the various marketing mix elements. The *sales-response function* describes this relationship. Figure 20-4 shows a hypothetical sales-response function. This function shows that the more the company spends in a given period on marketing, the higher its sales are likely to be. This particular function is S-shaped, although other shapes are possible. The S-shaped function says that low levels of marketing expenditure are not likely to produce much sales. Too few buyers will be reached, or reached effectively, by the company's marketing. Higher levels of marketing spending during the period will produce much higher levels of sales. But very high spending might not add much more sales because of eventually diminishing returns.

Diminishing returns to increases in marketing expenditures occur because there is an upper limit to the total potential demand for any product. As demand approaches this upper limit, it becomes increasingly expensive to attract the remaining, more reluctant buyers. Also, as the company steps up its marketing effort, competitors tend to do the same, so that each company faces more sales resistance.

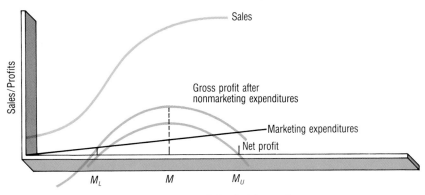

FIGURE 20-4
The sales-response function: the relationship between sales, marketing expenditures, and profits

How can marketing managers estimate the sales-response functions for their businesses? They can use one of three methods. Using the *statistical method*, the manager gathers data on past sales and marketing mix levels and estimates the sales-response functions with statistical techniques. Using the *experimental method*, the manager varies the marketing mix levels in matched samples and notes the resulting sales responses. Finally, using the *judgmental method*, experts are asked to make intelligent guesses about the needed relationships.[2]

Once estimated, how are sales-response functions used in profit optimization? Figure 20-4 shows the analysis for finding the optimal marketing expenditure. First, the marketing manager subtracts all nonmarketing costs from the sales-response function to find the gross-profit curve. Next, the marketing expenditures, shown by the straight line starting at the origin, are subtracted from the gross-profit curve to find the net-profit curve. The net-profit curve shows positive net profits with marketing expenditures between M_L and M_U, which could be defined as the range of rational marketing spending. The net-profit curve reaches a maximum at M. Therefore the marketing expenditure that would maximize net profit is $\$M$. The graphic solution can also be carried out mathematically; in fact, it has to be if sales volume is a function of more than one marketing mix variable.

This budgeting approach offers a good conceptual framework for studying relationships between marketing mix levels and the resulting sales and profits. Some marketers have developed complex models for estimating response curves and finding optimal budgets. Others prefer more practical, easier-to-use budgeting methods.[3]

*I*MPLEMENTATION

Planning good strategies is only a start toward successful marketing. A brilliant marketing strategy will count for little if the company fails to implement it properly. **Marketing implementation** is the process that turns marketing strategies and plans into marketing actions in order to accomplish strategic marketing objectives. Implementation involves day-to-day, month-to-month activities that effectively put the marketing plan to work. Whereas marketing planning addresses the *what* and *why* of marketing activities, implementation addresses the *who*, *where*, *when*, and *how*.

Many managers think that "doing things right" (implementation) is as important, or even more important, than "doing the right things" (strategy).

A surprisingly large number of very successful large companies . . . don't have long-term strategic plans with an obsessive preoccupation on rivalry. They concentrate on operating details and doing things well. Hustle is their style and their strategy. They move fast and they get it right. . . . Countless companies in all industries, young or old, mature or booming, are finally learning the limits of strategy and concentrating on tactics and execution.[4]

Yet implementation is difficult—it is often easier to think up good marketing strategies than to carry them out. And managers often have trouble diagnosing implementation problems. It is usually hard to tell whether poor performance was caused by poor strategy, poor implementation, or both.[5]

Reasons for Poor Implementation

Why do so many companies have trouble getting their marketing plans to work effectively? Several factors can cause implementation problems. *Isolated planning* is often a major cause. The company's planning often is carried out by high-level "professional planners" who have little direct contact with the marketing managers who must implement the plan. These planners are concerned with broad strategy and may prepare plans that are too general. Managers who face day-to-day operations may not fully understand the plans or they may resent what they see as unrealistic plans made up by "ivory-tower" planners. Many companies are cutting down their large central planning staffs and turning planning over to lower-level managers. In these companies, planners work directly with line managers to design more workable strategies.[6]

Another cause of poor implementation is management *tradeoffs between long-term and short-term objectives*. Company marketing strategies often cover *long-run* activities over three to five years. But the marketing managers who implement these strategies are usually rewarded for *short-run* sales, growth, or profits. When choosing between long-run strategy and short-run performance, managers usually favor the more rewarding short-run results. Some companies are taking steps to attain a better balance between short- and long-run goals. They are evaluating managers on both long-run and short-run performance and rewarding managers for reaching long-run strategic objectives.[7]

Natural *resistance to change* can cause implementation problems. The company's current operations have all been designed to implement past plans and strategies. New strategies requiring new company patterns and habits will be resisted. And the more different the new strategy from the old, the greater the resistance to implementing it.

Finally, implementation may fail for a *lack of specific implementation plans*. Some marketing planners leave the implementation details to managers, and the result is poor implementation or no implementation at all. Management cannot simply assume that its plans will be implemented. It must prepare a detailed implementation plan that shows the specific activities needed to put the plan into action. It must develop timetables and assign major implementation tasks to individual managers.

The Implementation Process

People at all levels of the marketing system must work together to implement marketing plans and strategies. People in the marketing department, in other company departments, and in outside organizations—all can help or hinder marketing implementation. The company must find ways to coordinate all these actors and their activities.

The implementation process is shown in Figure 20-5.[8] The figure shows that marketing strategy and marketing performance are linked by an implementation system consisting of five related elements: action programs, an organization structure, decision and reward systems, human resources, and managerial climate and company culture.

FIGURE 20-5
The marketing
implementation process

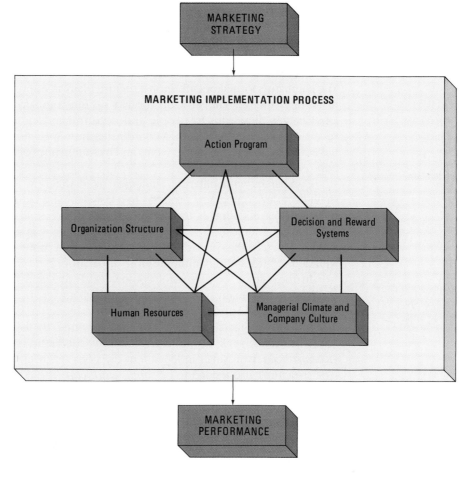

The Action Program

To implement marketing plans, people at all company levels make decisions and perform tasks. At Procter & Gamble, implementation of a plan to introduce a stream of high-quality new products requires day-to-day decisions and actions by thousands of people inside and outside the organization. In the marketing organization, marketing researchers test new product concepts and scan the marketplace for new product ideas. For each new product, marketing managers make decisions about target segments, branding, packaging, pricing, promoting, and distributing. Salespeople are hired, trained and retrained, directed, and motivated.

Marketing managers work with other company managers to get support for promising new products. They talk with engineering about product design. They talk with manufacturing about production and inventory levels. They talk with finance about funding and cash flows, with the legal staff about patents and product safety, and with personnel about staffing and training. Marketing managers also work with outside people. They meet with advertising agency people to plan ad campaigns and with the media to obtain publicity support. The salesforce urges retailers to advertise the new products, give them lots of shelf space, and use company displays.

The **action program** pulls all of these people and activities together; it identifies the decisions and actions needed to implement the marketing program. It also gives responsibility for these decisions and actions to specific people in the company. Finally, the action program gives a timetable that states when decisions must be made and when actions must be taken. The action program shows what must be done, who will do it, and how decisions and actions will be coordinated to reach the company's marketing objectives.

The Organization Structure

The company's formal organization structure plays an important role in implementing marketing strategy. The structure breaks up the company's work into well-defined jobs, assigns these jobs to people and departments, and allows efficiency through specialization. The structure then coordinates these specialized jobs by defining formal ties between people and departments and by setting lines of authority and communication.

Companies with different strategies need different organization structures. A small firm developing new products in a fast-changing industry might need a flexible structure that encourages individual action—a decentralized structure with lots of informal communication. A more established company in more stable markets might need a structure that provides more integration—a more centralized structure with well-defined roles and communication "through proper channels."

In their study of successful companies, Peters and Waterman found that the companies had many common structural characteristics that lead to successful implementation.[9] For example, their structures tended to be more *informal*—United Airline's MBWA (management by walking around), IBM's "open-door" policy, 3M's "clubs" to create small-group interaction. The successful companies' structures were *decentralized*, with small independent divisions or groups to encourage innovation. The structures also tended to be *simple and lean*. These simple structures are more flexible and allow the companies to adapt more quickly to changing conditions.

The excellent companies also have lean staffs, especially at higher levels. According to Peters and Waterman:

> It appears that most of our excellent companies have comparatively few people at the corporate level, and that what staff there is tends to be out in the field solving problems rather than in the home office checking on things. The bottom line is fewer administrators, more operators.[10]

In recent years, many large companies—General Motors, Polaroid, Du Pont, General Electric, Lever Brothers, and others—have cut back unneeded layers of management and restructured their organizations to reduce costs and increase marketing flexibility.

Some of the Peters and Waterman study conclusions have been questioned because the study focused on high-technology and consumer goods companies operating in rapidly changing environments.[11] The structures used by these companies may not be right for other types of firms in different situations. And many of the study's excellent companies will need to change their structures as their strategies and situations change. For example, the informal structure that made Hewlett-Packard so successful at the time of the study has caused problems for HP in recent years. The company has recently moved toward a more formal structure (see Marketing Highlight 20–1).

Decision and Reward Systems

Decision and reward systems include formal and informal operating procedures that guide such activities as planning, information gathering, budgeting, recruiting and training, control, and personnel evaluation and rewards. Poorly designed systems can work against implementation; well-designed systems can help implementation. Consider a company's compensation system. If it compensates managers for short-run results, they will have little incentive to work toward long-run objectives. Many companies are designing compensation systems that will overcome this problem. Here is an example:

> One company was concerned that its annual bonus system encouraged managers to ignore long-run objectives and focus on annual performance goals. To correct this, the company changed its bonus system to include rewards for both annual performance and for reaching "strategic milestones." Under the new plan, each manager works with planners to set two or three strategic objectives. At the end of the year, the manager's bonus is based on both operating performance and on reaching the strategic objectives. Thus the bonus system encourages managers to achieve more balance of the company's long- and short-run needs.[12]

Human Resources

Marketing strategies are implemented by people, so successful implementation requires careful human resources planning. At all levels, the company must fill its structure and systems with people who have the needed skills, motivation, and personal characteristics. Company personnel must be recruited, assigned, trained, and maintained. The selection and development of executives and other managers are especially important for implementation. Different strategies call for managers with different personalities and skills. New venture strategies need managers with entrepreneurial skills; holding strategies require managers with organizational and administrative skills; and retrenchment strategies call for managers with cost-cutting skills. Thus the company must carefully match its managers to the needs of the strategies to be implemented.

In recent years, more and more companies have recognized the importance of good people planning. Systematic, long-run human resources planning can give the company a strong competitive advantage.[13]

Managerial Climate and Company Culture

The company's managerial climate and company culture can make or break marketing implementation. **Managerial climate** involves the way company managers work with others in the company. Some managers take command, delegate little authority, and keep tight controls. Others delegate a lot, encourage their people to take initiative, and communicate informally. No one managerial style is best for all situations. Different strategies may require different leadership styles; which style is best varies with the company's structure, tasks, people, and environment.

Company culture is a system of values and beliefs shared by people in an organization. It is the company's collective identity and meaning. The culture informally guides the behavior of people at all company levels. Peters and Waterman found that excellent companies have strong and clearly defined cultures.

> Without exception, the dominance and coherence of culture proved to be an essential quality of the excellent companies. Moreover, the stronger the culture and the more it was directed toward the marketplace, the less need there was for policy manuals, organization charts, or detailed procedures and rules. In these companies, people way down the line know what they are supposed to do in most situations because the handful of guiding values is crystal clear. . . . Everyone at Hewlett-Packard knows that he or she is supposed to be innovative. Everyone at Procter & Gamble knows that product quality is the [norm].[14]

Marketing strategies that do not fit the company's style and culture will be difficult to implement. For example, a decision by Procter & Gamble to increase sales by reducing product quality and prices would not work well. It would be resisted by P&G people at all levels who identify strongly with the company's reputation for quality. Because managerial style and culture are so hard to change, companies

HEWLETT-PACKARD'S STRUCTURE EVOLVES

In 1939 two engineers—Bill Hewlett and Dave Packard—started Hewlett-Packard in a Palo Alto garage to build test equipment. At the start, Bill and Dave did everything themselves, from designing and building their equipment to marketing it. As the firm grew out of the garage and began to build more and different types of test equipment, Hewlett and Packard could no longer make all the necessary operating decisions by themselves. They assumed roles as top managers and hired functional managers to run various company activities. These managers were relatively autonomous, but still closely tied to the owners.

By the mid-1970s, Hewlett-Packard's 42 divisions employed more than 1,200 people. The company's structure evolved to support its heavy emphasis on innovation and autonomy. The structure was loose and decentralized. Each division operated as an autonomous unit and was responsible for its own strategic planning, product development, marketing programs, and implementation.

In 1982 Peters and Waterman, in their *In Search of Excellence*, cited HP's informal and decentralized structure as a major reason for the company's continued excellence. They praise HP's unrestrictive structure and high degree of informal communication (its MBWA—management by walking around—style). Peters and Waterman note that the HP structure de-

centralizes decision making and responsibility. In the words of one HP manager:

> Hewlett-Packard [should not] have a tight, military-type organization, but rather . . . give people the freedom to work toward [overall objectives] in ways they determine best for their own areas of responsibility.

The structure also decentralizes authority and fosters autonomy:

> The sales force does not have to accept a product developed by a division unless it wants it. The company cites numerous instances in which several million dollars of development funds were spent by a division, at which point the salesforce said, "No thanks."

But in recent years, though still profitable, Hewlett-Packard has met with some problems in the fast-changing microcomputer and minicomputer markets. According to *Business Week*:

> Hewlett-Packard's famed innovative culture and decentralization spawned such enormously successful products as its 3000 minicomputer, the handheld scientific calculator, and the ThinkJet nonimpact printer. But when a new climate required its fiercely autonomous divisions to cooperate in product development and marketing, HP's passionate devotion to the "autonomy and entrepreneurship" that Peters and Waterman advocate became a hindrance.

---

usually design strategies that fit their current cultures rather than trying to change their styles and cultures to fit new strategies.

Table 20-2 lists questions that companies should ask about each element of the implementation system. Successful implementation depends on how well the company blends the five activities into a cohesive program that supports its strategies.

MARKETING DEPARTMENT ORGANIZATION

The company must design a marketing department that can carry out marketing analysis, planning, implementation and control. In this section, we will focus on how marketing departments within companies are organized. If the company is very small, one person might end up doing all the marketing work—research, selling, advertising, customer service, and others. As the company expands, a marketing department organization emerges to plan and carry out marketing activities. In large companies, this department contains many marketing specialists. Thus General Mills has product managers, salespeople and sales managers, market researchers, advertising experts, and other specialists.

Hewlett-Packard began in this garage in 1939; now it operates around the world. Structure and culture changed with growth.

Thus Hewlett-Packard is finding that it must change its structure and culture to bring them in line with its changing situation. As *Business Week* puts it:

> To regain its stride, HP is being forced to abandon attributes of excellence for which it was praised. Its technology-driven, engineering-oriented culture, in which decentralization and innovation were a reli-

gion and entrepreneurs were the gods, is giving way to a marketing culture and growing centralization.

Sources: Based on information in Donald F. Harvey, *Business Policy and Strategic Management* (Columbus, OH: Charles E. Merrill, 1982), pp. 269–70; "Who's Excellent Now?" *Business Week*, November 5, 1984, pp. 76–78; and Thomas J. Peters and Robert H. Waterman, Jr., *In Search of Excellence: Lessons from America's Best-Run Companies* (New York: Harper & Row, 1982).

A company can have a marketing department and yet not operate as a modern marketing company. If company executives view the marketing function as primarily a selling function, they are missing the point. Only when they see that all the departments are "working for the customer" and that marketing is not just a department but part of a company philosophy will they become a modern marketing company.

Modern marketing departments can be arranged in several ways. A company will set up its marketing department in the way that best helps it meet its marketing objectives.

Functional Organization

The **functional organization** is the most common form of marketing organization. Marketing specialists are in charge of different marketing activities, or functions. Figure 20-6 shows five specialists: marketing administration manager, advertising and sales promotion manager, sales manager, marketing research manager, and new products manager. Other specialists might include a customer service manager, a marketing planning manager, and a distribution manager.

The main advantage of a functional marketing organization is that it is simple to administer. On the other hand, this form by itself is less and less effective as the

TABLE 20-2
Questions about the
Marketing
Implementation
System

Structure
What is the organization's structure?
What are the lines of authority and communication?
What is the role of task forces, committees, or similar mechanisms?

Systems
What are the important systems?
What are the key control variables?
How do product and information flow?

Tasks
What are the tasks to be performed and which are critical?
How are they accomplished, with what technology?
What strengths does the organization have?

People
What are their skills, knowledge, and experience?
What are their expectations?
What are their attitudes toward the firm and their jobs?

Culture
Are there shared values that are visible and accepted?
What are the shared values and how are they communicated?
What are the dominant management styles?
How is conflict resolved?

Fit
Does each component above support marketing strategy?
Do the various components fit together well to form a cohesive framework for implementing strategy?

Source: Adapted from David L. Aaker, *Strategic Market Management* (New York: Wiley, 1984), p. 151. © 1984, John Wiley & Sons, Inc.

company's products and markets grow. First, it becomes difficult to make plans for each different product or market, and products that are not favorites of the functional specialists get neglected. Second, as the functional groups compete with each other to gain more budget and status, top management has trouble coordinating all the marketing activities.

Geographic Organization

A company selling all across the country often uses a **geographic organization** for its salesforce. Figure 20-7 shows 1 national sales manager, 4 regional sales managers, 24 zone sales managers, 192 district sales managers, and 1,920 salespeople. Geographic organization allows salespeople to settle into a territory, get to know their customers, and work with a minimum of travel time and cost.

Product Management Organization

Companies with many products or brands often create a **product management organization.** The product management organization is headed by a products manager who supervises several product group managers who supervise product or brand managers in charge of specific products or brands (see Figure 20-8). The

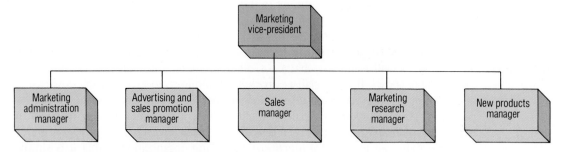

FIGURE 20-6 Functional organization

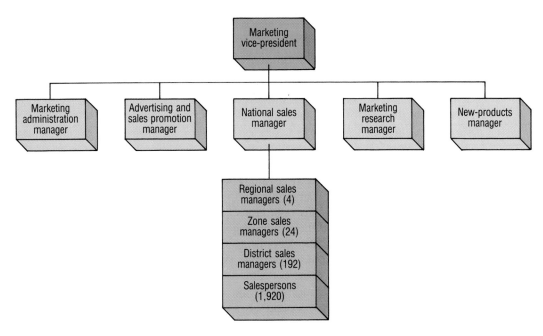

FIGURE 20-7   Geographic organization

product manager's job is to develop and implement a complete strategy and marketing program for a specific product or brand. A product management organization makes sense if the company has many very different products.

Product management first appeared in the Procter & Gamble Company in 1929. A new company soap, Camay, was not doing well, and a young P&G executive was assigned to give his exclusive attention to developing and promoting this product. He was successful, and the company soon added other product managers.[15]

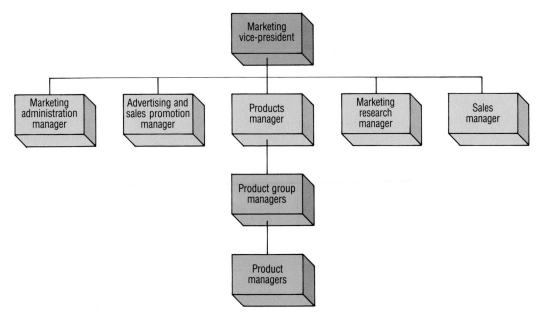

FIGURE 20-8   Product management organization

Since then, many firms, especially in the food, soap, toiletries, and chemical industries, have set up product management organizations. General Foods, for example, uses a product management organization in its Post Division. There are separate product group managers in charge of cereals, pet food, and beverages. Within the cereal product group, there are separate product managers for nutritional cereals, children's presweetened cereals, family cereals, and miscellaneous cereals. In turn, the nutritional cereal product manager supervises brand managers.

The product management organization has many advantages. The product manager coordinates the whole marketing mix for the product and can sense and react more quickly to product problems. Smaller brands get more attention than they would otherwise because they have their own product manager. Finally, product management is an excellent training ground for young executives—it involves them in almost every area of company operations.

But a price is paid for these advantages. First, product management creates some conflict and frustration. Product managers are often not given enough authority to carry out their responsibilities effectively. They are told they are "mini-presidents" but are often treated as low-level coordinators. Second, product managers become experts in their product but rarely become experts in any functions. This lack of expertise hurts products that depend on a specific function, such as advertising. Third, the product management system often costs more than expected. Originally, one manager is assigned to each major product. Soon product managers are appointed to manage even minor products. Each product manager gets an assistant brand manager, then later a brand assistant. With all these personnel, payroll costs climb. The company becomes saddled with a costly structure of product management people.

Many consumer package goods companies today are rethinking the role of the product manager. Product managers have long tended to be home-office people who planned long-term product strategy and watched over product profitability. But with the recent swing toward *regionalized marketing*—increased geographic segmentation, more localized marketing, greater use of point-of-sale pricing and sales promotion—the emphasis is shifting to local markets and shorter-term strategies. To effectively design and implement more localized strategies, already overworked product managers must now spend more time in the field. They must work with salespeople, learn what is happening in stores, and get closer to the customer. Some companies are trying new ways to deal with this problem. For example, Campbell Soup recently set up "brand sales managers," combination product managers and salespeople charged with handling brands in the field.[16]

Market Management Organization

Many companies sell one product line to many different types of markets. For example, Smith Corona sells its electric typewriters to consumer, business, and government markets. U.S. Steel sells its steel to the railroad, construction, and public utility industries. When different markets have different needs and preferences, a **market management organization** might be best for the company.

A market management organization is similar to the product management organization shown in Figure 20-8. Market managers are responsible for developing long-range and annual plans for the sales and profits in their markets. They have to coax help from marketing research, advertising, sales, and other functions. This system's main advantage is that the company is organized around the needs of specific customer segments.

Many companies have reorganized along market lines. The Heinz Company split its marketing organization into three groups: groceries, commercial restaurants, and institutions. Each group contains further market specialists. For example, the

Rethinking the role of the product manager: Campbell set up "brand sales managers."

institutional division contains separate market specialists who plan for schools, colleges, hospitals, and prisons.

Product Management/ Market Management Organization

Companies that produce many different products flowing into many different markets face a problem. They could use a product management system, which requires product managers to be familiar with highly diverse markets. Or they could use a market management system, which means that market managers would have to be familiar with the many diverse products bought by their markets. Or they could install both product and market managers in a *matrix organization*.

Figure 20-9 shows Du Pont's matrix organization. The product managers plan sales and profits for their respective fibers. They contact each market manager for estimates of how much fiber can be sold in each market. The market managers, on the other hand, develop profitable markets for existing and future Du Pont fibers. They contact the product managers to find out about prices and availabilities of different fibers.

This matrix organization assures that each product and market receives its share of management attention. But this system also has disadvantages. It adds costly layers of management and reduces organizational flexibility. And it generates additional conflict. For example, at Du Pont, should the nylon product manager have final authority for setting nylon prices in all markets? What happens if the men's wear market manager feels that nylon will lose out in this market unless special price concessions are made on nylon?

FIGURE 20-9
DuPont's product
management/market
management system

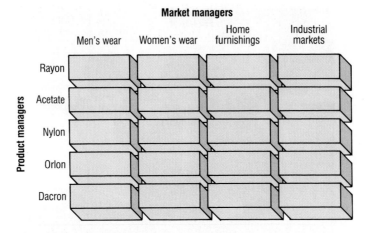

Most managers feel that only the more important products and markets justify separate managers. Some are not upset about the conflicts and costs and believe that the benefits of product and market specialization outweigh the costs.[17]

MARKETING CONTROL

Because many surprises will occur during the implementation of marketing plans, the marketing department has to engage in constant marketing control. **Marketing control** is the process of measuring and evaluating the results of marketing strategies and plans, and taking corrective action to assure that marketing objectives are attained.

There are three types of marketing control (see Table 20-3). *Annual plan control* involves checking ongoing performance against the annual plan, and taking corrective action when necessary. *Profitability control* involves determining the actual profitability of different products, territories, markets, and channels. *Strategic control* involves looking at whether the company's basic strategies are well matched to its opportunities.

Annual Plan Control

The purpose of **annual plan control** is to ensure that the company achieves the sales, profits, and other goals set out in its annual plan. It involves the four steps shown in Figure 20-10. First, management sets monthly or quarterly goals in the annual plan. Second, management measures its performance in the marketplace. Third, management evaluates the causes of any differences between expected and actual performance. Fourth, management takes corrective action to close the gaps between its goals and its performance. Doing so may require changing the action programs, or even changing the goals.

What specific control tools are used by management to check on performance? The four main tools are sales analysis, market-share analysis, marketing expense-to-sales analysis, and customer attitude tracking.

Sales analysis consists of measuring and evaluating actual sales in relation to sales goals. Such an analysis might involve finding out whether specific products and territories are producing their expected share of sales. Suppose the company sells in three territories where expected sales were 1,500 units, 500 units, and 2,000 units, respectively, adding up to 4,000 units. The actual sales volume was 1,400 units, 525 units, and 1,075 units. Thus territory A fell short by 7 percent; territory B had a 5 percent surplus; and territory C fell short by 46 percent! Territory C is causing most of the trouble. The sales vice-president can check into territory C to see why performance is poor.

TABLE 20-3
Types of Marketing
Control

TYPE OF CONTROL	PRIME RESPONSIBILITY	PURPOSE OF CONTROL	APPROACHES
Annual plan control	Top management Middle management	To examine whether the planned results are being achieved	Sales analysis Market-share analysis Marketing expense-to-sales ratios Customer attitude tracking
Profitability control	Marketing controller	To examine where the company is making and losing money	Profitability by: Product Territory Market segment Trade channel Order size
Strategic control	Top management Marketing auditor	To examine whether the company is pursuing its best marketing opportunities and doing this efficiently	Marketing audit

Company sales do not show how well the company is doing relative to competitors. A sales increase could be due to better economic conditions from which all companies gained, rather than to improved company performance in relation to its competitors. Management needs to use *market share analysis* to track the company's market share. If the company's market share goes up, it is gaining on competitors; if its market share goes down, it is losing to competitors.

Annual plan control requires making sure that the company is not overspending to achieve its sales goals. Thus, marketing control also includes *expense-to-sales analysis*. Watching the ratio of marketing expenses to sales will help keep marketing expenses in line.

Alert companies also use *customer attitude tracking* to check the attitudes of customers, dealers, and other marketing system participants. By watching changes in customer attitudes before they affect sales, management can take early action, if it is needed. The main customer attitude tracking systems are complaint and suggestion systems, customer panels, and customer surveys.

Profitability Control

Besides annual plan control, companies also need **profitability control** to measure the profitability of their various products, territories, customer groups, channels, and order sizes. This information will help management determine whether any products or marketing activities should be expanded, reduced, or eliminated. We will illustrate the steps in marketing profitability analysis with the following example: A lawnmower company wants to determine the profitability of selling its lawnmower through three types of retail channels: hardware stores, garden supply shops, and department stores. Its profit and loss statement is shown in Table 20-4A.

FIGURE 20-10
The control process

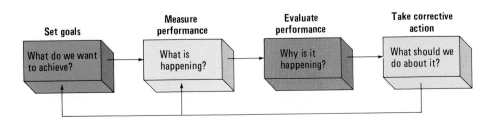

Keeping track of sales and expenses.

Step 1: *Identify functional expenses*. The company incurred the expenses listed in Table 20-4A to sell the product, advertise it, pack and deliver it, and bill and collect for it. Management must first measure how much of each expense was incurred for each activity. Suppose that most of the $9,300 in salary expense went to salespeople ($5,100); the rest went to an advertising manager ($1,200), packing and delivery help ($1,400), and office accounting people ($1,600). Table 20-4B shows the allocation of the salary expense to these four activities.

Table 20-4B also shows how rent of $3,000 is allocated to the four activities. Since the sales representatives work away from the office, the company allocates none of the building's rent expense to selling. The advertising manager and accounting manager use a small portion of floor space, but most of the floor space and equipment are rented for packing and delivery. Finally, the supplies expense covers promotional materials, packing materials, fuel purchases for delivery, and home-office stationery. The total of $3,500 in this account is reassigned to the four functions. Thus Table 20-4B summarizes how the company translates total expenses of $15,800 into functional expenses.

Step 2: *Assign functional expenses to channels*. The company next measures

TABLE 20-4A **A Simple Profit and Loss Statement**			
Sales			$60,000
Cost of goods sold			39,000
Gross margin			$21,000
Expenses			
Salaries		$9,300	
Rent		3,000	
Supplies		3,500	
			15,800
Net profit			$ 5,200

TABLE 20-4B
Translating Natural
Expenses into
Functional Expenses

NATURAL ACCOUNTS	TOTAL	SELLING	ADVERTISING	PACKING AND DELIVERY	BILLING AND COLLECTING
Salaries	$ 9,300	$5,100	$1,200	$1,400	$1,600
Rent	3,000	—	400	2,000	600
Supplies	3,500	400	1,500	1,400	200
	$15,800	$5,500	$3,100	$4,800	$2,400

how much functional expense goes for selling through each type of channel. It first calculates the number of sales made in each channel. Altogether, 275 sales calls were made during the period (see the Selling column of Table 20-4C). Since the total selling expense amounted to $5,500 (Table 20-4B), the selling expense per call averaged $20.

Similarly, the company allocates advertising expense according to the number of ads directed at each channel. Since there was a total of 100 ads, the average ad cost $31. Management allocates packing and delivery expense according to the number of orders placed by each channel; it uses the same basis for allocating billing and collection expense.

Step 3: Prepare a profit and loss statement for each channel. The company can now prepare a profit and loss statement for each channel (Table 20-4D). Since hardware stores accounted for one-half of total sales ($30,000 out of $60,000), the company charges this channel with half the cost of goods sold ($19,500 out of $39,000). This leaves a gross margin from hardware stores of $10,500. From this amount, the company must deduct the proportions of the functional expenses for hardware stores.

According to Table 20-4C, hardware stores received 200 out of 275 total sales calls. At $20 a call, hardware stores have to be charged with $4,000 selling expense. Hardware stores also received 50 ads. At $31 an ad, the hardware stores are charged with $1,550 of advertising. In the same way, the company computes the share of the other functional expenses to charge to hardware stores. In total, it allocates $10,050 of expenses to this channel. Subtracting this from the gross margin, the profit of selling through hardware stores is only $450.

The company repeats this analysis for the other channels. Management finds that it is losing money selling through garden supply shops and makes virtually all its profits in selling through department stores. Note that the gross sales through each channel do not reliably indicate the net profits being made in each channel.

What corrective action should the company take? It would be naive to conclude that management should drop garden supply shops and hardware stores in order

TABLE 20-4C
Allocating Functional
Expenses to Channels

CHANNEL TYPE		SELLING	ADVERTISING	PACKING AND DELIVERY	BILLING AND COLLECTING
		No. of Sales Calls in Period	No. of Advertisements	No. of Orders Placed in Period	No. of Orders Placed in Period
Hardware		200	50	50	50
Garden supply		65	20	21	21
Department stores		10	30	9	9
		275	100	80	80
Functional expense	=	$5,500	$3,100	$4,800	$2,400
No. of units		275	100	80	80
Cost per unit	=	$20	$31	$60	$30

TABLE 20-4D
Profit and Loss
Statements for
Channels

	HARDWARE	GARDEN SUPPLY	DEPT. STORES	WHOLE COMPANY
Sales	$30,000	$10,000	$20,000	$60,000
Cost of goods sold	19,500	6,500	13,000	39,000
Gross margin	$10,500	$ 3,500	$ 7,000	$21,000
Expenses				
Selling ($20 per call)	$ 4,000	$ 1,300	$ 200	$ 5,500
Advertising ($31 per advertisement)	1,550	620	930	3,100
Packing and delivery ($60 per order)	3,000	1,260	540	4,800
Billing ($30 per order)	1,500	630	270	2,400
Total expenses	$10,050	$ 3,810	$ 1,940	$15,800
Net profit (or loss)	$ 450	$ (310)	$ 5,060	$ 5,200

to concentrate on department stores. Several questions should be answered first. Would garden supply and hardware store buyers look for the brand in the remaining channel? What are the important trends regarding the three channels? For example, perhaps garden supply centers are growing, while department stores are declining. Has the company used the proper marketing with each channel?

Based on the answers, the company might take a number of alternative actions. It might drop only the weakest retailers in each channel. Or it might offer a program to train people in hardware and garden supply stores to sell lawnmowers more effectively. Or it could cut channel costs by reducing the number of sales calls and promotional aids going to garden supply shops and hardware stores. As a last resort, it could drop the less profitable channels altogether.

Strategic Control

From time to time, companies need **strategic control**, a critical review of their overall marketing effectiveness. Marketing strategies and programs can quickly become out of date. Each company should now and then reassess its overall approach to the marketplace, using a tool known as the marketing audit.[18] A **marketing audit** is a comprehensive, systematic, independent, and periodic examination of a company's environment, objectives, strategies, and activities to determine problem areas and opportunities and to recommend a plan of action to improve the company's marketing performance.

The marketing audit covers all major marketing areas of a business, not just a few trouble spots. It is normally conducted by an objective and experienced outside party who is independent of the marketing department. The marketing audit should be carried out periodically instead of only when there is a crisis. It promises benefits for the successful company as well as for the company in trouble.

The marketing auditor should be given freedom to interview managers, customers, dealers, salespeople, and others who might throw light on marketing performance. Table 20-5 shows the kinds of questions the marketing auditor will ask. Not all these questions are important in every situation. The auditor will develop a set of findings and recommendations based on this information. The findings may come as a surprise, and sometimes a shock, to management. Management decides which recommendations make sense, and how and when to implement them.

TABLE 20-5
Components of a
Marketing Audit

Part I. Marketing environment audit
Macroenvironment
A. Demographic
    1. What major demographic developments and trends pose opportunities or threats to this company?
    2. What actions has the company taken in response to these developments and trends?

TABLE 20-5 (Continued)

B. Economic
    1. What major developments in income, prices, savings, and credit will affect the company?
    2. What actions has the company been taking in response to these developments and trends?

C. Natural
    1. What is the outlook for the cost and availability of natural resources and energy needed by the company?
    2. What concerns have been expressed about the company's role in pollution and conservation, and what steps has the company taken?

D. Technological
    1. What major changes are occurring in product technology? In process technology? What is the company's position in these technologies?
    2. What major generic substitutes might replace this product?

E. Political
    1. What laws now being proposed could affect marketing strategy and tactics?
    2. What federal, state, and local actions should be watched? What is happening in the areas of pollution control, equal employment opportunity, product safety, advertising, price control, and so forth, that affects marketing strategy?

F. Cultural
    1. What is the public's attitude toward business and toward the products produced by the company?
    2. What changes in consumer and business life styles and values have a bearing on the company?

Task Environment

A. Markets
    1. What is happening to market size, growth, geographical distribution, and profits?
    2. What are the major market segments?

B. Customers
    1. How do customers and prospects rate the company and its competitors on reputation, product quality, service, salesforce, and price?
    2. How do different customer segments make their buying decisions?

C. Competitors
    1. Who are the major competitors? What are their objectives and strategies, their strengths and weaknesses, their sizes and market shares?
    2. What trends will affect future competition and substitutes for this product?

D. Distribution and Dealers
    1. What are the main trade channels for bringing products to customers?
    2. What are the efficiency levels and growth potentials of the different trade channels?

E. Suppliers
    1. What is the outlook for the availability of key resources used in production?
    2. What trends are occurring among suppliers in their pattern of selling?

F. Facilitators and Marketing Firms
    1. What is the cost and availability outlook for transportation services?
    2. What is the cost and availability outlook for warehousing facilities?
    3. What is the cost and availability outlook for financial resources?
    4. How effectively is the advertising agency performing?

G. Publics
    1. What publics represent particular opportunities or problems for the company?
    2. What steps has the company taken to deal effectively with each public?

Part II. Marketing strategy audit

A. Business Mission
    1. Is the business mission clearly stated in market-oriented terms? Is it feasible?

B. Marketing Objectives and Goals
    1. Are the corporate and marketing objectives stated in the form of clear goals to guide marketing planning and performance measurement?
    2. Are the marketing objectives appropriate, given the company's competitive position, resources, and opportunities?

C. Strategy
    1. What is the core marketing strategy for achieving the objectives? Is it sound?
    2. Are enough resources (or too much resources) budgeted to accomplish the marketing objectives?
    3. Are the marketing resources allocated optimally to market segments, territories, and products?
    4. Are the marketing resources allocated optimally to the major elements of the marketing mix— product quality, service, salesforce, advertising, promotion, and distribution?

Part III. Marketing organization audit

A. Formal Structure
    1. Does the marketing officer have adequate authority and responsibility over company activities that affect the customer's satisfaction?
    2. Are the marketing activities optimally structured along functional, product, end user, and territorial lines?

TABLE 20-5
(Continued)

B. Functional Efficiency
    1. Are there good communication and working relations between marketing and sales?
    2. Is the product management system working effectively? Are product managers able to plan profits or only sales volume?
    3. Are there any groups in marketing that need more training, motivation, supervision, or evaluation?
C. Interface Efficiency
    1. Are there any problems between marketing and manufacturing, R&D, purchasing, or financial management that need attention?

Part IV. Marketing systems audit
A. Marketing Information System
    1. Is the marketing intelligence system producing accurate, sufficient, and timely information about marketplace developments?
    2. Is marketing research being adequately used by company decision makers?
B. Marketing Planning System
    1. Is the marketing planning system well conceived and effective?
    2. Is sales forecasting and market potential measurement soundly carried out?
    3. Are sales quotas set on a proper basis?
C. Marketing Control System
    1. Are the control procedures adequate to ensure that the annual plan objectives are being achieved?
    2. Does management periodically analyze the profitability of products, markets, territories, and channels of distribution?
    3. Are marketing costs being periodically examined?
D. New Product Development System
    1. Is the company well organized to gather, generate, and screen new product ideas?
    2. Does the company do adequate concept research and business analysis before investing in new ideas?
    3. Does the company carry out adequate product and market testing before launching new products?

Part V. Marketing productivity audit
A. Profitability Analysis
    1. What is the profitability of the company's different products, markets, territories, and channels of distribution?
    2. Should the company enter, expand, contract, or withdraw from any business segments, and what would be the short- and long-term profit consequences?
B. Cost-Effectiveness Analysis
    1. Do any marketing activities seem to have excessive costs? Can cost-reducing steps be taken?

Part VI. Marketing function audits
A. Products
    1. What are the product line objectives? Are these objectives sound? Is the current product line meeting the objectives?
    2. Are there products that should be phased out?
    3. Are there new products that are worth adding?
    4. Would any products benefit from quality, feature, or style modifications?
B. Price
    1. What are the pricing objectives, policies, strategies, and procedures? To what extent are prices set on cost, demand, and competitive criteria?
    2. Do the customers see the company's prices as being in line with the value of its offer?
    3. Does the company use price promotions effectively?
C. Distribution
    1. What are the distribution objectives and strategies?
    2. Is there adequate market coverage and service?
    3. Should the company consider changing its degre of reliance on distributors, sales reps, and direct selling?
D. Advertising, Sales Promotion, and Publicity
    1. What are the organization's advertising objectives? Are they sound?
    2. Is the right amount being spent on advertising? How is the budget determined?
    3. Are the ad themes and copy effective? What do customers and the public think about the advertising?
    4. Are the advertising media well chosen?
    5. Is sales promotion used effectively?
    6. Is there a well-conceived publicity program?
E. Salesforce
    1. What are the organization's salesforce objectives?
    2. Is the salesforce large enough to accomplish the company's objectives?
    3. Is the salesforce organized along the proper principles of specialization (territory, market, product)?
    4. Does the salesforce show high morale, ability, and effort?
    5. Are the procedures adequate for setting quotas and evaluating performances?
    6. How is the company's salesforce rated in relation to competitors' salesforces?

SUMMARY

This chapter examines how marketing strategies are planned, implemented, and controlled.

Each business has to prepare marketing plans for its products, brands, and markets. The main components of a marketing plan are: executive summary, current marketing situation, threats and opportunities, objectives and issues, marketing strategies, action programs, budgets, and controls. The marketing budget section of the plan can be developed either by setting a target profit goal or by using sales-response functions to identify the profit-optimizing marketing plan.

It is often easier to plan good strategies than to carry them out. To be successful, companies must implement the strategies effectively. Implementation is the process that turns marketing strategies into marketing actions. Several factors can cause implementation failures—isolated planning, tradeoffs between long- and short-term objectives, natural resistance to change, and a failure to prepare detailed implementation plans.

The implementation process links marketing strategy and plans with marketing performance. The process consists of five related elements. The action program identifies crucial tasks and decisions needed to implement the marketing plan, assigns them to specific people, and sets up a timetable. The organization structure defines tasks and assignments and coordinates the efforts of the company's people and units. The company's decision and reward systems guide activities such as planning, information, budgeting, training, control, and personnel evaluation and rewards. Well-designed action programs, organization structures, and systems can encourage good implementation.

Successful implementation also requires careful human resources planning. The company must recruit, allocate, develop, and maintain good people. It must carefully match its managers to the requirements of the marketing programs being implemented. The company's managerial climate and company culture can make or break implemen-tation. Company climate and culture guide people in the company. Good implementation relies on strong and clearly defined cultures that fit the chosen strategy. Each element of the implementation system must fit company marketing strategy. Moreover, successful implementation depends on how well the company blends the five elements into a cohesive program that supports its strategies.

Most of the responsibility for implementation goes to the company's marketing department. Modern marketing departments are organized in a number of ways. The most common form is the functional marketing organization in which marketing functions are headed by separate managers reporting to the marketing vice-president. Another form is geographic organization in which sales and perhaps other functions specialize by geographic area. In the product management organization, products are assigned to product managers who work with functional specialists to develop and achieve their plans. In the market management organization, major markets are assigned to market managers who work with functional specialists. Some large companies use a product management and market management martix organization.

Marketing organizations carry out three types of marketing control. Annual plan control involves monitoring current marketing results to make sure that the annual sales and profit goals will be achieved. The main tools are sales analysis, market-share analysis, marketing expense-to-sales analysis, and customer attitude tracking. If poor performance is detected, the company can implement several corrective measures.

Profitability control calls for determining the actual profitability of the firm's products, territories, market segments, and channels. Strategic control makes sure that the company's marketing objectives, strategies, and systems fit the current and forecasted marketing environments. It uses the marketing audit to find marketing opportunities and problems and to recommend short-term and long-term actions to improve overall marketing performance.

QUESTIONS FOR DISCUSSION

1. A recently hired member of your staff wonders how a hundred-page marketing plan can be condensed into a one-page executive summary and also questions why an executive summary is needed at all. Describe to this staff member the purpose and contents of the executive summary section of the marketing plan.

2. Describe threats and opportunities facing McDonald's, Kentucky Fried Chicken, and other fast-food restaurant chains. What steps should these companies take to deal with the threats and take advantage of the opportunities that you have identified?

3. Can the objective-and-task approach for setting the promotional budget (described in Chapter 16) be adapted for use in setting the overall marketing budget? Outline how you would use the objective-and-task approach to set the marketing budget for Heinz ketchup.

4. Why is Anheuser-Busch more likely to use sales-response functions in trying to determine optimal marketing expenditures than is a small retailer who sells beer, wine, and other beverages? How confident can a manager be that this approach has led to the *optimal* marketing budget?

5. Describe the steps a company can take to avoid poor implementation of strategies. Do you think organization structure can affect a company's ability to implement its strategies? Why or why not?

6. A company owner requires his employees to dress conservatively yet expects people at his advertising agency to "look creative." What do these different expectations suggest about the owner's managerial climate and company culture?

7. Unisys sells a full range of computer systems to financial organizations, manufacturers, governments, and other customers in the United States and around the world. How should Unisys organize its marketing department—by function, geography, product, market, or some other way? Why?

8. A friend of yours who owns a restaurant thinks that it is not as profitable as it ought to be. What advice would you give your friend on the marketing control process as a way of helping a business succeed?

9. Why should a public university conduct a periodic marketing audit of itself? Who would conduct the audit? How would the findings of the audit be used? Briefly describe what you think an audit of your school would reveal.

10. Overall, which is the most important part of the marketing management process: planning, implementation, or control? Is a company that "does things right" more or less likely to succeed than a company that "does the right things"? Why or why not?

▮ KEY TERMS

Action program A detailed program that shows what must be done, who will do it, and how decisions and actions will be coordinated to implement marketing plans and strategy.

Annual plan control Evaluation and corrective action to ensure that the company achieves the sales, profits, and other goals set out in its annual plan.

Company culture A system of values and beliefs shared by people in an organization, the company's collective identity and meaning.

Company marketing opportunity An attractive arena for marketing action in which the company would enjoy a competitive advantage.

Functional organization An organization structure in which marketing specialists are in charge of different marketing activities or functions such as advertising, marketing research, sales management, and others.

Geographic organization An organization structure in which a company's national salesforce (and perhaps other functions) specializes by geographic area.

Managerial climate The company climate resulting from the way managers work with others in the company.

Market management organization An organization structure in which market managers are responsible for developing plans for sales and profits in their specific markets.

Marketing audit A comprehensive, systematic, independent, and periodic examination of a company's environment, objectives, strategies, and activities to determine problem areas and opportunities and to recommend a plan of action to improve the company's marketing performance.

Marketing control The process of measuring and evaluating the results of marketing strategies and plans, and taking corrective action to assure that marketing objectives are attained.

Marketing implementation The process that turns marketing strategies and plans into marketing actions in order to accomplish strategic marketing objectives.

Marketing strategy The marketing logic by which the business unit hopes to achieve its marketing objectives. It consists of specific strategies for target markets, the marketing mix, and the marketing budget.

Product management organization An organization structure in which product managers are responsible for developing and implementing marketing strategies and plans for a specific product or brand.

Profitability control Evaluation and corrective action to ensure the profitability of various products, territories, customer groups, trade channels, and order sizes.

Strategic control A critical review of the company's overall marketing effectiveness.

▮ REFERENCES

1. For more information, see "How the PC Project Changed the Way IBM Thinks," *Business Week*, October 3, 1983, pp. 86–90; Geoff Lewis, "Can Bill Lowe Put IBM's PC Unit in Pinstripes?" *Business Week*, January 20, 1986, pp. 83–84; and Peter Nulty, "IBM, Clonebuster," *Fortune*, April 27, 1987, p. 225.

2. For more on estimating and using sales-response functions, see Philip Kotler, *Marketing Management: Analysis, Planning, Implementation and Control*, 6th ed. (Englewood Cliffs, NJ: Prentice-Hall, 1988), Chap. 3.

3. For a detailed discussion of marketing budgeting, see Nigel F. Piercy, "The Marketing Budgeting Process: Marketing Management Implications," *Journal of Marketing*, October 1987, pp. 45–59.

4. Amar Bhide, "Hustle as Strategy," *Harvard Business Review*, September–October 1986, p. 59.

5. For more on diagnosing implementation problems, see Thomas V. Bonoma, "Making Your Marketing Strategy Work," *Harvard Business Review*, March–April 1984, pp. 70–71.

6. See "The New Breed of Strategic Planner: Number-Crunching Professionals Are Giving Way to Line Managers," *Business Week*, September 17, 1984, p. 62.

7. See Ray Stata and Modesto A. Maidique, "Bonus System for Balanced Strategy," *Harvard Business Review*, November–December 1980, pp. 156–63.

8. This figure is styled after several models of organizational design components. For examples, see Jay R. Galbraith, *Organizational Design* (Reading, MA: Addison-Wesley, 1977); Peter Lorange, *Implementation of Strategic Planning* (Englewood Cliffs, NJ: Prentice-Hall, 1982), p. 95; David L. Aaker, *Strategic Market Manage-*

ment (New York: Wiley, 1984), Chap. 9; and Carl R. Anderson, *Management: Skills, Functions, and Organization Performance* (Dubuque, IA: Wm. C. Brown, 1984), pp. 409–13.

9. See Thomas J. Peters and Robert H. Waterman, *In Search of Excellence: Lessons from America's Best-Run Companies* (New York: Harper & Row, 1982). For an excellent summary of the study's findings on structure, see Aaker, *Strategic Market Management*, pp. 154–57.

10. Peters and Waterman, *In Search of Excellence*, p. 311.

11. See "Who's Excellent Now?" *Business Week*, November 5, 1984, pp. 76–78; and Daniel T. Carroll, "A Disappointing Search for Excellence," *Harvard Business Review*, November–December 1983, pp. 78–79ff.

12. This example is adapted from one found in Robert M. Tomasko, "Focusing Company Reward Systems to Help Achieve Business Objectives," *Management Review* (New York: AMA Membership Publications Division, American Management Associations, October 1982), pp. 8–12.

13. For more on human resources planning, see D. Quinn Mills, "Planning With People in Mind," *Harvard Business Review*, July–August 1985, pp. 97–105; and Jason Hoerr, "Human Resources Managers Aren't Corporate Nobodies Anymore," *Business Week*, December 2, 1985, pp. 58–59.

14. Peters and Waterman, *In Search of Excellence*, pp. 75–76.

15. Joseph Winski, "One Brand, One Manager," *Advertising Age*, August 20, 1987, p. 86.

16. See Al Urbanski, "Repackaging the Brand Manager," *Sales and Marketing Management*, April, 1987, pp. 42–45.

17. For a more complete discussion of marketing organization approaches and issues, see Robert W. Ruekert, Orville C. Walker, Jr., and Kenneth J. Roering, "The Organization of Marketing Activities: A Contingency Theory of Structure and Performance," *Journal of Marketing*, Vol. 49 (Winter 1985), pp. 13–25.

18. For details, see Philip Kotler, *Marketing Management: Analysis, Planning, Implementation, and Control*, Chap. 25.

CASE 16

CLUB MED

Choosing the site of a new Club Med village is often as simple as going with what feels right. Jacques Giraud, president of New York–based Club Med, Inc., remembers how the company picked Huatulco as a village site. About two years ago, he was walking along a stretch of Mexican beach 300 miles south of Acapulco with a group that included Vice-Chairman Serge Trigano, the founder's son. Recalls Giraud: "Suddenly Serge stopped, took off his shoes, rolled up his pants, went into the water, and said, 'I want it here.'"

The instincts of Club Med officials have usually served them well. But a couple of slip-ups and some events beyond their control made 1987 a difficult year for the company that offers "the antidote for civilization." Club Med, Inc., 72% owned by France's Club Méditerranée, was spun off as a separate public company in 1984 to operate the villages in North America and Asia, the two fastest-growing markets in the worldwide system. By mid-December, the U.S. company will be running 27 resorts, including its first in Japan, on Hokkaido Island. But after two solidly profitable years, net income for the year ending October 31 is expected to decline 5% on revenues of $363 million. Even before the market crashed, its stock had fallen below the 52-week high of 29 ¼.

Copycats?

The trouble stems partly from consumer resistance to a 13% price hike last winter. Currency exchange losses have also hurt the bottom line. And political unrest and labor strife caused the temporary closing of resorts in Haiti and in the Turks and Caicos Islands—just when the popular Paradise Island village was shut down for renovations. That limited the company's offerings in 1987, driving some customers to take vacations elsewhere.

Those troubles were good news for Club Med's competitors—which are springing up all over. While resorts are the fastest-growing sector of the lodging industry, the business "has been somewhat besieged with an oversupply," says Gary B. Hedges, a resort specialist in the Phoenix office of Laventhol & Horwath, a leisure-time consulting firm. Hedges says 17% of the 23,900 lodging properties in the U.S. could be classified as resorts in 1987, up from 13% in 1985.

Some of those competitors are mimicking Club Med. In recent years a string of imitators—with such names as Hedonism II and Club Paradise—have appeared on Caribbean islands. And some of the hotel industry's biggest names are getting into the business. Resorts International, Inc., for example, built Club Paradise as a separate, all-inclusive resort adjacent to its hotel on Paradise Island.

These operators try to duplicate the Club Med formula, which combines an idyllic setting, a friendly, well-organized staff, and a single price that covers a wide range of activities. "There's no question that the people who are filling up these resorts are the right demographics to go to Club Med," says Thomas J. Garzilli, vice-president of Fly Fare Vacations, a New York travel wholesaler.

Open Domain

The increasing popularity of the $4 billion cruise industry is also cutting into Club Med's market. These days cruise vacations are being designed to appeal to a younger, more active clientele. "Cruising was once the domain of the rich, and the average age was deceased. Now cruising is open to everyone," says Robert H. Dickinson, senior vice-president for sales and marketing at Carnival Cruise Lines, Inc.

But Club Med executives insist that their villages are still in a class by themselves. Typical guests—*gentils membres*, or GMs, in the company vernacular—are baby boomers earning a median income of $60,000. Contrary to Club Med's reputation for catering to sybaritic singles, half the guests are married. And half are repeat visitors. Observes Ernest Levenstein, leisure-time analyst for Tucker, Anthony & R. L. Day, Inc., "Their objective is to get people to try the club. Once they do, they come back."

The company hopes to win more converts this year with new commercials created by Ammirati & Puris, Inc., the New York ad agency that six years ago dubbed Club Med "the antidote for civilization." One memorable commercial showed an overstressed businessman evolving into a relaxed human being in a week's time. Despite the success of that campaign, Club Med switched agencies and ad strategies in 1985.

The new agency, N. W. Ayer, Inc., used more of a direct-sell campaign, emphasizing the value of the one-price-for-everything Club Med vacation. It didn't work. "We can't advertise on price because we're more expensive than other resorts," says Giraud. "The Ayer ads had nice atmosphere, nice couples, but they didn't stand out as something different." So after much thought, Giraud went back to the agency he felt best understood the spirit of Club Med. A new Ammirati & Puris spot reports the world news, Club Med-style. Oil spills along the coast, for example, translate into a woman applying suntan lotion.

One-Day Jaunts

Club Med is taking other steps to shore up marketing. It just introduced a proprietary credit card with an interest rate tied to the prime, and it's giving better financial incentives to the most productive travel agents. More villages are offering family amenities such as "baby clubs," which provide child care for infants as young as six months. And for the 1989 Christmas season, the company intends to go head-to-head with the cruise lines by launching a 218-cabin sailing vessel to operate primarily in the Caribbean.

Club Med is also making greater efforts to fill its facilities during off-peak times. "We're satisfied with the winter and not with the summer," says Gilbert Trigano, chairman and founder of 33-year-old Club Méditerranée, which derives 25% of its revenues and profits from the U.S. company. With the weak U.S. dollar, Club Med successfully marketed its new Sandpiper village in Port St. Lucie, Fla., to French visitors in the summer—not a big season for American tourists to visit Florida. While most Club Med resorts require a week's stay, Sandpiper permits bookings by the day, attracting vacationers who have little time off. And the five-year-old corporate program, which allows companies to rent a village during the off-season, has boomed, with 1986 sales of $1.2 million swelling to $7.2 million in 1987.

In the meantime, Club Med is expanding steadily. Now that Sandpiper is up and running, the company will put United States development in high gear, especially on the West Coast. Plans call for the opening of two new villages a year in the United States and Asia, with more deluxe accommodations than in the past. So it looks as if Club Med officials will be rolling up their trousers and wading through the surf on a lot more virgin beaches.

1. Discuss Club Med's competitive environment.
2. Propose a competitive marketing strategy for Club Med.

Source: "Now Club Med Wants An Antidote For Competition." Reprinted from November 2, 1987, issue of *Business Week* by special permission, copyright © 1987 by McGraw-Hill, Inc.

CASE 17

THE ELECTRIC FEATHER PIROGUE

The Fin and Feather Products Company of Marshall, Texas, produces a line of small, versatile, lightweight boats called the Electric Feather Pirogue (pronounced pē rō). The term "feather" was chosen to emphasize the light weight of the boat and "electric" because it is propelled by an electric trolling motor. The name Pirogue refers to the historic small riverboats used on the Louisiana bayous. The kayak-shaped boat is 12 feet long, 38 inches wide, and 12 inches deep. It comes complete with motor and has a load capacity of about 540 pounds. Power is provided by a standard 12-volt automotive-type storage battery. The built-in Shakespeare motor is available with 18-pound or 24-pound thrust. The hull is handcrafted fiberglass, sturdily constructed by a hand-layup process.

The stable, flat-bottomed Pirogue can operate in very shallow water, so it is ideally suited for fishing, duck hunting, bird watching, or just leisure stream cruising. The propeller is protected from submerged objects by specially engineered motor guards on each side of the exposed drive unit. A 1½-inch sheet of polyurethane foam is built into the bottom to provide flotation. The boat is extremely simple to operate. A panel just below the wraparound gunwale contains two control switches—a forward-off-reverse switch and a low-medium-high speed switch. A horizontal lever just above the panel provides steering control. There is only one moving part in the entire control system. The three-speed, 18-pound thrust motor has a maximum speed of 10 miles an hour, and the four-speed, 24-pound thrust motor can attain a speed of 14 miles an hour. The company furnishes a one-year unlimited warranty on the boat, and the Shakespeare Company provides a similar warranty on the motor.

The company produced only one basic model of the boat but offered optional equipment that provided some variation within the product line. Retail prices ranged from approximately $490 to $650 depending on motor size and optional equipment. Although designed to accommodate two people, the standard model has only one molded plastic seat. The second seat, deluxe swivel seats, marine carpeting, and tonneau cover are the major optional items. No trailer is required because the boat fits nicely on the roof of even the smallest car or in the back of a station wagon or pickup truck. Without battery, the Pirogue weighs only about 80 pounds and can easily be handled by one person.

In year 1 (the base year), Mr. Bill Wadlington purchased controlling interest in, and assumed managerial control of, the seven-year-old Fin and Feather Products Company. One of Mr. Wadlington's first moves was to adopt a strict cash-and-carry policy; supplies and equipment were paid for at the time of purchase, and all sales were for cash prior to shipment whether shipment was to a dealer or directly to a customer. All shipments were F.O.B. the factory in Marshall, Texas. As a result of this policy, the firm has no accounts receivable and virtually no accounts payable. Mr. Wadlington anticipated sales of between 800 and 1000 units in year 1. This volume would approach plant capacity and produce a wholesale dollar volume of approximately $350,000 to $400,000. After only six months of operation Mr. Wadlington would not predict an exact annual net profit figure, but he was very optimistic about the first year's profit prospect. It was also difficult to predict exactly what future volume would be, but sales had shown a steady increase throughout the first half of the year. The flow of inquiries from around the United States and from several foreign countries made the future look bright.

The company hired no outside salespeople, and Mr. Wadlington was the only in-house salesman. There were 15 independent dealers around the country who bought at wholesale and assumed a standard markup. There was no formal agreement or contract between the company and the dealers, but to qualify as a dealer, an individual or firm's initial order had to be for at least five boats. Subsequent orders could be for any quantity desired. Dealers' orders had to be accompanied by a check for the entire amount of the purchase.

In addition to the dealers, the company had 20 agents who were authorized to take orders in areas outside the dealer territories. These agents accepted orders for direct shipment to customers and were paid a commission for the boats they sold. Agents were not assigned a specific territory but could not sell in the areas assigned to dealers. As with all sales, agent orders had to be prepaid. Direct orders from individuals were accepted at the factory when the customer lived outside a dealer territory. Most direct sales were the result of the company's advertisements in such magazines as *Ducks Unlimited, Outdoor Life, Argosy, Field and Stream,* and *Better Homes and Gardens.*

Mr. Wadlington had not established a systematic promotional program. The services of an out-of-state advertising agency were used to develop and place ads and to help with brochures and other promotional materials. Almost all negotiations with the agency were handled by phone or mail. The amount of advertising done at any time depended on existing sales volume. As sales declined, advertising was increased; when orders approached plant capacity, advertising was curtailed. Magazines were the primary advertising medium used. The dealers and agents were provided with attractive, professionally prepared brochures. The company had exhibited or had plans to exhibit, at boat shows in Texas, Ohio, and Illinois. Arrangements had been completed for Pirogues to be used as prizes on one of the more popular network game shows.

A detailed analysis of sales, in terms of who was buying the boats and for what purpose, had not been made. However, Mr. Wadlington did know that one of the most successful ads was in *Better Homes and Gardens.* An examination of orders produced by the ad indicated that they were primarily from women who were buying the boat for family use. There had been reports of the boats being used as utility boats for large houseboats and yachts, but the extent of such use was unknown. Although orders had been coming in from all parts of the country, the best sales areas had been in the eastern and southeastern parts of the United States. Mr. Wadlington attributed this, at least in part, to the fact that the company's past sales efforts had been concentrated almost exclusively in the southern and southwestern areas of the country. After the company began using national media, totally new markets were tapped. The Pirogue had virtually no direct competition, particularly outside the Texas-Louisiana area.

1. Identify the most likely target markets for the Pirogue.

2. Analyze the current distribution system for the Pirogue and suggest improvements.

3. Suggest other appropriate types of promotion for the Pirogue.

4. What do you think about scheduling advertising only when sales volume is below plant capacity?

5. Assess the current policy of requiring advance payment on all orders.

6. What data would Mr. Wadlington find useful for analyzing the effectiveness of his marketing program? How might he obtain these data?

7. Mr. Wadlington is opposed to changing his present marketing system. He contends that the plan is working because sales are strong and profit is satisfactory, and he asks, "Why change a winner?" How would you respond to his question?

Source: This case was prepared by Robert H. Solomon and Janelle C. Ashley of Stephen F. Austin State University as a basis for class discussion. Used with permission.

$\mathcal{21}$ International Marketing

FOR more than a hundred years, Eastman Kodak has been known for its easy-to-use cameras, high-quality film, and solid profits for investors. But during the past decade, Kodak's sales have flattened and its profits have declined. Perhaps complacent after its century of success, the company has been outpaced by more innovative competitors. In many cases, the competitors have been Japanese. Kodak dragged its feet in the 35-mm camera market and fell far behind Nikon, Canon, and Minolta. It lagged on video cameras and recorders and lost out to Sony, Matsushita, and Toshiba. And faster moving Japanese competitors grabbed up the market for self-contained, one-hour film-processing labs. So when another large Japanese competitor—Fuji Photo Film Company—moved in on Kodak's bread and butter color film business, Kodak took the challange seriously.

Fuji entered the U.S. film market in the early 1970s. It offered high-quality color films at 10 percent lower prices and beat Kodak to the market with high-speed films. Fuji pulled a major marketing coup by outbidding Kodak to become the official film of the 1984 Los Angeles Summer Olympic Games. Fuji's share of the huge U.S. color film market grew from just 2 percent in 1972 to over 8 percent in 1984, and it announced a 15 percent market share goal.

Fuji's U.S. sales grew at a rate of 20 percent a year, much faster than the market growth rate.

Kodak fought back fiercely to protect its whopping 85 percent share of the U.S. film market. It matched Fuji's new products and lower prices. It outspent Fuji by twenty to one on advertising and promotion and paid some $10 million to obtain sponsorship of the 1988 Summer Olympics in Seoul, South Korea. Most analysts agree that Kodak will successfully defend its U.S. market position. Fuji isn't likely to entice many consumers to abandon Kodak's familiar yellow and black film box to reach for Fuji green.

But Kodak is taking the battle a step further—it's attacking Japan, Fuji's home turf. Kodak is no stranger to international marketing: 40 percent of its $11 billion in sales come from 150 countries outside the United States. Kodak has been selling film in Japan since 1889. But until a few years ago, it didn't give the Japanese market much attention. Recently, however, Kodak has taken several aggressive steps to increase its Japanese presence and sales. It set up a separate subsidiary—Kodak Japan—and tripled its Japanese staff. It bought out a Japanese distributor and prepared to set up its own Japanese marketing and sales staff. It invested in a new technology center and a large Japanese research facility. And Kodak has greatly increased its Japanese promotion and publicity. Kodak Japan now sponsors everything from television talk shows to sumo wrestling tournaments.

Despite these strong efforts, it may be as hard for Kodak in Japan as for Fuji in the United States. Fuji, with over $3 billion in annual sales, has the resources to blunt Kodak's attack. The Japanese giant is firmly entrenched with a 70 percent share of the Japanese market versus Kodak's 15 percent. And high tariffs on foreign film protect Fuji's interests. Still, Kodak will gain several benefits from its stepped-up attack on Japan. First, Japan offers big opportunities for increased sales and profits—its $1.5 billion film and photo paper market is second only to the United States. Second, much of today's new photographic

technology comes out of Japan, so a greater presence in Japan will help Kodak to keep up with the latest developments. Third, ownership and joint ventures in Japan will help Kodak to better understand Japanese manufacturing and to obtain new products for the U.S. and other world markets. Kodak already sells many Japanese-made products under its own name in the United States. Kodak video cameras are made by Matsushita; its video tape is made by TDK Electronics. Kodak owns 10 percent of Chinon Industries, which makes the company's 35-mm cameras. Kodak sells film-processing labs made by Japanese manufacturers, and its medium-volume copiers are made by Canon.

Kodak reaps one more important benefit from its attack on the Japanese market. If Fuji must devote heavy resources to defending its Japanese home turf against Kodak's attacks, it will have fewer resources to use against Kodak in the United States.[1]

Chapter Objectives *After reading this chapter, you should be able to:*

1. Discuss how foreign trade, economic, political-legal, and cultural environments affect a company's international marketing decisions.
2. Describe three approaches to entering foreign markets.
3. Explain how companies might adapt their marketing mixes for foreign markets.
4. Identify the three forms of international marketing organization.

IN former times, American companies paid little attention to international trade. If they could pick up some extra sales through export, that might be okay. But the big market was at home, and it teemed with opportunities. The home market was much safer. Managers did not need to learn another language, deal with strange and changing currencies, face political and legal uncertainties, or adapt their products to different customer needs and expectations.

Today the situation is much different. The home market is no longer as rich in opportunity. Foreign firms are aggressively expanding into new international markets. What is worse, these firms have also entered the U.S. market, often with higher-quality products offering more value. The American firm that stays at home to play it safe might not only lose its chance to enter other markets, but also risks losing its home market.

Daily headlines tell about Japanese victories in the consumer electronics market and gains by Japanese, German, Swedish, and even Korean imports in the U.S. car market. They tell of Bic's successful attacks on Gillette; Nestle's gains in the coffee and candy markets; and the loss of textile and shoe markets to Third World imports.

Many American companies have made the world their market.

Such names as Sony, Toyota, Nestle, Perrier, Volvo, Norelco, Mercedes, and Panasonic have become household words. Other products that appear to be produced by American firms are really produced by foreign multinationals: Bantam Books, Baskin-Robbins Ice Cream, Capitol Records, Kiwi Shoe Polish, Lipton Tea, and Saks Fifth Avenue. America is also attracting huge foreign investments, in basic industries such as steel, and in tourist and real estate ventures—Japanese land purchases in Hawaii, Kuwait's resort development off the South Carolina coast, Arab purchases of Manhattan office buildings. One Saudi Arabian sheik even offered to buy the Alamo for his son. Few American industries are now safe from foreign competition.

Although some companies would like to stem the tide of foreign imports through protectionism, this response is only a temporary solution. In the long run it would raise the cost of living and protect inefficient U.S. firms. The answer is that more American firms must learn to move abroad and increase their competitiveness. Several

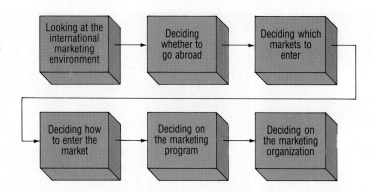

American companies have been successful at global marketing: Coca-Cola, McDonald's, IBM, Ford, Gillette, Kodak, Kellogg, Boeing, Xerox, Goodyear, and dozens of other American firms have made the world their market. But there are too few like them: In fact, just five U.S. manufacturers account for 17 percent of all manufacturing exports; 1,000 manufacturers (out of 300,000) account for 60 percent.

Ironically, while the need for companies to go abroad is greater, so are the risks. Several major problems confront companies that go global. Many countries that otherwise would be attractive markets—Mexico, Brazil, Poland, Romania, and many others—have built up such high foreign debt that they cannot even pay the interest on it. High debt, inflation, and unemployment in several countries have resulted in highly unstable governments and currencies, limiting trade and exposing U.S firms to many risks. Governments are placing more regulations on foreign firms; they are requiring joint ownership with domestic partners, the hiring of nationals, and limits on profits that can be taken from the country. And governments often impose unreasonably high tariffs or trade barriers in order to protect their own industries. Corruption is an increasing problem—officals in several countries often award business not to the best bidder, but to the highest briber.

You might conclude that companies are doomed whether they stay at home or go abroad. But we argue that companies selling "global products" have no choice but to internationalize their operations. And they must do so before the window closes on them, since firms from other countries are globalizing and achieving scale economies.

We might ask: Does international marketing involve any new marketing principles? In general the answer is no—the principles of setting marketing objectives, choosing target markets, developing marketing positions and mixes, and carrying out marketing control still apply. The principles are not new, but the differences among nations can be so great that the international marketer needs to understand foreign countries and how people in different countries respond to marketing efforts.

We will now look at the six decisions that a company faces in international marketing, as shown in Figure 21-1.

L OOKING AT THE INTERNATIONAL MARKETING ENVIRONMENT

A company has to learn many things before deciding whether to sell abroad. It must thoroughly understand the international marketing environment. That environment has changed very much in the last two decades, creating both new opportunities and new problems. World trade and investment have grown rapidly, with many attractive markets opening up in China, the USSR, Western Europe, and elsewhere. There has been a growth of global brands in autos, food, clothing, electronics, and many other categories. The number of **multinational companies**—companies that operate in many countries, and that have a major part of their operations outside their home country—has grown dramatically. Meanwhile, the United States's dominant position has declined. Other countries such as Japan and West Germany have increased their economic power in world markets (see Marketing Highlight 21–1). The interna-

MARKETING HIGHLIGHT 21–1

THE WORLD'S CHAMPION MARKETERS: THE JAPANESE?

Few dispute that the Japanese have performed an economic miracle since World War II. In a very short time, they have achieved global market leadership in many industries: autos, motorcycles, watches, cameras, optical instruments, steel, shipbuilding, computers, and consumer electronics. They are now making strong inroads into rubber tires, chemicals, machine tools, and even designer clothes and cosmetics. Some credit the global success of Japanese companies to their unique business and management practices. Others point to the help they get from Japan's government, powerful trading companies, and banks. Still others say Japan's success is based on low wage rates and unfair dumping policies.

But one of the main keys to Japan's success is its skillful use of marketing. The Japanese came to the United States to study marketing and went home understanding it better than many U.S. companies. They know how to select a market, enter it in the right way, build market share, and protect their share against competitors.

Selecting Markets. The Japanese work hard to identify attractive global markets. They look for industries that require high skills and high labor intensity but few natural resources. These include consumer electronics, cameras, watches, motorcycles, and pharmaceuticals. They like markets where consumers around the world would be willing to buy the same product designs. They look for industries where the market leaders are weak or complacent.

Entering Markets. Japanese study teams spend several months evaluating the target market, searching for market niches that are not being satisfied. Sometimes they start with a low-price, stripped-down version of a product, sometimes with a product that is as good as the competitions' but priced lower, sometimes with a product with higher quality or new features. The Japanese line up good distribution

in order to provide quick service to their customers. They use advertising to bring their products to the consumer's attention. Their entry strategy is to build market share rather than early profits. The Japanese often are willing to wait even a decade before realizing their profits.

Building Market Share. Once Japanese firms gain a market foothold, they begin to expand their market share. They pour money into product improvements and new models so that they can offer more and better things than the competition. They spot new opportunities through market segmentation, develop markets in new countries, and work to build a network of world markets and production locations.

Protecting Market Share. Once the Japanese achieve market leadership, they become defenders rather than attackers. Their defense strategy is to continue product development and refine market segmentation.

U.S. firms are now fighting back by adding new product lines, pricing more aggressively, streamlining production, buying or making components abroad, and forming strategic partnerships with other foreign companies. And many U.S. companies are operating successfully in Japan. American companies sell over 50,000 products in Japan, and many hold leading market shares—Coke leads in soft drinks (60 percent share), Schick in razors (71 percent), Polaroid in instant cameras (66 percent), and McDonald's in fast-food. Since the early 1980s, U.S. companies have increased their Japanese computer sales by 48 percent, pharmaceutical sales by 41 percent, and electronic parts sales by 63 percent.

Source: See Philip Kotler, Liam Fahey, and Somkid Jatusripitak, *The New Competition* (Englewood Cliffs, NJ: Prentice Hall, 1985); and Vernon R. Alden, "Who Says You Can't Crack Japanese Markets?" *Harvard Business Review*, January–February 1987, pp. 52–56.

tional financial system has become more complex and fragile, and U.S. companies face increasing trade barriers put up to protect domestic markets against foreign competition.

The International Trade System

The American company looking abroad must start by understanding the international trade system. When selling to another country, the American firm will face various trade restrictions. The most common is the **tariff,** which is a tax levied by a foreign government against certain imported products. The tariff may be designed to raise revenue or to protect domestic firms. The exporter may also face a **quota,** which sets limits on the amount of goods that the importing country will accept in certain product categories. The purpose of the quota is to conserve on foreign exchange and protect local industry and employment. An **embargo** is the strongest form of quota, under which some kinds of imports are totally banned.

American firms may face *exchange controls* which limit the amount of foreign exchange and the exchange rate against other currencies. The company may also face *nontariff barriers*, such as bias against American company bids or product standards that go against American product features.

> One of the cleverest ways the Japanese have found to keep foreign manufacturers out of their domestic market is to plead "uniqueness." Japanese skin is different, the government argues, so foreign cosmetics companies must test their products in Japan before selling there. The Japanese say their stomachs are small and have room for only the *mikan*, the local tangerine, so imports of U.S. oranges are limited. Now the Japanese have come up with what may be the flakiest argument yet: Their snow is different, so ski equipment should be too.[2]

At the same time, certain forces help trade between nations, or at least between some nations. Certain countries have formed **economic communities,** a group of nations organized to work toward common goals in the regulation of international trade. The most important economic community is the European Economic Community (EEC, also known as the Common Market). The EEC's members are the major Western European nations, with a combined population of over 300 million people, and they are working together to reduce tariffs, hold down prices, and expand employment and investment. EEC sets no tariffs on its members, but sets a uniform tariff for trade with nonmember nations. Since EEC's formation in 1958, other economic communities have been formed, such as the Latin American Integration Association (LAIA), the Central American Common Market (CACM), and the Council for Mutual Economic Assistance (CMEA) in Eastern Europe.

Each nation has unique features that must be understood. A nation's readiness for different products and services, and its attractiveness as a market to foreign firms, depend on its economic, political-legal, and cultural environments.

Economic Environment

In looking at foreign markets, the international marketer must study each country's economy. Two economic factors reflect the country's attractiveness as a market.

The first is the country's *industrial structure*. The country's industrial structure shapes its product and service needs, income levels, and employment levels. There are four types of industrial structures.

- *Subsistence economies*. In a subsistence economy the vast majority of people engage in simple agriculture. They consume most of their output and barter the rest for simple goods and services. They offer few market opportunities.

- *Raw-material-exporting economies*. These economies are rich in one or more natural resources but poor in other ways. Much of their revenue comes from exporting these resources. Examples are Chile (tin and copper), Zaire (rubber), and Saudi Arabia (oil).

These countries are good markets for large equipment, tools and supplies, and trucks. If there are many foreign residents and a wealthy upper class, they are also a market for luxury goods.

- *Industralizing economies.* In an industralizing economy, manufacturing accounts for between 10 and 20 percent of the country's economy. Examples include Egypt, India, and the Philippines. As manufacturing increases, the country needs more imports of textile raw materials, steel, and heavy machinery, and fewer imports of finished textiles, paper products, and automobiles. The industrialization creates a new rich class and a small but growing middle class, both demanding new types of imported goods.

- *Industrial economies.* Industrial economies are major exporters of manufactured goods and investment funds. They trade goods among themselves and also export them to other types of economies for raw materials and semifinished goods. The varied manufacturing activities of these industrial nations and their large middle class make them rich markets for all sorts of goods.

The second economic factor is the country's *income distribution*. The international marketer might find countries with five different income-distribution patterns: (1) very low family incomes, (2) mostly low family incomes, (3) very low, very high family incomes, (4) low, medium, high family incomes, and (5) mostly medium family incomes. Consider the market for Lamborghinis, an automobile costing $128,000. The market would be very small in countries with type 1 or type 2 income patterns. The largest single market for Lamborghinis turns out to be Portugal (income pattern 3), the poorest country in Europe, but one with enough wealthy, status-conscious families to afford them.

Political-Legal Environment

Nations differ greatly in their political-legal environments. At least four political-legal factors should be considered in deciding whether to do business in a given country.

Attitudes Toward International Buying

Some nations are very receptive to foreign firms, and others are very hostile. For example, Mexico for many years has been attracting foreign businesses by offering investment incentives and site-location services. On the other hand, India has bothered foreign businesses with import quotas, currency restrictions, and limits on the percentage of the management team that can be non-nationals. IBM and Coca-Cola left India because of all the "hassles." Pepsi, on the other hand, took positive steps to persuade the Indian government to allow it to do business in that country on reasonable terms (see Marketing Highlight 21–2).

Political Stability

Stability is another issue. Governments change hands, sometimes violently. Even without a change, a government may decide to respond to new popular feelings. The foreign company's property may be taken over; or its currency holdings may be blocked; or import quotas or new duties may be set. International marketers may still find it profitable to do business in an unstable country, but the situation will affect how they handle business and financial matters.

Monetary Regulations

Sellers want to take their profits in a currency of value to them. Ideally, the buyer can pay in the seller's currency or in other world currencies. Short of this, sellers might accept a blocked currency—one whose removal from the country is restricted by the buyer's government—if they can buy other goods in that country that they need or can sell elsewhere for a needed currency. Besides currency limits, a changing exchange rate also creates high risks for the seller.

BREAKING INTO AN UNRECEPTIVE MARKET

It is one thing to want to do business in a particular country, and another to be allowed into the country on reasonable terms. The problem of entering an unreceptive or blocked country calls for *megamarketing*, using economic, psychological, political, and public relations skills to gain the cooperation of several parties in order to enter and operate in a given market.

Pepsi-Cola used megamarketing in its attempt to enter the Indian market. After Coca-Cola was asked to leave India, Pepsi began to lay plans to enter this huge market. Pepsi worked with an Indian business group to seek government approval for its entry. Both domestic soft drink companies and anti-multinational legislators objected to letting Pepsi in, so Pepsi wanted to make an offer that the Indian government would find hard to refuse. It offered to help India export enough of its products to more than offset the outlay for importing soft drink syrup. Pepsi also promised to focus lots of selling effort on rural areas to help in their economic development. The company further offered to give food processing, packaging, and water treatment technology to India.

Clearly, Pepsi's strategy was to bundle a set of benefits that would win the support of all the various interest groups influencing the entry decision. Pepsi's marketing problem was not one of simply applying the 4Ps in a new market, but rather one of just getting into the market in the first place. In trying to win over the government and public groups, and to maintain a reasonable relationship once admitted, Pepsi had to add two more *Ps*—"politics" and "public opinion."

Many other large companies have learned that it pays to build good relations with host governments. Olivetti, for example, enters new markets by building housing for workers, supporting local arts and charities, and hiring and training local managers. IBM sponsors nutrition programs for Latin American children and gives agricultural advice to the Mexican government. Polaroid is helping Italy restore Leonardo da Vinci's *Last Supper*.

Sources: See Philip Kotler, "Megamarketing," *Harvard Business Review*, March–April 1986, pp. 117–24; Kenneth Labich, "America's International Winners," *Fortune*, April 14, 1986, p. 46; and Shelia Tefft, Cheryl Debes, and Dean Foust, "The Mouse That Roared at Pepsi," *Business Week*, September 7, 1987, p. 42.

Most international trade involves cash transactions. Yet many nations have too little hard currency to pay for their purchases from other countries. They want to pay with other items instead of cash. This need has led to a growing practice called **countertrade,** which now accounts for about 25 percent of all world trade. Countertrade takes several forms. *Barter* involves the direct exchange of goods or services, as when the West Germans built a steel plant in Indonesia in exchange for oil. Another form is *compensation* (or buyback), in which the seller sells a plant, equipment, or technology to another country and agrees to take payment in the resulting products. Thus Goodyear provided China with materials and training for a printing plant in exchange for finished labels. Another form is *counterpurchase*—the seller receives full payment in cash but agrees to spend some portion of the money in the other country within a stated time period. For example, PepsiCo sells its cola syrup to the USSR for rubles and agrees to buy Soviet vodka for sale in the United States.

Countertrade deals can be very complex. For example, Daimler-Benz recently agreed to sell 30 trucks to Romania in exchange for 150 Romanian jeeps, which it sold to Ecuador for bananas, which were in turn sold to a West German supermarket chain for German currency. Through this round-about process, Daimler-Benz finally obtained payment in German money.[3]

Government Bureaucracy

A fourth factor is the extent to which the host government runs an efficient system for helping foreign companies: efficient customs handling, good market information, and other factors that aid in doing business. A common shock to Americans is how quickly barriers to trade disappear if a suitable payment (bribe) is made to some official.

Cultural Environment

Each country has its own cultural environment—its own folkways, norms, and taboos. The way foreign consumers think about and use certain products must be checked by the seller before planning the marketing program. There are often surprises. For example, the average French man uses almost twice as many cosmetics and beauty aids as does his wife. The Germans and the French eat more packaged, branded spaghetti than the Italians. Italian children like to eat a chocolate bar between two slices of bread as a snack. And women in Tanzania will not give their children eggs for fear of making them bald or impotent.

Business norms and behavior also vary from country to country. U.S. business executives need to be briefed on these before dealing in another country. Here are some examples of different foreign business behavior:

- South Americans like to sit or stand very close to each other when they talk business—in fact, almost nose to nose. The American business executive keeps backing away as the South American moves closer. And both end up being offended.

- In face-to-face communications, Japanese business executives rarely say no to an American business executive. Americans are frustrated and do not know where they stand. Americans come to the point quickly. Japanese business executives find this offensive.

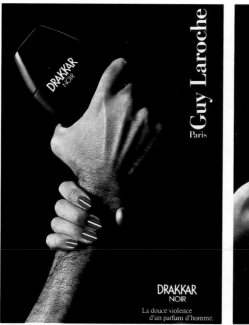

Adapting to the cultural environment: Compared with the European version of this ad (left), Guy Laroche tones down the sensuality in the Arab version (right). The man is clothed and the woman barely touches him.

- In France, wholesalers do not want to promote a product. They ask their retailers what they want, and they deliver it. If an American company builds its strategy around the French wholesaler's cooperating in promotions, it is likely to fail.

Each country and region has cultural traditions, preferences, and behaviors that the marketer must study.

DECIDING WHETHER TO GO ABROAD

Not all companies need to venture into foreign markets to survive. Many companies are local businesses that need only to market well in the local marketplace. Other companies, however, operate in global industries, where their strategic positions in major markets are strongly affected by their overall global positions. Thus IBM must organize globally if it is to gain purchasing, manufacturing, financial, and marketing advantages. Firms in a global industry must compete on a worldwide basis if they are to succeed.

Companies get involved in international marketing in one of two ways. Someone—a domestic exporter, a foreign importer, a foreign government—asks the company to sell abroad. Or the company starts to think on its own about going abroad. It might face overcapacity or see better marketing opportunities in other countries than at home.

Before going abroad, the company should try to define its international marketing objectives and policies. First, it should decide what volume of foreign sales it wants. Most companies start small when they go abroad. Some plan to stay small, seeing foreign sales as a small part of their business. Other companies have bigger plans, seeing foreign business as equal to or even more important than their domestic business.

Second, the company must choose between marketing in a few countries and marketing in many countries. The Bulova Watch Company made the latter choice and expanded into over one hundred countries. It spread itself too thin, made profits in only two countries, and lost around $40 million. Generally, it makes better sense to operate in fewer countries with deeper penetration in each.

Third, the company must decide on the types of countries to enter. Which countries are attractive will depend on the product, geographical factors, income and population, political climate, and other factors. The seller may prefer certain country groups or parts of the world.

DECIDING WHICH MARKETS TO ENTER

After listing possible international markets, the company will have to screen and rank them. Consider the following example:

> Many mass marketers dream of selling to China's one billion people. Some think of the market less elegantly as two billion armpits. To PepsiCo, though, the market is mouths, and the People's Republic is especially enticing: it is the most populous country in the world, and Coca-Cola does not yet dominate it.[4]

PepsiCo's decision to enter the huge Chinese market seems fairly simple and straightforward. China is a huge market without established competition. In addition to selling Pepsi soft drinks, the company hopes to build many of its Pizza Hut restaurants there. Yet we can question whether market size alone is reason enough for selecting China. PepsiCo must also consider other factors. Will the Chinese government be

Pepsi in China—a huge but risky market.

stable and supportive? Does China provide for the production and distribution technologies needed to produce and market Pepsi products profitably? Will Pepsi and pizza fit with Chinese tastes, means, and life styles?

Possible foreign markets should be ranked on several factors such as market size, market growth, cost of doing business, competitive advantage, and risk level. The goal is to figure out the market potential of each market, using indicators such as those shown in Table 21-1. Then the marketer must decide which markets will offer the greatest long-run return on investment.

TABLE 21-1
Indicators of Market Potential

1. Demographic characteristics	**4. Technological factors**
Size of population	Level of technological skill
Rate of population growth	Existing production technology
Degree of urbanization	Existing consumption technology
Population density	Education levels
Age structure and composition of the population	
	5. Socio-cultural factors
2. Geographic characteristics	Dominant values
Physical size of a country	Life style patterns
Topographical characteristics	Ethnic groups
Climate conditions	Linguistic fragmentation
3. Economic factors	**6. National goals and plans**
GNP per capita	Industry priorities
Income distribution	Infrastructure investment plans
Rate of growth of GNP	
Ratio of investment to GNP	

Source: Susan P. Douglas, C. Samual Craig, and Warren Keegan, "Approaches to Assessing International Marketing Opportunities for Small and Medium-Sized Business," *Columbia Journal of World Business,* Fall 1982, pp. 26–32.

DECIDING HOW TO ENTER THE MARKET

Once a company has decided to sell in a country, it must determine the best mode of entry. Its choices are *exporting*, *joint venturing*, and *direct investment* abroad. Each succeeding strategy involves more commitment, risk, control, and possible profits. The three market entry strategies are shown in Figure 21-2, along with the options under each.

Exporting   The simplest way to enter a foreign market is through **exporting.** The company may passively export its surpluses from time to time, or it may make an active commitment to expand exports to a particular market. In either case the company produces all its goods in the home country. It may or may not modify them for the export market. Exporting involves the least change in the company's product lines, organization, investments, or mission.

Companies typically start with *indirect exporting*, working through independent international marketing middlemen. Indirect exporting involves less investment—because the firm does not have to have an overseas salesforce or a set of contacts. It also involves less risk. International marketing middlemen—domestic-based export merchants or agents, cooperative organizations, export-management companies—bring know-how and services to the relationship, and the seller normally makes fewer mistakes.

Sellers eventually move into *direct exporting*, handling their own exports. The investment and risk are somewhat greater, but so is the potential return. The company can carry on direct exporting in several ways. First, it can set up a domestic export department which carries out export activities. Or it can set up an overseas sales branch which handles sales, distribution, and perhaps promotion. The sales branch gives the seller more presence and program control in the foreign market, and it often serves as a display center and customer service center. Or the company can send home-based salespeople abroad at certain times to find business. Finally, the company can do its exporting through foreign-based distributors who buy and own the goods or through foreign-based agents who sell the goods on behalf of the company.

Joint Venturing   A second method of entering a foreign market is through **joint venturing,** joining with foreign companies to produce or market a product or service. Joint venturing differs from exporting in that the company joins with a partner to sell or market abroad. It differs from direct investment in that an association is formed with someone in the foreign country. There are four types of joint venture.

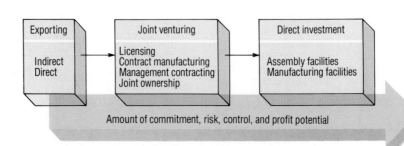

FIGURE 21-2
Market entry strategies

Licensing

Licensing is a simple way for a manufacturer to enter international marketing. The company enters into an agreement with a licensee in the foreign market, offering the right to use a manufacturing process, trademark, patent, trade secret, or other item of value for a fee or royalty. The company gains entry into the market at little risk; the licensee gains production expertise or a well-known product or name, without having to start from scratch. Coca-Cola markets internationally by licensing bottlers around the world and supplying them with syrup needed to produce the product. In Japan, Budweiser beer flows from Suntory breweries, Lady Borden ice cream is churned out at Meiji Milk Products dairies, and Marlboro cigarettes roll off production lines at Japan Tobacco Inc.[5]

Licensing has potential disadvantages. The firm has less control over the licensee than if it had set up its own production facilities. If the licensee is very successful, the firm has given up these profits, and if and when the contract ends, it may find it has created a competitor. To avoid these dangers, the company must create a mutual advantage for the licensee. A key to doing this is to remain innovative so that the licensee continues to depend on the company.

Contract Manufacturing

Another option **contract manufacturing** contracting with manufacturers in the foreign market to produce the product. Sears used this method in opening up department stores in Mexico and Spain. Sears found qualified local manufacturers to produce many of the products it sells. Contract manufacturing has the drawback of less control

Licensing: TOKYO DISNEYLAND is owned and operated by the Oriental Land Co., Ltd. (a Japanese development company) under license from Walt Disney Company.

over the manufacturing process and the loss of potential profits on manufacturing. On the other hand, it offers the company a chance to start faster, with less risk, and with the opportunity to form a partnership with or buy out the local manufacturer later.

Management Contracting

Under **management contracting,** the domestic firm supplies the management know-how to a foreign company that supplies the capital. The domestic firm exports management services rather than products. Hilton uses this arrangement in managing hotels around the world.

Management contracting is a low-risk method of getting into a foreign market, and it yields income from the beginning. The arrangement is very attractive if the contracting firm has an option to buy some share in the managed company later on. On the other hand, the arrangement is not sensible if the company can put its scarce management talent to better uses or if it can make greater profits by undertaking the whole venture. Management contracting prevents the company from setting up its own operations for a period of time.

Joint Ownership

Joint ownership ventures consist of the company joining with foreign investors to create a local business in which they share joint ownership and control. The company may buy an interest in a local firm, or the two parties may form a new business venture.

A jointly owned venture may be needed for economic or political reasons. The firm may lack the financial, physical, or managerial resources to undertake the venture alone. Or the foreign government may require joint ownership as a condition for entry.

Joint ownership has certain drawbacks. The partners may disagree over investment, marketing, or other policies. Whereas many American firms like to reinvest earnings for growth, local firms often like to take out these earnings. Whereas American firms give a large role to marketing, local investors may rely on selling.[6]

Direct Investment   The biggest involvement in a foreign market comes through **direct investment,** developing foreign-based assembly or manufacturing facilities. As a company gains experience in exporting, and if the foreign market is large enough, foreign production facilities offer many advantages. The firm may have lower costs in the form of cheaper labor or raw materials, foreign government investment incentives, and freight savings. The firm will gain a better image in the host country because it creates jobs. The firm develops a deeper relationship with government, customers, local suppliers, and distributors, letting it better adapt its products to the local market. And the firm keeps full control over the investment and can therefore develop manufacturing and marketing policies that serve its long-term international objectives.

The main disadvantage is that the firm faces many risks, such as restricted or devalued currencies, falling markets, or government takeover. In some cases, the firm has no choice but to accept these risks if it wants to operate in the host country.

DECIDING ON THE MARKETING PROGRAM

Companies that operate in one or more foreign markets must decide how much, if at all, to adapt their marketing mixes to local conditions. At one extreme are companies that use a **standardized marketing mix** worldwide. Standardization of the product, advertising, distribution channels, and other elements of the marketing mix promises the lowest costs because no major changes have been introduced. This thinking is behind the idea that Coca-Cola should taste the same around the world and that General Motors should produce a "world car" that suits the needs of most consumers in most countries.

At the other extreme is a **customized marketing mix.** The producer adjusts the marketing mix elements to each target market, bearing more costs but hoping for a larger market share and return. Nestle, for example, varies its product line and its advertising in different countries. Between the two extremes, many possibilities exist. Thus Levi Strauss can sell the same jeans worldwide but can vary the advertising theme in each country. The question of whether it is best to customize or standardize the marketing mix has been much debated in recent years (see Marketing Highlight 21–3).

We will now look at possible changes in a company's product, promotion, price, and distribution as it goes abroad.

Product   There are five strategies for adapting product and promotion to a foreign market (see Figure 21-3 on p. 567).[7] We will look at the three product strategies here, and later look at the two promotion strategies.

Straight extension means marketing the product in the foreign market without any change. Top management tells its marketing people: "Take the product as is and find customers for it." The first step, however, should be to find out whether the foreign consumers use that product and what form they prefer.

Straight extension has been successful in some cases but a disaster in others. Coca-Cola, Kellogg cereals, Heineken beer, McDonald's hamburgers—all are sold in about the same form around the world. But General Foods introduced its standard

Direct investment: General Motors owns production and marketing operations in many foreign countries.

MARKETING HIGHLIGHT 21–3

CUSTOMIZATION OR STANDARDIZATION?

Companies disagree on how much they should standardize their products and marketing programs across world markets. Most marketers believe that because consumers in different countries vary so much, marketing programs will be more effective if tailored to specific market needs. They point out that countries differ in economic, political, legal, and cultural respects. Consumers in different countries have varied geographic, demographic, economic, and cultural characteristics, resulting in different needs and wants, spending power, product preferences, and shopping patterns. Most marketers believe that these differences are hard to change, so they customize their products, prices, distribution channels, and promotion approaches to fit unique consumer desires in each country. They think that too much standardization places a company at a disadvantage against competitors who produce the goods that consumers want.

Recently, however, many companies have moved toward global standardization. They have created "world brands" which are manufactured and marketed in much the same way worldwide. These marketers believe that advances in communication, transportation, and travel are turning the world into a common marketplace. They claim that people around the world want the same products and lifestyles. Everyone wants things that make life easier and increase their free time and buying power. Common needs and wants create global markets for standardized products.

Instead of focusing on differences between markets and customizing products to meet these differences, marketers who standardize globally sell more or less the same product the same way to all consumers. They agree that there are differences in consumer wants and buying behavior and that these differences cannot be entirely ignored. But they think the wants are changeable. Despite what consumers *say* they want, all consumers want good products at lower prices.

> If the price is low enough, they will take highly standardized world products, even if these aren't exactly what mother said was suitable, what immemorial custom decreed was right, or what market research . . . asserted was preferred.

Thus the global corporation customizes products and marketing programs only when local wants cannot be changed or avoided. Standardization results in lower production, distribution, marketing, and management costs, letting the company offer consumers high quality and more reliable products at lower prices.

So which approach is best—customization or standardization? Clearly, global standardization is not an all-or-nothing proposition, but a matter of degree. Companies are justified in looking for more standardization to help keep costs and prices down. But they must remember that although standardization saves money, competitors are always ready to offer more of what consumers in each country want, and the company might pay dearly for replacing long-run marketing thinking with short-run financial thinking. One international marketer suggests that companies should "think globally but act locally to give the individual consumer more to say in what he or she wants." The corporate level gives strategic direction; local units focus on the individual consumer differences. Global marketing, yes; global standardization, no.

Source: See John A. Quelch and Edward J. Hoff, "Customizing Global Marketing," *Harvard Business Review*, May–June 1986, pp. 59–68; "Modular Marketing Cracks International Markets," *Marketing News*, April 27, 1984, p. 10; Julie Steur Hill and Joseph H. Winski, "Goodbye Global Ads," *Advertising Age*, November 16, 1987, p. 22; and Theodore Levitt, "The Globalization of Markets," *Harvard Business Review*, May–June 1983, pp. 92–102. Excerpt reprinted by permission of the *Harvard Business Review*. Copyright 1983 by the President and Fellows of Harvard College; all rights reserved.

powdered Jell-O in the British market only to find that British consumers prefer the solid-wafer or cake form. And Philips began to make a profit in Japan only after it reduced the size of its coffee makers to fit into smaller Japanese kitchens and its shavers to fit smaller Japanese hands. Straight extension is tempting because it involves no additional product development costs, manufacturing changes, or new promotion. But it can be costly in the long run.

FIGURE 21-3
Five international
product and promotion
strategies

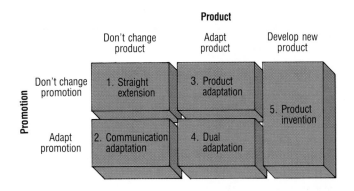

Product adaptation involves changing the product to meet local conditions or wants. Playtex uses the same overall marketing strategy and execution in different countries, but varies its product mix to satisfy local preferences. Heinz varies its baby-food products: In Australia it sells a baby food made from strained lamb brains; and in the Netherlands, a baby food made from strained brown beans. General Foods blends different coffees for the British (who drink their coffee with milk), the French (who drink their coffee black), and Latin Americans (who want a chicory taste).

Product invention consists of creating something new. This strategy can take two forms. It might mean reintroducing earlier product forms that happen to be well adapted to the needs of that country. The National Cash Register Company reintroduced its crank-operated cash register selling at half the price of a modern cash register and sold large numbers in the Orient, Latin America, and Spain. Or the company might create a new product to meet a need in another country. There is an enormous need in less-developed countries for low-cost, high-protein foods. Companies such as Quaker Oats, Swift, and Monsanto are researching the nutrition needs of these countries, creating new foods, and developing advertising campaigns to gain product trial and acceptance. Product invention can be costly, but the payoffs might make it worthwhile.

Promotion

Companies can adopt the same promotion strategy they used in the home market or change it for each local market.

Consider the message. Some multinational companies use a standardized advertising theme around the world. Exxon used "Put a tiger in your tank" and gained international recognition. The copy may be varied in a minor way to adjust for language differences. In Japan, where consumers have trouble pronouncing "snap, crackle, pop," the little Rice Krispies critters say "patchy, pitchy, putchy." Colors are sometimes changed to avoid taboos in other countries. Purple is associated with death in most of Latin America; white is a mourning color in Japan; and green is associated with jungle sickness in Malaysia. Even names have to be changed. In Sweden, Helene Curtis renamed Every Night Shampoo to Every Day because Swedes wash their hair in the morning. Kellogg had to rename Bran Buds cereal in Sweden, where the name roughly translates as "burned farmer."[8] (See Marketing Highlight 21–4 for more on language blunders in international marketing.)

Other companies ask their international divisions to fully adapt advertising messages to local markets. The Schwinn Bicycle Company might use a pleasure theme in the United States and a safety theme in Scandinavia. Kellogg ads in the United States promote the taste and nutrition of Kellogg's cereals versus competitors' brands.

Standardized advertising messages: Playtex uses about the same promotion approach in several different countries. Britain, West Germany, and Spain are shown here.

In France, where consumers drink little milk and eat little for breakfast, Kellogg's ads try to convince consumers that cereals are a tasty and healthful breakfast.

Media also need to be adapted internationally because media availability varies from country to country. TV advertising time is very limited in Europe, ranging from four hours a day in France to none in Scandinavian countries. Advertisers must buy time months in advance, and they have little control over when their ads will be shown. Magazines also vary in effectiveness; for example, they are a major medium in Italy and a minor one in Austria. Newspapers are national in the United Kingdom but only local in Spain.

Price Multinationals face many problems in setting their international prices. For example, how might Coca-Cola set its prices globally? It could set a uniform price everywhere, say 40 cents all around the world. But this amount would be too high a price in poor countries and not high enough in rich countries. Coca-Cola could charge what consumers in each country would bear. But this strategy ignores differences in the actual cost from country to country. The company could use a standard mark-up of their costs everywhere. But this approach might price Coca-Cola out of the market in some countries where its costs are high.

Regardless of how companies go about pricing their products, their foreign prices will probably be higher than their domestic prices. A Gucci handbag may

WATCH YOUR LANGUAGE!

Many U.S. multinationals have had difficulty crossing the language barrier, with results ranging from mild embarrassment to outright failure. Seemingly innocuous brand names and advertising phrases can take on unintended or hidden meanings when translated into other languages. And careless translations can make a marketer look downright foolish to foreign consumers. We've all run across examples when buying products from foreign countries—here's one from a firm in Taiwan attempting to instruct children on how to install a ramp on a garage for toy cars.

> Before you play with, please fix the waiting plate by yourself as per below diagram. But after you once fixed it, you can play with as is and no necessary to fix off again.

Many U.S. firms are guilty of similar atrocities when marketing abroad.

The classic language blunders involve standardized brand names that do not translate well. When Coca-Cola first marketed Coke in China in the 1920s, it developed a group of Chinese characters that, when pronounced, sounded like the product name. Unfortunately, the characters actually translated to mean "bite the wax tadpole." Today the characters on Chinese Coke bottles translate to "happiness in the mouth."

Several car makers have had similar problems when their brand names crashed into the language barrier. Chevy's Nova translated into Spanish as *no va*—"It doesn't go." GM changed the name to Caribe and sales increased. Ford introduced its Fiera truck only to discover that the name means "ugly old woman" in Spanish. And it introduced its Comet car in Mexico as the Caliente—slang for "streetwalker." Rolls-Royce avoided the name Silver Mist in German markets, where "mist" means "manure." Sunbeam, however, entered the German market with its Mist-Stick hair curling iron. As should have been expected, the Germans had little use for a "manure wand."

One well-intentioned firm sold its shampoo in Brazil under the name Evitol. It soon realized it was claiming to sell a "dandruff contraceptive." An American company reportedly had trouble marketing Pet milk in French-speaking areas. It seems that the word "pet" in French means, among other things, "to break wind."

Such classic boo-boos are soon discovered and corrected, and they may result in little more than embarrassment for the marketer. But countless other more subtle blunders may go undetected and damage product performance in less obvious ways. The multinational company must carefully screen its brand names and advertising messages to guard against those that might damage sales, make it look silly, or offend consumers in specific international markets.

Some of these and many other examples of language blunders are found in David A. Ricks. "Products That Crashed into the Language Barrier," *Business and Society Review*, Spring 1983, pp. 46–50.

---

sell for $60 in Italy and $240 in the United States. Why? Gucci has to add the cost of transportation, tariffs, importer margin, wholesaler margin, and retailer margin to its factory price. Depending on these added costs, as well as currency fluctuation risks, the product may have to sell for two to five times as much in another country to make the same profit.

Another problem involves the company setting a *transfer price* for goods that it ships to its foreign subsidiaries. Consider the following example:

> The Swiss pharmaceutical company Hoffman-Laroche charged its Italian subsidiary only $22 a kilo for librium in order to make high profits in Italy where the corporate taxes were lower. It charged its British subsidiary $925 per kilo for the same librium in order to keep the profits at home instead of in Britain where the corporate taxes were high. The British government sued Hoffman-LaRoche for back taxes and won.

If the company charges too high a price to a foreign subsidiary, it ends up paying higher tariff duties although it may pay lower income taxes in that country. If the company charges too low a price to its subsidiary, it can be charged with *dumping*. Dumping occurs when a company either charges less than its costs or less than it charges in its home market. Thus Harley-Davidson accused Honda and Kawasaki of dumping motorcycles on the United States market. The U.S. International Trade Commission agreed and responded with a special five-year tariff on Japanese heavy motorcycles, starting at 45 percent in 1983 and gradually dropping to 10 percent by 1988.[9] The Commission also recently ruled that Japan was dumping computer memory chips in the United States and laid stiff duties on future imports. Various governments are watching for dumping abuses and often force companies to set the price charged by other competitors for the same or similar products.

Last but not least, many multinationals face a *gray market* problem. For example; Minolta sold its cameras to Hong Kong distributors for less than it charged German distributors because of lower transportation costs and tariffs. Minolta cameras ended up selling at retail for $174 in Hong Kong and $270 in Germany. Some Hong Kong wholesalers noticed this price difference and shipped Minolta cameras to German dealers for less than the dealers were paying their German distributor. The German distributor could not sell its stock and complained to Minolta. Thus a company often finds some enterprising distributors buying more than they can sell in their own country, then shipping goods to another country to take advantage of price differences. Multinationals try to prevent gray markets by raising their prices to lower cost distributors, dropping those who cheat, or altering the product for different countries.

Distribution Channels

The international company must take a *whole-channel* view of the problem of distributing products to final consumers. Figure 21-4 shows the three major links between the seller and the final buyer. The first link, the seller's headquarters organization, supervises the channels and is part of the channel itself. The second link, channels between nations, gets the products to the borders of the foreign nations. The third link, channels within nations, gets the products from their foreign entry point to the final consumers. Too many American manufacturers think their job is done once the product leaves their hands. They should pay more attention to how it is handled within the foreign country.

Within-country channels of distribution vary a lot from country to country. There are large differences in the numbers and types of middlemen serving each foreign market. To get soap into Japan, Procter & Gamble has to work through what may be the most complex distribution system in the world. It must sell to a general wholesaler who sells to a basic product specialty wholesaler who sells to a specialty wholesaler who sells to a regional wholesaler who sells to a local wholesaler who finally sells to retailers. Use of all these levels may double or triple the consumer's price over the importer's price. Selling the same soap in tropical Africa, P&G sells

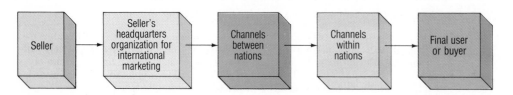

FIGURE 21-4 Whole-channel concept for international marketing

to an import wholesaler, who sells to several jobbers, who in turn sell to "petty traders" (mostly women) who sell the soap door to door.

Another difference lies in the size and character of retail units abroad. Whereas large-scale retail chains dominate the U.S. scene, most foreign retailing is done by many small independent retailers. In India, millions of retailers operate tiny shops or sell in open markets. Their markups are high, but the real price is brought down through price haggling. Supermarkets could offer lower prices, but they are difficult to start because of many economic and cultural barriers. People's incomes are low, and they prefer to shop daily for small amounts rather than weekly for large amounts. They lack storage and refrigeration to keep food for several days. Packaging is not well developed because it would add too much to the cost. These factors have kept large-scale retailing from spreading rapidly in developing countries.

DECIDING ON THE MARKETING ORGANIZATION

Companies manage their international marketing activities in at least three different ways. Most companies first organize an export department, then create an international division, and finally become a multinational organization.

Export Department

A firm normally gets into international marketing by simply shipping out the goods. If its international sales expand, the company organizes an export department with a sales manager and a few assistants. As sales increase, the export department expands to include various marketing services so that it can actively go after business. If the firm moves into joint ventures or direct investment, the export department will no longer be adequate.

International Division

Many companies get involved in several international markets and ventures. A company may export to one country, license to another, have a joint ownership venture in a third, and own a subsidiary in a fourth. Sooner or later it will create an international division or subsidiary to handle all its international activity.

International divisions are organized in a variety of ways. The international division's corporate staff consists of specialists in marketing, manufacturing, research, finance, planning, and personnel. They plan for and provide services to various operating units. The operating units may be organized in one of three ways. They may be *geographical organizations*, with country managers who are responsible for salespeople, sales branches, distributors, and licensees in their respective countries. Or the operating units may be *world product groups*, each responsible for worldwide sales of different product groups. Finally, the operating units may be *international subsidiaries*, each acting as a profit center.

Global Organization

Several firms have passed beyond the international division stage and become truly global organizations. They stop thinking of themselves as national marketers who sell abroad and start thinking of themselves as global marketers. The top corporate management and staff plan worldwide manufacturing facilities, marketing policies, financial flows, and logistical systems. The global operating units report directly to the chief executive or executive committee, not to the head of an international division. Executives are trained in worldwide operations, not just domestic *or* international. The company recruits from many countries; buys components and supplies where they cost the least; and invests where the expected returns are greatest.

Major companies must go more global in the 1990s if they hope to compete. As foreign companies successfully invade the domestic market, U.S. companies must move more aggressively into foreign markets. They will have to change from companies that treat their foreign operations as secondary to companies viewing the entire world as a single market.

■ SUMMARY

Companies today can no longer afford to pay attention only to their domestic market, no matter how large it is. Many industries are global industries, and those firms that operate globally achieve lower costs and higher brand awareness. Protectionist measures can only slow down the invasion of superior goods; the best company defense is a sound global offense.

At the same time, global marketing is risky because of changing exchange rates, unstable governments, protectionist tariffs and trade barriers, and several other factors. Given the potential gains and risks of international marketing, companies need a systematic way to make their international marketing decisions.

As a first step, the company must understand the international marketing environment, especially the international trade system. It must assess each foreign market's economic, political-legal, and cultural characteristics. Second, the company must consider what level of foreign sales it will seek, whether it will do business in a few or many countries, and what types of countries it wants to market in. Third, the company must decide which specific markets to enter. This decision calls for weighing the probable rate of return on investment against the level of risk. Fourth, the company has to decide how to enter each chosen market, whether through exporting, joint venturing, or direct investment. Many companies start as exporters, move to joint venturing, and finally make a direct investment. Companies must next decide how much their products, promotion, price, and channels should be adapted for each foreign market. Finally, the company must develop an effective organization for international marketing. Most firms start with an export department and graduate to an international division. A few pass to a global organization, which means that worldwide marketing is planned and managed by the top officers of the company.

■ QUESTIONS FOR DISCUSSION

1. With all the problems facing companies that "go global," why are so many companies choosing to expand internationally? What are the advantages of expanding beyond the domestic market?

2. When exporting goods to a foreign country, a marketer may be faced with various trade restrictions. Discuss the effects the following restrictions might have on an exporter's marketing mix: (a) tariffs, (b) quotas, and (c) embargoes.

3. Which of these will have the greatest impact on a soft-drink manufacturer's appraisal of a foreign nation's attractiveness as a market: the economic environment, the political-legal environment, or the cultural environment? Would your answer be the same for a manufacturer of pharmaceuticals? Why or why not?

4. What steps are involved in deciding which foreign markets to enter? Apply these steps to PepsiCo's decision to open Pizza Hut restaurants in Korea, and say whether you agree or disagree with the decision.

5. Discuss the steps an advertising agency could take in entering a foreign market. What types of joint ventures are possible? Compare the advantages and disadvantages

of a joint venture versus direct investment as ways of getting involved in a foreign country's advertising.

6. What product and promotion strategies might the Campbell Soup Company use in marketing canned soups in Brazil? Which combination of strategies would you recommend? Why?

7. The price of a product is often higher in foreign markets than in the domestic market, but there are many occasions when foreign prices are lower than domestic prices. Explain why foreign prices are sometimes higher and sometimes lower than domestic prices for the same product.

8. "Dumping" leads to price savings to the consumer. Why do governments make dumping illegal? What are the *disadvantages* to the consumer of dumping by foreign firms?

9. Which types of international marketing organization would you suggest for the following companies? (a) Huffy Bicycles, selling three models in the Far East; (b) a small manufacturer of toys, marketing its products in Europe; and (c) Dodge, planning to sell its full line of cars and trucks in Kuwait.

■ KEY TERMS

Contract manufacturing Joint-venturing to enter a foreign market by contracting with manufacturers in the foreign market to produce the product.

Countertrade International trade involving the direct or indirect exchange of goods for other goods instead of cash. Forms include barter, compensation (buy-back), and counterpurchase.

Customized marketing mix An international marketing strategy of adjusting the marketing mix elements to each international target market, bearing more costs but hoping for a larger market share and return.

Direct investment Entering a foreign market by developing foreign-based assembly or manufacturing facilities.

Economic community A group of nations organized to work toward common goals in the regulation of international trade; an example is the European Economic Community (EEC or Common Market).

Embargo A ban on the import of a certain product.

Exporting Entering a foreign market by exporting products and selling them through international marketing middlemen (indirect exporting) or through the company's own department, branch, or salespeople or agents (direct exporting).

Joint ownership Entering a foreign market by joining with foreign investors to create a local business in which the company shares joint ownership and control.

Joint venturing Entering foreign markets by joining with companies in the foreign country to produce or market a product or service.

Licensing A joint-venture method of entering a foreign market in which the company enters into an agreement with a licensee in the foreign market, offering the right to use a manufacturing process, trademark, patent, trade secret, or other item of value for a fee or royalty.

Management contracting A joint venture in which the domestic firm supplies the management know-how to a foreign company that supplies the capital; the domestic firm exports management services rather than products.

Multinational company A company that operates in many countries and that has a major part of its operations outside its home country.

Quota A limit on the amount of goods that an importing country will accept in certain product categories, designed to conserve on foreign exchange and protect local industry and employment.

Standardized marketing mix An international marketing strategy of using about the same product, advertising, distribution channels, and other elements of the marketing mix in all the company's international markets.

Tariff A tax levied by a government against certain imported products designed to raise revenue or protect domestic firms.

■ REFERENCES

1. See James B. Treec, Barbara Buell, and Jane Sasseen, "How Kodak is Trying to Move Mount Fuji," *Business Week*, December 2, 1985, pp. 62–64; Subrata N. Chakravarty and Ruth Simon, "Has the World Passed Kodak By?" *Forbes*, November 5, 1984, pp. 184–92; and Leslie Helm, "Has Kodak Set Itself Up for a Fall?" *Business Week*, February 22, 1988, pp. 134–38.

2. "The Unique Japanese," *Fortune*, November 24, 1986, p. 8.

3. For further reading, see John W. Dizard, "The Explosion of International Barter," *Fortune*, February 7, 1983; Leo G. B. Welt, *Trade Without Money: Barter and Countertrade* (New York: Harcourt Brace Jovanovich, 1984); and Demos Vardiabasis, "Countertrade: New Ways of Doing Business," *Business to Business*, December 1985, pp. 67–71.

4. Louis Kraar, "Pepsi's Pitch to Quench Chinese Thirsts," *Fortune*, March 17, 1986, p. 58. Also see Maria Shao,

"Laying the Foundation for the Great Mall of China," *Business Week*, January 25, 1988, pp. 68–69.

5. Larry Armstrong, "A Cheaper Dollar Doesn't Always Mean Cheaper American Goods," *Business Week*, May 5, 1986, p. 43.

6. For more on joint ventures, see "Are Foreign Partners Good for U.S. Companies?" *Business Week*, May 28, 1984, pp. 58–60; and Howard V. Perlmutter and David Heenan, "Cooperate to Compete Globally, *Harvard Business Review*, March–April, 1986, pp. 136–52.

7. See Warren J. Keegan, *Multinational Marketing Management*, 3rd Ed. (Englewood Cliffs, NJ: Prentice Hall, 1984), pp. 317–24.

8. See Kenneth Labich, "America's International Winners," *Fortune*, April 14, 1986, p. 44.

9. See Michael Oneal, "Harley-Davidson: Ready to Hit the Road Again," *Business Week*, July 21, 1986, p. 70.

22 Services Marketing and Nonprofit Marketing

TRADITIONALLY, hospitals had the problem of too many patients. But over the past decade, they began to face falling admissions and low occupancy. In the scramble to pull in new patients, many hospitals turned to marketing. The more they looked at the problem, the more complex the marketing challenges appeared. Most hospitals realized that they couldn't be all things to all people. Some began to focus on offering certain specialties—heart, pediatrics, burn treatment, psychiatry. Others focused on serving the special needs of certain demographic segments.

Century City Hospital in Los Angeles provides a good example of modern hospital marketing. It recently unveiled its "Century Pavilion," the hospital equivalent of a suite at the Ritz. The Pavilion consists of six luxury suites in which the area's affluent can get some of the finer things along with their health care. Since it opened, a steady stream of celebrities and other wealthy patients have lined up to pay the $1,000 per night required to stay in one of the classy Pavilion suites. From the moment they are whisked to their rooms by private elevator, Pavilion guests are pampered.

Century City did not stumble across the Pavilion idea by chance. The service is the result of a solid marketing program, headed by the hospital's marketing director. A research study of the hospital's primary market area showed that almost 50 percent of area residents were top income, highly educated professionals. Thirty-seven percent of the area population lives in homes worth over $200,000; over 7 percent have household incomes above $75,000. And there are over 40,000 millionaires in the Los Angeles–Long Beach area. Century City set out to capture this segment of well-heeled residents who had come to expect the best in food, accommodations, and service.

While cost efficiency is the battle cry in most health-care corners, the upscale patients wanted and could afford extras. Century City's research showed that this segment wanted privacy and exclusivity. So the hospital employed a noted interior-design firm to create suites with understated luxury, an elegant but quiet atmosphere. In these plush rooms, gourmet food is served on imported china and specially selected silver flatware. And since four of Pavilion's units come with a guest suite (for family, friends, and bodyguards), the units allow gracious hospitality. The hospital has even catered parties in the suites. And the units come with many other extras, such as secretarial services to help patients to keep up with their business tasks.

Century City decided against flashy institutional ads to promote the Pavilion. Instead, direct mail pieces were sent to about ten thousand households in Brentwood, Bel Aire, Beverly Hills, and wealthy areas of west Los Angeles. Direct mail was also used to reach eight hundred staff physicians, each of whom received a rose one day, a fancy notepad another, and a chocolate truffle in a third mailing, alerting them that the service was available for their prominent patients.

Century City uses a low-key approach to marketing. Other hospitals have used flashier, mass-selling tactics to drum up business. Sunrise Hospital in Las Vegas ran a large ad showing a ship with the caption: "Introducing the Sunrise Cruise. Win a Once-in-a-

Lifetime Cruise Simply by Entering Sunrise Hospital Any Friday or Saturday: Recuperative Cruise for Two." St. Lukes Hospital in Phoenix introduced nightly bingo games for all patients (except cardiac cases), producing immense patient interest and an annual profit of $60,000. A Philadelphia hospital served candlelight dinners with steak and champagne to parents of newborn children. Republic Health Corporation hospitals offer eleven branded "products, including Gift of Sight (cataract surgery), Miracle Moments (childbirth), and You're Becoming (cosmetic surgery).

Whatever the approach, most major hospitals now use some form of marketing. Many have become very good at it. According to Century City's director: "The Century Pavilion represents one element of what is happening in hospital marketing. Hospitals are becoming very sophisticated in defining who their patients are, what their needs are, and they're creating the kinds of services—whether it be luxury suites or same-day surgery—to meet those needs. In short, hospitals are definitely consumer oriented—a very large factor in health care today."[1]

Chapter Objectives   *After reading this chapter, you should be able to:*

1. Define service and identify four characteristics that affect the marketing of a service.
2. Describe the major marketing strategies for services.
3. Explain how organizations market themselves.
4. Discuss how persons and places are marketed.
5. Define social marketing and tell how social ideas are marketed.

MARKETING developed initially for spelling physical products such as toothpaste, cars, steel, and equipment. But this traditional focus on physical products may cause people to overlook the many other types of things that are marketed. In this chapter we will look at the special marketing requirements for services, organizations, persons, places, and ideas.

SERVICES MARKETING

One of the major trends in America has been the dramatic growth of services. Service jobs now account for 77 percent of total employment and 70 percent of GNP, and services will provide 90 percent of all new jobs in the next ten years.[2] Service jobs include not only people working in service industries—hotels, airlines, banks, and

The convenience industry: services that save you time—for a price.

others—but also people providing services in product-based industries, such as corporate lawyers, medical staff, and trainers. As a result of rising affluence, more leisure, and the growing complexity of products that require servicing, the United States has become the world's first service economy.

Service industries vary greatly. The government sector offers services through courts, employment services, hospitals, loan agencies, military services, police and fire departments, postal service, regulatory agencies, and schools. The private nonprofit sector offers services through museums, charities, churches, colleges, foundations, and hospitals. A good part of the business sector offers services through airlines, banks, hotels, insurance companies, consulting firms, medical and law practices, entertainment companies, real estate firms, advertising and research agencies, and retailers. Many workers in the manufacturing sector are really service providers, such as lawyers, computer operators, and accountants. Not only are there traditional service industries, but new types keep popping up all the time.

Want someone to fetch a meal from a local restaurant? In Austin, Texas, you can call EatOutIn. Plants need to be watered? In New York, you can call the Busy Body's Helper. Too busy to wrap and mail your packages? Stop by any one of the 72 outlets of Tender Sender, headquartered in Portland, Oregon. "We'll find it, we'll do it, we'll wait for it," chirps Lois Barnett, the founder of Personalized Services in Chicago. She and her crew of six will walk the dog, shuttle the kids to Little League, or wait in line for your theater tickets. Meet the convenience peddlers. They want to save you time. For a price, they'll do just about anything that's legal.[3]

Some service businesses are very large, with sales and assets in the trillions of dollars. Table 22-1 shows the five largest service companies in each of eight service categories. But there are also tens of thousands of smaller service providers. Selling services presents some special problems calling for special marketing solutions.[4] We will now look at the nature of services and their great variety; how the major characteristics of services affect their marketing; and how service firms can increase their differentiation, quality, and productivity.

Nature and Classification of Services

We define a service as follows:

A **service** is any activity or benefit that one party can offer to another that is essentially intangible and does not result in the ownership of anything. Its production may or may not be tied to a physical product.

TABLE 22-1
The Largest U.S.
Service Companies

COMMERCIAL BANKING	DIVERSIFIED FINANCIAL
Citicorp	American Express
Chase Manhattan	Federal National
Bank America	Mortgage Association
Chemical New York	Solomon
J. P. Morgan	Aetna Life & Casualty
	Merrill Lynch
LIFE INSURANCE	**RETAILING**
Prudential	Sears
Metropolitian	K mart
Equitable	Safeway
Aetna	Kroger
Teacher's Insurance	Wal-Mart
and Annuity	
TRANSPORTATION	**UTILITIES**
Allegis	GTE
United Parcel Service	BellSouth
Texas Air	NYNEX
CSX	Pacific Gas
AMR	and Electric
	Southwestern Bell
DIVERSIFIED SERVICES	**SAVINGS INSTITUTIONS**
Super Valu Stores	Financial Corporation
Fleming Companies	of American
McKesson	H. F. Ahmanson
Hospital Corporation	Great Western Financial
of America	Calfed
Ryder System	Meritor Financial Group

Source: "The Service 500," *Fortune*, June 6, 1988, pp. D3-D38.

Renting a hotel room, depositing money in a bank, traveling on an airplane, visiting a psychiatrist, getting a haircut, having a car repaired, watching a professional sport, seeing a movie, having clothes cleaned at a dry cleaner, getting advice from a lawyer— all involve buying a service.

Services can be classified in a number of ways. First, the service can be *people-based* or *equipment-based*. Equipment-based services vary depending on whether they are automated or monitored by unskilled or skilled operators. People-based services also vary by whether they are provided by unskilled, skilled, or professional workers. Figure 22-1 shows several industries that cluster in each group.

Some but not all services require the *client's presence*. A dental checkup involves the client's presence, but a car repair does not. If the client must be present, the service provider has to be considerate of his or her needs. Thus hair stylists will decorate their shops, play background music, and talk with customers, to make the service environment pleasant.

Services differ as to whether they meet a *personal* need (personal services) or a *business* need (business services). Doctors on a retainer with a company may charge the company employees less for a physical examination than they would charge their private patients. Service providers typically develop different marketing programs for personal and business markets.

Finally, what about the *service provider's objectives* (profit or nonprofit) and *ownership* (private or public)? These characteristics may be combined to produce quite different types of service organizations. For example, the marketing programs of a private investor hospital will differ sharply from those of a private charity hospital or a Veterans Administration hospital.[5]

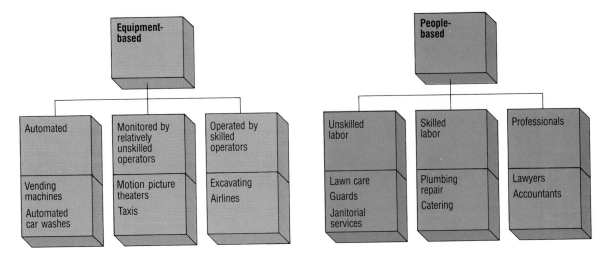

FIGURE 22-1   Types of service business

Source: Adapted by permission of the *Harvard Business Review.* An exhibit from "Strategy is Different in Service Business," by Dan R. E. Thomas (July–August 1978). Copyright © 1978 by the President and Fellows of Harvard College; all rights reserved.

Characteristics of Services and Their Marketing Implications

Whether public or private, profit or nonprofit, services have four major characteristics that greatly affect the design of marketing programs.

Intangibility

Services are **intangible**—they cannot be seen, tasted, felt, heard, or smelled before they are bought. People having cosmetic surgery cannot see the result before the purchase, and airline passengers have nothing but a ticket and the promise of safe delivery to their destinations.

To reduce uncertainty, buyers will look for signs of service quality. They will draw conclusions about quality from the place, people, equipment, communication material, and price that they see. Therefore the service provider's task is to make the service more tangible. Whereas product marketers try to add intangibles to their tangible offers, service marketers try to add tangibles to their intangible offers.[6]

Consider a bank that wants to convey the idea that its service is quick and efficient. It must "tangiblize" this positioning strategy in every aspect of customer contact. The bank's physical setting must suggest quick and efficient service: Its exterior and interior should have clean lines, internal traffic flow should be planned carefully, waiting lines should seem short, and background music should be light and upbeat. The bank's people should be busy and dressed appropriately. Its equipment—computers, copy machines, desks—should look modern. The bank's ads, brochures, and other communications should suggest efficiency, with clean and uncluttered designs and carefully chosen words and photos that communicate the bank's positioning. The bank should choose a name and symbol for its service that suggest speed and efficiency. Its pricing for various services should be kept simple and clear.

Inseparability

Physical goods are produced, then stored, later sold, and still later consumed. But services are first sold, then produced and consumed at the same time. Services are **inseparable** from their providers, whether the providers are persons or machines. If a person provides the service, then the person is a part of the service. Since the client is also present as the service is produced, provider-client interaction is a special feature of services marketing. Both the provider and the client affect the service outcome.

In the case of entertainment and professional services, buyers care a great deal about who provides the service. It is not the same service at a Kenny Rogers concert if Rogers gets sick and is replaced by Billy Joel. And a legal defense supplied by John Nobody differs from one supplied by F. Lee Bailey. When clients have strong provider preferences, price is used to ration the limited supply of the preferred provider's time.

Several strategies exist for getting around this limitation. The service provider can learn to work with larger groups. Some psychotherapists have moved from one-on-one therapy to small-group therapy to groups of over three hundred people in a large hotel ballroom. The service provider can learn to work faster—the psychotherapist can spend thirty minutes with each patient instead of fifty minutes and see more patients. The service organization can train more service providers and build up client confidence, as H&R Block has done with its national network of trained tax consultants.

Variability

Services are highly **variable**—their quality depends on who provides them and when and where they are provided. A tennis lesson from Jimmy Connors is likely to be of higher quality than one given by a local tennis pro. And Connors' lessons will vary with his energy and frame of mind at the time of each lesson. Service buyers are often aware of this high variability and talk to others before choosing a provider.

Service firms can take several steps toward quality control.[7] They can carefully select and train their personnel. Airlines, banks, and hotels spend large sums to train their employees to give good service. Consumers should find the same friendly and helpful personnel in every Marriott Hotel, for example. Service firms can provide employee incentives that emphasize quality, such as employee-of-the-month awards or bonuses based on customer feedback. They can make service employees more visible and accountable to consumers—auto dealerships can let customers talk directly with the mechanics working on their cars. The firm can regularly check customer satisfaction through suggestion and complaint systems, customer surveys, and comparison shopping. When poor service is found, it can be corrected. How the firm handles problems can dramatically affect customer perceptions of service quality. Here's a good example:

> A while back, we had a Federal Express package that, believe it or not, absolutely, positively didn't get there overnight. One phone call to Federal Express solved the problem. But that's not all. Pretty soon our phone rang, and one of Federal Express' senior executives was on the line. He wanted to know what happened and was very apologetic. Now that's service. With that one phone call, he assured himself of a customer for life.[8]

Perishability

Services are **perishable**—they cannot be stored. The reason many doctors charge patients for missed appointments is that the service value existed only at that point when the patient did not show up. The perishability of services is not a problem when demand is steady, because it is easy to staff the services in advance. When demand fluctuates, service firms have difficult problems. For example, public transportation companies have to own much more equipment because of rush hour demand than they would if demand were even throughout the day.

Service firms can use several strategies for producing a better match between demand and supply in a service business.[9] On the demand side, charging different prices at different times will shift some demand from peak to off-peak periods. Examples include low-early-evening movie prices and weekend discount prices for car rentals. Or nonpeak demand can be increased, as when McDonalds's offered its Egg McMuffin breakfast and hotels developed their mini-vacation weekends. Complementary services can be offered during peak time to provide alternatives to waiting customers, such as cocktail lounges to sit in while waiting for a table and automatic tellers in banks. Reservation systems can help to manage the demand level—airlines, hotels, and physicians use them a lot.

On the supply side, part-time employees can be hired to serve peak demand. Colleges add part-time teachers when enrollment goes up, and restaurants call in part-time waiters and waitresses when needed. Or peak-time demand can be handled more efficiently, having employees do only essential tasks during peak periods. Some tasks can be shifted to consumers, as when consumers fill out their own medical records or bag their own groceries. Or providers can share services, as when several hospitals share an expensive piece of medical equipment. Finally, the firm can plan ahead for expansion, as when an amusement park buys surrounding land for later development.

Marketing Strategies for Service Firms

Service firms typically lag behind manufacturing firms in their use of marketing.[10] Many service businesses are small (shoe repair, barbershops) and think marketing costs too much or is unneeded. There are also service businesses (legal, medical, and accounting practices) that still believe that it is unprofessional to use marketing. Other services businesses (colleges, hospitals) once had so much demand that they did not need marketing until recently.

Furthermore, service businesses are more difficult to manage using only a traditional marketing approach. In a product business, products are fairly standardized and sit on a shelf waiting for customers to reach for them. In a service business, the customer interacts with a service provider whose service quality is less certain and more variable. The service outcome is affected not just by the service provider, but by the whole "backroom" production process. Thus service marketing requires more than just traditional 4Ps marketing. In addition, it requires internal marketing and interactive marketing.[11]

Internal marketing means that the service firm must effectively train and motivate its customer contact employees and all the supporting service people to work as a team to provide customer satisfaction. For the firm to deliver consistently high service quality, everyone must practice a customer orientation. It is not enough to have a marketing department doing traditional marketing while the rest of the company goes its own way. Marketers must also get everyone else in the organization to practice marketing.[12]

Interactive marketing means that perceived service quality depends heavily on the quality of the buyer-seller interaction. In product marketing, product quality often depends little on how the product is obtained. But in services marketing, service quality depends on the service deliverer, especially in professional services. The customer judges service quality not just on technical quality (the success of the surgery) but also on its functional quality (whether the doctor showed concern and inspired confidence). Thus professionals cannot assume that they will satisfy the client simply by providing good technical service. They have to master interactive marketing skills as well.

Today, as competition increases, as costs rise, as productivity drops, and as service quality falls off, more service firms are taking an interest in marketing. Service companies face three major marketing tasks. They want to increase their *competitive differentiation*, *service quality*, and *productivity*.

Managing Differentiation

In these days of intense price competition, service marketers often complain that it is hard to differentiate their services from those of competitors. To the extent that customers view the services of different providers as similar, they care less about the provider than the price.

The solution to price competition is to develop a differentiated offer and image. The service firm can add *innovative features* to set its offer apart. For example, in the airline industry, companies have introduced such innovations as in-flight movies, advanced seating, air-to-ground telephone service, and frequent flyer award programs to differentiate their offers. Braniff once even featured scantily clad cabin crews, and Singapore Airlines added a piano bar. Unfortunately, most service innovations are easily copied. Still, the service company that regularly finds desired service innovations will gain a succession of temporary advantages, and by earning an innovative reputation may keep customers who want to go with the best.

Service companies can also work on differentiating their images through symbols and branding. The Harris Bank of Chicago adopted the lion as its symbol on its stationery, in its advertising, and even as stuffed animals offered to new depositors. The well known "Harris Lion" confers an image of strength to the bank. Humana, the nation's second-largest investor-owned system of hospitals and services, has developed a successful branding strategy. It standardized the names of all of its ninety

Service marketing strategies: UPS claims that greater efficiency and productivity allow it to offer high quality service at a low price.

hospitals with the "Humana" prefix, then built tremendous awareness and a reputation for quality around that name.

Managing Service Quality

One of the major ways to differentiate a service firm is for the firm to deliver consistently higher quality than competitors. The key is to meet or exceed the customers' service quality expectations. These expectations are based on past experiences, word-of-mouth, and service firm advertising. Customers compare *perceived service* of a given firm to *expected service*. If the perceived service meets or exceeds expected service, customers are apt to use the provider again.

Therefore the service provider needs to identify the expectations of target customers' concerning service quality. Unfortunately, service quality is harder to define and judge than product quality. It is harder to get agreement on the quality of a haircut than on the quality of a hair dryer. And service firms face trade-offs between customer satisfaction and company profitability—they will not always be able to meet the customers' wishes. What is important is that the service provider clearly defines and communicates the service level that will be provided, so that employees know what they must deliver and customers know what they will get.

Studies of well-managed service companies show that they share a number of common virtues regarding service quality. First, they have a history of *top management commitment to quality*. Management at companies such as Marriott, Disney, Delta, and McDonald's looks not only at financial performance but also at service performance. The best service providers *set high service quality standards*. Swissair, for example, aims to have 96 percent or more of its passengers rate its service as good or superior; otherwise it takes action. The top service firms *watch service performance closely*, both their own and that of competitors. They use such methods as comparison shopping, customer surveys, and suggestion and complaint forms. General Electric sends out 700,000 response cards a year to households to rate their service people's performance. Citibank takes regular measures of "ART"—accuracy, responsiveness, and timeliness—and sends out employees who act as customers to check on service quality. Finally, excellently managed service companies *satisfy employees as well as customers*. They believe that good employee relations will result in good customer relations. Management creates an environment of employee support, gives rewards for good service performance, and monitors employee job satisfaction.[13]

Managing Productivity

With their costs rising rapidly, service firms are under great pressure to increase productivity. There are several ways to improve service productivity. Service providers work harder or more skillfully for the same pay. Working harder is not a likely solution, but working more skillfully can result from better selection and training. Or the service provider can increase the quantity of service by giving up some quality. Doctors working for HMOs (health maintenance organizations) have moved toward handling more patients and giving less time to each patient. The provider can "industrialize the service" by adding equipment and standardizing production, as in McDonald's assembly-line approach to fast-food retailing. Commercial dishwashing, jumbo jets, multiple-unit motion picture theatres—all represent technological expansions of service.

Service providers can also increase productivity by designing more effective services. How-to-quit-smoking clinics and jogging may reduce the need for expensive medical services later on. Hiring paralegal workers reduces the need for expensive legal professionals. Providers can also give customers incentives to substitute company labor with their own labor. For example, business firms that sort their own mail before delivering it to the post office pay lower postal rates.

Companies must avoid pushing productivity so hard that it reduces perceived quality. Some productivity steps help standardize quality, increasing customer satisfaction. But other productivity steps lead to too much standardization and rob the consumers of customized service. In some cases, the service provider accepts reduced productivity to create more differentiation.

ORGANIZATION MARKETING

Organizations often carry out activities to "sell" the organization itself. **Organization marketing** consists of activities undertaken to create, maintain, or change attitudes and behavior of target audiences toward an organization. Both profit and nonprofit organizations do organization marketing. Business firms sponsor public relations or corporate advertising campaigns to polish up their images. Nonprofit organizations such as churches, colleges, charities, museums, and performing arts groups market their organizations in order to raise funds and attract members or patrons. Organization marketing calls for assessing the organization's current image and developing a marketing plan to improve its image.

Image Assessment

The first step in image assessment is to research the organization's current image among key publics. The way an individual or a group sees an organization is called its **organization image.** Different people can have different images of the same organization. The organization might be pleased with its public image or might find that it has serious image problems.

For example, suppose a bank does some marketing research to measure its image in the community. It finds its image to be that shown by the red line in Figure 22-2. Thus current and potential customers view the bank as somewhat small, noninnovative, unfriendly, and unknowledgeable. The bank will want to change this image.

Image Planning and Control

Next the organization should figure out what image it would like to have and can achieve. For example, the bank might decide that it would like the image shown by the blue line in Figure 22-2. It would like to be seen as giving more friendly and personal service and as being more innovative, knowledgeable, and larger.

The firm now develops a marketing plan to shift its actual image toward the

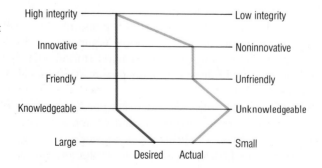

FIGURE 22-2
Image assessment

High integrity — Low integrity
Innovative — Noninnovative
Friendly — Unfriendly
Knowledgeable — Unknowledgeable
Large — Small
Desired   Actual

Ventilated Hush Puppies.

Will people ever stop panting over these shoes? Cool casuals, in mesh and breathable canvas.

Corporate image advertising: This ad attempts to reposition Hush Puppies as a modern, stylish brand.

desired one. Suppose the bank first wants to improve its image as giving friendly and personal service. The key step, of course, is to actually provide friendlier and more personal service. The bank can hire and train better tellers and others who deal with customers. It can change its decor to make the bank seem warmer. When the bank is certain that it has improved performance on the important image measures, it can design a marketing program to communicate the new image to customers. Using public relations, the bank can sponsor community activities, send its executives to speak to local business and civic groups, offer public seminars on household finances, and issue press releases on newsworthy bank activities. In its advertising, the bank can position itself as "your friendly, personal neighborhood bank."

Corporate image advertising is a major tool companies use to market themselves to various publics. In 1986, companies spent more than $785 million on image advertising.[14] Companies can use corporate advertising to build up or maintain a favorable image over many years. Or they can use it to counter events that might hurt their image. For example, Chrysler hired an image consultant firm to tell it how to keep its positive image after Lee Iococca moves on. Waste Management, the giant garbage disposal company, got into trouble a few years ago for dumping toxic wastes. It countered with an advertising campaign telling how the company has worked with various government agencies to help save a threatened species of butterfly.

Such organization marketing efforts can only work if the actual organization lives up to the projected image:

The experts on how to shine up a corporate image . . . agree that no amount of ballyhoo will fool anybody if the corporation behind it is trying to throw dust in the public eye.

The No. 1 rule is that you must match the reality with the image you are trying to create . . . you can't get away with dissonance between the image and the reality, or at least, not for long.[15]

Thus Waste Management's image campaign worked only because the company has worked to clean up toxic waste sites. Otherwise, even saving butterflies would not help the company's reputation.

The organization must resurvey its publics once in a while to see whether its activities are improving its image. Images cannot be changed overnight because of limited funds and the "stickiness" of public image. If the firm is making no progress, either its marketing offer or its marketing program will have to be changed.

PERSON MARKETING

Persons are also marketed. **Person marketing** consists of activities undertaken to create, maintain, or change attitudes or behavior toward particular persons. Two common forms of person marketing are celebrity marketing and political candidate marketing. A third form, personal marketing, used primarily to get a job, is described in Appendix 2, "Careers in Marketing."

Celebrity Marketing

Although celebrity marketing has a long history going back to the Caesars, in recent times we more often associate it with the buildup of athletes and entertainers. Actors hire agents to promote their stardom. The agent places news about the star in the mass media and schedules highly visible public appearances. One of the great promoters was the late Brian Epstein, who managed the Beatles' rise to stardom and received more money than any Beatle. Today celebrities are promoted by entire organizations. Many professional athletes employ agent companies to negotiate endorsement and advertising contracts, schedule personal appearances, issue press releases, and arrange other activities to promote the athlete's image and value.

Celebrity marketers cannot work miracles; much depends on the star. If the star is a born promoter, there is no limit. Singer Elton John, who has made more money than the Beatles or Elvis Presley, has worn over two hundred pairs of glasses, pounded the piano with his feet, batted tennis balls into the crowd, and hired actors to wander around the stage dressed as Frankenstein or Queen Elizabeth. Whether these were his ideas or his manager's, he carried them off well.

Celebrity marketers know that celebrity life cycles are quite varied and often short (see Figure 22-3). The head of marketing for Polygram, a major recording firm, likens a performer's career to a crate of strawberries that must be packaged, brought to the market, and sold before they spoil and become worthless. The national publicity director for Mercury Records describes a typical meeting: "We get together every six weeks. We'll go down our sales figures. If we decide a group is getting 'no action'—meaning no airplay or sales—we'll drop them. If promotion doesn't get results, you don't just throw away more money."[16] Some "has-been" celebrities will try to relaunch their careers, but most find it difficult to get back to the top.

Political Candidate Marketing

Political candidate marketing has become a major industry.[17] Every few years the public is treated to numerous campaigns for lcoal, state, and national offices. In these political campaigns, the candidates go into the voter market and use marketing research and advertising to maximize voter "purchasing."

Interest in the marketing aspects of elections has been stimulated by the spectacu-

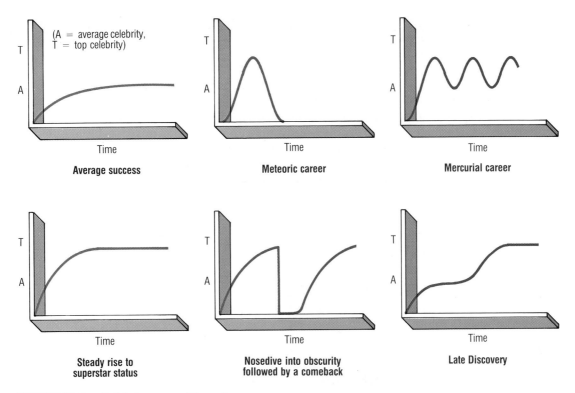

FIGURE 22-3   Celebrity career life cycles

Source: Charles Seton, "The Marketing of a Free Lance Fashion Photographer," unpublished paper, Northwestern University.

lar growth in political advertising, scientific opinion polling, computer analysis of voting patterns, and professional campaign management firms.

> The personal handshake, the local fund-raising dinner, the neighborhood tea, the rally, the precinct captain and the car pool to the polls are still very much with us . . . the new campaign has provided a carefully coordinated strategic framework within which the traditional activities are carried out in keeping with a Master Plan. It centers on a shift from the candidate-controlled, loosely knit, often haphazard "play-it-by-ear" approach to that of a precise, centralized "team" strategy for winning or keeping office. Its hallmarks include the formal strategic blueprint, the coordinated use of specialized propaganda skills, and a more subtle approach to opinion measurement and manipulation. And, though there is a world of difference between selling a candidate and merchandising soap or razor blades, some of the attributes of commercial advertising have been grafted onto the political process.[18]

*P*LACE MARKETING

Place marketing involves activities undertaken to create, maintain, or change attitudes or behavior toward particular places. There are four major types of place marketing: housing marketing, business site marketing, land investment marketing, and vacation marketing.

Housing Marketing

Housing marketing involves the sale or rental of single-family dwellings, apartments, and other types of housing units. It has traditionally relied on classified want ads

"THE GOODLIEST LAND": BUSINESS SITE MARKETING IN NORTH CAROLINA

In 1654, two English explorers returned to their homeland with news of "The Goodliest Land Under the Cope of Heaven"—they were describing what is now North Carolina. In recent years, numerous American and foreign companies have come to share this opinion of the Tar Heel state. In three successive *Business Week* surveys, North Carolina was named as first choice of the nation's top business executives for new plant location. The state does offer a number of economic and cultural advantages, but much credit for the state's popularity goes to the North Carolina Department of Commerce's Division of Industrial Development. The division employs a high-quality marketing program—including advertising, publicity, and personal selling—to convince targeted firms and industries to come to North Carolina.

The division's twenty-four industrial development representatives coordinate efforts with development professionals in more than 300 individual North Carolina communities. And the division provides extensive information to firms considering locating in the state—in-depth profiles of more than 325 communities, a computerized inventory of available industrial sites and building, estimates of state and local taxes for specific sites, analyses of labor costs and fringe benefits, details of transportation convenient to sites, and estimates of construction costs.

But the Division of Industrial Development does more than simply provide information—it aggressively seeks out firms and persuades them to locate in North Carolina. It invites groups of business executives to tour the state and hear presentations, and it sets up booths at industry trade fairs. Its representatives (sometimes including the state's governor) travel to other states to carry the North Carolina story to executives in attractive businesses and industries. The division also communicates and persuades through informational and promotional brochures delivered by mail, and through mass-media advertising. Ads and brochures such as that shown here tout North Carolina's benefits: a large and productive labor force, numerous educational and technical training institutions, low taxes, a good transportation network, low energy and construction costs, a good living environment, and plentiful government support and assistance.

The division's total budget runs only about $2 million a year, but the returns are great. From 1977 through 1987, new and expanding businesses announced investments of more than $20 billion in North Carolina, creating more than 310,000 new jobs.

Source: Based on information supplied by the North Carolina Department of Commerce, Division of Industrial Development.

---

and real estate agents. More advanced marketing has been used for condominium selling and the development of total communities. Large builders research housing needs and develop housing products aimed at the price ranges and wants of specific market segments. Some high-rise apartments have been built for the jet set, others for the geriatric set, filled with the features, symbols, and services appropriate to each. Entire housing communities have been designed for certain life-cycle or life-style groups.

Business Site Marketing

Business site marketing involves developing, selling, or renting business sites for such uses as factories, stores, offices, warehouses, and conventions. Large developers research companies' land needs and respond with real estate solutions, such as industrial parks, shopping centers, and new office buildings. Most states operate industrial development offices that try to sell companies on the advantages of locating new plants in their states (see Marketing Highlight 22–1). They spend large sums on advertising and offer to fly prospects to the site at no cost. Troubled cities, such as New York, Detroit, and Atlanta, have appointed task forces to improve the city's

With Bonuses Like This, No Wonder Our Workers Are 12% More Productive.

Obviously, happy workers are productive workers. And in a state with scenery and a climate like North Carolina's, there's certainly a lot to be happy about.

But perhaps the biggest reason we produce 12% more per production wage dollar than the U.S. average (which equals an extra hour's productivity each working day) has as much to do with quality of labor as with quality of life.

North Carolina is the tenth-largest state in population, yet we have the fifth-largest university system.

Our community colleges (there's one within 30 minutes

For the complete North Carolina story, just write North Carolina Department of Commerce, Office of Economic Development, Suite 000.

of 99% of the population) enroll over a half-million adults.

And our state-funded programs have trained workers for over 2,000 different industrial operations.

We employ the country's eighth-largest manufacturing force; we're now 13th in high-tech employment.

What's more, we're a right-to-work state. And stoppages here from labor disputes are the lowest in the nation.

Call us, and we'll tell you more about the workers who are considered to be highly skilled, highly motivated, and, in their lifestyle, highly fortunate. **North Carolina**

450 N. Salisbury Street, Raleigh, NC 22603. Or call (919) 733-4151.

North Carolina advertises to attract new business to the state.

image and draw new business to the area. They build large centers to house important conventions and business meetings. Foreign nations, such as Canada, Ireland, Greece, Mexico, and Turkey, have marketed their homeland as a good location for business investment.

Land Investment Marketing

Land investment marketing involves developing and selling land for investment. The buyers—corporations, doctors, small investors—hope to sell the land when it rises enough in value. Land investment marketing has played a major role in developing large parts of Florida and the Far West. Land developers have designed elaborate marketing programs involving mass-media advertising and publicity, direct mail, personal sales calls, free dinner meetings, and even free flights to the site.

Vacation Marketing

Vacation marketing involves attracting vacationers to spas, resorts, cities, states, and even entire nations. The effort is carried on by travel agents, airlines, motor clubs, oil companies, hotels, motels, and governmental agencies.

Today almost every city, state, and country markets its tourist attractions. Miami Beach is considering making gambling legal in order to attract more tourists. Texas advertises "Have a Big Time in Texas," and Michigan touts "YES M!CH!GAN." Philadelphia invites you to "Get To Know Us!" and Palm Beach, Florida, advertises "The Best of Everything" at low off-season prices. Some places, however, try to demarket themselves. Oregon has publicized its bad weather; Yosemite National Park may ban snowmobiling, conventions, and private cars; and Finland wants to discharge tourists from vacationing in certain areas where they feel the harm from mass tourism exceeds the revenues.

IDEA MARKETING

Ideas can also be marketed. In one sense, all marketing is the marketing of an idea, whether it be the idea of brushing your teeth, the idea that Crest is the most effective decay preventer, or anything else. Here we discuss only the marketing of social ideas, such as public health campaigns to reduce smoking, alcoholism, drug abuse, and overeating; environmental campaigns to promote wilderness protection, clean air, and conservation; and other campaigns such as family planning, human rights, and racial equality. This area has been called social marketing.[19] **Social marketing** is the design, implementation, and control of programs seeking to increase the acceptability of a social idea, cause, or practice in a target group.

Social marketers can pursue different objectives. They might want to produce understanding (knowing the nutritional value of different foods) or to trigger a one-time action (joining in a mass immunization campaign). They might want to change behavior (drunk-driving campaign) or change a basic belief (convincing employers that handicapped people can make strong contributions in the workforce). The Advertising Council of America has carried out dozens of social advertising campaigns, including "Smokey the Bear," "Keep America Beautiful," "Join the Peace Corps," "Buy Bonds," and "Go to College." But social marketing is much broader than just advertising. Many public advertising campaigns fail because they assign advertising the primary role and fail to develop and use all the marketing mix tools.

In designing effective social change strategies, social marketers go through a normal marketing planning process. First, they define the social change objective—for example, "to reduce the percentage of teenagers who drink and drive from 35 percent to 25 percent within 5 years." Next they analyze the attitudes, beliefs, values, and behavior of teenagers and the forces that support teenage drinking. They consider communication and distribution approaches that might prevent teenagers from driving while drinking (see Marketing Highlight 22–2), develop a marketing plan, and build a marketing organization to carry out the plan. Finally, they evaluate and adjust the program to make it more effective.

Social marketing is fairly new, and its effectiveness relative to other social change strategies is hard to evaluate. It is hard to produce social change with any strategy, let alone one that relies on voluntary response. Social marketing has mainly been applied to family planning, environmental protection, energy conservation, improved nutrition, auto driver safety, and public transportation—and there have been some encouraging successes. But more applications are needed before we can fully assess social marketing's potential for producing social change.

SOCIAL MARKETING OF SAFE AND SOBER DRIVING

In 1986, Reader's Digest Foundation, in partnership with the National Association of Secondary School Principals (NASSP), launched the first of a two-year, $1 million social marketing campaign to deliver a sober message to teenagers all across America. As part of the "Don't Drive and Drink Challenge," *Reader's Digest* magazine invited teams from leading advertising agencies to create posters against drinking and driving, with the winners receiving a Paris trip for two. More than 1000 teams from top agencies competed. Shown here are the 1986 and 1987 winning posters.

Reader's Digest Foundation distributed copies of the poster to 20,000 high schools. Students were challenged to compete for college scholarships by devising programs to promote sober driving. Over 700 schools submitted entries ranging from rock videos to puppet shows to anti-drunk-driving awareness weeks. One-hundred-fifteen winning schools received $500,000 in scholarships. The program was held a second year, with advertising agencies and schools again taking part and another $500,000 in scholarships awarded. Reader's Digest Foundation continues to offer copies of its posters and summaries of winning student programs as a resource to educators, the media, and community organizations.

Social marketing: marketing safe and sober driving.

SUMMARY

Marketing has been broadened in recent years to cover "marketable" entities other than products—namely, services, organizations, persons, places, and ideas.

As the United States moves increasingly toward a service economy, marketers need to know more about marketing services. Services are activities or benefits that one party can offer to another that are essentially intangible and do not result in the ownership of anything. Services are intangible, inseparable, variable, and perishable. Each characteristic poses problems and requires strategies. Marketers have to find ways to "tangiblize" the intangible; to increase the productivity of providers who are inseparable from the product; to standardize the quality in the face of variability; and to influence demand movements and supply capacities better in the face of service perishability.

Service industries have typically lagged behind manufacturing firms in adopting and using marketing concepts, but this is now changing. Services marketing strategy calls not only for external marketing but also for internal marketing to motivate employees and interactive marketing to create service delivery skills in service providers. To succeed, service marketers, must create competitive differentiation, offer high service quality, and find ways to increase service productivity.

Organizations can also be marketed. Organization marketing is undertaken to create, maintain, or change attitudes or behavior of target audiences toward an organization. It calls for assessing the organization's current image and developing a marketing plan for bringing about an improved image.

Person marketing consists of activities undertaken to create, maintain, or change attitudes or behavior toward particular persons. Two common forms are celebrity marketing and political candidate marketing.

Place marketing involves activities to create, maintain, or change attitudes or behavior toward particular places. The four most common types are housing marketing, business site marketing, land investment marketing, and vacation marketing.

Idea marketing involves efforts to market ideas. In the case of social ideas it is called social marketing and consists of the design, implementation, and control of programs seeking to increase the acceptability of a social idea, cause, or practice in a target group. Social marketing goes further than public advertising in coordinating advertising with the other elements of the marketing mix. The social marketer defines the social change objective, analyzes consumer attitudes and competitive forces, develops and tests alternative concepts, develops appropriate channels for the idea's communication and distribution, and finally, checks the results. Social marketing has been applied to family planning, environmental protection, energy conservation, and other public issues.

QUESTIONS FOR DISCUSSION

1. A "hot" concept in fast-food marketing is home delivery of everything from pizza to hamburgers to fried chicken. Why is demand for this service growing? How can marketers in other industries gain a competitive advantage by satisfying the growing demand for increased services?

2. Many banks have begun hiring marketing executives with consumer packaged-goods marketing experience. Why do you think this trend has started? What benefits and problems might banks experience as a result of this hiring practice?

3. What implications do the four major characteristics of services have for a movie theater chain? Give specific examples of how a theater can deal with the intangibility, inseparability, variability, and perishability of the service it provides.

4. Retail stores sell tangible products rather than services. Is interactive marketing an important concept to retailers? Why or why not? How can retailers use internal marketing to improve the quality of the buyer-seller interactions in their stores?

5. Why do organizations want to "sell" themselves and not just their products? List several reasons for organization marketing, and relate them to promotional campaigns of companies you are familiar with.

6. Many people feel that too much time and money are spent marketing political candidates and that modern political campaigns overemphasize image at the expense of issues. What is your opinion of political candidate marketing? Would some other approach to campaigning help consumers make better voting decisions?

7. News reports of questionable, high-pressure tactics in the sale of vacation homes are common. The "food processor" that one marketer used as an incentive to attract prospects turned out to be a fork! Why do you think unethical practices appear to be common in place marketing? What do these practices tell you about the adoption of the marketing concept by place marketers?

8. Social marketing is one approach to achieving social change. What other methods are available? Describe how these approaches could be used to reduce the amount of litter on the highways. What advantages and disadvantages does social marketing have, compared with these other approaches?

■ KEY TERMS

Inseparability A major characteristic of services—they are produced and consumed at the same time and cannot be separated from their providers, whether the providers are persons or machines.

Intangibility A major characteristic of services—they cannot be seen, tasted, felt, heard, or smelled before they are bought.

Organization image The way an individual or a group sees an organization.

Organization marketing Activities undertaken to create, maintain, or change attitudes and behavior of target audiences toward an organization.

Perishability A major characteristic of services—they cannot be stored for later sale or use.

Person marketing Activities undertaken to create, maintain, or change attitudes or behavior toward particular persons.

Place marketing Activities undertaken to create, maintain, or change attitudes or behavior toward particular places.

Service Any activity or benefit that one party can offer to another that is essentially intangible and does not result in the ownership of anything.

Social marketing The design, implementation, and control of programs seeking to increase the acceptability of a social idea, cause, or practice in target groups.

Variability A major characteristic of services—their quality may vary a lot, depending on who provides them and when and where they are provided.

■ REFERENCES

1. Portions adapted from Kevin T. Higgins, "Hospital Puttin' on the Ritz to Target High-End Market," *Marketing News*," January 17, 1986, p. 14.

2. See Norman Jonas, "The Hollow Corporation," *Business Week*, March 3, 1986, pp. 57–59; and Edward Prewitt and Sarah E. Morgenthau, "Flush Times for the Money Men," *Fortune*, June 8, 1987, pp. 192–94.

3. "Presto! The Convenience Industry: Making Life a Little Simpler," *Business Week*, April 27, 1987, p. 86.

4. See Leonard L. Berry, "Services Marketing is Different," *Business*, May–June 1980, pp. 24–30; Karl Albrecht and Ron Zembe, *Service America! Doing Business in the New Economy* (Homewood, IL: Dow-Jones-Irwin, 1985).

5. Further classifications of services are described in Christopher H. Lovelock, *Services Marketing* (Englewood Cliffs, NJ: Prentice Hall, 1984).

6. See Theodore Levitt, "Marketing Intangible Products and Product Intangibles," *Harvard Business Review*, May–June 1981, pp. 94–102.

7. For more discussion, see James L. Heskett, "Lessons in the Service Sector," *Harvard Business Review*, March–April 1987, pp. 122–24.

8. See Ray Lewis, "Whose Job is Service Marketing?" *Advertising Age*, August 3, 1987, pp. 14, 20.

9. See W. Earl Sasser, "Match Supply and Demand in Service Industries," *Harvard Business Review*, November–December 1976, pp. 133–40

10. See A. Parasuraman, Leonard L. Berry, and Valarie A. Zeithaml, "Service Firms Need More Marketing," *Business Horizons*, November–December 1983, pp. 28–31.

11. See Christian Gronroos, "A Service Quality Model and Its Marketing Implications," *European Journal of Marketing*, Vol. 18, No. 4, 1984, pp. 36–44.

12. See Leonard L. Berry, "Big Ideas in Services Marketing," *Journal of Consumer Marketing*, Spring 1986, pp. 47–51.

13. For more on service quality, see A. Parasuraman, Valarie A. Zeithaml, and Leonard L. Berry, "A Conceptual Model of Service Quality and Its Implications for Future Research," *Jorunal of Marketing*, Fall 1985, pp. 41–50.

14. Lori Kasler, "Corporate Image Advertising," *Advertising Age*, October 5, 1987, p. S1

15. Anne B. Fisher, "Spiffing Up the Corporate Image," *Fortune*, July 21, 1986, p. 69.

16. "In the Groove at Mercury Records," *Chicago Daily News*, Panorama Magazine, October 16, 1976.

17. See Joe McGinness, *The Selling of a President 1968* (New York: Trident Press, 1969): Daniel Burstein, "Presidential Timbre: Grooming the Candidates," *Advertising Age*, March 12, 1984, p. M4; and Patricia Sellers, "The Selling of the President in '88," *Fortune*, December 21, 1987, pp. 131–36.

18. See E. Glick, *The New Methodology* (Washington, DC: American Institute for Political Communication, 1967), p. 1. Also see Philip Kotler and Neil Kotler, "Business Marketing for Political Candidates," *Campaigns and Elections*, Summer 1981, pp. 24–33.

19. See Philip Kotler and Gerald Zaltman, "Social Marketing: An Approach to Planned Social Change," *Journal of Marketing*, July 1971, pp. 3–12.

23 *Marketing and Society*

GENERATIONS of parents have trusted the health and well-being of their babies to Gerber baby foods. Gerber sells over 1.3 billion jars of baby food each year, holding almost 70 percent of the market. But in early 1986, the company's reputation was threatened when over 250 customers in 30 states complained about finding glass fragments in Gerber baby food.

The company believed that these complaints were unfounded. Gerber plants are clean and modern, using many filters that would prevent such problems. There were no confirmed injuries from Gerber products. And the Food & Drug Administration had looked at more than 40,000 jars of Gerber baby food without finding a single major problem. Gerber suspected that the glass was planted by the people making the complaints and seeking publicity or damages. Yet the complaints received widespread media coverage, and many retailers pulled Gerber products from their shelves. The state of Maryland forbid the sales of some Gerber baby foods, and other states considered such bans.

The considerable attention given to the complaints may have resulted from the "Tylenol scares" in which Tylenol capsules laced with cyanide had caused consumer deaths. At the time, product tampering was a major public issue and consumer concern.

Gerber wanted to act responsibly, but social responsibility issues are rarely clear-cut. Some thought that, to ensure consumer safety, Gerber should quickly recall all its baby food products from store shelves until the problem was resolved. That was how the makers of such products as Tylenol, Contac, and Gatorade had reacted to tampering scares for their products. But Gerber executives did not think that a recall was best for consumers or for the company. After a similar scare in 1984, the company had recalled some 700,000 jars of baby food and had advertised heavily to reassure consumers. The isolated incident turned out to be the result of normal breakage during shipment. The recall cost Gerber millions of dollars in expenses and lost profits; the advertising caused unnecessary alarm and inconvenience to consumers. The company concluded that it had overreacted in its desire to be socially responsible.

So Gerber decided to do nothing, at least in the short-run. It refused to recall any products—in fact, it filed a $150 million suit against Maryland to stop the ban on the sales of Gerber products. It suspended its advertising, monitored sales and consumer confidence, reassured nervous retailers, and waited to see what would happen. This wait-and-see strategy could have been risky. If the complaints turned out to be well-founded, and Gerber's failure to act quickly caused consumer injuries or deaths, Gerber's reputation would be seriously damaged.

Finally, when research showed that consumer concern was spreading, Gerber aired a few television ads noting its concern about "rumors you may have heard" and assuring buyers that Gerber products "meet the highest standards." The company also mailed letters to about two million new mothers assuring them of Gerber's quality. In the end, the scare passed with little damage to Gerber's reputation or sales and with little consumer alarm or inconvenience.

Should Gerber have immediately recalled its products to prevent even the remote chance of consumer injury? Perhaps. But in many matters of social responsibility, the best course of action is unclear.[1]

Chapter Objectives   *After reading this chapter, you should be able to:*

1. List and respond to the social criticisms of marketing.
2. Define consumerism and environmentalism, and explain how they affect marketing strategies.
3. Describe the principles of socially responsible marketing.
4. Evaluate the role of ethics in marketing.
5. Discuss the principles that guide public policy toward marketing.

RESPONSIBLE marketers find out what consumers want and respond with the right products, priced to give good value to buyers and profit to the producer. The *marketing concept* is a philosophy of service and mutual gain. Its practice leads the economy by an invisible hand to satisfy the many and changing needs of millions of consumers.

Not all marketers follow the marketing concept. Some companies use questionable marketing practices. And some marketing actions that seem innocent in themselves strongly affect the larger society. Consider the sale of cigarettes. Ordinarily, companies should be free to sell cigarettes, and smokers should be free to buy them. But this transaction affects the public interest. First, the smoker may be shortening his or her own life. Second, smoking places a burden on the smoker's family and on society at large. Third, other people around the smoker may have to inhale the smoke and may suffer discomfort and harm. This is not to say that cigarettes should be banned. Rather, it shows that private transactions may involve larger questions of public policy.

This chapter looks at the social effects of private marketing practices. We will look at several questions. What are the most frequent social criticisms of marketing? What steps have private citizens taken to curb marketing ills? What steps have legislators and government agencies taken to curb marketing ills? And what steps have enlightened companies taken to carry out socially responsible marketing?

SOCIAL CRITICISMS OF MARKETING

Some social critics claim that marketing hurts individual consumers, society as a whole, and other business firms.

Marketing's Impact on Individual Consumers

Consumers have many concerns about how well the American marketing system serves their interests. Surveys usually show that consumers hold slightly unfavorable attitudes toward marketing practices.[2] A consumer survey conducted for Atlantic Richfield Company found that consumers are worried about high prices, poor-quality products, dangerous products, misleading advertising claims, and several other marketing-related problems (see Figure 23-1). Consumer advocates, government agencies, and other critics have accused marketing of harming consumers through high prices, deceptive practices, high-pressure selling, shoddy or unsafe products, planned obsolescence, and poor service to disadvantaged consumers.

High Prices

Many critics charge that the American marketing system causes prices to be higher than they would be under more "sensible" systems. They point to three factors—high costs of distribution, high advertising and promotion costs, and excessive markups.

HIGH COSTS OF DISTRIBUTION. A longstanding charge is that greedy middlemen mark up prices beyond the value of their services. Critics charge that there are too many middlemen or that middlemen are inefficient, provide unnecessary or duplicate services, and practice poor management and planning. As a result, distribution costs too much, and consumers pay for these excessive costs in the form of higher prices.

How do retailers answer these charges? They argue as follows: First, middlemen do work that would otherwise have to be done by manufacturers or consumers. Second, the rising markup reflects improved services that consumers want—more convenience, larger stores and assortments, longer store hours, return privileges, and others. Third, the costs of operating stores keep rising and force retailers to

FIGURE 23-1
Survey of consumer concerns
Source: Consumerism in the Eighties, poll of 1,252 adults, October 15–26, 1982, conducted by Louis Harris and Associates for ARCO. See Myrlie Evers, "Consumerism in the Eighties," reprinted with permission from the August 1983 issue of *Public Relations Journal*, copyright 1983, pp. 24–26.

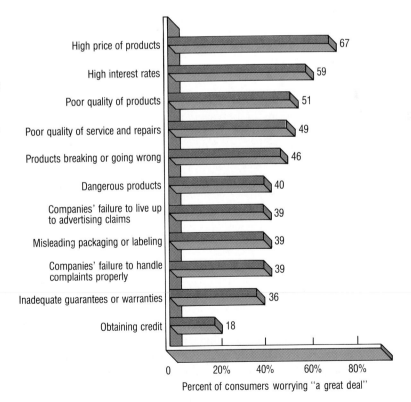

Percent of consumers worrying "a great deal"

raise their prices. Fourth, retail competition is so intense that margins are actually quite low. For example, supermarket chains are left with barely 1 percent profit on their sales after taxes.

HIGH ADVERTISING AND PROMOTION COSTS. Modern marketing is also accused of pushing up prices because of heavy advertising and sales promotion. For example, a dozen tablets of a heavily-promoted brand of aspirin sell for the same price as one hundred tablets of less-promoted brands. Critics feel that if many products were sold in bulk, their prices would be much lower. Differentiated products—cosmetics, detergents, toiletries—include costs of packaging and promotion that can amount to 40 percent or more of the manufacturer's price to the retailer. Much of the packaging and promotion adds only psychological rather than functional value to the product. Retailers use additional promotion—advertising, trading stamps, games—adding several cents more to retail prices.

Marketers answer these charges in several ways. First, consumers want more than the functional qualities of products. They also want psychological benefits such as feeling wealthy, beautiful, or special. Consumers can usually buy functional versions of products at lower prices, but they often are willing to pay more for products that also provide the wanted psychological benefits. Second, branding gives buyers confidence. A brand name means a certain quality, and consumers are willing to pay for well-known brands even if they cost a little more. Third, heavy advertising is needed to inform the millions of potential buyers of the merits of a brand. If consumers want to know what is available on the market, they must expect manufacturers to spend large sums of money on advertising. Fourth, heavy advertising and promotion are necessary for the firm when competitors are doing it. The business would lose "share of mind" if it did not match competitive spending. At the same time, companies are very cost conscious about promotion and try to spend their money wisely. And fifth, heavy sales promotion is needed from time to time because goods are produced ahead of demand in a mass-production economy. Special incentives have to be offered in order to sell inventories.

EXCESSIVE MARKUPS. Critics charge that some companies mark up goods excessively. They point to the drug industry, where a pill costing 5 cents to make may cost the consumer 40 cents. They point to the pricing tactics of funeral homes that prey on the emotions of bereaved relatives. They point to the high charges of television repair and auto repair people.

Marketers respond that most businesses try to deal fairly with consumers because they want repeat business. Most consumer abuses are unintentional. When shady marketers do take advantage of consumers, they should be reported to Better Business Bureaus and other consumer protection groups. Marketers also respond that consumers often do not understand the reason for high markups. For example, pharmaceutical markups must cover the costs of purchasing, promoting, and distributing existing medicines plus the high research and development costs of searching for new medicines.

Deceptive Practices

Marketers sometimes are accused of deceptive practices that lead consumers to believe they will get more value than they actually do. Some industries draw more complaints than others. Among the worst offenders are insurance companies (claiming that policies are "guaranteed renewable" or underwritten by the government), publishing companies (selling magazine subscriptions under false pretenses), mail order land sales organizations (misrepresenting land tracts or improvement costs), home improvement contractors (using bait-and-switch tactics), automotive repair shops (adver-

Some retailers use high markups, but higher prices cover services that consumers want—assortment, convenience, personal service, and return privileges.

tising low repair prices and then "discovering" a needed major repair), correspondence schools (overstating job opportunities), dance studios (signing up elderly people for lessons beyond their life expectancy), and companies selling medical devices (overstating therapeutic claims).

Deceptive practices fall into three groups. *Deceptive pricing* includes such practices as falsely advertising "factory" or "wholesale" prices or advertising a large price reduction from a high phony list price. *Deceptive promotion* includes such practices as overstating the product's features or performance, luring the customer to the store for a bargain that is out of stock, and running rigged contests. *Deceptive packaging* includes exaggerating package contents through subtle design, not filling the package to the top, using misleading labeling, and describing the size in misleading terms.

Deceptive practices have led to legislation and other consumer protection actions. In 1938 the Wheeler-Lea Act gave the FTC power to regulate "unfair or deceptive acts or practices." The FTC has published several guidelines listing deceptive practices. The toughest problem is defining what is deceptive. Shell Oil advertised that Super Shell with platformate gave more mileage than the same gasoline without platformate. Now this statement was true, but what Shell did not say is that almost all gasoline includes platformate. Its defense was that it had never claimed that platformate was found only in Shell gasoline. But even though the message was literally true, the FTC felt that the ad's intent was to deceive.

Marketers argue that most companies avoid deceptive practices because such practices harm their businesses in the long run. If consumers do not get what they expect, they will switch to more reliable products. Also, consumers usually protect themselves from deception. Most consumers recognize the marketer's selling intent and are careful when they buy, sometimes to the point of not believing completely true product claims. Levitt claims that some advertising puffery is bound to occur, and that it may even be desirable:

> There is hardly a company that would not go down in ruin if it refused to provide fluff, because nobody will buy pure functionality. . . . Worse, it denies . . . man's honest needs and values. . . . Without distortion, embellishment, and elaboration, life would be drab, dull, anguished, and at its existential worst. . . .[3]

High-Pressure Selling

Salespeople are sometimes accused of high-pressure selling that gets people to buy goods they had no thought of buying. It is often said that encyclopedias, insurance, real estate, and jewelry are sold, not bought. The salespeople are trained to deliver smooth canned talks to entice purchase. They sell hard because sales contests promise big prizes to those who sell the most.

Marketers know that buyers can often be talked into buying unwanted or unneeded things. Laws require door-to-door salespeople to announce that they are selling a product. Buyers also have a "three-day cooling-off period" in which they can cancel a contract after rethinking it. In addition, consumers can complain to Better Business Bureaus or state consumer protection agencies when they feel that undue selling pressure was applied.

Shoddy or Unsafe Products

Another criticism is that products lack the quality they should have. One complaint is that products are not made well. Automobiles bear many of the complaints—it seems that every new car has something wrong with it. Consumers grumble about rattles and pings, misalignments, dents, leaking, and creaking. Complaints have also been lodged against home and auto repair services, appliances, and clothing.

A second complaint is that some products deliver little benefit. Consumers got a shock on hearing that dry breakfast cereal may have little nutritional value. One nutrition expert told a Senate subcommittee: "In short, [the cereals] fatten but do little to prevent malnutrition. . . . The average cereal . . . fails as a complete meal even with milk added."[4] The expert added that consumers could often get more nutrition by eating the cereal package than the contents.

A third complaint concerns product safety. For years, Consumers Union has reported various hazards in tested products—electrical dangers in applicances, carbon monoxide poisoning from room heaters, finger risks in lawnmowers, and faulty steering in automobiles. Its testing and other activities have helped consumers to make better buying decisions and businesses to eliminate product flaws (see Marketing Highlight 23–1). Product quality has been a problem for several reasons, including manufacturer indifference, increased production complexity, poorly trained labor, and poor quality control.

On the other hand, most manufacturers want to produce quality goods. Consumers who are unhappy with one of the firm's products may avoid their other products and talk other consumers into doing the same. The way a company deals with product quality and safety problems can damage or help its reputation. Companies that sell poor-quality or unsafe products risk damaging conflicts with consumer groups. Unsafe products can result in product liability suits and large awards for damages.[5]

Planned Obsolescence

Critics have charged that some producers follow **planned obsolescence,** causing their products to become obsolete before they should actually need replacement. In many cases, they have been accused of continually changing consumer concepts

WHEN *Consumer Reports* Talks, Buyers Listen—and So Do Companies

Whether they're buying automobiles or life insurance, drain cleaner or refrigerators—or practically anything else—millions of shoppers won't plunk down their money until they consult *Consumer Reports*. For 51 years the publication of Consumers Union has been a fiercely independent arbiter of quality goods and an ardent advocate of consumer rights. It has published CU's ratings of thousands of products and services without ever losing a libel suit. And today, its monthly circulation is at an all-time high of 3.8 million.

A 90-member technical team puts products through their paces at CU's headquarters in Mount Vernon, N. Y. When they can, they use the same tests industry uses. They check the laundering power of washing machines, for example, by washing presoiled fabric swatches and measuring their brightness with optical instruments. If no standard tests exist, *Consumer Reports* invents them. To rate facial tissues, CU's technical team built a "sneeze machine" that squirts a controlled spray of water and air through a tissue mounted on embroidery hoops.

Open Book. CU describes its tests in detail when it rates products. But those explanations don't always placate the manufacturer whose product comes in last. If a company isn't happy with its rating, CU responds with an invitation to visit its labs.

Many companies have made changes in their products after getting a bad rating from CU. Although Whirlpool Corp. chafed at criticism that its washing-machine design made repair too difficult, on its new models the cabinet pops off to allow access to key parts.

In its April, 1973, issue, *Consumer Reports* rejected an entire category of products—microwave ovens—because doors on all 14 models tested were leaking radiation. Since then, ovenmakers have changed their designs. Today, "there's very little leakage around those doors," says CU technical director R. David Pittle.

Media Push. While *Consumer Reports* remains CU's major endeavor, the organization is branching out. In the last two years it has launched a travel newsletter, produced six home videocassettes,

Consumers Union's ninety-member technical team puts products through their paces.

spruced up its *Penny Power* children's magazine, and formed a book-publishing company. Since January, CU has been selling dealer's-cost listings for most auto models and options. Its media push also includes a thrice-weekly syndicated newspaper column, plus radio and television spots. All this has helped CU's bottom line. Last year it earned $3.4 million.

The prosperity has not diluted CU's activism. Founded by labor unionists in the 1930s, it was among the first organizations to urge consumers to boycott goods made in Nazi Germany. Now *Consumer Reports* is alarmed that many Americans are slipping into poverty. So it is kicking off a three-part series on the working poor. But will the outspoken judge of what's good comment on how well U.S. manufacturers stack up against the Japanese? No way, say Pittle. "Our purpose is to provide an objective evaluation of a product—regardless of who made it."

Source: Mimi Bluestone, "When *Consumer Reports* Talks, Buyers Listen—And So Do Companies," *Business Week*, June 8, 1987, p. 135. Reprinted by permission.

of acceptable styles in order to encourage more and earlier buying. An example is constantly changing clothing fashions. Producers have also been accused of holding back attractive functional features, then introducing them later to make older models obsolete. An example would be automobile manufacturers holding back safety and gasoline economy improvements. Finally, producers have been accused of using materials and components that will break, wear, rot, or rust sooner. For example, many drapery manufacturers are using a higher percentage of rayon in their drapes. They argue that rayon reduces the price of the drapes and has better holding power. Critics claim that rayon will cause the drapes to fall apart in two cleanings instead of four.

Marketers respond that consumers like style changes. They get tired of the old goods and want a new look in fashion or a new-styled car. No one has to buy the new look, and if not enough people like it, it will fail. Companies withhold new features when they are not fully tested, when they add more cost to the product than consumers are willing to pay, and for other good reasons. But they do so at the risk of having a competitor introduce the new feature and steal the market. Also, companies often put in new materials to lower their costs and prices. They do not design their products to break down earlier, because they do not want to lose their customers to other brands. Thus much of so-called planned obsolescence is the working of the competitive and technological forces in a free society, leading to ever-improving goods and services.

Poor Service to Disadvantaged Consumers

The American marketing system has been accused of poorly serving disadvantaged consumers. The urban poor often have to shop in smaller stores that carry inferior goods and charge higher prices. The former chairman of The Federal Trade Commission (FTC), Paul Rand Dixon, summarized a Washington, D.C., study:

> The poor pay more—nearly twice as much—for appliances and furniture sold in Washington's low-income area stores . . . Goods purchased for $100 at wholesale sold for $225 in the low-income stores compared with $159 in the general market stores. . . . Installment credit is a major marketing factor in selling to the poor . . . some low-income market retailers imposed effective annual finance charges as high as 33 percent. . . .[6]

Yet the merchants' profits were not too high:

> Low income market retailers have markedly higher costs, partly because of bad debt expenses, but to a greater extent because of higher selling, wage, and commission costs. These expenses reflect in part greater use of home demonstration selling, and expenses associated with the collection and processing of installment contracts. Thus, although their markups are often two or three times higher than general market retailers, on the average low-income market retailers do not make particularly high profits.[7]

Clearly, better marketing systems must be built in low-income areas, and low-income people need consumer protection. The FTC has taken action against merchants who advertise false values, sell old merchandise as new, or charge too much for credit. It is trying to make it harder for merchants to win court judgments against low-income people who were wheedled into buying something. Another hope is to get large retailers to open outlets in low-income areas.

Marketing's Impact on Society as a Whole

The American marketing system has been accused of adding to several "evils" in American society. Advertising has been a special target—so much so that the American Association of Advertising Agencies recently launched a campaign to defend advertising

ADVERTISING: ANOTHER WORD FOR FREEDOM OF CHOICE

During the past few years, the American Association of Advertising Agencies has run an advertising campaign featuring ads such as these to counter common criticisms of advertising. The association is concerned about research findings of negative public attitudes toward advertising. Two-thirds of the public recognizes that advertising provides helpful buying information, but a significant portion feels that advertising is exaggerated or misleading. The association believes that the ad campaign will increase general advertising credibility and make advertisers' messages more effective. Several media have agreed to run the ads as a public service.

The American Association of Advertising Agencies runs ads to counter common advertising criticisms.

against what it felt are common but untrue criticisms (see Marketing Highlight 23–2). Here we will examine claims that marketing creates false wants and too much materialism, too few social goods, cultural pollution, and too much political power.

False Wants and Too Much Materialism

Critics have charged that the marketing system urges too much interest in material possessions. People are judged by what they own rather than by what they are. To be considered successful, some say, people must own a suburban home, two cars, and the latest clothes and appliances. This drive for wealth and possessions appears to have increased in recent years.

> Money, money, money is the incantation of today. Bewitched by an epidemic of money enchantment, Americans in the Eighties wriggle in a St. Vitus's dance of materialism unseen since the Gilded Age of the Roaring Twenties. Under the blazing sun of money, all other values shine palely. . . . The evidence is everywhere. Open the scarlet covers of the Saks Fifth Avenue Christmas catalog, for starters, and look at what Santa Claus offers today's young family, from Dad's $1,650 ostrich-skin briefcase and Mom's $39,500 fur coat to Junior's $4,000, 15-mph miniature Mercedes.[8]

In a recent survey of teenage girls, 93 percent listed shopping as their favorite pastime, way ahead of dating, which placed sixth. In another poll, 80 percent of college freshman stated that it was very important for them to be very well-off financially, against only 40 percent who said developing a meaningful philosophy of life was an important objective.[9]

Critics do not view this interest in things as a natural state of mind but rather as false wants created by marketing. Business hires Madison Avenue to stimulate people's desires for goods, and Madison Avenue uses the mass media to create materialistic models of the good life. People work harder to earn the necessary money. Their purchases increase the output of American industry, and industry in turn uses Madison Avenue to stimulate more desire for the industrial output. Thus marketing is seen as creating false wants that benefit industry more than they benefit consumers.

These criticisms overstate the power of business to create wants. People have strong defenses against advertising and other marketing tools. Marketers are most effective when they appeal to existing needs rather than when they attempt to create new ones. Furthermore, people seek information when making important purchases and do not rely on single sources of information. Even minor purchases, which may be affected by advertising messages, lead to repeat purchases only if the product performs as promised. Finally, the high failure rate of new products shows that companies are not able to control demand.

On a deeper level, our wants and values are influenced not only by marketers, but also by family, peer groups, religion, ethnic background, and education. If Americans are highly materialistic, these values arose out of basic socialization processes that go much deeper than business and mass media could produce alone.

Too Few Social Goods

Business has been accused of overselling private goods at the expense of public goods. As private goods increase, they require more public services that are usually not forthcoming. For example, an increase in automobile ownership (private good) requires more highways, traffic control, parking spaces, and police services (public goods). The overselling of private goods results in "social costs." For cars, the social costs include excessive traffic congestion, air pollution, and deaths and injuries from car accidents.

A way must be found to restore a balance between private and public goods. Producers could be made to bear the social costs of their operations. For example, the government could require automobile manufacturers to build cars with additional safety features and better pollution control systems. The auto makers would then raise their prices to cover the extra costs. If buyers found the prices of some cars too high, the producers of these cars would disappear, and demand would move to those producers that could support the sum of the private and social costs.

Cultural pollution: People's senses are sometimes assaulted by commercial messages.

Cultural Pollution

Critics charge the marketing system with creating *cultural pollution*. People's senses are constantly being assaulted by advertising. Commercials interrupt serious programs; pages of ads obscure printed matter; billboards mar beautiful scenery. These interruptions continuously pollute people's minds with sex, materialism, power, or status. Though most people do not find advertising very annoying, and some even think it is the best part of television programming, some critics call for sweeping changes.

Marketers answer the charges of commercial noise with these arguments: First, they hope that their ads primarily reach the target audience. But because of mass-communication channels, some ads are bound to reach people who have no interest in the product and are therefore bored or annoyed. People who buy magazines addressed to their interests—such as *Vogue* or *Fortune*—rarely complain about the ads because they generally advertise products of interest. Second, the ads make television and radio free media and keep down the costs of magazines and newspapers. Most people think commercials are a small price to pay.

Too Much Political Power

Another criticism is that business wields too much political power. There are "oil," "cigarette," and "auto" senators who support an industry's interests against the public interest. Advertisers are accused of holding too much power over the mass media, limiting their freedom to report independently and objectively. One critic said: "How can *Life* . . . and *Reader's Digest* afford to tell the truth about the scandalously low nutritional value of most packaged foods . . . when these magazines are being subsidized by such advertisers as General Foods, Kellogg's, Nabisco, and General Mills? . . . The answer is *they cannot and do not*."[10]

American industries do promote and protect their interests. They have a right to representation in Congress and the mass media, although their influence could become too great. Fortunately, many powerful business interests thought to be untouchable have been tamed in the public interest. Standard Oil was broken up in 1911, and the meatpacking industry was disciplined in the early 1900s after exposures by Upton Sinclair. Ralph Nader caused legislation making the automobile industry build more safety into its cars, and the Surgeon General's Report resulted in cigarette companies putting health warnings on their packages. The media receive advertising revenues from many different advertisers, making it easier to resist the influence of one or a few of them. Too much business power tends to result in counter forces that check and offset these powerful interests.

Marketing's Impact on Other Businesses

Critics also charge that a company's marketing practices can harm other companies and reduce competition. Three problems are involved: acquisitions of competitors, marketing practices that create barriers to entry, and unfair competitive marketing practices.

Critics claim that firms are harmed and competition is reduced when companies expand by acquiring competitors rather than by developing their own new products. In the food industry alone during the last few years, R. J. Reynolds acquired Nabisco Brands, Philip Morris merged with General Foods, Procter and Gamble gobbled up Richardson-Vick, Beatrice joined Esmark, Nestle absorbed Carnation, and Quaker Oats bought Stokely-Van Camp.[11] These and large acquisitions in other industries have caused concern that vigorous young competitors will be absorbed and that competition will be reduced.

Acquisition is a complex subject. Acquisitions can sometimes be good for the society. The acquiring company may gain economies of scale leading to lower costs and lower prices. A well-managed company may take over a poorly managed company and improve its efficiency. An industry that was not very competitive might become more competitive after the acquisition. But acquisitions can also be harmful and therefore are closely regulated by the government.

Critics have also charged that marketing practices add barriers to the entry of new companies into an industry. Large marketing companies can use heavy promotion spending, patents, and tie-ups of suppliers or dealers to keep out or drive out competitors. People concerned with antitrust regulation recognize that some barriers are the result of the economic advantages of doing business on a large scale. Other barriers could be challenged by existing and new laws. For example, some critics have proposed a progressive tax on advertising spending to reduce the role of selling costs as a major barrier to entry.

Finally, some firms have used unfair competitive marketing practices with the intention of hurting or destroying other firms. They may set their prices below costs, threaten to cut off business with suppliers, or discourage the buying of the competitor's products. Various laws work to prevent such predatory competition. It is difficult, however, to prove that the intent or action was really predatory. In the classic A&P case, this large retailer was able to charge lower prices than small "mom and pop" grocery stores. The question is whether this was unfair competition or the healthy competition of a more efficient retailer against the less efficient.

CITIZEN ACTIONS TO REGULATE MARKETING

Because some people have viewed business as the cause of many economic and social ills, grassroots movements have arisen from time to time to keep business in line. The two major movements have been *consumerism* and *environmentalism*.

Consumerism   American business firms have been the target of organized consumer movements on three occasions. The first consumer movement took place in the early 1900s. It was fueled by rising prices, Upton Sinclair's writings on conditions in the meat industry, and ethical drug scandals. The second consumer movement, in the mid-1930s, was sparked by an upturn in consumer prices during the Depression and another drug scandal.

The third movement began in the 1960s. Consumers had become better educated; products had become more complex and hazardous; people were unhappy with American institutions; well-known writers accused big business of wasteful and unethical practices; President John F. Kennedy declared that consumers have the right to safety, to be informed, to choose, and to be heard; Congress investigated certain industries; and finally, Ralph Nader appeared on the scene to force many of the issues.

Since then many consumer groups have been organized and several consumer laws have been passed. Though the U.S. consumer movement has slowed somewhat in recent years, consumerism has spread internationally and has become very strong in several European countries.[12]

But what is the consumer movement? **Consumerism** is an organized movement of citizens and government to improve the rights and power of buyers in relation to sellers. The traditional sellers' rights include:

- The right to introduce any product in any size and style, provided it is not hazardous to personal health or safety; or, if it is, to include proper warnings and controls.

- The right to charge any price for the product, provided there is no discrimination among similar kinds of buyers.

Consumer desire for more information led to putting ingredients, nutrition, and dating information on product labels.

- The right to spend any amount to promote the product, provided it is not defined as unfair competition.
- The right to use any product message, provided it is not misleading or dishonest in content or execution.
- The right to use any buying incentive schemes, provided they are not unfair or misleading.

The traditional buyers' rights include:

- The right not to buy a product that is offered for sale.
- The right to expect the product to be safe.
- The right to expect the product to perform as claimed.

Comparing these rights, many believe that the balance of power lies on the sellers' side. True, the buyer can refuse to buy. But critics feel that the buyer has too little information, education, and protection to make wise decisions when facing sophisticated sellers. Consumer advocates call for the following additional consumer rights:

- The right to be well informed about important aspects of products.
- The right to be protected against questionable products and marketing practices.
- The right to influence products and marketing practices in ways that will improve the "quality of life."

Each right has led to proposals by consumerists. The right to be informed includes the right to know the true interest on a loan (truth-in-lending), the true cost per unit of a brand (unit pricing), the ingredients in a product (ingredient labeling), the nutrition in foods (nutritional labeling), product freshness (open dating), and the true benefits of a product (truth-in-advertising). The proposals related to consumer protection include strengthening consumer rights in cases of business fraud, requiring greater product safety, and giving more power to government agencies. The proposals relating to quality of life include controlling the ingredients that go into certain products (detergents) and packaging (soft-drink containers), reducing the level of advertising "noise," and putting consumer representatives on company boards to watch out for consumer interests.

Consumers have not only the right but also the responsibility to protect themselves instead of leaving this function to someone else. Consumers who feel they got a bad deal have several remedies available, including writing to the company president or to the media; contacting federal, state, or local agencies; and going to small-claims courts.

Environmentalism Whereas consumerists look at whether the marketing system is efficiently serving consumer wants, environmentalists look at how marketing affects the environment and at the costs of serving consumer needs and wants. During the past thirty years, several key books have promoted the cause of environmentalism by pointing out environmental dangers.[13] In 1962 Rachel Carson's *Silent Spring* told about pesticide pollution of the environment. It was no longer a matter of wasted resources, but of human survival. In 1970 the Ehrlichs coined the term "eco-catastrophe" to point out the harmful impact of certain American business practices on the environment. And in 1972 the Meadowses published *The Limits to Growth*, which warned people that the quality of life would decline in the face of unchecked population growth, spreading pollution, and uncontrolled use of natural resources.

These concerns are the basis for environmentalism. **Environmentalism** is an organized movement of concerned citizens and government to protect and improve people's living environment. Environmentalists are concerned with strip mining, forest depletion, acid rain, loss of the ozone layer in the atmosphere, toxic wastes,

African Elephant Genus: *Loxodonta* **Species:** *africana* **Adult size:** Length of head and body, male, 6-7.5m; female, 0.6m shorter; height, male, 3.3m; female, 2.4m **Adult weight:** Male, up to 6,000kg; female, 3,000kg **Habitat:** Savanna grassland and forest south of the Sahara **Surviving number:** Estimated at less than 1 million Photographed by Cynthia Moss

Wildlife as Canon sees it

One of the greatest roles of photography is to record and preserve images of the world around us worthy to be handed down as a heritage for all generations. A photograph of a family of African elephants peacefully crossing a wide-open grassland provides a memorable image that exemplifies the grandeur of the species.

Recent studies have revealed elephants to be the first land mammals known to communicate through infrasound. Learning more about this means of communication and their complex and highly structured social behavior could benefit the elephants' chances for survival. Unfortunately, elephant populations are declining rapidly due to poaching for valuable ivory. Stronger measures are required to control the killing of the animals in protected areas and stop the illegal ivory trade.

An invaluable research tool now being used in the long term study of elephants, photography can contribute to a better understanding of the species and help promote an awareness of the urgent need for greater efforts to protect this magnificent and irreplaceable part of our natural heritage.

And understanding is perhaps the single most important factor in saving the African elephant and all of wildlife.

EOS 620·650
The new autofocus SLR cameras
More than autofocus
More than ever

Canon

Canon shows societal concern by discussing the role of photography in creating long-run environmental benefits.

billboards, and litter; with the loss of recreational areas; and with the increase in health problems caused by bad air, polluted water, and chemically sprayed food.

Environmentalists are not against marketing and consumption; they simply want them to operate with more care for the environment. They feel that the marketing system's goal should not be to maximize consumption, consumer choice, or consumer satisfaction; the marketing system's goal should be to maximize life quality. And life quality means not only the quantity and quality of consumer goods and services, but also the quality of the environment. Environmentalists want environmental costs included in producer and consumer decision making.

Environmentalism has hit some industries hard. Steel companies and public utilities have had to invest billions of dollars in pollution-control equipment and costlier fuels. The auto industry has had to introduce expensive emission controls in cars. The packaging industry has had to find ways to reduce litter. The gasoline industry has had to create new low-lead and no-lead gasolines. These industries resent environmental regulations, especially when imposed too rapidly to allow the companies to make the proper adjustments. These companies have absorbed large costs as a result of environmentalism and have passed them on to buyers.

Marketers' lives also have become more complicated. Marketers must check into the ecological properties of the product and its packaging. They must raise prices to cover environmental costs, knowing that the product will be harder to sell. Yet environmental issues have become so important in our society that there

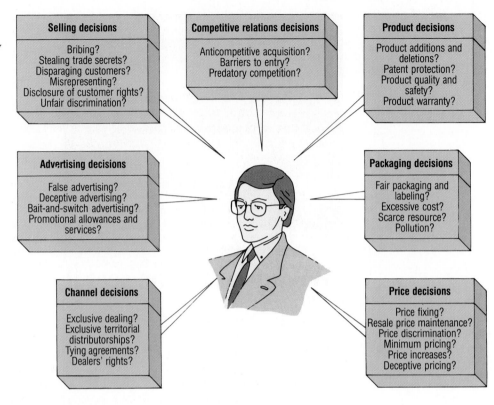

FIGURE 23-2
Major marketing decision areas that may be called into question under the law

Selling decisions

Bribing?
Stealing trade secrets?
Disparaging customers?
Misrepresenting?
Disclosure of customer rights?
Unfair discrimination?

Competitive relations decisions

Anticompetitive acquisition?
Barriers to entry?
Predatory competition?

Product decisions

Product additions and
deletions?
Patent protection?
Product quality and
safety?
Product warranty?

Advertising decisions

False advertising?
Deceptive advertising?
Bait-and-switch advertising?
Promotional allowances and
services?

Packaging decisions

Fair packaging and
labeling?
Excessive cost?
Scarce resource?
Pollution?

Channel decisions

Exclusive dealing?
Exclusive territorial
distributorships?
Tying agreements?
Dealers' rights?

Price decisions

Price fixing?
Resale price maintenance?
Price discrimination?
Minimum pricing?
Price increases?
Deceptive pricing?

is no turning back to the past when few managers worried about the effect of product and marketing decisions on environmental quality.

PUBLIC ACTIONS TO REGULATE MARKETING

Citizen concerns about marketing practices will usually lead to public attention and legislative proposals. New bills will be debated—many will be defeated, others will be modified, and a few will become workable laws.

We listed many of the laws affecting marketing in Chapter 3. The task is to translate these laws into the language that marketing executives understand as they make decisions about competitive relations, products, price, promotion, and channels of distribution. Figure 23-2 shows the major legal issues facing marketing management when making decisions.

BUSINESS ACTIONS TOWARD SOCIALLY RESPONSIBLE MARKETING

At first, many companies opposed consumerism and environmentalism. They thought the criticisms were either unfair or unimportant. But by now, most companies have come around to accepting the new consumer rights in principle. They might oppose some pieces of legislation as not being the best way to solve certain consumer problems, but they recognize the consumer's right to information and protection. Many of these companies have responded positively to consumerism and environmentalism in order to better serve consumer needs. Here we will look at responsible business responses to the changing marketing environment. We first outline a concept of enlightened marketing and then consider marketing ethics.

A Concept of Enlightened Marketing

The concept of **enlightened marketing** holds that the company's marketing should support the best long-run performance of the marketing system. Enlightened marketing consists of five principles: consumer-oriented marketing, innovative marketing, value marketing, sense-of-mission marketing, and societal marketing.

Consumer-Oriented Marketing

Consumer-oriented marketing means that the company should view and organize its marketing activities from the consumers' point of view. It should work hard to sense, serve, and satisfy the needs of a defined group of customers. Consider the following example:

> Barat College, a women's college in Lake Forest, Illinois, published a college catalog that openly spelled out Barat College's strong and weak points. Among the weak points it shared with applicants were the following: "An exceptionally talented student musician or mathematician . . . might be advised to look further for a college with top faculty and facilities in that field. . . . The full range of advanced specialized courses offered in a university will be absent. . . . The library collection is average for a small college, but low in comparison with other high-quality institutions."

The effect of "telling it like it is" is to build confidence so that applicants really know what they will find at Barat College and to emphasize that Barat College will strive to improve its consumer value as rapidly as time and funds permit.

Innovative Marketing

The principle of innovative marketing requires that the company continuously seek real product and marketing improvements. The company that overlooks new and better ways to do things will eventually lose out to a company that has found a better way. One of the best examples of an innovative marketer is Procter & Gamble:

> Wisk, a Lever Bros. product, has dominated liquid detergents for a generation, and liquids have been taking a growing share of the $3.2-billion-a-year detergent market. P&G tried to topple Wisk with run-of-the-laundry-room liquids called Era and Solo, but couldn't come close. Then it developed a liquid with 12 cleaning agents, twice the norm, and a molecule that traps dirt in the wash water. P&G christened it Liquid Tide and put it in a bottle colored the same fire-bright color as the ubiquitous Tide box. After just 18 months on the market, Liquid Tide is washing as many clothes as Wisk in the U.S., and the two are locked in a fierce battle for the No. 2 position, after powdered Tide, among all detergents.[14]

Value Marketing

According to the principle of value marketing, the company should put most of its resources into value-building marketing investments. Many things marketers do—one-shot sales promotions, minor packaging changes, advertising puffery—may raise sales in the short run, but add less value than improvements in the product's quality, features, or convenience. Enlightened marketing calls for building long-run consumer loyalty by continually improving the value consumers receive from the firm's marketing offer.

Sense-of-Mission Marketing

Sense-of-mission marketing means that the company should define its mission in broad social terms rather than narrow product terms. When a company defines a social mission, company people feel better about their work and have a clearer sense of direction. For example, defined in narrow product terms, International Minerals and Chemical Corporation's mission might be "to sell fertilizer." But the company states its mission more broadly:

We're not merely in the business of selling our brand of fertilizer. We have a sense of purpose, a sense of where we are going. The first function of corporate planning is to decide what kind of business the company is in. Our business is *agricultural productivity*. We are interested in anything that affects plant growth, now and in the future.[15]

Reshaping the basic task of producing fertilizer into the larger mission of improving agricultural productivity in order to feed the world's hungry gives a new sense of purpose to employees.

Societal Marketing

Following the principle of societal marketing, an enlightened company makes marketing decisions by considering consumers' wants, the company's requirements, consumers' long-run interests, and society's long-run interests. The company is aware that neglecting the last two factors is a disservice to consumers and society. Alert companies view societal problems as opportunities. As Drucker states: "Consumerism actually should be, must be, and I hope will be, the opportunity of marketing. This is what we in marketing have been waiting for."[16]

A societally-oriented marketer wants to design products that are not only pleasing but also salutary, beneficial. The difference is shown in Figure 23-3. Products can be classified according to their degree of immediate consumer satisfaction and long-run consumer benefit. **Desirable products** give both high immediate satisfaction and high long-run benefits. A desirable product, with immediate satisfaction and long-run benefits would be a tasty, nutritious breakfast food. **Pleasing products** give high immediate satisfaction but may hurt consumers in the long run. An example is cigarettes. **Salutary products** have low appeal but benefit consumers in the long run. Seat belts are salutary products. Finally, **deficient products,** such as bad-tasting yet ineffective medicine, have neither immediate appeal nor long-run benefits.

The challenge posed by pleasing products is that they sell very well, buy may end up hurting the consumer. The product opportunity, therefore, is to add long-run benefits without reducing the product's pleasing qualities. For example, Sears developed a phosphate-free laundry detergent that was very effective. The challenge posed by salutary products is to add some pleasing qualities so that they will become more desirable in the consumers' minds. For example, synthetic fats and fat substitutes, such as Procter & Gamble's Olestra and NutraSweet's Simplesse, promise to improve the appeal of more healthful low-calorie and low-fat foods.

Marketing Ethics

Even conscientious marketers face many moral dilemmas. The best thing to do is often unclear. Since not all managers have fine moral sensitivity, companies need to develop corporate marketing policies, broad guidelines that everyone in the organi-

FIGURE 23-3
Societal classification of new products

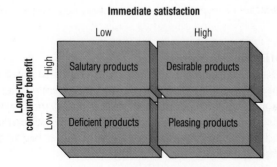

TABLE 23-1
Some Morally Difficult
Situations in
Marketing

1. You work for a cigarette company and up to now have not been convinced that cigarettes cause cancer. A report comes across your desk that clearly shows the link between smoking and cancer. What would you do?
2. Your R&D department has changed one of your products slightly. It is not really "new and improved," but you know that putting this statement on the package and in advertising will increase sales. What would you do?
3. You have been asked to add a stripped-down model to your line that could be advertised to pull customers into the store. The product won't be very good, but salespeople will be able to switch buyers up to higher-priced units. You are asked to give the green light for this stripped-down version. What would you do?
4. You are thinking of hiring a product manager who just left a competitor's company. She would be more than happy to tell you all the competitor's plans for the coming year. What would you do?
5. One of your top dealers in an important territory has had recent family troubles and his sales have slipped. It looks like it will take him a while to straighten out his family trouble. Meanwhile you are losing many sales. Legally, you can terminate the dealer's franchise and replace him. What would you do?
6. You have a chance to win a big account that will mean a lot to you and your company. The purchasing agent hints that a "gift" would influence the decision. Your assistant recommends sending a fine color television set to the buyer's home. What would you do?
7. You have heard that a competitor has a new product feature that will make a big difference in sales. The competitor will demonstrate the feature in a private dealer meeting at the annual trade show. You can easily send a snooper to this meeting to learn about the new feature. What would you do?
8. You have to choose between three ad campaigns outlined by your agency. The first (A) is a soft-sell, honest information campaign. The second (B) uses sex-loaded emotional appeals and exaggerates the product's benefits. The third (C) involves a noisy, irritating commercial that is sure to gain audience attention. Pretests show that the campaigns are effective in the following order: C, B, and A. What would you do?
9. You are interviewing a capable woman applicant for a job as salesperson. She is better qualified than the men just interviewed. At the same time, you know that some of your important customers prefer dealing with men, and you will lose some sales if you hire her. What would you do?
10. You are a sales manager in an encyclopedia company. Your competitor's salespeople are getting into homes by pretending to take a research survey. After they finish the survey, they switch to their sales pitch. This technique seems to be very effective. What would you do?

zation must follow. These policies should cover distributor relations, advertising standards, customer service, pricing, product development, and general ethical standards.

The finest guidelines cannot resolve all the difficult ethical situations the marketer faces. Table 23-1 lists some difficult ethical situations marketers could face during their careers. If marketers choose immediate sales-producing actions in all these cases, their marketing behavior might well be described as immoral or amoral. If they refuse to go along with *any* of the actions, they might be ineffective as marketing managers and unhappy because of the constant moral tension. Managers need a set of principles that will help them figure out the moral importance of each situation and how far they can go in good conscience.

But what principle should guide companies and marketing managers on issues of ethics and social responsibility? One philosophy is that such issues are decided by the free market or legal system. Under this principle, companies and their managers are not responsible for making moral judgments. Companies can in good conscience do whatever the system allows.

A second philosophy puts responsibility not with the system, but in the hands of individual companies and managers. This more enlightened philosophy suggests that a company should have a "social conscience." Companies and managers should apply high standards of ethics and morality when making corporate decisions, regardless of "what the system allows." History provides an endless list of examples of company actions that were legal and allowed but were highly irresponsible. Consider the following example:

Prior to the Pure Food and Drug Act, the advertising for a diet pill promised that a person taking this pill could eat virtually anything at any time and still lose weight. Too good to be true? Actually the claim was quite true; the product lived up to its billing with frightening efficacy. It seems that the primary active ingredient in this "diet supplement" was tapeworm larvae. These larvae would develop in the intestinal tract and, of course, be well fed; the pill taker would in time, quite literally, starve to death.[17]

Each company and marketing manager must work out a philosophy of socially responsible and ethical behavior. Under the societal marketing concept, each manager must look beyond what is legal and allowed and develop standards based on personal integrity, corporate conscience, and long-run consumer welfare. A clear and responsible philosophy will help the marketing manager deal with the many knotty questions posed by marketing and other human activities. Many industrial and professional associations have suggested codes of ethics, and many companies are now adopting their own codes of ethics and developing programs to teach managers about important ethics issues and to help them find the proper responses (see Marketing Highlight 23–3).[18]

But simply adopting a code of ethics will not solve the problem—social responsibility and ethics must be integrated into the corporate culture and the marketing management process.[19] Corporate values of profit and efficiency should be tempered by values of ethics and social responsibility. These values will then guide marketing management in setting marketing objectives, choosing target markets, developing the marketing mix, implementing marketing strategy, and controlling marketing efforts. Top management should try to create a company culture in which all employees know that the company is concerned with more than just how their actions affect profits, that it also cares about how these actions affect the environment and societal welfare.

MARKETING HIGHLIGHT 23–3

GENERAL DYNAMIC'S ETHICS PROGRAM

General Dynamic's ethics program is considered the most comprehensive in the industry. And little wonder—it was put together as generals from the Pentagon looked on. The program came about after charges that the company had deliberately overbilled the government on defense contracts.

Now at General Dynamics, a committee of board members reviews its ethics policies, and a corporate ethics director and steering group execute the ethics program. The company has set up hot lines to let any employee get instant advice on job-related ethical issues. Nearly all employees have attended ethics workshops; those for salespeople cover such topics as expense accounts and supplier relations.

The company also has a twenty-page code of ethics, which tells employees in detail how to conduct themselves. Here are some examples of rules for salespeople:

- If it becomes clear that the company must engage in unethical or illegal activity to win a contract, it will not pursue that business further.

- To prevent hidden interpretations or understandings, all information provided relative to products and services should be clear and concise.

- Receiving or soliciting gifts, entertainment, or anything else of value is prohibited.

- In countries where common practices indicate acceptance of conduct lower than that to which General Dynamics aspires, salespeople will follow the company's standards.

- Under no circumstances may an employee offer or give anything to customers or their representatives in an effort to influence them.

Source: Adapted from "This Industry Leader Means Business," *Sales and Marketing Management*, May 1987, p. 44.

Marketing executives of the 1990s will face many challenges. They will have abundant marketing opportunities because of technological advances in solar energy, home computers and robots, cable television, modern medicine, and new forms of transportation, recreation, and communication. At the same time, forces in the socio-economic environment will increase the limits under which marketing can be carried out. Those companies that are able to create new values and practice societally responsible marketing will have a world to conquer.

PRINCIPLES FOR PUBLIC POLICY TOWARD MARKETING

Finally, we want to propose several principles that might guide the formulation of public policy toward marketing and that will improve the marketing system's contribution to the quality of life. These principles reflect assumptions underlying much of modern American marketing theory and practice.

The Principle of Consumer and Producer Freedom

As much as possible, marketing decisions should be made by consumers and producers under relative freedom. Marketing freedom is important if a marketing system is to deliver a high standard of living. People can achieve satisfaction in their own terms rather than in terms defined by someone else. This freedom leads to greater fulfillment through a closer matching of products to desires. Freedom for producers and consumers is the cornerstone of a dynamic marketing system. But more principles are needed to implement this freedom and prevent abuses.

The Principle of Curbing Potential Harm

As much as possible, transactions freely entered into by producers and consumers are their private business. The political system curbs producer or consumer freedom only to prevent transactions that harm or threaten to harm the producer, consumer, or third parties. Transactional harm is a widely recognized ground for government intervention. The major issue is whether there is sufficient, actual or potential harm to justify the intervention.

The Principle of Meeting Basic Needs

The marketing system should serve disadvantaged consumers as well as affluent ones. In a free-enterprise system, producers make goods for markets that are willing and able to buy. Certain groups who lack purchasing power may go without needed goods and services, causing harm to their physical or psychological well-being. While preserving the principle of producer and consumer freedom, the marketing system should support economic and political actions to solve this problem. It should strive to meet the basic needs of all people, and all people should share to some extent in the standard of living it creates.

The Principle of Economic Efficiency

The marketing system strives to supply goods and services efficiently and at low prices. The extent to which a society's needs and wants can be satisfied depends on how efficiently its scarce resources are used. Free economies rely on active competition and informed buyers to make a market efficient. To make profits, competitors must watch their costs carefully while developing products, prices, and marketing programs that serve buyer needs. Buyers get the most satisfaction by finding out about different competing products, prices, and qualities and choosing carefully. The presence of active competition and well-informed buyers keeps quality high and prices low.

The Principle of Innovation	The marketing system encourages authentic innovation to bring down production and distribution costs and to develop new products to meet changing consumer needs. Much innovation is really imitation of other brands, with a slight difference to provide a talking point. The consumer may face ten very similar brands in a product class. But an effective marketing system encourages real product innovation and differentiation to meet the wants of different market segments.
The Principle of Consumer Education and Information	An effective marketing system invests heavily in consumer education and information to increase long-run consumer satisfaction and welfare. The principle of economic efficiency requires this investment, especially in cases where products are confusing because of their numbers and conflicting claims. Ideally, companies will provide enough information about their products. But consumer groups and the government can also give out information and ratings. Students in public schools can take courses in consumer education to learn better buying skills.
The Principle of Consumer Protection	Consumer education and information cannot do the whole job of protecting consumers. The marketing system must also provide consumer protection. Modern products are so complex that even trained consumers cannot evaluate them with confidence. Consumers do not know whether a microwave oven gives off too much radiation, whether a new automobile has safety flaws, or whether a new drug product has dangerous side effects. A government agency has to review and judge the safety levels of various foods, drugs, toys, appliances, fabrics, automobiles, and housing. Consumers may buy products but fail to understand the environmental consequences, so consumer protection also covers production and marketing activities that might harm the environment. Finally, consumer protection prevents deceptive practices and high-pressure selling techniques where consumers would be defenseless.

These seven principles are based on the assumption that marketing's goal is not to maximize company profits or total consumption or consumer choice but rather to maximize life quality. Life quality means meeting basic needs, having available many good products, and enjoying the physical and cultural environment. Properly managed, the marketing system can help to create and deliver a higher quality of life to people around the world.

■ SUMMARY

A marketing system should sense, serve, and satisfy consumer needs and improve the quality of consumers' lives. In working to meet consumer needs, marketers may take some actions that are not to everyone's liking or benefit. Marketing managers should be aware of the main criticisms.

Marketing's impact on consumer welfare has been criticized for high prices, deceptive practices, high-pressure selling, shoddy or unsafe products, planned obsolescence, and poor service to disadvantaged consumers. Marketing's impact on society has been criticized for creating false wants and too much materialism, too few social goods, cultural pollution, and too much political power. Marketing has also been accused of harming competitors and reducing competition through acquisitions, practices that create barriers to entry, and unfair competitive marketing practices.

Concerns about the marketing system have led to citizen action movements—consumerism and environmentalism. Consumerism is an organized social movement to strengthen the rights and power of consumers relative to sellers. Alert marketers view it as an opportunity to serve consumers better by providing more consumer information, education, and protection. Environmentalism is an organized social movement seeking to minimize the harm done to the environment and quality of life by marketing practices. It calls for curbing consumer wants when their satisfaction would create too much environmental cost.

Citizen action has led to the passage of many laws to protect consumers in the area of product safety, truth-in-packaging, truth-in-lending, and truth-in-advertising.

Many companies at first opposed these social movements and laws, but most of them now recognize a need for positive consumer information, education, and protection. Some companies have followed a policy of enlightened marketing based on the principles of consumer orientation, innovation, value creation, social mission, and societal orientation. Increasingly, companies are responding to the need to provide company policies and guidelines to help their managers deal with moral questions.

Future public policy must be guided by a set of principles that will improve the marketing system's contribution to the quality of life. These principles call for consumer and producer freedom, intervention only to prevent potential harm, arrangements to meet basic consumer needs adequately, the practice of economic efficiency, emphasis on authentic innovation, and the provision of consumer education, information, and protection.

■ QUESTIONS FOR DISCUSSION

1. Do you think that Gerber was right or wrong not to recall its baby food after customers complained of finding glass fragments in bottles? *Without* using hindsight, analyze the information about the situation facing Gerber in 1986, and say what action you would have recommended at the time.

2. Does distribution cost too much? If regulators limited the allowable number of levels in a channel of distribution or set a cap on the maximum markup a middleman could add to the price of a product, what impact would these practices have on consumers?

3. What evidence can you give that advertising does not add an excessive amount to the price of products? Does advertising affect marketers' willingness to innovate? Why or why not?

4. Does marketing *create* barriers to entry or *reduce* them? Describe how a small manufacturer of household cleaning products could use advertising to compete with Procter & Gamble.

5. If you were a marketing manager at Dow Chemical Company, which would you prefer: government regulations on acceptable levels of air and water pollution,

or a voluntary industry code suggesting target levels of emissions? Why?

6. Describe the five principles of enlightened marketing. Does Procter & Gamble practice these principles? Does your school? Give examples to support your answers.

7. Compare the marketing concept with the principle of societal marketing. Do you think marketers should adopt the societal marketing concept? What arguments can you give *against* the practice of societal marketing?

8. Choose three of the situations described in Table 23-1 and describe what you would do in each case. Would you make the same decision if your company were having severe financial troubles? What if your company did *not* have a policy supporting high ethical standards?

9. How well does the U.S. marketing system adhere to the principles described in the chapter? Give examples of marketing practices and companies that (a) have and (b) have not lived up to these principles.

10. If you had the power to change our marketing system in any way feasible, what improvements *would* you make? What improvements *can* you make as a consumer or entry-level marketing practitioner?

■ KEY TERMS

Consumerism An organized movement of citizens and government to improve the rights and power of buyers in relation to sellers.

Deficient products Products that have neither immediate appeal nor long-run benefits.

Desirable products Products that give both high immediate satisfaction and high long-run benefits.

Enlightened marketing A marketing philosophy that holds that the company's marketing should support the best long-run performance of the marketing system; its five principles include consumer-oriented marketing, innovative marketing, value marketing, sense-of-mission marketing, and societal marketing.

Environmentalism An organized movement of concerned citizens and government to protect and improve people's living environment.

Planned obsolescence A strategy of causing products to become obsolete before they should actually need replacement; it includes style obsolescence, functional obsolescence, and material obsolescence.

Pleasing products Products that give high immediate satisfaction but may hurt consumers in the long run.

Salutary products Products that have low appeal but benefit consumers in the long run.

■ REFERENCES

1. See Patricia Strnad, "Gerber Ignores Tylenol Textbook," *Advertising Age*, March 10, 1986, p. 3; Patricia Strnad, "Gerber Shifts Stance in 'Reassurance' Spots," *Advertising Age*, March 17, 1986, p. 8; and Felix Kessler, "Tremors from the Tylenol Scare Hit Food Companies," *Fortune*, March 31, 1986, pp. 59–62.

2. See John F. Gaski and Michael Etzel, "The Index of Consumer Sentiment Toward Marketing," *Journal of Marketing*, July 1986, pp. 71–81.

3. Excerpt from Theodore Levitt, "The Morality (?) of Advertising," *Harvard Business Review*, July–August 1970, pp. 84–92.

4. "The Breakfast of Fatties?" *Chicago Today*, July 24, 1970.

5. For more on product safety, see "Unsafe Products: The Great Debate over Blame and Punishment," *Business Week*, April 30, 1984, pp. 96–104; Michael Brody, "When Products Turn," *Fortune*, March 3, 1986, pp. 20–24; and Marisa Manley, "Product Liability: You're More Exposed Than You Think," *Harvard Business Review*, September–October 1987, pp. 28–40.

6. A speech delivered at Vanderbilt University Law School, reported in *Marketing News*, August 1, 1968, pp. 11, 15.

7. Ibid.

8. Myron Magnet, "The Money Society," *Fortune*, July 6, 1987, p. 26.

9. Ibid., p. 26. However, some social scientists predict a return to more basic values and social commitment. See Bill Barol, "The Eighties Are Over," *Newsweek*, January 4, 1988, pp. 40–48; and "Business Week's 1988 Hip Parade: Goodbye Greed, Hello Heartland," *Business Week*, January 18, 1988, p. 31.

10. From an advertisement for *Fact* magazine, which does not carry advertisements.

11. See Paul B. Brown, Zachary Schiller, Christine Dugas, and Scott Scredon, "New? Improved? The Brand-Name Mergers," *Business Week*, October 21, 1985, pp. 108–10; and Kenneth Dreyfack, "The Big Brands are Back in Style," *Business Week*, January 12, 1987, p. 74.

12. For more details, see Philip Kotler, "What Consumerism Means for Marketers," *Harvard Business Review*, May–June 1972, pp. 48–57; Paul N. Bloom and Stephen A. Greyser, "The Maturing of Consumerism," *Harvard Business Review*, November–December 1981, pp. 130–39; and Robert J. Samualson, "The Aging of Ralph Nader," *Newsweek*, December 16, 1985, p. 57.

13. See Rachel Carson, *Silent Spring* (Boston: Houghton Mifflin, 1962); Paul R. Ehrlich and Ann H. Ehrlich, *Population, Resources, Environment: Issues in Human Ecology* (San Francisco: W. H. Freeman, 1970); and Donnella H. Meadows, Dennis L. Meadows, Jorgen Randers, and William W. Behrens III, *The Limits to Growth* (New York: Universe Books, 1972).

14. Faye Rice, "The King of Suds Reigns Again," *Fortune*, August 4, 1986, p. 131.

15. Gordon O. Pehrson, quoted in "Flavored Algae from the Sea?" *Chicago Sun-Times*, February 3, 1965, p. 54.

16. Peter Drucker, "The Shame of Marketing," *Marketing/Communications*, August 1969, pp. 60, 64.

17. Dan R. Dalton and Richard A. Cosier, "The Four Faces of Social Responsibility," *Business Horizons*, May–June 1982, pp. 19–27.

18. For examples, see the American Marketing Association's code of ethics, discussed in "AMA Adopts New Code of Ethics," *Marketing News*, September 11, 1987, p. 1; and John A. Byrne, "Businesses Are Signing Up for Ethics 101," *Business Week*, February 15, 1988, pp. 56–57.

19. Donald P. Robin and R. Eric Reidenbach, "Social Responsibility, Ethics, and Marketing Strategy: Closing the Gap Between Concept and Application," *Journal of Marketing*, January 1987, pp. 44–58.

CASE 18

LIFELINE MAGAZINE

Sometimes target groups don't want to be reached. In that case, the only option is to communicate with those who can influence the target group.

That's what the National Foundation for Alcoholism Communications, Seattle, plans to do with its new magazine, *Alcoholism-Codependency-Addiction Lifeline*.

The publication should hit Waldenbooks' shelves next March. It is being billed as "America's answer book about alcoholism and addiction," focusing on prevention, treatment, and recovery.

"People and families in trouble with drugs and alcohol have many personal and pressing questions that are not being answered by public service announcements and government-sponsored campaigns," said Jerauld D. Miller, publisher and executive director of the foundation.

"Hundreds of thousands of Americans need help and answers and resources, not just political platitudes," he added. "They need a publication with names and numbers and case histories from people who have successfully kicked their habits, and we intend to make this information available to every American who needs to know."

The magazine's difficulties rest in trying to reach some of these people, namely the addicts or alcoholics themselves. Most people who have these dependencies either don't realize they have a problem or refuse to admit it exists, according to Bill Wipple, director of marketing and sales. "Our first marketing goal is to reach the addict," Wipple said. "But you can't reach the addict until he's reached the point of remorse."

This makes it almost impossible to reach most alcoholics or addicts when they need help the most. So the foundation has decided to target codependents (those who live with addicts and alcoholics) and those recovering from the diseases, he said.

The principle is similar to the one adopted by Al-Anon in its relationship to Alcoholics Anonymous (AA), Wipple said. Once codependents know the facts about the diseases and how to deal with the people suffering from the afflictions, they can set the dependents on the road to recovery.

But the magazine has an edge on Al-Anon, he said. Many codependents will not attend the group's meetings for fear that the addict will find out where they're going. A magazine is something they can use in the privacy of their offices or cars or when the dependent is not around. Besides providing education for codependents, it is hoped that addicts will find the magazines and get the clue that at least somebody thinks all is not well, Wipple said.

Codependents are not *Lifetime*'s only direct target audience, he said. The publication is also designed with recovering alcoholics and addicts in mind, partly because these people can spot others suffering from the diseases. For those going through the recovery process, the magazine features "articles of hope" about people who have pulled themselves out of the drinking or drug-use cycle.

Wipple said he believes the magazine will sell, largely because of the way it looks. It's kind of like *People*, with the first issue displaying a picture of Elizabeth Taylor on the cover and her tales of addiction inside.

It is hoped that once people are attracted to the celebrity cover, they will take note of the other articles within, including "10 Tips for Tempted Teens" and "Warning Signs of Relapse."

In addition to trying to sell the magazine to consumers, the foundation is attempting to sell it to ad agencies. To do so, the foundation is emphasizing that recovering addicts and alcoholics are a strong target market, especially for health-oriented products. "These people have a new lease on life and usually become interested in other, more healthy habits after they've given up their addictions," Wipple said.

More than 10 million books on alcoholism and other addictions were sold last year, Miller said. Millions of phone calls are logged each year by the hotlines, treatment programs, and self-help organizations. According to one Gallup survey, one out of every four American families has a member with a drug or drinking problem. Moreover, a survey conducted this summer by GMA Research Corp. indicated that among a sample of 100 recovering alcoholics and other dependents, more than 80% would buy *Lifeline*.

1. Define *Lifeline*'s target markets.

2. Can you think of any other appropriate target markets?

3. Discuss the difficulty of targeting groups that don't want to be reached.

4. If you were the advertising manager for a large consumer products company, would you consider advertising in *Lifeline*?

Source: Diane Schneidman, "New Magazine Targets A Segment That Might Not Want To Be Reached," *Marketing News*, Dec. 4, 1987. Reprinted with permission.

CASE 19

SEARS FINANCIAL NETWORK

Sears Financial Network is offering a broad range of consumer financial services through its financial network centers in nearly 300 Sears stores, with another 200 or more to be opened in the next few years. Sears is counting on attracting many of the nearly 40 million households that regularly shop at Sears to its in-store financial centers, which bring together in one location representatives of the Allstate Insurance Group, Coldwell Banker Real Estate Group, and Dean Witter Financial Services Group. In California, Sears Savings Bank is also represented. While store hours are observed, the center and its representatives operate independently of the store management, as Allstate in-store agents and concession operators (for example, optical departments) have done in the past.

Management needs to assess various potential customer groups; what consumer financial services it should offer and how they should be packaged; and how the centers and individual services should be promoted. Good planning calls for initially determining what would be sound for Sears before becoming overly concerned with legal restrictions and requirements because the latter vary from area to area and are subject to change. Good planning is especially important in this turbulent industry where changes are frequent, yet planning must be for the long haul.

Sears sees financial services as a growth opportunity suited to its capabilities and competitive strengths. Financial services are also attractive because they go beyond, but build upon, current business. Sears has continued to grow for over 100 years by finding new major growth opportunities that took the company beyond, but did not abandon, existing business. In each case, it took an outsider to provide the vision needed to see the new growth opportunity.

In the 1890s, when Richard Sears was finding it hard to keep his retail business afloat, Julius Rosenwald, a supplier of apparel to whom Sears owed money, saw an opportunity to become "buyer for the American farmer." He became a part of Sears Roebuck, and his mail-order concept launched the company on an era of tremendous prosperity.

By the 1920s, America's economic and social-structure had again changed drastically. The new growth opportunity seen by General Wood, another outsider, lay in the rapidly growing urban areas populated by an increasingly prosperous working class and a newly emerging white-collar middle class. To serve these new consumers, Wood developed a nationwide system of retail stores using the mail-order plant as jobbers and the catalog as a supplement to retail selling. A second enormously prosperous period for Sears ensued.

The American economy in its present stage is characterized by the inability of existing institutions to serve the country's growing needs for more efficient, accessible, and adequate financial and real estate services. This was seen by Arthur Wood, still another outsider who joined the firm as legal counsel and served as chairman just prior to Edward T. Telling. It was Mr. Telling who was responsible for working out the financial services concept and its implementation. The American people's confidence in Sears is perhaps its greatest asset, one that will serve the company well in fields where trust is essential.

The Sears Financial Network centers are a group of three separate but linked offices, each handling its own service—insurance, real estate, or stock and bond investments. Discounts on store merchandise are offered by Coldwell Banker in some situations. Consumer bank services are available in some California stores, and Sears is making every effort to acquire "consumer banks" so it can make this service available in other states where the legality is now in question.

J. C. Penney and K mart are in various stages of planning and offering financial centers. K Mart is considering adding several banking and brokerage services to a broad range of insurance offerings it tested in fifteen Texas and Florida stores. The exact mix of K mart in-store investment services is still being determined but "will look pretty similar to Sears," the company's executive vice-president for finance is reported to have said. In early 1985, ten "financial marts" in K mart stores were opened in the San Diego area jointly with First Nationwide, the nation's sixth-largest savings and loan. The Federal Home Loan Board approved the operation of limited-service branches in K mart stores. These branches offer money market accounts, individual retirement accounts, and short-term certificates of deposit.

In developing the full potential of the financial services opportunity, the first step is to develop each financial service independently, except for common location, common advertising, and legally permissible cross promotion. In this connection, Allstate's strategy should be considered for possible use by Coldwell Banker and Dean Witter in building business through their financial center activities.

The nucleus of the financial network is Allstate Insurance Company's strong customer base in life, home, and auto insurance, which was developed through a strategy centered on in-store company agents, who after building a list or "book" of clients, moved out into more widely dispersed new Allstate neighborhood sales offices, taking their clients with them. This opened the way for newly recruited agents, who went through the same process and thereby continued to expand the company's customer base. At present, it is not clear whether this process could or should be used with the stock brokerage or real estate services.

Financial services Sears might consider offering, or inviting concessionaires such as H&R Block to operate, are tax preparation, legal, financing planning, and asset management. Clustering these services affords a one-stop or financial supermarket arrangement, which is convenient for customers. The breadth of service available may increase the frequency of visits to the financial center. Where no Sears bank is available, "Cash Stations" or automatic tellers could be included by arrangement with a bank network, which again may increase customer convenience and frequency of visits. Other attractions can be designed for the center.

The long-term possible benefits from "bundling" financial services into a package (perhaps even including merchandise) must wait until the individual services are firmly established and the legal, competitive, and operational problems are clarified. But it is important that Sears develop several views of what the future will be like and plan how it can provide the needed individual and integrated services to consumers at a profit.

Transition plans are also necessary. Here is one possible plan. Most consumers in the Sears target group decide on specific financial transactions one at a time, with only a rough idea of an overall plan. They may seek advice from friends, relatives, lawyers, and others, but make their own decisions and administer their own affairs. There is an opportunity to develop a financial planning service to help customers coordinate their financial transactions. Trust and confidence are essential here. A *single service-based planner* such as an insurance agent or a stock broker is inclined to overemphasize his specific service and is frequently suspected of giving biased judgments. A financial planning service leads customers to other services, and if Sears can organize such a service so that customer and company *mutually benefit*, this service could become the core of the company's consumer financial services business. Ignoring for the moment any legal restrictions (which may well be lifted), plans should be developed that would be economically sound for Sears and its customers in the future.

1. What are the strengths and weaknesses of the present and suggested Sears Financial Network plans?

2. What is the underlying marketing strategy being used? Try to state it in as few words as possible.

3. What changes in the marketing aspects of the program would you recommend? Why?

CASE 20

MAYTAG COMPANY

The Maytag Company, a limited-line appliance manufacturer, has been one of the most profitable firms in the appliance business in recent years, with annual sales of over $500 million. Its basic strategy has been to make the best product and charge for it accordingly. Its sales have been primarily to the upper end of the replacement market. Neither the newly formed household market nor the builders' market has been targeted. Maytag's laundry equipment has the reputation of being trouble-free, and the company has enhanced this image by featuring "Ol' Lonely," the Maytag repairman with nothing to do, in its advertising. Changing conditions make it desirable for the company to consider whether its long-held strategy should be changed, especially in view of its recent acquisition of two cooking equipment manufacturers and the moves of industry leaders toward even fuller product lines.

Maytag acquired Hardwick Stove Company, makers and marketers of gas and electric ranges and microwave ovens sold through conventional outlets in medium- and low-price brackets. It also acquired Jenn-Air, a leading manufacturer of indoor electric barbeque grills and stove-top ventilation systems.

The cooking equipment market is fragmented and no brand is recognized as clearly a premium product. Maytag's president explained that while "cooking equipment is a mature market, it is an exciting one because product innovation is changing the traditional way people cook and broadening sales opportunities." At the same time, Maytag's entry into the cooking equipment industry is a gamble that some of its success in washers, dryers, and dishwashers will rub off on its ranges and ovens.

Maytag's laundry equipment is regarded as top of the line, but despite much effort and favorable ratings in *Consumer Reports*, many consumers and members of the industry consider its dishwasher to be second to Hobart's KitchenAid, long the leader in the high-quality, high-price niche. However, Maytag is narrowing the gap. The premium-quality niche for laundry and kitchen appliances targeted by both Maytag and KitchenAid may be eroding. Although there is no solid evidence of this, there is an increasingly frequent feeling in the trade and among consumers that while the quality difference between high-priced and medium-priced major laundry and kitchen appliances is becoming smaller, the price difference is becoming larger.

Microwave ovens for the home first caught on in the 1950s, but their growth was slow until the early 1970s. At that time microwave ovens had several problems: cooking was uneven, meats would not brown, foil-wrapped foods could not be put in the oven, few microwave cookbooks were available, and real or imagined radiation dangers were associated with microwaves. As soon as these problems were overcome, sales took off. By the late 1970s, counter-top microwave ovens were no longer considered a luxury. With more and more women working, the oven's appeal became stronger, and they are now being used in over 40 percent of U.S. households, as compared to 45 percent penetration for dishwashers. Microwave ovens, which range in price from $150 to $600, have been one of the hottest items in the appliance business. Industry forecasters foresee a penetration comparable to that of color television sets. Price competition and discounting are heavy. Premium prices are difficult to maintain.

Five of the forty or so producers of microwave ovens have well over 50 percent of the consumer market. Litton and Amana have been the leaders, but Sears, General Electric, and Sharp have been closing the gap. Maytag has a minor position in the fast-moving microwave market. Its recent acquisition of Hardwick provided no real help against the competition. Unless Maytag can find a niche where it has some competitive advantage, it is unlikely to make a profit from marketing microwave ovens.

The following are some of the major developments in the industry:

1. The structure of the major appliance industry is changing through mergers and acquisitions, with a few large full-line companies producing most of the industry output, a significant part of which is supplied to other companies for sale under their own brand names.

2. Competition, always keen in this industry, has become even more so. Low-cost producers, such as White Consolidated Industries, are constantly driving for lower costs. Heavy investments in factory automation are being made by GE and Whirlpool. Marketing efforts have been intensified, with greater emphasis on quick sales stimulants such as factory rebates, special factory-authorized sales, and additional incentives for consumers and dealers and their salespeople in the form of "spiffs."

3. Products are being designed with more electronic components to control operations. Microprocessors and other advanced technology require greater technological resources, not only for the design and manufacture of equipment, but also for service and repair. Touch-pad controls, digital readouts, more and better timers as well as flashing diagnostic readouts are being offered and readily accepted in top-of-the-line models.

4. Service is becoming a major problem. Special tools and more sophisticated service personnel are required for major repairs. Service calls are costly to make. The need for, and cost of, service calls are resented by consumers, especially when repairs are minor. Most companies would rather not be bothered with them. Few make a profit, although it is believed that the Sears service operation is profitable because of its large volume of maintenance contracts. GE and Whirlpool also have large service fleets and offer maintenance contracts. Consumer help is available from GE and Whirlpool by calling an 800 number.

5. Foreign competition now poses a serious threat. Compact refrigerators from Italy and France and microwave ovens from Japan already have significant market shares. Now a full line of full-size appliances, including refrigerators, freezers, electric ranges, dishwashers, and clothes washers and dryers, is being marketed in the United States under the Panasonic brand name. The products are made by U.S. firms, except for laundry equipment, which comes from the Far East. Sanyo is expected to follow Matsushita Electric Industrial Company, the parent of Panasonic. Two South Korean groups, Samsung and The Lucky-Goldstar, introduced low-priced compact microwave ovens to fit smaller living quarters and have done so well that they are establishing manufacturing facilities in the United States.

1. Describe Maytag's marketing mix prior to the acquisition of Hardwick Stove and Jenn-Air.

2. In what ways is Maytag's marketing mix different now than before the acquisition of Hardwick Stove and Jenn-Air?

3. Describe the target market strategy for Maytag. Discuss any changes you think should be considered.

4. Discuss the idea of a well-known, successful marketer of washers, dryers, and dishwashers adding ranges and ovens. Evaluate Maytag's decision to acquire established firms rather than developing its own products.

5. Identify other product items or lines Maytag should consider adding. Evaluate the pros and cons of each.

6. Maytag, Hardwick, and Jenn-Air each have unique marketing strategies. Should a common strategy be developed for the three brands?

1 *Marketing Arithmetic*

ONE aspect of marketing not discussed within the text is marketing arithmetic. The calculation of sales, costs, and certain ratios is important for many marketing decisions. The purpose of this appendix is to describe three major areas of marketing arithmetic: the operating statement, analytic ratios, and markups and markdowns.

OPERATING STATEMENT

The operating statement and the balance sheet are the two main financial statements used by companies. The balance sheet shows the assets, liabilities, and net worth of a company at a given time. The operating statement (also called profit and loss statement or income statement) is the more important of the two for marketing information. It shows company sales, cost of goods sold, and expenses during the time period. By comparing the operating statement from one time period to the next, the firm can spot favorable or unfavorable trends and take the appropriate action.

Table A1-1 shows the 1988 operating statement for Dale Parsons Men's Wear, a specialty store in the Midwest. This statement is for a retailer; the operating statement for a manufacturer would be somewhat different. Specifically, the section on purchases within the "cost of goods sold" area would be replaced by "cost of goods manufactured."

The outline of the operating statement follows a logical series of steps to arrive at the firm's $25,000 net profit figure:

Net sales	$300,000
Cost of goods sold	−175,000
Gross margin	$125,000
Expenses	−100,000
Net profit	$ 25,000

We will now look at major parts of the operating statement separately.

The first part of the operating statement details the amount that Parsons received for the goods the firm sold during the year. The sales figures consist of three items: gross sales, returns and allowances, and net sales. Gross sales is the total amount

TABLE A1-1
Operating Statement
for Dale Parsons Men's
Wear for the Year
Ending December 31,
1988

Gross sales			$325,000
Less: Sales returns and allowances			25,000
Net sales			$300,000
Cost of goods sold			
Beginning inventory, January 1, at cost		$ 60,000	
Gross purchases	$165,000		
Less: Purchase discounts	15,000		
Net purchases	$150,000		
Plus: Freight-in	10,000		
Net cost of delivered purchases		$160,000	
Costs of goods available for sale		$220,000	
Less: Ending inventory, December 31, at cost		$ 45,000	
Cost of goods sold			$175,000
Gross Margin			$125,000
Expenses			
Selling expenses			
Sales, salaries, and commissions	$ 40,000		
Advertising	5,000		
Delivery	5,000		
Total selling expenses		$ 50,000	
Administrative expenses			
Office salaries	$ 20,000		
Office supplies	5,000		
Miscellaneous (outside consultant)	5,000		
Total administrative expenses		$ 30,000	
General expenses			
Rent	$ 10,000		
Heat, light, telephone	5,000		
Miscellaneous (insurance, depreciation)	5,000		
Total general expenses		$ 20,000	
Total expenses			$100,000
Net profit			$ 25,000

charged to customers during the year for merchandise purchased in Parsons's store. As expected, some customers returned merchandise because of damage or a change of mind. If the customer gets a full refund or full credit on another purchase, we call this a *return*. Or the customer may decide to keep the item if Parsons will reduce the price; this is called an *allowance*. By subtracting returns and allowances from gross sales we arrive at net sales—what Parsons earned in revenue from a year of selling merchandise:

Gross sales	$325,000
Returns and allowances	−25,000
Net sales	$300,000

The second major part of the operating statement calculates the amount of sales revenue Dale Parsons has left after paying the costs of the merchandise. We start with the inventory in the store at the beginning of the year. During the year, Parsons bought $165,000 worth of suits, slacks, shirts, ties, jeans, and other goods. Suppliers gave the store discounts totaling $15,000, so that net purchases were $150,000. Because the store is located away from regular shipping routes, Parsons had to pay an additional $10,000 to get the products delivered, giving the firm a net cost of $160,000. Adding the beginning inventory, the cost of goods available for sale amounted to $220,000. The $45,000 ending inventory of clothes in the store on December 31 is then subtracted to come up with the $175,000 *cost of goods sold*. Here again we have followed a logical series of steps to figure out the cost of goods sold:

Amount Parsons started with (beginning inventory)	$ 60,000
Net amount purchased	+150,000
Any added costs to obtain these purchases	+ 10,000
Total cost of goods Parsons had available for sale during year	$220,000
Amount Parsons had left over (ending inventory)	− 45,000
Cost of goods actually sold	$175,000

The difference between what Parsons paid for the merchandise ($175,000) and what he sold it for ($300,000) is called the gross margin ($125,000).

In order to show the profit Parsons "cleared" at the end of the year, we must subtract from the gross margin the *expenses* incurred while doing business. The selling expenses included two sales employees, local newspaper and radio advertising, and the cost of delivering merchandise to customers after alterations. Selling expenses added up to $50,000 for the year. Administrative expenses included the salary for an office manager, office supplies such as stationery and business cards, and miscellaneous expenses including an administrative audit conducted by an outside consultant. Administrative expenses totaled $30,000 in 1988. Finally, the general expenses of rent, utilities, insurance, and depreciation came to $20,000. Total expenses were therefore $100,000 for the year. By subtracting expenses ($100,000) from the gross margin ($125,000), we arrive at the net profit of $25,000 for Dale Parsons Men's Wear during 1988.

*A*NALYTIC RATIOS

The operating statement provides the figures needed to compute some key ratios. Typically these ratios are called operating ratios—the ratio of selected operating statement items to net sales. They let marketers compare the firm's performance in one year to that in previous years (or to industry standards and competitors in the same year). The most commonly used operating ratios are the *gross margin percentage*, the *net profit percentage*, the *operating expense percentage*, and the *returns and allowances percentage*.

RATIO		FORMULA	COMPUTATION FROM TABLE A1-1
Gross margin percentage	=	$\dfrac{\text{gross margin}}{\text{net sales}}$	$= \dfrac{\$125,000}{\$300,000} = 42\%$
Net profit percentage	=	$\dfrac{\text{net profit}}{\text{net sales}}$	$= \dfrac{\$25,000}{\$300,000} = 8\%$
Operating expense percentage	=	$\dfrac{\text{total expenses}}{\text{net sales}}$	$= \dfrac{\$100,000}{\$300,000} = 33\%$
Returns and allowances percentages	=	$\dfrac{\text{returns and allowances}}{\text{net sales}}$	$= \dfrac{\$25,000}{\$300,000} = 8\%$

Another useful ratio is the *stockturn rate* (also called inventory turnover rate). The stockturn rate is the number of times an inventory turns over or is sold during a specified time period (often one year). It may be computed on a cost, selling, or unit price basis. Thus the formula can be:

$$\text{Stockturn rate} = \frac{\text{cost of goods sold}}{\text{average inventory at cost}}$$

or

$$\text{Stockturn rate} = \frac{\text{selling price of goods sold}}{\text{average selling price of inventory}}$$

or

$$\text{Stockturn rate} = \frac{\text{sales in units}}{\text{average inventory in units}}$$

We will use the first formula to calculate the stockturn rate for Dale Parsons Men's Wear:

$$\frac{\$175,000}{\frac{\$60,000 + \$45,000}{2}} = \frac{\$175,000}{\$52,500} = 3.3$$

That is, Parsons's inventory turned over 3.3 times in 1988. Normally the higher the stockturn rate, the higher the management efficiency and company profitability.

Return on investment (ROI) is frequently used to measure managerial effectiveness. It uses figures from the firm's operating statement and balance sheet. A commonly used formula for computing ROI is:

$$\text{ROI} = \frac{\text{net profit}}{\text{sales}} \times \frac{\text{sales}}{\text{investment}}$$

You may have two questions about this formula: Why use a two-step process when ROI could be computed simply as net profit divided by investment? And what exactly is "investment"?

To answer these questions, let's look at how each component of the formula can affect the ROI. Suppose Dale Parsons Men's Wear computed ROI as follows:

$$\text{ROI} = \frac{\$25,000 \text{ (net profit)}}{\$300,000 \text{ (sales)}} \times \frac{\$300,000 \text{ (sales)}}{\$150,000 \text{ (investment)}}$$

$$8.3\% \quad \times \quad 2 \quad = 16.6\%$$

Now, suppose that Parsons had worked to increase its share of the market. The firm could have had the same ROI if sales doubled while dollar profit and investment stayed the same (accepting a lower profit ratio to get a higher turnover and market share):

$$\text{ROI} = \frac{\$25,000 \text{ (net profit)}}{\$600,000 \text{ (sales)}} \times \frac{\$600,000 \text{ (sales)}}{\$150,000 \text{ (investment)}}$$

$$4.16\% \quad \times \quad 4 \quad = 16.6\%$$

Parsons might have increased its ROI by increasing net profit through more cost cutting and more efficient marketing:

$$\text{ROI} = \frac{\$50,000 \text{ (net profit)}}{\$300,000 \text{ (sales)}} \times \frac{\$300,000 \text{ (sales)}}{\$150,000 \text{ (investment)}}$$

$$16.6\% \quad \times \quad 2 \quad = 33.2\%$$

Another way to increase ROI is to find some way to get the same levels of sales and profits while decreasing investment (perhaps by cutting the size of Parsons' average inventory):

$$ROI = \frac{\$25{,}000 \text{ (net profit)}}{\$300{,}000 \text{ (sales)}} \times \frac{\$300{,}000 \text{ (sales)}}{\$75{,}000 \text{ (investment)}}$$

$$8.3\% \qquad \times \qquad 4 \qquad = 33.2\%$$

What is "investment" in the ROI formula? Investment is often defined as the total assets of the firm. But many analysts now use other measures of return to assess performance. These measures include return on net assets (RONA), return on stockholders equity (ROE), or return on assets managed (ROAM). Since investment is measured at a point in time, we usually compute ROI as the average investment between two time periods (say, January 1 and December 31 of the same year). We can also compute ROI as an "internal rate of return" by using discounted cash flow analysis (see any finance textbook for more on this technique). The objective in using any of these measures is to figure out how well the company has been using its resources. As inflation, competitive pressures, and cost of capital increase, the measures become increasingly important indicators of marketing and company performance.

MARKUPS AND MARKDOWNS

Retailers and wholesalers must understand the concepts of markups and markdowns. They must make a profit to stay in business, and the markup percentage affects profits. Markups and markdowns are expressed as percentages.

There are two different ways to compute markups—on *cost* or on selling *price*:

$$\text{Markup percentage on cost} = \frac{\text{dollar markup}}{\text{cost}}$$

$$\text{Markup percentage on selling price} = \frac{\text{dollar markup}}{\text{selling price}}$$

Dale Parsons must decide which formula to use. If Parsons bought shirts for $15 and wanted to mark them up $10, the markup percentage on cost would be $10/$15 = 67.7%. If Parsons based markup on selling price, the percentage would be $10/$25 = 40%. In figuring markup percentage, most retailers use the selling price rather than the cost.

Suppose Parsons knew the cost ($12) and desired markup on price (25%) for a man's tie and wanted to compute the selling price. The formula is:

Selling price = cost ÷ (1 − markup)
Selling price = $12 ÷ .75 = $16

As a product moves through the channel of distribution, each channel member adds a markup before selling the product to the next member. This "markup chain" is shown for a suit purchased by a Parsons customer for $200:

		$ AMOUNT	% OF SELLING PRICE
	Cost	$108	90%
Manufacturer	Markup	12	10%
	Selling price	$120	100%
	Cost	$120	80%
Wholesaler	Markup	30	20%
	Selling price	$150	100%
	Cost	$150	75%
Retailer	Markup	50	25%
	Selling price	$200	100%

The retailer whose markup is 25 percent does not necessarily enjoy more profit than a manufacturer whose markup is 10 percent. Profit also depends on how many items with that profit margin can be sold (stockturn rate) and on operating efficiency (expenses).

Sometimes a retailer wants to convert markups based on selling price to markups based on cost, and vice versa. The formulas are:

$$\text{Markup percentage on selling price} = \frac{\text{markup percentage on cost}}{100\% + \text{markup percentage on cost}}$$

$$\text{Markup percentage on cost} = \frac{\text{markup percentage on selling price}}{100\% - \text{markup percentage on selling price}}$$

Suppose that Dale Parsons found that a competitor was using a markup of 30 percent based on cost and wanted to know what this would be as a percentage of selling price. The calculation would be:

$$\frac{30\%}{100\% + 30\%} = \frac{30\%}{130\%} = 23\%$$

Since Parsons was using a 25 percent markup on the selling price for suits, he felt that the markup was suitable compared to that of the competitor.

Near the end of the summer Parsons still had an inventory of summer slacks in stock. Thus he decided to use a *markdown*, a reduction from the original selling price. Before the summer he had purchased twenty pairs at $10 each and had since sold ten pairs at $20 each. Parsons marked down the other pairs to $15 and sold five pairs. We compute the markdown ratio as follows:

$$\text{Markdown percentage} = \frac{\text{dollar markdown}}{\text{total net sales in dollars}}$$

The dollar markdown is $25 (5 pairs at $5 each) and total net sales are $275 (10 pairs at $20 + 5 pairs at $15). The ratio, then, is $25/$275 = 9%.

Larger retailers usually compute markdown ratios for each department rather than for individual items. The ratios provide a measure of relative marketing performance for each department and can be calculated and compared over time. Markdown ratios can also be used to compare the performance of different buyers and salespeople in a store's various departments.

2 *Careers in Marketing*

NOW that you have completed your first course in marketing, you have a good idea of what this field entails. You may have decided that you want to pursue a marketing career because it offers constant challenge, stimulating problems, work with people, and excellent advancement opportunities. Marketing is a broad field with a wide variety of tasks involving the analysis, planning, implementation, and control of marketing programs. You will find marketing positions in all types and sizes of institutions. This appendix will acquaint you with entry-level and higher-level marketing opportunities and list steps you might take to select a career path and better market yourself.

*D*ESCRIPTION OF MARKETING JOBS

Almost a third of all Americans are employed in marketing-related positions. The number of possible marketing careers is enormous. Because of the knowledge of products and consumers gained in these jobs, marketing positions provide excellent training for the highest levels in the organization. A recent study by an executive recruiting firm found that more top executives have come out of marketing than out of any other field—31 percent of the *Fortune* 1000 chief executives spent the bulk of their careers in marketing.[1]

Marketing salaries vary by company and position. Starting marketing salaries usually rank only slightly below those for engineering and chemistry and equal or exceed those for economics, finance, accounting, general business, and the liberal arts. If you succeed in an entry-level marketing position, you will quickly be promoted to higher levels of responsibility and salary.

Marketing has become an attractive career for some people who have not traditionally considered this field. One trend is the growing number of women entering marketing. Women have historically been employed in the retailing and advertising areas of marketing. But they have now moved into all types of sales and marketing positions. Women now pursue very successful sales careers in pharmaceutical companies, publishing companies, banks, consumer products companies, and an increasing number of industrial selling jobs. Their ranks are also growing in product and brand manager positions.

Another trend is the growing acceptance of marketing by nonprofit organizations. Colleges, arts organizations, libraries, and hospitals are increasingly applying marketing to their problems. They are beginning to hire marketing directors and marketing vice-presidents to manage their varied marketing activities.

Here are brief descriptions of some important marketing jobs.

Advertising

Advertising is an important business activity that requires skill in planning, fact gathering, and creativity. Although compensation for starting advertising people tends to be lower than that in other marketing fields, opportunities for advancement in advertising are usually greater because of less emphasis on age or length of employment. Typical jobs in advertising agencies are described below.[2]

Copywriters help find the concepts behind the written words and visual images of advertisements. They dig for facts, read avidly, and borrow ideas. They talk to customers, suppliers, and *anybody* who might give them clues about how to attract the target audience's attention and interest.

Art directors are the other part of the creative team. They translate copywriters' ideas into dramatic visuals called "layouts." Ad agency artists develop print layouts, package designs, television layouts (called "storyboards"), corporate logotypes, trademarks, and symbols. They specify style and size of typography, paste the type in place, and arrange all details of the ad so that it can be reproduced by engravers and printers. A very good art director or copy chief becomes the agency's creative director and oversees all the agency's advertising. The creative director is high in the ad agency's structure.

Account executives are the liaison between client and agency. They must know a lot about marketing and its components. They explain client plans and objectives to agency creative teams and supervise the development of the total advertising plan. Their main task is to keep the client happy with the agency! Because "account work" involves many personal relationships, account executives are usually personable, diplomatic, and sincere.

Media buyers select the best media for clients. Media representatives come to the buyer's office armed with statistics to prove that *their* numbers are better, *their* costs per thousand are less, and *their* medium delivers more ripe audiences than competitive media. Media buyers have to evaluate these claims. They must also bargain with the broadcast media for best rates and make deals with the print media for good ad positions.

Large ad agencies have active marketing research departments that provide market information needed to develop new ad campaigns and assess current campaigns. People interested in marketing research should consider jobs with ad agencies.

Brand and Product Management

Brand and product managers plan, direct, and control business and marketing efforts for their products. They are concerned with research and development, packaging, manufacturing, sales and distribution, advertising, promotion, market research, and business analysis and forecasting. In consumer goods companies, the newcomer (who usually needs an MBA) joins a brand team and learns the ropes by doing numerical analyses and watching the senior brand people. This person eventually heads the team and later moves on to manage a larger brand. Many industrial goods companies also have product managers. Product management is one of the best training grounds for future corporate officers.

Customer Affairs

Some large consumer goods companies have customer affairs people who act as a liaison between the customer and the firm. They handle complaints, suggestions, and problems concerning the company's products, determine what action to take, and coordinate the activities required to solve the problem. The position requires an empathetic, diplomatic, and capable person who can work with a wide range of people inside and outside the firm.

Industrial Marketing

People interested in industrial marketing careers can go into sales, service, product design, marketing research, or one of several other positions. They sometimes need a technical background. Most people start in sales and spend time in training and making calls with senior salespeople. If they stay in sales, they may advance to district, regional, and higher sales positions. Or they may go into product management and work closely with customers, suppliers, manufacturing, and sales engineering.

International Marketing

As U.S. firms increase their international business, they need people who are familiar with foreign languages and cultures and who are willing to travel to or relocate in foreign cities. For such assignments, most companies seek experienced people who have proved themselves in domestic operations. An MBA often helps but is not always required.

Marketing Management Science and Systems Analysis

People who have been trained in management science, quantitative methods, and systems analysis can act as consultants to managers facing difficult marketing problems such as demand measurement and forecasting, market structure analysis, and new product evaluation. Career opportunities exist mostly in larger marketing-oriented firms, management consulting firms, and public institutions concerned with health, education, or transportation. An MBA or an MS is often required.

Marketing Research

Marketing researchers interact with managers to define problems and identify the information needed to resolve them. They design research projects, prepare questionnaires and samples, analyze data, prepare reports, and present their findings and recommendations to management. They must understand statistics, consumer behavior, psychology, and sociology. A master's degree helps. Career opportunities exist with manufacturers, retailers, some wholesalers, trade and industry associations, marketing research firms, advertising agencies, and governmental and private nonprofit agencies.

New Product Planning

People interested in new product planning can find opportunities in many types of organizations. They usually need a good background in marketing, marketing research, and sales forecasting; they need organizational skills to motivate and coordinate others; and they may need a technical background. Usually the person works first in other marketing positions before joining the new product department.

Physical Distribution

Physical distribution is a large and dynamic field, with many career opportunities. Major transportation carriers, manufacturers, wholesalers, and retailers all employ physical distribution specialists. Coursework in quantitative methods, finance, accounting, and marketing will provide students with the necessary skills for entering the field.

Public Relations

Most organizations have a public relations person or staff to anticipate public problems, handle complaints, deal with media, and build the corporate image. People interested in public relations should be able to speak and write clearly and persuasively and should preferably have a background in journalism, communications, or the liberal arts. The challenges in this job are highly varied and very people-oriented.

Purchasing Purchasing agents are playing a growing role in firms' profitability during periods of rising costs, materials shortages, and increasing product complexity. In retail organizations, the job of purchasing agent—"buyer"—can be a good route to the top. Purchasing agents in industrial companies play a key role in holding down costs. A technical background is useful in some purchasing positions, along with a knowledge of credit, finance, and physical distribution.

Retailing Management Retailing provides people with an early opportunity to take on marketing responsibilities. Although retail starting salaries and job assignments have been lower than those in manufacturing or advertising, the gap is narrowing. The major routes to top management in retailing are merchandise management and store management. In merchandise management, a person moves from buyer trainee to assistant buyer to buyer to merchandise division manager. In store management, the person moves from management trainee to assistant department (sales) manager to department manager to store (branch) manager. Buyers are primarily concerned with merchandise selection and promotion; department managers are concerned with salesforce management and display. Large-scale retailing lets new recruits move in only a few years into the management of a branch or part of a store doing as much as $5 million in sales.

Sales and Sales Management Sales and sales management opportunities exist in a wide range of profit and nonprofit organizations and in product and service organizations, including financial, insurance, consulting, and government. People must carefully match their backgrounds, interests, technical skills, and academic training with available sales jobs. Training programs vary greatly in form and length, ranging from a few weeks to two years. Career paths lead from salesperson to district, regional, and higher levels of sales management, and in many cases, the top management of the firm.

Other Marketing Careers There are many other marketing-related jobs in areas such as sales promotion, wholesaling, packaging, pricing, and credit management. Information on these positions can be gathered from sources listed below.

CHOOSING AND GETTING A JOB

To choose and obtain a job, you must apply marketing skills, particularly marketing analysis and planning. Here are eight steps for choosing a career and finding that first job.

Make a Self-Assessment Self-assessment is the most important part of a job search. It involves honestly evaluating your interests, strengths, and weaknesses. What are your career objectives? What kind of organization do you want to work for? What do you do well and not so well? What sets you apart from other job seekers? Do the answers to these questions suggest which careers you should seek or avoid? For help in self-assessment, you might look at the following books, which raise many questions to consider:

1. *What Color Is Your Parachute?*, by Richard Bolles
2. *Three Boxes in Life and How to Get Out of Them*, by Richard Bolles
3. *Guerrilla Tactics in the Job Market*, by Tom Jackson

Also consult the career counseling, testing, and placement services at your school.

Examine Job Descriptions	Now look at various job descriptions to see what positions best match your interests, desires, and abilities. Descriptions can be found in the *Occupation Outlook Handbook* and the *Dictionary of Occupational Titles* published by the U.S. Department of Labor. These volumes describe what people in various occupations do, the specific training and education needed, the availability of jobs in each field, possibilities for advancement, and probable earnings.

Develop Job-Search Objectives

Your initial career shopping list should be broad and flexible. Look broadly for ways to achieve your objectives. For example, if you want a career in marketing research, consider the public as well as the private sector, and regional as well as national firms. Only after exploring many options should you begin to focus on specific industries and initial jobs. You need to set down a list of basic goals. Your list might say: "a job in a small company, in a large city, in the Sunbelt, doing marketing research, with a consumer products firm."

Examine the Job Market and Assess Opportunities

You must now look at the market to see what positions are available. For an up-to-date listing of marketing-related job openings, refer to the latest edition of the *College Placement Annual* available at school placement offices. This publication shows current job openings for hundreds of companies seeking college graduates for entry-level positions. It also lists companies seeking experienced or advanced-degree people. Use the services of your placement office to the fullest extent at this stage to find openings and set up interviews. Take the time to analyze the industries and companies in which you are interested. Consult business magazines, annual reports, business reference books, faculty members, school career counselors, and fellow students. Try to analyze the future growth and profit potential of the company and industry, chances for advancement, salary levels, entry positions, amount of travel, and other important factors.

Develop Search Strategies

How will you contact companies in which you are interested? There are several possible ways. One of the best ways is through on-campus interviews. But not all the companies that interest you will visit your school. Another good way is to phone or write the company directly. Finally, you can ask marketing professors or school alumni for contacts and references.

Develop Résumé and Cover Letter

Your resumé should persuasively present your abilities, education, background, training, work experience, and personal qualifications—but it also should be brief, usually one page. Its goal is to gain a positive response from potential employers.

The cover letter is, in some ways, more difficult to write than the resumé. It must be persuasive, professional, concise, and interesting. Ideally, it should set you apart from the other candidates for the position. Each letter should look and sound original, that is, individually typed and tailored to the specific organization being contacted. It should describe the position you are applying for, arouse interest, describe your qualifications, and tell how you can be contacted. Cover letters should be addressed to an individual rather than a title. You should follow up the letter with a telephone call.

Obtain Interviews

Here is some advice to follow before, during, and after your interviews.

Before the Interview

1. Interviewers have extremely diverse styles—the "chit chat, let's-get-to-know-each-other style"; the interrogation style of question after question; the tough-probing "why, why, why" style; and many others. Be ready for anything.

2. Practice being interviewed with a friend, and ask for a critique.

3. Prepare to ask at least five good questions that are not readily answered in the company literature.

4. Anticipate possible interview questions and prepare good answers ahead of time.

5. Avoid back-to-back interviews—they can be exhausting.

6. Dress conservatively and tastefully for the interview. Be neat and clean.

7. Arrive about ten minutes early to collect your thoughts before the interview. Check your name on the interview schedule, noting the name of the interviewer and the room number.

8. Review the major points you intend to cover.

During the Interview

1. Give a firm handshake in greeting the interviewer. Introduce yourself using the same form the interviewer uses. Make a good initial impression.

2. Retain your poise. Relax. Smile occasionally. Be enthusiastic throughout the interview.

3. Good eye contact, good posture, and distinct speech are musts. Don't clasp your hands or fiddle with jewelry, hair, or clothing. Sit comfortably in your chair. Do not smoke, even if asked.

4. Have extra copies of your resume with you.

5. Have your story down pat. Present your selling points. Answer questions directly. Avoid one-word answers, but don't be wordy.

6. Most times, let the interviewer take the initiative, but don't be passive. Find a good opportunity to direct the conversation to things you want the interviewer to hear.

7. The latter part of the interview is the best time to make your most important point or to ask a pertinent question, in order to end on a high note.

8. Don't be afraid to "close." You might say, "I'm very interested in the position and I have enjoyed this interview."

After the Interview

1. After leaving the interview, record the key points. Be sure to record who is to follow up on the interview and when a decision can be expected.

2. Objectively analyze the interview with regard to the questions asked, the answers given, your overall interview presentation, and the interviewer's response to specific points.

3. Send a thank-you letter mentioning any additional things and your willingness to supply further information.

4. If you do not hear within the time specified, write or call the interviewer to determine your status.

Follow-up   If you are successful in the initial interview, you will be invited to visit the organization. The in-company interview will run from a few hours to a whole day, and you may meet people from several departments. The company will examine your interest, maturity, enthusiasm, assertiveness, logic, and company and functional knowledge. You should ask questions about things that are important to you. Find out about the environment, job role, responsibilities, opportunity, current industrial issues, and the firm's personality. The company wants to find out if you are the right person for the job; and, as important, you want to find out if this is the right job for you.

■ REFERENCES

1. See E. S. Ely, "Room at the Top: American Companies Turn to Marketers to Lead Them Through the Eighties," *Madison Avenue*, September 1984, p. 57.

2. This description of advertising positions is based on Jack Engel, *Advertising: The Process and Practice* (New York: McGraw-Hill, 1980), pp. 429–34.

Glossary

Action program A detailed program that shows what must be done, who will do it, and how decisions and actions will be coordinated to implement marketing plans and strategy.

Administered VMS A vertical marketing system that co-ordinates successive stages of production and distribution, not through common ownership or contractual ties, but through the size and power of one of the parties.

Adoption The decision by an individual to become a regular user of a product.

Adoption process The mental process through which an individual passes from first hearing about an innovation to final adoption.

Advertising Any paid form of nonpersonal presentation and promotion of ideas, goods, or services by an identified sponsor.

Advertising goal A specific communication *task* to be accomplished with a specific *target* audience in a specific period of *time*.

Affordable method Setting the promotion budget at what management thinks the company can afford.

Agent A wholesaler who represents buyers or sellers on a more permanent basis, performs only a few functions, and does not take title to goods.

Alternative evaluation The stage of the buyer decision process in which the consumer uses information to evaluate alternative brands in the choice set.

Annual plan control Evaluation and corrective action to ensure that the company achieves the sales, profits, and other goals set out in its annual plan.

Atmospheres Designed environments that create or re-inforce the buyer's leanings toward buying a product.

Attitude A person's consistently favorable or unfavorable evaluations, feelings, and tendencies toward an object or idea.

Automatic vending Selling through vending machines.

Available market The set of consumers who have inter-est, income, and access to a particular product or service.

Baby boom The major increase in the annual birthrate following World War II and lasting until the early 1960s. The "baby boomers," now moving into middle age, are a prime target for marketers.

Basing-point pricing A geographic pricing strategy in which the seller designates some city as a basing point and charges all customers the freight cost from that city to the customer location, regardless of the city from which the goods are actually shipped.

BCG growth-share matrix A portfolio planning method that evaluates a company's strategic business units in terms of their market growth rate and relative market share. SBUs are classified as stars, cash cows, question marks, or dogs.

Behavior segmentation Dividing a market into groups based on their knowledge, attitude, use, or response to a product.

Belief A descriptive thought that a person holds about something.

Brand A name, term, sign, symbol, or design, or a combi-nation of them, intended to identify the goods or services of one seller or group of sellers and to differentiate them from those of competitors.

Brand image The set of beliefs consumers hold about a particular product.

Brand mark That part of a brand that can be recognized but is not utterable, such as a symbol, design, or distinctive coloring or lettering.

Brand name That part of a brand that can be vocalized—the utterable.

Breakeven pricing Setting price to break even on the costs of making and marketing a product or to make the desired profit. Also called target profit pricing.

Broker A wholesaler who does not take title to goods and whose function is to bring buyers and sellers together and assist in negotiation.

Business analysis A review of the sales, costs, and profit projections for a new product to find out whether they satisfy the company's objectives.

Business portfolio The collection of businesses and products that make up the company.

Buyer readiness states The stages consumers normally pass through on their way to purchase, including awareness, knowledge, liking, preference, conviction, or purchase.

Buyers People who make an actual purchase. People in an organization's buying center with formal authority to select the supplier and arrange terms of purchase; they may help shape product specifications but play their major role in selecting vendors and negotiating.

Buying center All the individuals and groups who participate in the buying decision process, who share common goals and the risks arising from the decisions.

Capital items Industrial goods that enter the finished product partly, including installations and accessory equipment.

Cash cows Low-growth, high-share businesses or products—established and successful units that generate cash which the company uses to pay its bills and support other business units that need investment.

Cash discount A price reduction to buyers who pay their bills promptly.

Catalog showroom A retail operation that sells a wide selection of high-markup, fast-moving, brand-name goods at discount prices.

Causal research Marketing research to test hypotheses about cause-and-effect relationships.

Chain stores Two or more outlets that are commonly owned and controlled, have central buying and merchandising, and sell similar lines of merchandise.

Company culture A system of values and beliefs shared by people in an organization; the company's collective identity and meaning.

Company marketing environment The actors and forces outside of marketing that affect marketing management's ability to develop and maintain successful transactions with its target customers.

Company marketing opportunity An attractive arena for marketing action in which the company would enjoy a competitive advantage.

Comparison advertising Advertising that compares one brand directly or indirectly to one or more other brands.

Competitive advantage An advantage over competitors gained by offering consumers lower prices than competitors for similar products or by providing more benefits that justify higher prices.

Competitive-parity method Setting the promotion budget to match competitors' outlays.

Competitive strategies Strategies that strongly position the company against competitors and that give the company the strongest possible strategic advantage.

Competitor analysis The process of identifying key competitors; assessing their objectives, strategies, strengths and weaknesses, and reaction patterns; and selecting which competitors to attack or to avoid.

Competitor-centered company A company whose moves are mainly based on competitors' actions and reactions; it spends most of its time tracking competitors' moves and market shares and trying to find strategies to counter them.

Concentrated marketing A market-coverage strategy in which the company goes after a large share of one or a few submarkets.

Concept testing Testing new product concepts with a group of target consumers to find out if the concept has strong consumer appeal.

Consumer cooperative A retail firm that is owned by its customers.

Consumer goods Goods bought by final consumers for personal consumption.

Consumer market All the individuals and households who buy or acquire goods and services for personal consumption.

Consumer promotion Sales promotion designed to stimulate consumer purchasing, including samples, coupons, rebates, prices-off, premiums, patronage rewards, displays, and contests and sweepstakes.

Consumerism An organized movement of citizens and government to improve the rights and power of buyers in relation to sellers.

Containerization Putting goods in boxes or trailers that are easy to transfer between two transportation modes. They are used in "multimode" systems commonly referred to as piggyback, fishyback, trainship, and airtruck.

Continuity Scheduling ads evenly within a given period.

Contract manufacturing Joint-venturing to enter a foreign market by contracting with manufacturers in the foreign market to produce the product.

Contractual VMS A vertical marketing system in which independent firms at different levels of production and distribution join together through contracts to obtain more economies or sales impact than they could achieve alone.

Convenience goods Consumer goods that the customer usually buys frequently, immediately, and with a minimum of comparison and buying effort.

Convenience store A small store, located near a residential area, open long hours seven days a week, and carrying a limited line of high-turnover convenience goods.

Conventional distribution channel A channel consisting of the independent producer(s), wholesaler(s), and retailer(s), each a separate business seeking to maximize its own profits, even at the expense of profits for the system as a whole.

Copyright The exclusive legal right to reproduce, publish, and sell the matter and form of a literary, musical, or artistic work.

Copy testing Measuring the communication effect of an advertisement before or after it is printed or broadcast.

Corporate VMS A vertical marketing system that combines successive stages of production and distribution under single ownership; channel leadership is established through common ownership.

Cost-plus pricing Setting price by adding a standard markup to the cost of a product.

Countertrade International trade involving the direct or indirect exchange of goods for other goods instead of cash. Forms include barter, compensation (buy-back), and counterpurchase.

Cultural environment Institutions and other forces that affect society's basic values, perceptions, preferences, and behaviors.

Culture The set of basic values, perceptions, wants, and behaviors learned by a member of society from family and other important institutions.

Customer-centered company A company that focuses on customer developments in designing its marketing strategies.

Customer salesforce structure A salesforce organization under which salespeople specialize in selling only to certain customers or industries.

Customer value analysis Analysis conducted to determine what benefits target customers value and how they rate the relative value of various competitors' offers.

Customized marketing mix An international marketing strategy of adjusting the marketing mix elements to each international target market, bearing more costs but hoping for a larger market share and return.

Deciders The people who ultimately make a buying decision or any part of it—whether to buy, what to buy, how to buy, or where to buy; people in an organization's buying center who have formal or informal power to select or approve the final suppliers.

Decline stage The product life-cycle stage in which a product's sales decline.

Deficient products Products that have neither immediate appeal nor long-run benefits.

Demand curve A curve that shows the number of units the market will buy in a given time period at different prices that might be charged.

Demands Human wants that are backed by buying power.

Demographic segmentation Dividing the market into groups based on demographic variables such as age, sex, family size, family life cycle, income, occupation, education, religion, race, and nationality.

Demography The study of human populations in terms of size, density, location, age, sex, race, occupation, and other statistics.

Department store A retail organization that carries a wide variety of product lines—typically clothing, home furnishings, and household goods; each line is operated as a separate department managed by specialist buyers or merchandisers.

Descriptive research Marketing research to better describe marketing problems, situations, or markets—such as the market potential for a product or the demographics and attitudes of consumers.

Desirable products Products that give both high immediate satisfaction and high long-run benefits.

Differentiated marketing A market-coverage strategy in which a company decides to target several segments and designs separate offers for each.

Direct investment Entering a foreign market by developing foreign-based assembly or manufacturing facilities.

Direct marketing Marketing through various advertising media that interact directly with consumers, generally calling for the consumer to make a direct response.

Discount store A retail institution that sells standard merchandise at lower prices by accepting lower margins and selling higher volume.

Discriminatory pricing Selling a product or service at two or more prices, where the difference in prices is not based on differences in costs.

Distribution center A large and highly automated warehouse designed to receive goods from various plants and suppliers, take orders, fill them efficiently, and deliver goods to customers as quickly as possible.

Distribution channel The set of firms and individuals that take title, or assist in transferring title, to a good or service as it moves from the producer to the final consumer or industrial user.

Diversification A strategy for company growth by starting up or acquiring businesses outside the company's current products and markets.

Dogs Low-growth, low-share businesses and products that may generate enough cash to maintain themselves, but do not promise to be a large source of cash.

Door-to-door retailing Selling door-to-door, office-to-office, or at home sales parties.

Durable goods Tangible goods that normally survive many uses.

Economic community A group of nations organized to work toward common goals in the regulation of international trade; an example is the European Economic Community (EEC or Common Market).

Economic environment Factors that affect consumer purchasing power and spending patterns.

Embargo A ban on the import of a certain product.

Emotional appeals Message appeals that attempt to stir up negative or positive emotions that will motivate purchase; examples include fear, guilt, shame, love, humor, pride, and joy appeals.

Enlightened marketing A marketing philosophy that holds that the company's marketing should support the best long-run performance of the marketing system; its five principles include consumer-oriented marketing, innovative marketing, value marketing, sense-of-mission marketing, and societal marketing.

Environmentalism An organized movement of concerned citizens and government to protect and improve people's living environment.

Events Designed occurrences that communicate messages to target audiences, such as news conferences, grand openings, or others.

Exchange The act of obtaining a desired object from someone by offering something in return.

Exclusive distribution Giving a limited number of dealers the exclusive right to distribute a company's products in their territories.

Experience curve The drop in the average per-unit production cost that comes with accumulated production experience. Also called the learning curve.

Experimental research The gathering of primary data by selecting matched groups of subjects, giving them different treatments, controlling related factors, and checking for differences in group responses.

Exploratory research Marketing research to gather preliminary information that will help to better define problems and suggest hypotheses.

Exporting Entering a foreign market by exporting products and selling them through international marketing middlemen (indirect exporting) or through the company's own department, branch, or salespeople or agents (direct exporting).

Extensive problem solving Buyer behavior in cases where buyers face complex buying decisions for more expensive, less frequently purchased products in an unfamiliar product class. Buyers engage in extensive information search and evaluation.

Fixed costs Costs that do not vary with production or sales level. Also called overhead.

FOB origin pricing A geographic pricing strategy in which goods are placed free on board a carrier, and the customer pays the freight from the factory to the destination.

Focus group interviewing Personal interviewing that consists of inviting six to ten people to gather for a few hours with a trained interviewer to talk about a product, service, or organization. The interviewer "focuses" the group discussion on important issues.

Forecasting The art of estimating future market demand by anticipating what buyers are likely to do under a given set of conditions.

Franchise A contractual association between a manufacturer, wholesaler, or service organization (a franchiser) and independent businesspeople (franchisees) who buy the right to own and operate one or more units in the franchise system.

Freight absorption pricing A geographic pricing strategy in which the company absorbs all or part of the actual freight charges in order to get the business.

Frequency The number of times the average person in the target market is exposed to an advertising message during a given period.

Functional discount A price reduction offered by the seller to trade channel members who perform certain functions such as selling, storing, and recordkeeping.

Functional organization An organization structure in which marketing specialists are in charge of different marketing activities or functions such as advertising, marketing research, sales management, and others.

Gatekeepers People in an organization's buying center who control the flow of information to others.

GE strategic business-planning grid A portfolio planning method that evaluates a company's strategic business units using indexes of industry attractiveness and the company's strength in the industry.

Geographic organization An organization structure in which a company's national salesforce (and perhaps other functions) specializes by geographic area.

Geographic segmentation Dividing a market into different geographical units such as nations, states, regions, counties, cities, or neighborhoods.

Going-rate pricing Setting price based largely on following competitors' prices rather than on company costs or demand.

Government market Governmental units—federal, state, and local—that purchase or rent goods and services for carrying out the main functions of government.

Growth stage The product life-cycle stage in which sales start climbing quickly.

Horizontal marketing system A channel arrangement in which two or more nonrelated companies at one level join together to follow a new marketing opportunity.

Human need A state of felt deprivation in a person.

Human want The form that a human need takes as shaped by culture and individual personality.

Idea generation The systematic search for new product ideas.

Idea screening Screening new product ideas in order to spot good ideas and drop poor ones as soon as possible.

Industrial goods Goods bought by individuals and organizations for further processing or for use in conducting a business.

Industrial market All the individuals and organizations that acquire goods and services that enter into the production of other products and services that are sold, rented, or supplied to others.

Industry The set of all sellers of a product. A group of firms that offer a product or class of products that are close substitutes for each other.

Influencers People whose advice or views carry some weight in making a final buying decision. People in an organiztion's buying center who affect the buying decision; they often help define specifications and also provide information for evaluating alternatives.

Information search The stage of the buyer decision process in which the consumer is aroused to search for more information; the consumer may simply have heightened attention or may go into active information search.

Initiator The person who first suggests or thinks of the idea of buying a particular product or service.

Inseparability A major characteristic of services—they are produced and consumed at the same time and cannot be separated from their providers, whether the providers are persons or machines.

Intangibility A major characteristic of services—they cannot be seen, tasted, felt, heard, or smelled before they are bought.

Intensive distribution Stocking a product in as many outlets as possible.

Introduction stage The product life cycle stage in which the new product is first distributed and made available for purchase.

Joint ownership Entering a foreign market by joining with foreign investors to create a local business in which the company shares joint ownership and control.

Joint venturing Entering foreign markets by joining with companies in the foreign country to produce or market a product or service.

Leading indicators Time series that change in the same direction but in advance of company sales.

Learning Changes in an individual's behavior arising from experience.

Licensing A joint-venture method of entering a foreign market in which the company enters into an agreement with a licensee in the foreign market, offering the right to use a manufacturing process, trademark, patent, trade secret, or other item of value for a fee or royalty.

Life style A person's pattern of living as expressed in his or her activities, interests, and opinions.

Limited problem solving Buying behavior in cases where buyers are aware of the product class but not familiar with all the brands and their features. Buyers engage in limited information search and evaluation.

Macroenvironment The larger societal forces that affect the whole microenvironment—demographic, economic, natural, technological, political, and cultural forces.

Management contracting A joint venture in which the domestic firm supplies the management know-how to a foreign company that supplies the capital; the domestic firm exports management services rather than products.

Managerial climate The company climate resulting from the way managers work with others in the company.

Manufacturers' sales branches and offices The wholesaling operations of sellers or buyers who do their own wholesaling rather than use independent wholesalers.

Market The set of actual and potential buyers of a product.

Market-centered company A company that pays balanced attention to both customers and competitors in designing its marketing strategies.

Market challengers A runner-up firm in an industry that is fighting hard to increase its market share.

Market development A strategy for company growth by identifying and developing new market segments for current company products.

Market follower A runner-up firm in an industry that simply wants to hold its market share without rocking the boat.

Market leader The firm in an industry with the largest market share; it usually leads other firms in price changes, new product introductions, distribution coverage, and promotion spending.

Market management organization An organization structure in which market managers are responsible for developing plans for sales and profits in their specific markets.

Market nichers Firms in an industry that serve small segments that the larger firms overlook or ignore.

Market penetration A strategy for company growth by increasing sales of current products to current market segments without changing the product in any way.

Market penetration pricing Setting a low price for a new product in order to attract a large number of buyers and a large market share.

Market positioning Arranging for a product to occupy a clear, distinctive, and desirable place relative to competing products in the minds of target consumers. Formulating a competitive positioning for a product and a detailed marketing mix.

Market segment A group of consumers who respond in a similar way to a given set of marketing stimuli.

Market segmentation The process of classifying customers into groups with different needs, characteristics, or behavior. Dividing a market into distinct groups of buyers who might require separate products or marketing mixes.

Market-skimming pricing Setting a high price for a new product to skim maximum revenue from the segments willing to pay the high price; the company makes fewer but more profitable sales.

Market targeting Evaluating each market segment's attractiveness and selecting one or more segments to enter.

Marketing A social and managerial process by which individuals and groups obtain what they need and want through creating and exchanging products and value with others.

Marketing audit A comprehensive, systematic, independent, and periodic examination of a company's environment, objectives, strategies, and activities to determine problem areas and opportunities and to recommend a plan of action to improve the company's marketing performance.

Marketing concept The marketing management philosophy which holds that achieving organizational goals depends on determining the needs and wants of target markets and delivering the desired satisfactions more effectively and efficiently than competitors.

Marketing control The process of measuring and evaluating the results of marketing strategies and plans, and taking corrective action to assure that marketing objectives are attained.

Marketing implementation The process that turns marketing strategies and plans into marketing actions in order to accomplish strategic marketing objectives.

Marketing information system (MIS) People, equipment, and procedures to gather, sort, analyze, evaluate, and distribute needed, timely, and accurate information to marketing decision makers.

Marketing intelligence Everyday information about developments in the marketing environment that helps managers prepare and adjust marketing plans.

Marketing intermediaries Firms that help the company to promote, sell, and distribute its goods to final buyers; they include middlemen, physical distribution firms, marketing service agencies, and financial intermediaries.

Marketing management The analysis, planning, implementation, and control of programs designed to create, build, and maintain beneficial exchanges with target buyers for the purpose of achieving organizational objectives.

Marketing management process The process of (1) analyzing marketing opportunities, (2) selecting target markets, (3) developing the marketing mix, and (4) managing the marketing effort.

Marketing mix The set of controllable marketing variables that the firm blends to produce the response it wants in the target market.

Marketing research The function that links the consumer, customer, and public to the marketer through information—information used to identify and define marketing opportunities and problems; generate, refine, and evaluate marketing actions; monitor marketing performance; and improve understanding of the marketing process.

Marketing strategy The marketing logic by which the business unit hopes to achieve its marketing objectives. It consists of specific strategies for target markets, marketing mix, and marketing budget.

Marketing strategy development Designing an initial marketing strategy for a new product based on the product concept.

Mass and selective media Print media (newspapers, magazines, direct mail), electronic media (radio, television), and display media (billboards, signs, posters) aimed at large, unsegmented audiences (mass media) or at selected audiences (selective media).

Materials and parts Industrial goods that enter the manufacturer's product completely, including raw materials and manufactured materials and parts.

Maturity stage The stage in the product life cycle in which sales growth slows or levels off.

Merchandising conglomerates Corporations that combine several different retailing forms under central ownership and that share some distribution and management functions.

Merchant wholesaler An independently owned business that takes title to the product it handles.

Microenvironment The forces close to the company that affect its ability to serve its customers—the company, marketing channel firms, customer markets, competitors, and publics.

Mission statement. A statement of the organization's purpose, what it wants to accomplish in the larger environment.

Monopolistic competition A market in which many buyers and sellers trade over a range of prices rather than a single market price.

Moral appeals Message appeals that are directed to the audience's sense of what is right and proper.

Motive (or drive) A need that is sufficiently pressing to direct the person to seek satisfaction of the need.

Multinational company A company that operates in many countries and that has a major part of its operations outside its home country.

Natural environment Natural resources that are needed as inputs by marketers or that are affected by marketing activities.

New product A good, service, or idea that is perceived by some potential customers as new.

New product development The development of original products, product improvements, product modifications, and new brands through the firm's own research and development efforts.

Nondurable goods Tangible goods normally consumed in one or a few uses.

Nonpersonal communication channels Media that carry messages without personal contact or feedback, including mass and selective media, atmospheres, and events.

Objective-and-task method Developing the promotion budget by (1) defining specific objectives, (2) determining the tasks that must be performed to achieve these objectives, and (3) estimating the costs of performing these tasks; the sum of these costs is the proposed promotion budget.

Observational research The gathering of primary data by observing relevant people, actions, and situations.

Off-price retailers Retailers who buy at less-than-regular wholesale prices and sell at less-than-retail, usually carrying a changing and unstable collection of higher quality merchandise, often leftover goods, overruns, and irregulars obtained from manufacturers at reduced prices. They include factory outlets, independents, and warehouse clubs.

Oligopolistic competition A market in which there are a few sellers who are highly sensitive to each other's pricing and marketing strategies.

Opinion leaders People within a reference group who, because of special skills, knowledge, personality, or other characteristics, exert influence on others.

Organization image The way an individual or a group sees an organization.

Organization marketing Activities undertaken to create, maintain, or change attitudes and behavior of target audiences toward an organization.

Organizational buying The decision-making process by which formal organizations establish the need for purchased products and services, and identify, evaluate, and choose among alternative brands and suppliers.

Packaging The activities of designing and producing the container or wrapper for a product.

Penetrated market The set of consumers who have already bought a particular product or service.

Perceived-value pricing Setting price based on buyers' perceptions of value rather than on the seller's cost.

Percentage-of-sales method Setting the promotion budget at a certain percentage of current or forecasted sales or as a percentage of the sales price.

Perception The process by which people select, organize, and interpret information into a meaningful picture of the world.

Perishability A major characteristic of services—they cannot be stored for later sale or use.

Person marketing Activities undertaken to create, maintain, or change attitudes or behavior toward particular persons.

Personal communication channels Channels through which two or more people communicate directly with each other, including face to face, person to audience, over the telephone, or through the mail.

Personal influence The effect of statements made by one person on another's attitude or probability of purchase.

Personal selling Oral presentation in a conversation with one or more prospective purchasers for the purpose of making sales.

Personality A person's distinguishing psychological characteristics that lead to relatively consistent and lasting responses to his or her own environment.

Physical distribution Planning, implementing, and controlling the physical flow of materials and final goods from points of origin to points of use to meet the needs of customers at a profit.

Place marketing Activities undertaken to create, maintain, or change attitudes or behavior toward particular places.

Planned obsolescence A strategy of causing products to become obsolete before they actually need replacement; it includes style obsolescence, functional obsolescence, and material obsolescence.

Pleasing products Products that give high immediate satisfaction but may hurt consumers in the long run.

Political environment Laws, government agencies, and pressure groups that influence and limit various organizations and individuals in society.

Postpurchase behavior The stage of the buyer decision process in which consumers take further action after purchase based on their satisfaction or dissatisfaction.

Potential market The set of consumers who profess some level of interest in a particular product or service.

Price The amount of money charged for a product or service, or the sum of the values consumers exchange for the benefits of having or using the product or service.

Price elasticity A measure of the sensitivity of demand to changes in price.

Primary data Information collected for the specific purpose at hand.

Primary demand The level of total demand for all brands of a given product or service—for example, the total demand for motorcycles.

Problem recognition The first stage of the buyer decision process in which the consumer recognizes a problem or need.

Product Anything that can be offered to a market for attention, acquisition, use, or consumption that might satisfy a need or want.

Product concept A detailed version of the new product idea stated in meaningful consumer terms.

Product concept philosophy The marketing management philosophy that consumers will favor products that offer the most quality, performance, and features, and therefore the organization should devote its energy to making continuous product improvements.

Product development Developing the product concept into a physical product in order to assure that the product idea can be turned into a workable product.

Product development strategy A strategy for company growth by offering modified or new products to current market segments.

Product idea An idea for a possible product that the company can see itself offering to the market.

Product image The way consumers picture an actual or potential product.

Product life cycle (PLC) The course of a product's sales and profits over its lifetime. It involves five distinct stages: product development, introduction, growth, maturity, and decline.

Product line A group of products that are closely related, either because they function in a similar manner, are sold to the same customer groups, are marketed through the same types of outlets, or fall within given price ranges.

Product management organization An organization structure in which product managers are responsible for developing and implementing marketing strategies and plans for a specific product or brand.

Product/market expansion grid A portfolio planning tool for identifying company growth opportunities through market penetration, market development, product development, or diversification.

Product mix The set of all product lines and items that a particular seller offers for sale to buyers. Also called product assortment.

Product position The way the product is defined by consumers on important attributes—the place the product occupies in consumers' minds relative to competing products.

Product salesforce structure A salesforce organization under which salespeople specialize in selling only a portion of the company's products or lines.

Production concept The marketing management philosophy that consumers will favor products that are available and highly affordable, and therefore management should focus on improving production and distribution efficiency.

Profitability control Evaluation and corrective action to ensure the profitability of various products, territories, customer groups, trade channels, and order sizes.

Promotion mix The specific mix of advertising, personal selling, sales promotion, and public relations that a company uses to pursue its advertising and marketing objectives.

Promotional allowance A payment or price reduction to reward dealers for participating in advertising and sales-support programs.

Promotional pricing Temporarily pricing products below the list price, and sometimes even below cost, to increase short-run sales.

Psychographic segmentation Dividing a market into different groups based on social class, life style, or personality characteristics.

Psychological pricing A pricing approach that considers the psychology of prices and not simply the economics—the price is used to say something about the product.

Public Any group that has an actual or potential interest in or impact on an organization's ability to achieve its objectives.

Public relations Building good relations with the company's various publics by obtaining favorable publicity, building up a good "corporate image," and handling or heading off unfavorable rumors, stories, and events. Major PR tools include press relations, product publicity, corporate communications, lobbying, and counseling.

Publicity Activities to promote a company or its products by planting news about it in media not paid for by the sponsor.

Pull strategy A promotion strategy that calls for spending a lot on advertising and consumer promotion to build up consumer demand; if the strategy is successful, consumers will demand the product from their retailers, who will demand it from wholesalers, who will in turn demand it from producers.

Pulsing Scheduling ads unevenly in bursts over a time period.

Purchase decision The stage of the buyer decision process in which the consumer actually buys the product.

Pure competition A market in which many buyers and sellers trade in a uniform commodity; no single buyer or seller has much affect on the going market price.

Pure monopoly A market in which there is a single seller—it may be a government monopoly, a private regulated monopoly, or a private nonregulated monopoly.

Push strategy A promotion strategy that calls for using the salesforce and trade promotion to push the product through the channels; the producer promotes the product to wholesalers, the wholesalers promote to retailers, and the retailers promote to consumers.

Qualified available market The set of consumers who have interest, income, access, and qualifications for a particular product or service.

Quantity discount A price reduction to buyers who buy large volumes.

Question marks Low-share business units in high-growth markets, which require a lot of cash to hold their share or build into stars.

Quota A limit on the amount of goods that an importing country will accept in certain product categories, designed to conserve on foreign exchange and protect local industry and employment.

Rational appeals Message appeals that relate to the audience's self-interest and show that the product will produce the claimed benefits; examples include appeals of product quality, economy, value, or performance.

Reach The percentage of people in the target market exposed to an ad campaign during the given period.

Reference groups Groups that have a direct (face-to-face) or indirect influence on the person's attitudes or behavior.

Reseller market All the individuals and organizations that acquire goods for the purpose of reselling or renting them to others at a profit.

Retailers Businesses whose sales come *primarily* from retailing.

Retailing All activities involved in selling goods or services directly to final consumers for their personal, non-business use.

Role The activities a person is expected to perform according to the people around him or her.

Routine response behavior Buying behavior in cases where buyers face simple buying decisions for low-cost, low-involvement, frequently purchased items in familiar product classes. Buyers do not give much thought, search, or time to the purchase.

Sales promotion Short-term incentives to encourage purchase or sales of a product or service.

Salesforce management The analysis, planning, implementation, and control of salesforce activities. It includes setting salesforce objectives; designing salesforce strategy; and recruiting, selecting, training, supervising, and evaluating the firm's salespeople.

Salesforce promotion Sales promotion designed to motivate the salesforce and make salesforce selling efforts more effective, including bonuses, contests, and sales rallies.

Salesperson An individual acting for a company who performs one or more of the following activities: prospecting, communicating, servicing, and information gathering.

Salutary products Products that have low appeal but benefit consumers in the long run.

Sample A segment of the population selected for marketing research to represent the population as a whole.

Sealed-bid pricing Setting price based on how the firm thinks competitors will price rather than solely on its own costs or demand; used when a company bids for jobs.

Seasonal discount A price reduction to buyers who buy merchandise or services out of season.

Secondary data Information that already exists somewhere, having been collected for another purpose.

Selective demand The demand for a given brand of a product or service—for example, the demand for a *Honda* motorcycle.

Selective distribution The use of more than one but less than all the middlemen who are willing to carry a company's products.

Selling concept The marketing management philosophy that consumers will not buy enough of the organization's products unless the organization undertakes a large selling and promotion effort.

Selling process The steps that the salesperson follows when selling, which include prospecting and qualifying, preapproach, approach, presentation and demonstration, handling objections, closing, and follow-up.

Served market (or target market) The part of the qualified available market the company decides to pursue.

Services Activities, benefits, or satisfactions that are offered for sale; they are essentially intangible and do not result in the ownership of anything.

Shopping center A group of retail businesses planned, developed, owned, and managed as a unit.

Shopping goods Consumer goods that the customer, in the process of selection and purchase, characteristically compares on such bases as suitability, quality, price, and style.

Social classes Relatively permanent and ordered divisions in a society whose members share similar values, interests, and behaviors.

Social marketing The design, implementation, and control of programs seeking to increase the acceptability of a social idea, cause, or practice in target groups.

Societal marketing concept The marketing management philosophy that the organization should determine the desired satisfactions more effectively and efficiently than competitors in a way that maintains or improves the consumer's and society's well-being.

Specialty goods Consumer goods with unique characteristics or brand identification for which a significant group of buyers is willing to make a special purchase effort.

Specialty store A retail outlet that carries a narrow product line with a deep assortment within that line.

Standardized marketing mix An international marketing strategy of using about the same product, advertising, distribution channels, and other elements of the marketing mix in all the company's international markets.

Stars High-growth, high-share businesses or products, which often require heavy investment to finance their rapid growth.

Statistical demand analysis A set of statistical procedures used to discover the most important real factors affecting sales and their relative influence; the most commonly analyzed factors are prices, income, population, and promotion.

Status The general esteem given to a role by society.

Strategic business unit (SBU) A unit of the company that has a separate mission and objectives, and that can be planned independently of other company businesses. An SBU can be a company division, a product line within a division, or sometimes a single product or brand.

Strategic control A critical review of the company's overall marketing effectiveness.

Strategic group A group of firms in an industry following the same or a similar strategy.

Strategic planning The process of developing and maintaining a strategic fit between the organization's goals and capabilities and its changing marketing opportunities. It relies on developing a clear company mission, supporting objectives, a sound business portfolio, and coordinated functional strategies.

Subculture A group of people with shared value systems based on common life experiences and situations.

Supermarkets Large, low-cost, low-margin, high-volume, self-service stores that carry a wide variety of food, laundry, and household products.

Superstore A store almost twice the size of a regular supermarket that carries a large assortment of routinely purchased food and nonfood items, and offers such services as laundry, dry cleaning, shoe repair, check cashing, bill paying, and bargain lunch counters.

Suppliers Firms and individuals that provide the resources needed by the company to produce goods and services.

Supplies and services Industrial goods that do not enter the finished product at all.

Survey research The gathering of primary data by asking people questions about their knowledge, attitudes, preferences, and buying behavior.

Systems buying Buying a whole solution to a problem and not making all the spearate decisions involved.

Tariff A tax levied by a government against certain imported products designed to raise revenue or protect domestic firms.

Technological environment Forces that affect new technologies, creating new product and market opportunities.

Territorial salesforce structure A salesforce organization that assigns each salesperson to an exclusive geographic territory in which the salesperson carries the company's full line.

Test marketing The stage of new product development in which the product and marketing program are tested in more realistic market settings.

Time-series analysis Breaking down past sales into trend, cycle, season, and erratic components, then recombining these components to produce a sales forecast.

Total costs The sum of the fixed and variable costs for any given level of production.

Total market demand The total volume of a product or service that would be bought by a defined consumer group in a defined geographic area in a defined time period in a defined marketing environment under a defined level and mix of industry marketing effort.

Trade promotion Sales promotion designed to gain reseller support and to improve reseller selling efforts, including discounts, allowances, free goods, cooperative advertising, push money, and conventions and trade shows.

Trade-in allowance A price reduction given for turning in an old item when buying a new one.

Trademark A brand or part of a brand that is given legal protection—it protects the seller's exclusive rights to use the brand name or brand mark.

Transaction A trade between two parties that involves at least two things of value, agreed upon conditions, a time of agreement, and a place of agreement.

Undifferentiated marketing A market-coverage strategy in which a company goes after the whole market with one market offer.

Uniform delivered pricing A geographic pricing strategy in which the company charges the same price plus freight to all customers regardless of their location.

Unsought goods Consumer goods that the consumer does not know about or knows about but does not normally think of buying.

Users The people who consume or use a product or service. Members of an organization's buying center who will use a product or service being purchased; users often initiate the buying proposal and help define product specifications.

Value analysis An approach to cost reduction in which components are carefully studied to determine if they can be redesigned or standardized or made by cheaper methods of production.

Variability A major characteristic of services—their quality may vary a lot, depending on who provides them and when and where they are provided.

Variable costs Costs that vary directly with the level of production.

Vertical marketing system (VMS) A distribution channel structure in which the producer(s), wholesaler(s), and retailer(s) act as a unified system; either one channel member owns the others, has contracts with them, or has so much power that they all cooperate.

Wholesalers Firms engaged *primarily* in wholesaling activity.

Wholesaling All activities involved in selling goods and services to those buying for resale or business use.

Zone pricing A geographic pricing strategy in which the company sets up two or more zones, all customers within a zone pay the same total price, and this price is higher in the more distant zones.

Acknowledgment of Illustrations

Packaged Foods Co.; **289** Kikkoman International, Inc.; **292** Sony Corporation of America; **294** Miller Brewing Company.

CHAPTER 12

300 Teri Stratford; **304** Sub-Zero Freezer Co., Inc.; **306** top; Ford Motor Company, bottom: Jaguar Cars, Inc.; **311** Photograph courtesy of Oscar Mayer Foods Corporation, Claussen is a registered trademark of Oscar Mayer Foods Corporation; **313** Fuddruckers, Inc.; **320** Waterford Wedgwood.

CHAPTER 13

324 Caterpillar Inc.; **327** Polaroid Corporation; **329** Snapper Power Equipment; **330** Hyatt Hotels Corporation; **332** AT&T; **338** Bausch & Lomb Professional Products Division; **338** Jean Patou Inc.

CHAPTER 14

346 Bolla & Bolla; **352** top left: The Coca-Cola Company, top right: Michael S. Yamashita/West Light, bottom left and right: The Coca-Cola Company; **359** McDonald's and Sears Roebuck and Co.; **361** left: Michael Rizza/Stock, Boston, right: Lee Lockwood/Black Star; **363** top: Chris Jones/The Stock Market, bottom: Christina Mufson/Comstock; **366** Frigidaire; **371** Xerox Corporation; **373** top left: Conrail, top right and bottom left: CSX Creative Services, bottom right: American Airlines.

CHAPTER 15

378 IKEA, Inc.; **382** Athletic Attic; **385** Ralph's Grocery Co./Studebaker; **387** 47th Street Photo; **390** Minneapolis Convention and Visitors Association; **392** Teri Stratford; **393** left: Home Shopping Network, right: Michael Mella; **397** Ted Hardin; **402** Fleming Companies, Inc., Oklahoma City, OK; **405** Foremost-McKesson.

CHAPTER 16

412 Quaker Oats Company; **419** Procter & Gamble Company; **422** General Foods; **426** John Lei/Stock, Boston; **427** McGraw-Hill, Inc.

CHAPTER 17

432 California Raisin Advisory Board; **439** Kraft, Inc.; **441** left: National Dairy Board, right: Star-Kist Foods, Inc.; **442** Warner Lambert Co.; **446** left: John M. Roberts, right: Ted Kappler; **447** Parking Meter Advertising; **451** Jayne Conte; **453** PepsiCo, Inc.; **457** Coleco; **459** Teri Stratford.

CHAPTER 18

464 top: Chemical New York Corp, bottom: Boeing; **468** left: Linda Bohm/Leo de Wys, right: Gabe Palmer/The Stock Market; **474** Rebecca Chao; **477** Wilson Learning Corporation, Eden Prairie, MN; **479** Hewlett-Packard; **482** Princess Cruises.

CHAPTER 19

490 A&W Beverages/Teri Stratford; **495** left: Procter & Gamble Company, right: DEP Corporation; **496** GE Appliances; **502** left: Johnson & Johnson Baby Products Company, right: Church & Dwight Co., Inc.; **506** left: Fuji Photo Film USA, Inc., right: reprinted courtesy of Eastman Kodak Company, © Eastman Kodak Company; **509** Teri Stratford.

CHAPTER 20

516 IBM; **522** State of Florida, Division of Economic Development, based on an original photographic concept by Arnold Zann/Black Star; **531** Hewlett-Packard; **535** © Mark Seliger; **538** D. Luria/FPG.

CHAPTER 21

548 Eastman Kodak Company; **551** top left: Nubar Alexanian/Stock, Boston, top right: Caroline Parsons, bottom left: Greg Davis/The Stock Market, bottom right: Paolo Fridman/Sygma; **557** Guy Laroche; **559** Pepsi-Cola International; **561** TOKYO DISNEYLAND is owned and operated by the Oriental Land Co., Ltd. (a Japanese Development company) under license from The Walt Disney Company, © 1986 The Walt Disney Company; **563** General Motors Corporation; **566** Playtex, Inc.

CHAPTER 22

572 Century City Hospital; **575** left: Robert Holmgren, right: John C. Hillery; **580** United Parcel Service of America; **583** Hush Puppies Division of Wolverine World Wide Inc.; **587** North Carolina Department of Commerce; **589** MADD, Mothers Against Drunk Driving, Milwaukee County, Wisconsin.

CHAPTER 23

592 © 1985 Marty Katz; **597** Katherine Lambert; **599** Rob Kinmonth; **601** American Association of Advertising Agencies; **603** Tom McHugh/Photo Researchers; **605** Campbell Soup Company; **607** Canon Inc.

Author Index

H

I

J

K

L

Subject Index

Q

Quaker Oats, 413–14, 456
Qualified available market, 198–99
Quality of life, 19
Quantity discounts, 331
Question marks, 32
Questionnaires, 104–6
Quota, 554

R

Railroad Retirement Board, 184
Railroads, 372, 374
Rational appeals, 418
Raw materials, shortages of, 68–69
RCA Corporation, 143, 195–96
Reach, 443
Rebates, 452
Reciprocity, 169–70
Red Baron Pizza Service, 456
Redbook magazine, 222
Reference groups, 121–24
References prices, 333
Regionalization, 218–19
Regionalized marketing, 534
Relative market share, 32
Reminder advertising, 438
Resale price maintenance, 316
Research and development, 71–73
Reseller market, 165
    buyer behavior, 182–84
Resumé, 631
Retailer cooperatives, 357, 389
Retailing, 379–400
    amount of service, 381–82
    careers in, 630
    control of outlets, 388–89
    defined, 380
    direct marketing, 391–94
    direct selling, 394–95
    future of, 398–400
    marketing decisions, 395–98
    product line sold, 382–85
    relative prices, 385–88
    type of store cluster, 390–91
Revlon, 241–42
Robinson-Patman Act of 1936, 75, 316
Role, 126
Role playing, 131
Roles in buyer decision processes, 143
Routine response buying behavior, 144

S

Saab, 230–31
Safety needs, 131–32
Sales analysis, 536–37
Sales presentations, 477–78
Sales promotion, 424, 426–29, 449–55
    award-winning, 456
    development of program, 454–55

objectives, 450
    tools, 451–54
Sales quotas, 481–82
Salesforce (*see* Personal selling)
Salesforce management, 468
Salesforce opinions, 207
Salesforce promotion, 450
Sales-response function, 524–25
Salient attributes, 149
Salutary products, 610
Samples, 103–4, 451
Schwinn Bicycle Company, 55–59
Sealed-bid pricing, 321–22
Searle, G. D., Company, 166
Sears Financial Network, 617–18
Sears Roebuck & Company, 19, 47, 79, 301–2
Seasonal discounts, 331
Secondary data, 97–99
Secondary groups, 121
SelectaVision, 143, 195–96
Selective demand, 200
Selective distortion, 133
Selective distribution, 364
Selective exposure, 132–33
Selective retention, 133–34
Self-actualization needs, 131–32
Self-assessment, 630
Self-concept, 130
Self-service retailing, 381
Self-sufficiency, 9
Seller's market, 10
Selling concept, 13–15
Selling process, 476–78
Seminar selling, 469
Senior consumers, 121
Sense-of-mission marketing, 609–10
Sentence completion, 131
Served market, 198–99, 507
Service retailers, 385
Services, 244–45
    defined, 575
    distribution channels in, 353
Services marketing, 574–82
    characteristics of, 577–79
    nature and classification of, 575–76
    strategies for, 579–82
Services mix, 397
Sex segmentation, 219–21
Shell Oil Company, 8
Sherman Antitrust Act of 1890, 74
Shopping centers, 390–91
Shopping goods, 245
Siemens Company, 19
Simulated test markets, 285–86
Singer Sewing Company, 48
Single sourcing, 177
Site location, 398, 404
Small Business Administration, 185
Social class:
    consumer behavior and, 120, 122
    market segmentation and, 221
Social criticisms of marketing, 594–604
Social goods, 602
Social marketing, 588–90
Social needs, 131–32
Socialist countries, marketing in, 19–20
Societal marketing, 15, 17, 610

Soft-drink market, 491–92
Sony Corporation, 19, 266, 505
Special-event pricing, 334
Specialty goods, 245
Specialty stores, 382–83
Spending patterns, changes in, 67–68
SRI values and life styles (VALS) typology, 128–29
Standard Industrial Classification (SIC), 202–3
Standard test markets, 284–85
Standardized marketing mix, 563
Star-Kist Foods, 456
Stars, 32
Statistical demand analysis, 209–10
Status, 126
Steelcase Company, 227–28
Stimulus object, 134
Store's atmosphere, 397–98
Straight extension, 563–64
Straight rebuy, 171
Strategic business-planning grid, 33–34
Strategic business units (SBUs), 31–34
Strategic control, 540–42
Strategic group, 495–96
Strategic planning, 28–40
    business portfolio, 31–37
    defined, 28
    mission statement, 28–30
    objectives and goals, 30–31
    planning functional strategies, 37–40
Structured surveys, 100
Style, 291
Subcultures, 77
    consumer behavior and, 119–21
Subliminal perception, 135
Supermarkets, 383–84
Superstores, 384
Supplier search, 180
Supplier selection, 180–81
Suppliers, 56
Supplies and services, 247–48
Survey research, 100–101
Surveys, of buyers' intentions, 206–7
Sweepstakes, 452, 453
Symbiotic marketing, 358
Systems analysis, 629
Systems buying and selling, 172

T

Tachistoscope, 105
Target marketing, 215
Target markets, 395–96
    selection, 40–45
Target profit planning, 523–24
Target profit pricing, 318–20
Tariff, 554
Technological environment, 70–73
Telecommunications, 111, 177
Telemarketing, 392–93, 480, 481
Telephone interviewing, 102
Television, 6
Television marketing, 393–94
Tennessee Valley Authority (TVA), 184

Territorial salesforce structure, 470
Test marketing, 284–87
Texas Instruments, 13, 309
3M Corporation, 4, 273–74, 528
Time pricing, 332
Time-series analysis, 209
Tobacco industry, 506
Top-down planning, 27
Total costs, 308–9
Total market demand, estimating, 199–201
Toyota, 19, 47
Trade-in allowances, 331
Trademark, 248
Trade promotion, 450
Trade shows, 287
Trainship, 374
Transactional harm, 613
Transportation, 372–74
Trucks, 372, 374
Truth-in-Lending Act of 1968, 75
Two-part pricing, 330
Tying agreements, 368
Tylenol, 457, 593

U

Undifferentiated marketing, 228–29
Uniform delivered pricing, 335
Unilever Corporation, 508–9
United Airlines, 528
Unsought goods, 245–46
Unstructured surveys, 100
Upgraded purchasing, 175
U.S. Postal Service, 21
Users, 143, 173
Utility function, 150

V

Vacation marketing, 587–88
Value analysis, 177, 179–80
Value marketing, 609
Values, 77
Variability of services, 578
Variable costs, 308
Vendor analysis, 181
Vernor's ginger ale, 491–92
Vertical marketing system (VMS), 355–58
Videotex, 394
Voluntary chains, 388–89

W

Wants, 4–7
Warehouse (wholesale) clubs, 386
Warehousing, 370–71
Warranties, 268
Waste management, 583–84
Water transportation, 373–74
Wheel of retailing concept, 399–400